The Deadline

Also by Jill Lepore

If Then:
How the Simulmatics Corporation Invented the Future

This America:
The Case for the Nation

These Truths:
A History of the United States

Joe Gould's Teeth

The Secret History of Wonder Woman

Book of Ages:
The Life and Opinions of Jane Franklin

The Story of America:
Essays on Origins

The Mansion of Happiness:
A History of Life and Death

The Whites of Their Eyes:
The Tea Party's Revolution and the Battle over American History

New York Burning:
Liberty, Slavery, and Conspiracy in Eighteenth-Century Manhattan

A Is for American:
Letters and Other Characters in the Newly United States

The Name of War:
King Philip's War and the Origins of American Identity

The
Deadline
—————————————— *Essays*

Jill Lepore

Liveright Publishing Corporation

A Division of W. W. Norton & Company
Celebrating a Century of Independent Publishing

For information about permission to reproduce selections from this book,
write to Permissions, Liveright Publishing Corporation, a division of
W. W. Norton & Company, Inc., 500 Fifth Avenue, New York, NY 10110

For information about special discounts for bulk purchases, please contact
W. W. Norton Special Sales atspecialsales@wwnorton.com or 800-233-4830

Manufacturing by Lakeside Book Company
Book design by Lovedog Studio
Production manager: Anna Oler

ISBN 978-1-63149-612-7

Liveright Publishing Corporation, 500 Fifth Avenue, New York, N.Y. 10110
www.wwnorton.com

W. W. Norton & Company Ltd., 15 Carlisle Street, London W1D 3BS

1 2 3 4 5 6 7 8 9 0

To H.F.

It changed, it shaped itself differently; it had become, she knew, giving one last look at it over her shoulder, already the past.

—Virginia Woolf, *To the Lighthouse*

Contents

Part Four
Just the Facts, Ma'am

Part Five
Battleground America

Part Six
The Disruption Machine

Part Ten
In Every Dark Hour

SOME OF THESE ESSAYS WERE PREVIOUSLY PUBLISHED under different titles. "The Ice Man" was previously reprinted in *The Mansion of Happiness*, published by Knopf. The remaining essays originally appeared in *The New Yorker*, and passages from some of them were included in *These Truths*, published by W. W. Norton. The introduction, "The Everyman Library," and "The Return of the Pervert" have not previously been published.

Introduction

ONE SUMMER DAY, THE SUN'S RAYS AS SPIKY AS A coronavirus, I went for a walk through a forest where pine trees poke out of a hill like pins from a pincushion. Somewhere along the trail, a black-legged deer tick dropped from a branch, crawled under my shirt and down my sweat-slick back, stopped, gnawed a hole in my skin, inserted a barbed nozzle, and began sucking my blood, unnoticed.

The fall semester was about to start, and I was busy tinkering with an American history syllabus, scratching off this, writing in that. In high school classrooms and on college campuses across the country, parents and students had been objecting to books, sources, assignments, demanding less coverage of this, more of that. Less poverty, more atrocity. More religion, less social justice. On the right, parents were banning books. On the left, students were clamoring for faculty to be fired. Meantime, I was putting together a U.S. history textbook: same problem. Either the history anyone was teaching or writing told of a past too ugly, too cruel, too unjust, or else it told of a past that was innocent and guileless, bloodless, witless. Conservative parents complained about their children reading *Maus*, Art Spiegelman's graphic novel about the Holocaust; progressive students refused to read the Supreme Court's majority opinion in 1857 in *Dred Scott*, the decision that sparked the Civil War. Too painful, they said. Except: history is racked with pain.

Classes started. It was hard to teach with a mask. I lost my breath. I couldn't sleep. I felt so dizzy, worse each day. My back hurt.

"Is it red?" I asked my husband, pulling up my shirt. "Did I scratch it or something?"

"Red as a bull's-eye," he said. "It's a tick."

He got the tweezers and the alcohol, struck a match, burned a needle, and yanked it off.

"Fat and squishy," he said, scientifically. "Like a pomegranate seed."
Might be Lyme disease.

"You need, like, a telehealth appointment."

"But I won't be able to show them my back."

"Just send them pictures."

He took a bunch of photographs and emailed them to me. I inspected them on my laptop, uploaded a few to my doctor's website, and went to bed. The next morning, I walked to class. In the lecture hall, getting ready to show a series of slides about *The Federalist Papers*, I plunked my laptop onto the podium and plugged it into the cable connecting it to the projector that hangs from the ceiling. A handful of students had shown up early, slinking out of their backpacks. When the projector blinked on, they gasped. I looked up. There, projected onto the giant screen behind me, loomed my desktop, and the last files I'd opened: a pair of photographs, close-ups of my fatty, menopausal back, two soft hills of vulnerable, pale flesh, each with a raised red welt in the middle, a seeming nipple, as if I'd just flashed my breasts. This, I thought, is how it ends.

HERE'S HOW IT BEGAN. I never set out to study history. I only ever set out to write. The history I read bugged me. About the only article I've ever written for an academic history journal is an essay called "Historians Who Love Too Much," in which I bang my head against the conventions of the discipline. I agreed with the heroine of Jane Austen's *Northanger Abbey*, when she complains about history, "It tells me nothing that does not either vex or weary me. The quarrels of popes and kings, with wars or pestilences, in every page; the men all so good for nothing, and hardly any women at all—it is very tiresome: and yet I often think it odd that it should be so dull, for a great deal of it must be invention." I have tried to write history differently.

But if the buttoned-up conventions of the discipline of history bugged me, when I started out, so did a very different kind of writing, the tits-out memoir, where the only authority the author holds—the only authority the author can imagine—is the authority of personal experience. I watched a lot of fascinating women—scholars, investigative reporters, novelists—who had all kinds of knowledge about all kinds of things end up writing, instead, about girlhood, womanhood, motherhood, and widowhood. I despise a lot of that writing and I also love a lot of that writing but, either way, my calculation was my own: there are few enough serious female intellectuals out there, getting column inches, that I should write like a man, write about wars and pestilences and the quarrels of popes and kings and presidents and constitutions. In graduate school, I at first planned to write a dissertation about the eighteenth-century culture of seduction. Noticing what happened to female scholars who wrote about sex, I decided instead to write a dissertation about a seventeenth-century war. When I got a job as an assistant professor, I learned that it was crucial, if you wanted to get tenure, to hide your children. ("The feminism of writers who are mothers is a fetish, but the motherhood of scholars is forbidden," I write in an essay in this book.) I hid everything. After I got tenure, I started to wobble on that commitment, but I was also planning to quit, walk away, stay home. In 2005, when I was first asked to write an essay for *The New Yorker,* I'd just had a baby, my third, facts I was determined to hide from my readers, and even from my editor, to whom this book is dedicated. I figured the rules of my department applied to the magazine. I steered clear of self-revelation. I avoided assignments that edged toward my actual life.

Here and there, I broke that rule. In 2009, I wrote a five-thousand-word essay called "Baby Food," about the history of breastfeeding, in which I remarked, in passing, about using a breast pump: "whether it's more boring or more lonesome I find hard to say." I got into the habit of sneaking in little asides like that, outing myself as a human being, and readers wrote to me, intimately, beautifully. In 2011, in "The Commandments," an essay about the U.S. Constitution, I described Benjamin Franklin's remarks at the Constitutional Convention this way: "Franklin liked to swaddle argument with affability, as if an argument were a colicky baby; the more forceful his argument, the more tightly he swaddled it." The domestic metaphors, the maternal asides: it became a compulsion, the unmasking of myself as a person who spends most of her time cooking, quilting, nursing, gardening, shoveling snow, and doing laundry. After my parents died, in 2012, I wrote an essay called "Prodigal Daughter." In 2019, on the twentieth anniversary of a death that shattered my life, I wrote "The Deadline," the title essay of this book: it explains why I write.

This collection gathers together essays written over the last decade or so, about everything from gun rights and police brutality to Bratz dolls and bicycles. Some of my older essays, not included here, appeared in two earlier anthologies of my writing: *The Mansion of Happiness*, essays about the history of the stages of life ("Baby Food" appears there), and *The Story of America*, essays on American history as myth (like "The Commandments"). All the essays I've collected in the book concern the hold of the dead over the living—the tug of time, as inevitable as gravity. I've organized these essays into ten parts. Aside from Part One, about my own life, and Part Two, a series of what I think of as Profiles of the Dead, the essays constitute reflections on the relationship between the American past and its fractious, violent present. With few exceptions, each is an attempt to yank a plant out of the ground and inspect its roots for grubs and rot and stunted growth. How did Americans become so polarized? Why do people believe in the gospel of disruptive innovation? How did the Bush administration justify torture? Why does impeachment no longer work? Why do race-riot commissions never fix anything? Most of the essays here concern law and politics but a lot have to do with technology, some with culture, and very many with constitutional rule, Trump and Trumpism. Part Ten amounts to a meditation on the experience of life under COVID.

The essays might seem to sort into two piles, the intimate and the intellectual. But I find that division wildly overdrawn, as if how people think about Congress draws on a different part of themselves than how they think about toddlers. To me it's all the same. In "The Shorebird," an essay about Rachel Carson, I tried to explain that I think she thought it was all the same, too, that she saw all organisms as part of an ecosystem, interdependent, because she knew what it felt like to need to be home to make dinner for her ailing mother and her adopted son. I, at least, have found that to be true.

There's no real way of avoiding stating the obvious here: I wrote these essays during a period of terrible, tragic decline in the United States, short, sharp years marked by rising political violence, endless vicious culture war, a series of constitutional crises, catastrophic climate change, and a global pandemic. It was a time that *felt* like a time, felt like history. (Most of the essays appear as originally written, even when developments have outpaced the narrative as I recorded it.) To essays on these subjects I mostly bring the vantage of scholarship, and snippets of archival evidence—I have a rule that every piece I write has to have, hidden within it, an archival Easter egg—but I also did my best to get out of the classroom and the library and go see what I could see, hoping to offer up some view of what the present looks like by way of the past. I set out, more than once, to report: to interview the head of the NRA, to meet with the founder of the Internet Archive, to attend the New Hampshire primaries, to watch presidential debates from the debate stage, to sit in the halls of nominating conventions. Finally, it needs saying that I wrote these essays during a time when I was also writing, and then revising, a sweeping history of the United States, a book called *These Truths*. I in fact wrote *These Truths* because of these essays, and so many more essays that are not included here, when I came to realize that, without intending to, I was, word by word, writing a very long history of the nation. That means that readers of *These Truths* might find passages in this collection familiar—in writing that book, I raided nearly every piece of political history I've ever written.

A "dead line" used to mean a line around a prison, a sort of invisible fence. This started in the 1860s: you see it all the time in the diaries of Civil War prisoners. If you went past the dead line, you were shot. Especially desperate Union soldiers, starving, would sometimes pass the dead line, knowing they'd get killed, as a way to end their lives. "Deadline" only started meaning a time by which you had to finish something—or else lose your job—in the early twentieth century. I don't know why, but I love nothing better than a deadline. It's a reason to write. I like being on time, writing about time. And I do generally write on deadline, in a rush, but I'm also haunted by another deadline, the river of time that divides the quick from the dead, and by what crosses that line, the remains, left behind. I can smell my father's tobacco in these essays, and my mother's soap. There are food stains on these pages, splotches of ketchup, spills of orange juice. They rumble with the gush of a running bath, the roar from the crowd at a Little League game. These essays aren't about those things, but my writing them from those places matters in how I see the world. A red thread runs through nearly all these essays, an unraveling spool, a worry about rule, every kind of rule, at every scale. Who rules? Do they rule well? Does this species of rule, within a family, a polity, a nation-state, distribute power fairly? Is it just? Can it be just? And what about a written constitution, by which the living are ruled by the dead?

In 1798, a few months after the English feminist Mary Wollstonecraft died, following the birth of a daughter who would go on to write *Frankenstein*, about a terrible birth, an American writer named Charles Brockden Brown published the first installments of a story, a tribute to Wollstonecraft's most famous book, *A Vindication of the Rights of Woman*. In Brown's story, a young American man goes to visit a learned lady. He asks her whether she's a Federalist, an advocate of the Constitution. She answers him, "What have I, as a woman, to do with politics? Even the government of our own country, which is said to be the freest in the world, passes over women as if they were not. We are excluded from all political rights without the least ceremony. Law-makers thought as little of comprehending us in their code of liberty, as if we were pigs, or sheep." She expounds on her view of the framers—men like James Madison, Alexander Hamilton, and John Jay, the authors of *The Federalist Papers*—who believed women ought only to "listen and obey." "It is not for me to smile at their tyranny, or receive, as my gospel, a code built upon such atrocious maxims," she says bitterly. "No, I am no federalist."

The day pictures of my tick-bitten back flashed on the screen in the lecture hall, that passage was on the slide I'd meant to use at the start of class: that learned lady, refusing to smile at tyranny, unwilling to countenance a constitution—"unjust and absurd"—that failed to count her as a human being. "I see myself, in my relation to society, regarded merely as a beast or an insect," she'd said.

I closed the laptop. I pulled the cord.

Part One

Prodigal Daughter

I was sick of silence, sick of attics and wallpaper, sick of blank pages and miniature rooms, sick of blighted girlhood.

The author at age seven. *Photograph by Marjorie Lepore*

PRODIGAL DAUGHTER

IN THE TRUNK OF HER CAR, MY MOTHER USED TO KEEP a collapsible easel, a clutch of brushes, a little wooden case stocked with tubes of paint, and, tucked into the spare-tire well, one of my father's old, tobacco-stained shirts, for a smock. She'd be out running errands, see something wonderful, pull over, and pop the trunk. I never knew anyone better prepared to meet with beauty.

"Fingers nimble, brush or thimble," my mother's college yearbook said about her. The cabinets in our kitchen used to be a murky green. One day, I came home from kindergarten to find that my mother had painted every cabinet sunflower yellow. "I was just so sick of that green," she said, washing up, briskly, at the kitchen sink. She stitched quilts; she painted murals. She had one dresser drawer filled with buttons and another with crayons. She once built me a dollhouse out of a stack of shoeboxes. She papered the rooms with scraps of wallpaper and lit them with strings of colored Christmas-tree lights as brightly as she lit my childhood with her trapped passion.

She'd grown up in a small town in Massachusetts, a devout Catholic. After college—a Catholic school in New Rochelle—she'd wanted to go places. It was 1949: the war was over; the world was wide. She got engaged to a man named Winstanley, who had a job with the State Department; she wanted to marry him because he was about to be posted to Berlin. That fell apart. For a while, she worked as a designer for the Milton Bradley Company, in Springfield, but she couldn't stand how, from her apartment, she could hear the keening of the polar bear in the city zoo. ("He had the smallest cage you ever saw," she told me. "All night, he cried.") Then she drove across the country in a jalopy and took a slow boat from San Diego to Honolulu. After that, she became a stewardess, so that she could see Europe. In 1955, she had to quit and come back home, to Massachusetts, to take care of her mother, who was dying. That's when she met my father, a junior high school principal: he hired her as an art teacher. Every day, he left a poem in her mailbox in the teachers' room. The filthiest ones are the best. ("Marjorie, Marjorie, let me park my car in your garagery.") He told her he wanted to live in Spain. He was courting; he was lying; no one hated to go anywhere more than my father; he almost never left town. Except for during the war, he had never lived anywhere but his mother's house.

My mother married my father in 1956. She was twenty-eight and he was thirty-one. She loved him with a fierce steadiness borne of loyalty, determination, and an unyielding dignity. On their honeymoon, in a cabin in Maine, for their first breakfast together, she made him blueberry pancakes. Pushing back his plate, he told her he didn't like blueberries. In fifty-five years of marriage, she never again cooked him breakfast.

Before I was born, my parents bought a house on Franklin Street. (My mother promptly planted a blueberry bush in the back yard.) The year I learned the alphabet, the letter *J*, the fishing hook, was my favorite, except for *F*. "I am four and my mother is forty-four and my father's name is Frank and my house is 44 Franklin Street," I would whisper, when no one was listening: I was the youngest.

THE STREET I GREW UP ON was named for Benjamin Franklin. For a long time, no name was more famous. "There have been as great Souls unknown to fame as any of the most famous," the man himself liked to say, shrugging it off.

Benjamin Franklin was born in Boston in 1706. He was the youngest of his father's ten sons. His sister Jane was born in 1712. She was the youngest of their father's seven daughters. Benny and Jenny, they were called, when they were little.

I never heard of Jane Franklin when I lived on Franklin Street. I only came across her name on a day, much later, when I sat down on the floor of a library to read the first thirty-odd volumes of Benjamin Franklin's published papers. I pulled one volume after another off the shelf, and turned the pages, astonished. She was everywhere, threaded through his life, like a slip stitch.

We "had sildom any contention among us," she wrote him, looking back at their childhood. "All was Harmony."

He remembered it differently. "I think our Family were always subject to being a little Miffy."

She took his hint. "You Introduce your Reproof of my Miffy temper so Politely," she wrote back, slyly, "won cant a Void wishing to have conquered it as you have."

He loved no one longer. She loved no one better. She thought of him as her "Second Self." No two people in their family were more alike. Their lives could hardly have been more different. Boys were taught to read and write, girls to read and stitch. Three in five women in New England couldn't even sign their names, and those who could sign usually couldn't actually write. Signing is mechanical; writing is an art.

Benjamin Franklin taught himself to write with wit and force and style. His sister never learned how to spell. What she did learn, he taught her. It was a little cruel, in its kindness, because when he left the lessons ended.

He ran away in 1723, when he was seventeen and she was eleven. The day he turned twenty-one, he wrote her a letter—she was fourteen—beginning a correspondence that would last until his death. (He wrote more letters to her than he wrote to anyone else.) He became a printer, a philosopher, and a statesman. She became a wife, a mother, and a widow. He signed the Declaration of Independence, the Treaty of Paris, and the Constitution. She strained to form the letters of her name.

He wrote the story of his life, about a boy who runs away from a life of poverty and obscurity in cramped, pious Boston to become an enlightened, independent man of the world: a free man. He meant it as an allegory about America.

"One Half the World does not know how the other Half lives," he once wrote. Jane Franklin was his other half. If his life is an allegory, so is hers.

"WRITE A BOOK ABOUT HER!" my mother said, when I told her about Jane Franklin. I thought she was joking. It would be like painting a phantom.

History's written from what can be found; what isn't saved is lost, sunken and rotted, eaten by earth. Jane kept the letters her brother sent her. But half the letters she sent him—three decades' worth—are miss-ing. Most likely, he threw them away. Maybe someone burned them. It hardly matters. A one-sided correspondence is a house without win-dows, a left shoe, a pair of spectacles, smashed.

My mother liked to command me to do things I found scary. I always wanted to stay home and read. My mother only ever wanted me to get away. She brought me with her wherever she went. She once sent me to live with my aunt in Connecticut. ("Just to see some-place different.") One year, she saved up to send me to a week of Girl Scout camp, the most exotic adventure I had ever heard of. I got homesick, and begged her to let me come home. "Oh, stop," she said. "And don't you dare call me again, either." When I was eleven, she took me to New York City, a place no one else in my family had ever been. It was the weekend of the annual gay-pride parade, on Chris-topher Street. "Isn't that interesting?" she said. She took a picture of me next to five men dressed in black leather carrying a banner that read COCKSUCKERS UNITE—this was 1978—so that I'd remember the existence of a world beyond Franklin Street. No one else in my fam-ily left home to go to college. My mother made sure I did. She might as well have written me a letter: "Run away, run away." By then, I didn't need a push.

JANE FRANKLIN NEVER RAN AWAY, and never wrote the story of her life. But she did once stitch four sheets of foolscap between two covers to make a little book of sixteen pages. In an archive in Boston, I held it in my hands. I pictured her making it. Her paper was made from rags, soaked and pulped and strained and dried. Her thread was made from flax, combed and spun and dyed and twisted. She dipped the nib of a pen slit from the feather of a bird into a pot of ink boiled of oil mixed with soot and, on the first page, wrote three words: "Book of Ages"—a lavish, calligraphic letter B, a graceful, slender, artful A. She would have learned this—an Italian round hand—out of a writing manual, like *The American Instructor: Or, Young Man's Best Companion*, a book her brother printed in Philadelphia.

At the top of the next page, in a much smaller and plainer hand, she began her chronicle:

> Jane Franklin Born on March 27-1712
> Edward Mecom Marryed to Jane Franklin the 27th of July 1727.

The Book of Ages: *her* age. Born, March 27, 1712; married, July 27, 1727. Fifteen years four months. She was a child. The legal age for marriage in Massachusetts was sixteen; the average age was twenty-four, which is the age at which her brother Benjamin married and, excepting Jane, the average age at which her sisters were married.

The man she married, Edward Mecom, was twenty-two. He was poor, he was a saddler, and he was a Scot. He wore a wig and a beaver hat. She never once wrote anything about him expressing the least affection.

She added another line:

> Josiah Mecom their first Born on Wednesday June the 4: 1729

She named this child, her first, for her father.

> and Died May the 18-1730.

The child of her childhood died three weeks shy of his first birthday.

"A Dead Child is a sight no more surprizing than a broken Pitcher," Cotton Mather preached, in a sermon called "Right Thoughts in Sad Hours." One in four children died before the age of ten. The dead were wrapped in linen dipped in melted wax while a box made of pine was built and painted black. Puritans banned prayers for the dead: at the grave, there would be no sermon. Nor, ministers warned, ought there to be tears. *A Token for Mourners or, The Advice of Christ to a Distressed Mother, bewailing the Death of her Dear and Only Son* cited Luke 7:13: "Weepe not."

What remains of a life? "Remains" means what remains of the body after death. But remains are also unpublished papers. And descendants are remains, too. The Boston Puritan poet Anne Bradstreet wrote about her children as "my little babes, my dear remains." But Bradstreet's poems were her children, as well: "Thou ill-form'd offspring of my feeble brain." Her words were all that her children would, one day, have left of her. "If chance to thine eyes shall bring this verse," she told them, "kiss this paper."

Jane didn't know how to write a poem. She couldn't have afforded a headstone. Instead, she went home, and wrote a book of remembrance. *Kiss this paper.*

COLLEGE WAS SOMETHING OF A BUST. It was the 1980s. On the one hand, Andrea Dworkin; on the other, Jacques Derrida. I took a job as a secretary, on the theory that it would give me more time to read what I wanted. "Is that working out?" my mother wanted to know. I wrote a graduate-school application essay about a short story of Isak Dinesen's called "The Blank Page." Very *A Room of One's Own.* Very *The Madwoman in the Attic.* ("I write now in my own litle chamber," Jane wrote, when she was sixty-four, "& nobod up in the house near me to Desturb me." She was very happy to have that room, but not having it sooner isn't why she didn't write more or better.) Then, suddenly, I realized that my life plan—bashful daughter of shackled artist reads "The Yellow Wallpaper"—was narrow, hackneyed, daffy.

I was sick of silence, sick of attics and wallpaper, sick of blank pages and miniature rooms, sick of blighted girlhood. I wanted to study war. I wanted to investigate atrocity. I wanted to write about politics. Really, I wanted to write about anything but Jane Franklin.

"What about beauty?" my mother pressed. I kept making excuses. I was pregnant. ("Edward Mecom Born on Munday the 29 March 1731.") I was too busy. ("My mind is keept in a contineual Agitation that I Dont know how to write," Jane once apologized.) I was pregnant again. ("Benjamin Mecom Born on Fryday the 29 of December 1732.") I was so tired. ("My litle wons are Interupting me Every miniut.") I was pregnant again. ("Ebenezer Mecom Born on May the 2 1735.") I felt rebuked, even by Jane herself. ("I was almost Tempted to think you had forgot me but I check those thoughts with the consideration of the dificulties you must labour under.") I hadn't forgotten her. I just couldn't bear to think about her, trapped in that house.

But Benjamin Franklin: I adored him. He was funny and brilliant and generous and fortunate. Every year of his life, his world got bigger. So did mine. When he had something to say, he said it. So did I.

My mother and I had got tangled up, like skeins. I wasn't the one who identified with Jane.

THE MORE I THOUGHT ABOUT JANE, the sadder it got. I tried to picture it. Her belly swelled, and emptied, and swelled again. Her breasts filled, and emptied, and filled again. Her days were days of flesh: the little legs and little arms, the little hands, clutched around her neck, the softness. A baby in her arms, she stared into kettles and tubs, swaying. The days passed to months, the months to years, and, in her Book of Ages, she pressed her children between the pages.

Her husband fell into debt. He may have gone mad. (Two of her sons became violently insane; they had to be locked up.) Jane and her children lived with her parents; she nursed them, in their old age. Josiah Franklin died in 1744. He was eighty-seven. In his will, he had divided his estate among his surviving children. Benjamin Franklin refused his portion: he gave it to Jane.

In 1751, Jane gave birth for the twelfth time. She was thirty-nine. She'd named her first baby for her father; she named this baby, her last, for her mother, Abiah Franklin:

Abiah mecom born augst 1st 1751.

The month Abiah Mecom was born, Benjamin Franklin took a seat in the Pennsylvania Assembly. His eighty-four-year-old mother wrote him a letter, with her daughter at her side. "I am very weeke and short bretht so that I Cant set to rite much," Abiah Franklin explained. She asked her daughter to write for her. Aside from Jane's Book of Ages, and notes she made in books she read, this is the only writing in her hand to survive, for the first four decades of her life:

P S Mother says she an't able and so I must tell you my self that I rejoyce with you and bles god for you in all your prosperity and doubt not but you will be grater blessings to the world as he bestows upon you grater honers.
J M

Mother says she an't able and so I must. They'd got tangled, too.

Jane's baby, Abiah Mecom, died within the year. So did Abiah Franklin:

my dear Mother Died May 8 1752.

She loved her; she washed her. She buried her. But it was Benjamin Franklin who paid for a gravestone, and wrote an epitaph:

JOSIAH FRANKLIN
AND ABIAH HIS WIFE
LIE HERE INTERRED.
THEY LIVED LOVINGLY TOGETHER IN WEDLOCK
FIFTY-FIVE YEARS.
. . . .
FROM THIS INSTANCE, READER,
BE ENCOURAGED TO DILIGENCE IN THY CALLING,
AND DISTRUST NOT PROVIDENCE.
HE WAS A PIOUS & PRUDENT MAN,
SHE A DISCREET AND VIRTUOUS WOMAN.
THEIR YOUNGEST SON,
IN FILIAL REGARD TO THEIR MEMORY,
PLACES THIS STONE.

This book of remembrance was a monument, not to his parents but to Franklin himself: prodigal son.

"DO THE RIGHT THING WITH SPIRIT," Jane once wrote. It's just the kind of thing my mother liked to say. One of Jane's sons became a printer. He once printed a poem called "The Prodigal Daughter": "She from her Mother in a Passion went, / Filling her aged Heart with Discontent."

My mother's heart began to fail. She had one heart attack, and then another. Surgery, and more surgery. Eventually, she had a defibrillator implanted in her chest. I'd visit her in the hospital; she'd send me away. All I wanted was to be there, with her, but that only made her remember going home to watch her mother die. "See? I'm fine," she'd say. "Now. Please: go. You have things to do."

I decided I had better read whatever of Jane's letters had survived. The first is one she wrote in 1758, when she was forty-five years old, to Franklin's wife, Deborah. This is her voice, gabby, frank, and vexed:

Dear Sister

for so I must call you come what will & If I dont Express my self proper you must Excuse it seeing I have not been acostomed to Pay my Complements to Governer & Baronets Ladys I am in the midst of a grate wash & Sarah still sick, & would gladly been Excused writing this Post but my husband says I must write & Give you Joy which we searly Joyn in; I sopose it will not be news to you, but I will tell you how I came by it, Mr Fluker Tould Cousen Williams & he Docter Perkins who Brought it to my Poor Son nedey who has a nother Relaps into Raising Blood & has not Done won stroke of work this month but was Just a going to begin when he was again taken Ill pray Pardon my Bad writing & confused composure & acept it as coming from your Ladyships affectionat Sister & most obedent

    Humble Servant

    Jane Mecom

She was in the middle of a great wash. One of her lodgers, Sarah, was ailing. Her poor son Edward (Neddy), who was married and a father, was sick again—weak and listless and coughing blood. But she had heard from Neddy, who heard it from her doctor, John Perkins, who heard it from Jonathan Williams Sr., the husband of Jane's friend Grace, who heard it from a Boston merchant, Thomas Flucker, that Benjamin Franklin had been given a baronetcy. Jane's husband told her she must send her congratulations, "searly"—surely. She was miffed. If this ridiculous rumor was true, why, for heaven's sake, was she the last to know about it?

"Your loving Sister," or "Your affectionate Sister," is how Jane usually signed off—not "your Ladyships affectionat Sister & most obedient Humble Servant." That was a jab. Must she curtsey?

By words on a page, she wanted to be carried away—out of her house, out of Boston, out into the world. The more details the better. "The Sow has Piged," a friend reported from Rhode Island, reminding her, "You told me to write you all." She loved gossip. "Cousen willames Looks soon to Lyin," she told Deborah, "she is so big I tell

Her she will have two." She once scolded her niece for writing letters that she found insufficiently chatty. "I want to know a Thousand litle Perticulars about your self yr Husband & the children such as your mother used to write me," Jane commanded, adding, "it would be Next to Seeing the little things to hear some of there Prattle (Speaches If you Pleas) & have you Describe there persons & actions tell me who they Look like." Stories, likenesses, characters: speeches.

MY MOTHER WASN'T MUCH of a letter writer. If she telephoned, she would yell, "This is your mother calling!" My sisters and my brother and I got her an iPad for her birthday. "If you call here keep talking as it takes us time to get to the phone," she emailed me. She had a cell phone, for emergencies; she brought it with her when she had to go to the hospital. Once, she was kept waiting on a gurney, in a hallway, for hours.

"This is your mother calling!"

"I know, Mom. Why haven't they gotten you a room?"

"Oh, I don't mind," she said. "The people here in the hallway are just *fascinating*." She was giggling.

"Mom. Did they give you something for the pain?"

"Oh, yes, it's wonderful."

"The people are interesting?"

"Oh, yes. It's like a soap opera here."

JANE, WRITING TO HER BROTHER, worried that she had spelled so badly, and expressed herself so poorly—"my Blundering way of Expresing my self," she called it—that he wouldn't be able to understand what she meant to say. "I know I have wrote and speld this worse than I do sometimes," she wrote him, "but I hope you will find it out."

To "find out" a letter was to decipher it, to turn writing back into speech. Jane knew that letters weren't supposed to be speeches written down; they were supposed to be more formal. Her brother warned her that she was too free with him. "You Long ago convinced me that there is many things Proper to convers with a Friend about that is not Proper to write," she confessed. But, then, he scolded her, too, for not being free enough. "I was allways too Difident," she said he had told her.

"Dont let it mortifie you that such a Scraw came from your Sister," she begged him.

"Is there not a little Affectation in your Apology for the Incorrectness of your Writing?" he teased her. "Perhaps it is rather fishing for Commendation. You write better, in my Opinion, than most American Women."

This was, miserably, true.

IT WAS THE DIFFIDENCE that got to me. Female demurral isn't charming. It's maddening. Half the time, I wanted to throttle her. Could she ever, would she never, express a political opinion?

I read on. And then, in the 1760s, a decade of riots, protests, and boycotts, something changed. Jane's whole family was sick. Her daughter Sally died; Jane took in Sally's four young children; then two of them died, only to be followed by Jane's husband and, not long after, by Jane's favorite daughter. "The Lord Giveth & the Lord taketh away," she wrote in her Book of Ages. "Oh may I never be so Rebelious as to Refuse Acquiesing & & saying from my hart Blessed be the Name of the Lord." And then: she put down her pen. She never wrote in her Book of Ages again.

"Realy my Spirits are so much Broken with this Last Hevey Stroak of Provedenc that I am not capeble of Expresing my self," she wrote to her brother. She did not think she could bear it. In the depth of her despair, she began to question Providence. Maybe her sons had failed not for lack of merit but because they were unable to overcome the disadvantage of an unsteadiness inherited from their father. Maybe her daughters and grandchildren had died because they were poor, and lived lives of squalor. Maybe not Providence but men in power—politics—determined the course of human events.

She wrote to her brother. She wanted to read "all the political Pieces" he had ever written. Could he please send them to her?

"I could as easily make a Collection for you of all the past Parings of my Nails," he wrote back. He sent what he could. She read, and I read.

She left home in 1775, after the battles of Lexington and Concord, when the British occupied Boston. For a while, she lived with her brother in Philadelphia. After he left for France, she spent the war as a fugitive. "I am Grown such a Vagrant," she wrote him. When peace came—after he helped negotiate it—he returned to Philadelphia, and she to Boston.

He gave her a house in the North End. She loved it. "I have this Spring been new planking the yard," she one day boasted, and "am Painting the Front of the House to make it look Decent that I may not be Ashamed when any Boddy Inquiers for Dr Franklins Sister."

She knew, for the first time, contentment. Except that she was starved for company. "I Injoy all the Agreable conversation I can come at Properly," she wrote to her brother, "but I find Litle, very Litle, Equal to that I have a Right to by Nature but am deprived of by Provedence."

It was a shocking thing to say: that she had a right to intelligent conversation—a natural right—but that Providence had deprived her of it. Before the war, she had favored independence from Britain. After it, she found her own kind of freedom. Once she started writing down her opinions, she could scarcely stop.

"I can not find in my Hart to be Pleasd at your Accepting the Government of the State and Therefore have not congratulated you on it," she wrote to her brother in 1786, when he accepted yet another political appointment. "I fear it will Fatigue you two much."

"We have all of us Wisdom enough to judge what others ought to do, or not to do in the Management of their Affairs," he wrote back. "Tis possible I might blame you as much if you were to accept the Offer of a young Husband."

She let that pass. "I have two favours to Ask of you," she begged him: "your New Alphabet of the English Language, and the Petition of the Letter Z."

"My new Alphabet is in a printed Book of my Pieces, which I will send you the first Opportunity I have," he answered. "The Petition of Z is inclos'd."

In "The Petition of the Letter Z," a satire about inequality, Z complains "That he is not only plac'd at the Tail of the Alphabet, when he had as much Right as any other to be at the Head but is, by the Injustice of his Enemies totally excluded from the Word WISE, and his Place injuriously filled by a little, hissing, crooked, serpentine, venomous Letter called S." In another essay, Franklin proposed a new alphabet. Jane found it cunning, especially since, as she explained, "I am but won of the Thousands & thousands, that write on to old Age and cant Learn."

"You need not be concern'd in writing to me about your bad Spelling," he wrote back, "for in my Opinion as our Alphabet now Stands, the bad Spelling, or what is call'd so, is generally the best." To illustrate, he told her a story: A gentleman receives a note that reads, "Not finding Brown at hom, I delivered your Meseg to his yf." When both the gentleman and his wife are unable to decipher the note, they consult their chambermaid, Betty. "Why, says she, y. f spells Wife, what else can it spell?"

Jane loved that. "I think Sir & madam were deficient in Sagasity that they could not find out y f as well as Bety," she wrote her brother, "but some times the Betys has the Brightst understanding."

"HOW'S THAT BOOK ABOUT Jane Franklin coming along?" my mother asked, every time I took her out. (We'd go to art museums, mostly. I'd race her around, in a wheelchair.) "Better," I said.

When Jane was seventy-four, she read a book called *Four Dissertations*, written by Richard Price, a Welsh clergyman and political radical. The first dissertation was called "On Providence." One objection to the idea that everything in life is fated by Providence, Price wrote, is the failure to thrive: "Many perish in the womb," and even more "are nipped in their bloom." An elm produces three hundred and thirty thousand seeds a year, but very few of those seeds ever grow into trees. A spider lays as many as six hundred eggs, and yet very few grow into spiders. So, too, for humans: "Thousands of Boyles, Clarks and Newtons have probably been lost to the world, and lived and died in ignorance and meanness, merely for want of being placed in favourable situations, and enjoying proper advantages." No one dies for naught, Price believed, but that doesn't mean suffering is fair, or can't be protested.

At her desk, with Price's *Four Dissertations* pressed open, Jane wrote a letter to her brother. "Dr Price thinks Thousand of Boyles Clarks and Newtons have Probably been lost to the world," she wrote. To this, she added an opinion of her own: "very few we know is Able to beat thro all Impediments and Arive to any Grat Degre of superiority in Understanding."

Benjamin Franklin knew, and his sister knew, that very few ever beat through. Three hundred thousand seeds to make one elm. Six hundred eggs to make one spider. Of seventeen children of Josiah Franklin, how many? Very few. Nearly none. Only one. Or, possibly: two.

BENJAMIN FRANKLIN DIED IN 1790. He was eighty-four. Jane died four years later. She was eighty-three. If she ever had a gravestone, it's long since sunken underground. She believed in one truth, above all: "The most Insignificant creature on Earth may be made some use of in the scale of Beings."

It wasn't until last year, sitting by my father in a room in intensive care in a hospital in the town where he'd been born eighty-seven years before, that I realized I had waited too long to write the only book my mother ever wanted me to write. From this Instance, Reader, Be encouraged to Diligence in thy Calling.

We buried my father. My mother ordered a single gravestone, engraved with both their names. I wrote as fast as I could. Meanwhile, I read my mother letters and told my mother stories. In a museum, I found a mourning ring Jane had owned; I told my mother about how, when no one was looking, I'd tried it on. (I didn't tell her that it didn't fit, and that I'd found this an incredible relief.) In a library not a dozen miles from Franklin Street, I found a long-lost portrait of Jane's favorite granddaughter: another Jenny, age nine. I brought my mother a photograph. She looked, for a long time, into that little girl's eyes. "She's beautiful," she said. She smiled. "I'm so glad you found her."

"That mother of yours," my father used to say, shaking his head, besotted. He knew he could never live without her. I never knew— never saw, never in the least suspected—that she couldn't live without him, either. But after his death, she didn't last out the year. She died at home, unexpectedly, and alone. She kept her paintbrushes in glass jars in my old bedroom. She was eighty-five.

I finished the last revisions. Too late for her to read it. I wrote the dedication.

Their youngest daughter. In filial regard. Places this stone.

—2013

THE DEADLINE

T HE PIPING ON THE RED SNOWSUIT WAS YELLOW, and on the green snowsuit it was blue: fire-engine red, sunflower yellow, summer-grass green, deep-ocean blue, the palette of preschool, the colors in a set of finger paints. I loved everything about those mail order snowsuits—the snap-off hoods, the ribbed cuffs—but I especially loved the piping, which ran, as thick as a pipe cleaner, across the yoke of each jacket and down each leg of the pants, like the stripes of a military uniform. Just what I'd have done if I'd sewn them myself. It made the boys look like soldiers from different regiments. The red-and-yellow brigade of the two-year-olds, the green-and-blue brigade of the four-year-olds. I still dream about them—the snowsuits, the little boys.

I sewed my first son his first snowsuit when I was pregnant with him, in the middle of a hard and terrible winter, the ramp-up to Y2K, the much anticipated end of the world. He wasn't due till the very beginning of April; it would be spring by then, thawed, even blooming. Still, wouldn't he be cold? He was coming out of me: didn't he need something to go into? I bought a yard of Kermit-green fleece and a matching zipper, and I stitched for him that sort of star-shaped sack Maggie Simpson wears. (Most of my ideas about parenting came from Marge, fretting beneath her blue beehive.) The zipper ran from the left foot to the right shoulder. I sewed on little flaps for his tiny hands to be tucked into, like letters into envelopes. I tried the snowsuit out on a stuffed bear the brown of the bark of a sugar maple. We named the bear Elly, for Eleanor Roosevelt, and I carried her around the house in her new fleece suit, practicing.

The doctors had to unzip the baby out of me. I couldn't push. Maybe I didn't want to, I don't know, I don't remember. When I was trying to deliver him, my best friend, Jane, was on her deathbed, more than a hundred miles away. We were historians, counters of years, markers of time, so in 2019, twenty years since that day, day of birth, day of death, I opened her computer, to honor the anniversary. We'd bought our first laptops together when we were in graduate school. It had taken her forever to pick out hers. No one hated change more. She dreaded disappointment like a disease. She was also superstitious: she hated jinxing anything with her own expectations. She spent eight months deciding on what kind of a phone to buy when her old one broke—not a smartphone, not a cell phone, mind you; this was a mere landline telephone—and when she got sick we were working on the three-year-long decision of whether or not she should get a dog. Her own decisions paralyzed her, but she was immediate and fierce with her advice to me, which never varied: my chapter drafts were always good, my haircuts always horrible.

A Macintosh PowerBook 160: she'd left it to me in her will, along with her books, but it had sat, plastic and inert, a thwarted life of the mind, her mind, a mind that I crammed into a box and stored in the back of the cupboard where I keep my fabric, yards of cambric and calico and gingham. Twenty years later, to the day, I yanked it out of the cupboard and hauled it out of the box. I plugged in a power cord attached to an adapter the size of a pound cake, but when I pried open the laptop sharp bits of steel-gray plastic broke off like chipped teeth, and the hinges cracked, and the screen fell away from the keyboard and dangled, like a mostly decapitated head, the Anne Boleyn of Apples. I propped the screen up against the wall and pressed the power button. It made that noise, the chime of Steve Jobs's doorbell, but nothing happened, so I pressed a bunch of keys and fussed with some parts that seemed to move, and I cursed, until my fourteen-year-old figured out that I had set the brightness to black. He fixed that, and the screen blinked at me, as if blinded by its own light, and then a square Macintosh computer face turned into a thick black arrow pointing at her hard drive, which, I discovered, she'd named Cooper, for my old dog, a lame yellow Lab, long since dead and buried.

All historians are coroners. I began my inquest. I hunted around this tiny-screen world of black and white, poking at the membrane of her brain. I clicked on a folder named "personal" and opened a file called "transitions notes." Microsoft Word version 5.1a 1992 popped up, copyrighted to the kid in graduate school we'd pirated our software from; she'd never updated hers. "Transitions" turned out to be notes she'd taken on a book published in 1980 called *Transitions: Making Sense of Life's Changes*, by William Bridges, who'd started out as a professor of American literature, a scholar of transcendentalism. She was always falling for this stuff, stuff I hated. The endless therapy, the what-color-is-your-parachute quizzes, the courage-to-heal to-do lists, the lifelong self-examination, the bottomless well. Bridges ended up a management consultant, an adviser to CEOs engaged in downsizing. Transitions? Joblessness. "Jane, that stuff is crap," I'd say, and she'd smile, and shrug, and go back to her book, Oprah for intellectuals, Freud for feminists, mother yourself, the latest claptrap.

I blinked. "Endings are like little deaths," she'd written in her notes on the Bridges book. "We forget that they can be entrances to the beginning of a new life." The computer began to bleat, a rumble of distress. The screen flickered, blindingly white, and then faded to black, and so, it embarrasses me to say, did I.

THE ONE TIME I LOST A BABY, I was alone, in a bathroom. I hadn't even known I was pregnant. I remember the color of the linoleum on the floor where I fell, beige, and the pattern, veined, and then the blood, and the tissue, a swirl of red and white: red-wine red, egg-white white. I remember the pain and the cold, I was so cold, and the membrane, diaphanous and wet, and the first convulsion of grief, and the second. I don't remember the rest.

I do remember that Jane took care of me afterward. When I got married, Jane stayed with us in a two-story cottage on an island. On the morning of the wedding, as everyone was getting dressed, a near-hurricane hit. The iron garden furniture flew away. Upstairs, one of the skylights blew open and the rain came pouring in, onto the wedding dress I'd sewn from a bargain bolt, brocade. Jane had just come out of the shower, but she reached up and pulled the skylight shut with one outstretched arm while, with the other, she held up her towel. "I'm the Statue of Liberty!" she screamed over the howl of the wind.

We met the first week of graduate school, when I gave her a ride home from a department picnic and she tested my knowledge of music, a test I failed. She was the sort of person who could draw anyone out, talk about anything, and forgive everything except pretension and pettiness. She was almost immoderately charming; she was irresistible. Go to a restaurant with her, and in five minutes she'd find out where the waitress had gone to high school. Go again, and she'd remember the name of that high school, and would pick up the conversation exactly where it had left off. Stop to get your dry cleaning with her only to discover that she knew the names of all the dry cleaner's children and the titles of their favorite picture books, and that she'd brought along another book, as a gift. She was dauntingly brilliant and she knew when to speak up, and who for. She had as many bad girlfriends as I had bad boyfriends. She loved to eat out and hated to eat in, and if she had you over for dinner she made you pasta with tomatoes, basil, and feta. She had an opinion on any movie. She had a crush on John Cusack. She loved to run. She drank coffee at any hour. She adored Jane Smiley. She was terrible at tennis. She had thick, curly dark-brown hair and very silly eyebrows and beautiful brown eyes, and she wore glasses that she called Official DC Congressional Intern Eyewear—round, wire-framed—and she'd had them since the 1980s, when they were a thing, but she was too attached to them to give them up. She was possibly the funniest person I ever met.

Jane knew everyone; I really only knew Jane. She was older; I was hungrier. "I trust her with almost everything," she'd typed about me into her computer, but there wasn't much else about me there, which was a relief. For most of the time I knew her, in the 1990s of Bill Clinton and Catharine MacKinnon, liberalism gone wrong, feminism gone bonkers, we talked on the telephone maybe half a dozen times a day, like ladies in a 1970s sitcom, Mary and Rhoda, Maude and Vivian. We discussed lunch: tuna fish or egg salad? We talked about what we were reading: Martin Amis, Zora Neale Hurston. We compared the soundtracks of our days: Richard Thompson, Emmylou Harris. We analyzed people. "He's a good egg," she'd always say about someone she liked. We talked about politics, elections, the war, all wars (I was writing about war), my dog, her cat, AIDS, Anita Hill. There wasn't much need to write to each other, although we once spent ages composing and revising a forty-word ad that she was determined to post in the back pages of a newspaper. It's still lurking in her computer:

Big-hearted cynic w/spiritual leanings & roving intellect
GWF, 36, Loves E. Dickinson, yoga, music, & my *New York Times.*
Passionate, smart, and seriously funny, with a soft spot for kids and
four-legged friends. Seeking similar, for friendship, maybe more.

Seeking similar, for friendship.

She tried Zoloft. She tried yoga. She kept the rain off me but it
always fell on her. All I could do was write; writing was what she
could not do. The year I finished my dissertation, she left graduate
school and spent a year at an ashram. "It's as if I am looking at my
work through the wrong end of binoculars," she wrote to me, after
we started emailing. I found on Cooper the hard drive a file called
"future visions," from 1995, a picture of what she imagined for herself in two years' time: "Clearly arrived somewhere, or at the very
least, well on the path to getting there." She wanted to finish her
dissertation. She wanted to become a writer. She wanted to have
children.

How do you do it? people sometimes ask me, people often ask me,
people always ask me. And why: Why the books? Why the babies?
Why the essays? Why so many, why so fast? What's the rush? Where's
the fire? Jane is the how, the why, the rush, and the fire. She never got
to do any of the things we both wanted. Only I did.

I found a file of commonplaces, her favorite thoughts typed out in
one long poem. Virginia Woolf: "Wander no more, I say; this is the
end." T. S. Eliot: "I said to my soul, be still." By 1997, when she hoped
to have arrived somewhere or, at the very least, to be on the path to
getting there, she hadn't. She'd fallen into another depression. "I can't
imagine spending my life fighting this," she emailed me. And, as it
turned out, she didn't have to.

A folder labeled "cancer stuff" contained a file called "treatment
options," with this list: cord-blood transplantation; mixed chimeric/
mini-transplant—Cytoxan up front, ATG, radiation to the thymus;
chemotherapy—azacitidine; full mismatched related transplant—full-
body radiation, course of idarubicin/Ara-C preparatory to infusion of
donor cells; haplo-identical transplant, T-cell depleted, full course of
chemo and radiation. Those were her very rotten choices.

She'd found out she had leukemia right about when I started trying to get pregnant. Her cells divided. My cells divided. Our selves divided. I'd taken her to the ER, that very first night, when she felt woozy, really woozy, scary woozy, but, even as she lay in a bed beneath a blanket made of paper, shrinking, she'd ended up engaging the doctor on call in a midnight analysis of the comparative narrative strategies of Quentin Tarantino and Spike Lee, and wondered whether they knew some of the same people in Tenafly, New Jersey; did he have cousins there? I was with her through terrifying treatments, each new unavailing misery. And she was with me through ultrasounds and feeling the baby's first kicks, each new impossible joy. She wrote to her doctors in August of 1998, when I was in my first trimester, and she was considering an experimental bone-marrow transplant, "How is 'success' defined? Is it simply living through the procedure?"

She lived through it. But living through it was not the definition of success. When she was sure she could not survive, when her doctors had given up, she decided to refuse to die until my baby came; she would wait to meet him, and only then would she let go. She wanted to wave to him on some kind of existential highway, driving in opposite lanes. It was like a game of chicken. Due date, death date—it gave a whole new meaning to the word "deadline." She tacked to her corkboard a passage from Edith Wharton's *Backward Glance*: "In spite of illness, in spite even of the arch-enemy sorrow, one can remain alive long past the usual date of disintegration if one is unafraid of change, insatiable in intellectual curiosity, interested in big things, and happy in small ways." But that, Jane, that is crap.

This resolution brought her unbearable pain, and it broke me. If I'm honest, the resolution wasn't entirely hers. I think I must have asked her not to die before the baby came. I probably begged her. I don't know, I don't remember. The whole year is a near-blackout, except that I remember how each day carried my baby closer to life and her closer to death. *I put her through this, I put her through this.* I sank to my knees under the weight. But she's the one who suffered for it, was flattened by it, flayed and tormented by it. After a bone marrow transplant from her sister failed, she left the hospital and went to live at our friend Denise's house, or, not to live there but to die there. On April 1, 1999, at a Passover Seder, Jane ate a bite of the matzo and the *maror*, the bitter herbs, the bread of life and the bitterness of affliction. The next day, she could no longer speak in sentences. "She tried and was frantic at first and what came out were words that almost made sense," Denise told me. My contractions had started. I went to the hospital. And I tried as hard as I could to push, but it felt as though I were pulling Jane to her death. Mainly, I screamed. They unzipped him out of me and sewed me up. Friends took a picture of the baby the minute he came out, a Polaroid, it slipped out of the camera like a tongue from a mouth, and then they ran down the hall and out into the parking garage and drove that hundred miles, childbed to deathbed. They showed Jane the photograph—she couldn't really see by that point, but Denise says she knew, she knew, she saw, she knew, she heard, she smiled—and then she died. She knew, she heard, she knew. Did she know? I don't know.

TWENTY YEARS AGO, I put my baby in his Kermit fleece and carried him out of the hospital. No one knows how these things will strike you, before they come to you, and I'd never taken care of a baby before, but I loved everything about it, everything about him. "When can we have another one?" is the first question I asked my doctor. I'd won a prize for my first book, a book about war. I didn't go to the award ceremony. I could not leave my baby. People were very mad at me: Why wasn't I more grateful? I went to Jane's memorial service instead, and delivered the eulogy, with my little frog.

The feminism of writers who are mothers is a fetish, but the motherhood of scholars is forbidden. When my son was four months old, I tried going to a conference. I missed him too much. I made a rule: no more conferences. People were very mad at me: Didn't I take my professional responsibilities seriously? I got an email from a fellow scholar who accused me of being an intellectual manqué. Didn't I want to get out there, hobnob, curry favor, court support, mix it up, do battle, become a gladiator? I did not. I got pregnant again and I dragged myself through the writing of a second book, figuring that either I'd get tenure or I'd quit. Jane would understand. I wrote in my acknowledgments about my oldest son, ridiculously, and regretted it when a reviewer mocked me. I adopted two new rules: never again read a review, and never show your colleagues your soft belly, ever.

I got tenure. Jane used to slouch around in a big black parka in the winter, with mittens I'd knitted for her, going on about her unfinished dissertation. She'd walk like Groucho Marx and slap her mittens together, with mock resolve. "I'm going to write a chapter this week!" she'd announce, never meaning it. She loved nothing more than a baby. I missed her like crazy.

I stitched quilts for my boys, Bear's Paw, North Wind. I bought them those piped snowsuits, the red-and-yellow one and the green-and-blue one, and knit them matching hats and mittens. I pushed them all over the city in their double stroller, their snow boots kicking out from under crocheted baby blankets, and I'd tell them stories about Jane. I pictured her scooping them into her arms. "She'd have eaten you up like English muffins," I told them.

When it was too cold and blustery to walk them to their day care center in the stroller, even with the snowsuits and the blankets, we had to drive the car. I'd pack their snow pants in a canvas bag, bring that to the driveway, and then carry the boys out, one in each arm, and buckle them into their seats, and we'd pretend they were astronauts. Once, after I backed out and started driving down the street, the car staggered, and I thought it was stuck on ice and snow. Then the rear of the car started smoking. I pulled to the side of the road. I'd run over the canvas bag; it was trapped in a tire well and was burning. I tugged it out and smothered it with snow. And then I collapsed sobbing on the sidewalk, staring at the red and the yellow and the green and the blue, turned black, as if the children themselves had been in a terrible accident, the piping broken open and white as bone.

I went to California to find out about a job in a place with no snow. I was writing a book about slavery. A professor whose work Jane and I had read together in a graduate seminar arranged for me to meet him at his apartment, because he wanted to show me his collection of rare books. "He's a bad egg," Jane had said, long ago, but I'd forgotten why. He showed me his inscribed first edition of *My Bondage and My Freedom* and told me he knew all about the size of Frederick Douglass's penis and the smallness of the vaginas of the white women with whom he had affairs. "Picture it," he said, stroking the spine of the book as he moved closer, pressing himself against me. I later learned that he'd been banned from campus. I felt sorry for him, in his sad, lonely apartment with his beautiful books and his grubby wretch of a self, or else I would've decked him. I decided against California.

I took a different job and moved into a house closer to preschool, so we could always walk, and never have to take the car again. I finished the book. I had another baby. Book, baby, book, baby, book, baby—another rule. I stitched another quilt. I started writing essays. I wrote about everything I thought Jane might ever have wanted to, but never did, never could, never would. I read books at Little League games. I wrote at the kitchen table, among piles of homework. I once went over a piece with a fact-checker, wearing headphones and hollering above the sound of street traffic, while riding to soccer practice on a tandem bicycle with a ten-year-old boy behind me who punched me in the back after the fact-checker asked me about the shape of an anatomical paperweight on a desk in a Planned Parenthood clinic and I shouted, "No, it wasn't a vulva. It was a uterus. What? No. It was a *uterus!*"

I suffered only for being so blessed, and for my cowardice. I dodged fights, I held my tongue, I minded my rules. Do the work. Deliver on deadline. Don't sweat the nonsense; you're not dead. I kept Jane's picture on my desk. Once, when I was walking home with a new baby strapped to my chest, my oldest son holding my hand and their brother squirming in a stroller whose underbelly was crammed with lunchboxes and library books, I ran into a colleague I adored. "Hey, how are you?" I asked. "So busy," he said, shaking his head importantly. "So much to juggle." He rushed past. I waved goodbye.

That baby never took a bottle. When he was a newborn, he nursed every forty-five minutes. Once, even though I was on maternity leave, I agreed to go to a meeting with a university president, because he'd asked for my opinion about something important. "Please let him know that I have to leave after forty minutes," I told his secretary. "*Or else I will leak,*" I whispered. He arrived twenty minutes late and started talking, holding forth, and when he didn't stop I finally interrupted him, reminded him that I had to leave, and offered my dissent.

"Professor Lepore, few people have the audacity to interrupt me," he said, "and fewer still have the temerity to do so in order to disagree with me."

I decided to stop hiding my soft belly. Fuck it.

TEN YEARS AFTER JANE'S DEATH, the beginning of the age of Obama, we had a big birthday party. Ten candles, cowboy hats and popguns. The next day, I went to the library where I'd deposited her papers. I opened up the archival box, expecting to find her. She wasn't in there. I flew to Michigan to interview a man who freezes the dead. He couldn't let go of people, either. For a long time, I wore her old, too-big shoes. I'd borrowed her gumption. It got as thin as a slipper. It's got thinner since.

Another ten years passed. Twenty years: a generation. The boys don't wear mittens anymore. Their feet are much bigger than mine, even bigger than Jane's. But I still miss their baby feet, and their patter, and the piffle of childhood. I reel at a baby's cry. I swoon at strollers. I don't understand why all the love songs aren't about babies. I wrote a very long book, a debt paid. I am tired of writing books. The books had always been for Jane. She heard, she knew. Did she know?

When my mother was the age I am now, and her children had grown up, she decided to clean the house, purging it of everything no longer needed: the cots in the attic, the board games in the basement. Somehow, she managed to cart to the dump an old coat box filled with the baby books she'd painstakingly kept, each book jacketed in a different shade of pastel, each page a clutter of annotations and photographs and locks of hair finer than thread. She'd thrown away the record of our childhood. She never forgave herself. But I'm not so sure it was an accident. My mother had been ambivalent about motherhood in a way that I never have been. It had confined her. It had saved me.

My friend Jane, bighearted cynic with spiritual leanings and roving intellect, loved ideas and books, and she loved babies, but she had a particular weakness for teenagers. Her mother died when she was sixteen, and she loved to watch people grow up and get past that age, and become stronger and better and wiser and glow bright and soar, like an Apollo rocket, to the moon and stars. Me, I have never understood what can possibly come next, here on earth. Why aren't all the sad songs about children leaving home? I keep a box of my sons' little knitted sweaters, cable, Argyle, zippered and buttoned, sunflower yellow, fire-engine red, in the closet where I've decided to stow Jane's computer, black and white and gray and mute and dead. It will not power on in the year 2029. *Wander no more, I say; this is the end.*

—2019

EASY RIDER

M Y FIRST BICYCLE WAS NOT, IN FACT, A BICYCLE. I rode it in 1968, when I was two years old and as tubby as a bear cub. It had four wheels, not two, and no pedals: strictly speaking, it was a scooter. But Playskool called it a Tyke Bike, so I say it qualifies, and aside from the matte-black, aluminum-alloy number that I've got now, which is called (by the manufacturer dead seriously, and by me aspirationally) the Bad Boy, the Tyke Bike may be the swankiest bicycle I've ever ridden. According to the box, Playskool's scooter—red and blue and white, with a yellow, leopard-spotted wooden seat, chrome handlebars, and black, white-walled wheels—offered "smart high style" for the "preschool jet set," as if a little girl in a diaper and a romper were about to scoot along the jetway to board a TWA flight bound for Zurich.

Before being handed down to me, my Tyke Bike, like most of the bicycles in my life, had belonged to my brother, Jack, and to both of my sisters, and, earlier still, to cousins or neighbors or some other family from Our Lady of Good Counsel, whose annual parish sale was where we always got our best stuff, bless the Virgin Mary. By the time I got the Tyke Bike, the paint was scuffed, the leopard spots had worn off, and the white plastic handlebar grips had been yanked off and lost, most likely buried in the back yard by the slobber-jawed neighborhood St. Bernard, a Christmas-present puppy whose name was Jingles and who was eventually run over by a car, like so many dogs on our street, which is another reason more people should ride bikes. I didn't mind about the missing handlebar grips. I tucked a stuffed bear into my red wagon, tied its rope to my seat post, and scooted down the sidewalk, dragging the wagon behind me, my first bike hack. Far from being a jet-setter, I have always been an unhurried bicyclist, something between deliberate and fretful. Jack, a speed demon and a danger mouse, but above all a gentleman, would wait for me at every telephone pole. *Jack and Jill went up the hill*, everyone would call out, as we wheeled past. *Phffttttt*, we'd raspberry back.

My current bicycle, the Cannondale Bad Boy, is said to be cloaked in "urban armor," looks as though it could fight in a regime-changing war, and is built for "traffic-slaying performance." I like the idea of being redoubtable on a roundabout, Mad Max on a mews, but, in truth, I have never slain any traffic. I have never slain anything. I once knew an old Polish man who called all drivers one of three things—"Cowboy!" "Old Woman!" "Teenager!"—which he'd shout out, raging, behind the steering wheel of his station wagon, in a heavily accented growl. I am, and have always been, Old Woman.

The Bad Boy is the only bike I've ever bought new. I paid an embarrassing amount of money for it in 2001, to celebrate getting tenure and maybe with the idea that I was finally going to be a badass, that all I needed was this James Dean mean-streets city bike. But the minute I got it home, I started hacking it, girling it out. I bolted a radio to the handlebars and listened to the news on my ride to work every day—I heard the war on terror unfold on that bicycle—until my friend Bruce told me I'd be exactly 74 percent happier if I listened to music instead. WERS. College radio. Indigo Girls. Dixie Chicks. He was right. For a long time, I had a baby seat strapped onto a rack in the back, molded gray plastic with a blue foam cushion seat and a nylon seat belt. Babies, not to say bad boys, would fall asleep back there, their nodding heads tipped over by the great weight of baby helmets covered in the spikes of a stegosaurus, poking into my back. I steered around potholes, ever so slowly, so as not to jolt them awake. Old Woman.

BICYCLES ARE THE WORKHORSES of the world's transportation system. More people get places by bicycle than by any other means, unless you count walking, which is also good for you, and for the planet, but you can travel four times faster on a bicycle than on foot, using only a fifth the exertion. People all over the world, and especially outside Western Europe and North America, get to school and work, transport goods, cart passengers, and even plow fields with bicycles. In many places, there isn't any other choice. Bikes are cheap, and easy to fix when they break, especially if you can keep track of your Allen keys and your tire levers. Mine are on the breakfast table, because, at the moment, I have a bike stand in the kitchen. For every car on earth, there are two bikes, one for every four people. (I refuse to count stationary bikes, including Pelotons, since they go nowhere.) "We live on a bicycle planet," Jody Rosen writes in *Two Wheels Good: The History and Mystery of the Bicycle*, a set of quirky and kaleidoscopic stories. But roads and parking lots and entire cities are still being built for cars, even though they're wrecking the world. Or, as bicycle advocates would have it, riffing on Orwell's *Animal Farm*, two wheels good, four wheels bad. Two wheels are better than two wings. In a contest of humans against all other animals in the efficiency of locomotion, humans on foot are about as ungainly, or gainly, as sheep. Condors come in first. But humans on bicycles beat even birds.

A few years back, the bicentennial of the bicycle wheeled past at breakneck, bike-messenger speed. In 1817, Baron Karl von Drais, the Master of the Woods and Forests to the Duke of Baden, invented a contraption called the *Laufmaschine*, or running machine. A climate crisis had led to a great dying off of livestock, including horses, especially in Germany. Drais meant for the *Laufmaschine* to be a substitute for the horse. It had a wooden frame, a leather saddle, two in-line wheels, and no pedals; you sort of scooted around on it, and a full-grown man could pick up pretty good speed. ("On descent it equals a horse at full speed," Drais wrote.) In England, *Laufmaschinen* were called "swiftwalkers." My Tyke Bike was a kind of *Laufmaschine*. I added the wagon, though.

In the history of the bicycle, ontogeny recapitulates phylogeny. Lately, posh toddlers, the newest preschool jet set, roll around on modern swiftwalkers, marketed as "wooden balance bikes." If you bike all your life, there's a fair chance you'll bike the whole history of bicycles. When I was three, I started riding a red metal tricycle, another hand-me-down from my brother. It had a chrome fender in the front, a red running board in the back, and, most crucial, pedals. The cranking of pedals converts downward motion into forward motion, with multiplying force. No one's quite sure who came up with this idea, or when—most historians place their bets on a French carriage maker, in 1855—but putting a crank on the axle of the front wheel, with pedals on either side of the hub, changed everything about bicycles, including their name: most people called the ones with pedals "velocipedes," which is, roughly, Latin for "fast feet." People expected velocipedes to replace horses. "We think the bicycle an animal, which will, in a great measure, supersede the horse," one American wrote in 1869. "It does not cost as much; it will not eat, kick, bite, get sick, or die."

My next bike, the red-and-yellow Big Wheel, had a lot in common with a velocipede known as the penny-farthing, which was invented in the 1870s. The penny-farthing, like the Big Wheel, had a much bigger wheel in front because, so long as the pedals cranked the front wheel, the bigger the wheel, the faster you could ride. "An ever saddled horse which eats nothing," a Boston penny-farthing manufacturer promised, boasting speeds of a mile in under three minutes. "The Big Wheels are rolling," the television ads of my childhood announced, "with the speed you need to win!" Big Wheels came and they went; they were made of plastic, and mine fell apart during a figure-eight race around a parking lot against the kids next door, when I skidded off course and crashed into a telephone pole. Penny-farthings were dangerous, too: riders pitched right over the top. (The Big Wheel debuted in 1969, and a fiftieth-anniversary edition came out in 2019. "It's just a really cheap piece of crap," a reviewer at Walmart.com reported.)

My first two-wheeled bicycle was a Schwinn, hyacinth-purple. My father, who seems to have spent most spring weekends raising and lowering bicycle seats, retrofitted it for me by bolting back on the rickety pair of training wheels that we kept on a shelf in the garage. Aside from the training wheels, everything on that purple Schwinn had been invented by the end of the 1880s: two wheels of about the same size, pneumatic tires, and pedals that drive the rear wheel by way of a chain and sprockets. This type of bike, in the 1880s, was marketed as a "safety." Unlike earlier models, it was surprisingly risk-free, mainly because, even without foot brakes, you could stop the bike by taking your feet off the pedals and skidding to a halt. That, as my mother liked to point out, was how I ruined all my sneakers.

The safety was the prototype of every modern bicycle. Most everything added to the bicycle since is just tinkering around the edges. During the bike craze of the 1890s, bicycles became an emblem of modernity; they were the epitome, as Paul Smethurst argued in *The Bicycle: Towards a Global History* (2015), of "the cult of speed, a lightness of being, a desire for existential freedom and a celebration of the future." That's how it felt to me, too, when I first pedaled away from home, without my training wheels, all on my own. My favorite bike ever, though, was my next bike, my sister's Sears knockoff of the Schwinn Sting-Ray. It had a green banana seat with glitter in the vinyl, monkey handlebars, and a sissy bar, which I had always understood to be the place where little sisters were supposed to sit. I added rainbow-colored covers to the spokes and rode to school, the library, the candy store, hitching my bike to posts with a combination lock attached to a cable as thin as yarn. No one ever stole it.

To ride a bike, Rosen points out, is to come as close to flying by your own power as humans ever will. No part of you touches the ground. You ride on air. Not for nothing were Orville and Wilbur Wright bicycle manufacturers when they first achieved flight, in Kitty Hawk, in 1903. Historically, that kind of freedom has been especially meaningful to girls and women. Bicycling, Susan B. Anthony said in 1896, "has done more to emancipate women than anything else in the world." I've always had a sneaking feeling that somehow I owe it to feminism to pedal hard, weave through traffic, crave speed, curse at cars. A guy in my neighborhood wears a T-shirt that reads CYCLOPATH. In my mind's eye, I'm that guy. Instead, I stop at yellow lights and smile at strangers, gushing with goodwill, giddy just to be out there.

Bicycles and bicyclists veer to the political left. Environmentalists ride bicycles. American suffragists rode bicycles. So did English socialists, who called the bicycle "the people's nag." Animal-welfare activists, who opposed the whipping of horses, favored bicycles. In 1896, the American preacher who coined the expression "What Would Jesus Do?" had this to say about bicycles: "I think Jesus might ride a wheel if He were in our place, in order to save His own strength and the beast of burden." But bicycles have also been used in warfare on six continents, and were favored by colonial officials during the age of empire. After the League of American Wheelmen started the Good Roads Movement, in 1880, the asphalt that paved the roads for bicyclists was mined in Trinidad, and the rubber for tires came from the Belgian Congo and the Amazon basin.

For a while, starting in the 1890s, the bicycle seemed likely to finally beat out the horse. Aside from not needing to be fed and not dying, bicycles are also quieter and cleaner than horses, something

I thought a lot about as a kid, because I had a job mucking out stables. But then along came the automobile. "There are some who claim the automobile will replace the bicycle, but this is rank nonsense," a Maine magazine reported in 1899. "Those who have become attached to their bicycles—there are several millions of bicycle riders—will not easily give up the pleasure of skimming along the country like a bird . . . for the more doubtful delight of riding in the cumbersome, ill-smelling automobile."

In 1899, 1.2 million bicycles were sold in the United States. Henry Ford's Model T made its debut in 1908. The next year, only a hundred and sixty thousand bicycles were sold in the U.S. In the absence of bike lanes, cyclists in all states but one have to follow the rules of something known as the Uniform Vehicle Code, first adopted in 1926. Like jaywalking, a crime invented by the automobile industry to criminalize being a pedestrian, the UVC treats bicycles as cars that go too slow. "It shall be unlawful for any person unnecessarily to drive at such a slow speed as to impede or block the normal and reasonable movement of traffic," the UVC decreed in 1930. E. B. White was among those who protested, calling for "a network of permanent bicycle paths." (Many paths were built under the direction of Robert Moses.) "A great many people have now reached forty years of age in this country, despite all the handicaps," White wrote in *The New Yorker* in 1933, when he was thirty-four, "and they are the ones who specially enjoy bicycling, the men being somewhat elated on discovering that they can still ride no hands." In 1944, in what became known as the Far to the Right law, the UVC stated that "any person operating a bicycle upon a roadway shall ride as near to the right side of the roadway as practicable," which could mean being driven off the road.

By the 1950s, when the League of American Wheelmen disbanded and bicycles were excluded from many roads (including all of the new federal highway system), bikes had been reinvented as toys, child's play. Grownups drove cars; kids rode bikes. Girls were supposed to ride girls' bikes, although when, at age twelve, I inherited a girl's three-speed Raleigh, I decided I hated girls' bikes. Twelve was when I first started to see clearly the price you had to pay for being a girl, the vulnerability, and right about then I got more scared of cars, too. A boy in my sixth-grade class was killed riding his bike home from school. I covered the frame of that feckless three-speed Raleigh with black duct tape, to make it meaner. It's bad enough being powerless, because of being a kid and, on top of it all, a girl; it's worse when the adults are riding around in cages made of three tons of metal. It felt then, and still feels now, like being a bird flying in a sky filled with airplanes: the deafening roar of their engines, their impossible speed, the cruelty of steel, the inescapable menace, the looming sense of catastrophe, your own little wings flapping in silence while theirs slice thunderously. Black duct tape is no defense, and no disguise, but it was all I could find in the kitchen drawer.

The first time I was ever hit by a car, I was riding home from school on a robin's-egg-blue Fuji ten-speed. I'd painted it polka-dot, strapped a milk crate to the back rack, and duct-taped a transistor radio to the crate, so I could listen to Red Sox games. Maybe I was distracted: ninth inning, pitching change. I don't remember. A station wagon hit me from behind; I broke its windshield, bounced off the hood, and tumbled onto the road, into oncoming traffic. I remember lying on the pavement, unable to move, watching a truck heading straight at me. Swerving to avoid me, it ran over my bike. A few minutes after I was taken away in an ambulance, my father happened to be driving by, on his way home from work, and saw my unmistakable polka-dot bike on the side of the road, its frame crushed and mangled, the milk crate and the transistor radio smashed. He fainted at the wheel and nearly crashed, too.

I've been hit more times since—doored, mainly, though that's enough to cost you your life if you fall into traffic. J. K. Rowling's left stiletto once nearly ended me; she swung open the door of a stretch limo and stepped out, pelican-legged, just as I was cruising by. I veered into traffic to avoid running over her foot and almost got mowed down by a bus. It doesn't matter how cautious you are on a bike. Cars and trucks can kill you just by bumping into you. People in my city are killed by trucks every year. After my first crash, my mother made me get a helmet. Jack, by then, had started fixing up cars. Sheet metal, rivets, Rust-Oleum, body wax, timing belts. He gave me his last bike, even though it was way too tall for me. I painted it and took it to college, where I got hit on College Avenue.

The biggest bicycle boom in American history, after the one in the

1890s, took place in the 1970s, even before the gas crisis. On the first Earth Day, April 22, 1970, bicycling activists staged protests all over the country. In San Jose, they buried a Ford. Later, in Chicago, they held a "pedal-in." Bike sales rose from nine million in 1971 to fourteen million in 1972, and more than half of those sales were to adults. *Time* announced a national bicycle shortage. "Look Ma, No Cars" was the motto of the New York–based group Action Against Automobiles in 1972. GIVE MOM A BIKE LANE, a placard read at a bike-in rally in San Francisco that year. The following year, as Carlton Reid reported in *Bike Boom: The Unexpected Resurgence of Cycling* (2017), more than two hundred pieces of bike legislation, including proposals to establish bike lanes, were introduced in forty-two states. In 1972, 1973, and 1974, bicycles outsold cars. Within a few years, though, the automobile lobby had bulldozed its way through state legislatures, and most proposals for bicycle infrastructure had been abandoned; by the time I was in college, in the 1980s, the boom was at an end.

Not for me. I biked through every last bicycle fad, with the same abandon with which, at age nine, I saved up S & H Green Stamps to buy a unicycle. In the 1990s, I got a used mountain bike. I traded it in for a hybrid. In London, I bought a folding bike. When I got married, my husband and I rented a tandem, and then decided to keep it. When our oldest kids were toddlers, we hitched a trailer to the rear wheel, and attached a construction-orange flag to the trailer, to wave a warning to cars, a prayer. Our family of bicycles kept growing. Today, two unicycles hang from hooks in our bike shed, relics of another bike-fanatic child.

The latest bicycle boom began with the pandemic. In March of 2020, New York City declared bicycle-repair shops "essential businesses." Pop-up bicycle lanes opened in cities all over the world. Roads were closed to cars and opened for bicycles. In the U.S., more than half the bicyclists riding for the first time during the pandemic, or returning to it, were women. More people riding bikes meant more bicycle accidents—the rate doubled. More than a quarter of cars that hit and killed bicyclists left them there to die alone. Bike lanes, bike shares, new bike-safety laws: the rate of bicycle fatalities keeps going up all the same. Cars and trucks refuse to yield. The bike boom of the pandemic, Rosen argues, was a lot like the worldwide rewilding. Bears on street corners, cougars on cul-de-sacs, bicycles on highways. These things happened. Briefly.

"Traffic, for all intents and purposes, is back to about 2019 levels," the head of highways in my state declared in June of 2021. The cars came back. By the end of that year, the bicycle boom had gone bust. "I don't think a lot of Americans are aware . . . how far behind we are on bicycle and pedestrian safety," Pete Buttigieg, the U.S. secretary of transportation, said. Republicans warned, "Democrats are coming for your cars." No one is coming for your cars.

Meanwhile, I am avoiding the inevitable e-bike. I still ride my very, very old Bad Boy, slowpoke and getting slower every year, towing a trailer to carry books, a radio bolted to the handlebars, rusting.

—2022

THE EVERYMAN LIBRARY

MY FATHER ONCE TOLD ME THAT HIS FATHER, Giovanni Lepore, used to bring sandwiches to Sacco and Vanzetti when they were in prison in Charlestown in the 1920s. He'd hitchhike there, carrying a rucksack stuffed with provolone and prosciutto on pumpernickel. I have no particular reason to believe this story is true, but it might be true. I can picture it. I can smell it. It *smells* true.

Nicola Sacco and Bartolomeo Vanzetti, Italian immigrants, had been arrested, tried, convicted, and executed for a crime they didn't commit. My grandfather had immigrated to the United States in 1907, the same year they did—*paesani*—and in the 1910s, he and Vanzetti had worked together in Clinton, Massachusetts, building a railroad and living, with all the other immigrant workers, in railroad sleeping cars in a part of town known as Little Italy. "Here I made many friends, whom I remember with the strongest emotion, with a love unaltered and unalterable," Vanzetti later wrote. I like to think that one of those friends was my grandfather. *Mio Gio.*

Still, I don't know. I don't know much about my grandfather. In 1919, he joined the U.S. Army and became an American citizen. His father, in Italy, Abruzzo, paid a scribe to write him a letter.

"Try to come back soon over on your mother's arms. Dear Son the way you said that your sick to stay all alone, we are feeling the same way because we get pretty old so I am pray you to come back . . . You can get wife and marry the girl you like."

My grandfather did go back to Italy, to find that wife, Concetta Cecchini, *Concettina*, and then never saw his homeland again. He never learned to speak English. He had strong views about the exploitation of immigrants, like him, who helped dig out the Wachusett Reservoir, not far from Little Italy, and build the Clinton dam, holding it all in. Once, when there was a rumor that Sacco and Vanzetti were going to blow up the Clinton dam, my grandfather sat in a tree over the reservoir and watched out for them all night. Or so my father told me. And later, when they were in prison, he brought them sandwiches. I have only my father's word for this. I never had the chance to ask my grandfather. He died during the Great Depression, more or less of poverty. At the funeral, my grandmother, *tristissima*, jumped into the pit and splayed herself on his coffin. My uncles had to drag her out. Later, when she found the money to get a family photograph taken, she had an old photograph of my grandfather pasted in next to her. He looks like a ghost.

I never fact-checked the Sacco and Vanzetti story with my grandmother. I don't speak Italian and she didn't speak English and we had a hard time with each other—she was hard and I am hard—and, anyway, I didn't think to ask until long after she'd died. My grandfather was something of a radical; but in sympathizing with Sacco and Vanzetti, he'd have been in good company. Five days after Sacco and Vanzetti went to the electric chair, in 1927, close to a quarter of a million people protested in Boston. Much was written about their political philosophy—like my grandfather, they were socialists, and maybe anarchists—and from prison, Vanzetti wrote the story of his life. As a boy in Italy, he'd spent seven years in school, from the ages of six to thirteen. Someone in town had a library, and Vanzetti had started reading St. Augustine. "The principles of humanism and equality of rights began to make a breach in my heart," he later wrote. He got ahold of Dante's *Commedia*. "My teeth were not made for such a bone," he wrote, but all the same, he "proceeded to gnaw it, desperately." He read history, literature, philosophy. In prison for seven years, Vanzetti read and read. "I feel the fever of knowledge in me," he wrote. He concluded: "the plague which besets humanity most cruelly is ignorance."

I like to think my grandfather read the same books and came to the same conclusions. I'm pretty sure he read Dante. Nicola Sacco, when he married and had a son, named him Dante. My grandfather, when he married and had a son, named him Dante, too. He had a second son, my father, and named him Francisco Amerigo, after his new home.

My father grew up in Clinton, with all of his cousins and aunts and uncles, who came over, in a tumble, from the same part of Italy. They had no heating or plumbing in his house and he liked to tell a story about how he first heard of toothpaste when a box of it fell off a truck and some kid in the neighborhood explained what it was for. He graduated from high school in June of 1941 and took a job as a janitor. In December, after the Japanese attack on Pearl Harbor, he joined the army. At Fort Devens, they pulled out most of his teeth: they were all rotten. After the war, he went to Clark University, in Worcester. If it hadn't been for the G.I. Bill, which paid his tuition, he'd never have gone to college. He didn't have a car, or enough money for the bus, so he hitchhiked. When he wasn't in class, he worked in Clinton at a bookbindery, to be close to books, as if he were young Benjamin Franklin, an apprentice at his brother's printing shop, which is something I thought about, many years later, at my father's deathbed, just me and him, where, as he slept, I read Carl Van Doren's biography of Franklin and then, when I looked up, he was gone.

My father always wanted to be a writer, Hemingway, Hemingway, with his bullfighters and his marlins, but never quite succeeded. Like Vanzetti, he once wrote an autobiography, never published. He called it *Diary of an Unknown*. He was not a marlin man, not a fisherman, not a bullfighter, not a hunter, not a boxer, not a man of the least violence. He did, though, smell the way I imagine Hemingway smelled. My father had an extraordinary affection for strange antique medicinals. Ointments, tinctures, elixirs. He smoked a pipe that he filled with Briggs tobacco, from a tin. He drank Moxie. He lathered himself with pHisoderm, a gentleman's soap, and splashed himself with Old Spice, an old man's aftershave. He had pocks all over his back; he told us they were bullet holes, from the war, but they were just pockmarks. He'd been a medic and had never been shot, had never seen combat, but what he meant to say, I think, was that he had been marked, indelibly, by the horror of war. It had left holes, drilled through his back.

My father kept a stack of books on his nightstand, mystery novels, mostly. He read them at night, lying in bed, while listening to the Red Sox on the radio. James Michener, Dick Francis. He was a public school teacher and a guidance counselor, a director of guidance, a guide. He wore plaid jackets and striped bow ties and he smoked, all day, and when girls got in trouble, he drove them to Boston, to get illegal abortions. And when boys got in trouble, he kept them out of prison, down to bribery. He never raised his voice. He only ever wanted to help, and to write, and to read in bed.

My father found himself in books, tucked in between the pages, like a bookmark or a silverfish. Mostly, he borrowed books, from the town library, or the library of the school where he taught. We never had very many books of our own around the house. Except, in his den, he kept a shelf of the first books he ever owned: his college textbooks. When he died, I inherited those books, a very little, very smoky library. Tiny books, held in one hand, all bound in cloth, and smelling of Briggs tobacco. Modern Library editions. Everyman editions. Viking Portable Library editions. Soft, and much pocked.

I once looked up his college transcript, and I found out that every one of these books was a book he bought for a class. *Julius Caesar*: in Shakespeare, sophomore year, my father got a C. God bless the days before grade inflation. An anthology of Ernest Hemingway, for The Short Story. B−. *Selections from the Poetical Works of Robert Browning*, for Romantic Poetry. C+. In the whole of Browning, my father has underlined only a single couplet, in pencil: "Ah, but a man's reach should exceed his grasp, / Or what's a heaven for?"

The most marked-up of all of the books in my father's little library is an edition of Virgil's *Aeneid*. He must have read it for a class called Roman Civilization (B+, his best grade). The *Aeneid* is also the only book my father put his name in. On the endpaper he stuck a return address sticker so that this book, if it ever got lost, would get back to him. This one book.

My father's copy of *Virgil's Works* is bound in green cloth, with a black leather insert on the cover. My father wrote all over it. Scribbles in the margins, underlines in the text, notes to himself, notes to Virgil. "Notice piety of Aeneas," he's written on page 39, and "Aeneas won't go without his father." *Seek we Crete and our forefathers*, he's underlined on page 47. On page 57, he's noted, in the right-hand margin, "They sight Italy!"

Virgil wrote the *Aeneid* in about 20 BC. My father's English translation begins this way: "I sing of arms and the man who came of old, a fated wanderer, from the coasts of Troy to Italy." Aeneas falls in love with Dido, an African queen, and then betrays her. He cries, all the time, about the suffering caused by war. As one world collapses, another is being built. "Happy are those whose walls are rising," Virgil writes. And yet everywhere is war: "Raw fear / Was everywhere, grief was everywhere, / Everywhere the many masks of death."

I picture my father—a very young man, who had lost his father, and seen war, and wandered the world—falling in love with this story of a homeland he had never seen, his father's Italy. My father, too, was looking for a home, when he took Roman Civilization in his senior year, in Worcester, in 1949. A job, a wife, a family, children. But he had found, too, a story of himself, and even of his past, in Virgil. A story of wandering, a story of war and of the sorrows of war. He found Aeneas, wearing the mask of death, carrying the burden of grief. Honoring the dead. Building a new home. Wondering why the good suffer, and why war endures. Sighting Italy. And finding beauty in poetry. *Seek we Crete and our forefathers.*

My father, who never knew toothpaste as a child. My father, who had all his teeth pulled by the U.S. Army. My father, who wore dentures from the age of eighteen. He'd stick them out at us, pretending to be a monster. My father, the gentlest man, the softest. I like to think I carry those books in a rucksack, with a provolone and prosciutto sandwich on pumpernickel. I pile them on a table, prop them up on a shelf, take them down, reread them. Loan them out, get them back. Head to the library. Get some more. Pass them on, every book a gift, every library an inheritance, a scroll, unfurling, like a newborn's tiny hand, opening, the child of a whole family, each of its ancestors.

He got ahold of those books when he went to college, books, the relics of the dead, hard books his father, with his hard life, had never owned. And he found that, after all, his teeth were made for these bones.

—2022

Part Two

Misjudged

Female heroes are in short supply not because women aren't brave but because female bravery is demeaned, no kind more than intellectual courage.

Rachel Carson in 1952.
U.S. Fish and Wildlife Service

IT'S STILL ALIVE

MARY WOLLSTONECRAFT GODWIN SHELLEY BEGAN writing *Frankenstein; or, the Modern Prometheus* when she was eighteen years old, two years after she'd become pregnant with her first child, a baby she did not name. "Nurse the baby, read," she had written in her diary, day after day, until the eleventh day: "I awoke in the night to give it suck it appeared to be sleeping so quietly that I would not awake it," and then, in the morning, "Find my baby dead." With grief at that loss came a fear of "a fever from the milk." Her breasts were swollen, inflamed, unsucked; her sleep, too, grew fevered. "Dream that my little baby came to life again; that it had only been cold, and that we rubbed it before the fire, and it lived," she wrote in her diary. "Awake and find no baby."

Pregnant again only weeks later, she was likely still nursing her second baby when she started writing *Frankenstein*, and pregnant with her third by the time she finished. She didn't put her name on her book—she published *Frankenstein* anonymously, in 1818, not least out of a concern that she might lose custody of her children—and she didn't give her monster a name, either. "This anonymous androdaemon," one reviewer called it. For the first theatrical production of *Franken-stein*, staged in London in 1823 (by which time the author had given birth to four children, buried three, and lost another unnamed baby to a miscarriage so severe that she nearly died of bleeding that stopped only when her husband had her sit on ice), the monster was listed on the playbill as "————."

"This nameless mode of naming the unnameable is rather good," Shelley remarked about the creature's theatrical billing. She herself had no name of her own. Like the creature pieced together from cadavers collected by Victor Frankenstein, her name was an assemblage of parts: the name of her mother, the feminist Mary Wollstonecraft, stitched to that of her father, the philosopher William Godwin, grafted onto that

of her husband, the poet Percy Bysshe Shelley, as if Mary Wollstonecraft Godwin Shelley were the sum of her relations, bone of their bone
and flesh of their flesh, if not the milk of her mother's milk, since her
mother had died eleven days after giving birth to her, mainly too sick
to give suck—*Awoke and found no mother.*

"It was on a dreary night of November, that I beheld the accomplishment of my toils," Victor Frankenstein, a university student, says,
pouring out his tale. The rain patters on the windowpane; a bleak
light flickers from a dying candle. He looks at the "lifeless thing" at
his feet, come to life: "I saw the dull yellow eye of the creature open;
it breathed hard, and a convulsive motion agitated its limbs." Having labored so long to bring the creature to life, he finds himself disgusted and horrified—"unable to endure the aspect of the being I had
created"—and flees, abandoning his creation, unnamed. "I, the miserable and the abandoned, am an abortion," the creature says, before, in
the book's final scene, he disappears on a raft of ice.

Frankenstein is four stories in one: an allegory, a fable, an epistolary
novel, and an autobiography, a chaos of literary fertility that left its
very young author at pains to explain her "hideous progeny." In the
introduction she wrote for a revised edition in 1831, she took up the
humiliating question "How I, then a young girl, came to think of,
and to dilate upon, so very hideous an idea" and made up a story in
which she virtually erased herself as an author, insisting that the story
had come to her in a dream ("I saw—with shut eyes, but acute mental vision,—I saw the pale student of unhallowed arts kneeling beside
the thing he had put together") and that writing it consisted of "making only a transcript" of that dream. A century later, when a lurch-
ing, grunting Boris Karloff played the creature in Universal Pictures'
brilliant 1931 production of *Frankenstein*, directed by James Whale,
the monster—prodigiously eloquent, learned, and persuasive in the
novel—was no longer merely nameless but all but speechless, too, as if
what Mary Wollstonecraft Godwin Shelley had to say was too radical
to be heard, an agony unutterable.

Every book is a baby, born, but *Frankenstein* is often supposed to
have been more assembled than written, an unnatural birth, as though
all that the author had done were to piece together the writings of
others, especially those of her father and her husband. "If Godwin's

daughter could not help philosophising," one mid-twentieth-century critic wrote, "Shelley's wife knew also the eerie charms of the morbid, the occult, the scientifically bizarre." This enduring condescension, the idea of the author as a vessel for the ideas of other people—a fiction in which the author participated, so as to avoid the scandal of her own brain—goes some way to explaining why *Frankenstein* has accreted so many wildly different and irreconcilable readings and restagings in the two centuries since its publication. For its 2018 bicentennial, the original, 1818 edition was reissued, as a trim little paperback, with an introduction by the distinguished biographer Charlotte Gordon, and as a beautifully illustrated hardcover keepsake, *The New Annotated Frankenstein* (Liveright), edited and annotated by Leslie S. Klinger. Universal is developing a new *Bride of Frankenstein* as part of a series of remakes from its backlist of horror movies. Filmography recapitulating politico-chicanery, the age of the superhero is about to yield to the age of the monster. But what about the baby?

FRANKENSTEIN, THE STORY OF a creature who has no name, has for two hundred years been made to mean just about anything. Lately, it has been taken as a cautionary tale for Silicon Valley technologists, an interpretation that derives less from the 1818 novel than from later stage and film versions, especially the 1931 film, and that took its modern form in the aftermath of Hiroshima. In that spirit, MIT Press has published an edition of the original text "annotated for scientists, engineers, and creators of all kinds," and prepared by the leaders of the Frankenstein Bicentennial Project, at Arizona State University, with funding from the National Science Foundation; they offer the book as a catechism for designers of robots and inventors of artificial intelligences. "Remorse extinguished every hope," Victor says, in Volume II, Chapter 1, by which time the creature has begun murdering everyone Victor loves. "I had been the author of unalterable evils; and I lived in daily fear, lest the monster whom I had created should perpetrate some new wickedness." The MIT edition appends, here, a footnote: "The remorse Victor expresses is reminiscent of J. Robert Oppenheimer's sentiments when he witnessed the unspeakable power of the atomic bomb. . . . Scientists' responsibility must be engaged before their creations are unleashed."

This is a way to make use of the novel, but it involves stripping out nearly all the sex and birth, everything female—material first mined by Muriel Spark, in a biography of Shelley published in 1951, on the occasion of the hundredth anniversary of her death. Spark, working closely with Shelley's diaries and paying careful attention to the author's eight years of near-constant pregnancy and loss, argued that *Frankenstein* was no minor piece of genre fiction but a literary work of striking originality. In the 1970s, that interpretation was taken up by feminist literary critics who wrote about *Frankenstein* as establishing the origins of science fiction by way of the "female gothic." What made Mary Shelley's work so original, Ellen Moers argued at the time, was that she was a writer who was a mother. Tolstoy had thirteen children, born at home, Moers pointed out, but the major female eighteenth- and nineteenth-century writers, the Austens and Dickinsons, tended to be "spinsters and virgins." Shelley was an exception.

So was Mary Wollstonecraft, a woman Shelley knew not as a mother but as a writer who wrote about, among other things, how to raise a baby. "I conceive it to be the duty of every rational creature to attend to its offspring," Wollstonecraft wrote in *Thoughts on the Education of Daughters*, in 1787, ten years before giving birth to the author of *Frankenstein*. As Charlotte Gordon notes in her dual biography *Romantic Outlaws*, Wollstonecraft first met her fellow political radical William Godwin in 1791, at a London dinner party hosted by the publisher of Thomas Paine's *Rights of Man*. Wollstonecraft and Godwin were "mutually displeased with each other," Godwin later wrote; they were the smartest people in the room, and they couldn't help arguing all evening. Wollstonecraft's *Vindication of the Rights of Woman* appeared in 1792, and the next year Godwin published *Political Justice*. In 1793, during an affair with the American speculator and diplomat Gilbert Imlay, Wollstonecraft became pregnant. ("I am nourishing a creature," she wrote Imlay.) Not long after Wollstonecraft gave birth to a daughter, whom she named Fanny, Imlay abandoned her. She and Godwin became lovers in 1796, and when she became pregnant they married, for the sake of the baby, even though neither of them believed in marriage. In 1797, Wollstonecraft died of an infection contracted from the fingers of a physician who reached into her uterus to remove the afterbirth. Godwin's daughter bore the name of his dead wife, as if she could be brought back to life, another afterbirth.

MARY WOLLSTONECRAFT GODWIN was fifteen years old when she met Percy Bysshe Shelley, in 1812. He was twenty, and married, with a pregnant wife. Having been thrown out of Oxford for his atheism and disowned by his father, Shelley had sought out William Godwin, his intellectual hero, as a surrogate father. Shelley and Godwin *fille* spent their illicit courtship, as much Romanticism as romance, passionately reading the works of her parents while reclining on Wollstonecraft's grave, in the St. Pancras churchyard. "Go to the tomb and read," she wrote in her diary. "Go with Shelley to the churchyard." Plainly, they were doing more than reading, because she was pregnant when she ran away with him, fleeing her father's house in the half-light of night, along with her stepsister, Claire Clairmont, who wanted to be ruined, too.

If any man served as an inspiration for Victor Frankenstein, it was Lord Byron, who followed his imagination, indulged his passions, and abandoned his children. He was "mad, bad, and dangerous to know," as one of his lovers pronounced, mainly because of his many affairs, which likely included sleeping with his half sister, Augusta Leigh. Byron married in January 1815, and a daughter, Ada, was born in December. But when his wife left him a year into their marriage, Byron was forced never to see his wife or daughter again, lest his wife reveal the scandal of his affair with Leigh. (Ada was about the age Mary Godwin's first baby would have been, had she lived. Ada's mother, fearing that the girl might grow up to become a poet, as mad and bad as her father, raised her instead to be a mathematician. Ada Lovelace, a scientist as imaginative as Victor Frankenstein, would in 1843 provide an influential theoretical description of a general-purpose computer, a century before one was built.)

In the spring of 1816, Byron, fleeing scandal, left England for Geneva, and it was there that he met up with Percy Shelley, Mary Godwin, and Claire Clairmont. Moralizers called them the League of Incest. By summer, Clairmont was pregnant by Byron. Byron was bored. One evening, he announced, "We will each write a ghost story." Godwin began the story that would become *Frankenstein*. Byron later wrote, "Methinks it is a wonderful book for a girl of nineteen—*not* nineteen, indeed, at that time."

During the months when Godwin was turning her ghost story into a novel, and nourishing yet another creature in her belly, Shelley's wife, pregnant now with what would have been their third child, killed herself; Clairmont gave birth to a girl—Byron's, though most people assumed it was Shelley's—and Shelley and Godwin got married. For a time, they attempted to adopt the girl, though Byron later took her, having noticed that nearly all of Godwin and Shelley's children had died. "I so totally disapprove of the mode of Children's treatment in their family—that I should look upon the Child as going into a hospital," he wrote, cruelly, about the Shelleys. "Have they *reared* one?" (Byron, by no means interested in rearing a child himself, placed the girl in a convent, where she died at the age of five.)

When *Frankenstein*, begun in the summer of 1816, was published eighteen months later, it bore an unsigned preface by Percy Shelley and a dedication to William Godwin. The book became an immediate sensation. "It seems to be universally known and read," a friend wrote to Percy Shelley. Sir Walter Scott wrote, in an early review, "The author seems to us to disclose uncommon powers of poetic imagination." Scott, like many readers, assumed that the author was Percy Shelley. Reviewers less enamored of the Romantic poet damned the book's Godwinian radicalism and its Byronic impieties. John Croker, a conservative member of Parliament, called *Frankenstein* a "tissue of horrible and disgusting absurdity"—radical, unhinged, and immoral.

BUT THE POLITICS OF *FRANKENSTEIN* are as intricate as its structure of stories nested like Russian dolls. The outermost doll is a set of letters from an English adventurer to his sister, recounting his Arctic expedition and his meeting with the strange, emaciated, haunted Victor Frankenstein. Within the adventurer's account, Frankenstein tells the story of his fateful experiment, which has led him to pursue his creature to the ends of the earth. And within Frankenstein's story lies the tale told by the creature himself, the littlest, innermost Russian doll: the baby.

The novel's structure meant that those opposed to political radicalism often found themselves baffled and bewildered by *Frankenstein*, as literary critics such as Chris Baldick and Adriana Craciun have pointed out. The novel appears to be heretical and revolutionary; it also appears to be counterrevolutionary. It depends on which doll is doing the talking.

If *Frankenstein* is a referendum on the French Revolution, as some critics have read it, Victor Frankenstein's politics align nicely with those of Edmund Burke, who described violent revolution as "a species of political monster, which has always ended by devouring those who have produced it." The creature's own politics, though, align not with Burke's but with those of two of Burke's keenest adversaries, Mary Wollstonecraft and William Godwin. Victor Frankenstein has made use of other men's bodies, like a lord over the peasantry or a king over his subjects, in just the way that Godwin denounced when he described feudalism as a "ferocious monster." ("How dare you sport thus with life?" the creature asks his maker.) The creature, born innocent, has been treated so terribly that he has become a villain, in just the way that Wollstonecraft predicted. "People are rendered ferocious by misery," she wrote, "and misanthropy is ever the offspring of discontent." ("Make me happy," the creature begs Frankenstein, to no avail.)

Mary Wollstonecraft Godwin Shelley took pains that readers' sympathies would lie not only with Frankenstein, whose suffering is dreadful, but also with the creature, whose suffering is worse. The art of the book lies in the way Shelley nudges readers' sympathy, page by page, paragraph by paragraph, even line by line, from Frankenstein to the creature, even when it comes to the creature's vicious murders, first of Frankenstein's little brother, then of his best friend, and, finally, of his bride. Much evidence suggests that she succeeded. "The justice is indisputably on his side," one critic wrote in 1824, "and his sufferings are, to me, touching to the last degree."

"Hear my tale," the creature insists, when he at last confronts his creator. What follows is the autobiography of an infant. He awoke, and all was confusion. "I was a poor, helpless, miserable wretch; I knew, and could distinguish, nothing." He was cold and naked and hungry and bereft of company, and yet, having no language, was unable even to name these sensations. "But, feeling pain invade me on all sides, I sat down and wept." He learned to walk, and began to wander, still unable to speak—"the uncouth and inarticulate sounds which broke from me frightened me into silence again." Eventually, he found shelter in a lean-to adjacent to a cottage alongside a wood, where, observing the cottagers talk, he learned of the existence of language: "I discovered the names that were given to some of the most familiar objects of discourse: I learned and applied the words *fire, milk, bread,* and *wood*." Watching the cottagers read a book, *Ruins of Empires,* by the eighteenth-century French revolutionary the Comte de Volney, he both learned how to read and acquired "a cursory knowledge of history"—a litany of injustice. "I heard of the division of property, of immense wealth and squalid poverty; of rank, descent, and noble blood." He learned that the weak are everywhere abused by the powerful, and the poor despised.

Shelley kept careful records of the books she read and translated, naming title after title and compiling a list each year—Milton, Goethe, Rousseau, Ovid, Spenser, Coleridge, Gibbon, and hundreds more, from history to chemistry. "Babe is not well," she noted in her diary while writing *Frankenstein.* "Write, draw and walk; read Locke." Or, "Walk; write; read the 'Rights of Women.'" The creature keeps track of his reading, too, and, unsurprisingly, he reads the books that Shelley read and reread most often. One day, wandering in the woods, he stumbles upon a leather trunk, lying on the ground, that contains three books: Milton's *Paradise Lost,* Plutarch's *Lives,* and Goethe's *The Sorrows of Young Werther*—the library that, along with Volney's *Ruins,* determines his political philosophy, as reviewers readily understood. "His code of ethics is formed on this extraordinary stock of poetical theology, pagan biography, adulterous sentimentality, and atheistical jacobinism," according to the review of *Frankenstein* most widely read in the United States, "yet, in spite of all his enormities, we think the monster, a very pitiable and ill-used monster."

Sir Walter Scott found this the most preposterous part of *Frankenstein*: "That he should have not only learned to speak, but to read, and, for aught we know, to write—that he should have become acquainted with *Werter,* with *Plutarch's Lives,* and with *Paradise Lost,* by listening through a hole in a wall, seems as unlikely as that he should have acquired, in the same way, the problems of *Euclid,* or the art of bookkeeping by single and double entry." But the creature's account of his education very closely follows the conventions of a genre of writing far distant from Scott's own: the slave narrative.

FREDERICK DOUGLASS, born into slavery the year *Frankenstein* was published, was following those same conventions when, in his autobiography, he described learning to read by trading with white boys for lessons. Douglass realized his political condition at the age of twelve, while reading the "Dialogue Between a Master and Slave," reprinted in *The Columbian Orator* (a book for which he paid fifty cents, and which was one of the only things he brought with him when he escaped from slavery). It was his coming of age. "The more I read, the more I was led to abhor and detest my enslavers," Douglass wrote, in a line that the creature himself might have written.

Likewise, the creature comes of age when he finds Frankenstein's notebook, recounting his experiment, and learns how he was created, and with what injustice he has been treated. It's at this moment that the creature's tale is transformed from the autobiography of an infant to the autobiography of a slave. "I would at times feel that learning to read had been a curse rather than a blessing," Douglass wrote. "It had given me a view of my wretched condition, without the remedy." So, too, the creature: "Increase of knowledge only discovered to me more clearly what a wretched outcast I was." Douglass: "I often found myself regretting my own existence, and wishing myself dead." The creature: "Cursed, cursed creator! Why did I live?" Douglass seeks his escape; the creature seeks his revenge.

Among the many moral and political ambiguities of Shelley's novel is the question of whether Victor Frankenstein is to be blamed for creating the monster—usurping the power of God, and of women—or for failing to love, care for, and educate him. The Frankenstein-is-Oppenheimer model considers only the former, which makes for a weak reading of the novel. Much of *Frankenstein* participates in the debate over abolition, as several critics have astutely observed, and the revolution on which the novel most plainly turns is not the one in France but the one in Haiti. For abolitionists in England, the Haitian revolution, along with continued slave rebellions in Jamaica and other West Indian sugar islands, raised deeper and harder questions about liberty and equality than the revolution in France had, since they involved an inquiry into the idea of racial difference. Godwin and Wollstonecraft had been abolitionists, as were both Percy and Mary Shelley, who, for instance, refused to eat sugar because of how it was produced. Although Britain and the United States enacted laws abolishing the importation of slaves in 1807, the debate over slavery in Britain's territories continued through the decision in favor of emancipation, in 1833. Both Shelleys closely followed this debate, and in the years before and during the composition of *Frankenstein* they together read several books about Africa and the West Indies. Percy Shelley was among those abolitionists who urged not immediate but gradual emancipation, fearing that the enslaved, so long and so violently oppressed, and denied education, would, if unconditionally freed, seek a vengeance of blood. He asked, "Can he who the day before was a trampled slave suddenly become liberal-minded, forbearing, and independent?"

Given Mary Shelley's reading of books that stressed the physical distinctiveness of Africans, her depiction of the creature is explicitly racial, figuring him as African, as opposed to European. "I was more agile than they, and could subsist upon coarser diet," the creature says. "I bore the extremes of heat and cold with less injury to my frame; my stature far exceeded theirs." This characterization became, onstage, a caricature. Beginning with the 1823 stage production of *Frankenstein*, the actor playing "———" wore blue face paint, a color that identified him less as dead than as colored. It was this production that George Canning, abolitionist, foreign secretary, and leader of the House of Commons, invoked in 1824, during a parliamentary debate about emancipation. Tellingly, Canning's remarks brought together the novel's depiction of the creature as a baby and the culture's figuring of Africans as children. "In dealing with the negro, Sir, we must remember that we are dealing with a being possessing the form and strength of a man, but the intellect only of a child," Canning told Parliament. "To turn him loose in the manhood of his physical strength, in the maturity of his physical passions, but in the infancy of his uninstructed reason, would be to raise up a creature resembling the splendid fiction of a recent romance." In later nineteenth-century stage productions, the creature was explicitly dressed as an African. Even the 1931 James Whale film, in which Karloff wore green face paint, furthers this figuring of the creature as Black: he is, in the film's climactic scene, lynched.

Because the creature reads as a slave, *Frankenstein* holds a unique place in American culture, as the literary scholar Elizabeth Young argued, a few years ago, in *Black Frankenstein: The Making of an American Metaphor.* "What is the use of living, when in fact I am dead," the Black abolitionist David Walker asked from Boston in 1829, in his *Appeal to the Colored Citizens of the World*, anticipating Eldridge Cleaver's *Soul on Ice* by a century and a half. "Slavery is everywhere the pet monster of the American people," Frederick Douglass declared in New York, on the eve of the American Civil War. Nat Turner was called a monster; so was John Brown. By the 1850s, Frankenstein's monster regularly appeared in American political cartoons as a nearly naked Black man, signifying slavery itself, seeking his vengeance upon the nation that created him.

MARY WOLLSTONECRAFT GODWIN SHELLEY was dead by then, her own chaotic origins already forgotten. Nearly everyone she loved died before she did, most of them when she was still very young. Her half sister, Fanny Imlay, took her own life in 1816. Percy Shelley drowned in 1822. Lord Byron fell ill and died in Greece in 1824, leaving Mary Wollstonecraft Godwin Shelley, as she put it, "the last relic of a beloved race, my companions extinct before me."

She chose that as the theme behind the novel she wrote eight years after *Frankenstein*. Published in 1826, when the author was twenty-eight, *The Last Man* is set in the twenty-first century, when only one man endures, the lone survivor of a terrible plague, having failed—for all his imagination, for all his knowledge—to save the life of a single person. *Nurse the baby, read. Find my baby dead.*

—2018

AHAB AT HOME

HERMAN MELVILLE SEEMS TO HAVE GOT THE IDEA to write a novel about a mad hunt for a fearsome whale during an ocean voyage, but he wrote most of *Moby-Dick* on land, in a valley, on a farm, in a house a-dither with his wife, his sisters, and his mother, a family man's *Walden*. He named the farm Arrowhead, after the relics he dug up with his plow, and he wrote in a second-floor room that looked out on mountains in the distance and, nearer by, on fields of pumpkins and corn, crops he sowed to feed his animals, "my friends the horse & cow." In the barn, he liked to watch them eat, especially the cow; he loved the way she moved her jaws. "She does it so mildly & with such a sanctity," he wrote, the year he kept on his desk a copy of Thomas Beale's *Natural History of the Sperm Whale*. On the door of his writing room, he installed a lock. By the hearth, he kept a harpoon; he used it as a poker.

There is no knowing Herman Melville. The year 2019 marked the two-hundredth anniversary of his birth and the hundredth anniversary of his revival. Born in 1819, he died in 1891, forgotten, only to be rediscovered around the centennial of his birth, in 1919. Since then, his fame has known no bounds, his reputation no rest, his life no privacy. His papers have been published, the notes he made in his books digitized, a log of his every day compiled, each movement traced, all utterances analyzed, every dog-eared page scanned and uploaded, like so much hay tossed up to a loft. And yet, as Andrew Delbanco wrote in a canny biography, *Melville: His World and Work* (2005), "the quest for the private Melville has usually led to a dead end."

On the road to that dead end there stands a barn, and it is on fire. Melville did not want his papers to be preserved. "It is a vile habit of mine to destroy nearly all my letters," he confessed. He burned his manuscripts. He shied from photographers: "To the devil with you and your Daguerreotype!" In *Pierre; or, The Ambiguities*, his freakishly autobiographical and, unless you take it seriously, deliriously funny gothic thriller set at a fictionalized Arrowhead and published in 1852—less than a year after *Moby-Dick*—a fevered, manic Pierre, having sunk himself into ruin and dragged his family into infamy, ponders his legacy:

> Hitherto I have hoarded up mementoes and monuments of the past; been a worshiper of all heirlooms; a fond filer away of letters, locks of hair, bits of ribbon, flowers, and the thousand-and-one minutenesses which love and memory think they sanctify:—but it is forever over now!

In a frenzy, Pierre proceeds to destroy his father's portrait, tearing the canvas from its frame, rolling it into a scroll, and committing it to the "crackling, clamorous flames," although, watching it blacken, he panics when, "suddenly unwinding from the burnt string that had tied it, for one swift instant, seen through the flame and smoke, the upwrithing portrait tormentedly stared at him in beseeching horror." But then he casts about the room, looking for more to burn:

> He ran back to the chest, and seizing repeated packages of family letters, and all sorts of miscellaneous memorials in paper, he threw them one after the other upon the fire.
> "Thus, and thus, and thus! . . . Now all is done, and all is ashes!"

Making kindling of correspondence appears to have been something of a Melville family tradition. Someone among Melville's ragged kin of landed aristocrats and wayward seamen and scheming bankrupts and gloomy widows destroyed the author's letters to his mother along with nearly all of his letters to his brothers and sisters. One of his nieces threw correspondence between her father and her uncle into a bonfire at Arrowhead, and, even though Melville's widow kept her husband's papers in a tin box, including his unpublished manuscripts (*Billy Budd*, tucked away in that box, wasn't published until 1924), Melville's letters to his wife, Elizabeth, appear to have been destroyed by their daughter, who refused to speak her father's name, possibly because, as some evidence suggests, Melville was insane. Elizabeth sometimes thought so, and critics said so, though the latter can scarcely be credited, on account of cruelty, and because what they meant was that his stories were nuts. "Herman Melville Crazy" was the headline of a now notorious review of *Pierre*. "N.B. *I aint crazy*," Melville wrote in a late-in-life postscript.

Maybe not, but he suffered horribly in the attic of his mind. After he finished *Moby-Dick* and was starting *Pierre*, he wrote, from Arrowhead, to Nathaniel Hawthorne—"Believe me, I am not mad!"—that he wished he could "have a paper-mill established at one end of the house, and so have an endless riband of foolscap rolling in upon my desk; and upon that endless riband I should write a thousand—a million— billion thoughts." He needed to write. He wanted to be read. He could not bear to be seen. His upwrithing portrait tormentedly stares at us in beseeching horror.

The plot of *Pierre* is set in motion by the arrival of a letter, handed to Pierre at a garden gate in the dark of a moonless night by an obscure, hooded figure:

> "For me!" exclaimed Pierre, faintly, starting at the strangeness of the encounter;—"methinks this is an odd time and place to deliver your mail!"

The letter is from Pierre's sister, the whale to his Ahab.

"Write direct to Pittsfield, Hermans care," Melville's sister Augusta instructed her correspondents when she moved to Arrowhead to live with him. Melville delivered the mail on his horse, Charlie, from a post office in the Berkshire village of Pittsfield, and carried it back, too. "Herman is just going to town & I have been obliged to make my pen fairly fly," Augusta apologized.

Augusta Melville was the most dutiful Melville letter writer, a role she appears to have been assigned by her mother. ("You had better write Herman on Thursday," the not-to-be-refused Mrs. Melville commanded.) She lived with her brother for most of her life—she never married—and served as his copyist, which made her his first reader. He often appears in her letters: "Herman just passed through the room. 'Who are you writing to Gus?'" And she appears in his scant surviving letters, too. "My sister Augusta begs me to send her sincerest regards both to you and Mr. Hawthorne," Melville wrote to Sophia Hawthorne, Nathaniel's wife.

Herman Melville was born in New York in 1819, his sister Augusta two years later. "Herman & Augusta improve apace as to growing & talking," their mother, Maria Gansevoort Melvill, wrote to her brother in 1824. Like Pierre Glendenning, the Pierre of *Pierre*, they were descended on both sides from Revolutionary War heroes, Thomas Melvill (it was Melville's mother who added the *e* to the family name) and Peter Gansevoort, the hero of the Siege of Fort Stanwix. "The patriots of the revolution stand first in every American's heart," Augusta wrote in a school essay. When Herman and Augusta were twelve and ten, their father died, raving mad; Herman watched him lose his mind, and he also, then or later, likely heard rumors of an illegitimate sister, all of which also happens to Pierre.

After his father's death, Melville left school and went to work as a clerk, spending a week in the summer at his uncle's farm near Pittsfield. In 1839, not yet twenty, Melville went to sea on a merchant ship, like Ishmael, before signing on to a whaling ship. He knew the world and came of age among close-quartered men. "Squeeze! squeeze! squeeze!" he writes, in *Moby-Dick*, about pressing the lumps out of sperm oil. "I squeezed that sperm till I myself almost melted into it; I squeezed that sperm till a strange sort of insanity came over me; and I found myself unwittingly squeezing my co-laborers' hands in it." In 1842, he deserted on an island in the South Pacific and lived for a month among a Polynesian people he called the Typee before signing on to an Australian whaling ship, and then a Nantucketer, returning to the United States in 1844, full of bowlegged sea stories and desperate for book learning. Pierre keeps a copy of *Hamlet* and Dante's *Inferno* on his writing desk. "I have swam through libraries," Melville wrote. Reading parts of *Moby-Dick* is like watching a fireworks in which Virgilian Roman candles, Old Testament sparklers, and Shakespearean bottle rockets pop off all at once, hissing and whistling; you get the feeling the stage manager is about to blow a finger off. If there's a showiness to Melville's pyrotechnics, his erudition was hard-won. But this was among the qualities of his *Moby-Dick* that reviewers found bonkers: "The style is maniacal—mad as a March hare."

Melville's first two books are narratives of his travels, *Typee*, published in 1846, and *Omoo*, in 1847, gripping adventure stories that made the young and dashing writer a celebrity, not least because of their lustiness, fifty shades of ocean spray, a quality not confined to his descriptions of half-naked Polynesian women, like Fayaway, in *Typee*—"Her full lips, when parted with a smile, disclosed teeth of a dazzling whiteness; and when her rosy mouth opened with a burst of merriment, they looked like the milk-white seeds of the 'arta,' a fruit of the valley, which, when cleft in twain, shows them reposing in rows on either side, embedded in the rich and juicy pulp"—but extending, as well, to the sea itself, the Pacific wind blowing "like a woman roused." All of this also happens to Pierre; he makes his dazzling debut as a literary heartthrob with a love sonnet called "The Tropical Summer."

Melville dedicated *Typee* to Lemuel Shaw, chief justice of the Massachusetts Supreme Judicial Court, the father of the woman he intended to marry, Elizabeth Shaw, who was a friend of Augusta's. After the wedding, in 1847, a New York newspaper ran this notice:

> Mr. HERMAN TYPEE OMOO MELVILLE has recently been united in lawful wedlock to a young lady of Boston. The fair forsaken FAYAWAY will doubtless console herself by sueing him for breach of promise.

The newlyweds settled in New York, renting a house with Lizzie's father's money. Lizzie, as guileless as she was wealthy, has a lot in common with Pierre's beloved Lucy. Melville's older brother, Gansevoort, had died in 1846, leaving Melville in charge of the family. His house was soon crammed to the rafters with his four sisters, his brother and his sister-in-law, and his mother, Maria, who lived with Herman for much of her widowhood, even though he gives every indication of having despised her. She bears an uncanny resemblance to Pierre's widowed mother, the sanctimonious and domineering Mary, whose unnatural attachment to her son—she calls him "brother" and he calls her "sister"—suggests incest, twice over (both mother-son and brother-sister!).

The Melvilles spent the summer on the farm near Pittsfield, a place Herman thought of as his "first love." He had a Linnaean cast of mind, the Sub-Sub-Sub-Librarian who in *Moby-Dick*, in a chapter titled "Cetology," divided "the whales into three primary BOOKS (subdivisible into CHAPTERS) . . . I. The FOLIO WHALE; II. The OCTAVO WHALE; III. The DUODECIMO WHALE." Delbanco considered Melville more of a New Yorker than any other American writer, so much so that reading the endlessly digressive Melville is "like strolling, or browsing, on a city street." But fields, too, teem and seethe and croak and shriek. On a wagon ride from the Pittsfield train station, Melville scribbled the names of all the grasses he knew: redtop, ribbon grass, finger grass, orchard grass, hair grass. He once wrote to Hawthorne about lying in a field on a summer's day: "Your legs seem to send out shoots into the earth. Your hair feels like leaves upon your head. This is the *all* feeling." He never loved any place more, not even the sea.

The Melvilles stayed in the city for less than three years, Lizzie in 1849 bearing the first of four children, Malcolm (a name Augusta, the family historian, found in the family tree), while Herman turned from travel writing to fiction. He'd been plagued by questions about the truthfulness of *Typee* and *Omoo*, and he felt shackled by having to stick to facts. "I began to feel an invincible distaste for the same; & a longing to plume my pinions for a flight," he explained. But critics disdained and readers declined his first avowed work of fiction, *Mardi*, leading him to write two more books in a matter of months, *Redburn* (1849) and *White-Jacket* (1850). He explained to his father-in-law, "They are two *jobs*, which I have done for money—being forced to it, as other men are to sawing wood."

Melville's prose is more usefully divided between nautical and non-nautical than between fact and fiction. In the first kind, except for Fayaway, who's about as real as a mermaid, there are hardly any women, and in the second kind, there's just the "one big, threatening woman," as John Updike put it, a glomming together of Melville's wife, mother, and sisters.

"Women have small taste for the sea," Melville told Sophia Hawthorne. But many of his readers were women; early on, they swooned for him. An 1849 issue of the *United States Magazine and Democratic Review* took notice of Melville's *Redburn* ("Once more Mr. Melville triumphs as the most captivating of ocean authors"). Augusta Melville, reading Ellis's book, found its characters implausible. "Whoever heard of such a man as that Mr. Ashley, & of such a woman, as that wife of his, & of such girls as those five daughters?—No one but Mrs. Ellis." She was the sort of female reader who had an appetite for adventure. "Have you seen Dr. May's new work 'The Barber'?" she asked a friend. "I read it in two sittings, but perhaps that is because life in Morocco was new to me, & my attention was arrested."

In 1849, Melville went to London to negotiate book contracts and to buy books, including Mary Shelley's *Frankenstein*—which ends with a mad, oceangoing pursuit. On his voyage back to New York, he got the idea for his own monster book. "The book is a romance of adventure, founded upon certain wild legends in the Southern Sperm Whale Fisheries," he announced. He began writing the book he called *The Whale* in New York, likely the part where Ishmael shares a bed at the Spouter Inn with a harpooner he believes to be a cannibal: "Upon waking next morning about daylight, I found Queequeg's arm thrown over me in the most loving and affectionate manner. You had almost thought I had been his wife."

In 1850, nearly without notice and absolutely without cash, Melville bought a hundred and sixty acres of land and moved his wife and the baby and Augusta and, off and on, his mother and his other sisters, to Pittsfield. Arrowhead is a museum now. The farmhouse, built in 1783, has been restored, and it's full of Melville bric-a-brac: Maria's sideboard, Lizzie's sewing stand, Herman's harpoon. In Herman and Lizzie's bedroom, on either side of the bedstead, there are two paneled doors, which lead to three tiny rooms. In these rooms, on the other side of the wall from their headboard, Melville's mother and sisters slept. There are no locks on the doors, and the only way to those rooms was through Herman and Lizzie's bedroom. There are similarly creepy sleeping arrangements in *Pierre*.

"**I HAVE A SORT OF SEA-FEELING** here in the country, now that the ground is all covered with snow," Melville wrote from Arrowhead, in December of 1850. "I look out my window in the morning when I rise as I would out of a port-hole of a ship in the Atlantic. My room seems a ship's cabin; & at nights when I wake up & hear the wind shrieking, I almost fancy there is too much sail on the house, & I had better go on the roof & rig the chimney."

Lizzie was probably nursing Malcolm when Melville began writing *Moby-Dick*, in which Ishmael spies, near the *Pequod*, whale cows nursing their calves, who, "as human infants while suckling will calmly and fixedly gaze away from the breast, as if leading two different lives." But for much of the time Melville was writing *Moby-Dick*, Lizzie was pregnant.

Locked in his study like Ahab in his cabin, the women his crew, Melville felt he had the whole book in his head; it was just a matter of getting it down. "Taking a book off the brain," he wrote to a friend, "is akin to the ticklish & dangerous business of taking an old painting off a panel—you have to scrape off the whole brain in order to get at it with due safety—& even then, the painting may not be worth the trouble." He rose at around eight in the morning and wrote until two thirty in the afternoon, when he took a break to eat, and to feed his horse and cow their dinner. He despised interruption. "Herman I hope returned home safe after dumping me & my trunks out so unceremoniously at the Depot," his furious mother wrote. "He hurried off as if his life had depended upon his speed."

Every day, on board the *Pequod*, Ishmael looks out for a glimpse of Ahab, his peg leg made out of whalebone. Finally, in chapter 28, the captain emerges:

He looked like a man cut away from the stake, when the fire has overrunningly wasted all the limbs without consuming them, or taking away one particle from their compacted aged robustness. His whole high, broad form, seemed made of solid bronze, and shaped in an unalterable mould, like Cellini's cast Perseus. Threading its way out from among his grey hairs, and continuing right down one side of his tawny scorched face and neck, till it disappeared in his clothing, you saw a slender rod-like mark, lividly whitish. It resembled that perpendicular seam sometimes made in the straight, lofty trunk of a great tree, when the upper lightning tearingly darts down it, and without wrenching a single twig, peels and grooves out the bark from top to bottom, ere running off into the soil, leaving the tree still greenly alive, but branded.

A half-inch hole had been drilled into the plank of the quarterdeck. "His bone leg steadied in that hole; one arm elevated, and holding by a shroud; Captain Ahab stood erect, looking straight out beyond the ship's ever-pitching prow." It might just be the best entrance in American literature. He's like one thing, he's like another, or another, or another, or yet another. To the devil with you and your daguerre-otype! Prose, man! Poetry! Philosophy! Meet thee evil! "For a Khan of the plank, and a king of the sea, and a great lord of Leviathans was Ahab." Melville wrote with sharpened bone. He meant his scope to be the whole great whale of the world.

Every day, Augusta Melville copied the pages her brother had written the day before, work that kept her from her own reading: "I quite sigh for leisure in which to satisfy my literary thirst." It inter-rupted her letter writing: "Herman came in with another batch of copying which he was most anxious to have as soon as possible." She sometimes thought about writing more than letters. "I really believe that I could at this moment write a sonnet," she confessed, stirred by the beauty of the Berkshires. "I declare it has made even prosaic me, poetical." A friend urged her to write about the goings-on beneath the roof of the Melvilles: "Guss suppose you write a novel founded on facts." But Augusta lived in a world where women had their brains, not their feet, bound. When her imagination threatened to break free of its bindings, she cinched it back up, like the time she had a dream that she refused to describe, explaining, "'Twas too strangely sad, too wildly sorrowful, for thine ears—& too intensely fantastic & airy for my pen."

Lizzie gave birth to a boy named Stanwix on October 22, 1851. The first reviews of *Moby-Dick* began to appear. "So much trash," accord-ing to one review. "Wantonly eccentric; outrageously bombastic." "Faulty as the book may be," it bears the marks of "unquestionable genius" was about the best that was generally said. "Captain Ahab is a striking conception," yet "if we had as much of Hamlet or Macbeth as Mr. Melville gives us of Ahab, we should be tired even of their sub-lime company." The book was too long, a leviathan. It was too ambi-tious, lurid with "a vile overdaubing with a coat of book-learning and mysticism." Too much of this, too much of that. "There is no method in his madness; and we must needs pronounce the chief feature of the volume a perfect failure, and the work itself inartistic." It was just . . . too much.

Late that fall, Melville, pondering *Pierre*, went to the forest to fell trees and chop firewood. Lizzie developed an excruciatingly painful infection in her left breast but did not wean the baby. (She was so light-headed from the pain that a sheet had to be hung on the wall next to her bed, because the floral wallpaper made her dizzy.) Her illness has occasioned some of the more ham-handed remarks of Melville's best-known biographers. Hershel Parker, on Melville's driving Lizzie to Boston to see the doctor: "He must have gone grudgingly. It had been bad enough to have to stop work on *Moby-Dick* to drive his sister Helen or his mother to the depot. Now he had to interrupt a book that again required intense concentration for long periods." Andrew Delbanco, on the inconvenience to the author of Lizzie's illness: "Perhaps the only thing one can say with confidence about Melville's married life is that when he took up sex as a literary theme in *Pierre*, he was experiencing sexual deprivation." Holy smokes.

During the years that he lived at Arrowhead, as the United States got closer to civil war, Melville wrote *Moby-Dick* (1851); *Pierre* (1852); *The Piazza Tales* (1856), a collection of short fiction that included "Bartleby, the Scrivener" and "Benito Cereno"; and *The Confidence-Man* (1857). He wrote epics; he wrote tales. He directed his readers' attention to acts of horror with a precise command of language and an uncontainable appetite for allegory, especially about whiteness. He indicted the mundane; he dismantled houses; he eviscerated imperialism; he pitied the whale; he hunted missionaries. He wrote about women as if he'd never met one.

Ralph Ellison once observed that Melville understood race as "a vital issue in the American consciousness, symbolic of the condition of Man," an understanding lost after the end of Reconstruction, when American literature decided to ignore "the Negro issue," pushing it "into the underground of the American conscience." Ellison didn't think that everyone ought to write about race. It just bugged him that when a writer had the need of a Black character or two, "up float his misshapen and bloated images of the Negro, like the fetid bodies of the drowned." That is what the women are like in Melville. They bob, and then they sink.

THE LETTER PIERRE RECEIVES at the beginning of *Pierre*, when he's seemingly engaged in an incestuous relationship with his mother, and on the verge of asking Lucy to marry him, is from his long-lost sister, Isabel. She tells him her life story. If *Moby-Dick* borrows from *Frankenstein*, *Pierre* borrows more, with its tale-within-a-tale, from the autobiography of Isabel. "I never knew a mortal mother," she begins. She remembers an old, ruined country house, where she was treated like an animal, not taught to speak, not knowing that she was human. And she never becomes fully human; she's a beautiful idiot: "I comprehend nothing, Pierre."

Pierre, feeling responsible for this subhuman sister but unwilling to cause his too beloved mother pain by revealing the existence of his dead father's illegitimate daughter, decides instead to pretend to marry Isabel, and they live together as husband and wife. (The literary critic Newton Arvin, who lost his job after being arrested for homosexuality, intimated that the incest in *Pierre* was a cover for a different taboo, Melville's unspeakable love for men.) Pierre loses his fortune and becomes a writer; Isabel becomes his diligent copyist. Eventually Lucy moves in, too.

Pierre, after his early success with "The Tropical Summer," decides to write "a comprehensive compacted work, to whose speedy completion two tremendous motives unitedly impelled;—the burning desire to deliver what he thought to be new, or at least miserably neglected Truth to the world; and the prospective menace of being absolutely penniless." So, too, Melville. After *Typee* and *Omoo*, none of Melville's books made much money. He fell further into debt. "What I feel most moved to write, that is banned,—it will not pay," he complained to Hawthorne. "Yet, altogether, write the *other* way I cannot. So the product is a final hash, and all my books are botches." He anticipated his fate: "Though I wrote the Gospels in this century, I should die in the gutter."

Melville looked upon *Moby-Dick* and *Pierre* as twins, each penetrating psychological depths, "still deep and deeper." Before plotting *Pierre*, he read *The Anatomy of Melancholy*, an edition inscribed "A. Melvill"—his father's own copy, sold at auction, after his father died, insane. Melville was haunted. He was fated. He was falling apart. By the time he finished writing *Pierre*, *Moby-Dick* had failed. In the final chapter of *Pierre*, the protagonist's publisher sends him a letter:

> SIR: You are a swindler. Upon the pretense of writing a popular novel for us, you have been receiving cash advances from us, while passing through our press the sheets of a blasphemous rhapsody.

A few wildly implausible paragraphs later, Pierre, Lucy, and Isabel all die in a heap, Shakespeare-style.

"*Pierre; or the Ambiguities* is, perhaps, the craziest fiction extant," one critic wrote, finding it more plausibly the product of "a lunatic hospital rather than from the quiet retreats of Berkshire." In 1860, Melville's father-in-law, knowing the extent of Melville's insolvency, put the family property in Lizzie's name. Melville published no more prose fiction in his lifetime. In 1863, he sold Arrowhead to his brother Allan. Before moving back to New York, where he became a customs inspector, he made a bonfire.

IN THE SPRING OF **1867**, a year after Melville published his first book of poetry, *Battle-Pieces*, his terrified wife nearly left him. Lizzie's family hatched a plot to all but kidnap her; Augusta may have been involved in the plan. Lizzie never left. Later that year, Malcolm Melville, aged eighteen, shot himself in the head, in his bedroom in his parents' house. After the funeral, Lizzie and Herman went to Arrowhead, where, by the chimney, there hung a sketch from *Paradise Lost*.

Augusta Melville died in April 1876, aged fifty-four, in her brother Tom's house on Staten Island, of what sounds like breast cancer. (Lizzie said that Augusta had long suffered from a "fibrous tumor" but had been too embarrassed to tell anyone about it.) In January, she'd begun collapsing from the pain, and had been heading to the city to stay with Herman and Lizzie when she received word that Melville refused to let her come, since he was busy proofing the pages of his epic poem, *Clarel*, for the publisher. He was a mess. "I am actually *afraid* to have any one here for fear that he will be upset entirely," Lizzie confided. *Clarel* was published that June, unappreciated, if more lately heralded, by critics including Helen Vendler, as a masterpiece. Melville's publisher pulped it.

Herman Melville died in New York, in 1891, at the age of seventy-two. "If the truth were known, even his own generation has long thought him dead," one New York obituary read. Few writers' critical acclaim has been more wholly posthumous.

Augusta Melville never wrote a novel about life among the Melvilles, but she did collect their papers, including more than five hundred letters that she stored in two trunks, which were in the Gansevoort family mansion when she died. Eventually, someone moved them into a barn. That's where they were in the 1980s, when an antique dealer found them. They ended up at the New York Public Library. In 2018, the library renamed the collection the Augusta Melville Papers. The library still has the trunks. They look like seaman's chests; they smell like horses.

At Arrowhead, the cellar of Melville's farmhouse, now an archive, holds a single letter of Augusta's, written in May of 1851, just as her brother was nearing the end of *Moby-Dick* and she was finishing copying it. She loved it. "That book of his will create a great interest I think," she wrote. "It is very fine."

The field where Melville grew pumpkins and corn for his horse and cow is a meadow, wild with violets, irises, daisies, clover, bee balm, Queen Anne's lace, vetch, and chickweed. Melville's apple trees still stand, nearly barren. The barn where he and Hawthorne went to escape the ladies has been turned into a gift shop where you can buy a T-shirt that says CALL ME ISHMAEL. The Wi-Fi there is Pequod, but I don't know the password. Some things are private.

—2019

THE FIREMAN

E UGENE VICTOR DEBS LEFT SCHOOL AT THE AGE OF fourteen, to scrape paint and grease off the cars of the Vandalia Railroad, in Indiana, for fifty cents a day. He got a raise when he was promoted to fireman, which meant working in the locomotive next to the engineer, shoveling coal into a firebox—as much as two tons an hour, sixteen hours a day, six days a week. Firemen, caked in coal dust, blinded by wind and smoke, had to make sure that the engine didn't explode, an eventuality they weren't always able to forestall. If they were lucky, and lived long enough, firemen usually became engineers, which was safer than being a switchman or a brakeman, jobs that involved working on the tracks next to a moving train, or racing across its top, in any weather, at the risk of toppling off and getting run over. All these men reported to the conductors, who had the top job, and, on trains owned by George Mortimer Pullman, one of the richest men in the United States, all of them—the engineers, the firemen, the brakemen, the switchmen, and even the scrapers—outranked the porters. Pullman porters were almost always Black men, and ex-slaves, and, at the start, were paid nothing except the tips they could earn by bowing before the fancy passengers who could afford the sleeping car, and who liked very much to be served with a shuffle and a grin, Dixie-style.

Every man who worked on the American railroad in the last decades of the nineteenth century became, of necessity, a scholar of the relations between the rich and the poor, the haves and the have-nots, the masters and the slaves, the riders and the ridden-upon. No student of this subject is more important to American history than Debs, half man, half myth, who founded the American Railway Union, turned that into the Social Democratic Party, and ran for president of the United States five times, including once from prison.

Debs, who wrote a lot about manliness, always said that the best kind of man was a sand man. "'Sand' means grit," he wrote in 1882, in *Firemen's Magazine*. "It means the power to hold on." When a train stalled from the steepness of the incline or the weight of the freight, railroad men poured sand on the tracks, to improve the grip of the wheels. Men need sand, too, Debs said: "Men who have plenty of 'sand' in their boxes never slip on the path of duty." Debs had plenty of sand in his box. He had, though, something of a morbid fear of ashes. Maybe that's a fireman's phobia, a tending-the-engine man's idea of doom. In prison—having been sentenced, brutally, to ten years of hard time at the age of sixty-three—he had a nightmare. "I was walking by the house where I was born," he wrote. "The house was gone and nothing left but ashes . . . only ashes—ashes!" The question today for socialism in the United States, which appears to be stoking its engines, is whether it's got enough sand. Or whether it'll soon be ashes, only ashes, all over again.

DEBS WAS BORN IN TERRE HAUTE, INDIANA, in 1855, seven years after Marx and Engels published *The Communist Manifesto*. His parents were Alsatian immigrants who ran a small grocery store. Debs worked for the railroads a little more than four years. In the wake of the Panic of 1873, he lost his job at Vandalia and tramped to East St. Louis looking for work; then, homesick, he tramped back to Terre Haute, where, in 1875, he took a job as a labor organizer, and, later, as a magazine editor, for the Brotherhood of Locomotive Firemen. He hung his old scraper on the wall, part relic, part badge, part talisman, of his life as a manual laborer.

Debs was a tall man, lanky and rubbery, like a noodle. He had deep-set blue eyes and lost his hair early, and he talked with his hands. When he gave speeches, he leaned toward the crowd, and the veins of his temples bulged. He was clean-shaven and favored bow ties and sometimes looked lost in crumpled, baggy suits. He had a way of hunching his shoulders that you often see, and admire, in tall men who don't like to tower over other people. In *Eugene V. Debs: A Graphic Biography*, drawn by Noah Van Sciver and written by Paul Buhle and Steve Max, Debs looks like an R. Crumb character, though not so bedraggled and neurotic.

People could listen to him talk for hours. "Debs! Debs! Debs!"

they'd cry, when his train pulled into a station. Crowds massed to hear him by the tens of thousands. But even though Debs lived until 1926, well into the age of archival sound, no one has ever found a recording of his voice. When Nick Salvatore wrote, in his comprehensive biography, *Eugene V. Debs: Citizen and Socialist*, in 1982, "His voice ran a gamut of tones: mock whisper to normal conversation to full stentorian power," you wonder how he knew. Debs could speak French and German and was raised in the Midwest, so maybe he talked like the Ohio-born Clarence Darrow, with a rasp and a drawl. Some of Debs's early essays and speeches were published in the first of six volumes of *The Selected Works of Eugene V. Debs*, edited by Tim Davenport and David Walters. Really, he wasn't much of a writer. The most delightful way to hear Debs is to listen to a recording made in 1979 by Bernie Sanders, in an audio documentary that he wrote and produced when he was thirty-seven years old and was the director of the American People's Historical Society, in Burlington, Vermont, two years before he became that city's mayor. In the documentary—available on YouTube and Spotify—Sanders, the Brooklyn-born son of a Polish Jew, performs parts of Debs's most famous speeches, sounding, more or less, like Larry David. It is not to be missed.

Debs began his political career as a Democrat. In 1879, when he was only twenty-three, he was elected city clerk of Terre Haute, as a Democrat; the city's Democratic newspaper called him "one of the rising young men of Terre Haute," and the Republican paper agreed, dubbing him "the blue-eyed boy of destiny." Debs looked back on these days less fondly. "There was a time in my life, before I became a Socialist, when I permitted myself as a member of the Democratic party to be elected to a state legislature," he later said. "I have been trying to live it down. I am as much ashamed of that as I am proud of having gone to jail." Throughout his life, he believed in individual striving, and he believed in the power of machines. "A railroad is the architect of progress," he said in a speech at the Grand Lodge of the Brotherhood of Locomotive Firemen in 1877, the year the president of the United States sent federal troops to crush a railroad workers' strike. The firemen's brotherhood was less a labor union than a benevolent society. "The first object of the association is to provide for the widows and orphans who are daily left penniless and at the mercy of public charity by the death of a brother," Debs explained. At the time, he was opposed to strikes. "Does the brotherhood encourage strikers?" he asked. "No—brotherhood."

For a long time, Debs disavowed socialism. He placed his faith in democracy, the franchise, and the two-party system. "The conflict is not between capital and labor," he insisted. "It is between the man who holds the office and the man who holds the ballot." But in the 1880s, when railroad workers struck time and time again, and as many as two thousand railroad men a year were killed on the job, while another twenty thousand were injured, Debs began to wonder whether the power of benevolence and fraternity was adequate protection from the avarice and ruthlessness of corporations backed up by armed men. "The strike is the weapon of the oppressed," Debs wrote in 1888. Even then he didn't talk about socialism. For Debs, this was Americanism, a tradition that had begun with the American Revolution. "The Nation had for its cornerstone a strike," he said. He also spent some time with a pencil, doing sums. Imagine, he wrote in an editorial, that a grandson of Cornelius Vanderbilt started out with two million dollars—a million from his grandfather and another million from his father. "If a locomotive fireman could work 4,444 years, 300 days each year, at $1.50 per day," Debs went on, "he would be in a position to bet Mr. Vanderbilt $2.50 that all men are born equal."

In 1889, Debs argued for an industrial union, a federation of all the brotherhoods of railroad workers, from brakemen to conductors, as equals. Samuel Gompers wanted those men to join his far less radical trade union, the American Federation of Labor, which he'd founded three years earlier, but in 1893 Debs pulled them into the American Railway Union. Soon it had nearly a hundred and fifty thousand members, with Debs, at its head, as their Moses. That's what got him into a battle with George Pullman, in 1894, and landed him, for the first time, in prison, where he read Marx's *Das Kapital*.

DEBS ONCE SAID THAT GEORGE PULLMAN was "as greedy as a horse leech," but that was unfair to leeches. In the aftermath of the Panic of 1893, Pullman slashed his workers' wages by as much as 50 percent, and, even though they lived in housing he provided, he didn't cut rents or the price of the food he sold them. Three thousand workers from the Pullman Palace Car Company, many of them American Railway Union members, had already begun a wildcat strike in May of 1894, a month before the ARU's first annual meeting, in Chicago. As Jack Kelly recounts, in *The Edge of Anarchy: The Railroad Barons, the Gilded Age, and the Greatest Labor Uprising in America*, Debs hadn't wanted the ARU to get involved, but the members of his union found the Pullman workers' plight impossible to ignore, especially after nineteen-year-old Jennie Curtis, who'd worked in the Pullman sewing department for five years, upholstering and making curtains, addressed the convention. Curtis explained that she was often paid nine or ten dollars for two weeks' work, out of which she paid Pullman seven dollars for her board and two or three more for rent. "We ask you to come along with us," she told Debs's men, because working for Pullman was little better than slavery. After hearing from her, the ARU voted for a boycott, refusing "to handle Pullman cars and equipment."

That Curtis had a voice at all that day was thanks in part to Debs, who had supported the admission of women to the ARU. He also argued for the admission of African Americans. "I am not here to advocate association with the negro, but I am ready to stand side by side with him," he told the convention. But, by a vote of 112 to 110, the assembled members decided that the union would be for whites only. If two votes had gone the other way, the history of the labor movement in the United States might have turned out very differently.

Black men, closed out of the ARU, formed the Anti-Strikers Railroad Union, to fill positions opened by striking whites. If working on a Pullman car was degrading, it was also, for decades, one of the best jobs available to African American men. Its perks included safe travel at a time when it was difficult for Black people to make their way between any two American cities without threat or harm. George Pullman's company was the nation's single largest employer of African American men. Thurgood Marshall's father was a Pullman porter. The ARU vote in 1894 set back the cause of labor for decades. The Brotherhood of Sleeping Car Porters achieved recognition from the Pullman Company only in 1937, after years of organizing by A. Philip Randolph.

The Pullman strike of 1894, one of the single biggest labor actions in American history, stalled trains in twenty-seven states. Debs's American Railway Union all but halted transportation by rail west of Detroit for more than a month—either by refusing to touch Pullman cars or by actively unhitching them from the trains. Whatever Debs's initial misgivings about the boycott, once his union voted for it he dedicated himself to the confrontation between "the producing classes and the money power." In the end, after a great deal of violence, George Pullman, aided by President Grover Cleveland, defeated the strikers. Pursued by a U.S. attorney general who had long served as a lawyer for the railroads, Debs and other ARU leaders were indicted and convicted of violating a federal injunction to stop "ordering, directing, aiding, assisting, or abetting" the uprising. The U.S. Supreme Court upheld Debs's conviction. He and seven other organizers were sentenced to time behind bars—Debs to six months, the others to three—and served that time in Woodstock, Illinois, in a county jail that was less a prison than a suite of rooms in the back of the elegant two-story Victorian home of the county sheriff, who had his inmates over for supper every night.

"The Socialist Conversion" is the title of the half-page panel depicting these six months in *Eugene V. Debs: A Graphic Biography*. It shows Debs in a prisoner's uniform, seated at a desk in a bare room, with a beady-eyed, billy-club-wielding prison guard looking on from the doorway, while a cheerful man in a suit, carrying *The Communist Manifesto*, approaches Debs, his speech bubble reading "This is a present from the Socialists of Milwaukee to you."

Very little of this is true. Debs's time in jail in Woodstock was remarkably comfortable. He ran the union office out of his cell. He was allowed to leave jail on his honor. "The other night I had to lock myself in," he told the *New York World* reporter Nellie Bly, when she went to interview him. "There was no sign of the prisoner about Mr. Debs' clothes," Bly reported. "He wore a well-made suit of grey tweed, the coat being a cutaway, and a white starched shirt with a standing collar and a small black and white scarf tied in a bow-knot." The Milwaukee socialist Victor Berger did bring Debs a copy of *Das Kapital*. And Debs and his fellow labor organizers dedicated most of their daily schedule to reading. "I had heard but little of Socialism" before the Pullman strike, Debs later claimed, insisting that the reading he did in jail brought about his conversion. But it's not clear what effect that reading really had on him. "No sir; I do not call myself a socialist," he told a strike commission that year. While in jail, he turned away overtures from socialists. And when he got out, in 1895, and addressed a crowd of more than a hundred thousand people who met him at the train station in Chicago, he talked about "the spirit of '76" and the Declaration of Independence and the Constitution, not Marx and Engels.

The next year, Debs endorsed the presidential candidate William Jennings Bryan, running on both the Democratic and the People's Party tickets. Only after Bryan's loss to William McKinley, whose campaign was funded by businessmen, did Debs abandon his devotion to the two-party system. The people elected Bryan, it was said, but money elected McKinley. On January 1, 1897, writing in the *Railway Times*, Debs proclaimed himself a socialist. "The result of the November election has convinced every intelligent wageworker that in politics, per se, there is no hope of emancipation from the degrading curse of wage-slavery," he wrote. "I am for socialism because I am for humanity. . . . Money constitutes no proper basis of civilization."

That June, at the annual meeting of the American Railway Union, Debs founded the Social Democracy of America party. When it splintered, within the year, Victor Berger and Debs joined what became the Social Democratic Party, and then, in 1901, the Socialist Party of America. For Debs, socialism meant public ownership of the means of production. "Arouse from your slavery, join the Social Democratic Party and vote with us to take possession of the mines of the country and operate them in the interest of the people," he urged miners in Illinois and Kansas in 1899. But Debs's socialism, which was so starry-eyed that his critics called it "impossibilism," was decidedly American, and had less to do with Karl Marx and communism than with Walt Whitman and Protestantism. "What is Socialism?" he asked. "Merely Christianity in action. It recognizes the equality in men."

The myth of Debs's Christlike suffering and socialist conversion in the county jail dates to 1900; it was a campaign strategy. At the Social Democratic Party convention that March, a Massachusetts delegate nominated Debs as the party's presidential candidate and, in his nominating speech, likened Debs's time in Woodstock to the Resurrection: "When he came forth from that tomb it was to a resurrection of life and the first message that he gave to his class as he came from his darkened cell was a message of liberty." Debs earned nearly ninety thousand votes in that year's election, and more than four times as many when he ran again in 1904. In 1908, he campaigned in thirty-three states, traveling on a custom train called the Red Special. As one story has it, a woman waiting for Debs at a station in Illinois asked, "Is that Debs?" to which another woman replied, "Oh, no, that ain't Debs—when Debs comes out you'll think it's Jesus Christ."

"This is our year," Debs said in 1912, and it was, in the sense that nearly a million Americans voted for him for president. But 1912 was also socialism's year in the sense that both the Democratic and the Republican parties embraced progressive reforms long advocated by socialists (and, for that matter, populists): women's suffrage, trust-busting, economic reform, maximum hour and minimum wage laws, the abolition of child labor, and the direct election of U.S. senators. As Debs could likely perceive a couple of years later, when the Great War broke out in Europe, 1912 was to be socialism's high-water mark in the United States. "You may hasten Socialism," he said, "you may retard it, but you cannot stop it." Except that socialism had already done most of what it would do in the United States in those decades: it had reformed the two major parties.

Debs was too sick to run in 1916. The United States declared war on Germany in April 1917; the Bolshevik Revolution swept Russia that November. Debs spoke out against the war as soon as it began. "I am opposed to every war but one," he said. "I am for that war with heart and soul, and that is the world-wide war of the social revolution. In that war I am prepared to fight in any way the ruling class may make necessary, even to the barricades." Bernie Sanders recorded this speech for his 1979 documentary. And, as a member of the Senate, Sanders said it again. "There is a war going on in this country," he declared on the floor of the Senate in 2010, in a speech of protest that lasted more than eight hours. "I am not referring to the war in Iraq or the war in Afghanistan. I am talking about a war being waged by some of the wealthiest and most powerful people against working families, against the disappearing and shrinking middle class of our country."

After Debs, socialism endured in the six-time presidential candidacy of his successor, Norman Thomas. But it endured far more significantly in Progressive Era reforms, in the New Deal, and in Lyndon Johnson's Great Society. In the decades since Ronald Reagan's election in 1980, many of those reforms have been undone, monopolies have risen again, and income inequality has spiked back up to where it was in Debs's lifetime. Socialism has been carried into the twenty-first century by way of Sanders, a Debs disciple, and by way of the utter failure of the two-party system. In 2018, a Gallup poll found that more Democrats view socialism favorably than view capitalism favorably. This brand of socialism has its own obsession with manliness, with its "Bernie bros" and allegations by women who worked on Sanders's 2016 presidential campaign of widespread sexual harassment and violence. Sanders's campaign manager, Jeff Weaver, then addressed some of these charges: "Was it too male? Yes. Was it too white? Yes." Hence the movement's new face, and new voice: the former Sanders campaign worker Alexandria Ocasio-Cortez.

Debs wrote its manifesto, but there's a certain timidity to the new socialism. It lacks sand. In 1894, one Pullman worker stated the nature of the problem: "We are born in a Pullman house, fed from the Pullman shops, taught in the Pullman school, catechized in the Pullman Church, and when we die we shall go to the Pullman Hell." We live in Amazon houses and eat Amazon groceries and read Amazon newspapers and when we die we shall go to an Amazon hell. In the meantime, you can buy your Bernie 2020 hats and AOC T-shirts on . . . Amazon.

DEBS WAS ARRESTED IN CLEVELAND in 1918, under the terms of the 1917 Espionage Act, for a speech protesting the war that he had given two weeks earlier, on June 16, in Canton, Ohio. "Debs Invites Arrest," the *Washington Post* announced. Most of the nation's newspapers described him as a dictator or a traitor, or both. And, because what he had said was deemed seditious, newspapers couldn't print it, and readers assumed the worst. But the speech was vintage Debs, from its vague blandishments and programmatic promises—"We are going to destroy all enslaving and degrading capitalist institutions and re-create them as free and humanizing institutions"—to its astute observations and forceful repetitions: "The working class who fight the battles, the working class who make the sacrifices, the working class who shed the blood, the working class who furnish the corpses, the working class have never yet had a voice in declaring war."

Debs was one of thousands of socialists jailed during the First World War and the Red Scare that followed, when the Justice Department effectively tried to outlaw socialism. His defense attorney compared him to Christ—"You shall know him by his works"—and called no one to the stand but Debs, who, during a two-hour oration, talked less about socialism than about the First Amendment. "I believe in free speech, in war as well as in peace," Debs told the court. "If the Espionage Law stands, then the Constitution of the United States is dead."

The socialist Max Eastman, watching him speak that day, described Debs's growing fervor. "His utterance became more clear and piercing, and it made the simplicity of his faith seem almost like a portent," Eastman wrote. But it's the speech Debs gave during his sentencing that would be his best-remembered address, his American creed: "While there is a lower class, I am in it; while there is a criminal element, I am of it; while there is a soul in prison, I am not free."

After being sentenced to ten years, he was taken by train from Cleveland to a prison in West Virginia, where he was held for two months before being transferred to the much harsher Atlanta Federal Penitentiary. On the wall of a cell that he shared with five other men, he hung a picture of Jesus, wearing his crown of thorns. Refusing to ask for or accept special treatment, he was confined to his cell for fourteen hours a day and was allotted twenty minutes a day in the prison yard. He wore a rough denim uniform. He ate food barely fit to eat. He grew gaunt and weak.

Debs came to think about the men he met in prison the way he'd once thought about men he'd worked with on the railroad. "A prison is a cross section of society in which every human strain is clearly revealed," he wrote, in a memoir called *Walls and Bars*. But if the railroad was a model of hierarchy, prison was a model of equality: "We were all on a dead level there."

He became an American folk hero, a champion of free speech. In his "from the jail house to the White House" campaign, in 1920, he earned nearly a million votes running for president as Convict No. 9653. But a vote for Debs in 1920 was not a vote for socialism; it was a vote for free speech.

Convict No. 9653 refused to ask for a pardon, even as he grew sicker, and leaner, and weaker. His reputation as a twentieth-century Christ grew. (Kurt Vonnegut's much beset narrator in *Hocus Pocus* says, "I am so powerless and despised now that the man I am named after, Eugene Debs, if he were still alive, might at last be somewhat fond of me.") His supporters began holding Free Debs rallies. President Woodrow Wilson refused to answer calls for amnesty. Warren Harding finally released him, on Christmas Day 1921. Debs never recovered. He lived much of what remained of his life in a sanatorium. In 1925, he said that the Socialist Party was "as near a corpse as a thing can be." He died the next year.

Debs understood capitalism best on a train, socialism best in prison. One of the last letters he wrote was to the judge who had sentenced him in 1918, asking whether his conviction had left him disenfranchised or whether he still had the right to vote.

—2019

THE SHOREBIRD

THE HOUSE, ON AN ISLAND IN MAINE, PERCHES ON A rock at the edge of the sea like the aerie of an eagle. Below the white-railed back porch, the sea-slick rock slopes down to a lumpy low tideland of eelgrass and bladder wrack, as slippery as a knot of snakes. Periwinkles cling to rocks; mussels pinch themselves together like purses. A gull lands on a shaggy-weeded rock, fluffs itself, and settles into a crouch, bracing against a fierce wind rushing across the water, while, up on the cliff, lichen-covered trees—spruce and fir and birch—sigh and creak like old men on a damp morning.

"The shore is an ancient world," Rachel Carson wrote from a desk in that house, a pine-topped table wedged into a corner of a room where the screen door trembles with each breeze, as if begging to be unlatched. Long before Carson wrote *Silent Spring*, her last book, published in 1962, she was a celebrated writer: the scientist-poet of the sea. "Undersea," her breakout essay, appeared in the *Atlantic* in 1937. "Who has known the ocean?" she asked. "Neither you nor I, with our earthbound senses, know the foam and surge of the tide that beats over the crab hiding under the seaweed of his tide-pool home; or the lilt of the long, slow swells of mid-ocean, where shoals of wandering fish prey and are preyed upon, and the dolphin breaks the waves to breathe the upper atmosphere." It left readers swooning, drowning in the riptide of her language, a watery jabberwocky of mollusks and gills and tube worms and urchins and plankton and cunners, brine-drenched, rock-girt, sessile, arborescent, abyssal, spine-studded, radiolarian, silicious, and phosphorescent, while, here and there, "the lobster feels his way with nimble wariness through the perpetual twilight."

Silent Spring, a landlubber, is no slouch of a book: it launched the environmental movement; provoked the passage of the Clean Air Act (1963), the Wilderness Act (1964), the National Environmental Policy Act (1969), the Clean Water Act and the Endangered Species Act (both

1972); and led to the establishment of the Environmental Protection Agency, in 1970. The number of books that have done as much good in the world can be counted on the arms of a starfish. Still, all of Carson's other books and nearly all of her essays concerned the sea. That Carson would be remembered for a book about the danger of back-yard pesticides like DDT would have surprised her in her younger years, when she was a marine biologist at the U.S. Bureau of Fisheries, writing memos about shad and pondering the inquiring snouts of whales, having specialized, during graduate school, in the American eel.

Carson was fiercely proud of *Silent Spring*, but, all the same, it's heartbreaking to see that a new collection, *Silent Spring and Other Writings on the Environment*, edited by Sandra Steingraber (Library of America), includes not one drop of her writing about the sea. Steingraber complains that, "while Carson's sea books occasionally allude to environmental threats, they call for no particular action," and, with that, sets them aside. Political persuasion is a strange measure of the worth of a piece of prose whose force lies in knowledge and wonder. In her first book, *Under the Sea-Wind* (1941), Carson wrote, "To stand at the edge of the sea, to sense the ebb and the flow of the tides, to feel the breath of a mist moving over a great salt marsh, to watch the flight of shore birds that have swept up and down the surf lines of the continents for untold thousands of years, to see the running of the old eels and the young shad to the sea, is to have knowledge of things that are as nearly eternal as any earthly life can be." She could not have written *Silent Spring* if she hadn't, for decades, scrambled down rocks, rolled up her pant legs, and waded into tide pools, thinking about how one thing can change another, and how, "over the eons of time, the sea has grown ever more bitter with the salt of the continents." She loved best to go out at night, with a flashlight, piercing the dread-black dark.

ALL CREATURES ARE MADE OF THE SEA, as Carson liked to point out; "the great mother of life," she called it. Even land mammals, with our lime-hardened skeletons and our salty blood, begin as fetuses that swim in the ocean of every womb. She herself could not swim. She disliked boats. In all her childhood, she never so much as smelled the ocean. She tried to picture it: "I used to imagine what it would look like, and what the surf sounded like."

Carson was born in 1907 in western Pennsylvania, near the Allegheny River, in a two-story clapboard house on a sixty-four-acre farm with an orchard of apple and pear trees and a barnyard of a pig, a horse, and some chickens and sheep, a place not unlike the one she conjures up in the opening lines of *Silent Spring*:

> There was once a town in the heart of America where all life seemed to live in harmony with its surroundings. The town lay in the midst of a checkerboard of prosperous farms, with fields of grain and hillsides of orchards where, in spring, white clouds of bloom drifted above the green fields. In autumn, oak and maple and birch set up a blaze of color that flamed and flickered across a backdrop of pines. Then foxes barked in the hills and deer silently crossed the fields, half hidden in the mists of the fall mornings.

The youngest of three children, she spent her childhood wandering the fields and hills. Her mother taught her the names of plants and the calls of animals. She read Beatrix Potter and *The Wind in the Willows*. At age eight, she wrote a story about two wrens, searching for a house. "I can remember no time, even in earliest childhood, when I didn't assume I was going to be a writer," she said. "I have no idea why." Stories she wrote in her teens chronicled her discoveries: "the bobwhite's nest, tightly packed with eggs, the oriole's aerial cradle, the framework of sticks which the cuckoo calls a nest, and the lichen-covered home of the humming-bird."

And then: something of the coal-pit blight of smokestacked Pittsburgh invaded Carson's childhood when her father, who never made a go of much of anything except the rose garden he tended, began selling off bits of the family's farm; meadows became shops. It wasn't the scourge of pesticides, but, to Carson, it was a loss that allowed her to write with such clarity, in the opening of *Silent Spring*, about the fate of an imagined American town sprayed with DDT:

> Then a strange blight crept over the area and everything began to change. Some evil spell had settled on the community: mysterious maladies swept the flocks of chickens; the cattle sickened and died. Everywhere was a shadow of death. The farmers spoke

of much illness among their families. In the town the doctors had become more and more puzzled by new kinds of sickness appearing among their patients. There had been several sudden and unexplained deaths, not only among the adults but even among children, who would be stricken suddenly while at play and die within a few hours.

Carson left home for the Pennsylvania College for Women, to study English. She sent poems to magazines—*Poetry*, the *Atlantic*, *Good Housekeeping*, the *Saturday Evening Post*—and made a collection of rejection slips, as strange as butterflies. Her mother sold apples and chickens and the family china to help pay the tuition and traveled from the farm to the college every weekend to type her daughter's papers (she later typed Carson's books, too), not least because, like so many mothers, she herself craved an education.

Carson, whose friends called her Ray, went to a college prom in 1928, but never displayed any romantic interest in men. She was, however, deeply passionate about her biology professor, Mary Scott Skinker. She changed her major, and followed Skinker to Woods Hole for a summer research project, which was how she came, at last, to see the ocean. By day, she combed the shore for hours on end, lost in a new world, enchanted by each creature. At night, she peered into the water off the docks to watch the mating of polychaete worms, bristles glinting in the moonlight.

Carson began graduate study in zoology at Johns Hopkins, completed a master's degree, and entered a PhD program in 1932. Her entire family moved to Baltimore to live with her: her mother, her ailing father, her divorced sister, and her two very young nieces. Carson, the family's only wage earner, worked as a lab assistant and taught biology and zoology at Johns Hopkins and at the University of Maryland. As the Depression deepened, they lived, for a while, on nothing but apples. Eventually, Carson had to leave graduate school to take a better-paying job, in the public education department of the Bureau of Fisheries, and brought in extra money by selling articles to the *Baltimore Sun*. Her best biographer, Linda Lear, writes gravely that one concerned oyster farming, while "three others continued her investigation into the plight of the shad."

Carson's father died in 1935, followed, two years later, by her older sister, leaving Carson to care for her mother and her nieces, ages eleven and twelve; she later adopted her grandnephew, when he was orphaned at the age of four. These obligations sometimes frustrated Carson, but not half as much as they frustrate her biographers. For Lear, the author of *Rachel Carson: Witness for Nature* (1997) and the editor of an excellent anthology, *Lost Woods: The Discovered Writing of Rachel Carson* (1998), Carson's familial obligations—in particular, the children—are nothing but burdens that "deprived her of privacy and drained her physical and emotional energy." Lear means this generously, as a way of accounting for why Carson didn't write more, and why, except for her *Sun* articles, she never once submitted a manuscript on time. But caring for other people brings its own knowledge. Carson came to see the world as beautiful, wild, animal, and vulnerable, each part attached to every other part, not only through prodigious scientific research but also through a lifetime of caring for the very old and the very young, wiping a dying man's brow, tucking motherless girls into bed, heating up dinners for a lonely little boy. The domestic pervades Carson's understanding of nature. "Wildlife, it is pointed out, is dwindling because its home is being destroyed," she wrote in 1938, "but the home of the wildlife is also our home." If she'd had fewer ties, she would have had less insight.

EARLY IN HER TIME at the Bureau of Fisheries, Carson drafted an eleven-page essay about sea life called "The World of Waters." The head of her department told her that it was too good for a government brochure and suggested that she send it to the *Atlantic*. After it was published, as "Undersea," Carson began writing her first book under the largesse of FDR's New Deal, in the sense that she drafted it on the back of National Recovery Administration stationery, while working for what became, in 1939, the U.S. Fish and Wildlife Service. *Under the Sea-Wind* appeared a few weeks before the Japanese bombed Pearl Harbor, and sank like a battleship.

Carson, who spent the meat-rationed war instructing housewives in how to cook little-known fish, grew restless. She pitched a piece to *Reader's Digest* about DDT. During the war, chemical companies had sold the pesticide to the military to stop the spread of typhus by killing lice. After the war, they began selling DDT and other pesticides commercially, to be applied to farms and gardens. Carson, reading government reports on fish and wildlife, became alarmed: DDT hadn't been tested for civilian use, and many creatures other than insects appeared to be dying. She proposed an article on the pesticide, investigating "whether it may upset the whole delicate balance of nature if unwisely used." *Reader's Digest* was not interested.

Writing at night, Carson began another book, hoping to bring to readers the findings of a revolution in marine biology and deep-sea exploration by offering an ecology of the ocean. "Unmarked and trackless though it may seem to us, the surface of the ocean is divided into definite zones," she explained. "Fishes and plankton, whales and squids, birds and sea turtles, are all linked by unbreakable ties to certain kinds of water." But the state of research also meant that mysteries abided: "Whales suddenly appear off the slopes of the coastal banks where the swarms of shrimplike krill are spawning, the whales having come from no one knows where, by no one knows what route."

Carson had taken on a subject and a field of research so wide-ranging that she began calling the book *Out of My Depth*, or *Carson at Sea*. She was haunted, too, by a sense of foreboding. In 1946, she'd had a cyst in her left breast removed. In 1950, her doctor found another cyst. After more surgery, she went to the seashore, Nags Head, North Carolina. "Saw tracks of a shore bird probably a sanderling, and followed them a little, then they turned toward the water and were soon obliterated by the sea," she wrote in field notes that she kept in spiral-bound notebooks. "How much it washes away, and makes as though it had never been."

When Carson finished the book, the *Atlantic* declined to publish an excerpt, deeming it too poetic. William Shawn, the managing editor of *The New Yorker*, did not share this reservation. *The Sea Around Us* appeared in the magazine, in 1951, as a three-part Profile of the Sea, *The New Yorker's* first-ever profile of something other than a person. Letters from readers poured in—"I started reading with an o-dear-now-whats-this attitude, and found myself entranced," one wrote—and many declared it the most memorable thing ever published in the magazine and, aside from John Hersey's *Hiroshima*, the best.

The Sea Around Us won the National Book Award, and remained on the *New York Times* bestseller list for a record-breaking eighty-six weeks. Reissued, *Under the Sea-Wind* became a bestseller, too. "Who is the author?" readers wanted to know. Carson's forcefully written work drew the supposition from male reviewers that its female author must be half-man. A reporter for the *Boston Globe* wrote, "Would you imagine a woman who has written about the seven seas and their wonders to be a hearty physical type? Not Miss Carson. She is small and slender, with chestnut hair and eyes whose color has something of both the green and blue of sea water. She is trim and feminine, wears a soft pink nail polish and uses lipstick and powder expertly, but sparingly."

Carson shrugged that off and, resigning from her government post, began to question federal policy. When Eisenhower's new secretary of the interior, a businessman from Oregon, replaced scientists in the department with political hacks, Carson wrote a letter to the *Washington Post:* "The ominous pattern that is clearly being revealed is the elimination from the Government of career men of long experience and high professional competence and their replacement by political appointees."

But the greatest change wrought by Carson's success came when, with the earnings from her biography of the ocean, she bought a tiny patch of land atop a rock in Maine, and built a small cottage there, a Walden by the sea. Carson once dived underwater, wearing an eighty-four-pound sea-diving helmet, and lasted, eight feet below, for only fifteen clouded minutes. Her real love was the shore: "I can't think of any more exciting place to be than down in the low-tide world, when the ebb tide falls very early in the morning, and the world is full of salt smell, and the sound of water, and the softness of fog." To fathom the depths, she read books; the walls of her house in Maine are lined with them, crammed between baskets and trays filled with sea glass and seashells and sea-smoothed stones. She wrote some of her next book, *The Edge of the Sea*, from that perch.

"My quarrel with almost all seashore books for the amateur," she reflected, "is that they give him a lot of separate little capsules of information about a series of creatures, which are never firmly placed in their environment." Carson's seashore book was different, an explanation of the shore as a system, an *ecosystem*, a word most readers had never heard before, and one that Carson herself rarely used but instead conjured, as a wave of motion and history:

> In my thoughts these shores, so different in their nature and in the inhabitants they support, are made one by the unifying touch of the sea. For the differences I sense in this particular instant of time that is mine are but the differences of a moment, determined by our place in the stream of time and in the long rhythms of the sea. Once this rocky coast beneath me was a plain of sand; then the sea rose and found a new shore line. And again in some shadowy future the surf will have ground these rocks to sand and will have returned the coast to its earlier state. And so in my mind's eye these coastal forms merge and blend in a shifting, kaleidoscopic pattern in which there is no finality, no ultimate and fixed reality—earth becoming fluid as the sea itself.

Paul Brooks, Carson's editor at Houghton Mifflin, once said that, as a writer, she was like "the stonemason who never lost sight of the cathedral." She was a meticulous editor; so was he. "Spent time on the Sand chapter with a pencil between my teeth," he wrote to her. But she didn't like being fixed up and straightened out, warning Brooks, "I am apt to use what may appear to be a curious inversion of words or phrases"—her brine-drenched jabberwocky—"but for the most part these are peculiar to my style and I don't want them changed."

Writing by the edge of the sea, Rachel Carson fell in love. She met Dorothy Freeman in 1953 on the island in Maine where Carson built her cottage and where Freeman's family had summered for years. Carson was forty-six, Freeman fifty-five. Freeman was married, with a grown son. When she and Carson weren't together, they maintained a breathless, passionate correspondence. "Why do I keep your letters?" Carson wrote to Freeman that winter. "Why? Because I love you!" Carson kept her favorite letters under her pillow. "I love you beyond expression," Freeman wrote to Carson. "My love is boundless as the Sea."

Both women were concerned about what might become of their letters. In a single envelope, they often enclosed two letters, one to be read to family (Carson to her mother, Freeman to her husband), one to be read privately, and likely destined for the "Strong box"—their code for letters to be destroyed. "Did you put them in the Strong box?" Carson would ask Freeman. "If not, please do." Later, while Carson was preparing her papers, which she'd pledged to give to Yale, Freeman read about how the papers of the writer Dorothy Thompson, recently opened, contained revelations about her relationships with women. Freeman wrote to Carson, "Dear, please, use the Strong box quickly," warning that their letters could have "meanings to people who were looking for ideas." (They didn't destroy all of them: those that survive were edited by Freeman's granddaughter and published in 1995.)

After the publication of *The Edge of the Sea* (1955), another bestseller that was also serialized in *The New Yorker*, Shawn wanted Carson to write a new book, to appear in the magazine, on nothing less than "the universe." And she might have tackled it. But when her niece Marjorie died of pneumonia, Carson adopted Marjorie's four-year-old son, Roger, a little boy she described as "lively as seventeen crickets." She set aside longer writing projects until, with some reluctance, she began work on a study whose title, for a long time, was *Man Against the Earth*.

IN JANUARY 1958, members of a citizens' Committee Against Mass Poisoning flooded newspapers in the Northeast with letters to the editor calling attention to the dire consequences of local and statewide insecticide aerial-spraying programs: the insects weren't dying, but everything else was. One Massachusetts housewife and bird-watcher, Olga Owens Huckins, who called the programs "inhumane, undemocratic and probably unconstitutional," wrote a letter to Carson. The committee had filed a lawsuit in New York, and Huckins suggested that Carson cover the story.

Carson had wanted to write about the destruction of the environment ever since the bombing of Hiroshima and the first civilian use of DDT, in 1945. Nevertheless, she couldn't possibly leave Roger and her ailing mother to report on a trial in New York. In February, she wrote to E. B. White, "It is my hope that you might cover these court hearings for *The New Yorker*." White demurred—he later told Carson that he didn't "know a chlorinated hydrocarbon from a squash bug"—

and said that she should write the story, forwarding Carson's letter to Shawn. In June, Carson went to New York and pitched the story to Shawn. "We don't usually think of *The New Yorker* as changing the world," he told her, "but this one time it might."

Freeman, wise woman, was worried that the chemical companies would go after Carson, relentlessly and viciously. Carson reassured her that she had taken that into account, but that, "knowing what I do, there would be no future peace for me if I kept silent." Marjorie Spock, the sister of the pediatrician, sent Carson reports from the trial, while Carson did her research from home, in Maryland and Maine, often with Roger at her side. She absorbed a vast scientific literature across several realms, including medicine, chemistry, physiology, and biology, and produced an explanation written with storybook clarity. Freeman wrote to Carson that she was "like the Mother Gull with her cheese sandwich," chewing it up before feeding it to her young. Carson wrote back, "Perhaps a subtitle of *Man Against the Earth* might be 'What the Mother Gull Brought Up.'"

In the fall of 1958, her mother had a stroke. Carson cared for her at home. Carson's mother had taught her birdsongs; the first time they visited Maine together, Carson had taken an inventory: "And then there were the sounds of other, smaller birds—the rattling call of the kingfisher that perched, between forays after fish, on the posts of the dock; the call of the phoebe that nested under the eaves of the cabin; the redstarts that foraged in the birches on the hill behind the cabin and forever, it seemed to me, asked each other the way to Wiscasset, for I could easily twist their syllables into the query, 'Which is Wiscasset? Which is Wiscasset?'"

Late in the autumn of Carson's mother's illness, Spock sent her a record album of birdsongs. Carson listened with Roger, teaching him each song. "He has a very sweet feeling for all living things and loves to go out with me and look and listen to all that goes on," she wrote to Spock. Carson's mother died that December, at the age of eighty-nine. The spring of 1959 was Carson's first spring without her mother. "Over increasingly large areas of the United States, spring now comes unheralded by the return of the birds, and the early mornings are strangely silent where once they were filled with the beauty of bird song," Carson would write. It was Paul Brooks who had the idea of using the title of the chapter on birds as the title for the entire book: *Silent Spring*. A season of grief.

And, still, Carson worried that she herself might be silenced. She grew sick; she and Freeman told hardly anyone, not even Brooks. Early in 1960, while immersed in a growing scientific literature on the consequences for humans "of the never-ending stream of chemicals of which pesticides are a part, chemicals now pervading the world in which we live, acting upon us directly and indirectly, separately and collectively," as if we were all fish, swimming in a poisoned sea, she found more lesions on her left breast.

On April 4, 1960, Carson had a radical mastectomy. Her surgeon provided her with no information about the tumors or the tissue he'd removed and recommended no follow-up treatment; when she asked him questions, he lied to her, as was common practice, especially with female patients. The surgery had been brutal and the recovery was slow. "I think I have solved the troublesome problem of the cancer chapters," she wrote to Brooks from Maine in September. But by November she'd found more lumps, this time on her ribs. She consulted another doctor, and began radiation treatments. In December, she finally confided in Brooks.

Carson kept her cancer secret because she was a private person, but also because she didn't want to give the chemical companies the chance to dismiss her work as having been motivated by her illness, and perhaps because, when the time came, she didn't want them to pull their punches; the harder they came after her, the worse they'd look. This required formidable stoicism. Beginning early in 1961, she was, on and off, in a wheelchair. One treatment followed another: more surgery, injections (one doctor recommended injections of gold). One illness followed another: the flu, staph infections, rheumatoid arthritis, eye infections. "Such a catalogue of illnesses!" she wrote to Freeman. "If one were superstitious it would be easy to believe in some malevolent influence at work, determined by some means to keep the book from being finished."

Early on, Carson was told that she had "a matter of months." She was afraid of dying, but she was terrified of dying before she could finish the book. Freeman, who thought the work itself was killing Carson, or at least impeding her ability to fight the cancer, urged her to abandon the book she'd planned and to produce, instead, something much shorter, and be done with it. "Something would be better than nothing, I guess," Carson mused, weighing the merits of recasting her pages into something "greatly boiled down" and "perhaps more philosophic in tone." She decided against it, and in January 1962 submitted to *The New Yorker* a nearly complete draft of the book.

Shawn called her at home to tell her that he'd finishing reading and that the book was "a brilliant achievement." He said, "You have made it literature, full of beauty and loveliness and depth of feeling." Carson, who had been quite unsure she'd survive to finish writing the book, was sure, for the first time, that the book was going to do in the world what she'd wanted it to do. She hung up the phone, put Roger to bed, picked up her cat, and burst into tears, collapsing with relief.

SILENT SPRING APPEARED IN THE NEW YORKER in three parts in June 1962 and as a book, published by Houghton Mifflin, in September. Everything is connected to everything else, she showed. "We poison the caddis flies in a stream and the salmon runs dwindle and die," Carson wrote:

> We poison the gnats in a lake and the poison travels from link to link of the food chain and soon the birds of the lake margins become its victims. We spray our elms and the following springs are silent of robin song, not because we sprayed the robins directly but because the poison traveled, step by step, through the now familiar elm-leaf-earthworm cycle. These are matters of record, observable, part of the visible world around us. They reflect the web of life—or death—that scientists know as ecology.

Its force was felt immediately. Readers wrote to share their own stories. "I can go into the feed stores here and buy, without giving any reason, enough poison to do away with all the people in Oregon," one gardener wrote. They began calling members of Congress. E. B. White wrote to Carson, declaring the pieces to be "the most valuable articles the magazine had ever published." At a press conference at the White House on August 29, a reporter asked President Kennedy whether his administration intended to investigate the long-range side effects of DDT and other pesticides. "Yes," he answered. "I know that they already are, I think particularly, of course, since Miss Carson's book."

"What she wrote started a national quarrel," *CBS Reports* announced in a one-hour special, "The Silent Spring of Rachel Carson," in which footage of Carson was intercut with footage of government and industry spokesmen, to create a de facto debate. (Carson refused to make any other television appearance.) In the program, Carson sits on the porch of her white-railed house in Maine, wearing a skirt and cardigan; the chief spokesman for the insecticide industry, Robert White-Stevens, of American Cyanamid, wears thick black-framed glasses and a white coat, standing in a chemistry lab, surrounded by beakers and Bunsen burners. White-Stevens questions Carson's expertise: "The major claims of Miss Rachel Carson's book, *Silent Spring*, are gross distortions of the actual fact, completely unsupported by scientific experimental evidence and general practical experience in the field."

Carson feigns perplexity: "Can anyone believe it is possible to lay down such a barrage of poisons on the surface of the earth without making it unfit for all life?"

White-Stevens fumes: "Miss Carson maintains that the balance of nature is a major force in the survival of man, whereas the modern chemist, the modern biologist and scientist believes that man is steadily controlling nature."

Carson rebuts: "Now, to these people, apparently, the balance of nature was something that was repealed as soon as man came on the scene. Well, you might just as well assume that you could repeal the law of gravity."

He may be wearing the lab coat, but, against Carson's serenity, it's White-Stevens who comes across as the crank. Carson wasn't so much calm, though, as exhausted. She was fifty-five; she looked twenty years older. (She told Freeman she felt ninety.) She begged Freeman not to tell anyone about the cancer: "There is no reason even to say I have not been well. If you want or think you need give any negative report, say I had a bad time with iritis that delayed my work, but it has cleared up nicely. And that you *never saw me look better.* Please say that." But if no one knew, it was not hard to see. When Carson was interviewed by CBS, she wore a heavy wig; she had lost her hair. She was not shown standing, which would have been difficult: the cancer had spread to her vertebrae; her spine was beginning to collapse. After the CBS reporter Eric Sevareid interviewed Carson, he told his producer Jay McMullen that the network ought to air the program as soon as possible. "Jay," he said, "you've got a dead leading lady."

In December, while shopping for a Christmas present for Roger—a record player—Carson fainted from pain and weakness. The tumors kept spreading. *CBS Reports* aired "The Silent Spring of Rachel Carson" in April 1963. The following month, Carson testified before Congress.

By fall, the cancer had moved into her pelvic bone. She wrote, "I moan inside—and I wake in the night and cry out silently for Maine." When Carson delivered what would be her final public speech, "Man Against Himself," hobbling to the stage with the use of a cane, a local newspaper described her as a "middle-aged, arthritis-crippled spinster." She wrote to Freeman that returning to Maine "is only a dream—a lovely dream."

Rachel Carson did not see the ocean again. Nor would she be remembered for what she wrote about the sea, from its shore to its depths. "The dear old *Sea Around Us* has been displaced," Freeman wrote, with sorrow. "When people talk about you they'll say 'Oh yes, the author of *Silent Spring*,' for I suppose there are people who never heard of *The Sea Around Us.*"

Early on the morning of April 14, 1964, Freeman wrote to Carson, wondering how she'd slept and wishing her the beauty of spring: "I can be sure you wake up to bird song." Carson died before dusk. Three weeks later, on their island in Maine, Freeman poured Carson's ashes into the sea. "Every living thing of the ocean, plant and animal alike, returns to the water at the end of its own life span the materials which had been temporarily assembled to form its body," Carson once wrote. Freeman sat on a rock and watched the tide go out.

Before Carson got sick, and even after, when she still believed she might get better, she thought that she'd take up, for her next book, a subject that fascinated her. "We live in an age of rising seas," she wrote.

"In our own lifetime we are witnessing a startling alteration of climate." She died before she could begin, wondering, till the end, about the swelling of the seas.

This spring, in the North Atlantic, not a single newborn right whale has been spotted: the water, it seems, is too warm; the mothers have birthed no calves. The sea is all around us. It is our home. And the last calf is our, inconsolable, loss.

—2018

MISJUDGED

RUTH BADER GINSBURG BLINKED BEHIND GIANT, round eyeglasses. It was the first day of her confirmation hearings, in July of 1993, the year after the Year of the Woman, and Joe Biden, the chairman of the Senate Judiciary Committee, was very pleased to see her. Keen to do penance for the debacle of the Clarence Thomas hearings, just two years before—the year before the Year of the Woman—when an all-male committee, chaired by Biden, failed to credit what Anita Hill had to say about George H. W. Bush's Supreme Court nominee, he could hardly have been friendlier to Bill Clinton's nominee, a much respected and widely admired sixty-year-old appellate judge. She sat with the stillness of a watchful bird. "Judge Ginsburg, welcome," Biden said heartily. "And, believe me, you are welcome here this morning."

He had more reasons, too, to beam at Ginsburg. Only weeks earlier, Clinton had withdrawn his nomination of Lani Guinier as assistant attorney general, an abandonment that had followed the very new president's unsuccessful nominations of two female attorneys general, Kimba Wood and Zoë Baird. Clinton and Biden needed a successful, high-profile female appointment, one without a discussion of pubic hair or video porn or nannies. On the way to work on the first day of the Ginsburg hearings, Biden had read the *New York Times* on the train and found that there was no mention of Ginsburg on page 1, or page 2, or page 3, which, he told Ginsburg, "was the most wonderful thing that has happened to me since I have been chairman of this committee." He flashed his movie star grin.

During that first session, scheduled for two and a half hours, the committee members—sixteen men and two lately added women— did nearly all the talking, delivering opening statements. Not until the outset of the second session did Biden sidle up to a question. "The Constitution has to be read by justices in light of its broadest and most fundamental commitments, commitments to liberty, commitments to individual dignity, equality of opportunity," he said, putting on his glasses, and taking them off again. Ginsburg blinked and stared and waited.

Biden's question concerned a recent speech, the Madison Lecture, in which Ginsburg had said that in making decisions concerning rights not listed in the Constitution judges should be "moderate and restrained" and avoid stepping "boldly in front of the political process," as he reminded her. "But, Judge," Biden said, "in your work as an advocate in the seventies you spoke with a different voice. In the seventies, you pressed for immediate extension of the fullest constitutional protection for women under the Fourteenth Amendment, and you said the Court should grant such protection notwithstanding what the rest of society, including the legislative branch, thought about the matter. . . . Can you square those for me or point out their consistency to me?"

What Biden was getting at has been mostly lost in the years since, years during which Ruth Bader Ginsburg, a distinguished justice, became a pop-culture feminist icon, a comic-book superhero. In the past year alone, the woman known to her fans as the Notorious RBG was the subject of a *Saturday Night Live* skit; a fawning documentary; a biopic, *On the Basis of Sex* (from a screenplay written by Ginsburg's nephew); a CNN podcast, *RBG Beyond Notorious*; and a biography, *Ruth Bader Ginsburg: A Life,* by Jane Sherron De Hart, an emeritus history professor at the University of California, Santa Barbara.

Such lavish biographical attention to a living Supreme Court justice is unusual, and new, even if that change is easy to lose sight of amid the intense scrutiny of the high school and college years of the Trump nominee Brett Kavanaugh, accused of sexual assault. (He denied the allegations.) Unlike candidates for political office, most sitting justices have preferred to remain, if not anonymous, largely unknown. The position is unelected, the appointment is for life, and the justices are not supposed to place themselves in the public eye, for fear of making themselves beholden to public opinion: arguably, the less attention to their personal lives the better. Before the past tumultuous decade, few, if any, justices who hadn't previously held an elected office had been the subject of a full-dress biography while still serving on the Court.

Writing a biography of a sitting justice introduces all kinds of problems of perspective, authority, and obligation. At the time De Hart was writing, Ginsburg had not deposited her papers in any archive and, having refused calls to resign under Obama's watch, insisted that she had no plans to retire. De Hart, who worked on the project for fifteen years, relied on published material, public records, and, extensively, interviews. Her publisher describes the book as "written with the cooperation of Ruth Bader Ginsburg." It would have been impossible to write the book without that cooperation, but it comes at no small cost.

Making De Hart's problems worse was Ginsburg's unprecedented judicial celebrity. On Matt Groening's animated series *Futurama*, Ginsburg appeared as an artificially preserved head, and although Antonin Scalia's severed head made a cameo or two as well, it was the Ginsburg character's catchphrase—"You Ruth Bader believe it!"—that ended up on T-shirts and coffee mugs, and is the thing your teenager says to you at the dinner table. At eighty-five, Ginsburg did her daily workout with Stephen Colbert on *The Late Show*. "I'm a huge fan!" Colbert said. Thurgood Marshall never lifted weights with Johnny Carson. Three goats were brought to Montpelier to eat the poison ivy spreading throughout the Vermont state capital: they were named Ruth, Bader, and Ginsburg. To my knowledge, no flock of sheep were ever named Oliver, Wendell, and Holmes.

God bless Ruth Bader Ginsburg, goats, bobbleheads, and all. But trivialization—RBG's workout tips! her favorite lace collars!—is not tribute. Female heroes are in short supply not because women aren't brave but because female bravery is demeaned, no kind more than intellectual courage. *Isn't she cute?* Ginsburg was a scholar, an advocate, and a judge of formidable sophistication, complexity, and, not least, contradiction and limitation. It is no kindness to flatten her into a paper doll and sell her as partisan merch.

Doing so also obscures a certain irony. Ginsburg often waxed nostalgic about her confirmation hearings, as she did when, regretting the partisan furor over Brett Kavanaugh—even before Christine Blasey Ford came forward—she said, "The way it was was right; the way it is is wrong." The second of those statements is undeniably and painfully true, but the first flattens the past. What Biden was getting at, in 1993, was what the president himself had said, dismissing the idea of nominating Ginsburg when it was first suggested to him. "The women," Clinton said, "are against her."

RUTH BADER WAS BORN in Brooklyn in 1933. At thirteen, she wrote a newspaper editorial, a tribute to the Charter of the United Nations. Her mother, an admirer of Eleanor Roosevelt, died when she was seventeen. Bader went to Cornell, where she liked to say that she learned how to write from Vladimir Nabokov. At Cornell, she also met Martin Ginsburg, and fell in love. They married in 1954 and had a baby, Jane, in 1955. Brilliant and fiercely independent, Ginsburg was devoted to Marty, to Jane, and to the law. At Harvard Law School, which first admitted women in 1950, she was one of only nine women in a class of some five hundred. In one of the first scenes in *On the Basis of Sex*, Erwin Griswold, the dean of the law school, asks each of those nine women, during a dinner party at his house, why she is occupying a place that could have gone to a man. In the film, Ginsburg, played by Felicity Jones, gives the dean an answer to which he can have no objection: "My husband, Marty, is in the second-year class. I'm at Harvard to learn about his work. So that I might be a more patient and understanding wife." This, which is more or less what Ginsburg actually said, was a necessary lie. It was possible for a woman to attend law school—barely—but it was not possible for her to admit her ambition.

In 1957, Marty was diagnosed with testicular cancer. During his illness and treatment—surgery followed by radiation—Ruth not only cared for him, and for the baby, but also covered all of his classes and helped him with his papers. She kept up an almost inhuman schedule, often working through the night. After Marty graduated, he took a job in New York, and Ruth transferred to Columbia. She graduated first in her class. "That's my mommy," four-year-old Jane said, when Ginsburg crossed the stage to accept her diploma.

Looking for work, Ginsburg confronted the limits of the profession's willingness to take female lawyers seriously. Felix Frankfurter, the first Supreme Court justice to hire an African American clerk, in 1948, refused to hire a woman, even after he was reassured that Ginsburg never wore pants. Stymied, Ginsburg went to Sweden to undertake a comparative study of Swedish and American law. On her return, in 1963, she accepted a position at Rutgers, teaching civil procedure. A year and a half later, when she found herself pregnant—given her husband's medical history, this blessing was unexpected—Ginsburg delayed informing the university, for fear of losing her position.

Ginsburg, in other words, had plenty of experience of what would now be called—because she called it this—discrimination on the basis of sex. In 1969, Ginsburg was promoted to full professor and her son, James, entered nursery school, rites of passage that freed her to explore a new interest: she began volunteering for the ACLU. Working with and eventually heading the ACLU's Women's Rights Project, Ginsburg pursued a series of cases designed to convince the Supreme Court, first, that there is such a thing as sex discrimination and, second, that it violates the Constitution.

Influenced by the pioneering constitutional analysis of Pauli Murray and Dorothy Kenyon, Ginsburg borrowed, too, from the strategy of Thurgood Marshall, who, as head of the NAACP's Legal and Educational Defense Fund beginning in 1940, had pursued his agenda step by step, case by case, over fourteen years, all the way to *Brown v. Board of Education*, decided in 1954. Erwin Griswold, notwithstanding his resentment of women law students, eventually dubbed Ginsburg "the Thurgood Marshall of gender equality law."

She prepared herself for litigation by teaching courses on women and the law, a subject that had rarely been taught. An undisputed leader of an emerging field, she soon left Rutgers. ("Columbia Snares a Prize in the Quest for Women Professors," the *Times* reported.) Unlike Marshall, who was very often on the front lines of civil unrest and political protest, Ginsburg worked full time as a law school professor, which placed constraints on her time and kept her at some remove from protests taking place on the streets. And, as De Hart observes, several crucial features distinguish their strategies. Marshall relied on the equal protection clause—"No State shall . . . deny to any person within its jurisdiction the equal protection of the laws"—of the Fourteenth Amendment, which was adopted after the Civil War in order to stop the former Confederate states from denying former slaves equal rights. Ginsburg also invoked the equal protection clause, but was left to argue only by analogy, suggesting that discrimination on the basis of sex is the same sort of thing. Finally, while there were plenty of rifts within the civil rights movement, Marshall never had to battle African Americans opposed to the very notion of equality under the law; Ginsburg, by contrast, faced a phalanx of conservative women, led by Phyllis Schlafly, who objected to equal rights altogether.

In one of the earliest of Ginsburg's antidiscrimination cases, *Reed v. Reed* (1971), she established that an Idaho law that gave preference to men over women in the administration of estates violated the equal protection clause. Ginsburg called her victory in *Reed* "a small, guarded step." She next hoped to bring to the Supreme Court a case called *Struck v. Secretary of Defense*. When Captain Susan Struck became pregnant, she decided to have the baby, but air force policy meant that she would lose her job unless she had an abortion. Ginsburg prepared to argue Struck's case on equal protection grounds: since no air force policy barred men from having children, the government was discriminating against Struck on the basis of sex. In choosing a case that would advance a desperately needed argument about reproductive autonomy, Ginsburg had cleverly selected one in which the litigant had chosen to have a baby, rather than to end a pregnancy, so that the Court's attention would be focused on the equality claims of women (and not on the politics of abortion). But the air force changed its policy and, in 1972, at the urging of then solicitor general Erwin Griswold, the case was dismissed, a decision that had profound consequences: the following year, the Court ruled on *Roe v. Wade* instead, and struck down anti-abortion legislation not on the ground of equal protection but on the ground of a much weaker constitutional doctrine, the right to privacy.

If *Struck* was Ginsburg's next, carefully placed stepping stone across a wide river, *Roe* was a rickety wooden plank thrown down across the water and—Ginsburg thought—likely to rot. In a lecture she delivered in 1984, she noted the political significance of the fact that the Court had treated sex discrimination as a matter of equal protection but reproductive autonomy as a matter of privacy. When the Court overturned laws on the basis of sex discrimination, no great controversy ensued, she observed, but *Roe v. Wade* remained "a storm center." She went on, "*Roe v. Wade* sparked public opposition and academic criticism, in part, I believe, because the Court ventured too far in the change it ordered and presented an incomplete justification for its action."

There are more what–ifs than there are stars in the sky. But *Roe* helped conservatives defeat the Equal Rights Amendment, which had passed Congress and appeared well on its way to ratification until Schlafly warned, starting in 1974, that the "ERA means abortion." Following Ginsburg's logic, it's impossible not to wonder whether, if the Court had heard *Struck* instead of *Roe*, the ERA would have passed, after which reproductive rights would have been recognized by the courts as a matter of equal protection. And the nation would not have become so divided. If, if.

Asked by the ACLU to take on litigation relating to the defense of *Roe*, Ginsburg declined. Instead, she continued to pursue antidiscrimination cases, and first appeared before the Supreme Court in *Frontiero v. Richardson*, in 1973, advocating for Sharron Frontiero, an air force lieutenant who had been denied benefits for her husband which were granted to men for their wives. "I ask no favor for my sex," Ginsburg told the nine men on the bench, quoting the nineteenth-century women's rights advocate Sarah Grimké. "All I ask of our brethren is that they take their feet off our necks." Ginsburg won, though the Court's holding was narrow. As she proceeded to try to widen that holding, she continued teaching at Columbia and writing law review articles. In 1979, after Jimmy Carter signed legislation expanding the federal judiciary, Ginsburg began pursuing a judgeship.

Carter was determined to appoint women and asked Sarah Weddington, the lawyer who had argued *Roe*, to help him find them. By 1970, only three in a hundred lawyers and fewer than two hundred of the nation's ten thousand judges were women. In 1971, Chief Justice Warren Burger, on hearing that Richard Nixon was considering nominating a woman to the Court, drafted a letter of resignation. "Feminist Picked for U.S. Court of Appeals Here," the *Washington Post* announced in December of 1979, even before Carter had officially named Ginsburg to the DC Circuit.

Strom Thurmond, whose office dismissed the nominee as a "one-issue woman," cast the lone vote against her nomination in the Senate Judiciary Committee, and she took a seat on the notoriously fractious DC court. There she became known as a consensus builder who adhered closely to precedent, wrote narrowly tailored decisions, and refused to join intemperately written opinions. A 1987 study showed that she voted more often with Republican appointees than with Democratic appointees. In *Dronenburg v. Zech* (1984), she voted against rehearing a case involving a sailor's allegation that the navy had discriminated against him by discharging him for homosexual conduct. She generally agreed with conservatives in opposing expanded regulation of corporate conduct. She insisted on the importance of not getting ahead of the law. In *Women's Equity Action League v. Cavazos* (1990), she dismissed a two-decades-old suit, arguing that the litigant groups' claim that federal agencies had failed to comply with their own antidiscrimination statutes "lacks the requisite green light from the legislative branch."

Of the fifty-seven people she hired as law clerks, interns, or secretaries during her time on the DC bench, not one was African American. Ginsburg was asked about this when she appeared before the Senate Judiciary Committee, and she promised, "If you confirm me for this job, my attractiveness to Black candidates is going to improve." But in her quarter century on the Supreme Court she hired only one African American clerk (a record that, distressingly, does not distinguish her from most of the bench). And, as both judge and justice, she frequently sided with conservatives on questions concerning criminal justice reform. In *Samson v. California* (2006), she joined an opinion, written by Clarence Thomas, upholding warrantless searches of people on parole; in *Davis v. Ayala* (2015), she declined to join an opinion condemning solitary confinement.

De Hart describes Ginsburg's thirteen years on the circuit court as something like a decontamination chamber, in which Ginsburg was rinsed and scrubbed of the hazard of her thirteen years as an advocate for women's rights. By 1993, she had been sufficiently depolarized to be appointed to the Supreme Court.

ON MARCH 9, 1993, seven weeks after Bill Clinton's inauguration, Ginsburg delivered the James Madison Lecture on Constitutional Law, at New York University. She took as her subject the importance of collegiality in decision-making and moderation in style. The lecture can be read as an indictment, not just of judicial excess but of the changing character of American political discourse. She inveighed against "too frequent resort to separate opinions and the immoderate tone of statements." Ginsburg had no use for grandstanding, or the cheeky remark, or even the snippy footnote. She offered a list of phrases used by dissenters who disparaged majority opinions by calling them "outrageous," or "inexplicable" or "Orwellian" or a "blow against the People." As an example of the sort of screeds she wished federal judges would stop writing, she cited a dissent that began this way: "Running headlong from the questions briefed and argued before us, my colleagues seek refuge in a theory as novel as it is questionable."

One measure of how politics has descended into acrimony since then is that the Notorious RBG came to be celebrated for just this kind of blistering, contemptuous dissent, as if spitting had become a virtue. Consider a Bustle.com feature, "4 Epic Ginsburg Dissents That Prove She's a Badass," or the signature line of Kate McKinnon's RBG: "That's a Ginsburn!" In fact, there really aren't many Ginsburns to be found in the records of the Supreme Court. Ginsburg produced forcefully written dissents, especially as the Court moved to the right, but they are not themselves immoderate. Instead, they scold her colleagues for their immoderacy, as when, in 2013, objecting to the majority's decision to overturn much of the 1965 Voting Rights Act, she complained, "The Court's opinion can hardly be described as an exemplar of restrained and moderate decisionmaking."

Early in 1993, less than two weeks after Ginsburg delivered her Madison Lecture, Justice Byron White notified President Clinton of his intention to retire. The White House counsel, Bernard Nussbaum, gave the president a list of some forty possible nominees. No Democratic president had appointed a Supreme Court justice since Lyndon Johnson named Thurgood Marshall, in 1967. Clinton, as in so many things, proved indecisive; he was also distracted, and still staffing his Justice Department. He conferred with senators, but relied on seventy-five (unnamed) DC lawyers for advice. He contemplated Mario Cuomo and George J. Mitchell, the Senate majority leader. Most presidential selection processes—in the days before Trump's *Survivor*-style public charades—took place secretly, and quickly. Clinton's process was open, and interminable. The longer he took to make his decision the more interest groups were able to influence the process, not least because the White House invited them in. Over eighty-seven days and nights, Clinton asked all sorts of people their opinions. Kim Gandy, the executive vice president of the National Organization for Women, told the historian Richard Davis that her conduit to the president was the press: "We were frequently asked, 'What do you think about Bruce Babbitt for the Supreme Court?' and 'What do you think about Breyer?'" He just couldn't make up his mind.

Janet Reno, Clinton's very new attorney general, urged him to name a woman. But Ginsburg, for all that she had done to advance women's rights during the 1970s, was apparently not on the lists sent to the White House by women's groups. In her Madison Lecture, Ginsburg cited *Roe* to illustrate a crucial problem in judicial decision-making—"doctrinal limbs too swiftly shaped, experience teaches, may prove unstable." It would have been better, she thought, if the Court had decided *Struck* instead. Saying this took courage. In 1993, Operation Rescue ("If you believe abortion is murder, act like it's murder") was protesting outside abortion clinics. Other feminists disagreed with the reasoning behind *Roe*—just as some feminists today lament the tactics of the #MeToo movement—but calling *Roe* into question in public when abortion clinics were being bombed seemed beyond the pale. Many also found Ginsburg's counterfactual implausible. "Coulda, woulda, shoulda," NOW's president, Patricia Ireland, said; pro-life activists "don't care about the legal theory—they care about stopping abortion and controlling women's lives."

And so when Clinton, eager to please, entertained names proposed by women's groups, he learned that some of them refused to support Ginsburg, because they were worried that she might be willing to overturn *Roe* (which is not what she had written, but one gathers that the Madison Lecture was more often invoked than read). At one point, Clinton asked Senator Daniel Patrick Moynihan to suggest a woman. "Ruth Bader Ginsburg," Moynihan answered. "The women are against her" was the president's reply. Moynihan called Martin Ginsburg and said, "You best take care of it."

Ginsburg, a prominent and well-connected tax lawyer, was already running a behind-the-scenes campaign, without his wife's knowledge. In February 1993, he'd organized a breakfast meeting with the president of a leading women's group in DC to seek her support for his plan to get his wife nominated as solicitor general. He did not succeed. He had the same experience at a meeting in New York. In April and

May, he courted the press and solicited at least thirty-four letters of support, largely from the legal academy, where Ginsburg, an excellent scholar, was widely admired. Fourteen members of the faculty of NYU Law School—people who had been in the room when Ginsburg delivered the Madison Lecture—wrote a joint letter to say that they were "distressed that her remarks at NYU have been misconstrued as anti-choice and anti-women."

All spring, the Ginsburg family kept up the campaign, which involved bringing the lack of support among women's groups out into the open, so that it could be countered. The Brookings Institution fellow Stephen Hess, a cousin of Ginsburg's, warned reporters, including the *New York Times* columnist Anthony Lewis, that feminists were opposed to Ginsburg, and mailed them copies of the Madison Lecture. "I do not know Judge Ginsburg," Lewis wrote in his column on May 10. "I do not support or oppose her as a possible choice for the Supreme Court. I just find the knee-jerk arguments invoked against her—and against others who have been mentioned—depressing."

Nine days later, the heads of the National Women's Law Center, the Women's Legal Defense Fund, and NOW's Legal Defense and Education Fund (on whose board Ginsburg had served) sent Nussbaum a remarkable joint statement: "It has been reported that the women's movement would oppose the nomination of Judge Ruth Bader Ginsburg to the Supreme Court. We want to be certain there is no confusion about where our organizations stand: at this stage in the process, we have not taken any position in favor or in opposition to any candidate." It was hardly a ringing endorsement. Nussbaum faxed a copy of the letter to Marty Ginsburg, who later recalled, "I saw it as a pearl beyond price," since it would allow him to expose and embarrass the authors. He sent copies of the letter to members of the press. Eventually, key women's groups, which had been unwilling to oppose Ginsburg publicly, ceased opposing her privately, especially after May 29, when Clinton hired David Gergen as a senior adviser. Women's groups believed that Gergen was steering Clinton toward Bruce Babbitt and Stephen Breyer. "One minute there were all these female nominees," Kim Gandy said. "And then, as soon as David Gergen gets there, suddenly all the nominees look like David Gergen."

Summoned to the White House on Sunday, June 13, Ginsburg met with the president for ninety minutes. He made his decision later that day and, after watching a Chicago Bulls game that went into three overtimes, called her nearly at midnight. The *Wall Street Journal* posited a rule: "When Bill Clinton is doing the picking, it's better to be last than first." The *Washington Post* applauded Clinton for valuing "reputation rather than celebrity." The next day, in the Rose Garden, Clinton announced his nomination, and Ginsburg delivered a moving acceptance speech. Her daughter had written in her high school yearbook in 1973, under "Ambition": "To see her mother appointed to the Supreme Court. If necessary, Jane will appoint her." Ginsburg told the crowd, "Jane is so pleased, Mr. President, that you did it instead."

When Ginsburg finished, Brit Hume, then at ABC News, asked a question:

> The withdrawal of the Guinier nomination, sir, and your apparent focus on Judge Breyer, and your turn, late it seems, to Judge Ginsburg, may have created an impression, perhaps unfair, of a certain zigzag quality in the decision-making process here. I wonder, sir, if you could kind of walk us through it, perhaps disabuse us of any notion we might have along those lines. Thank you.

If you watch the footage today, the question comes across as gentlemanly, even Edwardian. But Clinton turned beet red and said:

> I have long since given up the thought that I could disabuse some of you of turning any substantive decision into anything but political process. How you could ask a question like that after the statement she just made is beyond me.

And then he took no more questions.

It was a month later, riding the train into the capital, that Biden was thrilled to discover no mention of Ginsburg's nomination hearings on the front pages of the *Times*. She was an excellent nominee. "My approach, I believe, is neither liberal nor conservative," Ginsburg told the committee. The Senate voted to confirm her 96–3, with one abstention. But the idea that her appointment was uncontroversial is almost entirely a myth.

Few justices have been better prepared to appear before the Senate Judiciary Committee than Ginsburg, who had made an academic study of the history of the process. As she had related in a law review article, it was in many respects surprising that the executive would play so great a role in shaping the judiciary. At the Constitutional Convention in 1787, the Senate was initially granted the exclusive power to appoint Supreme Court justices; that measure, proposed on June 13, was accepted without objection. A proposal made on July 18 for the president to name justices and for the Senate to provide advice and consent was defeated. Only on September 7, ten days before the final draft, did the convention revisit this question, and adopt the proposed sharing of power.

In 1988, taking stock of two hundred years of Supreme Court nominations, Ginsburg observed that more than a hundred men and one woman had served on the Court, and the Senate had rejected twenty-eight, of whom only five had been blocked in the twentieth century. No nominee was questioned before the Senate Judiciary Committee until 1925, when Harlan Stone made a brief appearance to answer questions specifically about the Teapot Dome scandal. The next nominee to appear before the committee was Felix Frankfurter, in 1939, who announced: "While I believe that a nominee's record should be thoroughly scrutinized by this committee, . . . I should think it not only bad taste but inconsistent with the duties of the office for which I have been nominated for me to attempt to supplement my past record by present declarations. That is all I have to say."

He relented, but largely for the purpose of denying that he was a communist. Only since 1955 have nominees routinely appeared before the committee. All followed some version of the Frankfurter rule, placing strict limits on what they would discuss, until Robert Bork, who said, on the first day of his confirmation hearings, "I welcome this opportunity to come before the committee and answer whatever questions the members might have." He quickly clarified that, although he said he was happy to discuss his "judicial philosophy," he would demur on specific cases—a distinction, as Ginsburg observed, that "blurred as the questions and answers wore on," not least because Bork, Nixon's former solicitor general and the last man standing after the Saturday Night Massacre in 1973, seemed delighted by the attention.

Bork's confirmation hearings were both the last episode of the Watergate scandal and the first episode of a new and enduring scandal, the blurring of the legislative and judicial branches of the federal government. Bork's nomination elicited paid television advertisements, as if he were running for an elected office. Since then, the distance between the judiciary and the political process has almost entirely eroded. With Merrick Garland, Senate Republicans, acting with breathtaking heedlessness, abandoned the constitutional principle that a Supreme Court nomination is meant to be insulated from public opinion, Mitch McConnell arguing that the American people, not the sitting American president, would name the next Supreme Court justice. "I wish I could wave a magic wand and have it go back to the way it was," Ginsburg said in September, after the first Kavanaugh hearings. Partisanship has corrupted the confirmation process. The legitimacy of the Court has declined. Women have yet to gain the equal protection of the law. And there is no wand.

IN THE SUMMER OF 1993, when Biden finally sidled up to his question, he was asking Ginsburg to explain the distance between her 1973 *Frontiero* brief and her 1993 Madison Lecture. How could she at one point say that the Court can move ahead of public opinion and at another point say that it shouldn't? The transcript reads:

> THE CHAIRMAN: Can you square those for me or point out their consistency to me?
> JUDGE GINSBURG: Yes.
> THE CHAIRMAN: That is a good answer. Now we will go on to the next question. [*Laughter*]

Biden pressed; Ginsburg evaded. "I saw my role in those days as an advocate," she said, talking about *Reed*, and those stepping stones.

"Judge, I don't mean to cut you off," Biden said. "I am trying to square, though, your—I understand your position as an advocate. Then you became an appellate court judge, and you gave a lecture this year called the Madison Lecture. . . ."

Biden found her charming. And she *was* charming, and she was smart, and she was much better prepared than he was. He could not nail her down. Ginsburg answered with a precision that was characteristic of her briefs, of her oral arguments, and of her opinions from the federal appellate court, but also with a self-control honed by decades of experience arguing with people who underestimated her.

"My time is up, Judge," Biden eventually said, wearily. "You have been very instructive about how things have moved, but you still haven't—and I will come back to it—squared for me the issue of whether or not the Court can or should move ahead of society." Ginsburg offered a short sermon about reticence:

> We cherish living in a democracy, and we also know that this Constitution did not create a tricameral system. Judges must be mindful of what their place is in this system and must always remember that we live in a democracy that can be destroyed if judges take it upon themselves to rule as Platonic guardians.

She never answered Biden's question. Instead, she established her own rule: the Ginsburg precedent, a rule of restraint. But there are very few rules left anymore, and even less restraint.

—2018

Postscript: Ruth Bader Ginsburg died in 2020.

Part Three

Valley of the Dolls

Rot is always a problem for the living dead,
which is why resurrectionists borrow a good deal
from methods used in preserving food.

A Bratz doll. *bobo / Alamy Stock Photo*

THE ODDYSSEY

ROBERT L. RIPLEY, WHO WAS HEAVYSET AND DAINTY, wore his dark widow's peak slicked back flat and had teeth so jutting and crooked that, until he got some of them yanked out and straighter fakes jammed back in (which hurt like hell), he looked remarkably like a vampire. He had a girlfriend called Okie and a dog named Dokie. Among his prized possessions was a bullet that a man had coughed up forty-nine years after being shot in the chest. Ripley traveled all over the world to collect what he called "queeriosities": the skull of a Tibetan man, the shrunken head of an Ecuadoran woman, the penis of a whale. "Has a fish that swims backward," Geoffrey T. Hellman wrote of Ripley in his notebook when he interviewed him for a Profile, in *The New Yorker*, in 1940. That wasn't the screwiest thing in Hellman's jumble of notes about Ripley's quirks. Consider: "Likes to polish totem poles." Or: "Loves outwitting Armenian rug merchants." Then, there's the fact, reported by Hellman, that Ripley—a fifty-year-old bachelor at the time—was happiest when wearing nothing but his bathrobe and his dead mother's wedding ring. "Doesn't like to work w clothes on," Hellman noted. Ripley was fabulously wealthy. He stored his treasures in three houses, and the overflow on a fifty-six-foot-long red-yellow-and-blue Chinese junk. Still, even the man who has everything is not without his little foibles. "Cant drive a car," Hellman jotted down in his notebook. "Has a horror of freaks."

Ripley's catchphrase, "Believe It or Not!," came with its own punctuation, lest the requisite enthusiasm prove unforthcoming. Believe It or Not! was also the name of Ripley's corporation, headquartered in New York, on East Forty-Fifth Street; of his radio show, broadcast coast to coast on a national network; of his movie shorts, produced by Warner Bros.; and of his best-selling books, published by Simon & Schuster. But, before all that, *Believe It or Not!* was the title of Ripley's cartoons and comic strips, printed in three hundred and twenty-five newspapers in thirty-eight countries and seventeen languages. Hellman, in his notes, summed up his subject: "Probly best known man in world."

To research the Profile, Hellman visited Ripley's twenty-seven-room mansion, in Mamaroneck, New York. The house was perched on a tiny island that Ripley had named Bion (it's an acronym). Ripley, graciously, dressed for the occasion: "R. wears blue green blouse and slacks." Aside from staged eccentricity, freak tourism, and eye-popping spectacle, Ripley trafficked in anachronism, hyperbole, and casuistry. Believe it or not: "Christmas was forbidden in Massachusetts for 22 years." Strange as it may seem: "The surgeon Dr. Politman, a native of Lorraine, died at the age of 140, having been drunk each day since he was 25 years old." Did you know: "A JUNE BUG IS NOT A BUG. (It is a May beetle.)" Hellman intimated delicately, "A good many of Ripley's eye-openers rest on rather minute technicalities."

Ripley's believe-it-or-nots came with a guarantee: "On request, sent with stamped, addressed envelope, Mr. Ripley will furnish proof of anything depicted or described by him." No one promised a speedy reply: Ripley told Hellman that he had a million unopened letters in his attic. He took handfuls with him when he traveled. He liked to drop them out of airplanes while flying over, say, north-central Africa, to see how long they would take to come back to him. He thought there was no question they would.

At the house in Mamaroneck, Ripley took Hellman on a tour. "Persian beauty kit in sunroom," Hellman dutifully reported in his notebook. "Buddhist prayer wheel in Blue room. Nangpu bed in guestroom." The Aztec mask room: "This room just completed." Here and there: steins, tapestries, a Japanese shrine. Elsewhere: a replica of the Taj Mahal, wired with lights that could glow either yellow or pink ("This is strictly Hindu"). In a "chamber of horrors" hidden behind the bar and blasted out of boulder, Hellman scribbled a list: "Skeleton of two headed baby. Pix of deformed people. R. grinning w old leper woman. Pregnancy belt of split bamboo. Chastity belt w lock. Iron maid of Nuremberg." He had a full-sized figure of a Japanese sculptor, Hananuma Masakichi, a self-portrait so lifelike that, for materials, the artist used his own hair and fingernails and toenails and even his own teeth.

"I only deal in oddities," Ripley explained to his guest. "Not freaks." Hellman enlarged upon this nicety in his Profile:

> He thinks the word "freak" has an unpleasant connotation and insists that the two-headed fishes, human pincushions, fork-tongued ladies, eyeless infants, four-footed chickens, and three-headed calves to which he has drawn international attention are not freaks. "An oddity is a high-class freak," he once said guardedly, when pinned down.

The interview drew to a close. Maybe they were standing by the door. "The most unusual thing in the house is Mr. Ripley," Ripley's German housekeeper, Almuth Dold, said, as if on cue. Hellman wrote that down in his notebook, and used it in the piece. He made no mention of the whale penis, though. He was picky about shtick.

NEAL THOMPSON'S BIOGRAPHY, *A Curious Man: The Strange and Brilliant Life of Robert "Believe It or Not!" Ripley*, is, unbelievably, boring. Thompson has written three other books: a biography of the astronaut Alan Shepard, a history of Nascar, and an account of the fate of a New Orleans high school football team during and after Hurricane Katrina. His biography of Ripley is published by Crown Archetype, a division of Random House, and promoted and sold by Ripley Entertainment, a global media conglomerate that is the successor to Ripley's Believe It or Not! *A Curious Man* is part book, part stunt.

Ripley Entertainment, according to its website, controls "over 90 exciting attractions in 10 countries, along with best-selling books, a network television series in more than 70 countries, and the longest continuously published newspaper comic in history." Its properties include the Guinness World Records Museums and the Louis Tussaud's Waxworks. Its headquarters are in Orlando, where it houses the papers of the man who started it all. As Thompson explains, Ripley Entertainment gave him "unfettered access to the climate-controlled room containing the company's archives, a one-stop-shopping trove of Ripley's personal and business papers, journals, photographs, home movies, letters, and more." (You can see a selection of 1930s and '40s photographs from that three-hundred-foot-long collection in a terrific coffee-table book published in 1993: *Dear Mr. Ripley: A Compendium of Curioddities from the Believe It or Not! Archives*.) Thompson also had at his disposal the Doug and Hazel Anderson Storer Collection, donated to the University of North Carolina. It contains letters, travel diaries, films, photographs, contracts, and radio scripts. Doug Storer was Ripley's agent and producer. When Ripley died, Storer became the president of Believe It or Not! Thompson's sources are the guardians of Ripley's legacy.

Despite this astonishing cache of almost-never-before-seen-if-possibly-slightly-fishy documents, Thompson's account of Ripley's life relies, too, and at times heavily, on press clippings, including "Odd Man," Hellman's two-part *New Yorker* Profile of Ripley. It comes, then, as a bit of a slap when Thompson says that "Odd Man" is derivative, that Hellman "summarized the Ripley legend" and "rehashed vignettes of Ripley's charmed career." Thompson didn't investigate Hellman's sources, so far as I can tell; he had no particular reason to. For the record, though, Hellman's typed-up research notes are filed with his papers at the Fales Library, at New York University. One thing you can find out by reading them is that Ripley wanted Hellman to write his biography. Hellman did not.

Meanwhile, *A Curious Man*, a book whose author had at his fingertips materials that few other historians have seen, reads as though it were written not by Ripley's biographer but by his publicist. Over three decades, Ripley showed the world to more Americans than any reporter or ambassador ever did. Thompson argues that Ripley was "a voice for the people, bringing the world's weirdness to their doorsteps." He was "the country's know-it-all professor of history, geography, science, and anthropology," Thompson writes. "His offbeat lessons gave people hope." That's not history; that's advertising copy. Hope, while occasionally the thing with feathers, is not usually a two-headed pickled fetus from Sri Lanka.

LeRoy Ripley was born in Santa Rosa, California, in 1890. His family called him Roy; other people called him Rip. He was gentle and shy, endearingly shy. His teeth protruded so badly that speech was difficult; there were some sounds he just couldn't make. He stammered and stuttered. He spent much of his childhood drawing pictures and playing baseball. (He played, very briefly, on a semiprofessional team.) His father died when he was fifteen. Ripley sold his first cartoon three years later. He never finished high school. In 1909, when he was eighteen, he took a job as a sports cartoonist for the *San Francisco Bulletin*. In 1912, he moved to New York, where he was hired by the *Globe*, on the condition that he drop the name LeRoy. ("We don't want any pansies around here," his editor told him, or at least that's how Ripley explained it to Hellman.) He took his middle name, Robert, as his first.

One day in December of 1918, stumped for sports news, Ripley drew a cartoon for the *Globe* illustrating nine strange athletic firsts; e.g., "J. Darby of England jumped backwards 12 feet 11 inches (with weights)," and "Ed Lamy broadjumped on ice 25 feet 7 inches." He later titled this collage of incredible sports facts "Believe It or Not!" Readers begged for more.

In 1919, in the first flush of fame, Ripley married a Ziegfeld Follies girl. They lived together less than a year. She divorced him, citing cruelty. Ripley began his travels in 1922, when the newspaper sent him on a trip: "Ripley's Rambles 'Round the World." Only peace had made this journey possible. Ripley started out taking a train to San Francisco and, next, a steamer to Hawaii, Japan, China, the Philippines, and Singapore. From every stop, he cabled dispatches. "I went to bed and slept with a Dutch wife," he reported from Java, only to explain, in the next day's dispatch, that a Dutch wife is a kind of pillow. In Ripley, the foreign is weird and the weird is foreign.

"I have traveled 20,000 miles and have seen no place which so baffles description as this," Ripley reported from India. "Cows are sacred, little girls are married at the age of three, the dead are fed to vultures, holy men sleep on beds of nails, and a man may marry as many wives as he wants." Ripley's drawings, documenting his rambles and his discoveries, are energetic, but it was their subject more than their style that captivated readers. He drew the head and torso of a woman. Below it he wrote, "THE HALF WOMAN. 'Violetta,' as she prefers to be known, was born without arms or legs, of normal parents less than thirty years ago in Germany." He drew a swarthy, beret-wearing man with hands that looked like squid: "THE VILLAGE OF MANY FINGERS. Every inhabitant of the village of Cervera de Buitrago, in the Province of Madrid, Spain, has a multiplicity of fingers and toes." Was he selling sympathy? Was he selling Schadenfreude? Sixteen million people had died in the Great War; another twenty million had been wounded. No one wanted to live in the Village of Many Fingers.

In 1923, Ripley returned to New York, where he worked for various newspapers, including the *Evening Post*. (The *Globe* had folded.) By now, he had embarked on a series of affairs, both at home and abroad; the longest would eventually be with Okie, whose real name was Ruth Ross. Ripley met her in Europe. In 1925, he went on a Ramble 'Round South America. "I have traveled the world over searching for strange and unbelievable things," he told his readers. "I have seen white negroes, purple white men, and I know a man who was hanged and still lives." This time, on Ripley's return, Max Schuster, of Simon & Schuster, wrangled a *Believe It or Not!* collection out of him. Published in 1929, it was a knockout. William Randolph Hearst sent his editors a two-word telegram: "HIRE RIPLEY." Hearst picked up Ripley's strip and ran it in his newspaper syndicate, King Features. This deal netted Ripley more than a hundred thousand dollars a year. The Warner Bros. movie shorts started in 1930, the weekly radio program that same year. Ripley got big, and then he got bigger. Letters reached him even if there was no address on the envelope, only a slight tear—a "rip."

The movies allowed Ripley to offer his readers a kind of proof that he couldn't put in a drawing. In the shorts—each is about ten minutes long—he'd usually draw a picture of something he'd seen. Then he'd leave his easel and introduce another kind of evidence: a photograph of an African man who had horns growing out of his head, footage of a fish that could walk, a performance by a woman who could say more than eight words a second. The shorts are immensely charming. The best part about them is Ripley: in three-piece suit and spats, bungling his lines, walking as if on tiptoe, his teeth poking out of his mouth. Watching Ripley introduce a freak is like watching a crippled man throw down his crutches and dance like Fred Astaire. Everything about Ripley is awkward, except this one waltz.

GEOFFREY T. HELLMAN STARTED WRITING for *The New Yorker* in 1929. He was tall and fair and princely: Yale, the Grolier Club, the Social Register. He wrote his first Profile in 1931. Not long afterward, he went to work for Henry Luce. In 1936, he became an editor at *Life*. The following year, *Life* ran a lavish, fawning photo-story about Ripley's house in Mamaroneck, called "Believe It or Not: This Is Where Robert L. Ripley Lives." Hellman didn't much like *Life;* he wanted to go back to *The New Yorker*. But there was a hitch: *The New Yorker*'s editor, Harold Ross, kept killing Hellman's stories, which tended to be sardonic, even cruel.

In 1939, Hellman traveled to Hollywood. While there, he pitched to *The New Yorker* a story about Lee Zavitz, a special-effects man who was about to burn Atlanta for *Gone with the Wind* but who specialized in weather. ("He produces fogs, tempests, blizzards etc at will," Hellman wrote to his editor.) The Zavitz piece, published at the beginning of 1940, ends this way: "He says the most temperate effects are often the most taxing. 'You can't imagine the trouble it takes to make a little breeze,' he said."

Hellman pondered the gentleness of a breeze. He picked up copies of Ripley's books. In one, he read about Violetta, the half woman. In his notes, Hellman copied down what Ripley had written: "She can dress herself, comb her own hair, thread a needle, sew, and perform other feats apparently bordering on the impossible." There follows a query: "HOW?" Hellman went to Ripley's Odditorium, at 1600 Oddway (a street more generally, if less imaginatively, known as Broadway). It boasted "currioddities from 200 countries," along with "40 living Ripley radio oddities." Young women wore nurses' uniforms with RIPLEY stitched into their caps and coats. Fainting was common. Hellman bought a ticket for the show. There was a man without a stomach, a man who drove spikes into his head, and a woman who swallowed a neon tube bolted to a rifle, which she then fired. "Mr. Hubbard will first attach hooks to his eyelids," the master of ceremonies called out. "Dr. May-field, chemist immune to heat and fire, inhales gas, puts torch in mouth," Hellman wrote in his notes. There follows a query: "WHERE THESE PEOPLE LIVE? EAT?"

Hellman went to Ripley's house in Mamaroneck. "His favor-ite expression is 'I'm just a boy,'" Hellman wrote in his notes. He asked Ripley how he spent his days. "Rises 6.30, works till 11, then starts moving furniture," Hellman jotted down. "Moves statues and tables constantly."

Ripley was restless. War in Europe had curtailed his travels. All he could do was move the movables and polish the totem poles. He drank too much; he ate too much; he bought too much. He was trapped. He couldn't even get his teeth fixed. "The teeth used to stick out even more than they do now," Hellman remarked. "But by the time he felt rich enough to have them straightened he had decided that his expression was so widely known that people would miss seeing them, and so he had them straightened only part-way."

Hellman was far too clever not to wonder whether he and Ripley were in the same racket. Ripley once drew a man he met in India who had been staring at the sun every day for fifteen years; he had long since gone blind. Hellman once pitched a Profile of the astrophysicist Charles Greeley Abbot. "He is the world's greatest authority on the effect of solar radiation on the earth," Hellman told his editor. Each had a sun man. Ripley collected freaks; Hellman collected characters. Ripley drew oddities; Hellman profiled them. Ripley was fascinated by the Human Inchworm and the Child Cyclops; Hellman by Joe Crane, the national parachute champion, and Charles Nessler, the inventor of the artificial eyelash. Ripley planned to compile an Oddcyclopedia. Hellman hoped to publish a book of essays titled *Hellmania*.

There is another query in Hellman's notes about Ripley. It reads, "WHERE DOES HE DRAW THE LINE?" This could have been asked about either of them.

There, though, the likeness ends. Hellman got under people's skin; Ripley was purely a skin man. For Ripley, the fact that Miss Zelma George, of Canton, Ohio, could write two different sentences, one with each hand, at the same time, upside down and backward, said it all. You could turn Hellman's brilliantly witty twenty-thousand-word Profiles into one-liners: "When he is not with close friends, Le Corbusier often displays a lively sense of his own importance," or "Knopf is at once Olympian and dressy; few literary men can stare him down." But a more sensible way to spend an afternoon would be to drive a spike into your head.

"Odd Man," Hellman's Profile of Ripley, begins like this: "The consuming passion of Robert L. Ripley, whose 'Believe It or Not' cartoons daily widen the horizon of some sixty million people, is to become a citizen of the world in the largest geographical sense of the word."

By the time Hellman met him, Ripley had visited 201 countries out of a possible 253. "Germany's expansion has confused him," Hellman wrote, ruefully. "If Hitler continues to swallow up territory at his recent rate, in a few years Ripley may even be in a position to state truthfully that he has visited more countries than exist."

Ripley liked to call himself "the modern Marco Polo." His wanderings began just after the Great War and ended during the Cold War. They span years darkened by fascism, Nazism, civil wars, revolutions, and the atomic bomb. They cover an era that featured the birth of commercial aviation, the rise of Communist China, the emergence of postcolonialism, and the founding of the United Nations. Between Ripley's first ramble and his last, Americans' ideas about their nation's place in the world turned nearly upside down.

You wouldn't know it from reading Ripley's *Believe It or Not!* Even his travel diaries prove unrevealing, at least as Thompson quotes from them. "Can India offer more wonders than Japan or China, especially China?" Ripley asks. "It seems impossible." He thinks Canton is "a vast rabbit warren of slant-eyed humanity." He laments that Nairobi is full of "stupid white people trying to change the age-old habits of the Africans." He finds Tehran "much overrated"; in Baghdad, he likes the food.

Thompson finds Ripley cosmopolitan. Hellman found him provincial. "Speaks no foreign languages," Hellman wrote in his notes. But Ripley managed to be both provincial and cosmopolitan in the same two-headed way that he managed to be both heavyset and dainty. In the 1940s, Ripley collected in his house in Mamaroneck a harem of women from all over the world: Hungary, England, Germany, Russia, and Japan. (He required some of them to sign a waiver before moving in; it stated that they were doing so voluntarily.) He'd have parties and his guests would be people like Joe Laurello, who could turn his head all the way around, like an owl.

"All people are good," Ripley told Hellman. "All people are fundamentally all right." That never made it out of Hellman's notebook.

Hellman didn't buy it. Ripley collected people; he didn't necessarily like them. His world was teeming with humanity and stalked by horror. It was hardly hopeful.

"I FEEL PERFECTLY AT HOME when I travel," Ripley told Hellman, that day they met, in a house filled with shrunken heads and skeletons. "When I come back, everything is just where I left it." Robert L. Ripley died, of a heart attack, on May 27, 1949. He was fifty-nine. That August, his estate was auctioned at the Plaza Art Galleries, in New York, on East Fifty-Ninth Street. Gothic torches, Eskimo harpoons, camel's bells, Aztec masks, Baroque armchairs, lacquered Buddhas—everything went on the block. The auction, of nearly a thousand objects, took four days and brought in nearly ninety thousand dollars. Harry Richman, a song-and-dance man, bought a portion of Ripley's collection of beer steins, including one made out of an elephant's tusk. Having no better place to put the steins in his Brooklyn apartment, he kept them in his bathroom. A collector named John Arthur nudged Richman out of the bidding for a stein made from the tusk of a walrus. ("I could cry," Richman told *Life*.) Arthur also bought Ripley's chastity belt and his iron maiden; he spent, in all, fifty thousand dollars. He planned to open a floating museum on Ripley's Chinese junk. He said, "You can show this stuff in Timbuktu."

Hellman didn't attend the auction; he was in Europe. But *The New Yorker* covered the event in its Talk of the Town. The auction catalogue stated the claim that Ripley had traveled, in his lifetime, six hundred thousand miles. *The New Yorker* raised an eyebrow: "No one man could have accumulated that stuff in so short a distance."

—2013

THE ICE MAN

Robert C. W. Ettinger, who thinks death is for chumps, drives a rusty white Chevy Lumina with a bumper sticker on the rear that reads Choose Life! Ettinger is ninety-one years old, bent and crooked. His face is splotched, his goatee grizzled, his gray hair wispy and unkempt. He leans on a worn wooden cane and wears a thick orthopedic shoe on his left foot. His legs were smashed when he was hit by German mortar fire in November 1944, just before the Battle of the Bulge. He spent four years in an army hospital, where he had bone grafts and skin grafts; antibiotics saved his life. More recently, he has undergone angioplasty, cataract surgery, a hemorrhoidectomy, and prostate surgery, twice. That Ettinger endures is a miracle of science. Actuarially, chances are good that he'll be dying soon, and, if the going gets much tougher, he'll kill himself. He has planned that down to the last detail. He has one concern. "The problem, of course, with suicide is that if you don't do it right you face autopsy," he told me. "And then you're no good for freezing."

Ettinger is a founder of the cryonics movement. When he dies, the blood will be drained from his body, antifreeze will be pumped into his arteries, and holes will be drilled into his skull, after which he will be stored in a vat of liquid nitrogen at −320 degrees Fahrenheit. He expects to be defrosted, sometime between fifty and two hundred years from now, by scientists who will make him young and strong and tireless. Ettinger has already frozen his mother and his two wives, along with ninety-two other people who await resurrection inside giant freezers in a building five minutes away from his house, in Clinton Township, Michigan.

I went out to Michigan to meet Ettinger one May. Clinton Township—population 95,648 at the last census, 95,743 if you count the corpses at the Cryonics Institute ("Our patients are not truly dead in any fundamental sense," Ettinger says)—lies twenty miles northeast of

Detroit. The township is named for New York's Erie Canal–building governor, DeWitt Clinton; Easterners began arriving in droves soon after the canal was completed, in 1825. Ground was broken for a canal to Kalamazoo in 1838, a year after Michigan joined the Union, but then the railroad came. At the Clinton Township Historic Village, which consists of a log cabin, an old meetinghouse, and a wishing well, the grass was squishy, as if someone had left the sprinklers on too long; actually, it was the old, abandoned Clinton-Kalamazoo Canal, oozing up. The past has a way of doing that.

There are only three ways to go when you die. You can be buried, burned, or frozen. If there is no God, Ettinger says, your only chance at an afterlife is Option 3. I decided to take a closer look at Options 1 and 2. Driving along Cass Avenue, I passed the First Presbyterian Church, where a sign out front read:

LIFE IS SHORT
SO PRAY HARD

Down the road, I stopped at Clinton Grove Memorial Park, which was established in 1855 and is the oldest burial ground around. A canopy of oaks and elms shelters six thousand nineteenth-century dead. Vacancies remain. A flashing sign cycled through three messages: CREMATION SPACE $395 . . . MONUMENTS SOLD HERE . . . THINK SPRING!

Across the street are two tombstone firms: "Lincoln Granite, family owned and operated since 1903"; and "Clinton Grove Granite Works, est. 1929." Both offices were closed, so I browsed through the outdoor displays, gravestones of pink and gray granite, their borders engraved with stock sentiments: FOREVER IN OUR HEARTS, inside two valentines; IN GOD'S CARE, on a banner beneath a cross. In the middle of each stone, a polished, empty space awaits only a pair of dates and someone's name. I tried to think spring.

THE CRYONICS INSTITUTE OCCUPIES A seven-thousand-square-foot brick-fronted warehouse in an industrial park behind the township's water and sewerage building. Past a shabby waiting room is the small office of Andy Zawacki. Andy constitutes half of CI's full-time staff. He is also one of CI's more than eight hundred members, which means that he plans to be frozen when he dies. ("Life-time members" pay $1,250 to join and $28,000 upon "death"; they are encouraged to pay by making the institute the beneficiary of their life insurance policies.) On C.I.'s website, Andy wears a lab coat, as if he were a scientist or a doctor, but, mostly, he's a handyman. He has been working for CI since he graduated from high school. He's lumpy and balding and soft-spoken but, other than that, not a bit like Peter Lorre.

He answered the door and took me into the office, where Robert Ettinger was waiting. I started to say hello. "You want to see it?" Ettinger asked.

Andy led us down the hall and through a door into a storage area with fluorescent lights and sixteen-foot-high ceilings. Almost every-thing in the room was white or silver, like the inside of a refrigera-tor just off the truck from Sears. It sounded like a refrigerator, too, a faintly throbbing *hrrrmmm*. There were fourteen cylindrical freezers. They looked like propane tanks, the kind you attach to your gas grill, except that they were about ten feet tall and six feet wide. Each held six patients. All but four were filled. There were also three older, rect-angular freezers, and then there was a stainless-steel thermos about the size of a rain barrel, and that's where Ettinger was headed. He lifted the lid. Liquid nitrogen wafted out.

"Cats," he said. He blew into the container and waved his hand, trying to clear the vapor. "Can't see much, I guess."

I peered in. I blew. We blew together. I couldn't see a thing.

"Cats in there?" I asked, peering, blowing.

"Yup."

"How many?"

"Don't know."

Andy interjected, "We've got about sixty pets. Mostly dogs and cats."

"A few birds," Ettinger added. He closed the lid.

I stared at the giant freezers. "Are they upside down?" Better for the brain on thawing, I guess. I pictured hibernating bats.

"Well, not the first ones," Ettinger explained. "We put them in hor-izontally. Everyone else—in the cylinders—is upside down."

"And, in . . . cannisters or something, within the cylinders?"

"No." He shook his head. "In sleeping bags."

"Just regular sleeping bags? Like, from Kmart?"

"No," Andy said. "Walmart."

Ettinger, leaning on his cane, surveyed the room.

"Your mother, and your two wives," I began hesitantly. "Are they all in this room?"

"Yes."

"And . . . where?"

"No idea." He shrugged. "My mother and my first wife used to be over there," he said, pointing to one corner of the room. "But we moved them over there"—he pointed to the cylinders. "Andy, do you know where they are?"

"That one." Andy indicated one of the cylinders with his chin. "Or maybe that one. One of those two. I can check."

Ettinger, slightly sheepish: "We have a chart."

ROBERT ETTINGER WAS BORN IN ATLANTIC CITY in December of 1918. His mother's family came from Odessa; his father was born in Germany. In about 1922, the Ettingers moved to Detroit. Ettinger's father ran a furniture store, and the family lived in a house on Calvert Street, where, in 1927, when he was eight years old, Ettinger started reading *Amazing Stories*, the first magazine of what its editor, Hugo Gernsback, called "scientifiction": "Extravagant Fiction Today . . . Cold Fact Tomorrow." Much in Gernsback's stories has come true: rockets, television, computers, cell phones. Gernsback's stories also revisited a literary perennial: immortality.

Stories about immortality are ancient; they are part of every religion; they riddle myths and legends. And they always contain an argument with history, because to live forever is to conquer time as much as it is to conquer death. About a century and a half ago, stories about immortality got mixed up with stories about scientists. In 1845, Edgar Allan Poe wrote "The Facts in the Case of M. Valdemar," about a mesmerist who hypnotizes a dying man at the instant of his death and keeps him in a trance for seven months. When he tries to lift the trance, the poor man cries, "For God's sake!—quick!—quick!—put me to sleep—or, quick!—waken me!—quick!—I say to you that I am dead!" and promptly melts into a pool of putrescence. In "A Thousand Deaths," an early Jack London short story, from 1899, the narrator's mad-scientist father repeatedly kills and revives him, leaving him dead for longer and longer stretches: "Another time, after being suffocated, he kept me in cold storage for three months, not permitting me to freeze or decay."

Rot is always a problem for the living dead, which is why resurrectionists borrow a good deal from methods used in preserving food. In 1766, the Scottish surgeon John Hunter tried to animate frozen fish. Benjamin Franklin thought that if he could be preserved in a vat of Madeira wine he would have liked very much to see what the world was like in a century or two. People used to eat their food fresh, canned, or salted, until someone got the idea to sell pond ice, and then those who could afford it paid to have ice delivered by the iceman. Starting in the 1890s, housewives could rent lockers in cold-storage warehouses. All this made for some fantastic scientifiction. In January 1930, Gernsback published "The Corpse That Lived": a man who dies in a plane crash in the year 2025 is immersed in a bathtub of ice cubes and brought back to life by an electric pulse. The next month's issue included "The Ice Man": Marcus Publius, frozen in Rome in 59 BCE, is defrosted in 1928 by a professor who's remarkably handy with an electric blanket.

Ettinger dates his interest in immortality to 1931, when, at the age of twelve, he read "The Jameson Satellite," in which a dying professor has himself entombed in a rocket and launched into the cold storage of space. Forty million years pass, whereupon a race of mechanical men transplant Jameson's brain into a body like theirs—steel head, probing tentacles—so that he, too, can be an everlasting Zorome.

"I grew up with the expectation that one day we would learn how to reverse aging," Ettinger has said. Immortality is no good if you're doomed to decrepitude. When Ettinger was shot, in the Second World War, he thought, naturally, about death. In the hospital, he wrote the kind of fiction that he had read as a boy. "The Penultimate Trump" was published in 1948, in a Gernsback knockoff called *Startling Stories*, and tells of H. D. Haworth, who is ninety-two years old and survives only because his doctors have managed to cobble him together. "They gave him gland extracts, they gave him vitamins, they gave him blood transfusions. They gave him false teeth, eye-glasses, arch-supports. They cut out his varicose veins, his appendix, one of his kidneys." Haworth, pursuing immortality with the same ruthlessness with which he had pursued an ill-gotten fortune, pays a brilliant young scientist to put him "to sleep in a nice refrigerator until people really know something about the body." The scientist says, "We'd better put the vault in Michigan—very safe country, geologically."

MICHIGAN IS ALSO WHERE freezers come from. In 1923, the year after the Ettingers moved to Detroit, a company called Frigidaire, owned by General Motors and based in Detroit, began selling refrigerators in cabinets for home use. A chemist hired by General Motors developed Freon-12. In the 1930s, General Foods launched Birds Eye frozen foods. By 1944, more than 85 percent of American homes had refrigerators; when the war ended, Americans had babies and built suburbs and bought appliances. Two hundred thousand freezers were manufactured in 1946, and twice that many the following year.

H. D. Haworth makes his arrangements in secret, convinced that if anyone found out what he was doing "everyone would demand a frigidaire instead of a coffin." He dies; the scientist puts him in a freezer. Three centuries later, he awakens, naked, in a room with a beautiful woman doctor, and observes that he is young, strong, and, to his astonished delight, ready: "A long-forgotten stimulus performed its ancient function." Unfortunately, things don't turn out as well as he had hoped. Word had got out, and everybody had started going into the "freezatoria." In the absence of any expectation of heaven, people had begun behaving very badly. Scientists had therefore invented the Farbenstein Probe, to find out if a Sleeper had ever sinned; after scanning Haworth's brain, the probe sentences him to a penal colony on a planet that used to be called Mars. What do they call it now? he asks. "Now they call it Hell."

INSIDE THE CRYONICS INSTITUTE, I stood with Ettinger, contemplating Haworth and finding it hard not to think about "The Cerebral Library," which appeared in *Amazing Stories* two months before "The Jameson Satellite," and which involves a mad scientist who hires a Chinese surgeon to help him collect five hundred brains in glass jars. This place reminded me of a library, too, or, more, of an archive, a place where people deposit their papers—the contents of their heads—

when they're dead, so that someone, some future historian, can find them and bring them back to life.

"Have you got any neuros?" I asked.

A neuro is a severed head; the theory is that scientists in the future, like the Zoromes, will give you a new body, so why bother saving the old one if your brain is all they'll need? In 2002, when Red Sox baseball great Ted Williams died, his head was sawed off and frozen. It is now stored at the Alcor Life Extension Foundation, in Scottsdale, Arizona. Alcor, with some nine hundred members and eighty-nine patients, is CI's chief rival, although it charges a great deal more for eternal life. After Williams died, his oldest daughter insisted that her father had not wanted to be frozen, and produced a will in which he stated that he wished to be cremated, whereupon his son found, in the trunk of Williams's car, a piece of scrap paper that said something about "biostasis."

Ettinger has appeared on *ABC World News Tonight*, and has been interviewed by the *New York Times*, where he was referred to as "Dr. Ettinger"; elsewhere, reporters have called him "a Michigan physics professor." Ettinger has two master's degrees, one in physics and the other in mathematics, both from Wayne State University, which he attended on the G.I. Bill after the war. Many decades ago, he taught at Highland Park Community College, a school that no longer exists. He doesn't call himself "Doctor" or "Professor," but he does consider himself a scientist, insofar as he has "a scientific attitude."

"Neuropreservation" has a scientific attitude, too, but that doesn't make it a science; it's more like extremely optimistic cosmetic surgery. It promises to cure hair loss, wrinkles, senescence, impotence, and death, all at once. Ah, yes, but will it work? It would be going too far to say that stranger things have happened, because they haven't. Reanimating and rejuvenating the dead would be several orders of magnitude stranger than, say, landing on the moon. But it does boast a handful of somewhat prominent promoters and a much larger group of defenders, whose position amounts to: What the hell, it's worth a try. Ralph Merkle, a former professor of computer science at Georgia Tech who now teaches at a place called Singularity University, serves on Alcor's board of directors. (Merkle happens to be the grandnephew of Fred Merkle, whose base-running error—he failed to touch second—

cost the New York Giants the National League pennant in 1908, an error known forever after as Merkle's Boner.) The MIT professor Marvin Minsky, who will await resurrection at Alcor, emailed me, in lieu of an explanation, this helpful chart:

Cryonics	It works	It doesn't work
Sign up	Live	Die, lose life insurance
Do nothing	Die	Die

Which looks a lot like this chart—

God	Exists	Doesn't exist
Pray hard	Live	Die
Do nothing	Die	Die

—and which, while altogether different from faith, is another way of trying to cover all the bases.

As for its scientific plausibility: credentialed laboratory scientists who conduct peer-reviewed experiments having to do with the storage of organic tissue at very low temperatures (embryos, for instance, or organs for transplant) don't generally think the dead will one day awaken. The consensus appears to be that when you try to defrost a frozen corpse you get mush. And even if, in the future, scientists could repair the damage done to cells by freezing and thawing, what they would have, at best, is a cadaver. Merkle believes that nanotechnology will solve this problem—microscopic robots will repair the cells, one by one—but, as Ettinger himself points out, anyone wanting to resurrect and rejuvenate the dead must complete four tasks: cure the person of what killed her, reverse the decay that set in between death and freezing, repair the damage done by the freezing itself, and make her young again. Even Orpheus would be daunted.

And, of course, success would also seem to depend on whether the people doing the freezing are doing it well. On August 18, 2003, *Sports Illustrated* published an investigative report by Tom Verducci. Using tapes, photographs, and documents provided by Larry Johnson, Alcor's chief operating officer at the time, Verducci described how Williams's head had been "shaved, drilled with holes, accidentally cracked as many as 10 times and moved among three receptacles," until it was finally put in "a liquid-nitrogen-filled steel can that resembles a lobster pot." (Alcor denies that the head was mishandled.)

"No." Ettinger declared. "We don't do neuros."

"But—" Andy began.

"Oh, right." In 1999, a cryonics firm called CryoCare went under.

"We do have heads," Ettinger said. "Transfers."

ROBERT ETTINGER ANNOUNCED the dawn of what he called the Freezer Era at the height of the Cold War. In 1949, he met his first wife, Elaine, at a Zionist meeting. In the 1950s, they moved to the suburbs and had two children. In the basement of their house in Oak Park, Michigan, Ettinger built a fallout shelter and waited for a scientist to read "Penultimate Trump" and turn today's extravagant fiction into tomorrow's cold fact. Finally, he decided to do it himself. In 1962, he wrote a sixty-page manifesto and sent a copy to Frederik Pohl, the editor of the science fiction magazine *Worlds of Tomorrow*. Pohl, who was a regular guest on an all-night New York AM-radio broadcast, *The Long John Nebel Show*, arranged for Ettinger to be invited. One thing led to another, and eventually Thomas McCormack, a junior editor at Doubleday, agreed to publish Ettinger's manifesto.

The Prospect of Immortality appeared in 1964, the year *Dr. Strangelove* hit theaters. Through that lens, mortality begins to look rather a lot like mutual assured destruction and immortality, at 320 below, like nothing so much as a fabulously air-conditioned fallout shelter. In *Strangelove*, the world faces nuclear Armageddon. On orders from a U.S. Air Force general who is convinced of a communist conspiracy to "sap and impurify all of our precious bodily fluids," American airmen have dropped a bomb on Russia, thereby triggering the Soviets' Doomsday Machine. Everyone on the planet is about to die. From the war room in Washington, the U.S. president (played by Peter Sellers) entertains proposals made by his scientific adviser, Dr. Strangelove (also Sellers):

> STRANGELOVE: Mister President, I would not rule out the chance
> to preserve a nucleus of human specimens. It would be quite
> easy, at the bottom of some of our deeper mineshafts. . . .

PRESIDENT: How long would you have to stay down there?

STRANGELOVE (*PULLS OUT A CIRCULAR SLIDE RULE*): Well, let's see now. . . . Hmm. I would think possibly, uh, one hundred years.

After the Manhattan Project, after Sputnik, after dishwashers and electric mixers, either scientists and engineers were on the verge of solving everything (in which case, go into the freezer, because the world will be even better when you wake up) or someone was about to launch an atomic bomb (in which case, go into the freezer, because maybe you'll survive). "Before long," Ettinger predicted, "the objectors will include only a handful of eccentrics."

Ettinger conceded that the logistics of freezing the dead might prove difficult at first, especially in the "retarded nations," where "makeshifts may be necessary to stretch the rupees, pesos, etc." In poor, hot countries, "bodies will be stored in pits insulated with straw and cooled with dry ice"—where, in all likelihood, they will simply rot. No worries. "It will not at first greatly matter how skillfully the bodies are preserved, so long as *hope* is preserved." But if no one ever dies, won't there be too many people on the planet? "The people could simply agree to share the available space in shifts," Ettinger suggested, "going into suspended animation from time to time to make room for others." There will be no childbirth. Fetuses will be incubated in jars. "Essentially, motherhood will be abolished." Then, too, eugenics will help keep the birthrate down, and deformed babies could be frozen against the day that someone might actually want them, or figure out how to fix them. "Cretins," for instance, or babies born with cerebral palsy: "Would not early freezing be a true mercy?" For the weak-minded, who might find making such a decision difficult, Ettinger offered a philosophical rule of thumb: Ask yourself, "If the child were *already* frozen, and it were within my power to return him to deformed life, would I do so? If the answer is negative, then probably the freezer is where he belongs."

ON THE FLOOR IN FRONT OF THE FREEZERS at the Cryonics Institute are four slotted boxes painted white, with a black number in each slot, like the slots in a company mailroom.

"What's this?"

Ettinger looked away. Andy explained that the numbers refer to the patients, most of whom choose to remain anonymous, and the box is for their families. Over the years, a half dozen have sent flowers, mostly roses, long dead. Attached to one bouquet was a card in an unopened envelope. It turns out that staring at an unopened envelope inside a freezatorium is substantially more depressing than looking at the blank space on a tombstone. Thoughts of spring eluded me.

"Do patients' families ever visit?" I asked.

"Not many," Andy said. Ettinger had wandered off toward the office, passing a half-open door that I hadn't noticed before.

"What's in there?"

"A storeroom," Ettinger called over his shoulder. "Used to be a library."

We sat down in the conference room. Along the wall hung twenty-eight eight-by-ten-inch photographs of patients, beginning with Ettinger's mother. His father, who died in 1984 at the age of eighty-nine, was not among them. "He's in a mausoleum," Ettinger said, shaking his head. "I tried very hard to get him to be frozen, but his second wife was against it. He was too wimpy to stand up to her." Ettinger's brother, who died ten years ago, proved to be as weak as his father. "In his last illness, he became depressed and told his children that he didn't want to be frozen. I told them they should freeze him anyway, but I couldn't get them to and he was lost." This was how Ettinger always spoke of the unfrozen dead. His uncle Herman died in a car accident: "That was a shame. He was lost."

When *Prospect of Immortality* was published, Ettinger became something of a star. He claims, plausibly, that nearly everyone now active in cryonics first heard about it, directly or indirectly, from him. Ben Best, CI's current president, picked up a copy at a health-food store. Stanley Kubrick read it, Ettinger says, and then arranged to meet with him. But when Kubrick died, in 1999, he was lost. He is buried in Hertfordshire.

Ettinger said that he was interviewed by David Frost, Steve Allen, Merv Griffin, and Johnny Carson.

"Did these people take you seriously?" I asked.

"Talk-show hosts don't take anything seriously. They're idiots." He told me that he was once on a show with William F. Buckley Jr.

"What did Buckley make of you?"

"He was aghast at everything I said." This was the first time I'd seen Ettinger smile. "He thought it was immoral, unethical, unsanitary, against the will of God!" He laughed. "Buckley understood nothing."

THE FIRST HUMAN BEING was frozen in 1966; it went badly, and, a few months later, the body had to be buried. The following year, Ettinger held a press conference when a man named James Bedford was frozen by an organization that later became the Cryonics Society of California. (What with one snafu and another, most of the people who were frozen in California rotted.) Alcor was founded in 1972. The same year, St. Martin's Press, where Thomas McCormack had moved, published Ettinger's second book, *Man into Superman: The Startling Potential of Human Evolution—And How to Be a Part of It*. It begins, "By working hard and saving my money, I intend to become an immortal superman." The following year, *Sleeper* came out. Miles Monroe (Woody Allen), who runs a health-food restaurant in Greenwich Village, goes into the hospital for an ulcer, but when the surgery goes awry he is covered in "Bird's-Eye wrapper" and stuck in a freezer for two hundred years. When he wakes up, he's peevish, especially after his doctor tells him that his resurrection is a miracle of science:

> MILES (PACING): To me, a miracle of science is, like, going to the hospital for a minor operation, I come out the next day, my rent isn't two thousand months overdue. That's a miracle of science. This is what I call a cosmic screwing. And then: where am I anyhow? I mean, what happened to everybody? Where are all my friends?
> DOCTOR: You must understand that everyone you knew in the past has been dead nearly two hundred years.
> MILES: But they all ate organic rice!

In *Man into Superman*, Ettinger throws around a lot of Nietzsche and George Bernard Shaw but shows more evidence of having whiled away the hours reading *Penthouse*, which began publication in 1965. The world of tomorrow will be unimaginably better than the world of today. How? There will be transsex and supersex! Scientists will invent a "sexual superwoman . . . with cleverly designed orifices of various kinds, something like a wriggly Swiss cheese, but shapelier and more fragrant." Animals will be bred as sex slaves; even incest might be allowed. Also, scientists will likely equip men with wings, built-in biological weapons, body armor made of hair, and "telescoping, fully adjustable" sexual organs. (Hold on. That last one. Doesn't the existing model already come with that?)

Ettinger saw Allen's film when it came out. "He has a lot of good things to say about death, but, as far as I know, he's never done anything about it," he said.

"Like what?"

"Like sign up."

For a very long time, no one signed up. Ettinger's first patient was his mother, Rhea. He froze her in 1977.

"Did she want to be frozen?"

"I don't know if she was really enthusiastic about it, but she was willing."

His second patient was his first wife, who died in November 1987. What did she think about the prospect of being frozen?

"She never talked much about it. It was just taken for granted."

He remarried the following year. One month after Ettinger froze his wife, Saul Kent froze the head of his mother, Dora, at the Alcor facility. Kent, the author of *Future Sex* (1974) and *The Life-Extension Revolution* (1980), had become a convert to cryonics after reading *Prospect of Immortality* on the beach. He had also founded the vitamin-peddling Life Extension Foundation, in Hollywood, Florida, which was raided by the Food and Drug Administration in 1987. (The FDA later dropped all charges.) For a time, there was some question whether Dora Kent was actually dead when her head was cut off.

Ettinger's second wife, Mae, suffered a stroke in Scottsdale, Arizona, in 2000. Ettinger was with her. It was horrible. She was helpless; he was helpless. "All she was able to do was move one arm," he said, his voice quavering. Mae knew that she would be frozen; Ettinger had paid a local funeral home a retainer to "practice once a year." She died the day after the stroke. Ettinger takes comfort in what happened next. He acted fast. "I pronounced death—anyone can do that in Arizona—and the funeral people were there in a few minutes. We had already started packing her in ice, and the funeral people started right away." She was flown to Detroit. She is Patient No. 34. She was not lost.

ETTINGER FINDS NOTHING SO UNINTERESTING as history. "When the future expands," he wrote, "the past shrinks." In the golden age, no one will read Shakespeare: "Not only will his work be far too weak in intellect, and written in too vague and puny a language, but the problems which concerned him will be, in the main, no more than historical curiosities." Still, Ettinger told me, when I asked, that his mother and both his wives kept photo albums and that they're at the institute, in that storeroom that was once a library, somewhere. He promised that we could look for them on the second day of my visit, even though he was baffled by my interest. The future, so gleamy and white. How could anyone possibly care about the musty, dusty past?

The storeroom was a mess. There was an old StairMaster and some folding tables. The bookshelves housed a set of the Encyclopædia Britannica, someone's college textbooks—*Organic Chemistry*—and a T-shirt with the periodic table. Along one wall stood a bank of file drawers.

"What's in there?"

"Any patient who wants to can buy a drawer, to put things in," Andy said.

"Really?"

"But not many of them ask."

Mae Ettinger did. She kept a diary and requested that it be stored here, marked "Not to be read until and unless it is deemed useful for the revival." It won't survive, though. Paper turns to dust.

Andy riffled through drawer after drawer. At last, he found them: ten bulky albums with flesh-toned covers, pink, brown, and beige. He and I lugged them back to the table in the conference room. And then Ettinger and I sat for a good hour, maybe more, and turned pages. The albums were mostly photographs, but there were old documents in there, too: a military ID, a college transcript, newspaper clippings. Ettinger hadn't wanted to drag these albums out, but now that he had decided to indulge me he was determined to be thorough. He didn't skip a single photograph, even prying apart pages that had got stuck. He was bored before we began; I could have looked at that stuff forever.

The earliest albums belonged to his mother: sepia pictures of his babyhood. He offered names: "That's Leo. . . . That's Pee Wee Russell. He married my mother's sister, Mary." He remembered people from his early years best. He was very sharp on the names of his cousins, growing up, and he never missed the name of a dog. He plans to freeze the one he has now, Mugsy. Mae will like that. His father appeared in a picture or two, then disappeared. There followed photographs of Ettinger in uniform (handsome, smiling, promising) and, on the next pages, in casts, in wheelchairs, on crutches—a young man cut down. Here was his wedding, under a chuppah. The next albums were Elaine's: snapshots of postwar suburbia—the paddle pool, the tricycle, boys with crew cuts, girls in checkered dresses.

And then there was a long gap, until Mae's albums started. There were a handful of pictures of Ettinger, but many more of a sweetly happy Mae, surrounded by people—her bowling league, her children and grandchildren from her first marriage. "That's one of Pat's kids," he'd say. Or, more often than not, "Who the hell is that? I don't know who the hell that is."

"When you wake up, nearly everyone in these albums will be gone," I said. "Won't you miss them?"

"I hope to see the people I knew before, and that I loved before." Ettinger sighed. "Most of the people I grew up with are already gone. That's been true for a long time. Most of the people that anybody grows up with they lose track of. We lose them."

Unless we save them, in the freezer, in an archive, in our children, forever in our hearts, in God's care. We had gone through one of the albums, two, five, eight. I asked why cryonics is, by any objective measure, a failure. Ettinger talked about something that he calls the "legacy effect," the crippling hold of the past. If not for that, the Freezer Era would have dawned in 1964, when it was supposed to.

And then, as abruptly as we began, we were done. He pulled himself up to standing, grabbed his cane, and tapped the last page of the final photo album. "Someone should have put labels on these things," he muttered.

JUST AFTER I LEFT MICHIGAN, Ettinger self-published a new book, *Youniverse: Toward a Self-Centered Philosophy of Immortalism and Cryonics* (you are the most important person in the universe; no one else matters), and the Cryonics Institute admitted a new patient. Patient No. 93 was born Billie Joe Bonsall but had had his name legally changed to William Constitution O'Rights. He had no known occupation, although he liked to dress up as a priest. Bill O'Rights was forty-three when he "deanimated," in a hospital in Maine; the next day, his body was flown to Detroit in an icebox. At the Faulmann and Walsh funeral home, Jim Walsh opened the body and pumped in eight liters of ethylene glycol. Then he brought it to CI, where Andy put it into a Walmart sleeping bag and placed it in a cooling box. A few days later, Patient No. 93 was hoisted up on a forklift and lowered into a freezer, head first, like a hibernating bat, beside invisible cats, inside a seven-thousand-square-foot building in an industrial park in the heart of America, where some of the sorriest ideas of a godforsaken and alienated modernity endure.

Robert C. W. Ettinger might be the institute's next patient, but, for now, he's holding on. The longer he lives, the better his chances, because in the golden age, or what used to be called hell, scientists choosing which patients to thaw will follow a simple rule: last in, first out.

—2010

Postscript: Robert Ettinger died in 2011 at the age of ninety-two. His remains are stored at the Cryonics Institute.

VALLEY OF THE DOLLS

BRATZ DOLLS HAVE SWOLLEN HEADS, POUTY LIPS, spindly limbs, and chunky-heeled shoes. Their waists are barely wider than their necks. Their eyes and heads are so big and their noses so small that if it weren't for their *Penthouse* makeup (icy eye shadow, cat-eye liner, glistening lip gloss, and eyelashes as long as their fingers) and their come-hither clothes (crop tops, hot pants, micro-minis, and kinky boots), they'd look like emaciated babies, Kewpie dolls in a time of famine. Carter Bryant was thirty-one and working at Mattel in August of 2000, designing clothes for Barbie, when he created Bratz, though he later said—and his legal defense turned on this claim—that he'd got the idea for the dolls while on a seven-month break from Mattel, two years earlier. He drew some sketches of clothes-obsessed, bratty-looking teenagers—"The Girls with a Passion for Fashion!" he called them—and made a prototype by piecing together bits and bobs that he found in a trash bin at work and in his own collection at home: a doll head, a plastic body, and Ken boots. He meant for his Bratz to come in pick-your-own skin colors and to have monetizably vague ethnic names. Two weeks before Bryant quit Mattel, he sold his idea to a Mattel competitor, MGA Entertainment, which brought out four Bratz girls in 2001—Jade, Cloe, Yasmin, and Sasha—the first dolls to successfully rival Barbie since she made her debut, in 1959, in a zebra-striped swimsuit and stilettos, eyebrows arched, waist pinched.

Mattel sued Bryant; Mattel sued MGA; MGA sued Mattel. In the course of years of legal wrangling, hundreds of millions of dollars changed hands, but I'm afraid I couldn't possibly tell you exactly how much because, as talking Barbie used to say, her pull string wriggling, "Math class is tough!"

The feud between Barbie and Bratz occupied the narrow space between thin lines: between fashion and porn, between originals and copies, and between toys for girls and rights for women. In 2010, Alex Kozinski, then the chief judge of the U.S. Court of Appeals for the Ninth Circuit, who presided over *Mattel v. MGA*, wrote in his opinion that most of what makes a fashion doll desirable is not protectable intellectual property, because there are only so many ways to make a female body attractive. "Little girls buy fashion dolls with idealized proportions which means slightly larger heads, eyes and lips; slightly smaller noses and waists; and slightly longer limbs than those that appear routinely in nature," Kozinski wrote, giving "slightly" a meaning I never knew it had. But only so much exaggeration is possible, he went on. "Make the head too large or the waist too small and the doll becomes freakish." I'd explain how it is that anyone could look at either a Barbie or a Bratz doll and not find it freakish, except that such an explanation is beyond me. As a pull-string Barbie knockoff once told Lisa Simpson, "Don't ask me! I'm just a girl!"

In 2017, Orly Lobel, a professor at the University of San Diego School of Law, published *You Don't Own Me: How Mattel v. MGA Entertainment Exposed Barbie's Dark Side*. For the book, a hair-raising account of a Barbie Dreamhouse–size Jarndyce and Jarndyce, Lobel interviewed Judge Kozinski over lunch and happened to mention that, when she was a girl, her mother, a psychologist, told her that Barbie dolls were bad for girls' body image. Kozinski professed astonishment. "The only thing wrong that I saw when I held Barbie," he said, joking, "is when I lift her skirt there is nothing underneath." In 2017, Kozinski resigned from the federal judiciary after more than a dozen women, including two of his own former law clerks, accused him of inappropriate behavior. Justice is hard!

BEFORE BARBIE, DOLLS WERE BABIES, to be fed and burped and bathed and wheeled around in prams and put down for naps. Barbie, who has hips and breasts, was a ripoff of a magnificently racy German doll called Lilli. Lilli was inspired by the title character in a *Playboy*-style comic strip; she works as a secretary but is usually barely dressed, like the time she shows up at the office in a bikini. "So dumb!" she says. "When I wake up in the morning, I think I'm still on vacation!" ("Gentlemen prefer Lilli," her slogan went.) Ruth Handler, who cofounded Mattel with her husband in 1945, bought more than a dozen Lillis while on a tour of Europe with her children, Barbara and Ken, in 1956. She had the dolls shipped back home to California, and charged the Mattel designer Jack Ryan, a lesser Hugh Hefner, with making an American Lilli. Handler's husband declared that she was "anatomically perfect." Mattel introduced its doll as Barbie, Teen Age Fashion Model.

Ruth Handler elaborated on Barbie's German origins only after Ryan, a man she called "the world's greatest swinger," began claiming that the idea for Barbie was his, not hers. ("He couldn't think of anything original," Handler said about Ryan, "but once you led him, and said what he should make, then he figured out how to make it happen.") Handler said she named the doll after her daughter, but Ryan insisted that he was the one who named her, after a different Barbara, his wife. (Another of Ryan's five wives, Zsa Zsa Gabor, claimed, after divorcing him, that she hadn't been able to bear the fur-lined sex dungeon in his Bel Air mansion.) In 1961, Lilli's manufacturer sued Mattel, charging that the company had copied Lilli "one to one," having modified her "only very slightly; et voilà, Barbie was created." Handler liked to say that Lilli was a freak, that she had an "elongated and distorted kind of look," while Barbie was entirely natural. "I wanted an American teen-ager, but I wanted a narrow waist, narrow ankles, and boobs," Handler said. In fact, the two dolls are nearly identical. Mattel settled the case out of court, and bought Lilli's copyright in 1964. In 1978, Handler, having been investigated by the Securities and Exchange Commission, was indicted for fraud; she maintained her innocence but pleaded no contest. Two years later, Ryan sued Mattel; Mattel settled. In 1991, after suffering a stroke, Ryan shot himself in the head. Handler, who, after battling breast cancer, had founded a company, Nearly Me, that made prosthetic breasts, died in 2002, the year Bratz won the Toy of the Year Award.

Notwithstanding her lurid origins, Barbie was the world's top-selling toy for girls for a half century. Mattel is believed to have sold nearly a billion Barbie dolls. Sales have lately been falling (despite Mattel's introduction, in 2016, of "body diversity" Barbies that come in different sizes, shapes, and colors). Still, nine in ten American girls between the ages of three and ten own at least one Barbie doll, and, even without counting those buried in landfills, there might well be more Barbies in the United States than there are people.

Barbie is both a relic from another era and a bellwether of changing ideas about women and work, sex, and men. Her 1959 debut coincided with the release of the erotically charged film *Pillow Talk*. Doris Day, who looks something like Barbie, plays an extravagantly fashionable interior decorator obliged to share a party line with a rakish playboy (Rock Hudson). They flirt over the phone. "This career girl had everything but love," the film's trailer announced, introducing "the most sparkling sexcapade that ever winked at convention." The playboy has a switch in his apartment with which he can lock the door from the couch, so that his dates can't escape. The interior decorator, who fends off all manner of advances from her clients, wants nothing more than to be carried into the playboy's lair. (Much of the winking at convention had to do with Hudson's sexuality: at one point, he plays a straight man pretending to be a gay man; at another point, he is taken for a pregnant man.)

In 1961, Barbie began dating Ken, a Rock Hudson look-alike named after Ruth Handler's son. Their sexcapade sparkled. "I have a date tonight!" an early talking Barbie said in 1968. "Would you like to go shopping?" Originally marketed to girls between the ages of nine and twelve, the career girl and her beach-blanket-bingo boyfriend weathered the women's movement and the sexual revolution by appealing, each year, to younger and younger children, which also made Barbie appear, each year, older and older. By the 1990s, when three out of four women between twenty-five and fifty-four worked outside the home and Mattel was taking in a billion dollars annually in Barbie sales alone, Barbie had become a plaything for three-year-olds—girls who wore footie pajamas and pull-up diapers and who drank out of sippy cups, girls who were still toddlers. Barbie wasn't their baby; Barbie wasn't the teenager they wanted to grow up to be; Barbie was their mommy.

If *Pillow Talk* marked the advent of Barbie, the movie version of *Bridget Jones's Diary*, released in theaters in 2001, marked the debut of Bratz. At a failing London publishing house, another career girl, played by Renée Zellweger, works for Daniel Cleaver, played by

Hugh Grant. Much of their office flirting, conducted not by telephone but by email, concerns her clothes: microminis and see-through blouses—Bratz clothes.

> *DANIEL:* If walking past my office was attempt to demonstrate presence of skirt, can only say that it has failed parlously—Cleave.
> *BRIDGET:* Shut up, please. I am very busy and important. P.S. How dare you sexually harass me in this impertinent manner?
> *DANIEL:* Message Jones. Mortified to have caused offense. Will avoid all non-P.C. overtones in future. Deeply apologetic. P.S. Like your tits in that top.

MGA sold ninety-seven million dollars' worth of Bratz dolls in 2001 and a billion dollars' worth in 2003. Mattel began to panic. To the press, as Lobel recounts, Isaac Larian, MGA's CEO, offered all sorts of explanations about where the idea for Bratz had come from, including from a focus group or from his daughter, Jasmine. Eventually, according to Lobel, an anonymous letter tipped Mattel off to the truth: Bratz had been created not by Isaac Larian or by any of his children but by Carter Bryant, who, when he was hired by Mattel, had signed an intellectual property agreement: everything he created during his employment at Mattel, it said, belonged to Mattel.

"WHAT DOES IT MEAN TO OWN AN IDEA?" Oren Bracha, a professor at the University of Texas School of Law, asks in *Owning Ideas: The Intellectual Origins of American Intellectual Property, 1790–1909.* Intellectual property takes the form of patents and copyrights, legal instruments derived from the practices of fifteenth-century Italian republics. In Anglo-American law, the first patents and copyrights were issued in the sixteenth century, although they weren't rights; they were privileges, favors granted by the Crown, such as the patent that Elizabeth I granted to Sir Walter Raleigh in 1584 for the "discoverie" of Virginia and to "Have holde & enjoye the saide Land," or the copyright that James I granted in 1611 to printers of what became known as the King James Bible. As Bracha pointed out, early patents and copyrights were not understood to involve ideas. That transformation came in the course of the eighteenth century, when the courts began to understand ideas as things that could be owned and ownership of them as having the characteristics of property rights.

In 1787, patents and copyrights had only lately taken on this meaning and force in English common law when the U.S. Constitution granted Congress the power "to promote the progress of science and useful arts by securing for limited times to Authors and Inventors the exclusive rights to their respective writings and discoveries." In the late eighteenth century, a property in ideas came to rest in authors and inventors, on the theory, foundational to possessive individualism, that the act of creation is the act of an individual. Not everyone agreed with this premise, which pits the property rights of authors and inventors against a public interest in books and inventions. Benjamin Franklin famously refused to patent any of his inventions, on the ground that, he explained, "as we enjoy great advantages from the inventions of others, we should be glad of an opportunity to serve others by any invention of ours; and this we should do freely and generously."

Few followed his lead. Instead, nineteenth-century Americans "democratized invention," according to the economist Zorina Khan, granting to ordinary people, as a universal right, what had once been a privilege granted to an elite few. They also adopted a Romantic notion of authorship—fetishizing the originality of the fevered, Byronic genius—though jurists like the Supreme Court justice Joseph Story found the standard of unstained originality all but useless for adjudicating copyright disputes. "No man creates a new language for himself, at least if he be a wise man," Story wrote. "Virgil borrowed much from Homer . . . and even Shakespeare and Milton, so justly and proudly our boast as the brightest originals, would be found to have gathered much from the abundant stores of current knowledge and classical studies in their days."

The reason to protect a property in ideas, at least originally, was to promote creativity both by rewarding authors and inventors for what they do and by, after a fixed time, releasing their ideas to the world. The standard of originality in intellectual property has, historically, been low, because everything, to some degree, copies at least part of something else. Good ideas are cobbled together out of other ideas, even bad ideas, and, for people to keep having new ideas, old ideas have to be set free. As Louis Brandeis explained in 1918, "The general rule of law is, that the noblest of human productions—knowledge, truths ascertained, conceptions, and ideas—become, after voluntary communication to others, free as the air to common use."

The reign of authors and inventors began coming to a close in the 1880s, with the rise of corporate liberalism. Authors and inventors there might still be, but, when they were employees, their employers owned their ideas. Corporate ownership of ideas, the dramatic extension of the terms of copyright, and a wild expansion of what counts as protectable intellectual property have together undermined the original purpose of intellectual property law. Nine out of ten patents granted in the United States are now owned by corporations. Congress passed ten copyright-extension acts in the course of the twentieth century; copyright now lasts for seventy years after the death of the author. Corporations have attempted to claim exclusive legal rights to everything from yoga moves to genetic sequences. Lucasfilm, George Lucas's company, sued two lobbying groups over the use of the phrase "star wars" to refer to the Reagan administration's proposed missile-defense system, and licenses the word "droid" to Verizon, even though it was coined in the 1950s, twenty years before Lucasfilm used it in *Star Wars*. By the 1990s, especially after the passage of the soi-disant Mickey Mouse Protection Act, in 1998, a growing number of legal scholars had begun to question the basic assumptions of intellectual property law, wondering whether it has ever done what it was meant to do. Insisting on a "freedom to copy," they argued that the private rights of corporations were overrunning the public interest.

"The central narrative of intellectual property law, that legal protection against copying is necessary in order to promote creative behavior, has been subjected to surprisingly little scrutiny," Kate Darling and Aaron Perzanowski observed in *Creativity Without Law: Challenging the Assumptions of Intellectual Property*, a collection of essays that looked at creative artists whose work has thrived outside the regime of intellectual property—including chefs, bartenders, pornographers, and tattoo and graffiti artists. Tattoos are protectable intellectual property, but nearly all tattoo artists operate outside that legal realm, following, instead, a set of industry norms. Pornography, which has historically been the first to adopt and adapt to new technologies, is generally lax about copyright enforcement and has instead devised a new business model, based on sharing not content but experiences. By operating outside intellectual property law, each of these industries has thrived, both creatively and economically. A counter case could be made that industries that are vigilant about copyright infringement—action-figure franchises, say, or television sitcoms—may have made a lot of money for the corporations that own them, but the results have not generally been distinguished for their creativity.

Calls for reform, often sounded, have not been heeded. One of the loudest and sharpest critics of the intellectual property corporate rampage was Judge Kozinski. "Overprotecting intellectual property is as harmful as underprotecting it," he wrote, long before issuing his opinion in *Mattel v. MGA*. As Lobel reports, Kozinski is that rare bird—a judicial celebrity. He hobnobs with Hollywooders, and kept his own IMDb page, where he had personally rated more than a thousand films. A movie buff and a libertarian, Kozinski was also a free-speech advocate, a position that extends to both pornography and intellectual property. In one notable opinion, a dissent in a copyright case in which the producers of *Wheel of Fortune* had complained about a Vanna White robot in a Samsung ad, Kozinski wrote, "We call this creativity, not piracy."

Kozinski, in other words, would appear to agree with Joseph Story and Louis Brandeis. "Nobody writes anything from scratch," he said in an interview in 2006. "We all build on the past from a shared public domain of ideas." In one of the darker ironies of this saga, Kozinski, a jurist known for his promotion of the freedom to copy, was felled by a social movement that involves the repetition of endlessly similar stories and calls itself #MeToo.

"THEY CANNOT KEEP MAKING DOLLS LIKE THIS! Something has to be done!" Lisa Simpson fumes, hopelessly, in a 1994 episode of *The Simpsons*. If sexy dolls for little girls have never strayed far from either pornography or debates about intellectual property, they've also never strayed far from the politics of the workplace. When Lisa and Marge visit the doll company to complain, a man in a suit whistles from a boardroom to their tour guide, "Hey, Jiggles! Grab a pad and back that gorgeous butt in here!" Miffed, Lisa comes up with her own idea for a doll, a doll with "the tenacity of Nina Totenberg and the common sense of Elizabeth Cady Stanton and, to top it off, the down-to-earth good looks of Eleanor Roosevelt." She sells exactly . . . one. Her intellectual property is worthless. As Kozinski would write in his opinion in *Mattel v. MGA*, it's possible to make dolls that don't look like porn stars but "there's not a big market for fashion dolls that look like Patty and Selma Bouvier"—a reference to Lisa Simpson's big-nosed, wide-waisted, thick-ankled aunts.

In 2004, which, as it happens, was the year that the Ninth Circuit Court judge Alex Kozinski was rated the No. 1 male Superhottie of the federal judiciary, by the now defunct legal-gossip blog Underneath Their Robes (John Roberts, then a judge for the DC Circuit Court, was ranked No. 5), Mattel sued MGA. As the case slowly made its way to trial, Bratz sales continued to soar. Marketed as "multiethnic," and often described as "urban," and "street," Bratz dolls were celebrated for racial and ethnic diversity and greeted as markers of the "browning of America." Their popularity in Middle American suburbia tracked the spreading influence of hip-hop and rap, including hip-hop and rap's representation of girls and women. ("Cutie the bomb, met her at a beauty salon," Kanye West rapped in the chart-topping "Gold Digger" in 2005, a best-selling Bratz year. "She went to the doctor, got lipo with your money.") Mattel had been far worse than tone-deaf on race: it once released a doll called Oreo Barbie, which came in both Black and white versions. But Bratz made race into a consumer accessory, and, as the cultural critic Lisa Guerrero has pointed out, Jade, Cloe, Yasmin, Sasha, and the rest of the Bratz never work; they only shop. By 2006, the year the activist Tarana Burke founded an organization called Just Be Inc. to raise awareness about the sexual abuse of Black and brown girls, using the slogan "Me Too," Bratz dolls were outselling Barbies in England, Australia, and South Africa and competing well in the United States, where sales of Barbie dolls were down 13 percent, notwithstanding the introduction of the truly porny collectors' edition Lingerie Barbie, who, in a pink bustier and peekaboo peignoir, looks like nothing so much as a heavily drugged Marilyn Monroe about to pass out.

Mattel v. MGA finally reached a California district court in 2008, the year that Judge Kozinski—who, if the stories told about him are to be believed, appears to have fancied himself a "like your tits in that top" sort of boss—was the subject of a judicial inquiry for posting pornographic images to his public website, alex.kozinski.com. The images included, according to the *Los Angeles Times*, "a photo of naked women on all fours painted to look like cows." Perhaps inevitably, pornography played a role in the Mattel case, too. During the discovery phase of the initial trial, Lobel reports, a California district court judge granted Mattel's attorneys permission to scan Carter Bryant's computer for evidence. On that computer, they found pornography, and also software used to wipe hard drives. During the trial, the judge allowed Mattel's lawyers to introduce the pornography as evidence, and to question him about it. In the end, the district court jury ruled in Mattel's favor, awarding the company a hundred million dollars, a tenth of the one billion that Mattel had sought. Kozinski, meanwhile, was reprimanded for posting pornography, but, after apologizing and shutting down his website, he remained on the bench, which is how he came to adjudicate the doll wars when, on appeal, *Mattel v. MGA* went to Kozinski's court in 2009, Barbie's fiftieth birthday.

"Who owns Bratz?" Kozinski asked at the opening of his landmark opinion. Not Mattel, was his answer, in a ruling in which he listed a series of errors made by the lower court, including its finding that the features of an idealized female body were ideas that anyone could own. "America thrives on competition," Kozinski declared. "Barbie, the all-American girl, will, too."

Kozinski's ruling sent the case back to the district court for a second trial, where, as Lobel expertly explains, much turned on MGA's lawyer Jennifer Keller's questioning of the Mattel CEO, Robert Eckert.

"Say I am eighteen, doodling away. I place my doodles in my parents' house in one of the drawers of my teenage closet," Keller said. "Twenty years later, I am hired by Mattel. I visit my parents' home and find the doodles. Does Mattel own them?"

"Yes," Eckert said. "Probably, yes."

Aghast at Mattel's absurd overreach, the jury not only found against Mattel but found in favor of MGA's countersuit. The judge awarded MGA more than three hundred million dollars in damages.

Some legal scholars thought that an appeal of Kozinski's opinion might carry *Barbie v. Bratz* to the Supreme Court. That never happened, but the legal battle went on with yet another lawsuit. The intellectual property issues raised by the case have not been resolved, nor have the weightier matters of the intellectual independence of girls or the relationship between men and women at work.

Once told to be hotties (even judges wanted to be hotties!), girls were next told to empower themselves by being hot employees, as both the culture and corporations set aside long-standing concerns about sexual harassment in the workplace—abandoning possible societal, industry-wide, or even governmental remedies—in favor of sex-positive corporate feminism. The 2013 publication of Sheryl Sandberg's *Lean In* marked a steepening in the decline of structural efforts to reform workplaces. Instead of fighting for equal pay, equal work, and family leave, women were told that they needed to empower themselves, one by one, through power dressing and personal exertion. Unsurprisingly, Barbie and Bratz leaned in, too. MGA relaunched Bratz with the latest mindless lingo of corporate-friendly girl power in a box. "We have doctors, lawyers, journalists," MGA's CEO, Isaac Larian, told *Forbes*. "Now more than ever before, Bratz empowers girls." The rebranded dolls, though, had no discernible interest in such careers. Instead, the Bratz, who, like Barbie, started out as teenagers, now came with hobbies, including yoga and running, and wardrobes newly inspired by study-abroad travel. Mattel ran its own Sandbergian campaign—"When a Girl Plays with Barbie, She Imagines Everything She Can Become"—and promoted Doctor Barbie, who, with her stethoscope, wears stilettos, a miniskirt, and a white lab coat embroidered, in pink thread, BARBIE.

Empowerment feminism is a cynical sham. As Margaret Talbot once noted in *The New Yorker*, "To change a Bratz doll's shoes, you have to snap off its feet at the ankles." That is pretty much what girlhood feels like. In a 2014 study, girls between four and seven were asked about possible careers for boys and girls after playing with either Fashion Barbie, Doctor Barbie, or, as a control, Mrs. Potato Head. The girls who had played with Mrs. Potato Head were significantly more likely to answer yes to the question "Could you do this job when you grow up?" when shown a picture of the workplaces of a construction worker, a firefighter, a pilot, a doctor, and a police officer. The study had a tiny sample size, and, like most slightly nutty research in the field of social psychology, has never been replicated, or scaled up, except that, since nearly all American girls own a Barbie, the population of American girls has been the subject of the scaled-up version of that experiment for nearly six decades.

#MeToo arises from the failure of empowerment feminism. Women have uncannily similar and all too often harrowing and even devastating stories about things that have happened to them at work because men do very similar things to women; leaning in doesn't help. There's more copying going on, too: pornography and accounts of sexual harassment follow the same script. Nobody writes anything from scratch. Abandoning structural remedies and legislative reform for the politics of personal charm—leaning in, dressing for success, being Doctor Barbie—left women in the workplace with few choices but to shut up and lean in more and to dress better. It's no accident that #MeToo started in the entertainment and television news businesses, where women are required to look as much like Barbie and Bratz dolls as possible, with the help of personal trainers, makeup artists, hair stylists, personal shoppers, and surgeons. Unfortunately, an extrajudicial crusade of public shaming of men accused of "sexual misconduct" is no solution, and a poor kind of justice, not least because it brooks no dissent, as if all that women are allowed to say about #MeToo is "Me, too!" The pull string wriggles.

Inevitably, the doll wars met up with the sex wars. *The only thing wrong that I saw when I held Barbie is when I lift her skirt there is nothing underneath.* In December, Kozinski resigned from the bench after the *Washington Post* reported on allegations of sexual harassment made by at least fifteen women. In a statement, Kozinski referred to his "broad sense of humor" and said, "It grieves me to learn that I caused any of my clerks to feel uncomfortable." Two of his former clerks assert that he asked them to look at pornography with him in his chambers. "What do single girls in San Francisco do for sex?" he allegedly asked another clerk, which is the sort of thing Rock Hudson's *Pillow Talk* character would say. Dahlia Lithwick, *Slate*'s legal correspondent, met Kozinski in 1996, when she was clerking for another judge. "I cannot recall what we talked about," Lithwick later wrote. "I remember only feeling quite small and very dirty." Kozinski sounds like the sort of person who may have snapped a lot of people's feet off at the ankles. No results of any formal investigation have been announced.

"Would you please let me know if I owe you?" Ruth Handler wrote, once upon a time, to the store in Germany where she'd placed an order for a shipment of Lilli dolls, their breasts pert, lips plump. The consequences of that purchase remain incalculable. Mattel owns Barbie. MGA owns Bratz. And corporations still own the imaginations of little girls.

—2018

THE MAN IN THE BOX

BEHIND THE DOOR LABELED STUDIO FOUR, WHERE *Doctor Who* is filmed, it smells of glue and paint. Industrial-gauge steel chains hang from the ceiling, which is painted black and is so impossibly high that it feels more like a night sky than like the underside of a roof, the chains like falling stars. The only light is artificial, slanted, and green. The concrete floor is speckled and spattered. Surrounding the set, cameras, lights, and microphones stand on tripod legs of smeared chrome like an army of giant arthropod invaders, patiently waiting. In the stillness, a stagehand wearing a black hooded sweatshirt and black cargo pants rummages through a Tupperware storage box, making an awful clatter. He pulls out something metal and rusted, cradling in his tattooed hands the part that would roll away if you were to guillotine a robot. "This, this," he mutters in quiet triumph, "is the head we need."

Doctor Who is the most original science fiction television series ever made. It is also one of the longest-running television shows of all time. (Virtually every other marathoner is a soap opera.) It was first broadcast in 1963, three years before *Star Trek*, and, with apologies to Gene Roddenberry, is smarter and, better yet, sillier. The USS *Enterprise*, for all its talking computers and swooshing doors, is a crabbed and pious Puritan village; Doctor Who tumbles through time and space in the *Tardis*, a ship that from the outside looks like an early twentieth-century British police box, painted blue and bearing a sign on its door that reads POLICE TELEPHONE. FREE FOR USE OF PUBLIC. ADVICE AND ASSISTANCE OBTAINABLE IMMEDIATELY. Inside (it's bigger on the inside), the *Tardis* has something of the character of the reading room of the British Library, if the British Library had a swimming pool and were a pub designed by someone who adored Frank Gehry, Lewis Carroll, and typewriters with missing keys.

On November 23, 2013, *Doctor Who* celebrated its fiftieth anniversary with a seventy-five-minute, 3D special called *The Day of the Doctor*, which BBC Worldwide billed as a "global simulcast," meaning that it will be seen at the same time in almost eighty countries—a new frontier in the history of television. For many people around the world, *Doctor Who* was the face of the BBC. At the height of its first run, which ended in 1989, *Doctor Who* was seen by 110 million viewers in fifty-four nations, including the United States, where, beginning in the 1970s, it was broadcast by PBS and watched by the kind of quisling American kid who hadn't the heart for *Happy Days*.

"*Doctor Who* is the story of a lovely world in which a kind man saves everyone from harm," Steven Moffat says. Moffat, a fifty-one-year-old Scot, started watching *Doctor Who* when he was a little boy and is now its executive producer and head writer. He says that it has two things: "scary monsters and a funny doctor." Every week, it's the same: the *Tardis* lands; the funny doctor pops out; he meets scary monsters; and then he defeats them, because he is very, very clever.

From the start, *Doctor Who* was meant to be a "loyalty program," a show that people reliably tune in to every week. Fifty years later, TV people scheduled around what was known as "event television," and it wasn't necessarily a weekly affair; instead, it was often a one-off, like the instant-to-internet Netflix release of all thirteen episodes of the first season of the American adaptation of the BBC's *House of Cards*. *Doctor Who* began as family television: a show that kids and their parents and grandparents can all watch, maybe even together, on the sofa. But the industry term "3G TV" didn't mean television enjoyed by three generations of your family; it meant television you could watch on a mobile telephone with third-generation wireless data service. *Doctor Who* became BBC Worldwide's top-selling iTunes download. In the United States, *Doctor Who* aired on BBC America, but here and around the world viewers watched the series on platforms that defy programming schedules and that didn't require families or sofas, or even TVs.

The fiftieth anniversary of *Doctor Who* marked an end to an era in the history of television: the end of the age of the box. In 1999, when *Doctor Who* was off the air (if thriving in fan fiction), Moffat wrote a spoof called *Doctor Who—The Curse of Fatal Death*, starring everyone from Rowan Atkinson to Hugh Grant, in which one character tells the

Doctor, "You're like Father Christmas, the Wizard of Oz, and Scooby Doo!" But Doctor Who is also Great Britain. The world's longest-running science fiction television series is, among other things, a fable about British history: the Doctor halts every invasion and averts every atrocity, except when he can't. Doesn't that story ever get old?

"AN UNEARTHLY CHILD," the first episode of *Doctor Who*, was broadcast—live, in black-and-white—from a BBC studio in London on November 23, 1963, one day after John F. Kennedy was shot in Dallas. The BBC had never before done anything like it.

Doctor Who was the brainchild of Sydney Newman, a Canadian who became head of the BBC's drama department in 1962. Newman, who'd created *The Avengers,* for ITV, in 1961, was brought in to produce television that could meet the BBC's remit as a government-owned broadcasting service as well as its need to win viewers from ITV, a commercial rival that had begun broadcasting in 1955. By 1960, the BBC had not a single program among the top ten ratings earners. Newman had an idea for something that could be both educational and entertaining: science fiction. His department commissioned a report on the state of the genre. It proved discouraging. "Several facts stand out a mile," the report began. "The first is that SF is overwhelmingly American in bulk." Also, "SF is not itself a wildly popular branch of fiction—nothing like, for example, detective and thriller fiction." In particular, "It doesn't appeal much to women." Then, too, "SF is largely a short story medium," in which, as Kingsley Amis had pointed out, the heroes are ideas, not people, and the ideas are often "so bizarre as to sustain conviction only with difficulty over any extended treatment." In other words: adapting for television an existing work of science fiction was impossible and hiring any science fiction writer inadvisable.

Newman decided to flout the genre's conventions. In a flurry of memos (now stored in the BBC's archives in Reading), members of his staff explored the possibilities. "The essence of S.F. is that the wonder or fairytale element shall be given a scientific or technical explanation," one reported. "To do this there must be at least one character capable of giving the explanation." It might not be a bad idea if this character were to have something "of the feeling of Sherlock Holmes."

But, if so, he ought to have a female Watson, because "S.F. is deliberately unsexual; women are not really necessary to it"—and so it would be wise to "add feminine interest."

A time machine was first suggested at a meeting held on March 26, 1963. From an educational point of view, this device had a significant advantage: a hero who travels through time and space can offer lessons in both history and science. *Doctor Who* is distinctly British, and indebted to H. G. Wells. It was also influenced by the 1951 Hollywood film *The Day the Earth Stood Still*, in which an alien who travels with a shiny metal robot lands a flying saucer on the Washington Mall, in the hope of ending war on Earth. But the series, as it developed, was meant to appeal to women as much as to men, to adults as much as to children, and to revolve around a hero who is a fully realized dramatic character, not a disembodied idea. A flying saucer was proposed and rejected. "Bug-Eyed Monsters" and "Tin Robots" were discouraged (a suggestion not always honored). And a narrative structure was adopted that allows not only for extended but for infinite treatment.

Newman hired Verity Lambert as a producer. He'd worked with her on ITV's acclaimed *Armchair Theatre* (a forerunner of PBS's *Masterpiece*). Lambert was the only female producer of television drama at the BBC, and, at twenty-seven, also the youngest. She cast a fifty-five-year-old character actor named William Hartnell as the Doctor. (He never gives his name. *Doctor Who* was meant to sound groovy: the first James Bond film, *Dr. No*, had just been released.) To play the Doctor, Hartnell wore long white hair, a ribbon tie, a striped waistcoat with a watch fob, a dark cloak, a streaming white scarf, and, on top of his head, a black hat that, according to a BBC America blog post titled "How to Dress Like the First Doctor," "looks a little like a tea cosy."

Hartnell's doctor, mincing and fusty, was more Micawber than Holmes, more Dickens than Conan Doyle. The Doctor was supposed to be hundreds of years old, and it was important that Hartnell look and act antique, so that the Doctor's relationship with his traveling companion, a spunky, wide-eyed teenage girl, would be unimpeachable. (Another long-standing *Doctor Who* dictum: no hanky-panky in the *Tardis*.) To this end, it was also decided that the girl ought to be the Doctor's granddaughter.

Most of what works best in *Doctor Who* comes out of ancient forms of serial historical writing, from the *Odyssey* to the Old Testament. The Doctor and his granddaughter are part of a diaspora. "We are not of this race," he explains. "We are not of this Earth. We are wanderers in the fourth dimensions of space and time, cut off from our own planet and our own people."

The first episode of *Doctor Who* opens in present-day London. "An Unearthly Child" begins with a bobby walking down a foggy street. He enters an abandoned warehouse; he finds a police box. Title credits then dissolve to a school where Barbara, a history teacher, and Ian, a science teacher, are puzzled by one of their students, fifteen-year-old Susan: she knows a great deal more about history and science than they do. Following her home after school, Barbara and Ian discover that Susan lives with her grandfather inside the police box.

Why a police box? It was bizarre. It needed explaining. "Therefore here is some phoney science," one of Lambert's staff wrote, offering the sort of gobbledygook you'd come across in an Arthur C. Clarke story: "The outside appearance of the machine is a police box because when the machine is made and before it goes critical it is given an anchor in a definite age and space, without which there can be neither past nor future, and the time/space traveler would go mad—or meet God." Lambert let that pass. Instead, she has the Doctor and Susan explain that the *Tardis* is supposed to change its shape to blend in with the local surroundings but that its chameleon circuit is broken, so it's stuck being a police box. The real problem, it was widely believed, was that Lambert's production budget could not possibly accommodate building a new ship for every adventure.

That's how the *Tardis* got stuck as a police box, but it doesn't explain why it started out that way. That explanation may lie in the history of policing. Beat policing is a British invention. British police are called bobbies because the London Metropolitan Police, a model for police forces all over the world, was created by Home Secretary Sir Robert (Bobby) Peel, in 1829. Doctor Who polices worlds. The idea of a world's policeman dates to the First World War and began to come into common usage near the end of the Second. In 1943, during a birthday dinner for Winston Churchill, FDR called upon the allied powers—the United States, Great Britain, the Soviet Union, and China—to serve as the world's "four policemen." In 1945, the four policemen became the United Nations Security Council.

Doctor Who is, unavoidably, a product of mid-twentieth-century debates about Britain's role in the world as its empire unraveled. It is also one of the stranger means by which British culture has reckoned with the horrors of the Second World War, the apocalyptic doomsaying of the Cold War, and the lasting madness of twenty-first-century terrorism. Superman, who first appeared in 1938, thwarted gangsters and thugs and criminal masterminds. But Doctor Who, created in the postwar, postcolonial, atomic age, inherited the agony of helplessness: he believes he can use his power to travel through time and space to undo unspeakable slaughter, only to find that, very often, he cannot. "Imagine you were in Pompeii and you tried to save them but in doing so you make it happen," he says, trying to explain to a woman who is about to die in a nuclear explosion that he is powerless to prevent it. "Everything I do just makes it happen." (He tries anyway. Moments after he saves her life, she kills herself.)

Doctor Who is a chronicle of the impossibility of rescue. Yet it contains within it both a liberal fantasy about the heroism of the West in opposing atrocity and a conservative politics of self-congratulation, which, in the end, amount to the same thing. "You act like such a radical," an alien said to the Doctor, not long ago, "and yet all you want to do is preserve the old order."

Doctor Who is also a TV show about TV: a fantasy about the bounds of fantasy. In "An Unearthly Child," after Susan's teachers force their way inside the police box, she explains that the *Tardis*—the name is her acronym for Time and Relative Dimension in Space—exists in a different dimension from the outside. When Barbara and Ian still can't understand how a box so small can contain so much, the Doctor instructs them by way of an analogy. "You say you can't fit an enormous building into one of your smaller sitting rooms," he points out, "but you've discovered television, haven't you?"

By 2013, *Doctor Who* was no longer produced in London; it was produced at BBC Wales, in Cardiff. Roath Lock, a 170,000-square-foot facility housing nine state-of-the-art studios, is one of the BBC's largest television production centers. It opened in 2012. So did the Doctor Who Experience, a tourist stop next door: an all-in-one interactive entertainment center, museum, and gift shop in a building that, from the outside, looks like a giant blue tube of toothpaste. It is not bigger on the inside.

Roath Lock is *Doctor Who* HQ. Its neo-faux-retro-Edwardian facade is a tribute to *Doctor Who*'s hammy, psychedelic kookiness. Its corridors are sized to accommodate, side by side, two Daleks, the half-robot, half-mutant monsters from the planet Skaro who have been stalking the Doctor since Lyndon B. Johnson strode the halls of the White House. And some of the building's porthole windows are frosted so that the fans can't see into the ground-floor cafeteria, where, I hereby report, actors dressed as the metallic cyborgs known as Cybermen can indeed be found eating Cornish pasties.

Backstage in the gloaming of Studio Four, four Cybermen have collapsed onto folding metal chairs, resting in between takes. They stretch their legs wide. They are very hot. An intern comes by with a fan, but the rotator is broken so he waves it around by hand. He announces, "I am the Oscillator-in-Chief."

I share a toolbox, by way of a bench, with Ailsa Berk, the show's choreographer. Berk has pale, spiky hair and rimless glasses and is so elegant and lithe that she looks as if she had pipe cleaners where her bones are supposed to be. She was an exoreptilian bounty hunter in *Star Wars: The Return of the Jedi*. In *Greystoke: The Legend of Tarzan*, she played a female ape. For the BBC's *Chronicles of Narnia*, she worked the animatronic Aslan. She arranges the choreography for most of the monsters in *Doctor Who*. I ask which is her favorite. She thinks it over carefully.

"The Ood are very beautiful," she says. (The Ood are telepaths from the thirty-ninth century who have tentacles growing out of their noses and hold one of their two brains in their hands.) "And the scarecrows are very scary. Because it's something so familiar." (The scarecrows are scarecrows.) She leans closer. She whispers, "I don't do Daleks."

UPSTAIRS AND ALONG THE HALL from Studio Four, I sit down with Steven Moffat in the Dalek Room, where the walls are papered with blueprints of the original Daleks. Moffat is wearing a black suit and a blue striped shirt. He has to do a lot of swanning about on behalf of *Doctor Who*. Comic-Con. The TV Choice Awards. Talk shows. This is how event TV works: buzz, buzz, tweet, tweet. "Every day here is a day away from writing," he complains to me.

Moffat is thickset and funny and full of *Doctor Who* bluster. "In the history of all science fiction," he says, "the Dalek is the best alien that's ever been done. Everything else is just a guy in a suit."

The Daleks were invented by Terry Nation, who was born in Cardiff in 1930. His mother was an air-raid warden. In 1941, he survived the Cardiff Blitz. In 1955, he moved to London and started writing for the radio comedy program *The Goon Show*. He took a job writing for *Doctor Who* in 1963. He once said that he got the name "Dalek" from an encyclopedia volume that ran from "dal" to "lek." He made that up. ("It's absolute rubbish," he confessed.) Really, he was just trying to think up a word that sounded super-creepy. He'd been through a blitz; he'd been close to people in the Campaign for Nuclear Disarmament. He invented a race of creatures mutated by an apocalyptic nuclear war who, in order to survive, live inside robotic shells and are so convinced of their own purity that their object is to exterminate every other race.

"I've had this brilliant idea for some baddies," he said to his wife. "I'm going to call them Daleks."

She said, "Drink your tea while it's hot."

The original Daleks were designed by Raymond P. Cusick, who got the job when Ridley Scott, then a set designer at the BBC, left the corporation. Lambert had four monsters built and then tried them out in a car park, actors crouched inside, scooching along on hidden casters. The Daleks made their first appearance in *Doctor Who* in a seven-part series that began on December 21, 1963. It attracted an average of nearly nine million viewers, catapulting *Doctor Who* into the top twenty rated programs. The first Daleks were about five feet high. They have no legs; instead, they're built of what look like shiny, polka-dotted skirts about the size and shape of the base of an industrial-grade floor-waxing machine. One arm looks like a plunger and the other like a whisk. If they weren't psychotic mutant alien murderers, a Dalek would be useful to have around the house, unclogging drains, scrambling eggs, and polishing the floors.

As the show was originally conceived, the Doctor could travel in three directions: to the past, to the future, and sideways (for instance, a parallel universe). The future was expensive. So was sideways. The past was cheap, especially when stock footage was available. The episode called "The Time Meddler" uses footage shot during a 1949 reenactment to show Vikings landing off the northeast coast of England in 1066. Also, at least originally, the history was meant to be real history and, because the science was nonsense, the educational value of *Doctor Who* derived almost entirely from its exploration of the past. The Time Meddler, who is disguised as a monk, is from Doctor Who's home planet (his *Tardis*, which has a functioning chameleon circuit, is disguised as a Saxon sarcophagus). Like the Doctor, the monk can't stand to see suffering. He would like to thwart the Norman Conquest.

"I want to improve things," he says.

"Improve what?" the Doctor asks.

"King Harold, I know he'd be a good king. There wouldn't be all those wars in Europe, those claims over France went on for years and years."

There's a fair bit of history here. But an audience survey reported that viewers found the historical episodes boring. One housewife said, "The sooner he gets back to the future the better."

The first installment of a story line called "Dalek Invasion of Earth" aired on November 21, 1964. It bound together a cherished national narrative about the Second World War—Britain is the last defense against totalitarianism—with panic-induced Cold War preparedness. In 1964, the Home Service began broadcasting what was known as the Civil Defence Information Bulletin: seven short films about what to do in case of a nuclear attack. In "Dalek Invasion of Earth," the year is 2164; the Daleks roll all over a postapocalyptic London, raising their plunger-arms in Third Reich salutes and screeching about the Final Solution. More than twelve million people tuned in.

"Please, please will you tell us what happened in last Saturday's episode of Dr. Who," one letter in the BBC archives reads. "We were away from here & missed it. The Thorne Family." At Roath Lock, I had to sign a nondisclosure agreement to get past the Dalek who guards the door. Lambert had a different approach to spoilers. When a little boy from Canterbury wrote that he was going to miss the end of "Dalek Invasion" because his family was going on holiday to America, Lambert wrote back, "I am sorry you are going to miss the end of '*DOCTOR WHO.*' I cannot give you any detailed information on how it ends, but if you promise not to tell anybody . . ." And then she told him.

Soon there were Dalek costumes, stuffed Daleks, and blow-up Dalek beach toys. The Daleks went on tour. They visited Cardiff. "Thousands of children lined the route—12 deep at times," BBC Wales reported to Lambert. "The Beatles had nothing like this." Trading on Dalekmania, the BBC was able to sell *Doctor Who* to affiliates all over the world. By 1965, the show could be seen in places as far-flung as Australia, Gibraltar, Singapore, Barbados, Sierra Leone, New Zealand, and Nigeria.

There have been complaints over the years that *Doctor Who* is too violent, and the Daleks, in particular, are too scary. Moffat finds this exasperating. "There's always this nonsense in which people say, 'Watch out because kids may not know it's not real!'" he says. "As if kids don't know what playing is." In 1964, a pint-size Dalek was the must-have Christmas gift. Children wrote to Lambert begging for Daleks to visit their birthday parties. Sometimes she sent them. One woman wrote, about her four-year-old son, "He was heartbroken last Saturday when they were all killed off." At the height of the Cold War, three years after Eichmann was tried in Jerusalem, while Britain prepared for an atomic day of doom, radiation-damaged Nazi robots became inflatable bath toys.

ONE REASON THAT *DOCTOR WHO* SPANNED a half century is a casting trick written into the plot. When William Hartnell could no longer play the role, it was decided that the Doctor would be able to regenerate when he is on the verge of death, returning to life in another body. Between 1963 and 1989, seven actors played the Doctor. The show earned a cult following. A *Doctor Who* Appreciation Society was founded in 1975; a magazine called *The Doctor Who Weekly* began appearing four years later. In the 1980s, *Doctor Who* got campy; then it grew threadbare. By the time it went off the air, the production budget for an episode of *Doctor Who* was about a seventh of the budget for an episode of *Star Trek: The Next Generation*. It showed.

But the fate of *Doctor Who* in the 1980s and '90s is characterized less by decline and disappearance than by preservation. By the time it began to look as though the series might be canceled, video recorders had become available for home use. Nostalgic fans began trying to collect old episodes. In the 1960s and '70s, the BBC had customarily wiped tapes after broadcast. Collectors discovered that the BBC had sometimes made copies of the tapes first; these had been sent to the former British colonies, where they had not always been destroyed. "The Time Meddler" was found at a television station in Nigeria. At the urging of fans, the BBC began releasing old episodes, first on videocassette, next on DVD, and, finally, online. For the BBC, the archive has been a gold mine. As part of the fiftieth-anniversary media blitz, the BBC announced that nine missing episodes from the late 1960s had been discovered. (Ninety-seven episodes remain at large.)

Doctor Who was canceled in 1989. The series that began in 2005 is usually referred to as the *Doctor Who* "reboot." A trick, with a series that has an archive of more than six hundred episodes, is that the next episode needs to be fun to watch even if you've never seen the show before. Moffat calls himself a "demented, hard-core fan," but he figures that the only possible thing he can do, as a writer, is to ignore people like him. "If we really hate it, we'll only watch it thirty-five times," he says. The audience that Moffat's really after has barely heard of *Doctor Who*. He has told reporters, "The guy who wrote *The Wire* said, 'Fuck the casual viewer.' And I understand that. The casual viewer cannot catch up with a show like that, or *Breaking Bad*. 'He's a chemistry teacher? Huh?' But on a show like this, we want the casual viewer."

Moffat started writing for *Doctor Who* in 2005, when the series was revived by Russell T. Davies, who read *The Doctor Who Weekly* as a kid. Davies cast, as the ninth doctor, Christopher Eccleston, who had played the Messiah in a TV miniseries that Davies wrote and produced called *The Second Coming*. (The eighth doctor appeared in a TV movie in 1996.) Before *Doctor Who*, Davies was best known for creating the series *Queer As Folk*. (Conservatives worried that he would bring a "gay agenda" to the show.) The biggest change that Davies made concerns the Doctor's backstory. He decided that the Doctor's home planet had been destroyed by Daleks in the Great Time War, leaving the Doctor the last of his race.

The rebooted *Doctor Who* has a different vantage on British history from the original. For a long time, Britain, like the rest of the world, paid not a great deal of attention to the slaughter of Jews during the Second World War. It isn't that no one reported on it; it's that there was a public relations preference and a popular prejudice for depicting the victims as nonspecific. In 1945, when the British Ministry of Information hired Alfred Hitchcock to make a film about the extermination camps, he was instructed, in a memo, "It is especially desirable to document the extent to which non-Jewish German nationals were the victims of the German concentration camp system." (The film was never shown.) In the 1960s, after Eichmann's trial was widely reported, by, among others, Hannah Arendt in *The New Yorker*, "the Holocaust," as it was now called, became something of an American obsession. Not so in Britain, where, in 1961, even a small exhibit about the Holocaust in Coventry Cathedral proved controversial. In the 1970s and '80s, while the Holocaust became "the benchmark of oppression and atrocity" in the American imagination, as the historian Peter Novick has argued, it was largely ignored in the United Kingdom. The 1990s saw a reversal; schools in Britain became more dedicated to teaching the Holocaust than schools in the United States. But this schoolroom treatment often works the same way as that memo sent to Hitchcock: the story of the Holocaust becomes not the story of a particular people but everyone's story, an all-purpose atrocity.

The revival of *Doctor Who* makes that move as well. When Doctor Who, a character who operates as an allegory for Britain, becomes a remnant of a nearly exterminated race, a timeless atrocity is folded into the national narrative. Davies's Doctor is consumed by grief, regret, and compassion. In one episode, he meets a space pirate who has murdered the inhabitants of an ark, the last survivors of a doomed planet.

"Piracy and genocide," the Doctor says, grimly.

"Very emotive words, Doctor," the pirate says.

"I'm a very emotive man."

H. G. Wells used science fiction to critique industrial-era class relations. A century later, a campaign of racial extermination became the go-to sci-fi plotline. The *Tardis* lands, the funny doctor pops out, and bears witness to genocide.

THE FIRST DOCTOR WHO STORY that Steven Moffat wrote for Davies is "The Empty Child." The *Tardis* lands in London in 1941. The Doctor looks around. He makes a speech. "Right now, not very far from here, the German war machine is rolling up the map of Europe. Country after country, falling like dominoes. Nothing can stop it— nothing. Until one tiny, damp little island says, 'No, no. Not here.'" There's other trouble brewing. An alien spaceship, which turns out to be a medical-supply ship, has crashed nearby; a robotic cloud of nano-genes, attempting to save the life of a mortally injured little boy, have altered his DNA so that his face has become melded to the gas mask he was wearing when he was hit by a falling bomb. The boy-monster wanders the city asking everyone he meets, "Are you my mummy?" If you let him touch you, you become a monster, too. The Doctor fixes everything but he also fixes nothing: no one who has endured a blitz can entirely take that gas mask off, ever again. "The Empty Child" is a haunting story about damage.

An acute tenderness toward children pervades Moffat's stories. (Moffat has two children at home.) Davies has said that the difference between his *Doctor Who* and Moffat's is that Moffat's stories are all about being a parent. I asked Moffat about that. "I'm good at writing about what I'm doing," he says. "I used to write about dating. Then about being married. I'm good at writing about what I'm doing. I don't say, 'I shall now do a giant space metaphor about what it's like to be a dad.'"

In "Blink," another story written by Moffat, the monsters are weeping angels, statues who come to life the second you close your eyes, send you back in time, and then, as the Doctor explains, "consume the energy of all the days you might have had." When the weeping angels steal the *Tardis* and send the Doctor back to 1969, he effects his rescue by making a video recording and sending it to the future. "Blink," which Moffat wrote not long after the 7/7 London bombings, might seem to lend itself to a reading about terrorism, sleeper cells, and surveillance. Moffat says that *Doctor Who* never offers any commentary: *Doctor Who* is a fairy tale, and nothing more. "Our science is mad science," he insists. "Our history is mad history." If you keep your eyes shut.

STEVEN MOFFAT HAS GOT THE ICONS OF British genre fiction sewed up in his two pockets. The train ride from London to

Cardiff lasts about two and a half hours; it was during that ride, while working for Davies, that Moffat and another *Doctor Who* writer, Mark Gatiss, got the idea of reviving Sherlock Holmes. *Sherlock*, starring Benedict Cumberbatch and Martin Freeman, debuted in 2010. It is jointly produced by WGBH, in Boston, for Masterpiece, and, for the BBC, by Hartswood Films. Hartswood Films is run by Moffat's wife, Sue Vertue, and her mother, Beryl Vertue, who in the 1960s was Terry Nation's literary agent.

"*Sherlock* is *Doctor Who* an hour later," Moffat likes to say. I asked him how he keeps the two characters separate in his head. They've even got a similar archnemesis. Moffat says that he has to pretend to be two writers, except that, really, he doesn't have to because—and here he cites Sydney Newman, because Steven Moffat is a crackerjack *Doctor Who* historian—Sherlock Holmes and Doctor Who are the same character: the Edwardian amateur. Their stories follow the same formula. Moffat loves the formula, and each of its rules. "Could there be a Bond film in which Bond does not go to M's office?" he asks. Moffat likes a hero who comes with plot constraints. "The best story ever told is the story of Clark Kent," he says. "He can do everything except this one thing: be with the woman he loves. Why don't they ever make the movie *Kent*?"

There is no movie called *Kent* because American filmmakers prefer superheroes who remain changelessly invincible, the diminished status of the world's last superpower notwithstanding. Doctor Who, on the other hand, is a creature of history. Iraq and Afghanistan wound him. At Syria, he pauses. Should he really be meddling with time? He has begun to think that maybe he only ever makes everything worse. Financial meltdown, suicide attacks, chemical weapons, cyberwar. The more vulnerable Britain, the more vulnerable the Doctor.

Moffat also shot stories in the United States. In "The Angels Take Manhattan," the Statue of Liberty is revealed to be a very scary monster from another planet. But there's no risk of *Doctor Who* becoming American. "This show is British," Moffat says. "We make a British show because we're British."

In 2012, Moffat had to cast a new Doctor. Christopher Eccleston left *Doctor Who* after one season. The tenth Doctor was David Tennant, who had played the lead in Davies's television series *Casanova*. When

Tennant left, Moffat, having taken over from Davies, cast Matt Smith as the eleventh Doctor; Smith was twenty-seven when he started, making him the youngest Doctor ever. Smith has said that he would not return. The BBC announced that the twelfth Doctor would be Peter Capaldi, best known for playing Malcolm Tucker in the British political satire *The Thick of It*, a character he introduced to American audiences in the 2009 film *In the Loop*.

Capaldi, at fifty-five, is the oldest Doctor since William Hartnell. He is the only actor Moffat auditioned. Moffat says, "He came round to my house. I made him coffee. And then he capered about, being the Doctor for a bit. It's not that you need to see if he can act. You want to see, Can *Doctor Who* dialogue come out of that mouth?" Sure it can. Capaldi is tremendously talented. But Moffat took some guff for not casting a woman, and he's testy about it. He's also sick of hearing that nearly all of the Doctor's companions are a version of spunky fifteen-year-old Susan, from 1963, with her miniskirts and bobby socks and doe eyes, but they are. The latest companion, Clara Oswald (played by Jenna Coleman), could have turned out differently; in some past, future, or other world—it's as yet unclear which—she'd been transformed into a Dalek. She likes to say that everyone's an android now, anyway. In an episode aired and set in 2013, the Doctor discovers that aliens are using wireless internet service to upload the contents of computer users' heads.

"Human souls trapped like flies in the World Wide Web!" he cries.

Clara shrugs. "Isn't that basically Twitter?"

"The story of technology going bad really works as a *Doctor Who* story," Moffat says. "I can get a scary robot out of that."

Doctor Who has been around for almost as long as there's been TV. "Oh, this is a brilliant year!" the Doctor announces as he bounds out of his box and gets his bearings in an episode written by Mark Gatiss. The *Tardis* has landed in London in 1953. The Doctor takes stock of the moment in time: "A nation throwing off the shackles of war and looking forward toward a happier, brighter future!" Nearby, inside a row house, a grandmother warns a boy about a newfangled machine known as a television: "I hear they rot your brains, rot them into soup, and your brain comes pouring out of your ears. That's what television does." Meanwhile, Mr. Magpie, a TV salesman, is doing a brisk business because everyone is buying TVs to watch the coronation of the queen. Mr. Magpie says cheerfully, "We may be losing the Empire but we can still be proud!"

It turns out that Mr. Magpie is being controlled by a scary alien. And the TVs he's installing really *are* sucking people's brains out.

The *Tardis* is always broken. There's never a world policeman around when you need one. The Doctor can go anywhere in space and time. There is only one thing he cannot do. He cannot stop the killing.

Weeping angels have invaded Manhattan. People wear earbuds. Cybermen are coming, uploading, downloading. And we carry our televisions in our hands, like an Ood, cradling its second brain.

—2013

NO, WE CANNOT

HERE ARE THE PLOTS OF SOME DYSTOPIAN NOVELS, set in the near future. The world got too hot, so a wealthy celebrity persuaded a small number of very rich people to move to a makeshift satellite that, from orbit, leaches the last nourishment the earth has to give, leaving everyone else to starve. The people on the satellite have lost their genitals, through some kind of instant mutation or super-quick evolution, but there is a lot of sex anyway, since it's become fashionable to have surgical procedures to give yourself a variety of appendages and openings, along with decorative skin grafts and tattoos, there being so little else to do. There are no children, but the celebrity who rules the satellite has been trying to create them by torturing women from the earth's surface. ("We are what happens when the seemingly unthinkable celebrity rises to power," the novel's narrator says.) Or: North Korea deployed a brain-damaging chemical weapon that made everyone in the United States, or at least everyone in LA, an idiot, except for a few people who were on a boat the day the scourge came, but the idiots, who are otherwise remarkably sweet, round up and kill those people, out of fear. Led by a man known only as the Chief, the idiots build a wall around downtown to keep out the Drifters and the stupidest people, the Shamblers, who don't know how to tie shoes or button buttons; they wander around, naked and barefoot. Thanks, in part, to the difficulty of clothing, there is a lot of sex, random and unsatisfying, but there are very few children, because no one knows how to take care of them. (The jacket copy bills this novel as "the first book of the Trump era.")

Or: Machines replaced humans, doing all the work and providing all the food, and, even though if you leave the city it is hotter everywhere else, some huffy young people do, because they are so bored, not to mention that they are mad at their parents, who do annoying things like run giant corporations. The runaways are called walkaways. (I gather they're not in a terribly big hurry.) They talk about revolution, take a lot of baths, upload their brains onto computers, and have a lot of sex, but, to be honest, they are very boring. Or: Even after the coasts were lost to the floods when the ice caps melted, the American South, defying a new federal law, refused to give up fossil fuels, and seceded, which led to a civil war, which had been going on for decades, and was about to be over, on Reunification Day, except that a woman from Louisiana who lost her whole family in the war went to the celebration and released a poison that killed a hundred million people, which doesn't seem like the tragedy it might have been, because in this future world, as in all the others, there's not much to live for, what with the petty tyrants, the rotten weather, and the crappy sex. It will not give too much away if I say that none of these novels have a happy ending (though one has a twist). Then again, none of them have a happy beginning, either.

Dystopias follow utopias the way thunder follows lightning. Lately, the thunder is roaring. But people are so grumpy, what with the petty tyrants and such, that it's easy to forget how recently lightning struck. "Whether we measure our progress in terms of wiredness, open-mindedness, or optimism, the country is moving in the right direction, and faster, perhaps, than even we would have believed," a reporter for *Wired* wrote in May 2000. "We are, as a nation, better educated, more tolerant, and more connected because of—not in spite of—the convergence of the internet and public life. Partisanship, religion, geography, race, gender, and other traditional political divisions are giving way to a new standard—wiredness—as an organizing principle." Nor was the utopianism merely technological, or callow. In January 2008, Barack Obama gave a speech in New Hampshire, about the American creed:

> It was a creed written into the founding documents that declared the destiny of a nation: Yes, we can. It was whispered by slaves and abolitionists as they blazed a trail towards freedom through the darkest of nights: Yes, we can. It was sung by immigrants as they struck out from distant shores and pioneers who pushed westward against an unforgiving wilderness: Yes, we can. . . . Yes, we can heal this nation. Yes, we can repair this world.
>
> Yes, we can.

That was the lightning, the flash of hope, the promise of perfectibility. The argument of dystopianism is that perfection comes at the cost of freedom. Every new lament about the end of the republic, every column about the collapse of civilization, every new novel of doom: these are its answering thunder. Rumble, thud, rumble, *ka-boom*, *KA-BOOM*!

A UTOPIA IS A PARADISE, a dystopia a paradise lost. Before utopias and dystopias became imagined futures, they were imagined pasts, or imagined places, like the Garden of Eden. "I have found a continent more densely peopled and abounding in animals than our Europe or Asia or Africa, and, in addition, a climate milder and more delightful than in any other region known to us," Amerigo Vespucci wrote, in extravagant letters describing his voyages across the Atlantic, published in 1503 as "Mundus Novus," a new world. In 1516, Thomas More published a fictional account of a sailor on one of Vespucci's ships who had traveled just a bit farther, to the island of Utopia, where he found a perfect republic. (More coined the term: "utopia" means "nowhere.") *Gulliver's Travels* (1726) is a satire of the utopianism of the Enlightenment. On the island of Laputa, Gulliver visits the Academy of Lagado, where the sages, the first progressives, are busy trying to make pincushions out of marble, breeding naked sheep, and improving the language by getting rid of all the words. The word "dystopia," meaning "an unhappy country," was coined in the 1740s, as the historian Gregory Claeys points out in a shrewd study, *Dystopia: A Natural History*. In its modern definition, a dystopia can be apocalyptic, or postapocalyptic, or neither, but it has to be anti–utopian, a utopia turned upside down, a world in which people tried to build a republic of perfection only to find that they had created a republic of misery. *A Trip to the Island of Equality*, a 1792 reply to Thomas Paine's *Rights of Man*, is a dystopia (on the island, the pursuit of equality has reduced everyone to living in caves), but Mary Shelley's 1826 novel, *The Last Man*, is not dystopian; it's merely apocalyptic.

The dystopian novel emerged in response to the first utopian novels, like Edward Bellamy's best-selling 1888 fantasy, *Looking Backward*, about a socialist utopia in the year 2000. *Looking Backward* was so successful that it produced a dozen anti-socialist, anti-utopian replies, including *Looking Further Backward* (in which China invades the United States, which has been weakened by its embrace of socialism) and *Looking Further Forward* (in which socialism is so unquestionable that a history professor who refutes it is demoted to the rank of janitor). In 1887, a year before Bellamy, the American writer Anna Bowman Dodd published *The Republic of the Future*, a socialist dystopia set in New York in 2050, in which women and men are equal, children are reared by the state, machines handle all the work, and most people, having nothing else to do, spend much of their time at the gym, obsessed with fitness. Dodd describes this world as "the very acme of dreariness." What is a dystopia? The gym. (That's still true. In a 2011 episode of *Black Mirror*, life on earth in an energy-scarce future has been reduced to an interminable spin class.)

Utopians believe in progress; dystopians don't. They fight this argument out in competing visions of the future, utopians offering promises, dystopians issuing warnings. In 1895, in *The Time Machine*, H. G. Wells introduced the remarkably handy device of traveling through time by way of a clock. After that, time travel proved convenient, but even Wells didn't always use a machine. In *When the Sleeper Awakes* (1899), his hero simply oversleeps his way to the twenty-first century, where he finds a world in which people are enslaved by propaganda, and "helpless in the hands of the demagogue." That's one problem with dystopian fiction: forewarned is not always forearmed.

Sleeping through the warning signs is another problem. "I was asleep before," the heroine of *The Handmaid's Tale* says in the new Hulu production of Margaret Atwood's 1986 novel. "That's how we let it happen." But what about when everyone's awake, and there are plenty of warnings, but no one does anything about them? *NK3*, by Michael Tolkin, is an intricate and cleverly constructed account of the aftermath of a North Korean chemical attack; the NK3 of the title has entirely destroyed its victims' memories and has vastly diminished their capacity to reason. This puts the novel's characters in the same position as the readers of all dystopian fiction: they're left to try to piece together not a whodunnit but a howdidithappen. Seth Kaplan, who'd been a pediatric oncologist, pages through periodicals left in a seat back on a Singapore Airlines jet, on the ground at LAX. The periodicals, like the plane, hadn't moved since the plague arrived. "It confused Seth that the plague was front-page news in some but not all of the papers," Tolkin writes. "They still printed reviews of movies and books, articles about new cars, ways to make inexpensive costumes for Halloween." Everyone had been awake, but they'd been busy shopping for cars and picking out movies and cutting eyeholes in paper bags.

THE LATEST BLIGHTED CROP OF dystopian novels is pessimistic about technology, about the economy, about politics, and about the planet, making it a more abundant harvest of unhappiness than most other heydays of downheartedness. The internet did not stitch us all together. Economic growth has led to widening economic inequality and a looming environmental crisis. Democracy appears to be yielding to authoritarianism. "Hopes, dashed" is, lately, a long list, and getting longer. The plane is grounded, seat backs in the upright position, and we are dying, slowly, of stupidity.

Pick your present-day dilemma; there's a new dystopian novel to match it. Worried about political polarization? In *American War*, Omar El Akkad traces the United States' descent from gridlock to barbarism as the states of the former Confederacy (or at least the parts that aren't underwater) refuse to abide by the Sustainable Future Act, and secede in 2074. Troubled by the new Jim Crow? Ben H. Winters's *Underground Airlines* is set in an early twenty-first-century United States in which slavery abides, made crueler and more inescapable by the giant, unregulated slave-owning corporations that deploy the surveillance powers of modern technology, so that even escaping to the North (on underground airlines) hardly offers much hope, since free blacks in cities like Chicago live in segregated neighborhoods with no decent housing or schooling or work and it's the very poverty in which they live that defeats arguments for abolition by hardening ideas about race. As the book's narrator, a fugitive slave, explains, "Black gets to mean poor and poor to mean dangerous and all the words get murked together and become one dark idea, a cloud of smoke, the smokestack fumes drifting like filthy air across the rest of the nation."

Radical pessimism is a dismal trend. The despair, this particular publishing season, comes in many forms, including the grotesque. In *The Book of Joan*, Lidia Yuknavitch's narrator, Christine Pizan, is forty-nine, and about to die, because she's living on a satellite orbiting the earth, where everyone is executed at the age of fifty; the wet in their bodies constitutes the colony's water supply. (Dystopia, here, is menopause.) Her body has aged: "If hormones have any meaning left for any of us, it is latent at best." She examines herself in the mirror: "I have a slight rise where each breast began, and a kind of mound where my pubic bone should be, but that's it. Nothing else of woman is left." Yuknavitch's Pizan is a resurrection of the medieval French scholar and historian Christine de Pisan, who in 1405 wrote the allegorical *Book of the City of Ladies*, and, in 1429, *The Song of Joan of Arc*, an account of the life of the martyr. In the year 2049, Yuknavitch's Pizan writes on her body, by a torturous process of self-mutilation, the story of a twenty-first-century Joan, who is trying to save the planet from Jean de Men (another historical allusion), the insane celebrity who has become its ruler. In the end, de Men himself is revealed to be "not a man but what is left of a woman," with "all the traces: sad, stitched-up sacks of flesh where breasts had once been, as if someone tried too hard to erase their existence. And a bulbous sagging gash sutured over and over where . . . life had perhaps happened in the past, or not, and worse, several dangling attempts at half-formed penises, sewn and abandoned, distended and limp."

Equal rights for women, emancipation, Reconstruction, civil rights: so many hopes dashed; so many causes lost. Pisan pictured a city of women; Lincoln believed in union; King had a dream. Yuknavitch and El Akkad and Winters unspool the reels of those dreams, and recut them as nightmares. This move isn't new, or daring; it is, instead, very old. The question is whether it's all used up, as parched as a postapocalyptic desert, as barren as an old woman, as addled as an old man.

A UTOPIA IS A PLANNED SOCIETY; planned societies are often disastrous; that's why utopias contain their own dystopias. Most early twentieth-century dystopian novels took the form of political parables, critiques of planned societies, from both the left and the right. The utopianism of communists, eugenicists, New Dealers, and fascists produced the Russian novelist Yevgeny Zamyatin's *We* in 1924, Aldous Huxley's *Brave New World* in 1935, Ayn Rand's *Anthem* in 1937, and George Orwell's *1984* in 1949. After the war, after the death camps, after the bomb, dystopian fiction thrived, like a weed that favors shade.

"A decreasing percentage of the imaginary worlds are utopias," the literary scholar Chad Walsh observed in 1962. "An increasing percentage are nightmares."

Much postwar pessimism had to do with the superficiality of mass culture in an age of affluence, and with the fear that the banality and conformity of consumer society had reduced people to robots. "I drive my car to supermarket," John Updike wrote in 1954. "The way I take is superhigh, / A superlot is where I park it, / And Super Suds are what I buy." Supersudsy television boosterism is the utopianism attacked by Kurt Vonnegut in *Player Piano* (1952) and by Ray Bradbury in *Fahrenheit 451* (1953). Cold War dystopianism came in as many flavors as soda pop or superheroes and in as many sizes as nuclear warheads. But, in a deeper sense, the midcentury overtaking of utopianism by dystopianism marked the rise of modern conservatism: a rejection of the idea of the liberal state. Rand's *Atlas Shrugged* appeared in 1957, and climbed up the *Times* bestseller list. It has sold more than eight million copies.

The second half of the twentieth century, of course, also produced liberal-minded dystopias, chiefly concerned with issuing warnings about pollution and climate change, nuclear weapons and corporate monopolies, technological totalitarianism and the fragility of rights secured from the state. There were, for instance, feminist dystopias. The utopianism of the Moral Majority, founded in 1979, lies behind *The Handmaid's Tale* (a book that is, among other things, an updating of Harriet Jacobs's 1861 *Incidents in the Life of a Slave Girl*). But rights-based dystopianism also led to the creation of a subgenre of dystopian fiction: bleak futures for bobby-soxers. Dystopianism turns out to have a natural affinity with American adolescence. And this, I think, is where the life of the genre got squeezed out, like a beetle burned up on an asphalt driveway by a boy wielding a magnifying glass on a sunny day. It sizzles, and then it smokes, and then it just lies there, dead as a bug.

Dystopias featuring teenage characters have been a staple of high school life since *The Lord of the Flies* came out, in 1954. But the genre only really took off in the aftermath of Vietnam and Watergate, when distrust of adult institutions and adult authority flourished, and the publishing industry began producing fiction packaged for "young adults," ages twelve to eighteen. Some of these books are pretty good. M. T. Anderson's 2002 YA novel, *Feed*, is a smart and fierce answer to the "Don't Be Evil" utopianism of Google, founded in 1996. All of them are characterized by a withering contempt for adults and by an unshakable suspicion of authority. *The Hunger Games*, whose first installment appeared in 2008, has to do with economic inequality, but, like all YA dystopian fiction, it's also addressed to readers who feel betrayed by a world that looked so much better to them when they were just a bit younger. "I grew up a little, and I gradually began to figure out that pretty much *everyone* had been lying to me about pretty much *everything*," the high school–age narrator writes at the beginning of Ernest Cline's best-selling 2011 YA novel, *Ready Player One*.

Lately, even dystopian fiction marketed to adults has an adolescent sensibility, pouty and hostile. Cory Doctorow's novel *Walkaway* begins late at night at a party in a derelict factory with a main character named Hubert: "At twenty-seven, he had seven years on the next oldest partier." The story goes on in this way, with Doctorow inviting grownup readers to hang out with adolescents, looking for immortality, while supplying neologisms like "spum" instead of "spam" to remind us that we're in a world that's close to our own, but weird. "My father spies on me," the novel's young heroine complains. *Walkaway* comes with an endorsement from Edward Snowden. Doctorow's earlier novel, a YA book called *Little Brother*, told the story of four teenagers and their fight for internet privacy rights. With *Walkaway*, Doctorow pounds the same nails with the same bludgeon. His walkaways are trying to turn a dystopia into a utopia by writing better computer code than their enemies. "A pod of mercs and an infotech goon pwnd everything using some zeroday they'd bought from scumbag default infowar researchers" is the sort of thing they say. "They took over the drone fleet, and while we dewormed it, seized the mechas."

EVERY DYSTOPIA IS A HISTORY of the future. What are the consequences of a literature, even a pulp literature, of political desperation? "It's a sad commentary on our age that we find dystopias a lot easier to believe in than utopias," Atwood wrote in the 1980s. "Utopias we can only imagine; dystopias we've already had." But what was really happening then was that the genre and its readers were sorting themselves out by political preference, following the same path—to the same ideological bunkers—as families, friends, neighborhoods, and the news. In the first year of Obama's presidency, Americans bought half a million copies of *Atlas Shrugged*. In the first month of the administration of Donald ("American carnage") Trump, during which Kellyanne Conway talked about alternative facts, *1984* jumped to the top of the Amazon bestseller list. (Steve Bannon is a particular fan of a 1973 French novel called *The Camp of the Saints*, in which Europe is overrun by dark-skinned immigrants.) The duel of dystopias is nothing so much as yet another place poisoned by polarized politics, a proxy war of imaginary worlds.

Dystopia used to be a fiction of resistance; it's become a fiction of submission, the fiction of an untrusting, lonely, and sullen twenty-first century, the fiction of fake news and Infowars, the fiction of helplessness and hopelessness. It cannot imagine a better future, and it doesn't ask anyone to bother to make one. It nurses grievances and indulges resentments; it doesn't call for courage; it finds that cowardice suffices. Its only admonition is: despair more. It appeals to both the left and the right, because, in the end, it requires so little by way of literary, political, or moral imagination, asking only that you enjoy the company of people whose fear of the future aligns comfortably with your own. Left or right, the radical pessimism of an unremitting dystopianism has itself contributed to the unraveling of the liberal state and the weakening of a commitment to political pluralism. "This isn't a story about war," El Akkad writes in *American War*. "It's about ruin." A story about ruin can be beautiful. Wreckage is romantic. But a politics of ruin is doomed.

—2017

BUZZ

IN 1976, AT THE TAIL END OF THE FORD ADMINISTRA-tion, hippies no longer hip, Sue Vargo and Molly Mead decided that they wanted to drive to the Florida Keys in a Volkswagen bus. They were best friends, in their twenties, living in a women-only commune in Massachusetts: muddy boots, acoustic guitars, mercurial vegetarians. They bought a beat-up VW bus, circa 1967, red and white, with a split windshield, a stick shift that sprouted up from the floor like a sturdy sapling, a big, flat, bus-driver steering wheel half the size of a hula hoop, and windshield wipers that waved back and forth—cheerful and eager, like a puppy—without wiping anything away. The bus had no suspension. "You just bounced along," Vargo said, bobbing her head. *"Boing, boing, boing."*

In 2022, Volkswagen is bringing back the bus—souped-up, tricked-out, and no longer bouncy—as the ID. Buzz. "ID." stands for "intelligent design," and "Buzz" means that it's electric. It might be the most anticipated vehicle in automotive history. Volkswagen has been teasing a return of the classic, iconic, drive-it-to-the-Grateful-Dead bus for more than two decades. (I'm one of the people who've been counting the days.) The company keeps announcing that it's coming, and then it never comes. Finally, it really is coming, and not only is it electric but it can also be a little bit psychedelic, two-toned, in the colors of a box of Popsicles: tangerine, lime, grape, lemon. It's on sale in Europe in 2022 and will be available in the United States in 2024. (One reason for the wait is that Volkswagen is making a bigger one for the U.S. market, with three rows of seats instead of two.) Volkswagen expects the Buzz, which has a range of something like two hundred and sixty miles, to be the flagship of a fast-growing electric fleet. The CEO of Volkswagen of America said that the demand for the Buzz in the U.S. is unlike anything he's seen before. "The Buzz has the ability to rewrite the rules," *Top Gear* reported in 2022, naming it Electric Car of the Year.

Bus nuts are busting out of their pop-tops. "I want one!" is more or less the vibe online. But not all bus nuts are on board. Sue Vargo is dubious. The Buzz, in the way of new EVs, is more *swoosh* than *boing*, less a machine you operate—pulling levers, cranking wheels, pumping brakes—than a computer you ride around in while its screen flashes officious little reminders at you. This is what new cars do, what they are. It's not what old cars did, or what they were. The bus was cheap; the Buzz is pricey. (The base U.S. version is expected to cost around forty-five thousand dollars.) Also, the front end of the bus, famously, had a face, a loopy, goofy, smiling face: the eyes two perfectly round, bug-eyed headlights, the nose a swooping piece of chrome trim, the mouth a gently curving bumper. The Buzz has a face, too, but its eyes, hard and angular, look angry, as if beneath a furrowed brow, and its smile is a smirk. "If this is the future," someone on the VW Bus Junkies Facebook page posted, "I'd rather live in the past."

The future of the automobile is, undeniably, swoosh and buzz and smart—smart this, smart that. But is it appealing? VW's pitch for the Buzz marries nostalgia with moral seriousness about climate change, a seriousness that, for VW, is a particular necessity. Volkswagen dominated the diesel vehicle industry with its "clean diesel" cars and trucks until, in 2015, it admitted to tampering with the software on more than ten million vehicles in order to cheat on emissions tests. The scandal shattered the company and led to the resignation of Martin Winterkorn, then the VW Group's CEO. He still faces criminal charges in Germany; another VW executive was given a prison sentence by an American court. Civil suits are ongoing. Just this May, Volkswagen agreed to pay nearly two hundred and fifty million dollars to settle claims filed in England and Wales.

Sue Vargo and her wife used to own a diesel VW Golf. "After the scandal, we brought it back to the dealer and traded it in for a new, gas Golf, for basically nothing," she told me, but she doesn't trust VW. A lot of people feel that way. The scandal likely sped up Volkswagen's plans to go electric. In 2021, the company launched its Way to Zero initiative, gunning for Tesla and pledging net carbon emissions of zero by 2050 at the latest. The pledge involves not only the cars that it makes but how it makes them: VW is investing in wind farms all over Europe and one of the largest solar plants in Germany. By 2030, half of Volkswagen's U.S. sales are expected to come from EVs. No carmaker is investing so much in the jump to electric. Even Elon Musk has conceded that although Tesla leads the EV-tech race, Volkswagen places a very respectable second.

The Volkswagen ID. Buzz, then, isn't just any electric car. It's a bid for Volkswagen's redemption. Is it also the car that can usher in an EV revolution, a true turn of the wheel in the long history of the automobile?

IN THE SPRING, I went to see the Buzz at the New York International Auto Show, at the Javits Center, a glass-and-steel K'nex box of a building that has exactly as much charm as an airport. Walking there, down West Thirty-Eighth Street, I passed a four-story brick stable, with thirty-six horses housed on the second floor and a carriage parked out front, near a sign that read SHARE THE ROAD: HORSES PAVED THE WAY. Actually, when road paving began, it was for bicycles. The New York auto show didn't start out as an auto show; it started out, in the 1890s, as the New York bicycle show. Bicycles, at the time, were known as "silent horses," just as cars became known as "horseless carriages." Then cars drove bicycles off the road. Many of those cars were electric. In 1899, when the bicycle show became the bicycle and automobile show, nearly every automobile it displayed was electric. The *Times* predicted that every vehicle in the city would soon be "propelled by the wonderful motive power which was discovered as controllable, years and years ago, by the ever illustrious Benjamin Franklin." In 1900, the tens of thousands of New Yorkers who turned up for the bicycle and auto show got a chance to see more than twenty electric cars—manufactured by firms that included the American Electric Vehicle Co., the General Electric Automobile Co., and the Indiana Bicycle Co.—alongside two gasoline-powered runabouts, two steam-powered carriages, one gas-run wagon, and one Auto-Quadricycle. The first New York auto show, held later that year, featured an indoor track, made of wooden planks, that you could race the cars around, and General Electric's coin-operated "electrant," or electric hydrant, a four-foot-tall charging station, where, for a quarter, you could get a twenty-five-mile recharge. The *Times* reported, "It is expected that these automatic devices will be installed in suburban villages and places on the main lines of travel between important points where an electric vehicle might otherwise become stalled for lack of power." (Today, there still aren't anywhere near enough charging stations around.)

By the turn of the century, one of every three motorcars in the U.S. was electric. As an electric-car manufacturer remarked, gas engines "belch forth from their exhaust pipe a continuous stream of partially unconsumed hydrocarbons in the form of a thin smoke with a highly noxious odor." He couldn't fathom anyone tolerating them for long: "Imagine thousands of such vehicles on the streets, each offering up its column of smell." Electric cars didn't pose this problem; they were also quieter, easier to drive, and simpler to repair. The problem was the storage capacity of the battery. A lot of people put their faith in a collaboration between the Edison Storage Battery Company, founded in 1901, and the Ford Motor Company, founded in 1903. "The fact is that Mr. Edison and I have been working for some years on an electric automobile which would be cheap and practicable," Henry Ford told the *Times* in 1914. But by 1917 the collaboration had fallen apart, and by 1920 the gas engine had won. The EV dark age had begun.

That dark age may be ending. At the 2022 New York auto show, half the floor space was devoted to EVs. Downstairs, on an EV test track powered by Con Edison, you could ride around in more than twenty-five different electric cars; upstairs, you could test-drive Ford's new electric pickup truck, the F-150 Lightning. It was as if the marriage between Edison and Ford had, at last, been consummated. Still, there was plenty of shtick. Subaru had the greenest display—fake pine trees, fake rocks, potted evergreens, hanging vines, a real dog run, ferns, fake logs, "bear-resistant" trash containers, and a new SUV called the Outback Wilderness—but only one actual electric car, the Solterra, parked in a fake forest. (The Wilderness runs on gasoline, twenty-two city miles to the gallon.)

Volkswagen displayed its gleaming fleet in a back corner of the main show floor, where the Buzz was parked on a platform behind a plastic half wall and roped off, like a work of art. It was one of the few cars at the show that you couldn't climb into or touch. People were curious about it, took pictures, pointed it out to their kids. "I think it's sharp," they'd say. "Is it a Bulli?" (That's what the VW bus is called in Germany.) Or, "Oh, a Kombi!" (what it's called in much of Latin America). Technically, the Buzz is the start of a whole new line, but sentimentally it's the eighth generation of a very old car.

VOLKSWAGEN'S FIRST CAR, THE TYPE 1, is better known as the VW Beetle. It dates to the company's origins in Nazi Germany. Hitler wanted a "people's car," and in 1934 the Reich commissioned the designer Ferdinand Porsche to develop it. The Type 1 was manufactured at a factory in Wolfsburg whose workers, in the early 1940s, consisted mostly of *Dienstverpflichtete*, forced laborers, including Polish women; Soviet, Italian, and French prisoners of war; and concentration camp prisoners. (In the 1990s, Volkswagen paid reparations.) After the war, the Volkswagen factory in Wolfsburg was one of the few sites of industrial production not razed by bombing, and the Allies set about supporting its operation as a way to bolster West Germany's economic redevelopment. The first postwar Beetles were sold in 1945. Not long afterward, a Dutch importer noticed that workers at Wolfsburg had used spare parts—Type 1 chassis, piles of boards, steering wheels—to put together makeshift *Plattenwagen*, flatbed carts, to carry their tools. He had the idea that if you put a box on top of the chassis, instead of just a platform, you'd have a pretty neat little bus. This became the Type 2, the original VW bus, also known as the T1, the first-generation Transporter. It was first sold in 1950, and six years later VW opened a factory in Hanover that was entirely dedicated to building the new model. In the argot of kids' flicks, the Type 1 is Herbie, from the 1968 Disney movie *The Love Bug*; the Type 2 is Fillmore, from the 2006 Pixar film *Cars*. (George Carlin did Fillmore's voice.)

The T1 and T2 sold like crazy. In Europe, the VW bus could do anything: it was used as a fire truck, an ambulance, a delivery vehicle, a taxi. It didn't have a lot of power, but it could go anywhere and park in any spot, and it could carry a lot more than you'd think. People loved it for camping, especially if they got the Westfalia, a model that came with two beds, a hammock, a refrigerator, a stove, a kitchen cabinet, and a dining table. *Motor Trend* wrote, "More a way of life than just another car, the VW Bus, when completely equipped with the ingenious German-made Kamper kit, can open up new vistas of freedom (or escape) from humdrum life." In the U.S., the bus wasn't at first called a bus—it was called a station wagon—and was marketed as the ideal car for the suburban family. The hippie part came later. You get the sense that something was changing, a mood shifting, in a TV ad from 1963. The camera pans around a VW Samba, a model with twenty-one windows, while a man's voice asks:

> If your TV set broke down right now, could your wife find something to talk about? Is she the kind of wife that can bake her own bread? Does she worry about the arms race? Do the neighbors' kids wish they had her for a mother? Will your wife say yes to a camping trip after fifty straight weeks of cooking? Will she let your daughter keep a pet snake in the back yard? Can you show up very late for dinner without calling first, with two old friends? Will your wife let the kids eat frankfurters for breakfast? Would she name a cat Rover? Would she let you give up your job with a smile and mean it? Congratulations. You have the right kind of wife for the Volkswagen station wagon.

A year or so later, the VW bus had become the iconic image of the counterculture. You could go to concerts in it, or to protests. You could smoke pot in it, or fool around. You could sleep there on the cheap. You could plot a revolution, or you could store your surfboard. Still, for all the cult of the counterculture, the fate of the VW bus, starting in the 1960s, mainly had to do with the price of chicken.

Here's where I need to explain about the Chicken War. In the 1950s, the factory farming of poultry by Big Agribusiness exploded, leading to a plunge in the price of chicken and a boom in the market for it. American farmers exported staggering numbers of cheap frozen chicken parts to Europe, so many that chicken became one of the most valuable U.S. exports—much to the distress of German farmers. "In Bavaria and Westphalia, protectionist German farmers' associations stormed that U.S. chickens are artificially fattened with arsenic and should be banned," *Time* reported in 1962. "The French government did ban U.S. chickens, using the excuse that they are fattened with estrogen. With typical Gallic concern, Frenchmen hinted that such hormones could have catastrophic effects on male virility." Members of

Europe's Common Market raised tariffs on imported chicken. "Everyone is preoccupied with Cuba, Berlin, Laos—and chickens," one German minister reported after a visit to the U.S. The German chancellor, describing two years of diplomatic talks with President Kennedy, said, "I guess that about half of it has been about chickens." Americans were furious: there was talk, for a time, of pulling U.S. troops out of NATO unless the chicken tax was dropped. Instead, in December 1963, President Johnson, eyeing the next year's election and needing the support of the United Auto Workers, not least for his civil rights agenda, retaliated in kind. Volkswagen had started selling a Type 2 pickup truck that was becoming popular. The UAW was threatening a strike. Johnson, whose secretary of defense was Robert McNamara, the former CEO of Ford Motors, imposed a 25 percent tax on imported light trucks. It was aimed at Volkswagen, but it applied to everyone. It has never been lifted.

Because of the tax, Volkswagen couldn't sell the Type 2 in the United States as any kind of truck—not as a pickup, not as a panel van, not as any vehicle that could be construed as commercial. It could only be a passenger van, a family car. Although Dodge is usually given credit for inventing the minivan, if "credit" is the word, it's really Volkswagen that invented it, out of necessity. As the 1960s wore on, though, driving around a pile of people came to mean something different, something about community. There's the faded-green rusted rear door of a 1966 Type 2 in the Smithsonian National Museum of African American History and Culture: it was used by civil rights activists in South Carolina to take Black children to school. Painted on it, in wobbly white letters, are the words LOVE IS PROGRESS.

SUE VARGO GOT HER FIRST CAR, a used VW Beetle, in 1973, the year she graduated from Michigan State. The bus and the Beetle have the same engine, toylike and in the back, and she learned how to fix it by reading *How to Keep Your Volkswagen Alive: A Manual of Step by Step Procedures for the Compleat Idiot*, a guidebook with R. Crumb–style illustrations. "It told you what six wrenches you needed, and how to make a timing light out of a twelve-volt bulb and some alligator clips," she told me. "You had to set the valves every six thousand miles." Anyone could do it.

Vargo's friend Molly Mead got her first VW bus, brand-new, all blue, in 1971. The next year, she and a friend added a cooler, a two-burner propane stove, an eight-track player, and a transistor radio and camped in that bus for four months, with two golden retrievers in the back, driving through Colorado, Wyoming, Montana, and Vancouver, and over to Vancouver Island and back, then down the West Coast, while Richard Nixon ran for reelection. "In Seattle, I cast my mail-in ballot for McGovern," Mead told me. They listened to Led Zeppelin, Cream. The VW bus was famously underpowered. Thirty horsepower. (The ID. Buzz has more than six times that.) Two dogs, two women, the Rockies: the bus could barely make it, creeping uphill like a slug.

Volkswagen made millions of T2s, including an electric model. It stopped making T2s in 1979. My first Volkswagen bus, which was made in 1987, was a T3, known in the U.S. as a Vanagon. It was almost twenty years old when my husband bought it. ("You have the right kind of wife for the Volkswagen station wagon.") It was rusty and brown, with a stick shift, and the locks didn't work and it smelled like smoke, except more like a campfire than like cigarettes, and we took it camping and pushed down the seats to make a bed and slept inside, with two toddlers and a baby and a Great Dane, and we all fit, even with fishing poles and Swiss Army knives and battery-operated lanterns and binoculars and Bananagrams and bug spray and a beloved, pint-size red plastic suitcase full of the best pieces from our family's Lego collection. It was, honestly, the dream. If you took it to the beach, you could just slide open the door and pop up the table—the five seats in back faced one another—and eat peanut butter and jelly sandwiches while watching the waves or putting a baby down for a nap. The carpet would get covered with sand and crushed seashells. Weeks later, the whole van would still smell like a cottage by the sea.

After the Vanagon engine stopped turning over, we got a ten-year-old 2002 Volkswagen Eurovan, a camper with a pop-top. Technically, it's a T4. It's also the last bus that Volkswagen sold in the U.S. (That decision was mainly due to the decline of the dollar against the deutsche mark in the 1990s. In much of the rest of the world, you can still buy a T5, a T6, or a T7, which is a hybrid, and the fact that you can't buy any of these in the U.S. is one reason for all the pent-up American demand for the updated bus.) We bought our T4 in California, at a place called Pop-Top Heaven. The day we drove it off the lot, half the dashboard warning lights came on. Check engine! Brake failure! Check tire level! Engine overheating! The T4 is a lot harder to fix yourself than the T3. We had to make an emergency stop at Auto-Zone for a gadget called an onboard diagnostics detector. We plugged it in and most of the lights went off, and so we drove the bus across the country, camping with three boys, who slept below, with the two of us sleeping in the pop-top. Or not exactly sleeping. Resting. Or watching the first four seasons of *The Simpsons* on a portable DVD player. Or listening to *The Penderwicks* on audiocassette. One of our kids had taken a vow not to listen to a single piece of music produced after the year 1985, and he's the one who gets carsick, so he got to sit in front, which meant that he controlled the radio, so there was a lot of Fleetwood Mac, the Ramones, the Beatles, the Police. Just past Death Valley, we needed a jump start. At the Grand Canyon, we dug the first aid kit out from under the spare tire to treat lacerations from tumbling down a trail. In Cleveland, we rolled up to the Rock & Roll Hall of Fame blasting Little Richard. And then we were home—filthy, unbroken, proven.

It still runs. The locks keep getting stuck; the heating doesn't work; three seasons out of four, the sliding door won't budge. We can't bear to sell it. We've taken out all the seats. We just use it to haul stuff around, not so much an empty nest as an empty shell.

Every VW bus ever owned by Sue Vargo and Molly Mead, every VW bus I've owned: they were all built at the factory in Hanover, Germany. The ID. Buzz is being built there, too. When it started, I flew to Germany and drove to Hanover in a rental car, a Volkswagen Tiguan. New Volkswagens have more than thirty different "driver-assistance programs." On the Autobahn, if I tried to change lanes without signaling, the car balked. Driver assist is different from power locks and power steering and an automatic transmission. It's more like having another driver in the car. It's like when, in a driver's-ed car, the teacher has his own brake pedal in the front passenger seat, and if you roll through a stop sign he pumps the brakes himself. Your onboard computer can park your car. It can tell you when it's safe to pass. You get the feeling you're not needed anymore. You might like that feeling, or you might not.

The Hanover factory is the size of a hundred and fifty-two soccer fields, or the size of a small town. Its gray concrete-and-metal floor is painted with white and yellow traffic stripes, and to the right there's a lane for pedestrians. I took a tour riding in the back seat of a T6 with its top cut off, painted a royal blue that I think of as VW blue. It felt like riding in the Popemobile. The factory's fourteen thousand workers—mostly men, mostly wearing blue jeans and VW-blue T-shirts—use bicycles to get around, as if (the genius of German engineering!) they'd reinvented the bicycle as the best and easiest mode of transportation. Everything and everyone was on the move, an exploded version of Richard Scarry's *Busy, Busy World*. Workers would bike by, eyeing us a little suspiciously. Parts are moved from place to place not with *Plattenwagen* but with autonomous vehicles, R2-D2-ish beeping carts—the ugly, clumsy ancestors of a new species of sleeker, prettier driverless cars, the dinosaurs to those birds. They stopped, politely, at every intersection, their cameras looking both ways before crossing the road.

Thomas Hahlbohm runs the plant. He's got a graying beard and wears his curly red hair pulled back in a bun. Improbably, he's a Pittsburgh Steelers fan. His father worked in this factory decades ago, and Hahlbohm started out on the assembly line. During my tour, he stood in the front of the T6, turning around to talk to me over a never-ending thrum of metal hammering metal. The basic project of building a car is unchanged. A car starts out, in the press shop, as a roll of sheet metal, unfurled into a press that stamps out parts: side panels, front panels. Those get put together in the body shop, to form a ghostly husk, which is sent to the paint shop and dipped in a series of pools, then rolled around to the assembly shop, where everything else is fitted into it. At a spot called the wedding station, the chassis comes up from the basement and is screwed to the body.

But if the basics remain unchanged, every detail is different. Most of Hahlbohm's job involves overseeing ceaseless adjustment: replacing software; installing new, more fully automated equipment; and retraining the workforce. "This is the old body shop of the T6," he said, as we wheeled past. It was built twenty years ago. "And, as you know, if you try to use now a computer from 2000?" He rolled his eyes. You can only replace the software for so long; after a while, you just need a new computer. Volkswagen will retire this body shop soon and build a new one. The art of automotive innovation is the acceleration of evolution.

The Hanover factory is making three different cars, the T6, the T7, and the Buzz, all on the trickiest parts of assembly: attaching the hatchback. It's plastic, instead of metal, to help keep the vehicle's weight down. Plastic is unforgiving. As a Buzz is rolled along the conveyor belt, a worker wearing gloves climbs inside the back, and three workers on the belt help a robot arm nudge the hatchback into place. It's a ballet, and a big challenge for an aging workforce. "We have to bring the people from the past to the future," Hahlbohm said. He's trying to get his workforce excited about the vehicles. One is on display in front of the factory; soon, workers will be able to take them out for rides.

Everywhere in the plant, the machinery is color-coded: orange for the T6, green for the T7, and yellow for the Buzz. Volkswagen will phase out the T6 before long, and introduce other variations of the Buzz, including the bigger, American version. In Europe, especially in smaller cities, the Buzz will be used as a police car, a school bus, a delivery van, a postal truck, and an actual bus, something between public transport and a multi-passenger ride-hailing service. Eventually, a version of the Buzz is intended to establish the first fleet of self-driving taxis and shuttles. But the chicken tax means that, in the U.S., the Buzz can't be sold as anything but a passenger car. If the Buzz is the vehicle of the future, its future in the U.S. is shackled to a deal LBJ brokered with the UAW more than half a century ago.

Once you're set up to make EVs, they're easier to build than combustion engine cars. "Because it's simpler, we will save ten hours per car," Hahlbohm said. With every new iteration of the production cycle, more parts of the process are automated. Every change is also meant to make the work less physically demanding for humans. The cars are on a conveyor belt, and so are the workers, riding along it on rolling chairs. The key to production, Hahlbohm said, is reduction of effort. Reduction of effort has lately become the key to driving, too.

TO PICTURE THE BUZZ, imagine that a Toyota Sienna got pregnant by a Tesla. At the New York auto show, I sounded out people staring at the Buzz on its pedestal. Kenneth Pearl, a New Yorker in fleece and jeans, who comes to the show every year, told me that his sister used to have a VW bus. He's not sure the Buzz will capture the attention of young people. And he'd never get an EV, he said, because he'd have no way to charge it. I asked Sonya Fitzmaurice, a jewelry designer from River Vale, New Jersey, if she thought it looked like the bus. "Sort of?" she said. "Like the Scooby-Doo van. The Mystery Van." She was wearing an embroidered motorcycle jacket. She figures she'll get an EV at some point, but when she does she won't buy the Buzz. It's too big, she said. "And we're downsizing."

It struck me that the sort of people who go to auto shows might not be the sort of people who are on the verge of buying a high-fashion EV, nostalgia or no. Tesla often doesn't bother with auto shows. Instead, Elon Musk stages his own shows. For better or worse, Volkswagen doesn't have a Musk. But the launch of the Buzz has been a little Teslish. In March 2022, the Buzz made its world premiere in Paris, and since then Volkswagen has been trotting it around to all the swankiest places, the tech-debut equivalents of the Met Gala: South by Southwest, in Austin, Texas; the World Economic Forum, in Davos, Switzerland. I asked to test it, and, amazingly, the company brought one to me, in my hometown. It was loaded onto a semi, along with a 1969 bus, and driven to the parking lot behind Harvard Stadium. Then I was sent a photo, and a message: "Your chariots await."

I pulled into the parking lot in my beat-up, emptied-out, pine-green Eurovan. I eyed my chariots.

The difference between driving the bus and driving the Buzz is the difference between beating eggs with a whisk and pressing the On button of a mixer. There's just very little to do. The accelerator has a triangle on it, a Play button; the brake has two vertical lines on it, for Pause.

I shifted into reverse, hit Play.

I began pulling out, but a physicist I know walked by and waved me down. She was with a friend, a German biologist, who'd been waiting for the Buzz for well over a year. I pulled over so they could look inside. "I'm totally in love with it," he said. They wanted a ride. It was as if I'd shown up in a spaceship. Heads turned. Everyone waved, everyone honked. Everyone wanted a ride. We didn't have room. I'd brought some teenagers along.

"This is insane, dog," one said to another.

"We got so much cred right now."

There were a lot of gadgets to investigate.

"Are there, like, a hundred USB ports?"

"It's crazy quiet in here."

I drove around the block, gliding, almost floating, noiselessly, effortlessly. I hit Pause.

In 1976, when Sue Vargo and Molly Mead decided to go on a road trip together, Mead saw an ad for that '67 VW bus and showed up with cash. They named their bus Billie Jean. "We dyked it out, built a platform in the back with two-by-fours, put in a bed, parked it by the side of the road at night, and got rousted out of places where we weren't supposed to camp," Vargo said. "It was a blast." It was also the ideal lesbian-road-trip car. You never needed to check into a hotel. It made it down to Florida—*boing, boing, boing*—and almost back, before the engine nearly sputtered out.

For a while in the seventies, Vargo worked as a mechanic, a wrench, at a four-bay shop called Mecca Motors. Her other car was a motorcycle, a Honda 350. Later, she got a doctorate in psychology. For years, she worked part time at the auto shop and part time at her psychotherapy practice. "They were both fixing things," she said. "But the time frame in the garage was way shorter. Something came in, it was broken, you fixed it, and it went back, same day."

For the Buzz that's coming to the United States in 2024, you won't need to tighten the distributor cap or jury-rig a timing belt in a pinch. There will be no quirkily illustrated, *Whole Earth Catalog*–style *How to Keep Your Volkswagen Buzz Alive*. You won't recognize the innards, and you won't be able to fix them, not even with an onboard diagnostics detector. In the new world of cars, only machines learn.

Molly Mead once had a minivan, a Dodge Caravan, when her kids were little. Sue Vargo used to have a Prius. Mead thinks she might get an EV—her wife's a pastor, and has a long commute—but, she says,

"I'm not going to be buying a Tesla." Neither of them wants a Buzz; it's too big for them, and they don't think it looks fun to drive.

I still want one, though. Or maybe I just want those road trips back, the Ramones, *The Simpsons*, the fishing poles, the sleeping bags, and that pint-size red plastic suitcase full of Legos. Only love is progress.

—2022

Part Four

Just the Facts, Ma'am

The past has not been erased, its erasure has not been forgotten, the lie has not become truth. But the past of proof is strange and, on its uncertain future, much in public life turns.

Rosalind Russell in *His Girl Friday*, 1940.
PictureLux / The Hollywood Archive / Alamy Stock Photo

JUST THE FACTS, MA'AM

WHAT MAKES A BOOK A HISTORY? IN THE EIGHteenth century, novelists called their books "histories," smack on the title page. No one was more brash about this than Henry Fielding, who, in his 1749 *History of Tom Jones, a Foundling*, included a chapter called "Of Those Who Lawfully May, and of Those Who May Not Write Such Histories as This." Fielding insisted that what flowed from his pen was "true history"; fiction was what historians wrote.

"I shall not look on myself as accountable to any Court of Critical Jurisdiction whatever: For as I am, in reality, the Founder of a new Province of Writing," Fielding explained. Tom Jones's claim to truth is different from Margaret Jones's. Some years back, Jones, also known as Margaret Seltzer, tried to pass off a gangland bildungsroman as the story of her life. Pulped days after it was published, the book, titled *Love and Consequences*, is a fraud; *Tom Jones* is not. Fielding was playing; Seltzer was just lying.

But Fielding meant it when he said that *Tom Jones* was true, and there's a sense in which he was right. History matters, but the best novels boast a kind of truth that even the best history books can never claim. And when history books are wrong they can be miserably, badly, ridiculously wrong, a point that wasn't lost on Jane Austen, who, in 1791, when she was sixteen, wrote a brilliant parody of Oliver Goldsmith's four-volume, march-of-the-monarchs *History of England, from the Earliest Times to the Death of George II*. (Goldsmith, the author of the novel *The Vicar of Wakefield*, wrote history to keep out of debtors' prison.) Austen called her parody *The History of England from the Reign of Henry the 4th to the Death of Charles the 1st, by a Partial, Prejudiced & Ignorant Historian*. It consisted of thirteen perfectly dunderheaded character sketches of crowned heads of England. Of Henry V, she wrote, "During his reign, Lord Cobham was burnt alive, but I forget what for." Of the Duke of Somerset: "He was beheaded, of which he might with reason have been proud, had he known that such was the death of Mary Queen of Scotland; but as it was impossible that he should be conscious of what had never happened, it does not appear that he felt particularly delighted with the manner of it." Of the allegation that Lady Jane Grey, Edward VI's cousin, read Greek: "Whether she really understood that language or whether such a study proceeded only from an excess of vanity for which I believe she was always rather remarkable, is uncertain." Once in a great while, Austen happened to bump into a fact or two, for which she apologized: "Truth being I think very excusable in an Historian."

Historians and novelists are kin, in other words, but they're more like brothers who throw food at each other than like sisters who borrow each other's clothes. The literary genre that became known as "the novel" was born in the eighteenth century. History, the empirical sort based on archival research and practiced in universities, anyway, was born at much the same time. Its novelty is not as often remembered, though, not least because it wasn't called "novel." In a way, history is the anti-novel, the novel's twin, though which is Cain and which is Abel depends on your point of view.

Among the ancients, history was a literary art, as John Burrow illustrates in his fascinating compendium *A History of Histories: Epics, Chronicles, Romances and Inquiries from Herodotus and Thucydides to the Twentieth Century.* Invention was a hallmark of ancient history, which was filled with long, often purely fictitious speeches of great men. It was animated by rhetoric, not by evidence. Even well into the eighteenth century, not a few historians continued to understand themselves as artists, with license to invent. Eager not to be confused with antiquarians and mere chroniclers, even budding empiricists confessed a certain lack of fussiness about facts. In *Letters on the Study and Use of History* (1752), Henry St. John, Viscount Bolingbroke condemned those who "store their minds with crude unruminated facts and sentences; and hope to supply, by bare memory, the want of imagination and judgment."

THE TRANSFORMATION OF HISTORY into an empirical science began as early as the sixteenth century and became entrenched only in the nineteenth century. By the time the American Historical Association was founded, in 1884, the "cult of the fact" (as the intellectual historian Peter Novick has called it) had achieved ascendancy. Ever since, generations of historians have defined themselves by a set of standards that rest on the distinction between truth and invention, even when that has meant scorning everyone who came before them. Between 1834 and 1874, the American statesman and historian George Bancroft, much influenced by Sir Walter Scott, produced a ten-volume *History of the United States*. It is romantic and opinionated; it has a gritty voice and a passionate point of view. It's a little . . . novel-ish. In the 1870s, one Young Turk suggested that a better title for it would be *The Psychological Autobiography of George Bancroft, As Illustrated by Incidents and Characters in the Annals of the United States*. A generation later, Bancroft's monumental accomplishment looked even worse: now it was, as the Yale historian Charles McLean Andrews put it, "nothing less than a crime against historical truth."

But is "historical truth" truer than fictional truth? The difference between history and poetry, Aristotle argued, is that "the one tells what has happened, the other the kind of things that can happen. And in fact that is why the writing of poetry is a more philosophical activity, and one to be taken more seriously, than the writing of history." Historians have turned this thinking on its head. History, not literature, is the serious stuff.

In the 1980s and '90s, many historians worried that the seriousness of history, its very integrity as a discipline, was in danger of being destroyed by literary theorists who insisted on the constructedness, the fictionality, of all historical writing—who suggested that the past is nothing more than a story we tell about it. The field seemed to be tottering on the edge of an epistemological abyss: If history is fiction, if history is not true, what's the use? (The panic has since died down, but it hasn't died out. Donald Kagan, in his 2005 Jefferson lecture, "In Defense of History," grumbled about the perils of "pseudo-philosophical mumbo-jumbo.") In 1990, Sir Geoffrey Elton called postmodern literary theory "the intellectual equivalent of crack." The next year, the eminent American historian Gordon Wood, writing in *The New York Review of Books,* warned that if things were to keep on this way historians would soon "put themselves out of business." Reviewing Simon Schama's *Dead Certainties (Unwarranted Speculations)*—a history book in which Schama indulged in flights of fancy, fully disclosed as such—Wood wrote, "His violation of the conventions of history writing actually puts the integrity of the discipline of history at risk." That review, along with twenty more (including one of a book of mine), appears in Wood's book *The Purpose of the Past: Reflections on the Uses of History*; each review has an afterword, and in an introduction the author catalogues the failings of "unhistorical historians."

Revisiting his review of *Dead Certainties*, Wood takes the trouble to reproach Schama again for having "forgotten that he was not Walter Scott or E. L. Doctorow," and for ignoring "both the epistemological climate of the early 1990s and the devastating effects such a work by such a distinguished historian could have on the conventions of the discipline." As Wood sees it, these conventions need protecting because their novelty—"They are scarcely more than a century old"— makes them fragile. But they're sturdier than he thinks. Margaret Jones is accountable to a court of jurisdiction in a way that Tom Jones was not. Historians and critics, readers and writers, haven't given up on truth. And postmodernism turns out to be a bit of a bugbear. It's premodernism that's got all the teeth.

IN THE EIGHTEENTH CENTURY, the boundary between history and fiction was different from what it is now. For one thing, plenty of people wrote both history books and novels, including Voltaire, Fielding, Tobias Smollett, Oliver Goldsmith, Daniel Defoe, William Godwin, Mary Wollstonecraft, and Charles Brockden Brown. The century's most influential historians, David Hume and Edward Gibbon, happen to have been particular fans of Fielding's novels (and Fielding considered reading history essential preparation for writing novels). History books and novels alike aimed at seducing readers through plot and even suspense. "History, like tragedy, requires an exposition, a central action, and a dénouement," Voltaire wrote in 1752. "My secret is to force the reader to wonder: Will Philip V ascend the throne?"

Eighteenth-century novels also pretended that they were true. Not only did they call themselves "histories"; they also often took the form of counterfeit historical documents, usually letters or journals—a form that was *itself* a parody of the conventions of historical writing. In the preface to *The Life and Strange Surprizing Adventures of Robinson Crusoe*

(1719), Daniel Defoe insisted, "The Editor believes the thing to be a just History of Fact; neither is there any Appearance of Fiction in it." But of course Defoe was not the editor of a journal kept by a man named Crusoe; there was no journal. Defoe made it up. What Defoe meant by this imposture, one critic wrote, "I know not; unless you would have us think, that the Manner of your telling a Lie will make it a Truth."

It's easy to think that Defoe was joking, as if Robinson Crusoe's journal were as much a gimmick as *Esquire*'s "diary" of Heath Ledger, but Defoe, like Fielding, was making a (mostly) straight-faced epistemological argument. And less playful novelists did the same thing. Samuel Richardson insisted that he was merely the editor of Pamela's letters, first published in England in 1740 as *Pamela; or, Virtue Rewarded* (and published by Benjamin Franklin in Philadelphia two years later). This was a lie, but not a hoax; Richardson wanted his novels to be read with "Historical Faith," since they contained, he believed, the truth of the possible, the truth of human nature. The first American novels weren't published until the 1780s and '90s, but they cluttered their title pages with the same claims: "FOUNDED ON FACT"; "A Tale of *Truth*."

What this implies is nicely illustrated by David Hume (who, in his lifetime, was better known as a historian than as a philosopher). In "Of the Study of History" (1741), Hume told a story about how the same book can be read as both history and fiction. A "young beauty" asked Hume to send her some novels; instead, he sent her some history books—*Plutarch's Lives*—but told her they were novels, assuring her "that there was not a word of truth in them from beginning to end." She read them avidly, at least "'till she came to the lives of ALEXAN-DER and CAESAR, whose names she had heard of by accident; and then returned me the book, with many reproaches for deceiving her." As fiction, *Plutarch's Lives* was delightful; as history, it was unbearable. Hume toyed with the opposite idea in *A Treatise of Human Nature* (1739–40): two books, one a history, and one a novel, might contain the same truth. "If one person sits down to read a book as a romance, and another as a true history," he wrote, "they plainly receive the same ideas, and in the same order; nor does the incredulity of the one, and the belief of the other hinder them from putting the very same sense upon their author. His words produce the same ideas in both."

If a history book can be read as if it were a novel, and if a reader can find the same truth in a history book and a novel, what, finally, is the difference between them? This is a difficult question, Hume admitted. Maybe it just *feels* different—more profound—to read what we believe to be true (an idea assented to) than what we believe to be false (a fancy): "An idea assented to feels different from a fictitious idea, that the fancy alone presents to us."

But there's more between them. A novel, as Defoe put it, is a "private History," a history of private life. "I will tell you in three words what the book is," Laurence Sterne wrote in *The Life and Opinions of Tristram Shandy*, published beginning in 1759. He was talking about Locke's account of how the mind worked and, by extension, his own. "It is a history.—A history! of who? what? where? when? Don't hurry yourself.—It is a history-book, Sir, (which may possibly recommend it to the world) of what passes in a man's own mind." Fielding went farther. He called his writing "true history." It is "our Business to relate Facts as they are," Fielding told his reader, classing himself among historical writers who draw their materials not from records but from "the vast authentic Doomsday-Book of Nature."

For Fielding, there are two kinds of historical writing: history based in fact (whose truth is founded in documentary evidence), and history based in fiction (whose truth is founded in human nature). Maybe—to take some license with Jane Austen's *Pride and Prejudice* (1813)—these two manners of writing bear the same relationship to one another as Mr. Darcy and Mr. Wickham: "One has got all the truth, and the other all the appearance of it." The question is: Which is which?

"DISMISS ME FROM THE FALSEHOOD and impossibility of history, and deliver me over to the reality of romance," the English writer William Godwin pleaded in "Of History and Romance," in 1797. (Not for nothing had Godwin called his novel written a few years earlier *Things as They Are*.) There is not and never can be any such thing as true history, Godwin insisted: "Nothing is more uncertain, more contradictory, more unsatisfactory than the evidence of facts." Every history is incomplete; every historian has a point of view; every historian relies on what is unreliable—documents written by people who were not under oath and cannot be cross-examined. (That is to say, even the best historian has a good deal in common with Jane Austen's *Partial, Prejudiced & Ignorant Historian*.) Before his imperfect sources, the historian is powerless: "He must take what they choose to tell, the broken fragments, and the scattered ruins of evidence." He could decide merely to reproduce his sources, to offer a list of facts: "But this is in reality no history. He that knows only on what day the Bastille was taken and on what spot Louis XVI perished, knows nothing."

Fortunately, there is yet another kind of history, Godwin argued, "the noblest and most excellent species of history": the novel, or romance. The novelist is the better historian—and especially better than the empirical historian—because he *admits* that he is partial, prejudiced, and ignorant, and because he has not forsaken passion: "The writer of romance is to be considered as the writer of real history; while he who was formerly called the historian, must be contented to step down into the place of his rival, with this disadvantage, that he is a romance writer, without the arduous, the enthusiastic and the sublime licence of imagination that belong to that species of composition."

Godwin's essay wasn't published until the twentieth century, which makes it all the more remarkable that the Philadelphian Charles Brockden Brown put forth a look-alike argument in "The Difference Between History and Romance," an essay published in the *Monthly Magazine and American Review* in April 1800. (To be sure, Brown was very much influenced by Godwin. Carl Van Doren once wrote, "His novels all bear the marks of haste, immaturity, and Godwin.") "History and romance are terms that have never been very clearly distinguished from each other," Brown began. "It should seem that one dealt in fiction, and the other in truth; that one is a picture of the *probable* and certain, and the other a tissue of untruths; that one describes what *might* have happened, and what has *actually* happened, and the other what never had existence." Yet these distinctions are not as helpful as they at first appear: history concerns facts, but, because these have to be arranged and explained, the historian "is a dealer, not in certainties, but probabilities, and is therefore a romancer."

In an 1806 essay called "Historical Characters Are False Representations of Nature," Brown suggested that the historian's grossest deception is promoting the idea that only the great are good: "Popular prejudice assists the illusion, and because we are accustomed to behold public characters occupy a situation in life that few can experience, we are induced to believe that their capacities are more enlarged, their passions more refined, and, in a word, that nature has bestowed on them faculties denied to obscurer men." But great characters are *not* superior to obscure men, who are, alas, condemned to obscurity by history itself. "If it were possible to read the histories of those who are doomed to have no historian, and to glance into domestic journals as well as into national archives," Brown speculated, "we should then perceive the unjust prodigality of our sympathy to those few names, which eloquence has adorned with all the seduction of her graces."

Fiction, in other words, can do what history doesn't but should: it can tell the story of ordinary people. The eighteenth century's fictive history (not to be confused with what we call "historical fiction") is the history of private life; the history of what passes in a man's own mind; true to the Book of Nature; and written in plain, simple style, exhibiting both judgment and invention. And it is the history of obscure men. Who are these obscure men? Well, a lot of them are women.

FOR EVERY TOM JONES AND ROBINSON CRUSOE, there were a dozen Clarissas, Pamelas, and Charlotte Temples. If eighteenth-century novels are history, they're women's history. And they were adored, above all, by women readers. "Novel Reading, a Cause of Female Depravity" was the revealing title of an essay published in England in 1797 and in Boston five years later. Everyone from preachers to politicians damned novels as corrupting of both public and private virtue and, above all, of women's virtue. "Novels not only pollute the imaginations of young women," one American magazine writer insisted in 1798; they give them "false ideas of life."

What, pray, was the remedy for this grave social ill? Reading *history*. "There is nothing which I would recommend more earnestly to my female readers than the study of history," Hume wrote in "Of the Study of History" (which is why he gave his lady friend *Plutarch's Lives*, and told her it was a novel). But on the whole, women were not particularly interested in reading history. Hume attributed this to the fair sex's "aversion to matter of fact" and its "appetite for falsehood." Men "allow us Poetry, Plays, and Romances," Mary Astell wrote in 1705, "and when they would express a particular Esteem for a Woman's Sense, they recommend History." But why read it? "For tho' it may be of Use to Men who govern Affairs, to know how their Fore-fathers Acted, yet what is this to us?" Much as writers of history tried to woo women readers, they made very little headway. Near the end of the century, Mary Wollstonecraft was left to ask of women: "Is it surprising that they find the reading of history a very dry task?" (After publishing her *Vindication of the Rights of Women*, in 1792, Wollstonecraft started writing a novel, *Maria; or, the Wrongs of Women*, to make sure that her arguments would reach women readers. Her husband, William Godwin, had it published in 1798, after she died, in childbirth.)

Women were not only not interested in history; they didn't trust it. In *Northanger Abbey* (completed by 1803), Jane Austen's comic heroine, who adores novels, confesses that she finds history both boring and impossible to credit: "It tells me nothing that does not either vex or weary me. The quarrels of popes and kings, with wars or pestilences, in every page; the men all so good for nothing, and hardly any women at all—it is very tiresome: and yet I often think it odd that it should be so dull, for a great deal of it must be invention." Austen saw fit to echo this exchange in *Persuasion* (1818). "All histories are against you," Captain Harville insists, when Austen's levelheaded heroine, Anne Elliot, argues that women are more constant than men. "But perhaps you will say, these were all written by men," Harville guesses, and Anne agrees. "Men have had every advantage of us in telling their own story," she observes, saying, "I will not allow books to prove any thing."

By the end of the eighteenth century, not just novel readers but most novel writers were women, too. And most historians, along with their readers, were men. As the discipline of history, the anti-novel, emerged, and especially as it professionalized, it defined itself as the domain of men. (Women might write biography, or dabble in genealogy.) Eighteenth-century observers, in other words, understood the distinction between history and fiction not merely and maybe not even predominantly as a distinction between truth and invention but as a distinction between stories by, about, and of interest to men and stories by, about, and of interest to women. Women read novels, women wrote novels, women were the heroines of novels. Men read history, men wrote history, men were the heroes of history. (When men wrote novels, Godwin suggested, this was regarded as "a symptom of effeminacy.")

As Burrow's *A History of Histories* and Wood's *Purpose of the Past* make clear, however, much of what distinguished eighteenth-century fiction from eighteenth-century history is now part of how academic historians write history. Most of the popular history books you'll find in Barnes & Noble celebrate the public lives of famous men, but the history books that many academics have been writing for the past half century concern the private lives of ordinary people. (Memoirs constitute a related but distinct genre, chronicling the lives of both the famous and the not so famous, and borrowing from the conventions of history and of fiction. Fake memoirs, like Margaret Jones's or Misha Defonesca's, borrow from those genres, but without achieving the legitimacy of either.) "By the 1970s," Wood writes, "this new social history of hitherto forgotten people had come to dominate academic history writing." Maybe the topics that have seized professional historians' attention—family history, social history, women's history, cultural history, "microhistory"—constitute nothing more than an attempt to take back territory they forfeited to novelists in the eighteenth century. If so, historians have reclaimed from novelists nearly everything except the license to invent . . . and women readers. Today, publishers figure that men buy the great majority of popular history books; most fiction buyers are women.

Is "history at risk"? If women barely read it at all, and if men mostly read books with titles like *Guts and Guns*, it just might be. *A History of Histories* and *The Purpose of the Past* offer a useful reminder that history is a long and endlessly interesting argument, where evidence is everything and storytelling is everything else. But, as for telling stories, maybe historians still have a few things to learn from novelists. Reading Jane Austen being I think very excusable in an Historian.

—2008

BAD NEWS

IN THE 1930S, ONE IN FOUR AMERICANS GOT THEIR news from William Randolph Hearst, who lived in a castle and owned twenty-eight newspapers in nineteen cities. Hearst's papers were all alike: hot-blooded, with leggy headlines. Page 1 was supposed to make a reader blurt out, "Gee whiz!" Page 2: "Holy Moses!" Page 3: "God Almighty!" Still, you can yank people around for only so long. Wonder ebbs. Surprise is fleeting. Even rage abates. In 1933, Hearst turned seventy. He started to worry. How would the world remember him when he could no longer dictate the headlines? Ferdinand Lundberg, a reporter for the *New York Herald Tribune*, was beginning work on a book about him; no one expected it to be friendly. Hearst therefore did what many a rich, aging megalomaniac has done before and since: he hired a lackey to write an authorized biography, preemptively.

In 2010, one in four Americans got the news from Fox News. That year, Roger Ailes, its head, turned seventy. Gabriel Sherman, an editor and reporter for *New York* magazine, was beginning work on a book about him. Sherman interviewed more than six hundred people for *The Loudest Voice in the Room*. Ailes, who is known for menace, was not among them. "Take your best shot at me," Ailes is said to have told another *New York* writer, "and I'll have the rest of my life to go after you." Unwilling to sit down for an interview with Sherman, Ailes met instead with Zev Chafets, a former columnist for the *Daily News,* a contributor to the *New York Times Magazine,* and the author of a biography of Rush Limbaugh. Chafets shadowed Ailes at Fox News; watched his son play basketball; walked with him, flanked by his bodyguard; and visited his home, in Garrison, New York, where Ailes has bought up not only the land around his nine-thousand-square-foot mansion but also the local newspaper, to which he named, as publisher, his wife.

"I got a closer, more prolonged look at Roger Ailes than any journalist ever has," Chafets writes in *Roger Ailes: Off Camera,* which appeared, preemptively, a year before Sherman's book. Ailes, Chafets says, looks like "a small-town banker in a Frank Capra movie." That sounds disapproving, but in this particular Bedford Falls we are meant to admire Mr. Potter and each of his little witticisms. Ailes on Gingrich: "Newt's a prick." Biden: "He's dumb as an ashtray." Maddow: "Rachel is good and she will get even better when she discovers that there are people on earth who don't share every one of her beliefs." Krugman: "He's a dope but nobody wants to say it because he's won awards." There's plenty of obloquy in Chafets's book. There's also a great deal of what might be termed the testicular imagination. Rupert Murdoch says, of meeting Ailes, "I thought, Either this man is crazy or he has the biggest set of balls I've ever seen." Chafets adds, by way of aside, "Ailes was thinking pretty much the same thing." Holy Moses.

WILLIAM RANDOLPH HEARST NEEDED A MOUTHPIECE; he couldn't trust an actual biographer—he was convinced that most people who wrote serious books for a living were communists. In the fall of 1934, he ordered his editors to send reporters posing as students to college campuses, to find out which members of the faculty were Reds. Many of the people Hearst thought were communists thought Hearst was a fascist. This charge derived, in part, from the fact that Hearst had professed his admiration for Hitler and Mussolini. It was easy to despise Hearst. It was also lazy. Hating some crazy old loudmouth who is a vindictive bully and lives in a castle is far less of a strain than thinking about the vulgarity and the prejudices of his audience. In 1935, the distinguished war correspondent and radio broadcaster Raymond Gram Swing observed, "People who are not capable of disliking the lower middle class in toto, since it is a formidable tax on their emotions, can detest Hearst instead." Ailes haters, take note.

Swing despaired over what had happened to journalism under Hearst, and said so, which took courage. Hearst attacked his critics in his papers relentlessly and ferociously. Some fought back. "Only cowards can be intimidated by Hearst," the historian Charles Beard said. Beard had resigned from Columbia in 1917, after the university began firing professors who opposed U.S. involvement in the war. (Beard himself favored American involvement; what he opposed was the university's assault on intellectual freedom.) He'd been elected president of the American Political Science Association in 1925 and, in 1933, president of the American Historical Association. He wasn't someone Hearst could easily crush, or daunt. In February of 1935, Beard addressed an audience of nine hundred schoolteachers in Atlantic City. "William Randolph Hearst has pandered to depraved tastes and has been an enemy of everything that is noblest and best in the American tradition," he said. "No person with intellectual honesty or moral integrity will touch him with a ten-foot pole." The crowd gave Beard a standing ovation.

To write the story of his life, Hearst turned to a woman named Cora Baggerly Older. Her husband, Fremont Older, was one of Hearst's editors; the Olders had often visited Hearst at his 165-room castle, San Simeon. In December of 1935, Older, at work on the biography, alerted Hearst's office that she had learned "that a hostile book called THE LORD OF SAN SIMEON written by Oliver Carlson and Ernest Sutherland Bates is soon to be published by the Viking Press." Lundberg's biography was about to come out, too. It was called *Imperial Hearst*. A preface was supplied by Charles Beard.

ROGER AILES WAS BORN IN WARREN, OHIO, in 1940. He has hemophilia, which didn't stop his father from beating him with an electrical cord. A story Ailes has told—"his Rosebud story," according to Stephen Rosenfield, who worked with Ailes in the 1970s—is about a lesson he learned in his bedroom as a boy. His father, holding out his arms, told him to jump off the top bunk and then deliberately failed to catch him, saying, "Don't ever trust anybody."

Ailes went to Ohio University, where he majored in television and radio, and worked for the campus radio station, WOUB. While he was in college, his parents divorced; his mother told the court that her husband had threatened to kill her. After graduation, Ailes took a job at KYW-TV, in Cleveland, working for *The Mike Douglas Show*.

"Roger Ailes was a legend at a very young age," according to Marvin Kalb, and by all accounts Ailes was an exceptionally talented television producer. In 1967, he met Joe McGinniss, then a columnist for the *Philadelphia Inquirer*, who wrote about him in *The Selling of the President 1968*, an account of Nixon's presidential campaign, and catapulted him to celebrity. The book's turning point comes when, one day in

1967, in the greenroom of *The Mike Douglas Show*, Nixon says to Ailes, "It's a shame a man has to use gimmicks like this to get elected." Ailes says, "Television is not a gimmick." Ailes became Nixon's television producer. In McGinniss's telling, Ailes more or less got Nixon elected.

After the election, Ailes moved to New York and worked as a television consultant, talent agent, and Off Broadway producer. Entertainment slid into politics, politics into entertainment. Ailes began making issue ads and advising candidates. One of his clients was Philip Morris. Ailes insisted that he had no partisan loyalties. "I don't have this burning thing to elect all Republicans," he told the *Washington Post* in 1972. That year, he helped run the North Carolina gubernatorial campaign of Jim Holshouser Jr., a Republican who supported busing. "If you don't do an antibusing spot on TV, you will lose the election," Ailes told Holshouser. "Now, if I were you, I'd do the fucking spot, win the election, and then, once you're in office, do whatever you think is right." Holshouser did the spot and won. ("And what did he do about busing?" Chafets asks Ailes. Ailes answers, "I have no idea.")

In 1974, Ailes was hired as a consultant for Television News Inc., or TVN, a news service funded by Joseph Coors. Six months later, he became TVN's news director. "He didn't know anything about news," Reese Schonfeld, a TVN executive and, later, a cofounder of CNN, told Sherman. "He knew television." In 1975, the *Columbia Journalism Review* called Ailes "the only man in history to run a national news organization while owning an entertainment industry consulting firm." TVN folded later that year.

In the 1980s, Ailes's politics grew more conservative, as did the GOP. Between 1980 and 1986, Ailes helped get thirteen Republican senators and eight members of Congress elected, including Dan Quayle and Mitch McConnell. He also played a crucial role in the presidential campaigns of Ronald Reagan and George H. W. Bush. He urged Reagan to disarm Walter Mondale in debate by promising not to make age an issue. "I am not going to exploit, for political purposes, my opponent's youth and inexperience," Reagan said. Ailes calmed Bush's nerves before his first debate against Michael Dukakis. "If you get in trouble out there, just call him an animal fucker," Ailes whispered. According to a team of reporters from *Newsweek*, Ailes had proposed an ad, which never ran, called "Bestiality." It would have featured a screen of text—"In 1970, Governor Michael Dukakis introduced legislation in Massachusetts to repeal the ban on sodomy and bestiality"—shown over a soundtrack of barnyard animals, bleating.

"HAVE NOT SEEN BOOK BUT JACKET IS COLOR OF SAN SIMEONS INDOOR POOL," Cora Baggerly Older wrote in a telegram to Hearst on February 7, 1936, the day *William Randolph Hearst: American* appeared. The reviews were not kind. One critic observed, "Mrs. Older writes an authorized biography, and the result is about what one would look for." Chafets compares Ailes to Rudyard Kipling and Teddy Roosevelt. "Likenesses between William Randolph Hearst and Napoleon, Charlemagne, the Louis of France and the Popes of Rome are noted in Mr. Hearst's official biography," a reviewer remarked about Older's book, "yet it is possible that Mrs. Fremont Older, the biographer, is amazed at her own moderation."

Both Carlson and Bates's and Lundberg's Hearst biographies appeared a couple of months later, in April 1936. Carlson was a historian of journalism, Bates an English professor; their account is a story of Hearst's life as a decline into a savage cynicism, to the point that his "so-called 'news' papers are little more than a gigantic chain-store, selling political patent medicines and adulterated economics." Lundberg called for a congressional inquiry into Hearst's enterprises. *The New Yorker* called Beard's introduction "as juicy a piece of invective as you will find in several months of Sundays." Beard had, in fact, got rather exercised. "Hearst's fate is ostracism by decency in life, and oblivion in death," he wrote. "It goes with him to the vale of shadows." He was badly provoked, of course. Still, one prefers, as a rule, to stop short of cursing a man to eternal damnation.

IN 1988, Ailes cowrote a book called *You Are the Message.* Its premise is that everyone, at every moment, is not so much communicating as broadcasting. You have only seven seconds to be likable before someone changes the channel. "It's what I call the like factor," the book explains. (Today, this hooey has gone online: Like me! Follow me!)

Ailes met Limbaugh in 1991. Limbaugh was the host of the nation's most successful right-wing radio talk show, an entertainment genre made possible by Reagan's 1987 repeal of the FCC's Fairness Doctrine, which had been established in 1949. Ailes began producing a Limbaugh television show. In 1994, Ailes launched America's Talking, an affiliate of NBC's cable outlet, CNBC. Its twelve-hour all-talk lineup included a call-in show called *Am I Nuts?* and *Pork*, a program about government waste. As Sherman tells it, among the factors that contributed to its demise, less than two years later, was Ailes's tendency to insult his colleagues. On the radio, he said of Mary Matalin and Jane Wallace, the hosts of a show called *Equal Time*, that they were "girls who if you went into a bar around seven, you wouldn't pay a lot of attention but get to be tens around closing time." In a meeting, Ailes allegedly called his CNBC associate David Zaslav "a little fucking Jew prick." NBC commissioned an investigation, which concluded that Ailes had a "history of abusive, offensive, and intimidating statements/threats and personal attacks made to and upon a number of other people."

Ailes called the charges "false and despicable" (and Zaslav later recanted), but in November 1995, Ailes agreed to NBC's stipulation that he would "not engage in conduct that a reasonable employee would perceive as intimidating or abusive." A month later, NBC and Microsoft announced the creation of MSNBC, which was assigned the slot that America's Talking had occupied on the cable dial. Zaslav was hired to help launch it.

Fox News, owned by Murdoch and run by Ailes, got its start in 1996. "I left politics a number of years ago," Ailes said at a press conference. "We expect to do fine, balanced journalism." CNN had sixty million subscribers. MSNBC had twenty-five million. Fox News debuted in October 1996, with seventeen million.

The best thing that ever happened to Fox News was the Monica Lewinsky story, which, together with other Clinton scandals, led to a 400 percent increase in prime-time ratings. Much of Fox's lineup was already in place, but when the Lewinsky scandal broke, early in 1998, Ailes launched Brit Hume's 6:00 p.m. newscast, *Special Report*, and moved *The O'Reilly Report* to 8:00 p.m. By the beginning of 1999, Fox News was beating MSNBC.

During the 2000 election, Ailes relied on John Ellis, a first cousin of George W. Bush, to head Fox News's "decision desk." "Jebbie says we got it!" Ellis said at around 2:10 a.m. on Election Night, after getting off the phone with the governor of Florida. Fox called the election for Bush. Later, before a House subcommittee, Ailes was asked if there had been anything inappropriate in his employing Ellis. "Quite the contrary," he said. "I see this as a good journalist talking to his very high-level sources on Election Night."

Fox News's coverage of 9/11 and the war in Iraq improved its ratings, demonstrated its influence, and intensified the controversy over its practices. Critics charged that Fox News didn't report the war; it promoted it. When CBS's Morley Safer questioned Fox News about the flag pins worn by its anchors and reporters, Ailes said, "I'm a little bit squishy on killing babies, but when it comes to flag pins I'm pro-choice." By January of 2002, Fox was beating CNN.

In the years since, Fox News has steered the conservative movement. "That's a hard-hitting ad," Sean Hannity said, airing the attack on John Kerry by the Swift Boat Veterans for Truth, in 2004. In 2009, Glenn Beck's show, which debuted the day before Obama's inauguration, helped boost the channel's ratings and fueled the Tea Party movement.

"You don't get me," Ailes told Sherman, when they met at a party. "You don't get me" is what Fox News viewers across the country have been saying to the Washington press corps since the channel started, and fair enough. Still, in the end, the overturning of American journalism hasn't served their interests, or anyone's. Well-reported news is a public good; bad news is bad for everyone.

Sherman sees Ailes as a kingmaker, which isn't entirely convincing. Ailes is an entertainer. He's also a bogeyman. Raymond Gram Swing noticed that Hearst was largely a projection of his readers: "If he ever indulges in introspection his tragedy must be in seeing that for all his power, for all his being the biggest publisher in the world, he is not a leader, never has been a leader and never could be a leader." Hearst died in 1951. Between 1952 and 1988, an era marked by the Fairness Doctrine (and, according to conservatives, a liberal media), Republicans won seven out of ten presidential elections. Between 1988 and 2012, during the ascendancy of conservative media, Republicans won only three out of seven presidential elections. When Mitt Romney lost, Ailes blamed the party. "The GOP couldn't organize a one-car funeral," he said. Another explanation is that the conservative media drove the party into a graveyard.

No one reads Mrs. Older anymore. Hearst endures, instead, in *Citizen Kane*, a 1941 film that bears enough of a resemblance to Lundberg's book that Lundberg sued. "I had never seen or heard of the book *Imperial Hearst* by Mr. Lundberg," Orson Welles insisted in a deposition. A trial ended in a hung jury; the case was settled out of court.

Lundberg's evidence was good, but Welles made a persuasive argument that Kane wasn't a character; he was a type—an American sultan. If Xanadu looked like San Simeon, that's because men like Kane always wall themselves off in "one of those enormous imitation feudal kingdoms." A man like Kane, Welles said, believes that "politics as the means of communication, and indeed the nation itself, is all there for his personal pleasuring." The audience he craves he also hates. "Such men as Kane always tend toward the newspaper and entertainment world," Welles said. "They combine a morbid preoccupation with the public with a devastatingly low opinion of the public mentality and moral character."

Nothing could be more natural than that a man like that would attempt to dictate his place in history. And nothing could be more unavailing. History is the shadow cast by the dead. So long as there's light, the shadow will fall.

—2014

Postscript: In 2016, six women who had worked at Fox News, including two prominent anchors, filed sexual harassment charges against Ailes. He resigned in 2017 and died later that year.

AFTER THE FACT

T ED CRUZ'S CAMPAIGN AUTOBIOGRAPHY IS CALLED
A Time for Truth. "This guy's a liar," Donald Trump said at
a 2016 GOP debate, pointing at Cruz. Trump thought a lot of people
were liars, especially politicians (Jeb Bush: "Lying on campaign trail!")
and reporters ("Too bad dopey @megynkelly lies!"). Not for nothing
was he called the Human Lie Detector. And not for nothing was he
called a big, fat Pinocchio with his pants on fire by the fact-checking
teams at the *Times*, the *Washington Post*, and PolitiFact, whose careful reports apparently had little influence on the electorate, because,
as a writer for *Politico* admitted, "Nobody but political fanatics pays
much mind to them." "You lied," Marco Rubio said to Trump during
another truth-for-tat debate. Cruz tried to break in, noting that Rubio
had called him a liar, too. Honestly, there was so much loudmouthed
soothsaying that it was hard to tell who was saying what. A line from
the transcript released by CNN reads:

UNIDENTIFIED MALE: I tell the truth, I tell the truth.

Eat your heart out, Samuel Beckett.

On the one hand, not much of this is new. "Gen. Jackson is incapable
of deception," Andrew Jackson's supporters insisted, in 1824. "Among
all classes in Illinois the *sobriquet* of 'honest Abe' is habitually used by
the masses," a Republican newspaper reported of Lincoln, in 1860. The
tweets at #DumpTrump—"This man is a hoax!"—don't quite rise to
the prose standard of the arrows flung at supporters of John Adams,
who Jeffersonians said engaged in "every species of villainous deception, of which the human heart, in its last stage of depravity is capable."

"When a president doesn't tell the truth, how can we trust him to
lead?" a Mitt Romney ad asked in 2012, during an election season
in which the Obama campaign assembled a so-called Truth Team to

point out Romney's misstatements of fact. Remember the Swift Boat Veterans for Truth, from 2004? This kind of thing comes and goes, and, then again, it comes. Cast back to Nixon: *Among all classes, the sobriquet of "Tricky Dick" was habitually used by the masses.* "Liar" isn't what opponents generally called Ford or Carter or the first George Bush, but a Bob Dole ad, in 1996, charged that "Bill Clinton is an unusually good liar," and much the same was said of Hillary Clinton, dubbed "a congenital liar" by William Safire. A Bernie Sanders campaign ad referred to him, pointedly, as "an honest leader"; his supporters were less restrained. At a rally in Iowa, they chanted, "She's a liar!"

On the other hand, some of this actually is new. When a sitting member of Congress called out "You lie!" during the president's remarks before a joint session in 2009, that, for instance, was new. ("That's not true," Obama replied.) John Oliver's #MakeDonaldDrumpfAgain campaign is both peerless and unprecedented. On HBO, Oliver checked Trump's facts, called Trump a "litigious serial liar," and dared him to sue. Also newish in 2016 was the rhetoric of unreality, the insistence, chiefly by Democrats, that some politicians were incapable of perceiving the truth because they had an epistemological deficit: they no longer believed in evidence, or even in objective reality.

To describe this phenomenon, Democrats in 2016 went very often to the Orwellian well: "The past was erased, the erasure was forgotten, the lie became truth." Hillary Clinton had a campaign ad called "Stand for Reality." "I'm just a grandmother with two eyes and a brain," she says, which is an awfully strange thing for a former First Lady, U.S. senator, and secretary of state to say. But what she meant, I guess, was that even some random old lady can see what Republican aspirants for the Oval Office can't: "It's hard to believe there are people running for president who still refuse to accept the settled science of climate change."

The past has not been erased, its erasure has not been forgotten, the lie has not become truth. But the past of proof is strange and, on its uncertain future, much in public life turns. In the end, it comes down to this: the history of truth is cockamamie, and during the 2016 U.S. presidential campaign, it got cockamamier.

MOST OF WHAT IS WRITTEN ABOUT TRUTH is the work of philosophers, who explain their ideas by telling little stories about experiments they conduct in their heads, like the time Descartes tried to convince himself that he didn't exist, and found that he couldn't, thereby proving that he did. Michael P. Lynch is a philosopher of truth. His fascinating book *The Internet of Us: Knowing More and Understanding Less in the Age of Big Data* begins with a thought experiment: "Imagine a society where smartphones are miniaturized and hooked directly into a person's brain." As thought experiments go, this one isn't much of a stretch. ("Eventually, you'll have an implant," Google's Larry Page promised, "where if you think about a fact it will just tell you the answer.") Now imagine that, after living with these implants for generations, people grow to rely on them, to know what they know and forget how people used to learn—by observation, inquiry, and reason. Then picture this: overnight, an environmental disaster destroys so much of the planet's electronic communications grid that everyone's implant crashes. It would be, Lynch says, as if the whole world had suddenly gone blind. There would be no immediate basis on which to establish the truth of a fact. No one would really know anything anymore, because no one would know how to know. I Google, therefore I am not.

Lynch thought we were frighteningly close to this point: blind to proof, no longer able to know. After all, we were already no longer able to agree about how to know. (See: climate change, above.) Lynch wasn't terribly interested in how we got here. He began at the arrival gate. But altering the flight plan would seem to require going back to the gate of departure.

Historians don't rely on thought experiments to explain their ideas, but they do like little stories. When I was eight or nine years old, a rotten kid down the street stole my baseball bat, a Louisville Slugger that I'd bought with money I'd earned delivering newspapers, and on whose barrel I'd painted my last name with my mother's nail polish, peach-plum pink. "Give it back," I told that kid when I stomped over to his house, where I found him practicing his swing in the back yard. "Nope," he said. "It's mine." Ha, I scoffed. "Oh, yeah? Then why does it have my name on it?" Here he got wily. He said that my last name was also the name of his baseball team in the town in Italy that he was from, and that everyone there had bats like this. It was a dumb story. "You're a liar," I pointed out. "It's mine." "Prove it," he said, poking me in the chest with the bat.

The law of evidence that reigns in the domain of childhood is essentially medieval. "Fight you for it," the kid said. "Race you for it," I countered. A long historical precedent stands behind these judicial methods for the establishment of truth, for knowing how to know what's true and what's not. In the West, for centuries, trial by combat and trial by ordeal—trial by fire, say, or trial by water—served both as means of criminal investigation and as forms of judicial proof. Kid jurisprudence works the same way: it's an atavism. As a rule, I preferred trial by bicycle. If that kid and I had raced our bikes and I'd won, the bat would have been mine, because my victory would have been God-given proof that it had been mine all along: in such cases, the outcome is itself evidence. Trial by combat and trial by ordeal place judgment in the hands of God. Trial by jury places judgment in the hands of men. It requires a different sort of evidence: facts.

A "fact" is, etymologically, an act or a deed. It came to mean something established as true only after the church effectively abolished trial by ordeal in 1215, the year that King John pledged, in Magna Carta, "No free man is to be arrested, or imprisoned . . . save by the lawful judgment of his peers or by the law of the land." In England, the abolition of trial by ordeal led to the adoption of trial by jury for criminal cases. This required a new doctrine of evidence and a new method of inquiry, and led to what the historian Barbara Shapiro called "the culture of fact": the idea that an observed or witnessed act or thing—the substance, the *matter*, of fact—is the basis of truth and the only kind of evidence that's admissible not only in court but also in other realms where truth is arbitrated. Between the thirteenth century and the nineteenth, the fact spread from law outward to science, history, and journalism.

What were the facts in the case of the nail-polished bat? I didn't want to fight, and that kid didn't want to race. I decided to wage a battle of facts. I went to the library. Do they even have baseball in Italy? Sort of. Is my name the name of a baseball team? Undeterminable, although in Latin it means "hare," a fact that, while not dispositive, was so fascinating to me that I began to forget why I'd looked it up.

I never did get my bat back. Forget the bat. The point of the story is that I went to the library because I was trying to pretend that I was a grownup, and I had been schooled in the ways of the Enlightenment. Empiricists believed they had deduced a method by which they could discover a universe of truth: impartial, verifiable knowledge. But the movement of judgment from God to man wreaked epistemological havoc. It made a lot of people nervous, and it turned out that not everyone thought of it as an improvement. For the length of the eighteenth century and much of the nineteenth, truth seemed more knowable, but after that it got murkier. Somewhere in the middle of the twentieth century, fundamentalism and postmodernism, the religious right and the academic left, met up: either the only truth is the truth of the divine or there is no truth; for both, empiricism is an error. That epistemological havoc has never ended: much of contemporary discourse and pretty much all of American politics is a dispute over evidence. An American presidential debate has a lot more in common with trial by combat than with trial by jury, which is what people are talking about when they say these debates seem "childish": the outcome is the evidence. The ordeal endures.

THEN CAME THE INTERNET. The era of the fact is coming to an end: the place once held by "facts" is being taken over by "data." This is making for more epistemological mayhem, not least because the collection and weighing of facts require investigation, discernment, and judgment, while the collection and analysis of data are outsourced to machines. "Most knowing now is Google-knowing—knowledge acquired online," Lynch wrote in *The Internet of Us* (his title is a riff on the ballyhooed and bewildering Internet of Things). We now only rarely discover facts, Lynch observes; instead, we download them. Of course, we also upload them: with each click and keystroke, we hack off tiny bits of ourselves and glom them onto a data leviathan.

"The Internet didn't create this problem, but it is exaggerating it," Lynch wrote, and it's an important and understated point. Blaming the internet is shooting fish in a barrel—a barrel that is floating in the sea of history. It's not that you don't hit a fish; it's that the issue is the ocean. No matter the bigness of the data, the vastness of the web, the freeness of speech, nothing could be less well settled in the twenty-first century than whether people know what they know from faith or from facts, or whether anything, in the end, can really be said to be fully proved.

Lynch has been writing about this topic for a long time, and passionately. The root of the problem, as he saw it, is a well-known paradox: reason can't defend itself without resort to reason. In his 2012 book *In Praise of Reason*, Lynch identified three sources of skepticism about reason: the suspicion that all reasoning is rationalization, the idea that science is just another faith, and the notion that objectivity is an illusion. These ideas have a specific intellectual history, and none of them are on the wane. Their consequences, he believed, are dire: "Without a common background of standards against which we measure what counts as a reliable source of information, or a reliable method of inquiry, and what doesn't, we won't be able *to agree on the facts,* let alone values. Indeed, this is precisely the situation we seem to be headed toward in the United States." Hence, truthiness. "I'm no fan of dictionaries or reference books: they're elitist," Stephen Colbert said in 2005, when he coined "truthiness" while lampooning George W. Bush. "I don't trust books. They're all fact, no heart. And that's exactly what's pulling our country apart today."

The origins of no other nation are as wholly dependent on the empiricism of the Enlightenment, as answerable to evidence. "Let facts be submitted to a candid world," Thomas Jefferson wrote in the Declaration of Independence. Or, as James Madison asked, "Is it not the glory of the people of America, that whilst they have paid a decent regard to the opinions of former times and other nations, they have not suffered a blind veneration for antiquity, for custom, or for names, to overrule the suggestions of their own good sense, the knowledge of their own situation, and the lessons of their own experience?" When we Google-know, Lynch argued, we no longer take responsibility for our own beliefs, and we lack the capacity to see how bits of facts fit into a larger whole. Essentially, we forfeit our reason and, in a republic, our citizenship. You could see how this works every time you tried to get to the bottom of a story by reading the news on your smartphone. Or you could see it in a GOP debate when Rubio said that Trump had hired Polish workers, undocumented immigrants, and Trump called him a liar:

TRUMP: That's wrong. That's wrong. Totally wrong.
RUBIO: That's a fact. People can look it up. I'm sure people are googling it right now. Look it up. "Trump Polish workers," you'll see a million dollars for hiring illegal workers on one of his projects.

In the hour after the debate, Google Trends reported a 700 percent spike in searches for "Polish workers." "We rate Rubio's claim Half True," PolitiFact reported. But what you saw when you Google "Polish workers" was a function of, among other things, your language, your location, and your personal web history. Reason can't defend itself. Neither can Google.

TRUMP DIDN'T REASON. He was a lot like that kid who stole my bat. He wanted combat. Cruz's appeal was to the judgment of God. "Father God, please . . . awaken the body of Christ, that we might pull back from the abyss," he preached on the campaign trail. Rubio's appeal was to Google.

Is there another appeal? People who care about civil society have two choices: find some epistemic principles other than empiricism on which everyone can agree or else find some method other than reason with which to defend empiricism. Lynch suspected that doing the first of these things is not possible, but that the second might be. He thought the best defense of reason is a common practical and ethical commitment. I believe he means popular sovereignty. That, anyway, is what Alexander Hamilton meant in *The Federalist Papers*, when he explained that the United States is an act of empirical inquiry: "It seems to have been reserved to the people of this country, by their conduct and example, to decide the important question, whether societies of men are really capable or not of establishing good government from reflection and choice, or whether they are forever destined to depend for their political constitutions on accident and force." The evidence is not yet in.

—2016

Postscript: Trump won the nomination and the election in 2016, and when he lost in 2020, his former Republican challengers failed to dispute his claim, a lie, that he had, in fact, won.

HARD NEWS

T HE WOOD-PANELED TAILGATE OF THE 1972 OLDS-
mobile station wagon dangled open like a broken jaw, making a wobbly bench on which four kids could sit, eight legs swinging.
Every Sunday morning, long before dawn, we'd get yanked out of bed
to stuff the car's way-back with stacks of twine-tied newspapers, clam-
ber onto the tailgate, cut the twine with my mother's sewing scissors,
and ride around town, bouncing along on that bench, while my father
shouted out orders from the driver's seat. "Watch out for the dog!" he'd
holler between draws on his pipe. "Inside the screen door!" "Mailbox!" As the car crept along, never stopping, we'd each grab a paper
and dash in the dark across icy driveways or dew-drunk grass, crash-
ing, seasonally, into unexpected snowmen. "Back porch!" "Money
under the mat!" He kept a list, scrawled on the back of an envelope,
taped to the dashboard: the Accounts. "They owe three weeks!" He
didn't need to remind us. We knew each Doberman and every debt.
We'd deliver our papers—*Worcester Sunday Telegrams*—and then run
back to the car and scramble onto the tailgate, dropping the coins we'd
collected into empty Briggs tobacco tins as we bumped along to the
next turn, the newspaper route our Sabbath.

The *Worcester Sunday Telegram* was founded in 1884, when a telegram meant something fast. Two years later, it became a daily. It was
never a great paper but it was always a pretty good paper: useful, gos-
sipy, and resolute. It cultivated talent. The poet Stanley Kunitz was a
staff writer for the *Telegram* in the 1920s. The *New York Times* reporter
Douglas Kneeland, who covered Kent State and Charles Manson,
began his career there in the 1950s. Joe McGinniss reported for the
Telegram in the 1960s before writing *The Selling of the President*. From
bushy-bearded nineteenth-century politicians to baby-faced George
W. Bush, the paper was steadfastly Republican, if mainly concerned
with scandals and mustachioed villains close to home: overdue repairs

to the main branch of the public library, police raids on illegal betting establishments—"Worcester Dog Chases Worcester Cat Over Worcester Fence," as the old Washington press corps joke about a typical headline in a local paper goes. Its pages rolled off giant, thrumming presses in a four-story building that overlooked city hall the way every city paper used to look out over every city hall, the Bat-Signal over Gotham.

Most newspapers like that haven't lasted. Between 1970 and 2016, the year the American Society of News Editors quit counting, five hundred or so dailies went out of business; the rest cut news coverage, or shrank the paper's size, or stopped producing a print edition, or did all of that, and it still wasn't enough. The newspaper mortality rate is old news, and nostalgia for dead papers is itself pitiful at this point, even though, I still say, there's a principle involved. "I wouldn't weep about a shoe factory or a branch-line railroad shutting down," Heywood Broun, the founder of the American Newspaper Guild, said when the *New York World* went out of business, in 1931. "But newspapers are different." And the bleeding hasn't stopped. Between January 2017 and April 2018, a third of the nation's largest newspapers, including the *Denver Post* and the *San Jose Mercury News*, reported layoffs. In a newer trend, so did about a quarter of digital-native news sites. *BuzzFeed News* laid off a hundred people in 2017; speculation is that *BuzzFeed* is trying to dump it. The *Huffington Post* paid most of its writers nothing for years, upping that recently to just above nothing, and yet, despite taking in tens of millions of dollars in advertising revenue in 2018, it failed to turn a profit.

Even veterans of august and still thriving papers are worried, especially about the fake news that's risen from the ashes of the dead news. "We are, for the first time in modern history, facing the prospect of how societies would exist without reliable news," Alan Rusbridger, for twenty years the editor in chief of the *Guardian*, writes in *Breaking News: The Remaking of Journalism and Why It Matters Now*. "There are not that many places left that do quality news well or even aim to do it at all," Jill Abramson, a former executive editor of the *New York Times*, writes in *Merchants of Truth: The Business of News and the Fight for Facts*. Like most big-paper reporters and editors who write about the crisis of journalism, Rusbridger and Abramson are interested in national and international news organizations. The local story is worse.

First came conglomeration. Worcester, Massachusetts, the second-largest city in New England, used to have four dailies: the *Telegram*, in the morning, and the *Gazette*, in the evening (under the same ownership), the *Spy*, and the *Post*. Now it has one. The last great laying waste to American newspapers came in the early decades of the twentieth century, mainly owing to (a) radio and (b) the Depression; the number of dailies fell from 2,042 in 1920 to 1,754 in 1944, leaving 1,103 cities with only one paper. Newspaper circulation rose between 1940 and 1990, but likely only because more people were reading fewer papers, and, as A. J. Liebling once observed, nothing is crummier than a one-paper town. In 1949, after yet another New York daily closed its doors, Liebling predicted, "If the trend continues, New York will be a one- or two-paper town by about 1975." He wasn't that far off. In the 1980s and '90s, as Christopher B. Daly reports in *Covering America: A Narrative History of the Nation's Journalism*, "the big kept getting bigger." Conglomeration can be good for business, but it has generally been bad for journalism. Media companies that want to get bigger tend to swallow up other media companies, suppressing competition and taking on debt, which makes publishers cowards. In 1986, the publisher of the *San Francisco Chronicle* bought the *Worcester Telegram* and the *Evening Gazette*, and, three years later, right about when Time and Warner became Time Warner, the *Telegram* and the *Gazette* became the *Telegram & Gazette*, or the *T&G*, smaller fries but the same potato.

Next came the dot-coms. Craigslist went online in the Bay Area in 1996 and spread across the continent like a weed, choking off local newspapers' most reliable source of revenue: classified ads. The *T&G* tried to hold on to its classified advertising section by wading into the shallow waters of the internet, at telegram.com, where it was called, acronymically, and not a little desperately, "TANGO!" Then began yet another round of corporate buyouts, deeply leveraged deals conducted by executives answerable to stockholders seeking higher dividends, not better papers. In 1999, the New York Times Company bought the *T&G* for nearly three hundred million dollars. By 2000, only three hundred and fifty of the fifteen hundred daily newspapers left in the United States were independently owned. And only one out of every hundred American cities that had a daily newspaper was anything other than a one-paper town.

Then came the fall, when papers all over the country, shackled to mammoth corporations and a lumbering, century-old business model, found themselves unable to compete with the upstarts—online news aggregators like the *Huffington Post* (est. 2005) and Breitbart News (est. 2007), which were, to readers, free. News aggregators also drew display advertisers away from print; Facebook and Google swallowed advertising accounts whole. Big papers found ways to adapt; smaller papers mainly folded. Between 1994 and 2016, years when the population of Worcester County rose by more than a hundred thousand, daily home delivery of the *T&G* declined from more than a hundred and twenty thousand to barely thirty thousand. In one year alone, circulation fell by 29 percent. In 2012, after another round of layoffs, the *T&G* left its building, its much reduced staff small enough to fit into two floors of an office building nearby. The next year, the owner of the Boston Red Sox bought the newspaper, along with the *Boston Globe*, from the New York Times Company for seventy million dollars, only to unload the *T&G* less than a year later, for seventeen million dollars, to Halifax Media Group, which held it for only half a year before Halifax itself was bought, flea market–style, by an entity that calls itself, unironically, the New Media Investment Group.

The numbers mask an uglier story. In the past half century, and especially in the past two decades, journalism itself—the way news is covered, reported, written, and edited—has changed, including in ways that have made possible the rise of fake news, and not only because of mergers and acquisitions, and corporate ownership, and job losses, and Google Search, and Facebook and *BuzzFeed*. There's no shortage of amazing journalists at work, clear-eyed and courageous, broad-minded and brilliant, and no end of fascinating innovation in matters of form, especially in visual storytelling. Still, journalism, as a field, is as addled as an addict, gaunt, wasted, and twitchy, its pockets as empty as its nights are sleepless. It's faster than it used to be, so fast. It's also edgier, and needier, and angrier. It wants and it wants and it wants. But what does it need?

THE DAILY NEWSPAPER IS THE TAPROOT of modern journalism. Dailies mainly date to the 1830s, the decade in which the word "journalism" was coined, meaning daily reporting, the *jour* in journalism. Early dailies depended on subscribers to pay the bills. The press was partisan, readers were voters, and the news was meant to persuade (and voter turnout was high). But by 1900 advertising made up more than two-thirds of the revenue at most of the nation's eighteen thousand newspapers, and readers were consumers (and voter turnout began its long fall). "The newspaper is not a missionary or a charitable institution, but a business that collects and publishes news which the people want and are willing to buy," one Missouri editor said in 1892. Newspapers stopped rousing the rabble so much because businesses wanted readers, no matter their politics. "There is a sentiment gaining ground to the effect that the public wants its politics 'straight,'" a journalist wrote the following year. Reporters pledged themselves to "facts, facts, and more facts," and, as the press got less partisan and more ad-based, newspapers sorted themselves out not by their readers' political leanings but by their incomes. If you had a lot of money to spend, you read the *St. Paul Pioneer Press*; if you didn't have very much, you read the *St. Paul Dispatch*.

Unsurprisingly, critics soon began writing big books, usually indictments, about the relationship between business and journalism. "When you read your daily paper, are you reading facts or propaganda?" Upton Sinclair asked on the jacket of *The Brass Check*, in 1919. In *The Disappearing Daily*, in 1944, Oswald Garrison Villard mourned "what was once a profession but is now a business." The big book that inspired Jill Abramson to become a journalist was David Halberstam's *The Powers That Be*, from 1979, a history of the rise of the modern, corporate-based media in the middle decades of the twentieth century. Halberstam, who won a Pulitzer Prize in 1964 for his reporting from Vietnam for the *New York Times*, took up his story more or less where Villard left off. He began with FDR and CBS radio; added the *Los Angeles Times*, Time Inc., and CBS television; and reached his story's climax with the *Washington Post* and the *New York Times* and the publication of the Pentagon Papers, in 1971.

Halberstam argued that between the 1930s and the 1970s radio and television brought a new immediacy to reporting, while the resources provided by corporate owners and the demands made by an increasingly sophisticated national audience led to harder-hitting, investigative, adversarial reporting, the kind that could end a war and bring down a president. Richard Rovere summed it up best: "What the *Los Angeles Times*, the *Washington Post*, *Time* and CBS have in common is that, under pressures generated internally and externally, they moved from venality or parochialism or mediocrity or all three to something approaching journalistic excellence and responsibility." That move came at a price. "Watergate, like Vietnam, had obscured one of the central new facts about the role of journalism in America," Halberstam wrote. "Only very rich, very powerful corporate institutions like these had the impact, the reach, and above all the resources to challenge the President of the United States."

There's reach, and then there's reach. When I was growing up, in the 1970s, nobody I knew read the *New York Times*, the *Washington Post*, or the *Wall Street Journal*. Nobody I knew even read the *Boston Globe*, a paper that used to have a rule that no piece should ever be so critical of anyone that its "writer could not shake hands the next day with the man about whom he had written." After journalism put up its dukes, my father only ever referred to the *Globe* as "that communist rag," not least because, in 1967, it became the first major paper in the United States to come out against the Vietnam War.

The view of the new journalism held by people like my father escaped Halberstam's notice. In 1969, Nixon's vice president, Spiro Agnew, delivered a speech drafted by the Nixon aide Pat Buchanan accusing the press of liberal bias. It's "good politics for us to kick the press around," Nixon is said to have told his staff. The press, Agnew said, represents "a concentration of power over American public opinion unknown in history," consisting of men who "read the same newspapers" and "talk constantly to one another." How dare they. Halberstam waved this aside as so much PR hooey, but, as has since become clear, Agnew reached a ready audience, especially in houses like mine.

Spiro who? "The press regarded Agnew with uncontrolled hilarity," Arthur Schlesinger Jr. observed in 1970, but "no one can question the force of Spiro T. Agnew's personality, nor the impact of his speeches." No scholar of journalism can afford to ignore Agnew anymore. In *On Press: The Liberal Values That Shaped the News*, the historian Matthew Pressman argues that any understanding of the crisis of journalism in the twenty-first century has to begin by vanquishing the ghost of Spiro T. Agnew.

For Pressman, the pivotal period for the modern newsroom is what Abramson calls "Halberstam's golden age," between 1960 and 1980, and its signal feature was the adoption not of a liberal bias but of liberal values: "Interpretation replaced transmission, and adversarialism replaced deference." In 1960, nine out of every ten articles in the *Times* about the presidential election were descriptive; by 1976, more than half were interpretative. This turn was partly a consequence of television— people who simply wanted to find out what happened could watch television, so newspapers had to offer something else—and partly a consequence of McCarthyism. "The rise of McCarthy has compelled newspapers of integrity to develop a form of reporting which puts into context what men like McCarthy have to say," the radio commentator Elmer Davis said in 1953. Five years later, the *Times* added "News Analysis" as a story category. "Once upon a time, news stories were like tape recorders," the *Bulletin of the American Society of Newspaper Editors* commented in 1963. "No more. A whole generation of events had taught us better—Hitler and Goebbels, Stalin and McCarthy, automation and analog computers and missiles."

These changes weren't ideologically driven, Pressman insists, but they had ideological consequences. At the start, leading conservatives approved. "To keep a reporter's prejudices out of a story is commendable," Irving Kristol wrote in 1967. "To keep his judgment out of a story is to guarantee that the truth will be emasculated." After the *Times* and the *Post* published the Pentagon Papers, Kristol changed his spots. Journalists, he complained in 1972, were now "engaged in a perpetual confrontation with the social and political order (the 'establishment,' as they say)." By 1975, after Watergate, Kristol was insisting that "most journalists today . . . are 'liberals.'" With that, the conservative attack on the press was off and running, all the way to Trumpism—"the failing New York Times," "CNN is fake news," the press is "the true enemy of the people"—and, in a revolution-devouring-its-elders sort of way, the shutting down of William Kristol's *Weekly Standard*, in December 2018. "The pathetic and dishonest Weekly Standard . . . is flat broke and out of business," Trump tweeted. "May it rest in peace!"

WHAT MCCARTHY AND TELEVISION were for journalism in the 1950s, Trump and social media would be in the 2010s: license to change the rules. Halberstam's golden age, or what he called "journalism's high-water mark," ended about 1980. Abramson's analysis in *Merchants of Truth* begins with journalism's low-water mark, in 2007, the year after Facebook launched its News Feed, "the year everything began to fall apart."

Merchants of Truth isn't just inspired by *The Powers That Be*; it's modeled on it. Abramson's book follows Halberstam's structure and mimics its style, chronicling the history of a handful of nationally prominent media organizations—in her case, *BuzzFeed*, *Vice*, the *Times*, and the *Washington Post*—in alternating chapters that are driven by character sketches and reported scenes. The book is saturated with a lot of gossip and glitz, including details about the restaurants the powers that be frequent, and what they wear ("Sulzberger"—the *Times*'s publisher—"dressed in suits from Bloomingdale's, stylish without being ostentatiously bespoke, and wore suspenders before they went out of fashion"), alongside crucial insights about structural transformations, like how web and social media publishing "unbundled" the newspaper, so that readers who used to find a fat newspaper on their front porch could, on their phones, look, instead, at only one story. "Each individual article now lived on its own page, where it had a unique URL and could be shared, and spread virally," Abramson observes. "This put stories, rather than papers, in competition with one another."

This history is a chronicle of missed opportunities, missteps, and lessons learned the hard way. As long ago as 1992, an internal report at the *Washington Post* urged the mounting of an "electronic product": "The *Post* ought to be in the forefront of this." Early on, the *Guardian* started a New Media lab, which struck a lot of people as frivolous, Rusbridger writes, because, at the time, "only 3 per cent of households owned a PC and a modem," a situation not unlike that at the *Guardian*'s own offices, where "it was rumored that downstairs a bloke called Paul in IT had a Mac connected to the internet." A 1996 business plan for the *Guardian* concluded that the priority was print, and the London *Times* editor Simon Jenkins predicted, "The Internet will strut an hour upon the stage, and then take its place in the ranks of the lesser media." In 2005, the *Post* lost a chance at a 10 percent investment in Facebook, whose returns, as Abramson points out, would have floated the newspaper for decades. The CEO of the Washington Post Company, Don

Graham, and Mark Zuckerberg shook hands over the deal, making a verbal contract, but, when Zuckerberg weaseled out of it to take a better offer, Graham, out of kindness to a young fella just starting out, simply let him walk away. The next year, the *Post* shrugged off a proposal from two of its star political reporters to start a spinoff website; they went on to found *Politico*. The *Times*, Abramson writes, declined an early chance to invest in Google, and was left to throw the kitchen sink at its failing business model, including adding a Thursday Style section to attract more high-end advertising revenue. Bill Keller, then the newspaper's editor, said, "If luxury porn is what saves the Baghdad bureau, so be it."

More alarming than what the *Times* and the *Post* failed to do was how so much of what they did do was determined less by their own editors than by executives at Facebook and *BuzzFeed*. If journalism has been reinvented during the past two decades, it has, in the main, been reinvented not by reporters and editors but by tech companies, in a sequence of events that, in Abramson's harrowing telling, resemble a series of puerile stunts more than acts of public service.

Who even are these people? *Merchants of Truth* has been charged with factual errors, including by people Abramson interviewed, especially younger journalists. She can also be maddeningly condescending. She doffs her cap at Sulzberger, with his natty suspenders, but dismisses younger reporters at places like *Vice* as notable mainly for being "impossibly hip, with interesting hair." This is distracting, and too bad, because there is a changing of the guard worth noting, and it's not incidental: it's critical. All the way through to the 1980s, all sorts of journalists, including magazine, radio, and television reporters, got their start working on daily papers, learning the ropes and the rules. Rusbridger started out in 1976 as a reporter at the *Cambridge Evening News*, which covered stories that included a petition about a pedestrian crossing and a root vegetable that looked like Winston Churchill. In the UK, a reporter who wanted to go to Fleet Street had first to work for three years on a provincial newspaper, pounding the pavement. Much the same applied in the U.S., where a cub reporter did time at the *Des Moines Register*, or the *Worcester Telegram*, before moving up to the *New York Times* or the *Herald Tribune*. Beat reporting, however, is not the backstory of the people who, beginning in the 1990s, built the New Media.

Jonah Peretti started out soaking up postmodern theory at UC Santa Cruz in the mid-1990s, and later published a scholarly journal article about the scrambled, disjointed, and incoherent way of thinking produced by accelerated visual experiences under late capitalism. Or something like that. Imagine an article written by that American Studies professor in Don DeLillo's *White Noise*. Peretti thought that watching a lot of MTV can mess with your head—"The rapid fire succession of signifiers in MTV style media erodes the viewer's sense of temporal continuity"—leaving you confused, stupid, and lonely. "Capitalism needs schizophrenia, but it also needs egos," Peretti wrote. "The contradiction is resolved through the acceleration of the temporal rhythm of late capitalist visual culture. This type of acceleration encourages weak egos that are easily formed, and fade away just as easily." Voilà, a business plan!

Peretti's career in viral content began in 2001, with a prank involving email and Nike sneakers while he was a graduate student at the MIT Media Lab. (Peretti ordered custom sneakers embroidered with the word "sweatshop" and then circulated Nike's reply.) In 2005, a year the New York Times Company laid off five hundred employees and the *Post* began paying people to retire early, Peretti joined Andrew Breitbart, a Matt Drudge acolyte, and Ken Lerer, a former PR guy at AOL Time Warner, in helping Arianna Huffington, a millionaire and a former anti-feminist polemicist, launch the *Huffington Post*. Peretti was in charge of innovations that included a click-o-meter. Within a couple of years, the *Huffington Post* had more web traffic than the *Los Angeles Times*, the *Washington Post*, and the *Wall Street Journal*. Its business was banditry. Abramson writes that when the *Times* published a deeply reported exclusive story about WikiLeaks, which took months of investigative work and a great deal of money, the *Huffington Post* published its own version of the story, using the same headline—and beat out the *Times* story in Google rankings. "We were learning that the internet behaved like a clattering of jackdaws," Rusbridger writes. "Nothing remained exclusive for more than two minutes."

Pretty soon, there were jackdaws all over the place, with their schizophrenic late-capitalist accelerated signifiers. Breitbart left the *Huffington Post* and started Breitbart News around the same time that Peretti left to focus on his own company, Contagious Media, from which he launched *BuzzFeed*, where he tested the limits of virality with offerings like the seven best links about gay penguins and "YouTube Porn Hacks." He explained his methods in a pitch to venture capitalists: "Raw buzz is automatically published the moment it is detected by our algorithm," and "the future of the industry is advertising as content."

Facebook launched its News Feed in 2006. In 2008, Peretti mused on Facebook, "Thinking about the economics of the news business." The company added its Like button in 2009. Peretti set likability as *BuzzFeed*'s goal, and, to perfect the instruments for measuring it, he enlisted partners, including the *Times* and the *Guardian*, to share their data with him in exchange for his reports on their metrics. Lists were liked. Hating people was liked. And it turned out that news, which is full of people who hate other people, can be crammed into lists.

Chartbeat, a "content intelligence" company founded in 2009, launched a feature called Newsbeat in 2011. Chartbeat offers real-time web analytics, displaying a constantly updated report on web traffic that tells editors what stories people are reading and what stories they're skipping. The *Post* winnowed out reporters based on their Chartbeat numbers. At the offices of Gawker, the Chartbeat dashboard was displayed on a giant screen.

In 2011, Peretti launched *BuzzFeed News*, hiring a thirty-five-year-old *Politico* journalist, Ben Smith, as its editor in chief. Smith asked for a "scoop-a-day" from his reporters, who, he told Abramson, had little interest in the rules of journalism: "They didn't even know what rules they were breaking." In 2012, *BuzzFeed* introduced three new one-click ways for readers to respond to stories, beyond "liking" them—LOL, OMG, and WTF—and ran lists like "10 Reasons Everyone Should Be Furious About Trayvon Martin's Murder," in which, as Abramson explains, *BuzzFeed* "simply lifted what it needed from reports published elsewhere, repackaged the information, and presented it in a way that emphasized sentiment and celebrity." *Buzz-Feed* makes a distinction between *BuzzFeed* and *BuzzFeed News*, just as newspapers and magazines draw distinctions between their print and their digital editions. These distinctions are lost on most readers. *Buzz-Feed News* covered the Trayvon Martin story, but its information, like *BuzzFeed*'s, came from Reuters and the Associated Press.

Even as news organizations were pruning reporters and editors,

Facebook was pruning its users' news, with the commercially appealing but ethically indefensible idea that people should see only the news they want to see. In 2013, Silicon Valley began reading its own online newspaper, the Information, its high-priced subscription peddled to the information elite, following the motto "Quality stories breed quality subscribers." Facebook's goal, Zuckerberg explained in 2014, was to "build the perfect personalized newspaper for every person in the world." Ripples at Facebook create tsunamis in newsrooms. The ambitious news site Mic relied on Facebook to reach an audience through a video program called Mic Dispatch, on Facebook Watch; after Facebook suggested that it would drop the program, Mic collapsed. Every time Facebook News tweaks its algorithm—tweaks made for commercial, not editorial, reasons—news organizations drown in the undertow. An automated Facebook feature called Trending Topics, introduced in 2014, turned out to mainly identify junk as trends, and so "news curators," who tended to be recent college graduates, were given a new, manual mandate, "massage the algorithm," which meant deciding, themselves, which stories mattered. The fake news that roiled the 2016 election? A lot of that was stuff on Trending Topics. (In 2018, Facebook discontinued the feature.)

BuzzFeed surpassed the Times website in reader traffic in 2013. BuzzFeed News is subsidized by BuzzFeed, which, like many websites—including, at this point, those of most major news organizations—makes money by way of "native advertising," ads that look like articles. In some publications, these fake stories are easy to spot; in others, they're not. At BuzzFeed, they're in the same font as every other story. BuzzFeed's native-advertising bounty meant that BuzzFeed News had money to pay reporters and editors, and it began producing some very good and very serious reporting, real news having become something of a luxury good. By 2014, BuzzFeed employed a hundred and fifty journalists, including many foreign correspondents. It was obsessed with Donald Trump's rumored presidential bid, and followed him on what it called the "fake campaign trail" as early as January 2014. "It used to be the New York Times, now it's BuzzFeed," Trump said wistfully. "The world has changed." At the time, Steve Bannon was stumping for Trump on Breitbart. Left or right, a Trump presidency was just the sort of story that could rack up the LOLs, OMGs, and WTFs. It still is.

In March 2014, the *Times* produced an "Innovation" report, announcing that the newspaper had fallen behind in "the art and science of getting our journalism to readers," a field led by *BuzzFeed*. That May, Sulzberger fired Abramson, who had been less than all-in about the *Times* doing things like running native ads. Meanwhile, *BuzzFeed* purged from its website more than four thousand of its early stories. "It's stuff made at a time when people were really not thinking of themselves as doing journalism," Ben Smith explained. Not long afterward, the *Times* began running more lists, from book recommendations to fitness tips to takeaways from presidential debates.

The *Times* remains unrivaled. It staffs bureaus all over the globe and sends reporters to some of the world's most dangerous places. It has more than a dozen reporters in China alone. Nevertheless, *Buzz-Feed News* became more like the *Times*, and the *Times* became more like *BuzzFeed*, because readers, as Chartbeat announced on its endlessly flickering dashboards, wanted lists, and luxury porn, and people to hate.

THE GUARDIAN, founded as the *Manchester Guardian* in 1821, has been held by a philanthropic trust since 1936, which somewhat insulates it from market forces, just as Jeff Bezos's ownership now does something similar for the *Post*. By investing in digital-readership research from the time Rusbridger took charge, in 1995, the *Guardian* became, for a while, the online market leader in the UK. By 2006, two-thirds of its digital readers were outside the UK. In 2007, the *Guardian* undertook what Rusbridger calls "the Great Integration," pulling its web and print parts together into a single news organization, with the same editorial management. It also developed a theory about the relationship between print and digital, deciding, in 2011, to be a "digital-first organization" and to "make print a slower, more reflective read which would not aspire to cover the entire waterfront in news."

Rusbridger explains, with a palpable grief, his dawning realization that the rise of social media meant that "chaotic information was free: good information was expensive," which meant, in turn, that "good information was increasingly for smaller elites" and that "it was harder for good information to compete on equal terms with bad." He takes these circumstances as something of a dare: "Our generation had been handed the challenge of rethinking almost everything societies had, for centuries, taken for granted about journalism."

Has that challenge been met? The *Guardian's* own success is mixed. As of 2018, it was in the black, partly by relying on philanthropy, especially in the U.S. "Reader revenue," in the form of donations marked not as subscriptions but as voluntary "memberships," is expected to overtake advertising revenue before long. Raising money from people who care about journalism has allowed the *Guardian* to keep the website free. It's also broken some big stories, from the Murdoch papers phone hacking scoop to the saga of Edward Snowden, and provided riveting coverage of ongoing and urgent stories, especially climate change. But, for all its fine reporting and substantive "long reads," the paper consists disproportionately of ideologically unvarying opinion essays. By some measures, journalism entered a new, Trumpian, gold-plated age during the 2016 campaign, with the Trump bump, when news organizations found that the more they featured Trump the better their Chartbeat numbers, which, arguably, is a lot of what got him elected. The bump swelled into a lump and, later, a malignant tumor, a carcinoma the size of Cleveland. Within three weeks of the election, the *Times* added 132,000 new subscribers. (This effect hasn't extended to local papers.) News organizations all over the world now advertise their services as the remedy to Trumpism, and to fake news; fighting Voldemort and his Dark Arts is a good way to rake in readers. And scrutiny of the administration has produced excellent work, the very best of journalism. "How President Trump Is Saving Journalism," a 2017 post on Forbes.com, marked Trump as the Nixon to today's rising generation of Woodwards and Bernsteins. Superb investigative reporting is published every day, by news organizations both old and new, including *BuzzFeed News*.

By the what-doesn't-kill-you line of argument, the more forcefully Trump attacks the press, the stronger the press becomes. Unfortunately, that's not the full story. All kinds of editorial decisions are now outsourced to Facebook's News Feed, Chartbeat, or other forms of editorial automation, while the hands of many flesh-and-blood editors are tied to so many algorithms. For one reason and another, including twenty-first-century journalism's breakneck pace, stories now routinely appear that might not have been published a generation ago, prompting contention within the reportorial ranks. In 2016, when *BuzzFeed News* released the Steele dossier, many journalists disapproved, including CNN's Jake Tapper, who got his start as a reporter for the *Washington City Paper*. "It is irresponsible to put uncorroborated information on the internet," Tapper said. "It's why we did not publish it, and why we did not detail any specifics from it, because it was uncorroborated, and that's not what we do." The *Times* veered from its normal practices when it published an anonymous opinion essay by a senior official in the Trump administration. And *The New Yorker* posted a story online about Brett Kavanaugh's behavior when he was an undergraduate at Yale, which Republicans in the Senate pointed to as evidence of a liberal conspiracy against the nominee.

There's plenty of room to argue over these matters of editorial judgment. Reasonable people disagree. Occasionally, those disagreements fall along a generational divide. Younger journalists often chafe against editorial restraint, not least because their cohort is far more likely than senior newsroom staff to include people from groups that have been explicitly and viciously targeted by Trump and the policies of his administration, a long and growing list that includes people of color, women, immigrants, Muslims, members of the LGBTQ community, and anyone with family in Haiti or any of the other countries Trump deemed "shitholes." Sometimes younger people are courageous and sometimes they are heedless and sometimes those two things are the same. "The more 'woke' staff thought that urgent times called for urgent measures," Abramson writes, and that "the dangers of Trump's presidency obviated the old standards." Still, by no means is the divide always or even usually generational. Abramson, for instance, sided with *BuzzFeed News* about the Steele dossier, just as she approves of the use of the word "lie" to refer to Trump's lies, which, by the *Post*'s reckoning, came at the rate of more than a dozen a day in 2018.

The broader problem is that the depravity, mendacity, vulgarity, and menace of the Trump administration put a lot of people, including reporters and editors, off their stride. The Trump-era crisis, which was nothing less than a derangement of American life, has caused many people in journalism to make decisions they regret, or might yet. In the age of Facebook, Chartbeat, and Trump, legacy news organizations, hardly less than startups, violated or changed their editorial standards in ways that contributed to political chaos and epistemological mayhem. Did editors sit in a room on Monday morning, twirl the globe, and decide what stories are most important? Or did they watch Trump's Twitter feed and let him decide? It often felt like the latter. Sometimes what doesn't kill you doesn't make you stronger; it makes everyone sick. The more adversarial the press, the more loyal Trump's followers, the more broken American public life. The more desperately the press chased readers, the more our press resembled our politics.

The problems are well understood, the solutions harder to see. Good reporting is expensive, but readers don't want to pay for it. The donation-funded *ProPublica*, "an independent, nonprofit newsroom that produces investigative journalism with moral force," employed more than seventy-five journalists. Good reporting is slow, good stories unfold, and most stories that need telling don't involve the White House. The Correspondent, an English-language version of the Dutch website De Correspondent, tried to "unbreak the news." It didn't run ads. It didn't collect data (or at least not much). It didn't have subscribers. Like NPR, it was free for everyone, supported by members, who paid what they could. "We want to radically change what news is about, how it is made, and how it is funded," its founders stated. Push-notifications-on news is bad for you, they say, "because it pays more attention to the sensational, exceptional, negative, recent, and incidental, thereby losing sight of the ordinary, usual, positive, historical, and systematic." What would the Correspondent look like? It would stay above the fray. It might sometimes be funny. It was slated to debut sometime in 2019. Aside from the thing about ads, it sounds a lot like a magazine, when magazines came in the mail.

AFTER WE'D SHOVED THE LAST, fat *Worcester Sunday Telegram* inside the last, unlatched screen door, we'd head home, my father taking turns a little too fast, so that we'd have to clutch at one another and at the lip of the tailgate, to keep from falling off. "Dad, slow down!" we'd squeal, not meaning it. Then he'd make breakfast, hot chocolate with marshmallows in the winter, orange juice from a can of frozen concentrate in the summer, and on my plate I'd make wedges of cantaloupe into Viking ships sailing across a sea of maple syrup from the Coast of Bacon to Pancake Island. After breakfast, we'd dump the money from the tobacco tins onto the kitchen table and count coins, stacking quarters and nickels and dimes into wrappers from the Worcester County Institution for Savings, while my father updated the Accounts, and made the Collection List.

Going collecting was a drag. You had to knock on people's doors and ask your neighbors for money—"*Telegram!* Collecting!"—and it was embarrassing, and, half the time, they'd ask you in, and before you knew it you'd be helping out, and it would take all day. "So long as you're here, could you hold the baby while I take a quick shower?" "Honey, after this, could you bring my mail down to the post office on that cute little bike of yours?" I came to understand that the people who didn't leave the money under the mat hadn't forgotten to. They just liked having a kid visit on Sunday afternoon.

The death of a newspaper is sometimes like other deaths. The Mrs. and the Miss, a very, very old woman and her very old daughter, lived in a crooked green house on top of a rise and wore matching house-coats and slippers. The Miss followed the Mrs. around like a puppy, and, if you found them in the parlor reading the paper, the Mrs. would be poring over the opinion pages while the Miss cut pictures out of the funnies. "The Miss can't think straight," my father said. "Her head's scrambled. So be gentle with her. Nothing to be afraid of. Be sure to help them out." Once when I biked over there, the Miss was standing, keening, noise without words, sound without sense. The Mrs. wasn't moving, and she wasn't ever going to move again. I called for help and held the Miss's hand, waiting for the wail of sirens. I didn't know what else to do.

—2019

Part Five

Battleground America

When carrying a concealed weapon for self-defense is understood not as a failure of civil society, to be mourned, but as an act of citizenship, to be vaunted, there is little civilian life left.

Brooklyn, 1964.

Photograph by Stanley Wolfson / Library of Congress

BATTLEGROUND AMERICA

JUST AFTER SEVEN THIRTY ON THE MORNING OF FEB-
ruary 27, 2012, a seventeen-year-old boy named T. J. Lane
walked into the cafeteria at Chardon High School, about thirty miles
outside Cleveland. It was a Monday, and the cafeteria was filled with
kids, some eating breakfast, some waiting for buses to drive them to
programs at other schools, some packing up for gym class. Lane sat
down at an empty table, reached into a bag, and pulled out a .22-caliber
pistol. He stood up, raised the gun, and fired. He said not a word.

Russell King, a seventeen-year-old junior, was sitting at a table with
another junior, Nate Mueller. King, shot in the head, fell face first
onto the table, a pool of blood forming. A bullet grazed Mueller's ear.
"I could see the flame at the end of the gun," Mueller said later. Daniel Parmertor, a sixteen-year-old snowboarder, was shot in the head.
Someone screamed "Duck!" Demetrius Hewlin, sixteen, was also shot
in the head, and slid under the table. Joy Rickers, a senior, tried to
run; Lane shot her as she fled. Nickolas Walczak, shot in his neck, arm,
back, and face, fell to the floor. He began crawling toward the door.

Ever since the shootings at Columbine High School, in a Denver
suburb, in 1999, American schools have been preparing for gunmen.
Chardon started holding drills in 2007, after the Virginia Tech massacre, when twenty-three-year-old Seung-Hui Cho, a college senior,
shot fifty-seven people in Blacksburg.

At Chardon High School, kids ran through the halls screaming
"Lockdown!" Some of them hid in the teachers' lounge; they bar-
ricaded the door with a piano. Someone got on the school's public-
address system and gave instructions, but everyone knew what to do.
Students ran into classrooms and dived under desks; teachers locked the
doors and shut off the lights. Joseph Ricci, a math teacher, heard Walczak, who was still crawling, groaning in the hallway. Ricci opened
the door and pulled the boy inside. No one knew if the shooter had

more guns, or more rounds. Huddled under desks, students called 911 and texted their parents. One tapped out, "Prayforus."

From the cafeteria, Frank Hall, the assistant football coach, chased Lane out of the building, and he ran off into the woods.

Moments later, four ambulances arrived. EMTs raced Rickers and Walczak to Chardon's Hillcrest Hospital. Hewlin, Parmertor, and King were flown by helicopter to a trauma center at MetroHealth Medical Center, in Cleveland. By eight thirty, the high school had been evacuated.

At a quarter to nine, police officers with dogs captured Lane, about a mile from the school.

"I hate to say it, but we trained for exactly this type of thing, a school emergency of this type," Dan McClelland, the county sheriff, said.

Danny Parmertor died that afternoon. That evening, St. Mary's Church opened its doors, and the people of Chardon sank to their knees and keened. At the town square, students gathered to hold a vigil. As night fell, they lit candles. Drew Gittins, sixteen, played a Black Eyed Peas song on his guitar. "People killin', people dyin'," he sang. "People got me, got me questionin', Where is the love?"

Russell King had been too badly wounded. A little after midnight, doctors said that they couldn't save him.

IN 2012, there were nearly three hundred million privately owned firearms in the United States: a hundred and six million handguns, a hundred and five million rifles, and eighty-three million shotguns. That works out to about one gun for every American. The gun that T. J. Lane brought to Chardon High School belonged to his uncle, who had bought it in 2010, at a gun shop. Both of Lane's parents had been arrested on charges of domestic violence over the years. Lane found the gun in his grandfather's barn.

The United States is the country with the highest rate of civilian gun ownership in the world. (The second highest is Yemen, where the rate is nevertheless only half that of the U.S.) No civilian population is more powerfully armed. Most Americans do not, however, own guns, because three-quarters of people with guns own two or more. According to the General Social Survey, conducted by the National Policy Opinion Center at the University of Chicago, the prevalence of gun ownership has declined steadily in the past few decades. In 1973, there were guns in roughly one in two households in the United States; in 2010, one in three. In 1980, nearly one in three Americans owned a gun; in 2010, that figure had dropped to one in five.

Men are far more likely to own guns than women are, but the rate of gun ownership among men fell from one in two in 1980 to one in three in 2010, while, in that same stretch of time, the rate among women remained one in ten. What may have held that rate steady in an age of decline was the aggressive marketing of handguns to women for self-defense, which is how a great many guns are marketed. Gun ownership is higher among whites than among blacks, higher in the country than in the city, and higher among older people than among younger people. One reason that gun ownership was declining, nationwide, might be that high school shooting clubs and rifle ranges at summer camps were no longer common.

Although rates of gun ownership, like rates of violent crime, were falling, the power of the gun lobby was not. Between 1980 and 2012, forty-four states passed some form of law that allows gun owners to carry concealed weapons outside their homes for personal protection. (Five additional states had these laws before 1980. Illinois was the sole holdout.) A federal ban on the possession, transfer, or manufacture of semiautomatic assault weapons, passed in 1994, was allowed to expire in 2004. In 2005, Florida passed the Stand Your Ground law, an extension of the so-called castle doctrine, exonerating from prosecution citizens who use deadly force when confronted by an assailant, even if they could have retreated safely; Stand Your Ground laws expand that protection outside the home to any place that an individual "has a right to be." Twenty-four states soon passed similar laws.

The day before T. J. Lane shot five high school students in Ohio, another high school student was shot in Florida. The *Orlando Sentinel* ran a three-paragraph story. On February 26, seventeen-year-old Trayvon Martin left a house in a town outside Orlando and walked to a store. He was seen by a twenty-eight-year-old man named George Zimmerman, who called 911 to report that Martin, who was black, was "a real suspicious guy." Zimmerman got out of his truck. Zimmerman was carrying a 9 mm pistol; Martin was unarmed. What happened next has not been established, and is much disputed. Zimmerman told the police that Martin attacked him. Martin's family has said that the boy, heard over a cell phone, begged for his life.

Zimmerman shot Martin in the chest. Martin did not survive. Zimmerman was not immediately charged. Outside Orlando, the story was not reported.

THE DAY AFTER THE SHOOTING IN OHIO, I went to a firing range. I'd signed up for a lesson the week before. Once, when I was in Air Force ROTC for a year, I spent an afternoon studying how to defeat a sniper, but I'd never held a gun before.

The American Firearms School sits in an industrial park just north of Providence, in a beige stucco building topped with a roof of mint-green sheet metal. From the road, it looks like a bowling alley, but from the parking lot you can tell that it's not. You can hear the sound of gunfire. It doesn't sound like thunder. It doesn't sound like rain. It sounds like gunfire.

Inside, there's a shop, a pistol range, a rifle range, a couple of class-rooms, a locker room, and a place to clean your gun. The walls are painted police blue up to the wainscoting, and then white to the ceiling, which is painted black. It feels like a clubhouse, except, if you've never been to a gun shop before, that part feels not quite licit, like a porn shop. On the floor, there are gun racks, gun cases, holsters, and gun safes. Rifles hang on a wall behind the counter; handguns are under glass. Most items, including the rifles, come in black or pink: there are pink handcuffs, a pink pistol grip, a pink gun case, and pink paper targets. Above the pink bull's-eye, which looks unnervingly like a breast, a line of text reads, CANCER SUCKS.

The American Firearms School is run by Matt Medeiros, a Rhode Island firefighter and EMT. Medeiros is also a leader of the Rhode Island chapter of Pink Heals, a nonprofit organization of emergency and rescue workers who drive pink fire trucks and pink police cars to raise money for cancer research and support groups. When Pink Heals opened a women's center in West Warwick, Medeiros held a fundraiser at the Firearms School.

Unlike many firing ranges, which are private clubs, the American Firearms School is open to the public. Most mornings, federal, state, and local law enforcement agencies, as well as private security firms, rent out the ranges for training and target practice. Classes, from beginner to advanced, are held in the afternoons, and are run by certified instructors.

In many states, to purchase a gun from a licensed dealer you need a permit, which requires you to complete firearms safety training, not unlike driver's education. But even if all states required this, not everyone who buys a gun would have to take a class. That's because 40 percent of the guns purchased in the United States are bought from private sellers at gun shows, or through other private exchanges, such as classified ads, which fall under what is known as the "gun show loophole" and are thus unregulated.

At the American Firearms School, the Learn to Shoot program, for novices, costs forty dollars for ninety minutes: a lesson, a gun rental, range time, two targets, and two boxes of bullets. This doesn't constitute sufficient instruction for a gun permit in the state, but the school offers a one-day, ninety-nine-dollar course that does: Basic Firearms Safety includes shooting fundamentals, a discussion of firearms law, and guidance in safe firearms storage.

The idea that every man can be his own policeman, and every woman hers, has necessitated revisions to the curriculum: civilians now receive training once available only to law enforcement officers, or the military. A six-hour class on concealed carrying includes a lesson in "engaging the threat." NRA Basic Personal Protection in the Home teaches "the basic knowledge, skills, and attitude essential to the safe and efficient use of a handgun for protection of self and family" and provides "information on the law-abiding individual's right to self-defense," while NRA Basic Personal Protection Outside the Home is a two-day course. A primer lasting three hours provides "a tactical look at civilian life." This raises the question of just how much civilian life is left.

As I waited for my lesson, I paged through a stack of old magazines while watching Fox News on a flat-screen television. In Michigan and Arizona, Mitt Romney and Rick Santorum were competing in that day's Republican primaries. At the top of the hour came the headlines: in Ohio, Demetrius Hewlin had just died. For a tick, the news announcer fell silent.

I put down *Field and Stream* and picked up *American Rifleman*, a publication of the NRA. The magazine includes a regular column called The Armed Citizen. A feature article introduced David Keene, the NRA's president. Keene is a longtime conservative political strategist. Grover Norquist once called him "a conservative Forrest Gump." The 2012 presidential election, Keene told *American Rifleman*, is "perhaps the most crucial election, from a Second Amendment standpoint, in our lifetimes."

THE SECOND AMENDMENT READS, "A well-regulated militia being necessary to the security of a free State, the right of the people to keep and bear arms shall not be infringed." Arms are military weapons. A firearm is a cannon that you can carry, as opposed to artillery so big and heavy that you need wheels to move it, or people to help you. Cannons that you can carry around didn't exist until the Middle Ages. The first European firearms—essentially, tubes mounted on a pole—date to the end of the fourteenth century and are known as "hand cannons." Then came shoulder arms (that is, guns you can shoulder): muskets, rifles, and shotguns. A pistol is a gun that can be held in one hand. A revolver holds a number of bullets in a revolving chamber, but didn't become common until Samuel Colt patented his model in 1836. The firearms used by a well-regulated militia, at the time the Second Amendment was written, were mostly long arms that, like a smaller stockpile of pistols, could discharge only once before they had to be reloaded. In size, speed, efficiency, capacity, and sleekness, the difference between an eighteenth-century musket and the gun that George Zimmerman was carrying is roughly the difference between the first laptop computer—which, not counting the external modem and the battery pack, weighed twenty-four pounds—and an iPhone.

A gun is a machine made to fire a missile that can bore through flesh. It can be used to hunt an animal or to commit or prevent a crime. Enough people carrying enough guns, and with the will and the training to use them, can defend a government, or topple one. For centuries before the first English colonists traveled to the New World, Parliament had been regulating the private ownership of firearms. (Generally, ownership was restricted to the wealthy; the principle was that anyone below the rank of gentleman found with a gun was a poacher.) England's 1689 Declaration of Rights made a provision that "subjects which are Protestants may have arms for their defence suitable to their condition and as allowed by law"; the Declaration was an attempt to resolve a struggle between Parliament and the Crown, in which Parliament wrested control of the militia from the Crown.

In the United States, Article VI of the Articles of Confederation, drafted in 1776 and ratified in 1781, required that "every state shall always keep up a well regulated and disciplined militia, sufficiently armed and accoutred, and shall provide and constantly have ready for use, in public stores, a due number of field pieces and tents, and a proper quantity of arms, ammunition and camp equipage." In early America, firearms and ammunition were often kept in public arsenals. In 1775, the British Army marched to Concord with the idea of seizing the arsenal where the colonial militia stored its weapons. In January of 1787, a Massachusetts resident named Daniel Shays led eleven hundred men, many of them disaffected Revolutionary War veterans, in an attempt to capture an arsenal in Springfield; they had been protesting taxes, but they needed guns and ammunition. Springfield had been an arsenal since 1774. In 1777, George Washington, at the urging of Henry Knox, made it his chief northern arsenal. By 1786, Springfield housed the largest collection of weapons in the United States. In the winter of 1787, the governor of Massachusetts sent the militia to suppress the rebellion; the Springfield arsenal was defended. That spring, the Constitutional Convention met in Philadelphia. Among the matters the delegates were to take up was granting to the federal government the power to suppress insurgencies like Shays's Rebellion. From Boston, Benjamin Franklin's sister Jane wrote to him with some advice for "such a Number of wise men as you are connected with in the Convention": no more weapons, no more war. "I had Rather hear of the Swords being beat into Plow-shares, and the Halters used for Cart Roops, if by that means we may be brought to live Peaceably with won a nother."

The U.S. Constitution, which was signed in Philadelphia in September of 1787, granted Congress the power "to provide for calling forth the Militia to execute the Laws of the Union, suppress Insurrections and repel Invasions," the power "to provide for organizing, arming, and disciplining the Militia, and for governing such Part of them as may be employed in the Service of the United States, reserving to the States respectively, the Appointment of the Officers, and the Authority of training the Militia according to the discipline prescribed by Congress," and the power "to raise and support Armies, but no Appropriation of Money to that Use shall be for a longer Term than two Years."

Ratification was an uphill battle. The Bill of Rights, drafted by James Madison in 1789, offered assurance to Anti-Federalists, who feared that there would be no limit to the powers of the newly consti-tuted federal government. Since one of their worries was the prospect of a standing army—a permanent army—Madison drafted an amend-ment guaranteeing the people the right to form a militia. In Madison's original version, the amendment read, "The right of the people to keep and bear arms shall not be infringed; a well armed and well reg-ulated militia being the best security of a free country: but no person religiously scrupulous of bearing arms shall be compelled to render military service in person." This provision was made in the same spirit as the Third Amendment, which forbids the government to force you to have troops billeted in your home: "No Soldier shall, in time of peace be quartered in any house, without the consent of the Owner, nor in time of war, but in a manner to be prescribed by law."

None of this had anything to do with hunting. People who owned and used long arms to hunt continued to own and use them; the Second Amendment was not commonly understood as having any relevance to the shooting of animals. As Garry Wills once wrote, "One does not bear arms against a rabbit." Meanwhile, militias continued to muster— the Continental army was disbanded at the end of the Revolutionary War—but the national defense was increasingly assumed by the United States Army; by the middle of the nineteenth century, the United States had a standing army, after all. Harpers Ferry was the U.S. Army's south-ern armory, Springfield its northern. In 1859, when John Brown and his men raided Harpers Ferry, they went there to get guns.

AT THE AMERICAN FIREARMS SCHOOL, you can either rent a gun or bring your own. It's like an ice-skating rink that way, except that renting skates when you don't know how to skate is different from renting a gun when you don't know how to shoot. The guys who work at the school don't take any chances. In the twelve years since the school opened, there has never been an accident. "You can't do anything here without us watching you," Tom Dietzel told me. "In a swimming pool, there are lifeguards. And this place is a lot more dangerous than a swimming pool."

Dietzel, who is twenty-four and has long dark hair, is one of the few instructors at the school who isn't ex-military, ex-police, or ex-rescue. He led me to a classroom, opened a case, and took out a .22-caliber Mark III Target Rimfire pistol. Dietzel studied history in college, and on weekends he gives tours of the Freedom Trail, in Boston. We talked about the eighteenth-century portraits in the new wing of the Museum of Fine Arts; we debated the oratory of Joseph Warren. Dietzel owns a flintlock musket; he's a Revolutionary War reenactor, with the Thirteenth Continental Regiment. He showed me a photograph of himself in costume: a cocked hat, a mustard-colored scarf of flax. He could have been painted by Gilbert Stuart.

Dietzel is a skilled and knowledgeable teacher, steady, patient, and calm. He had written safety rules on a whiteboard: Never point your gun at anyone. Keep your finger off the trigger. Don't trust the safety. Assume every gun is loaded.

He explained how to load the magazine. "This is a semiautomatic," he said. "After you fire, it will load the next bullet, but you have to pull the trigger again to fire. We don't have automatics here." Automatic weapons are largely banned by the federal government. "An automatic, you pull the trigger and it keeps shooting." Dietzel shook his head. "Because: Why? Why?"

Gun owners may be more supportive of gun safety regulations than is the leadership of the NRA. According to a 2009 Luntz poll, for instance, requiring mandatory background checks on all purchasers at gun shows is favored not only by 85 percent of gun owners who are not members of the NRA but also by 69 percent of gun owners who are.

Dietzel rose. "Stand like a shortstop about to field a ball," he said.

He showed me how to hold the .22.

Every day, Dietzel goes to work and, at some point, has to hand a gun to a perfect stranger who has never used one. He went over the rules again.

We got earplugs and headgear and ammunition and went to the

range. I fired a hundred rounds. Then Dietzel told me to go wash my hands, to get the gunpowder off, while he went to clean the gun.

The halls at the American Firearms School are decorated with framed prints: Monet's *Impression, Sunrise*; Van Gogh's *Irises*. A sign on the door of the women's restroom reads EVERY TUESDAY IS LADIES NIGHT. LADIES GET FREE RANGE TIME FROM 5:00 PM TO 9:00 PM.

I opened the door, and turned on the tap. T. J. Lane had used a .22-caliber Mark III Target Rimfire pistol. For a long time, I let the water run.

ON MARCH 8, 2012, Trayvon Martin's father, Tracy Martin, held a press conference in Orlando. "We feel justice has not been served," he said. He demanded the release of recordings of calls to 911. "Family Wants Answers in Teen's Death," the Associated Press reported.

Two days later, the biggest gun show in New England was held in West Springfield, Massachusetts, in an exposition center the size of an airport hangar. (Nationwide, there are about five thousand gun shows annually.) Early in the morning, men with guns lined up to have them inspected at the door: two policemen made sure that every gun was unloaded; a plastic bucket on the floor, half filled with sand, was for dumping ammunition, like the bin at airport security where TSA officers make you chuck your toothpaste. Tickets cost eleven dollars, but there was no charge for children younger than twelve.

Inside was a flea market: hundreds of folding tables draped with felt tablecloths and covered with guns, along with knives, swords, and a great deal of hunting gear. Long guns stood on their stocks, muzzles up. Handguns rested under glass, like jewelry. CASH FOR GUNS, the sign at the Tombstone Trading Company read. Ammunition was sold outdoors, in cartons, as in the fastener aisle of a hardware store. At the NRA booth, membership came with a subscription to one of the NRA's three magazines, an NRA baseball hat, twenty-five hundred dollars of insurance, "and the most important benefit of all— protecting the Constitution."

I stopped at the table of Guns Inc., which advertises itself as the largest firearms dealer in western Massachusetts. Guns Inc. is also an arsenal: a place where people who don't want to keep their guns at home can pay to have them stored.

IN THE NINETEENTH CENTURY, the Springfield Armory grew to become the single biggest supplier of long arms to the U.S. Army. It shut its doors in 1968. A National Historic Site now, it houses about ten thousand weapons, most of which are shoulder arms. A sign on the door warns that no firearms are allowed inside. "People ask about that," Richard Colton, a park ranger and the site's historian, told me when I visited, "but we have plenty of guns here already."

The story of the Springfield Armory illustrates a shift in the manufacture and storage of firearms: from public to private. In 1974, a family in Illinois founded a company devoted to arms manufacturing and import called Springfield Armory Inc. The firm, "the first name in American firearms," is one of the largest of its kind in the United States. Dennis Reese, the current CEO, and his brother Tom have staunchly opposed gun regulation. I asked Brian Pranka, of Guns Inc., if he had any Springfield Armory guns. He said, "You can't buy a Springfield handgun in Springfield." The company does not make handguns that conform to all the gun safety regulations in states like Massachusetts, New York, and California, and in Illinois they have lobbied the legislature, successfully defeating a state ban on assault weapons. In 2008, the Illinois State Rifle Association gave the Reeses the Defenders of Freedom Award.

On the first day of the Springfield gun show, Trayvon Martin's parents appeared on *Good Morning America*. On March 19, the Department of Justice, responding to growing protests, announced that it would conduct an investigation. On March 23, President Obama answered questions about the shooting at a press conference. "If I had a son, he'd look like Trayvon," the president said. Later that day, Rick Santorum spoke outside a firing range in West Monroe, Louisiana, where he'd just shot fourteen rounds from a Colt .45. He told the crowd, "What I was able to exercise was one of those fundamental freedoms that's guaranteed in our Constitution, the right to bear arms."

IN THE TWO CENTURIES FOLLOWING the adoption of the Bill of Rights, in 1791, no amendment received less attention in the courts than the Second, except the Third. As Adam Winkler, a constitutional law scholar at UCLA, demonstrates in a remarkably nuanced book, *Gunfight: The Battle Over the Right to Bear Arms in America*, firearms have been regulated in the United States from the start. Laws banning the carrying of concealed weapons were passed in Kentucky and Louisiana in 1813, and other states soon followed: Indiana (1820), Tennessee and Virginia (1838), Alabama (1839), and Ohio (1859). Similar laws were passed in Texas, Florida, and Oklahoma. As the governor of Texas explained in 1893, the "mission of the concealed deadly weapon is murder. To check it is the duty of every self-respecting, law-abiding man."

Although these laws were occasionally challenged, they were rarely struck down in state courts; the state's interest in regulating the manufacture, ownership, and storage of firearms was plain enough. Even the West was hardly wild. "Frontier towns handled guns the way a Boston restaurant today handles overcoats in winter," Winkler writes. "New arrivals were required to turn in their guns to authorities in exchange for something like a metal token." In Wichita, Kansas, in 1873, a sign read LEAVE YOUR REVOLVERS AT POLICE HEADQUARTERS, AND GET A CHECK. The first thing the government of Dodge did when founding the city, in 1873, was pass a resolution that "any person or persons found carrying concealed weapons in the city of Dodge or violating the laws of the State shall be dealt with according to law." On the road through town, a wooden billboard read THE CARRYING OF FIREARMS STRICTLY PROHIBITED. The shoot-out at the O.K. Corral, in Tombstone, Arizona, Winkler explains, had to do with a gun control law. In 1880, Tombstone's city council passed an ordinance "to Provide against the Carrying of Deadly Weapons." When Wyatt Earp confronted Tom McLaury on the streets of Tombstone, it was because McLaury had violated that ordinance by failing to leave his gun at the sheriff's office.

The National Rifle Association was founded in 1871 by two men, a lawyer and a former reporter from the *New York Times*. For most of its history, the NRA was chiefly a sporting and hunting association. To the extent that the NRA had a political arm, it opposed some gun control measures and supported many others, lobbying for new state laws in the 1920s and '30s, which introduced waiting periods for handgun buyers and required permits for anyone wishing to carry a concealed weapon. It also supported the 1934 National Firearms Act—the first major federal gun control legislation—and the 1938 Federal

Firearms Act, which together created a licensing system for dealers and prohibitively taxed the private ownership of automatic weapons ("machine guns"). The constitutionality of the 1934 act was upheld by the U.S. Supreme Court in 1939, in *United States v. Miller*, in which Franklin Delano Roosevelt's solicitor general, Robert H. Jackson, argued that the Second Amendment is "restricted to the keeping and bearing of arms by the people collectively for their common defense and security." Furthermore, Jackson said, the language of the amendment makes clear that the right "is not one which may be utilized for private purposes but only one which exists where the arms are borne in the militia or some other military organization provided for by law and intended for the protection of the state." The Court agreed, unanimously. In 1957, when the NRA moved into new headquarters, its motto, at the building's entrance, read FIREARMS SAFETY EDUCATION, MARKSMANSHIP TRAINING, SHOOTING FOR RECREATION. It didn't say anything about freedom, or self-defense, or rights.

THE MODERN GUN DEBATE BEGAN with a shooting. In 1963, Lee Harvey Oswald bought a bolt-action rifle—an Italian military surplus weapon—for $19.95 by ordering it from an ad that he found in *American Rifleman*. Five days after Oswald assassinated President Kennedy, Thomas Dodd, a Democratic senator from Connecticut, introduced legislation restricting mail order sales of shotguns and rifles. The NRA's executive vice president, Franklin L. Orth, testified before Congress, "We do not think that any sane American, who calls himself an American, can object to placing into this bill the instrument which killed the president of the United States."

Gun rights arguments have their origins not in eighteenth-century Anti-Federalism but in twentieth-century liberalism. They are the product of what the Harvard law professor Mark Tushnet has called the "rights revolution," the pursuit of rights, especially civil rights, through the courts. In the 1960s, gun ownership as a constitutional right was less the agenda of the NRA than of Black nationalists. In a 1964 speech, Malcolm X said, "Article number two of the constitutional amendments provides you and me the right to own a rifle or a shotgun." Establishing a constitutional right to carry a gun for the purpose of self-defense was part of the mission of the Black Panther Party for Self-Defense, which was founded in 1966. "Black People can develop Self-Defense Power by arming themselves from house to house, block to block, community to community throughout the nation," Huey Newton said.

In 1968, as Winkler relates, the assassinations of Robert Kennedy and Martin Luther King Jr. gave the issue new urgency. A revised Gun Control Act banned mail order sales, restricted the purchase of guns by certain high-risk people (for example, those with criminal records), and prohibited the importation of military surplus firearms. That law, along with a great deal of subsequent law-and-order legislation, was intended to fight crime, control riots, and solve what was called, at the time, the "Negro problem." The regulations that are part of these laws—firearms restrictions, mandatory sentencing guidelines, abolition of parole, and the "war on drugs"—are now generally understood to be responsible for the dramatic rise in the U.S. incarceration rate.

The NRA supported the 1968 Gun Control Act, with some qualms. Orth was quoted in *American Rifleman* as saying that although some elements of the legislation "appear unduly restrictive and unjustified in their application to law-abiding citizens, the measure as a whole appears to be one that the sportsmen of America can live with."

DAVID KEENE, THE NRA'S PRESIDENT, is the former chairman of the American Conservative Union. In his office in Washington, he has a photograph of Ronald Reagan on the wall and a view of Pennsylvania Avenue out the window. Keene has white hair, blue eyes, and an air of plainspoken geniality. When he was eight or nine, he says, his grandfather taught him how to shoot by aiming a .22 at squirrels and rabbits.

Keene's parents were labor organizers. They never once voted for a Republican. "My first political activity was going door to door passing out pamphlets for JFK in the snows of Wisconsin," Keene told me. In the 1950s, he said, "Lionel Trilling considered conservatism to be a political pathology." Keene became a conservative in high school, when he read *The Constitution of Liberty*, by Friedrich Hayek. In 1960, at the Republican National Convention, Barry Goldwater said, "Let's grow up conservatives, if we want to take this party back, and I think we can someday. Let's get to work." Four years later, Keene volunteered for Goldwater's campaign.

After Goldwater's defeat, Keene finished college and went on to law school. He became the national chairman of the Young Americans for Freedom. "What brought conservatism to dominance was the Great Society," Keene argues, because Johnson's vision represented "the culmination of the thinking that you could solve everything with money, and nothing worked." Keene went to DC to work for Spiro Agnew, and then for Richard Nixon.

On Election Day in 1970, Keene was at the White House. Joseph Tydings, a Democratic senator from Maryland who had introduced a Firearms Registration and Licensing Act, was running for reelection. "The returns were coming in, and someone said, 'What's going on in Maryland?'" Keene recalled. "And someone answered, 'I can tell you this: everywhere except Baltimore, there are long lines of pickup trucks at the polls. He's going down over gun control.'"

IN THE 1970s, the NRA began advancing the argument that the Second Amendment guarantees an individual's right to carry a gun, rather than the people's right to form armed militias to provide for the common defense. Fights over rights are effective at getting out the vote. Describing gun safety legislation as an attack on a constitutional right gave conservatives a power at the polls that, at the time, the movement lacked. Opposing gun control was also consistent with a larger anti-regulation, libertarian, and anti-government conservative agenda. In 1975, the NRA created a lobbying arm, the Institute for Legislative Action, headed by Harlon Bronson Carter, an award-winning marksman and a former chief of the U.S. Border Control. But then the NRA's leadership decided to back out of politics and move the organization's headquarters to Colorado Springs, where a new recreational-shooting facility was to be built. Eighty members of the NRA's staff, including Carter, were ousted. In 1977, the NRA's annual meeting, usually held in Washington, was moved to Cincinnati, in protest of the city's recent gun control laws. Conservatives within the organization, led by Carter, staged what has come to be called the Cincinnati Revolt. The bylaws were rewritten and the old guard was pushed out. Instead of moving to Colorado, the NRA stayed in DC, where a new motto was displayed: "The Right of the People to Keep and Bear Arms Shall Not Be Infringed."

Ronald Reagan was the first presidential candidate whom the NRA had endorsed. David Keene ran Reagan's southern campaign. Reagan's election, in 1980, made it possible for conservatives to begin turning a new interpretation of the Second Amendment into law. As the legal scholar Reva B. Siegel has chronicled, Orrin Hatch became the chair of the Subcommittee on the Constitution, and commissioned a history of the Second Amendment, which resulted in a 1982 report, "The Right to Keep and Bear Arms." The authors of the report claimed to have discovered "clear—and long-lost—proof that the Second Amendment to our Constitution was intended as an individual right of the American citizen to keep and carry arms in a peaceful manner, for protection of himself, his family, and his freedoms."

In March of 1981, John Hinckley Jr. shot Reagan, the White House press secretary, James Brady, a DC policeman, and a Secret Service agent. He used a .22 that he had bought at a pawnshop. A month later, the *Times* reported that Harlon Carter, then the NRA's executive vice president, had been convicted of murder in Laredo, Texas, in 1931, at the age of seventeen. Carter had come home from school to find his mother distressed. She told him that three teenage boys had been loitering nearby all afternoon, and that she suspected them of having been involved in stealing the family's car. Carter left the house with a shotgun, found the boys, and told them that he wanted them to come back to his house to be questioned. According to the trial testimony of twelve-year-old Salvador Peña, Ramón Casiano, fifteen, the oldest of the boys, said to Carter, "We won't go to your house, and you can't make us." Casiano took out a knife and said, "Do you want to fight me?" Carter shot Casiano in the chest. At Carter's trial for murder, the judge, J. F. Mullally, instructed the jury, "There is no evidence that defendant had any lawful authority to require deceased to go to his house for questioning, and if defendant was trying to make deceased go there for that purpose at the time of the killing, he was acting without authority of law, and the law of self-defense does not apply." Two years later, Carter's murder conviction was overturned on appeal; the defense argued that the instructions to the jury had been improper.

When the *Times* broke the Casiano murder story, Carter at first denied it, saying the trial record concerned a different man with a similar name. He later said that he had "nothing to hide" and was "not going to rehash that case or any other that does not relate to the National Rifle Association."

James Brady and his wife, Sarah, went on to become active in the gun control movement, but neither the assassination attempt nor Carter's past derailed the gun rights movement. In 1986, the NRA's interpretation of the Second Amendment achieved new legal authority with the passage of the Firearms Owners Protection Act, which repealed parts of the 1968 Gun Control Act by invoking "the rights of citizens . . . to keep and bear arms under the Second Amendment." This interpretation was supported by a growing body of scholarship, much of it funded by the NRA. According to the constitutional law scholar Carl Bogus, at least sixteen of the twenty-seven law review articles published between 1970 and 1989 that were favorable to the NRA's interpretation of the Second Amendment were "written by lawyers who had been directly employed by or represented the NRA or other gun rights organizations." In an interview, former chief justice Warren Burger said that the new interpretation of the Second Amendment was "one of the greatest pieces of fraud, I repeat the word 'fraud,' on the American public by special interest groups that I have ever seen in my lifetime."

The debate narrowed, and degraded. Political candidates who supported gun control faced opponents whose campaigns were funded by the NRA. In 1991, a poll found that Americans were more familiar with the Second Amendment than they were with the First: the right to speak and to believe, and to write and to publish, freely.

"IF YOU HAD ASKED, IN **1968,** will we have the right to do with guns in 2012 what we can do now, no one, on either side, would have believed you," David Keene said.

Between 1968 and 2012, the idea that owning and carrying a gun is both a fundamental American freedom and an act of citizenship gained wide acceptance and, along with it, the principle that this right is absolute and cannot be compromised; gun control legislation was diluted, defeated, overturned, or allowed to expire; the right to carry a concealed handgun became nearly ubiquitous; Stand Your Ground legislation passed in half the states; and, in 2008, in *District of Columbia v. Heller*, the Supreme Court ruled, in a 5–4 decision, that the District's 1975 Firearms Control Regulations Act was unconstitutional. Justice Scalia wrote, "The Second Amendment protects an individual right to possess a firearm unconnected with service in a militia." Two years later, in another 5–4 ruling, *McDonald v. Chicago*, the Court extended *Heller* to the states.

Nevertheless, Keene says that all of these gains are fragile, because President Obama—who in his first term has not only failed to push for gun control but has signed legislation extending gun rights—has been hiding his true convictions. (From 1994 to 2002, Obama served on the board of the Chicago-based Joyce Foundation, which funds pro-gun-control advocacy and research.) "If this president gets a second term, he will appoint one to three Supreme Court justices," Keene says. "If he does, he could reverse *Heller* and *McDonald*, which is unlikely, but, more likely, they will restrict those decisions."

This issue has been delivering voters to the polls since 1970. Conservatives hope that it will continue to deliver them in 2012. Keene, in his lifetime, has witnessed a revolution. "It's not just the conservative political victories, the capture of the Republican Party, the creation of a conservative intellectual elite," he said, "but the whole change in the way Americans look at government." No conservative victories will last longer than the rulings of this Supreme Court.

One in three Americans knows someone who has been shot. As long as a candid discussion of guns is impossible, unfettered debate about the causes of violence is unimaginable. Gun control advocates say the answer to gun violence is fewer guns. Gun rights advocates say that the answer is more guns: things would have gone better, they suggest, if the faculty at Columbine, Virginia Tech, and Chardon High School had been armed. That is the logic of the concealed-carry movement; that is how armed citizens have come to be patrolling the streets. That is not how civilians live. When carrying a concealed weapon for self-defense is understood not as a failure of civil society, to be mourned, but as an act of citizenship, to be vaunted, there is little civilian life left.

In 2002, Keene's son David Michael Keene was driving on the George Washington Memorial Parkway when, in a road rage incident, he fired a handgun at another motorist. He was sentenced to ten years in prison for "using, brandishing, and discharging a firearm in a crime of violence." I asked Keene if this private tragedy had left him uncertain about what the NRA had wrought. He said no: "You break the law, you pay the price."

I asked Keene if any public atrocity had given him pause. He explained that it is the NRA's policy never to comment on a shooting.

I asked him how he would answer critics who charge that no single organization has done more to weaken Americans' faith in government, or in one another, than the NRA.

"We live in a society now that's balkanized," Keene said. "But that has nothing to do with guns."

ON MONDAY, MARCH 26, 2012, thousands of students rallied in Atlanta, carrying signs that read I AM TRAYVON MARTIN, and DON'T SHOOT! One week later, in Oakland, a forty-three-year-old man named One Goh walked into Oikos University, a small Christian college. He was carrying a .45-caliber semiautomatic pistol and four magazines of ammunition. He grabbed Katleen Ping, a receptionist, and dragged her into a classroom. Nearby, Lucas Garcia, a thirty-three-year-old ESL teacher, heard a voice call out, "Somebody's got a gun!" He helped his students escape through a back door. Dechen Yangdon, twenty-seven, turned off the lights in her classroom and locked the door. She could hear Ping screaming, "Help, help, help!" "We were locked inside," Yangdon said later. "We couldn't help her."

Goh ordered the students to line up against the wall. He said, "I'm going to kill you all."

They had come from all over the world. Ping, twenty-four, was born in the Philippines. She was working at the school to support her parents, her brother, two younger sisters, and her four-year-old son, Kayzzer. Her husband was hoping to move to the United States. Tshering Rinzing Bhutia, thirty-eight, was born in Gyalshing, India, in the foothills of the Himalayas. He took classes during the day; at night, he worked as a janitor at San Francisco International Airport. Lydia Sim, twenty-one, was born in San Francisco, to Korean parents; she wanted to become a pediatrician. Sonam Choedon, thirty-three, belonged to a family living in exile from Tibet. A Buddhist, she came to the United

States from Dharamsala, India. She was studying to become a nurse. Grace Eunhea Kim, twenty-three, was putting herself through school by working as a waitress. Judith Seymour was fifty-three. Her parents had moved back to their native Guyana; her two children were grown. She was about to graduate. Doris Chibuko, forty, was born in Enugu, in eastern Nigeria, where she practiced law. She immigrated in 2002. Her husband, Efanye, works as a technician for AT&T. They had three children, ages eight, five, and three. She was two months short of completing a degree in nursing.

Ping, Bhutia, Sim, Choedon, Kim, Seymour, and Chibuko: Goh shot and killed them all. Then he went from one classroom to another, shooting, before stealing a car and driving away. He threw his gun into a tributary of San Leandro Bay. Shortly afterward, he walked into a grocery store and said, "I just shot some people."

A multilingual memorial service was held at the Allen Temple Baptist Church. Oakland's mayor, Jean Quan, said, "Oakland is a city of dreams." A friend of Choedon's said, "Mainly, we're praying for her next life, that she can have a better one." In Gyalshing, Bhutia's niece, Enchuk Namgyal, asked that her uncle's body be sent home to be cremated in the mountains above the village, across the world from the country where he came for an education, religious freedom, and economic opportunity, and was shot to death.

Kids in Chardon High are back in school. Nickolas Walczak is in a wheelchair. There are Trayvon Martin T-shirts. Oikos University is closed. The NRA has no comment.

In an average year, roughly a hundred thousand Americans are killed or wounded with guns. On April 6, the police found One Goh's .45. Five days later, George Zimmerman was charged with second-degree murder. In May, T. J. Lane will appear at a hearing. Trials are to come. In each, introduced as evidence, will be an unloaded gun.

—2012

Postscript: No meaningful gun safety legislation has been passed in the ten years that have passed since I wrote this piece. The mass shootings continued. And in 2022, the Supreme Court sanctioned the reading of the Second Amendment the NRA had for so long been fighting for.

BLOOD ON THE GREEN

PHILLIP LAFAYETTE GIBBS MET DALE ADAMS WHEN they were in high school, in Ripley, Mississippi, a town best known as the home of William Faulkner's great-grandfather, who ran a slave plantation, fought in the Mexican-American War, raised troops that joined the Confederate Army, wrote a best-selling mystery about a murder on a steamboat, shot a man to death and got away with it, and was elected to the Mississippi legislature. He was killed before he could take his seat, but that seat would have been two hundred miles away in the state capitol, in Jackson, a city named for Andrew Jackson, who ran a slave plantation, fought in the War of 1812, was famous for killing Indians, shot a man to death and got away with it, and was elected president of the United States. Phillip Gibbs's father and Dale Adams's father had both been sharecroppers: they came from families who had been held as slaves by families like the Jacksons and the Faulkners, by force of arms.

In 1967, after Gibbs and Adams started dating, he'd take her out to the movies in a car that he borrowed from his uncle, a car with no key; he had to jam a screwdriver into the ignition to start it up. After Dale got pregnant, they were married, at his sister's house. They named the baby Phillip Jr.; Gibbs called him his little man. Gibbs went to Jackson State, a historically Black college, and majored in political science. In 1970, his junior year, Gibbs decided that he'd like to study law at Howard when he graduated. He was opposed to the war in Vietnam, but he was also giving some thought to joining the air force, because that way, at least, he could provide his family with a decent apartment. "I really don't want to go to the air force but I want you and my man to be staying with me," he wrote to Dale, after she and the baby had moved back home to Ripley to save money.

The Jackson State campus was divided by a four-lane road called Lynch Street, named for Mississippi's first Black congressman, John

Roy Lynch, who was elected during Reconstruction, in 1872, though a lot of people thought that the street honored another Lynch, the slaveholding judge whose name became a verb. It was on Lynch Street, just after midnight, on May 15, 1970, that policemen in riot gear shot and killed Phillip Gibbs. He was twenty-one. In a barrage—they fired more than a hundred and fifty rounds in twenty-eight seconds—they also fatally shot a seventeen-year-old high school student named James Earl Green, who was walking down the street on his way home from work. Buckshot and broken glass wounded a dozen more students, including women watching from the windows of their dormitory, Alexander Hall. Phillip Gibbs's sister lived in that dormitory.

That night, as the historian Nancy K. Bristow recounts in *Steeped in the Blood of Racism: Black Power, Law and Order, and the 1970 Shootings at Jackson State College*, students at Jackson State had been out on Lynch Street protesting, and young men from the neighborhood had been throwing rocks and setting a truck on fire, partly because of something that had happened ten days before and more than nine hundred miles away: at Kent State University, the Ohio National Guard had shot and killed four students and wounded nine more. They fired as many as sixty-seven shots in thirteen seconds. "Four dead in Ohio," Crosby, Stills, Nash & Young would sing, in a ballad that became an anthem. "Shot some more in Jackson," the Steve Miller Band sang, in 1970, in the "Jackson-Kent Blues." In the days between the shootings at Kent State and Jackson State, police in Augusta, Georgia, killed six unarmed Black men, shot in the back, during riots triggered by the death of a teenager who had been tortured while in police custody. At a march on May 19, protesters decorated coffins with signs: 2 KILLED IN JACKSON, 4 KILLED IN KENT, 6 KILLED IN AUGUSTA.

Two, plus four, plus six, plus more. In 1967, near Jackson State, police killed a twenty-two-year-old civil rights activist—shot him in the back and in the back of the head—after the Mississippi National Guard had been called in to quell student demonstrations over concerns that ranged from police brutality to the Vietnam War. And in 1968, at South Carolina State, police fatally shot three students and wounded dozens more, in the first mass police shooting to take place on an American college campus. Four dead in Ohio? It's time for a new tally.

MAY 2020 MARKED THE FIFTIETH ANNIVERSARY of the Kent State shootings, an occasion explored in Derf Backderf's deeply researched and gut-wrenching graphic nonfiction novel, *Kent State: Four Dead in Ohio.* Backderf was ten years old in 1970, growing up outside Kent; the book opens with him riding in the passenger seat of his mother's car, reading *Mad,* and then watching Richard Nixon on television. *Kent State* reads, in the beginning, like a very clever college newspaper comic strip—not unlike early *Doonesbury,* which debuted that same year—featuring the ordinary lives of four undergraduates, Allison Krause, Jeff Miller, Sandy Scheuer, and Bill Schroeder, their roommate problems, their love lives, their stressy phone calls with their parents, and their fury about the war. As the violence intensifies, Backderf's drawings grow darker and more cinematic: the intimate, moody panels of smart, young, good people, muddling through the inanity and ferocity of American politics yield to black-backed panels of institutional buildings, with the people around them saying completely crazy things, then to explosive splash pages of soldiers, their guns locked and loaded, and, finally, to a two-page spread of those fateful thirteen seconds: "*BOOM!*" "*BANG!*" "*BANG! BANG! POW!*"

Backderf's publisher billed his book as telling "the untold story of the Kent State shootings," but the terrible story of what happened at Kent State on May 4, 1970, has been told many times before, including by an extraordinary fleet of reporters and writers who turned up on campus while the blood was still wet on the pavement. Joe Eszterhas and Michael Roberts, staff writers for the *Cleveland Plain Dealer,* both of whom had reported on Vietnam, reached campus within forty-five minutes of the first shot—they rushed in to cover the growing campus unrest—and stayed for three months to report *Thirteen Seconds: Confrontation at Kent State,* their swiftly published book. Eszterhas went on to become a prominent screenwriter. Philip Caputo, a twenty-eight-year-old *Chicago Tribune* reporter who later won a Pulitzer Prize and wrote a best-selling memoir about his service in Vietnam, was driving to Kent State, from the Cleveland airport, when the news about the shots came over the radio. "I remember stepping on the gas," he writes, in the introduction to *13 Seconds: A Look Back at the Kent State Shootings,* a series of reflections on his earlier reporting. "I entered the picture late," the best-selling novelist James A. Michener wrote. "I arrived by car in early August." He stayed for months. *Reader's Digest* had hired him to write *Kent State: What Happened and Why*, providing him with reams of research from on-the-spot reporters. The political commentator I. F. Stone cranked out a short book—really, a long essay—titled *The Killings at Kent State: How Murder Went Unpunished*. So many books were published about the shooting, so fast, that when NBC's *Today* show featured their authors the result was a screaming match. Before introducing them, the host, Hugh Downs, gave a grave, concise, newsman's account of the sequence of events:

> On Thursday, April 30th, 1970, President Richard Nixon announced that American forces were moving into Cambodia. On Friday, May 1st, students at Kent State University in Kent, Ohio, expressed their displeasure at the President's announcement. That night, there was violence in the streets of Kent. On Saturday, May 2nd, the ROTC building was burned, National Guardsmen moved onto the campus. On Sunday, May 3rd, students and Guardsmen traded insults, rocks, and tear gas. On Monday, May 4th, the confrontations continued. There was marching and counter-marching. Students hurled rocks and Guardsmen chased students, firing tear gas. The Guardsmen pursued the students up an area called Blanket Hill. Some Guardsmen pointed their rifles menacingly. And suddenly, it happened.

Nearly all accounts of what happened at Kent State begin the way the *Today* show did, on April 30, 1970, when, in a televised address, Nixon announced that the United States had sent troops into Cambodia, even though, only ten days earlier, he had announced the withdrawal of a hundred and fifty thousand troops from Vietnam. Students on college campuses had been protesting the war since 1965, beginning with teach-ins at the University of Michigan. By 1970, it had seemed as though U.S. involvement in the war in Vietnam was finally winding down; now, with the news of the invasion of Cambodia, it was winding back up. Nixon, who had campaigned on a promise to restore law and order, warned Americans to brace for protest. "My fellow Americans, we live in an age of anarchy, both abroad and at home," he said. "Even here in the United States, great universities are being systematically destroyed."

Nixon's Cambodia speech led to antiwar protests at hundreds of colleges across the country. Campus leaders called for a National Student Strike. Borrowing from the Black Power movement, they used a Black fist as its symbol. The number of campuses involved grew by twenty a day. Most demonstrations were peaceful, but others were violent, even terrifying. In some places, including Kent, students rioted, smashing shop windows, pelting cars, setting fires, and throwing firebombs. In Ohio, the mayor of Kent asked the governor to send in the National Guard.

Nixon hated the student protesters as much in private as he did in public. "You see these bums, you know, blowing up the campuses," he said the day after the Cambodia speech. He had long urged a hard line on student protesters: antiwar protesters, civil rights activists, all of them. So had Ronald Reagan, who ran for governor of California in 1966 on a promise to bring law and order to Berkeley, a campus he described as "a rallying point for communists and a center for sexual misconduct." In 1969, he ordered the California Highway Patrol to clear out a vacant lot near the Berkeley campus which student and local volunteers had turned into a park. Police fired shots, killing one onlooker, and injuring dozens of people. Reagan called in the National Guard. Weeks before Nixon's Cambodia speech stirred up still more protest, Reagan, running for reelection, said that he was ready for a fight. "If it takes a bloodbath," he said, "let's get it over with."

MAY 4, 1970, THE DAY OF THAT BLOODBATH, fell on a Monday. The Guardsmen at Kent State started firing not long after noon, while students were crossing campus; there seems to be some chance that they mistook the students spilling out of buildings for an act of aggression, when, actually, they were leaving classes. Bill Schroeder, a sophomore, was an ROTC student. "He didn't like Vietnam and Cambodia but if he had to go to Vietnam," his roommate said later, "he would have gone." Schroeder was walking to class when he was shot in the back. Jeff Miller, a junior from Plainview, Long Island, hated the war, and went out to join the protest; he was shot in the mouth. Sandy Scheuer had been training to become a speech therapist. Shot in the neck, she bled to death. Allison Krause, a freshman honor student from outside Pittsburgh, was about to transfer. She'd refused to join groups like Students for a Democratic Society, which, by 1969, had become increasingly violent. (Her father told a reporter that she had called them "a bunch of finks.") But she became outraged when the National Guard occupied the campus. On a final exam, she had tried to answer the question "What is the point of history?" "Dates and facts are not enough to show what happened in the past," she wrote. "It is necessary to analyze and delve into the human side of history to come up with the truth." She had lost her naivete, she told her professor, in a reflection that she wrote at the end of the exam: "I don't take the books as 'the law' anymore." Her professor wrote back, "A happy thing—that." She had gone out to protest the invasion of Cambodia.

Thirteen seconds later, with four students on the ground, the shooting seemed likely to start up again, until Glenn Frank, a middle-aged geology professor, grabbed a megaphone. "Sit down, please!" he shouted at the students, his voice frantic, desperate. "I am begging you right now. If you don't disperse right now, they're going to move in, and it can only be a slaughter. Would you please listen to me? Jesus Christ, I don't want to be a part of this!" Finally, the students sat down.

Students elsewhere stood up. Campuses across the country erupted. Demonstrations took place in four out of every five colleges and universities. One in five simply shut down, including the entire University of California system, and sent their students home. Students marched on administration buildings, they burned more buildings, they firebombed, they threw Molotov cocktails. And they marched on Washington. *The New Yorker* declared it "the most critical week this nation has endured in more than a century."

BUT ONE OF THE MOST VIOLENT PROTESTS was a counterprotest, as David Paul Kuhn points out in his riveting book *The Hardhat Riot: Nixon, New York City, and the Dawn of the White Working-Class Revolution.* For all the talk of tragedy in the nation's newspapers and magazines, a majority of Americans blamed the students. They'd had it with those protests: the destruction of property, the squandering of an education. Hundreds of thousands of U.S. servicemen were fighting in Vietnam, young people who hadn't dodged the draft; most of them came from white, blue-collar families. Kent State students were shattering shop windows and burying the Constitution and telling National Guardsmen to go fuck themselves? Four dead in Ohio? Fifty thousand servicemen had already died in Vietnam, and more were dying every day. (It's worth noting that both Trump and Biden avoided the draft: Trump said he had bone spurs; Biden got five student deferments and later cited asthma.)

On May 7, three days after the shooting at Kent State, as many as five thousand students thronged the Manhattan funeral service of Jeff Miller. As the mourners marched through the city, scattered groups of construction workers, up on girders, threw beer cans at them. The mayor, John Lindsay, had declared May 8 a "day of reflection," and closed the city's public schools. A thousand college students turned up for an antiwar rally, hoping to shut down Wall Street: "One-two-three-four. We don't want your fuckin' war! Two-four-six-eight. We don't want your fascist state!" They were met by construction workers, many of whom had come down from the Twin Towers and not a few of whom had buried their soldier sons, or their neighbors' sons, in flag-draped coffins.

Joe Kelly, six feet four and from Staten Island, was working on building the elevators at the World Trade Center. He said he'd reached his "boiling point," and headed over to the protest during his lunch hour, joining hundreds of workers in yellow, red, and blue hard hats, some carrying American flags, many chanting, "Hey, hey, whaddya say? We support the USA!" and "Love it or leave it!" Kelly thought the students looked "un-American." The students called the hard hats "motherfucking fascists." Kelly punched a kid who, he said, swung at him and knocked the kid down. While police officers looked on, more or less approvingly, the workers attacked the protesters, clubbing them with tools, kicking them as they lay on the ground. Some of the policemen dragged hippies out of the fight by their hair. Even some Wall Street guys, in suits and ties, joined the hard hats. Lindsay had called for the flag at city hall to be lowered to half-mast. The construction workers swarmed the building and forced city workers to raise the flag back up. Other workers chased undergraduates from Pace University back to campus, breaking into a building on which students had draped a white banner that read VIETNAM? CAMBODIA? KENT STATE? WHAT NEXT? Pace was next. Students tried to barricade the buildings while construction workers broke windows and leaped inside, shouting, "Kill those long-haired bastards!"

Two weeks later, at the White House, Nixon received a memo from his aide Patrick Buchanan. "A group of construction workers came up Wall Street and beat the living hell out of some demonstrators who were desecrating the American flag," Buchanan reported. "The most insane suggestion I have heard about here in recent days was to the effect that we should somehow go prosecute the hard hats to win favor with the kiddies." He advised the opposite tack: abandon the kiddies, and court the hard hats. The day before, a hundred and fifty thousand New York construction workers, teamsters, and longshoremen marched through the streets of the city. The *Daily News* called it a "Parade for Nixon." They were trying to make America great again. Nixon invited the march's leaders to the White House, where they gave hard hats as a gift. Nixon was well on his way to becoming the hero of the white working class, men and women, but especially men, who left the Democratic Party for the GOP. "These, quite candidly, are *our people now*," Buchanan told Nixon. They were Nixon's, and they were Reagan's, and they are Trump's.

ON MAY 7, the day of Jeff Miller's funeral in New York, signs were posted all over the Jackson State campus:

BE CONCERNED
MEET IN FRONT THE DINING HALL
AT 2:00 P.M. TODAY
TO DISCUSS CAMBODIA.

A small crowd showed up. Two days later, only about a dozen Jackson State students went to a rally in downtown Jackson. One student leader recalled, "The kids at Kent State had become second-class niggers, so they had to go." They had found out what he and his classmates had known their whole lives: what happens when the police think of you as Black.

It's not clear that Phillip Gibbs went to any of those rallies, but in high school, in Ripley, he'd joined sit-ins aiming to integrate the town swimming pool, an ice-cream shop, and the Dixie Theatre. In *Lynch Street: The May 1970 Slayings at Jackson State College*, published in 1988, Tim Spofford argued that Jackson State had never been a particularly political campus. But Jackson had in fact been very much in the fray of the civil rights, antiwar, and Black Power movements. In 1961, students at Mississippi's Tougaloo College—another historically Black school—had held a sit-in in an attempt to desegregate the Municipal Library, in nearby Jackson. After the Tougaloo students were arrested, students at Jackson State marched down Lynch Street, toward the jail where the Tougaloo protesters were being held; they were stopped by police with tear gas, billy clubs, and attack dogs. Two years later, the civil rights activist Medgar Evers was assassinated at his home in Jackson. The next year, his brother, Charles Evers, who had replaced Medgar as head of the state's NAACP, tried to calm campus protesters after a female student was nearly killed by a hit-and-run as she crossed Lynch Street. Police came and shot at the students, wounding three. The local press was not inclined to support the protesters. "Did you hear about the new NAACP doll?" a columnist for the *Jackson Daily News* had asked. "You wind it up and it screams, 'police brutality.'"

A lot of students at Jackson State couldn't afford to get involved. In the wake of the 1970 shootings, one student said, "Mothers are out scrubbing floors for white folks and sending these kids to Jackson State. 'You're doin' better than I ever did,' they tell the kids. 'You better stay outta that mess.'"

Still, by May 13, 1970, five days after the Hard Hat Riot in New York, there were plans, or at least rumors about plans, to burn the Jackson State ROTC building. That night, students threw rocks at cars driving down Lynch Street. "Havin' nigger trouble on Lynch Street?" one squad car asked over the police radio. When students started setting fires, the governor called in the Mississippi National Guard, but, before they could arrive, the all-white Mississippi Highway Patrol turned up. Jackson State's president, an alumnus, met with students the next morning; they told him that they were angry about Cambodia, the draft, and Kent State, and also about the curfew for students in the women's dormitory and the lack of a pedestrian bridge over Lynch Street. He called the police chief and asked him to close Lynch Street overnight; the police chief initially refused.

That night, a rumor spread that Charles Evers, who was now the mayor of Fayette, Mississippi, and who had a daughter at Jackson State, had been shot. As the National Guard had done at Kent State, the authorities at Jackson State insisted that the police and patrolmen had identified a sniper. (No evidence has ever corroborated these claims.) A few minutes after midnight, law enforcement officers began firing. In the morning, the college president closed the campus and sent the students home.

"So we'll film the show without an audience, and edit in the gasps of wonder later."

Time called what happened in Mississippi "Kent State II." After Phillip Gibbs's wife, Dale, learned that her husband had been killed, she found out she was pregnant, with her second child. This one, Demetrius, graduated from Jackson State in 1995, and has had a hard time explaining what happened to the father he never knew. "If I try to tell people about the shootings at Jackson State, they don't know about it," he has said. "They don't know until I say, 'Kent State.'"

In *Steeped in the Blood of Racism*, Bristow insists, "Jackson State was not another Kent State." Bristow blames white liberals for failing to understand the shootings at Jackson State as a legacy of the Jim Crow South's brutal regime of state violence, and for deciding, instead, that what happened at Jackson State was just like what happened at Kent State. She faults the Beach Boys, for instance, for a track on their 1971 album, *Surf's Up*; even though they had noted the specific racial nature of the events at Jackson State ("The violence spread down South to where Jackson State brothers / Learned not to say nasty things about Southern policemen's mothers"), these lines appeared in a song called "Student Demonstration Time," which, Bristow laments, "told listeners the Jackson State shootings belonged in a litany of crises on college campuses."

That was more or less the verdict of the President's Commission on Campus Unrest, appointed by Nixon in June 1970. It wasn't a bunch of whitewashers. The nine-person commission, chaired by William

Scranton, the former Republican governor of Pennsylvania, included the president of Howard University; a Black member of the Harvard Society of Fellows studying the history of racism; and, as its only active military member, the first African American air force general, a former commander of the Tuskegee Airmen. After holding public hearings in Kent and Jackson, the Scranton Commission concluded that most campus unrest had been peaceful, that it was a response to racial inequality and the war in Vietnam, that it wasn't mayhem, and, also, that it wasn't unusual. "It is not so much the unrest of the past half-dozen years that is exceptional as it is the quiet of the 20 years which preceded them," the report asserted, noting that Americans who attended college from the 1940s to the early 1960s had formed a "silent generation." As far as the commission was concerned, the modern era of campus unrest began on February 1, 1960, when four students from North Carolina Agricultural and Technical College sat down at a "Whites Only" lunch counter in Greensboro. Nixon rejected the report.

It's this argument—that white and Black student protesters can be understood to have been involved in a single movement, for racial justice, free speech, and peace, led by the fight for civil rights—that Bristow, bizarrely, rejects as a white-liberal fantasy. If it was a fantasy, it was also Martin Luther King Jr.'s fantasy. In 1967, after King first spoke out against the war in Vietnam, people asked him why, saying, "Peace and civil rights don't mix." Their response saddened him, he said, because it suggested that "they do not know the world in which they live."

A QUESTION, LATELY, IS: Which world do Americans remember? The Scranton Commission concluded that the shootings at both Kent State and Jackson State had been unjustified. It did not, however, urge the prosecution of the shooters, something that a lot of people who wrote books about Kent State urged but that James Michener opposed. "It would be an exercise in futility," he said during his commencement address at Kent State, in December 1970. In his five-hundred-page *Kent State: What Happened and Why*, Michener blamed the protesters and, especially, outside radical agitators, who, like the snipers, seem to have been mostly an invention of the authorities. Joe Eszterhas and

Michael Roberts called Michener's book "a Magical Mystery Tour of innuendo, half-truth, carefully-structured quotation and anonymous attribution." They concluded that the National Guardsmen, exhausted, poorly trained, and badly led, had committed murder. "There was death, but not murder," Michener insisted.

A week short of the first anniversary of the shootings at Kent State, Michener, Eszterhas, Roberts, and I. F. Stone appeared on that panel on the *Today* show. "Hugh—obviously, this will be a free-swinging affair," Downs's producer noted, in the show overview. By the end of the hour, the guests had nearly come to blows. "Jim, don't you believe in American justice?" Eszterhas asked, after Michener continued to insist that a federal grand jury investigation would be a waste of time, because no jury would convict the Guardsmen. "How do you know that?" Roberts asked. Michener: "Because it has been the history throughout our country. The law doesn't run its course." At this point, even Downs jumped in: "Aren't you in effect indicting the American system of justice?" Stone tried to read out loud from a statement by Kent students. Michener shouted him down: "I won't let you read that."

That spring, the *New York Times* ran a long investigative piece, "Jackson State a Year After," by Stephan Lesher, a legal affairs correspondent. Alexander Hall was still pockmarked with bullet holes. Lynch Street had been closed to traffic, but with a tall chain-link fence, which made the campus feel like a prison. "No one has been punished," Lesher wrote. "No one is going to be":

> No one—least of all Jackson's blacks—expected a different outcome. . . . Yet, there is a barely perceptible chance that the Jackson State violence will be remembered as more than simply another brutal chapter in Mississippi's disregard for Black humanity.

No one has been punished, and no one is going to be. Except everyone's been punished, the whole nation has suffered, and will keep on suffering, until the shooting stops. That will take a political settlement, a peace, that the nation has needed for a half century. And it will require a history that can account for Greensboro, and Berkeley, and Kent State, and the Hard Hats, and Jackson State, all at once. King made a prediction: "If we do not act, we shall surely be dragged down the long, dark, and shameful corridors of time reserved for those who possess power without compassion, might without morality, and strength without sight." It turns out that the corridor of time is longer than he could have known.

—2020

Postscript: The 2020 anniversary of Kent State was largely ignored. Three weeks later, George Floyd was killed in Minneapolis.

THE LONG BLUE LINE

T O POLICE IS TO MAINTAIN LAW AND ORDER, BUT the word derives from *polis*—the Greek for "city," or "polity"—by way of *politia*, the Latin for "citizenship," and it entered English from the Middle French *police*, which meant not constables but government. "The police," as a civil force charged with deterring crime, came to the United States from England and is generally associated with monarchy—"keeping the king's peace"—which makes it surprising that, in the antimonarchical United States, it got so big, so fast. The reason is, mainly, slavery.

"Abolish the police," as a rallying cry, dates to 1988 (the year that N.W.A recorded "Fuck tha Police"), but long before anyone called for its abolition, someone had to invent the police: the ancient Greek polis had to become the modern police. "To be political, to live in a *polis*, meant that everything was decided through words and persuasion and not through force and violence," Hannah Arendt wrote in *The Human Condition*. In the polis, men argued and debated, as equals, under a rule of law. Outside the polis, in households, men dominated women, children, servants, and slaves, under a rule of force. This division of government sailed down the river of time like a raft, getting battered, but also bigger, collecting sticks and mud. Kings asserted a rule of force over their subjects on the idea that their kingdom was their household. In 1769, William Blackstone, in his *Commentaries on the Laws of England*, argued that the king, as "pater-familias of the nation," directs "the public police," exercising the means by which "the individuals of the state, like members of a well-governed family, are bound to conform their general behavior to the rules of propriety, good neighbourhood, and good manners; and to be decent, industrious, and inoffensive in their respective stations." The police are the king's men.

History begins with etymology, but it doesn't end there. The polis is not the police. The American Revolution toppled the power of the king over his people—in America, "the law is king," Thomas Paine wrote—but not the power of a man over his family. The power of the police has its origins in that kind of power. Under the rule of law, people are equals; under the rule of police, as the legal theorist Markus Dubber has written, we are not. We are more like the women, children, servants, and slaves in a household in ancient Greece, the people who were not allowed to be a part of the polis. But for centuries, through struggles for independence, emancipation, enfranchisement, and equal rights, we've been fighting to enter the polis. One way to think about "Abolish the police," then, is as an argument that, now that all of us have finally clawed our way into the polis, the police are obsolete.

BUT ARE THEY? The crisis in policing is the culmination of a thousand other failures—failures of education, social services, public health, gun regulation, criminal justice, and economic development. Police have a lot in common with firefighters, EMTs, and paramedics: they're there to help, often at great sacrifice, and by placing themselves in harm's way. To say that this doesn't always work out, however, does not begin to cover the size of the problem. The 2020 killing of George Floyd, in Minneapolis, cannot be wished away as an outlier. Every year between 2015 and 2020, police in the United States killed roughly a thousand people. (During each of those same years, about a hundred police officers were killed in the line of duty.) One study suggests that, among American men between the ages of fifteen and thirty-four, the number who were treated in emergency rooms as a result of injuries inflicted by police and security guards was almost as great as the number who, as pedestrians, were injured by motor vehicles. Urban police forces are nearly always whiter than the communities they patrol. The victims of police brutality are disproportionately Black teenage boys: children. To say that many good and admirable people are police officers, dedicated and brave public servants, which is, of course, true, is to fail to address both the nature and the scale of the crisis and the legacy of centuries of racial injustice. The best people, with the best of intentions, doing their utmost, cannot fix this system from within.

In 2020, there were nearly seven hundred thousand police officers in the United States, about two for every thousand people, a

rate that is lower than the European average. The difference is guns.
Police in Finland fired six bullets in all of 2013; in an encounter on
a single day in the year 2015, in Pasco, Washington, three policemen
fired seventeen bullets when they shot and killed an unarmed thirty-
five-year-old orchard worker from Mexico. Five years ago, when the
Guardian counted police killings, it reported that "in the first 24 days
of 2015, police in the US fatally shot more people than police did
in England and Wales, combined, over the past 24 years." American
police are armed to the teeth, with more than seven billion dollars'
worth of surplus military equipment off-loaded by the Pentagon to
eight thousand law enforcement agencies since 1997. At the same
time, they face the most heavily armed civilian population in the
world. Gun violence undermines civilian life and debases everyone.
A study found that, given the ravages of stress, white male police
officers in Buffalo have a life expectancy twenty-two years shorter
than that of the average American male. The debate about policing
also has to do with all the money that's spent paying heavily armed
agents of the state to do things that they aren't trained to do and that
other institutions would do better. History haunts this debate like a
bullet-riddled ghost.

THAT HISTORY BEGINS IN ENGLAND, in the thirteenth century, when maintaining the king's peace became the duty of an officer
of the court called a constable, aided by his watchmen: every male adult
could be called on to take a turn walking a ward at night and, if trouble came, to raise a hue and cry. This practice lasted for centuries. (A
version endures: George Zimmerman, when he shot and killed Trayvon Martin, in 2012, was serving on his neighborhood watch.) The
watch didn't work especially well in England—"The average constable
is an ignoramus who knows little or nothing of the law," Blackstone
wrote—and it didn't work especially well in England's colonies. Rich
men paid poor men to take their turns on the watch, which meant
that most watchmen were either very elderly or very poor, and very
exhausted from working all day. Boston established a watch in 1631.
New York tried paying watchmen in 1658. In Philadelphia, in 1705,
the governor expressed the view that the militia could make the city
safer than the watch, but militias weren't supposed to police the king's

subjects; they were supposed to serve the common defense—waging wars against the French, fighting Native peoples who were trying to hold on to their lands, or suppressing slave rebellions.

The government of slavery was not a rule of law. It was a rule of police. In 1661, the English colony of Barbados passed its first slave law; revised in 1688, it decreed that "Negroes and other Slaves" were "wholly unqualified to be governed by the Laws . . . of our Nations," and devised, instead, a special set of rules "for the good Regulating and Ordering of them." Virginia adopted similar measures, known as slave codes, in 1680:

> It shall not be lawfull for any negroe or other slave to carry or arme himselfe with any club, staffe, gunn, sword or any other weapon of defence or offence, nor to goe or depart from of his masters ground without a certificate from his master, mistris or overseer, and such permission not to be granted but upon perticuler and necessary occasions; and every negroe or slave soe offending not haveing a certificate as aforesaid shalbe sent to the next constable, who is hereby enjoyned and required to give the said negroe twenty lashes on his bare back well layd on, and soe sent home to his said master, mistris or overseer . . . that if any negroe or other slave shall absent himself from his masters service and lye hid and lurking in obscure places, comitting injuries to the inhabitants, and shall resist any person or persons that shalby any lawfull authority be imployed to apprehend and take the said negroe, that then in case of such resistance, it shalbe lawfull for such person or persons to kill the said negroe or slave soe lying out and resisting.

In eighteenth-century New York, a person held as a slave could not gather in a group of more than three; could not ride a horse; could not hold a funeral at night; could not be out an hour after sunset without a lantern; and could not sell "Indian corn, peaches, or any other fruit" in any street or market in the city. Stop and frisk, stop and whip, shoot to kill.

Then there were the slave patrols. Armed Spanish bands called *hermandades* had hunted runaways in Cuba beginning in the 1530s, a practice that was adopted by the English in Barbados a century later. It had a lot in common with England's posse comitatus, a band of stout men that a county sheriff could summon to chase down an escaped criminal. South Carolina, founded by slaveowners from Barbados, authorized its first slave patrol in 1702; Virginia followed in 1726, North Carolina in 1753. Slave patrols married the watch to the militia: serving on patrol was required of all able-bodied men (often, the patrol was mustered from the militia), and patrollers used the hue and cry to call for anyone within hearing distance to join the chase. Neither the watch nor the militia nor the patrols were "police," who were French, and considered despotic. In North America, the French city of New Orleans was distinctive in having *la police:* armed City Guards, who wore military-style uniforms and received wages, an urban slave patrol.

In 1779, Thomas Jefferson created a chair in "law and police" at the College of William & Mary. The meaning of the word began to change. In 1789, Jeremy Bentham, noting that "police" had recently entered the English language, in something like its modern sense, made this distinction: police keep the peace; justice punishes disorder. ("No justice, no peace!" Black Lives Matter protesters cry in the streets.) Then, in 1797, a London magistrate named Patrick Colquhoun published *A Treatise on the Police of the Metropolis.* He, too, distinguished peace kept in the streets from justice administered by the courts: police were responsible for the regulation and correction of behavior and "the PREVENTION and DETECTION OF CRIMES."

It is often said that Britain created the police, and the United States copied it. One could argue that the reverse is true. Colquhoun spent his teens and early twenties in colonial Virginia, had served as an agent for British cotton manufacturers, and owned shares in sugar plantations in Jamaica. He knew all about slave codes and slave patrols. But nothing came of Colquhoun's ideas about policing until 1829, when Home Secretary Robert Peel—in the wake of a great deal of labor unrest, and after years of suppressing Catholic rebellions in Ireland, in his capacity as Irish Secretary—persuaded Parliament to establish the Metropolitan Police, a force of some three thousand men, headed by two civilian justices (later called "commissioners"), and organized like an army, with each superintendent overseeing four inspectors, sixteen sergeants, and a hundred and sixty-five constables, who wore coats and pants of blue with black top hats, each assigned a numbered badge and a baton. Londoners came to call these men "bobbies," for Bobby Peel.

It is also often said that modern American urban policing began in 1838, when the Massachusetts legislature authorized the hiring of police officers in Boston. This, too, ignores the role of slavery in the history of the police. In 1829, a Black abolitionist in Boston named David Walker published an *Appeal to the Coloured Citizens of the World*, calling for violent rebellion: "One good black man can put to death six white men." Walker was found dead within the year, and Boston thereafter had a series of mob attacks against abolitionists, including an attempt to lynch William Lloyd Garrison, the publisher of *The Liberator*, in 1835. Walker's words terrified Southern slaveowners. The governor of North Carolina wrote to his state's senators, "I beg you will lay this matter before the police of your town and invite their prompt attention to the necessity of arresting the circulation of the book." By "police," he meant slave patrols: in response to Walker's *Appeal*, North Carolina formed a statewide "patrol committee."

New York established a police department in 1844; New Orleans and Cincinnati followed in 1852, then, later in the 1850s, Philadelphia, Chicago, and Baltimore. Population growth, the widening inequality brought about by the Industrial Revolution, and the rise in such crimes as prostitution and burglary all contributed to the emergence of urban policing. So did immigration, especially from Ireland and Germany, and the hostility to immigration: a new party, the Know-Nothings, sought to prevent immigrants from voting, holding office, and becoming citizens. In 1854, Boston disbanded its ancient watch and formally established a police department; that year, Know-Nothings swept the city's elections.

American police differed from their English counterparts: in the U.S., police commissioners, as political appointees, fell under local control, with limited supervision; and law enforcement was decentralized, resulting in a jurisdictional thicket. In 1857, in the Great Police Riot, the New York Municipal Police, run by the mayor's office, fought on the steps of city hall with the New York Metropolitan Police, run by the state. The Metropolitans were known as the New York Mets. That year, an amateur baseball team of the same name was founded.

Also, unlike their British counterparts, American police carried guns, initially their own. In the 1860s, the Colt Firearms Company began manufacturing a compact revolver called a Pocket Police Model, long before the New York Metropolitan Police began issuing service weapons. American police carried guns because Americans carried guns, including Americans who lived in parts of the country where they hunted for food and defended their livestock from wild animals, Americans who lived in parts of the country that had no police, and Americans who lived in parts of North America that were not in the United States. Outside big cities, law enforcement officers were scarce. In territories that weren't yet states, there were U.S. marshals and their deputies, officers of the federal courts who could act as de facto police, but only to enforce federal laws. If a territory became a state, its counties would elect sheriffs. Meanwhile, Americans became vigilantes, especially likely to kill indigenous peoples, and to lynch people of color. Between 1840 and the 1920s, mobs, vigilantes, and law officers, including the Texas Rangers, lynched some five hundred Mexicans and Mexican Americans and killed thousands more, not only in Texas but also in territories that became the states of California, Arizona, Nevada, Utah, Colorado, and New Mexico. A San Francisco vigilance committee established in 1851 arrested, tried, and hanged people; it boasted a membership in the thousands. An LA vigilance committee targeted and lynched Chinese immigrants.

The U.S. Army operated as a police force, too. After the Civil War, the militia was organized into seven new departments of permanent standing armies: the Department of Dakota, the Department of the Platte, the Department of the Missouri, the Department of Texas, the Department of Arizona, the Department of California, and the Department of the Columbian. In the 1870s and '80s, the U.S. Army engaged in more than a thousand combat operations against Native peoples. In 1890, at Wounded Knee, South Dakota, following an attempt to disarm a Lakota settlement, a regiment of cavalrymen massacred hundreds of Lakota men, women, and children. Nearly a century later, in 1973, FBI agents, SWAT teams, and federal troops and state marshals laid siege to Wounded Knee during a protest over police brutality and the failure to properly punish the torture and murder of an Oglala Sioux man named Raymond Yellow Thunder. They fired more than half a million rounds of ammunition and arrested more than a thousand people. Today, according to the CDC, Native Americans are more likely to be killed by the police than any other racial or ethnic group.

MODERN AMERICAN POLICING BEGAN IN 1909, when August Vollmer became the chief of the police department in Berkeley, California. Vollmer refashioned American police into an American military. He'd served with the Eighth Army Corps in the Philippines in 1898. "For years, ever since Spanish-American War days, I've studied military tactics and used them to good effect in rounding up crooks," he later explained. "After all we're conducting a war, a war against the enemies of society." Who were those enemies? Mobsters, bootleggers, socialist agitators, strikers, union organizers, immigrants, and Black people.

To domestic policing, Vollmer and his peers adapted the kinds of tactics and weapons that had been deployed against Native Americans in the West and against colonized peoples in other parts of the world, including Cuba, Puerto Rico, and the Philippines, as the sociologist Julian Go has demonstrated. Vollmer instituted a training model imitated all over the country, by police departments that were often led and staffed by other veterans of the United States wars of conquest and occupation. A "police captain or lieutenant should occupy exactly the same position in the public mind as that of a captain or lieutenant in the United States army," Detroit's commissioner of police said. (Today's police officers are disproportionately veterans of U.S. wars in Iraq and Afghanistan, many suffering from post-traumatic stress. The Marshall Project, analyzing data from the Albuquerque police, found that officers who are veterans are more likely than their non-veteran counterparts to be involved in fatal shootings. In general, they are more likely to use force, and more likely to fire their guns.)

Vollmer-era police enforced a new kind of slave code: Jim Crow laws, which had been passed in the South beginning in the late 1870s and upheld by the Supreme Court in 1896. William G. Austin became Savannah's chief of police in 1907. Earlier, he had earned a Medal of Honor for his service in the U.S. Cavalry at Wounded Knee; he had also fought in the Spanish-American War. By 1916, African American churches in the city were complaining to Savannah newspapers about the "whole scale arrests of negroes because they are negroes—arrests that would not be made if they were white under similar circumstances." African Americans also confronted Jim Crow policing in the Northern cities to which they increasingly fled. James Robinson, Philadelphia's chief of police beginning in 1912, had served in the infantry during the Spanish-American War and the Philippine-American War. He based his force's training on manuals used by the U.S. Army at Leavenworth. Go reports that, in 1911, about 11 percent of people arrested were African American; under Robinson, that number rose to 14.6 percent in 1917. By the 1920s, a quarter of those arrested were African Americans, who, at the time, represented just 7.4 percent of the population.

Progressive Era, Vollmer-style policing criminalized Blackness, as the historian Khalil Gibran Muhammad argued in his 2010 book, *The Condemnation of Blackness: Race, Crime, and the Making of Modern Urban America.* Police patrolled Black neighborhoods and arrested Black people disproportionately; prosecutors indicted Black people disproportionately; juries found Black people guilty disproportionately; judges gave Black people disproportionately long sentences; and, then, after all this, social scientists, observing the number of Black people in jail, decided that, as a matter of biology, Black people were disproportionately inclined to criminality.

More recently, between the New Jim Crow and the criminalization of immigration and the imprisonment of immigrants in detention centers, this reality has only grown worse. "By population, by per capita incarceration rates, and by expenditures, the United States exceeds all other nations in how many of its citizens, asylum seekers, and undocumented immigrants are under some form of criminal justice supervision," Muhammad writes in a preface to a new edition. "The number of African American and Latinx people in American jails and prisons today exceeds the entire populations of some African, Eastern European, and Caribbean countries."

Policing grew harsher in the Progressive Era, and, with the emergence of state police forces, the number of police grew, too. With the rise of the automobile, some, like California's, began as "highway patrols." Others, including the state police in Nevada, Colorado, and Oregon, began as the private paramilitaries of industrialists which employed the newest American immigrants: Hungarians, Italians, and Jews. Industrialists in Pennsylvania established the Iron and Coal Police to end strikes and bust unions, including the United Mine Workers; in 1905, three years after an anthracite coal strike, the Pennsylvania State Police started operations. "One State Policeman should be able to handle one hundred foreigners," its new chief said.

The U.S. Border Patrol began in 1924, the year that Congress restricted immigration from southern Europe. At the insistence of southern and western agriculturalists, Congress exempted Mexicans from its new immigration quotas in order to allow migrant workers to enter the United States. The Border Patrol began as a relatively small outfit responsible for enforcing federal immigration law, and stopping smugglers, at all of the nation's borders. In the middle decades of the twentieth century, it grew to a national quasi-military focused on policing the southern border in campaigns of mass arrest and forced deportation of Mexican immigrants, aided by local police like the notoriously brutal LAPD, as the historian Kelly Lytle Hernández has chronicled. What became the Chicano movement began in Southern California, with Mexican immigrants' protests of the LAPD during the first half of the twentieth century, even as a growing film industry cranked out features about Klansmen hunting Black people, cowboys killing Indians, and police chasing Mexicans. More recently, you can find an updated version of this story in *L.A. Noire*, a video game set in 1947 and played from the perspective of a well-armed LAPD officer, who, driving along Sunset Boulevard, passes the crumbling, abandoned sets from D. W. Griffith's 1916 film *Intolerance*, imagined relics of an unforgiving age.

TWO KINDS OF POLICE APPEARED on midcentury American television. The good guys solved crime on prime-time police procedurals like *Dragnet*, starting in 1951, and *Adam-12*, beginning in 1968 (both featured the LAPD). The bad guys shocked America's conscience on the nightly news: Arkansas state troopers barring Black students from entering Little Rock Central High School, in 1957; Birmingham police clubbing and arresting some seven hundred Black children protesting segregation, in 1963; and Alabama state troopers beating voting rights marchers at Selma, in 1965. These two faces of policing help explain how, in the 1960s, the more people protested police brutality, the more money governments gave to police departments.

In 1965, President Lyndon Johnson declared a "war on crime," and asked Congress to pass the Law Enforcement Assistance Act, under which the federal government would supply local police with military-grade weapons, weapons that were being used in the war in Vietnam. During riots in Watts that summer, law enforcement killed thirty-one people and arrested more than four thousand; fighting the protesters, the head of the LAPD said, was "very much like fighting the Viet Cong." Preparing for a Senate vote just days after the uprising ended, the chair of the Senate Judiciary Committee said, "For some time, it has been my feeling that the task of law enforcement agencies is really not much different from military forces; namely, to deter crime before it occurs, just as our military objective is deterrence of aggression."

As Elizabeth Hinton reported in *From the War on Poverty to the War on Crime: The Making of Mass Incarceration in America*, the "frontline soldiers" in Johnson's war on crime—Vollmer-era policing all over again—spent a disproportionate amount of time patrolling Black neighborhoods and arresting Black people. Policymakers concluded from those differential arrest rates that Black people were prone to criminality, with the result that police spent even more of their time patrolling Black neighborhoods, which led to a still higher arrest rate. "If we wish to rid this country of crime, if we wish to stop hacking at its branches only, we must cut its roots and drain its swampy breeding ground, the slum," Johnson told an audience of police policymakers in 1966. The next year, riots broke out in Newark and Detroit. "We ain't rioting agains' all you whites," one Newark man told a *Life* magazine reporter not long before being shot dead by police. "We're riotin' agains' police brutality." In Detroit, police arrested more than seven thousand people.

Johnson's Great Society essentially ended when he asked Congress to pass the Omnibus Crime Control and Safe Streets Act, which had the effect of diverting money from social programs to policing. *The New Yorker* called it "a piece of demagoguery devised out of malevolence and enacted in hysteria." James Baldwin attributed its "irresponsible ferocity" to "some pale, compelling nightmare—an overwhelming collection of private nightmares." The truth was darker, as the sociologist Stuart Schrader chronicled in his 2019 book, *Badges Without Borders: How Global Counterinsurgency Transformed American Policing*. During the Cold War, the Office of Public Safety at the USAID provided assistance to the police in at least fifty-two countries, and training to officers from nearly eighty, for the purpose of counterinsurgency—the suppression of an anticipated revolution, that collection of private nightmares; as the OPS reported, it contributed "the international dimension to the Administration's War on Crime." Counterinsurgency boomeranged, and came back to the United States, as policing.

In 1968, Johnson's new crime bill established the Law Enforcement Assistance Administration, within the Department of Justice, which, in the next decade and a half, disbursed federal funds to more than eighty thousand crime control projects. Even funds intended for social projects—youth employment, for instance, along with other health, education, housing, and welfare programs—were distributed to police operations. With Richard Nixon, any elements of the Great Society that had survived the disastrous end of Johnson's presidency were drastically cut, with an increased emphasis on policing, and prison-building. More Americans went to prison between 1965 and 1982 than between 1865 and 1964, Hinton reports. Under Ronald Reagan, still more social services were closed, or starved of funding until they died: mental hospitals, health centers, jobs programs, early childhood education. By 2016, eighteen states were spending more on prisons than on colleges and universities. Activists who today call for defunding the police argue that, for decades, Americans have been defunding not only social services but, in many states, public education itself. The more frayed the social fabric, the more police have been deployed to trim the dangling threads.

The blueprint for law enforcement from Nixon to Reagan came from the Harvard political scientist James Q. Wilson between 1968, in his book *Varieties of Police Behavior*, and 1982, in an essay in the *Atlantic* titled "Broken Windows." On the one hand, Wilson believed that the police should shift from enforcing the law to maintaining order, by patrolling on foot, and doing what came to be called "community policing." (Some of his recommendations were ignored: Wilson called for other professionals to handle what he termed the "service functions" of the police—"first aid, rescuing cats, helping ladies, and the like"—which is a reform people are asking for today.) On the other hand, Wilson called for police to arrest people for petty crimes, on the theory that they contributed to more serious crimes. Wilson's work informed programs like Detroit's STRESS (Stop the Robberies, Enjoy Safe Streets), begun in 1971, in which Detroit police patrolled the city undercover, in disguises that included everything from a taxi driver to a "radical college professor," and killed so many young Black men that an organization of Black police officers demanded that the unit be disbanded. The campaign to end STRESS arguably marked the very beginnings of police abolitionism. STRESS defended its methods. "We just don't walk up and shoot somebody," one commander said. "We ask him to stop. If he doesn't, we shoot."

FOR DECADES, THE WAR ON CRIME was bipartisan, and had substantial support from the Congressional Black Caucus. "Crime is a national defense problem," Joe Biden said in the Senate, in 1982. "You're in as much jeopardy in the streets as you are from a Soviet missile." Biden and other Democrats in the Senate introduced legislation that resulted in the Comprehensive Crime Control Act of 1984. A decade later, as chairman of the Senate Judiciary Committee, Biden helped draft the Violent Crime Control and Law Enforcement Act, whose provisions included mandatory sentencing. In May 1991, two months after the Rodney King beating, Biden introduced the Police Officers' Bill of Rights, which provided protections for police under investigation. In 1988, eight years after the NRA first endorsed a presidential candidate, Reagan, the Fraternal Order of Police, the nation's largest police union, first endorsed a presidential candidate, George H. W. Bush. In 1996, it endorsed Bill Clinton.

Partly because of Biden's record of championing law enforcement, the National Association of Police Organizations endorsed the Obama-Biden ticket in 2008 and 2012. In 2014, after police in Ferguson, Missouri, shot Michael Brown, the Obama administration established a task force on policing in the twenty-first century. Its report argued that police had become warriors when what they really should be is guardians. Most of its recommendations were never implemented.

In 2016, the Fraternal Order of Police endorsed Donald Trump, saying that "our members believe he will make America safe again." Police unions lined up behind Trump again in 2020. "We will never abolish our police or our great Second Amendment," Trump said at Mt. Rushmore, on the occasion of the Fourth of July. "We will not be intimidated by bad, evil people."

Trump is not the king; the law is king. The police are not the king's men; they are public servants. And, no matter how desperately Trump would like to make it so, policing really isn't a partisan issue. Out of the stillness of the shutdown, the voices of protest have roared like summer thunder. An overwhelming majority of Americans, of both parties, support major reforms in American policing. And a whole lot of police, defying their unions, also support those reforms.

Those changes won't address plenty of bigger crises, not least because the problem of policing can't be solved without addressing the problem of guns. But this much is clear: the polis has changed, and the police will have to change, too.

—2020

THE RIOT REPORT

O N FEBRUARY 14, 1965, BACK FROM A TRIP TO LOS Angeles, and a week before he was killed in New York, Malcolm X gave a speech in Detroit. "Brothers and sisters, let me tell you, I spend my time out there in the street with people, all kind of people, listening to what they have to say," he said. "And they're dissatisfied, they're disillusioned, they're fed up, they're getting to the point of frustration where they are beginning to feel: What do they have to lose?"

That summer, President Lyndon B. Johnson signed the Voting Rights Act. In a ceremony at the Capitol Rotunda attended by Martin Luther King Jr., Johnson invoked the arrival of enslaved Africans in Jamestown, in 1619: "They came in darkness and they came in chains. And today we strike away the last major shackles of those fierce and ancient bonds." Five days later, Watts was swept by violence and flames, following a protest against police brutality. The authorities eventually arrested nearly four thousand people; thirty-four people died. "How is it possible, after all we've accomplished?" Johnson asked. "How could it be? Is the world topsy-turvy?"

Two years later, after thousands of police officers and National Guard troops blocked off fourteen square miles of Newark and nearly five thousand troops from the 82nd and the 101st Airborne were deployed to Detroit, where seven thousand people were arrested, Johnson convened a National Advisory Commission on Civil Disorders, chaired by Illinois's governor, Otto Kerner Jr., and charged it with answering three questions: "What happened? Why did it happen? What can be done to prevent it from happening again and again?" Johnson wanted to know why Black people were still protesting, after Congress had finally passed landmark legislation, not only the Voting Rights Act but also the Civil Rights Act of 1964, and a raft of anti-poverty programs.

Or maybe he really didn't want to know why. When the Kerner Commission submitted its report, the president refused to acknowledge it.

There's a limit to the relevance of the so-called race riots of the 1960s to the protests of the Black Lives Matter movement. But the tragedy is: they're not irrelevant. Nor is the history that came before. The language changes, from "insurrection" to "uprising" to the bureaucratic "civil disorder," terms used to describe everything from organized resistance to mayhem. But, nearly always, they leave a bloody trail in the historical record, in the form of government reports. The Kerner Report followed centuries of official and generally hysterical government inquiries into Black rebellion, from the unhinged *A Journal of the proceedings in the Detection of the Conspiracy formed by some White People, in conjunction with Negro and other Slaves, for burning the City of New-York in America, and murdering the Inhabitants*, in 1744, to the largely fabricated *Official Report of the Trials of Sundry Negroes, charged with an attempt to raise an insurrection in the state of South-Carolina*, in 1822. The white editor of the as-told-to (and highly dubious) "The Confessions of Nat Turner, the Leader of the Late Insurrection in Southampton, Va. . . . also, An Authentic Account of the Whole Insurrection, with Lists of the Whites Who Were Murdered . . . ," in 1831, wrote, "Public curiosity has been on the stretch to understand the origin and progress of this dreadful conspiracy, and the motives which influences its diabolical actors." What happened? Why did it happen? What can be done to prevent it from happening again and again?

AFTER RECONSTRUCTION, IDA B. WELLS, in *Southern Horrors: Lynch Law in All Its Phases*, which appeared in 1892, turned the genre on its head, offering a report on white mobs attacking Black men, a litany of lynchings. "Somebody must show that the Afro-American race is more sinned against than sinning, and it seems to have fallen upon me to do so," Wells wrote in the book's preface, after a mob burned the offices of her newspaper, the *Free Speech*. White mob violence against Black people and their homes and businesses was the far more common variety of race riot, from the first rising of the KKK, after the Civil War, through the second, in 1915. And so the earliest twentieth-century commissions charged with investigating "race riots" reported on the riots of white mobs, beginning with the massacre in East St. Louis, Illinois, in 1917, in which, following labor unrest, as many as three thousand white men roamed the city, attacking, killing, and lynching Black people, and burning their homes. Wells wrote that as many as a hundred and fifty men were killed, while police officers and National Guardsmen either looked on or joined in. Similar riots took place in 1919, in twenty-six cities, and the governor of Illinois appointed an interracial commission to investigate. "This is a tribunal constituted to get the facts and interpret them and to find a way out," he said.

The Chicago Commission on Race Relations, composed of six whites and six Blacks, who engaged the work of as many as twenty-two whites and fifteen Blacks, heard nearly two hundred witnesses and, in 1922, published a seven-hundred-page report, with photographs, maps, and color plates: *The Negro in Chicago: A Study of Race Relations and a Race Riot*. It paid particular attention to racial antipathy: "Many white Americans, while technically recognizing Negroes as citizens, cannot bring themselves to feel that they should participate in government as freely as other citizens." Much of the report traces how the Great Migration brought large numbers of blacks from the Jim Crow South to Chicago, where they faced discrimination in housing and employment, and persecution at the hands of local police and the criminal justice system:

> The testimony of court officials before the Commission and its investigations indicate that Negroes are more commonly arrested, subjected to police identification, and convicted than white offenders, that on similar evidence they are generally held and convicted on more serious charges, and that they are given longer sentences. . . . These practices and tendencies are not only unfair to Negroes, but weaken the machinery of justice and, when taken with the greater inability of Negroes to pay fines in addition to or in lieu of terms in jail, produce misleading statistics of Negro crime.

Very little came of the report. In 1935, following riots in Harlem, yet another hardworking commission weighed in:

This sudden breach of the public order was the result of a highly emotional situation among the colored people of Harlem, due in large part to the nervous strain of years of unemployment and insecurity. To this must be added their deep sense of wrong through discrimination against their employment in stores which live chiefly upon their purchases, discrimination against them in the school system and by the police, and all the evils due to dreadful overcrowding, unfair rentals and inadequate institutional care. It is probable that their justifiable pent-up feeling, that they were and are the victims of gross injustice and prejudice, would sooner or later have brought about an explosion.

Who was to blame?

The blame belongs to a society that tolerates inadequate and often wretched housing, inadequate and inefficient schools and other public facilities, unemployment, unduly high rents, the lack of recreation grounds, discrimination in industry and public utilities against colored people, brutality and lack of courtesy of the police.

In Detroit in 1943, after a riot left twenty-five blacks and nine whites dead and led to the arrest of nearly two thousand people, Michigan's governor appointed the commissioner of police and the attorney general to a panel that concluded, without conducting much of an investigation, that responsibility for the riots lay with Black leaders, and defended the police, whom many had blamed for the violence. A separate, independent commission, led by Thurgood Marshall, then chief counsel for the NAACP, conducted interviews, hired private detectives, and produced a report titled "The Gestapo in Detroit." The group called for a grand jury, arguing that "much of the blood spilled in the Detroit riot is on the hands of the Detroit police department." No further investigation took place, and no material reforms were implemented.

That's what usually happens. In a 1977 study, "Commission Politics: The Processing of Racial Crisis in America," Michael Lipsky and David J. Olson reported that, between 1917 and 1943, at least twenty-one commissions were appointed to investigate race riots, and, however sincerely their members might have been interested in structural change, none of the commissions led to any. The point of a race-riot commission, Lipsky and Olson argue, is for the government that appoints it to appear to be doing something, while actually doing nothing.

THE CONVULSIONS THAT LED to the Kerner Commission began in Los Angeles, in 1965. Between 1960 and 1964, the nation enjoyed unrivaled prosperity, but in Watts, among the poorest neighborhoods of LA, one in three men had no work. In Los Angeles, as Mike Davis and Jon Wiener write in Set the Night on Fire: L.A. in the Sixties, "the LAPD operated the nation's most successful negative employment scheme." Police stopped Black men for little or no reason, and, if they talked back, they got arrested; left with an arrest record, they became unemployable.

On August 11, 1965, a Wednesday, a motorcycle cop pulled over a car with a driver and a passenger, two brothers, Ronald and Marquette Frye, about a block from their house, near 116th Street. Their mother, Rena, all of five feet tall, came over. Marquette resisted handcuffs—he would strike those fierce and ancient shackles. The motorcycle cop called for backup; twenty-six police vehicles raced to the scene, sirens screaming. "Does it take all these people to arrest three people?" an onlooker asked. When Rena Frye tried to stop the police from beating her sons with billy clubs, they pinned her to the hood of a patrol car and, after a crowd had gathered, arrested another of her sons and dragged her away. "Goddam! They'd never treat a white woman like that!" someone called out. The crowd protested, and grew, and protested, and grew. What came to be known as the Watts riot lasted for six days and spread across nearly fifty square miles. On Friday night, a man said:

I was standing in a phone booth watching. A little kid came by carrying a lamp he had taken out of a store. Maybe he was about twelve. He was with his mother. I remember him saying: "Don't run Mommy. They said we could take the stuff because they're going to burn the store anyway." Then, suddenly, about five police cars stopped. There were about 20 cops in them and they all got out. One came up to the booth I was standing in. The cop hit me on the leg with his club. "Get out of here, nigger," he yelled at me. I got out of the booth. Another cop ran up to the boy and hit him in the head with the butt of a shotgun. The kid dropped like a stone. The lamp crashed on the sidewalk. I ran out of the phone booth and grabbed the cop by the arm. I was trying to stop him from beating the boy. Two cops jumped on my back. Others struck the boy with their clubs. They beat that little kid's face to a bloody pulp. His mother and some others took him away. That's when I thought, white people are animals.

Johnson could barely speak about what was happening in Watts. An aide said, "He refused to look at the cable from Los Angeles describing the situation. He refused to take the calls from the generals who were requesting government planes to fly in the National Guard. . . . We needed decisions from him. But he simply wouldn't respond."

The same Friday, the National Guard arrived. "More Americans died fighting in Watts Saturday night than in Vietnam that day," an observer wrote. On Sunday, fifteen police officers fired eleven shotgun rounds into Aubrey Griffith, inside his own house, where he and his wife had been in bed while their son, on leave from the air force, was watching TV. The officers banged on the door, and Griffith told his wife to call the police. An inquest ruled his death—and every other death at the hands of the National Guard or the police during the days of protest—a justifiable homicide.

Martin Luther King Jr. arrived on Tuesday. "All we want is jobs," a man said to him, at a community meeting in Watts. "We get jobs, we don't bother nobody. We don't get no jobs, we'll tear up Los Angeles, period." Later, King recalled that one man told him, "We won!" King had replied, "What do you mean, 'We won'? Thirty-some people dead, all but two are Negroes. You've destroyed your own. What do you mean, 'We won'?" The man said, "We made them pay attention to us."

Paying attention, at that point, only ever really took this form: the governor appointed a commission, this time headed by John A. McCone, a lavishly wealthy and well-connected California industrialist who, in 1961, had been made director of the CIA by President

Kennedy but had resigned in April 1965, in part because he objected to Johnson's reluctance to engage in a wider war in Vietnam. The McCone Commission report, titled "Violence in the City," celebrated the City of Angels: "A Negro in Los Angeles has long been able to sit where he wants in a bus or a movie house, to shop where he wishes, to vote, and to use public facilities without discrimination. The opportunity to succeed is probably unequaled in any other major American city." It called for the creation of fifty thousand new jobs, but, first, "attitudinal training." It blamed the riots on outside agitators and civil rights activists: "Although the commission received much thoughtful and constructive testimony from Negro witnesses, we also heard statements of the most extreme and emotional nature. For the most part our study fails to support—and indeed the evidence disproves—most of the statements made by the extremists." Fundamental to the McCone thesis was the claim that peaceful demonstrations produce violent riots, and should therefore be discouraged. In a devastating rebuttal, Bayard Rustin laid this argument to waste:

> It would be hard to frame a more insidiously equivocal statement of the Negro grievance concerning law enforcement during a period that included the release of the suspects in the murder of the three civil rights workers in Mississippi, the failure to obtain convictions against the suspected murderers of Medgar Evers and Mrs. Violet Liuzzo . . . and the police violence in Selma, Alabama. . . . And surely it would have been more to the point to mention that throughout the nation Negro demonstrations have almost invariably been non-violent, and that the major influence on the Negro community of the civil-rights movement has been the strategy of discipline and dignity.

By the summer of 1967, amid the protests in Newark and Detroit, Johnson was facing a conservative backlash against his Great Society programs, and especially against the Fair Housing Act, which was introduced in Congress in 1966. He'd also been trying to gain passage of a Rat Extermination Act, to get rid of urban infestations; Republicans called it the Civil Rats Bill. Johnson had long since lost the right; now he was losing the left. By April, King had come out against the war in Vietnam. Beleaguered and defensive, Johnson launched an "Optimism Campaign," in an effort to convince the public that the U.S. was winning the war in Vietnam. George Romney, the Republican governor of Michigan, who was expected to run against Johnson in 1968, asked for federal troops to be sent to Detroit, which would be the first time since FDR sent them in 1943. Johnson wavered. "I'm concerned about the charge that we cannot kill enough people in Vietnam so we go out and shoot civilians in Detroit," he said. In the end, he decided to authorize the troops, and to blame Romney, announcing, on television, that there was "undisputed evidence that Governor Romney of Michigan and the local officials in Detroit have been unable to bring the situation under control." Twenty-seven hundred army paratroopers were deployed to Detroit, with Huey helicopters that most Americans had seen only in TV coverage of the war in Vietnam.

On July 27, 1967, Johnson gave a televised speech on "civil disorders," announcing his decision to form a national commission to investigate race riots. Protests had taken place, and turned violent, in more than a hundred and fifty cities that summer, and they were being televised. Were they part of a conspiracy? Johnson suspected so, even though his advisers told him that he was wrong. "I don't want to foreclose the conspiracy theory now," he said. "Keep that door open."

Johnson loved presidential commissions: people called him, not affectionately, "the great commissioner." In the first decade after the Second World War, U.S. presidents appointed an average of one and a half commissions a year. Johnson appointed twenty. In *Separate and Unequal: The Kerner Commission and the Unraveling of American Liberalism*, Steven M. Gillon observes that "commissions became a convenient way for presidents to fill the gap between what they could deliver and what was expected of them." To his new commission, Johnson appointed a Noah's ark of commissioners, two by two: two congressmen, one Republican, one Democrat; one business leader, one labor leader. Roy Wilkins, the executive director of the NAACP, was, with Edward Brooke, a Republican senator from Massachusetts, one of two African Americans. The commission included no political radicals, no protesters, and no young people. The president expected the commission to defend his legislative accomplishments and agenda, and to endorse his decision to send the National Guard to Detroit. When he called Fred Harris, the thirty-six-year-old Oklahoma senator, to discuss the appointment, he told Harris to remember that he was a "Johnson man." Otherwise, Johnson said, "I'll take out my pocket knife and cut your peter off." Nearly as soon as he convened the commission, Johnson regretted it, and pulled its funding.

OTTO KERNER, BORN IN CHICAGO in 1908, went to Brown and then Northwestern, for law school, and, in the 1930s and into the Second World War, served in the Illinois National Guard for twenty years, retiring in 1954 with the rank of major general. Under his leadership, as Bill Barnhart and Gene Schlickman report in their biography, *Kerner: The Conflict of Intangible Rights*, the Illinois guard had the nation's highest percentage of African Americans. A former district attorney, later elected to a county judgeship, Kerner had a reputation for strict personal integrity, earning him the nickname Mr. Clean. He was elected governor of Illinois in 1960, and it is possible that his coattails delivered the state to John F. Kennedy, in one of the closest presidential races in American history. He had a strong record on civil rights, and was an adamant supporter of fair housing, declaring, in 1968, "Civil disorders will still be the order of the day unless we create a society of equal justice."

After Kerner got the call from Johnson, he announced, "Tomorrow, I go to Washington to help organize this group of citizens for the saddest mission that any of us in our careers have been asked to pursue—why one American assaults another, why violence is inflicted on people of our cities, why the march to an ideal America has been interrupted by bloodshed and destruction. We are being asked, in a broad sense, to probe into the soul of America."

Kerner wanted open hearings. "My concern all the time about this commission has been that at the conclusion our greatest problem is going to be to educate the whites, rather than the Negro," he said. Kerner did not prevail on this point. J. Edgar Hoover testified on the first day, to say that the FBI had found no evidence of a conspiracy behind the riots, and that he thought one good remedy for violence would be better gun laws. "You have to license your dog," he said. Why not your gun? Martin Luther King Jr. told the commission, "People who are completely devoid of hope don't riot."

Maybe the most painful testimony came from Kenneth B. Clark, the African American psychologist, at the City College of New York, whose research on inequality had been pivotal to the Supreme Court's decision in *Brown v. Board of Education*. He told the commission:

> I read that report . . . of the 1919 riot in Chicago, and it is as if I were reading the report of the investigating committee on the Harlem riot of '35, the report of the investigating committee on the Harlem riot of '43, the report of the McCone Commission on the Watts riot. I must again in candor say to you members of this Commission—it is a kind of Alice in Wonderland—with the same moving picture re-shown over and over again, the same analysis, the same recommendations, and the same inaction.

The historical trail is blood spilled in a deeply rutted road.

John V. Lindsay, the handsome liberal mayor of New York who served as vice-chair of the commission, got most of the media attention. But Kerner did his work. When the commission traveled, Kerner went out on the street to talk to people. He went for a walk in Newark, and talked to a group of people who told him they had three concerns: police brutality, unemployment, and the lack of a relocation program for displaced workers. One man told the governor that he hadn't had a job in eight years.

After months of hearings and meetings, the commission began assembling its report. Kerner wanted it to be moving, and beautifully written. John Hersey was asked to write it, perhaps in the style of *Hiroshima*; Hersey said no. (Instead, much of the report was drafted by the commission's executive director, David Ginsburg, who later helped write Hubert Humphrey's campaign platform.) Toward the end of the commission's deliberations, Roy Wilkins offered emotional personal testimony that greatly informed a draft by Lindsay, describing "two societies, one black, one white." Another draft contained a passage that was later stricken: "Past efforts have not carried the commitment, will or resources needed to eliminate the attitudes and practices that have maintained racism as a major force in our society. Only the dedication of every citizen can generate a single American identity and a single American community." Every word of the report was read aloud, and every word was unanimously agreed on. The final draft did include this passage: "Race prejudice has shaped our history decisively; it now threatens to affect our future. White racism is essentially responsible for the explosive mixture which has been accumulating in our cities since the end of World War II." In the final report, as the historian Julian Zelizer writes in an introduction to a 2016 edition, "no institution received more scrutiny than the police." That's been true of every one of these reports since 1917.

Johnson, when he got the report, was so mad that he refused to sign the letters thanking the commissioners for their service. "I'd be a hypocrite," he said. "Just file them . . . or get rid of them."

THE KERNER REPORT WAS PUBLISHED on March 1, 1968, but first it was leaked (probably by Ginsburg) to the *Washington Post*, which ran a story with the headline "Chief Blame for Riots Put on White Racism." It became an overnight bestseller. It sold more copies than the Warren Commission report, three-quarters of a million copies in the first two weeks alone. Released in a paperback edition by Bantam, it was said to be the fastest-selling book since *Valley of the Dolls*.

Civil rights activists, expecting a whitewash, were stunned. "It's the first time whites have said, 'We're racists,'" the head of CORE declared. Republicans rejected it. "One of the major weaknesses of the president's commission is that it, in effect, blames everybody for the riots except the perpetrators of the riots," Nixon said from the campaign trail. "I think this talk . . . tends to divide people, to build a wall in between people." Conservatives deemed it absurd. "What caused the riots," William F. Buckley Jr. wrote, "isn't segregation or poverty or frustration. What caused them is a psychological disorder which is tearing at the ethos of our society as a result of boredom, self-hatred, and the arrogant contention that all our shortcomings are the result of other people's aggressions upon us."

Johnson came up with his own explanation for what had happened in America during his presidency: "I've moved the Negro from D+ to C−. He's still nowhere. He knows it. And that's why he's out in the streets. Hell, I'd be there, too." In 1969, Harry McPherson, Johnson's chief speechwriter, tried to explain what had so bothered Johnson about the Kerner Report. "It hurt his pride," McPherson said, because it made it clear that Johnson had not, somehow, saved the Negro. But there was a bigger, sounder reason, he believed: "The only thing that held any hope for the Negro was the continuation of the coalition between labor, Negroes, intellectuals, . . . big city bosses and political machines and some of the urban poor. . . . In other words, it required keeping the Polacks who work on the line at River Rouge in the ball park and supporting Walter Reuther and the government as they try to spend a lot of money for the blacks." Middle-class whites didn't give a damn, he thought, but blacks needed poor and working-class whites on their side. "Then a Presidential commission is formed and goes out and comes back, and what does it say? Who's responsible for the riots? 'The other members of the coalition. They did it. Those racists.' And thereupon, the coalition says . . . 'we'll go out and find ourselves a guy like George Wallace, or Richard Nixon.'"

That spring, Martin Luther King Jr. was killed, and then Robert F. Kennedy. In July, five months after the release of the report, Kerner wrote his own reflections, looking back at the response to the maelstrom that had followed King's assassination, and arguing against the militarization of the police: "Armored vehicles, automatic weapons and armor-piercing machine guns are for use against an enemy, and not a lawbreaker. . . . If you come out with a show of force, you in a sense challenge the other side to meet you. Force begets force."

Still, Johnson fulfilled Kerner's wish to be appointed to the federal bench. During Kerner's confirmation hearings, he was questioned by Strom Thurmond about the conclusions of the report that bore his name:

> THURMOND: Why do you say "white racism" caused these riots?
> KERNER: I beg your pardon.
> THURMOND: Why do you want to blame the white people . . . for this trouble?
> KERNER: Because we say this has developed over a period of time, and the people in the Negro ghettos indicated that the rebellion was against the white establishment. . . .
> THURMOND: . . . What does that term mean? What did you think it meant when you put it in this report or approved of it?
> KERNER: I thought it meant this—that over a period of years the

Negro was kept within a certain area economically and geographically and he was not allowed to come out of it.

In 1971, Kerner became involved in a scandal connected with his ownership of stock in a racetrack; he was eventually charged and convicted of mail fraud. Sentenced to three years in prison, he went to the Federal Correctional Institution, a minimum security prison in Fayette County, Kentucky, on July 29, 1974, two weeks before Nixon resigned. He insisted that his conviction was one of Nixon's "dirty tricks." "I have reason to believe I was one of the victims of this overall plan," he wrote. He suspected Nixon of punishing him for his role in Kennedy's victory in 1960. In his cell, Kerner kept a journal. "So frequently I sit here alone," he wrote, thinking thoughts that inmates have thought since the beginning of prisons:

> I wonder of what use is our prison system—as I have often wondered when I was seeking an alternative to this inhuman manner of restraining those who have violated the law. The waste of man power—both by the restrainers and the one restrained. Removing the individual from the outside world really accomplishes nothing of a positive nature. The restraint builds up frustrations and a smothering of the will. It kills motivation and completely removes decision ability.

With an ailing heart and what was soon discovered to be lung cancer, Kerner was paroled after serving seven months. He spent what time he had left urging prison reform. He died in 1976. Not long before his death, asked about the Kerner Report, he said, "The basis for the report, I think, is as valid today as the day we sent it to the government printing office."

ON JUNE 1, 2020, IN WASHINGTON, DC, police in riot gear cleared Lafayette Square of peaceful protesters by force. ("Take off the riot gear, I don't see no riot here," protesters chanted.) The purpose was to allow President Trump to stride to St. John's Church, accompanied by the attorney general and the chairman of the Joint Chiefs of Staff, and be photographed holding a Bible. The next day, Ohio's

Republican senator, Rob Portman, called for a national commission on race relations. "It would not be a commission to restate the problem but to focus on solutions and send a strong moral message that America must live up to the ideal that God created all of us as equal," Portman said. He suggested that it might be co-chaired by former presidents Barack Obama and George W. Bush.

The United States does not need one more commission, or one more report. A strong moral message? That message is being delivered by protesters every day, on street after street after street across the nation. *Stop killing us.* One day, these reports will lie archived, forgotten, irrelevant. Meanwhile, they pile up, an indictment, the stacked evidence of inertia. In the summer of 1968, the civil rights leader Whitney Young published an essay titled "The Report That Died," writing, "The report is still there, it still reads well, but practically nothing is being done to follow its recommendations." It was as it had ever been. It is time for it to be something else.

—2020

Part Six

The Disruption Machine

Disruptive innovation is competitive strategy for an age seized by terror.

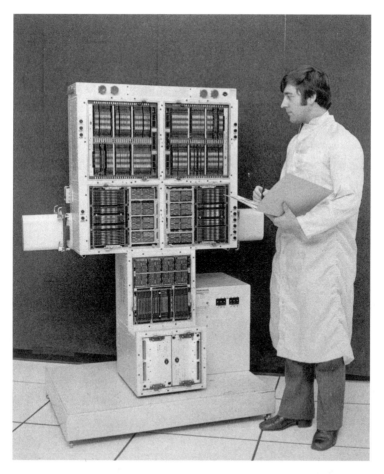

The UNIVAC 1832, 1974.
Bettmann via Getty Images

THE COBWEB

Malaysia Airlines Flight 17 took off from Amsterdam at 10:31 a.m. GMT on July 17, 2014, for a twelve-hour flight to Kuala Lumpur. Not much more than three hours later, the plane, a Boeing 777, crashed in a field outside Donetsk, Ukraine. All 298 people on board were killed. The plane's last radio contact was at 1:20 p.m. GMT. At 2:50, Igor Girkin, a Ukrainian separatist leader also known as Strelkov, or someone acting on his behalf, posted a message on VKontakte, a Russian social media site: "We just downed a plane, an AN-26." (An Antonov 26 is a Soviet-built military cargo plane.) The post includes links to video of the wreckage of a plane; it appears to be a Boeing 777.

Two weeks before the crash, Anatol Shmelev, the curator of the Russia and Eurasia collection at the Hoover Institution, at Stanford, had submitted to the Internet Archive, a nonprofit library in California, a list of Ukrainian and Russian websites and blogs that ought to be recorded as part of the archive's Ukraine Conflict collection. Shmelev is one of about a thousand librarians and archivists around the world who identify possible acquisitions for the Internet Archive's subject collections, which are stored in its Wayback Machine, in San Francisco. Strelkov's VKontakte page was on Shmelev's list. "Strelkov is the field commander in Slaviansk and one of the most important figures in the conflict," Shmelev had written in an email to the Internet Archive on July 1, and his page "deserves to be recorded twice a day."

On July 17, at 3:22 p.m. GMT, the Wayback Machine saved a screenshot of Strelkov's VKontakte post about downing a plane. Two hours and twenty-two minutes later, Arthur Bright, the Europe editor of the *Christian Science Monitor*, tweeted a picture of the screenshot, along with the message "Grab of Donetsk militant Strelkov's claim of downing what appears to have been MH17." By then, Strelkov's VKontakte page had already been edited: the claim about shooting down a plane was deleted. The only real evidence of the original claim lies in the Wayback Machine.

The average life of a web page is about a hundred days. Strelkov's "We just downed a plane" post lasted barely two hours. It might seem, and it often feels, as though stuff on the web lasts forever, for better and frequently for worse: the embarrassing photograph, the regretted blog (more usually regrettable not in the way the slaughter of civilians is regrettable but in the way that bad hair is regrettable). No one believes any longer, if anyone ever did, that "if it's on the web it must be true," but a lot of people do believe that if it's on the web it will stay on the web. Chances are, though, that it actually won't. In 2006, David Cameron gave a speech in which he said that Google was democratizing the world, because "making more information available to more people" was providing "the power for anyone to hold to account those who in the past might have had a monopoly of power." Seven years later, Britain's Conservative Party scrubbed from its website ten years' worth of Tory speeches, including that one. In 2014, *BuzzFeed* deleted more than four thousand of its staff writers' early posts, apparently because, as time passed, they looked stupider and stupider. Social media, public records, junk: in the end, everything goes.

Web pages don't have to be deliberately deleted to disappear. Sites hosted by corporations tend to die with their hosts. When Myspace, GeoCities, and Friendster were reconfigured or sold, millions of accounts vanished. (Some of those companies may have notified users, but Jason Scott, who started an outfit called Archive Team—its motto is "We are going to rescue your shit"—says that such notification is usually purely notional: "They were sending email to dead email addresses, saying, 'Hello, Arthur Dent, your house is going to be crushed.'") Facebook has been around for only a decade; it won't be around forever. Twitter is a rare case: it has arranged to archive all of its tweets at the Library of Congress. In 2010, after the announcement, Andy Borowitz tweeted, "Library of Congress to acquire entire Twitter archive—will rename itself Museum of Crap." Not long after that, Borowitz abandoned that Twitter account. You might, one day, be able to find his old tweets at the Library of Congress, but not anytime soon: the Twitter Archive is not yet open for research. Meanwhile, on the web, if you click on a link to Borowitz's tweet about the Museum of Crap, you get this message: "Sorry, that page doesn't exist!"

The web dwells in a never-ending present. It is—elementally—ethereal, ephemeral, unstable, and unreliable. Sometimes when you try to visit a web page what you see is an error message: "Page Not Found." This is known as "link rot," and it's a drag, but it's better than the alternative. More often, you see an updated web page; most likely the original has been overwritten. (To overwrite, in computing, means to destroy old data by storing new data in their place; overwriting is an artifact of an era when computer storage was very expensive.) Or maybe the page has been moved and something else is where it used to be. This is known as "content drift," and it's more pernicious than an error message, because it's impossible to tell that what you're seeing isn't what you went to look for: the overwriting, erasure, or moving of the original is invisible. For the law and for the courts, link rot and content drift, which are collectively known as "reference rot," have been disastrous. In providing evidence, legal scholars, lawyers, and judges often cite web pages in their footnotes; they expect that evidence to remain where they found it as their proof, the way that evidence on paper—in court records and books and law journals—remains where they found it, in libraries and courthouses. But a 2013 survey of law and policy-related publications found that, at the end of six years, nearly 50 percent of the URLs cited in those publications no longer worked. According to a 2014 study conducted at Harvard Law School, "more than 70% of the URLs within the Harvard Law Review and other journals, and 50% of the URLs within United States Supreme Court opinions, do not link to the originally cited information." The overwriting, drifting, and rotting of the web is no less catastrophic for engineers, scientists, and doctors. Last month, a team of digital library researchers based at Los Alamos National Laboratory reported the results of an exacting study of three and a half million scholarly articles published in science, technology, and medical journals between 1997 and 2012: one in five links provided in the notes suffers from reference rot. It's like trying to stand on quicksand.

The footnote, a landmark in the history of civilization, took centuries to invent and to spread. It has taken mere years nearly to destroy. A footnote used to say, "Here is how I know this and where I found it." A footnote that's a link says, "Here is what I used to know and where I once found it, but chances are it's not there anymore." It doesn't matter whether footnotes are your stock-in-trade. Everybody's in a pinch. Citing a web page as the source for something you know—using a URL as evidence—is ubiquitous. Many people find themselves doing it three or four times before breakfast and five times more before lunch. What happens when your evidence vanishes by dinnertime?

The day after Strelkov's "We just downed a plane" post was deposited into the Wayback Machine, Samantha Power, the U.S. ambassador to the United Nations, told the UN Security Council, in New York, that Ukrainian separatist leaders had "boasted on social media about shooting down a plane, but later deleted these messages." In San Francisco, the people who run the Wayback Machine posted on the Internet Archive's Facebook page, "Here's why we exist."

THE ADDRESS OF THE INTERNET ARCHIVE is archive.org, but another way to visit is to take a plane to San Francisco and ride in a cab to the Presidio, past cypresses that look as though someone had drawn them there with a smudgy crayon. At 300 Funston Avenue, climb a set of stone steps and knock on the brass door of a Greek Revival temple. You can't miss it: it's painted wedding-cake white and it's got, out front, eight Corinthian columns and six marble urns.

"We bought it because it matched our logo," Brewster Kahle told me when I met him there, and he wasn't kidding. Kahle is the founder of the Internet Archive and the inventor of the Wayback Machine. The logo of the Internet Archive is a white, pedimented Greek temple. When Kahle started the Internet Archive, in 1996, in his attic, he gave everyone working with him a book called *The Vanished Library*, about the burning of the Library of Alexandria. "The idea is to build the Library of Alexandria Two," he told me. (The Hellenism goes further: there's a partial backup of the Internet Archive in Alexandria, Egypt.) Kahle's plan is to one-up the Greeks. The motto of the Internet Archive is "Universal Access to All Knowledge." The Library of Alexandria was open only to the learned; the Internet Archive is open to everyone. In 2009, when the Fourth Church of Christ, Scientist, decided to sell its building, Kahle went to Funston Avenue to see it, and said, "That's our logo!" He loves that the church's cornerstone was laid in 1923: everything published in the United States before that date lies in the public domain. A temple built in copyright's year zero seemed fated. Kahle hops, just slightly, in his shoes when he gets excited. He says, showing me the church, "It's *Greek!*"

Kahle is long-armed and pink-cheeked and public-spirited; his hair is gray and frizzled. He wears round wire-rimmed eyeglasses, linen pants, and patterned button-down shirts. He looks like Mr. Micawber, if Mr. Micawber had left Dickens's London in a time machine and landed in the Pacific, circa 1955, disguised as an American tourist. Instead, Kahle was born in New Jersey in 1960. When he was a kid, he watched *The Rocky and Bullwinkle Show*; it has a segment called "Peabody's Improbable History," which is where the Wayback Machine got its name. Mr. Peabody, a beagle who is also a Harvard graduate and a Nobel laureate, builds a WABAC machine—it's meant to sound like a UNIVAC, one of the first commercial computers—and he uses it to take a boy named Sherman on adventures in time. "We just set it, turn it on, open the door, and there we are—or *were*, really," Peabody says.

When Kahle was growing up, some of the very same people who were building what would one day become the internet were thinking about libraries. In 1961, in Cambridge, J. C. R. Licklider, a scientist at the technology firm Bolt, Beranek and Newman, began a two-year study on the future of the library, funded by the Ford Foundation and aided by a team of researchers that included Marvin Minsky, at MIT. As Licklider saw it, books were good at displaying information but bad at storing, organizing, and retrieving it. "We should be prepared to reject the schema of the physical book itself," he argued, and to reject "the printed page as a long-term storage device." The goal of the project was to imagine what libraries would be like in the year 2000. Licklider envisioned a library in which computers would replace books and form a "network in which every element of the fund of knowledge is connected to every other element."

In 1963, Licklider became a director at the Department of Defense's Advanced Research Projects Agency (now called DARPA). During his first year, he wrote a seven-page memo in which he addressed his colleagues as "Members and Affiliates of the Intergalactic Computer Network," and proposed the networking of ARPA machines. This sparked the imagination of an electrical engineer named Lawrence Roberts, who later went to ARPA from MIT's Lincoln Laboratory. (Licklider had helped found both BBN and Lincoln.) Licklider's two-hundred-page Ford Foundation report, *Libraries of the Future*, was published in 1965. By then, the network he imagined was already being built, and the word "hyper-text" was being used. By 1969, relying on a data transmission technology called "packet-switching" which had been developed by a Welsh scientist named Donald Davies, ARPA had built a computer network called ARPAnet. By the mid-1970s, researchers across the country had developed a network of networks: an internetwork, or, later, an "internet."

Kahle enrolled at MIT in 1978. He studied computer science and engineering with Minsky. After graduating, in 1982, he worked for and started companies that were later sold for a great deal of money. In the late eighties, while working at Thinking Machines, he developed Wide Area Information Servers, or WAIS, a protocol for searching, navigating, and publishing on the internet. One feature of WAIS was a time axis; it provided for archiving through version control. (Wikipedia has version control; from any page, you can click on a tab that says "View History" to see all earlier versions of that page.) WAIS came before the web, and was then overtaken by it. In 1989, at CERN, the European Particle Physics Laboratory, in Geneva, Tim Berners-Lee, an English computer scientist, proposed a hypertext transfer protocol (HTTP) to link pages on what he called the World Wide Web. Berners-Lee toyed with the idea of a time axis for his protocol, too. One reason it was never developed was the preference for the most up-to-date information: a bias against obsolescence. But the chief reason was the premium placed on ease of use. "We were so young then, and the web was so young," Berners-Lee told me. "I was trying to get it to go. Preservation was not a priority. But we're getting older now." Other scientists involved in building the infrastructure of the internet are getting older and more concerned, too. Vint Cerf, who worked on ARPAnet in the seventies, and now holds the title of Chief Internet Evangelist at Google, has started talking about what he sees as a need for "digital vellum": long-term storage. "I worry that the twenty-first century will become an informational black hole," Cerf emailed me. But Kahle has been worried about this problem all along.

"I'm completely in praise of what Tim Berners-Lee did," Kahle told me, "but he kept it very, very simple." The first web page in the United States was created at SLAC, Stanford's linear accelerator center, at the end of 1991. Berners-Lee's protocol—which is not only usable but also elegant—spread fast, initially across universities and then into the public. "Emphasized text like *this* is a hypertext link," a 1994 version of SLAC's web page explained. In 1991, a ban on commercial traffic on the internet was lifted. Then came web browsers and e-commerce: both Netscape and Amazon were founded in 1994. The internet as most people now know it—web-based and commercial—began in the mid-nineties. Just as soon as it began, it started disappearing.

AND THE INTERNET ARCHIVE began collecting it. The Wayback Machine is a web archive, a collection of old web pages; it is, in fact, *the* web archive. There are others, but the Wayback Machine is so much bigger than all of them that it's very nearly true that if it's not in the Wayback Machine it doesn't exist. The Wayback Machine is a robot. It crawls across the internet, in the manner of Eric Carle's very hungry caterpillar, attempting to make a copy of every web page it can find every two months, though that rate varies. (It first crawled over *The New Yorker*'s home page, newyorker.com, in November 1998, and since then has crawled the site nearly seven thousand times, lately at a rate of about six times a day.) The Internet Archive is also stocked with web pages that are chosen by librarians, specialists like Anatol Shmelev, collecting in subject areas, through a service called Archive It, at archive-it.org, which also allows individuals and institutions to build their own archives. (A copy of everything they save goes into the Wayback Machine, too.) And anyone who wants to can preserve a web page, at any time, by going to archive.org/web, typing in a URL, and clicking "Save Page Now." (That's how most of the twelve screenshots of Strelkov's VKontakte page entered the Wayback Machine on the day the Malaysia Airlines flight was downed: seven captures that day were made by a robot; the rest were made by humans.)

I was on a panel with Kahle a few years ago, discussing the relationship between material and digital archives. When I met him, I was struck by a story he told about how he once put the entire World Wide Web into a shipping container. He just wanted to see if it would fit.

How big is the web? It turns out, he said, that it's twenty feet by eight feet by eight feet, or at least it was on the day he measured it. How much did it weigh? Twenty-six thousand pounds. He thought that *meant* something. He thought people needed to *know* that.

Kahle put the web into a storage container, but most people measure digital data in bytes. This essay is about two hundred thousand bytes. A book is about a megabyte. A megabyte is a million bytes. A gigabyte is a billion bytes. A terabyte is a million million bytes. A petabyte is a million gigabytes. In the lobby of the Internet Archive, you can get a free bumper sticker that says "10,000,000,000,000,000 BYTES ARCHIVED." Ten petabytes. It's obsolete. That figure is from 2012. Since then, it's doubled.

The Wayback Machine has archived more than four hundred and thirty billion web pages. The web is global, but, aside from the Internet Archive, a handful of fledgling commercial enterprises, and a growing number of university web archives, most web archives are run by national libraries. They collect chiefly what's in their own domains (the Web Archive of the National Library of Sweden, for instance, includes every web page that ends in ".se"). The Library of Congress has archived nine billion pages, the British Library six billion. Those collections, like the collections of most national libraries, are in one way or another dependent on the Wayback Machine; the majority also use Heritrix, the Internet Archive's open-source code. The British Library and the Bibliothèque Nationale de France backfilled the early years of their collections by using the Internet Archive's crawls of the .uk and .fr domains. The Library of Congress doesn't actually do its own web crawling; it contracts with the Internet Archive to do it instead.

The church at 300 Funston Avenue is twenty thousand square feet. The Internet Archive, the building, is open to the public most afternoons. It is, after all, a library. In addition to housing the Wayback Machine, the Internet Archive is a digital library, a vast collection of digitized books, films, television and radio programs, music, and other stuff. Because of copyright, not everything the Internet Archive has digitized is online. In the lobby of the church, there's a scanning station and a listening room: two armchairs, a coffee table, a pair of bookshelves, two iPads, and two sets of headphones. "You can listen to anything here," Kahle says. "We can't put all our music on the internet, but we can put everything here."

Copyright is the elephant in the archive. One reason the Library of Congress has a very small web page collection, compared with the Internet Archive, is that the Library of Congress generally does not collect a web page without asking, or at least giving notice. "The Internet Archive hoovers," Abbie Grotke, who runs the Library of Congress's web archive team, says. "We can't hoover, because we have to notify site owners and get permissions." (There are some exceptions.) The Library of Congress has something like an opt-in policy; the Internet Archive has an opt-out policy. The Wayback Machine collects every web page it can find, unless that page is blocked; blocking a web crawler requires adding only a simple text file, "robots.txt," to the root of a website. The Wayback Machine will honor that file and not crawl that site, and it will also, when it comes across a robots.txt, remove all past versions of that site. When the Conservative Party in Britain deleted ten years' worth of speeches from its website, it also added a robots.txt, which meant that, the next time the Wayback Machine tried to crawl the site, all its captures of those speeches went away, too. (Some have since been restored.) In a story that ran in the *Guardian*, a Labour Party MP said, "It will take more than David Cameron pressing delete to make people forget about his broken promises." And it would take more than a robots.txt to entirely destroy those speeches: they have also been collected in the UK Web Archive, at the British Library. The UK has what's known as a legal deposit law; it requires copies of everything published in Britain to be deposited in the British Library. In 2013, that law was revised to include everything published on the UK web. "People put their private lives up there, and we actually don't want that stuff," Andy Jackson, the technical head of the UK Web Archive, told me. "We don't want anything that you wouldn't consider a publication." It is hard to say quite where the line lies. But Britain's legal deposit laws mean that the British Library doesn't have to honor a request to stop collecting.

Legal deposit laws have been the standard in western Europe for centuries. They provide national libraries with a form of legal protection unavailable to the Library of Congress, which is not strictly a national library; also, U.S. legal deposit laws have exempted online-only works. "We are citadels," Gildas Illien, the former web archivist at the Bibliothèque Nationale de France, told me. The Internet Archive is an invaluable public institution, but it's not a national library, either, and, because the law of copyright has not kept up with technological change, Kahle has been collecting websites and making them freely available to the public without the full and explicit protection of the law. "It's extremely audacious," Illien says. "In Europe, no organiza-tion, or very few, would take that risk." There's another feature to legal deposit laws like those in France, a compromise between advocates of archiving and advocates of privacy. Archivists at the BnF can capture whatever web pages they want, but those collections can be used only in the physical building itself. (For the same reason, you can't check a book out of the Bibliothèque Nationale de France; you have to read it there.) One result is that the BnF's web archive is used by a handful of researchers, a few dozen a month; the Wayback Machine is used by hundreds of thousands of people a day.

In 2002, Kahle proposed an initiative in which the Internet Archive, in collaboration with national libraries, would become the head of a worldwide consortium of web archives. (The Internet Archive col-lects from around the world, and is available in most of the world. Currently, the biggest exception is China—"I guess because we have materials on the archive that the Chinese government would rather not have its citizens see," Kahle says.) This plan didn't work out, but from that failure came the International Internet Preservation Con-sortium, founded in 2003 and chartered at the BnF. It started with a dozen member institutions; there are now fifty-three.

Something else came out of that consortium. I talked to Illien two days after the massacre in Paris at the offices of *Charlie Hebdo*. "We are overwhelmed, and scared, and even taking the subway is terrify-ing, and we are scared for our children," Illien said. "The library is a target." When we spoke, the suspects were still at large; hostages had been taken. Illien and his colleagues had started a web archive about the massacre and the world's response. "Right now the media is full of it, but we know that most of that won't last," he said. "We wrote to our colleagues around the world and asked them to send us feeds to these URLs, to websites that were happening, right now, in Paris, so that we could collect them and historians will one day be able to see." He was very quiet. He said, "When something like that happens, you wonder what you can do from where you sit. Our job is memory."

The plan to found a global internet archive proved unworkable, partly because national laws relating to legal deposit, copyright, and privacy are impossible to reconcile, but also because Europeans tend to be suspicious of American organizations based in Silicon Valley ingesting their cultural inheritance. Illien told me that, when faced with Kahle's proposal, "national libraries decided they could not rely on a third party," even a nonprofit, "for such a fundamental heritage and preservation mission." In this same spirit, and in response to Google Books, European libraries and museums collaborated to launch Europeana, a digital library, in 2008. The Googleplex, Google's headquarters, is thirty-eight miles away from the Internet Archive, but the two could hardly be more different. In 2009, after the Authors Guild and the Association of American Publishers sued Google Books for copyright infringement, Kahle opposed the proposed settlement, charging Google with effectively attempting to privatize the public library system. In 2010, he was on the founding steering committee of the Digital Public Library of America, which is something of an American version of Europeana; its mission is to make what's in libraries, archives, and museums "freely available to the world . . . in the face of increasingly restrictive digital options."

Kahle is a digital utopian attempting to stave off a digital dystopia. He views the web as a giant library, and doesn't think it ought to belong to a corporation, or that anyone should have to go through a portal owned by a corporation in order to read it. "We are building a library that is us," he says, "and it is ours."

WHEN THE INTERNET ARCHIVE bought the church, Kahle recalls, "we had the idea that we'd convert it into a library, but what does a library look like anymore? So we've been settling in, and figuring that out."

From the lobby, we headed up a flight of yellow-carpeted stairs to the chapel, an enormous dome-ceilinged room filled with rows of oak pews. There are arched stained glass windows, and the dome is a stained glass window, too, open to the sky, like an eye of God. The chapel seats seven hundred people. The floor is sloped. "At first, we thought we'd flatten the floor and pull up the pews," Kahle said, as he gestured around the room. "But we couldn't. They're just too beautiful."

On the wall on either side of the altar, wooden slates display what, when this was a church, had been the listing of the day's hymn numbers. The archivists of the internet have changed those numbers. One hymn number was 314. "Do you know what that is?" Kahle asked. It was a test, and something of a trick question, like when someone asks you what's your favorite B track on the White Album. "Pi," I said, dutifully, or its first three digits, anyway. Another number was 42. Kahle gave me an inquiring look. I rolled my eyes. Seriously? But it is serious, in a way. It's hard not to worry that the Wayback Machine will end up like the computer in Douglas Adams's *Hitchhiker's Guide to the Galaxy*, which is asked what is the meaning of "life, the universe, and everything," and, after thinking for millions of years, says, "Forty-two." If the internet can be archived, will it ever have anything to tell us? Honestly, isn't most of the web trash? And, if everything's saved, won't there be too much of it for anyone to make sense of any of it? Won't it be useless?

The Wayback Machine is humongous, and getting humongouser. You can't search it the way you can search the web, because it's too big and what's in there isn't sorted, or indexed, or catalogued in any of the many ways in which a paper archive is organized; it's not ordered in any way at all, except by URL and by date. To use it, all you can do is type in a URL, and choose the date for it that you'd like to look at. It's more like a phone book than like an archive. Also, it's riddled with errors. One kind is created when the dead web grabs content from the live web, sometimes because web archives often crawl different parts of the same page at different times: text in one year, photographs in another. In October 2012, if you asked the Wayback Machine to show you what cnn.com looked like on September 3, 2008, it would have shown you a page featuring stories about the 2008 McCain-Obama presidential race, but the advertisement alongside it would have been for the 2012 Romney-Obama debate. Another problem is that there is no equivalent to what, in a physical archive, is a perfect provenance. When the computer scientist Michael Nelson tweeted the archived screenshots of Strelkov's page, a man in St. Petersburg tweeted back,

"Yep. Perfect tool to produce 'evidence' of any kind." Kahle is careful on this point. When asked to authenticate a screenshot, he says, "We can say, 'This is what we know. This is what our records say. This is how we received this information, from which apparent website, at this IP address.' But to actually say that this happened in the past is something that we can't say, in an ontological way." Nevertheless, screenshots from web archives have held up in court, repeatedly. And, as Kahle points out, "They turn out to be much more trustworthy than most of what people try to base court decisions on."

You can do something more like keyword searching in smaller subject collections, but nothing like Google searching (there is no relevance ranking, for instance), because the tools for doing anything meaningful with web archives are years behind the tools for creating those archives. Doing research in a paper archive is to doing research in a web archive as going to a fish market is to being thrown in the middle of an ocean; the only thing they have in common is that both involve fish.

The web archivists at the British Library had the brilliant idea of bringing in a team of historians to see what they could do with the UK Web Archive; it wasn't all that much, but it was helpful to see what they *tried* to do, and why it didn't work. Gareth Millward, a young scholar interested in the history of disability, wanted to trace the history of the Royal National Institute for the Blind. It turned out that the institute had endorsed a talking watch, and its name appeared in every advertisement for the watch. "This one advert appears thousands of times in the database," Millward told me. It cluttered and bogged down nearly everything he attempted. In 2014, the Internet Archive made an archive of its .gov domain, tidied up and compressed the data, and made it available to group of scholars, who tried very hard to make something of the material. It was so difficult to recruit scholars to use the data that the project was mostly a wash. Kahle says, "I give it a B." Stanford's web archivist, Nicholas Taylor, thinks it's a chicken-and-egg problem. "We don't know what tools to build, because no research has been done, but the research hasn't been done because we haven't built any tools."

The footnote problem, though, stands a good chance of being fixed by a tool called Perma.cc. It was developed by the Harvard Library

Innovation Lab, and its founding supporters included more than sixty law school libraries, along with the Harvard Berkman Center for Internet and Society, the Internet Archive, the Legal Information Preservation Alliance, and the Digital Public Library of America. Perma. cc promises "to create citation links that will never break." It works something like the Wayback Machine's "Save Page Now." If you're writing a scholarly paper and want to use a link in your footnotes, you can create an archived version of the page you're linking to, a "permalink," and anyone later reading your footnotes will, when clicking on that link, be brought to the permanently archived version. Perma. cc has already been adopted by law reviews and state courts; it's only a matter of time before it's universally adopted as the standard in legal, scientific, and scholarly citation.

Perma.cc is a patch, an excellent patch. Herbert Van de Sompel, a Belgian computer scientist then at the Los Alamos National Laboratory, tried to reweave the fabric of the web. It's not possible to go back in time and rewrite the HTTP protocol, but Van de Sompel's work involves adding to it. He and Michael Nelson are part of the team behind Memento, a protocol that you can use on Google Chrome as a web extension, so that you can navigate from site to site, and from time to time. He told me, "Memento allows you to say, 'I don't want to see this link where it points me to today; I want to see it around the time that this page was written, for example.'" It searches not only the Wayback Machine but also every major public web archive in the world, to find the page closest in time to the time you'd like to travel to. ("A world with one archive is a really bad idea," Van de Sompel points out. "You need redundance.") The Memento group is launching a web portal called Time Travel. Eventually, if Memento and projects like it work, the web will have a time dimension, a way to get from now to then, effortlessly, a fourth dimension. And then the past will be inescapable, which is as terrifying as it is interesting.

AT THE BACK OF THE CHAPEL, up a short flight of stairs, there are two niches, arched alcoves the same shape and size as the stained glass windows. Three towers of computers stand within each niche, and ten computers are stacked in each tower: black, rectangular, and humming. There are towers like this all over the building; these are only six of them. Still, this is *it*.

Kahle stands on his tiptoes, sinks back into his sneakers, and then bounds up the stairs. He is like a very sweet boy who, having built a very fine snowman, drags his mother outdoors to see it before it melts. I almost expect him to take my hand. I follow him up the stairs.

"Think of them as open stacks," he says, showing me the racks. "You can walk right up to them and touch them." He reaches out and traces the edge of one of the racks with the tip of his index finger. "If you had all the words in every book in the Library of Congress, it would be about an inch, here," he says, measuring the distance between his forefinger and thumb.

Up close, they're noisy. It's mainly fans, cooling the machines. At first, the noise was a problem: a library is supposed to be quiet. Kahle had soundproofing built into the walls.

Each unit has a yellow and a green light, glowing steadily: power indicators. Then, there are blue lights, flickering.

"Every time a light blinks, someone is uploading or downloading," Kahle explains. Six hundred thousand people use the Wayback Machine every day, conducting two thousand searches a second. "You can *see* it." He smiles as he watches. "They're glowing books!" He waves his arms. "They glow when they're being read!"

One day last summer, a missile was launched into the sky and a plane crashed in a field. "We just downed a plane," a soldier told the world. People fell to the earth, their last passage. Somewhere, someone hit "Save Page Now."

Where is the internet's memory, the history of our time?

"It's right *here*!" Kahle cries.

The machine hums and is muffled. It is sacred and profane. It is eradicable and unbearable. And it glows, against the dark.

—2015

THE DISRUPTION MACHINE

In the last years of the 1980s, I worked not at startups but at what might be called finish-downs. Tech companies that were dying would hire temps—college students and new graduates—to do what little was left of the work of the employees they'd laid off. This was in Cambridge, near MIT. I'd type users' manuals, save them onto 5.25-inch floppy disks, and send them to a line printer that yammered like a set of prank-shop chatter teeth, but, by the time the last perforated page coiled out of it, the equipment whose functions those manuals explained had been discontinued. We'd work a month here, a week there. There wasn't much to do. Mainly, we sat at our desks and wrote wishy-washy poems on keyboards manufactured by Digital Equipment Corporation, left one another sly messages on pink While You Were Out sticky notes, swapped paperback novels—Kurt Vonnegut, Margaret Atwood, Gabriel García Márquez, that kind of thing—and, during lunch hour, had assignations in empty, unlocked offices. At Polaroid, I once found a Bantam Books edition of *Steppenwolf* in a clogged sink in an employees' bathroom, floating like a raft. "In his heart he was not a man, but a wolf of the steppes," it said on the bloated cover. The rest was unreadable.

Not long after that, I got a better assignment: answering the phone for Michael Porter, a professor at Harvard Business School. I was an assistant to his assistant. In 1985, Porter had published a book called *Competitive Advantage*, in which he elaborated on the three strategies—cost leadership, differentiation, and focus—that he'd described in his 1980 book, *Competitive Strategy*. I almost never saw Porter, and when I did, he was dashing, affably, out the door, suitcase in hand. My job was to field inquiries from companies that wanted to book him for speaking engagements. *The Competitive Advantage of Nations* appeared in 1990. Porter's ideas about business strategy reached executives all over the world.

Porter was interested in how companies succeed. The scholar who in some respects became his successor, Clayton M. Christensen, entered a doctoral program at Harvard Business School in 1989 and joined the faculty in 1992. Christensen was interested in why companies fail. In his 1997 book, *The Innovator's Dilemma*, he argued that, very often, it isn't because their executives made bad decisions but because they made good decisions, the same kind of good decisions that had made those companies successful for decades. (The "innovator's dilemma" is that "doing the right thing is the wrong thing.") As Christensen saw it, the problem was the velocity of history, and it wasn't so much a problem as a missed opportunity, like a plane that takes off without you, except that you didn't even know there was a plane, and had wandered onto the airfield, which you thought was a meadow, and the plane ran you over during takeoff. Manufacturers of mainframe computers made good decisions about making and selling mainframe computers and devising important refinements to them in their R&D departments—"sustaining innovations," Christensen called them— but, busy pleasing their mainframe customers, one tinker at a time, they missed what an entirely untapped customer wanted, personal computers, the market for which was created by what Christensen called "disruptive innovation": the selling of a cheaper, poorer-quality product that initially reaches less profitable customers but eventually takes over and devours an entire industry.

Ever since *The Innovator's Dilemma*, everyone is either disrupting or being disrupted. There are disruption consultants, disruption conferences, and disruption seminars. In 2014, the University of Southern California is opening a new program: "The degree is in disruption," the university announced. "Disrupt or be disrupted," the venture capitalist Josh Linkner warns in a new book, *The Road to Reinvention*, in which he argues that "fickle consumer trends, friction-free markets, and political unrest," along with "dizzying speed, exponential complexity, and mind-numbing technology advances," mean that the time has come to panic as you've never panicked before. Larry Downes and Paul Nunes, who blog for *Forbes*, insist that we have entered a new and even scarier stage: "big bang disruption." "This isn't disruptive innovation," they warn. "It's devastating innovation."

Things you own or use that are now considered to be the product of disruptive innovation include your smartphone and many of its apps, which have disrupted businesses from travel agencies and record stores to mapmaking and taxi dispatch. Much more disruption, we are told, lies ahead. Christensen has cowritten books urging disruptive innovation in higher education (*The Innovative University*), public schools (*Disrupting Class*), and health care (*The Innovator's Prescription*). His acolytes and imitators, including no small number of hucksters, have called for the disruption of more or less everything else. If the company you work for has a chief innovation officer, it's because of the long arm of *The Innovator's Dilemma*. If your city's public school district has adopted an Innovation Agenda, which has disrupted the education of every kid in the city, you live in the shadow of *The Innovator's Dilemma*. If you saw the episode of the HBO sitcom *Silicon Valley* in which the characters attend a conference called TechCrunch Disrupt 2014 (which is a real thing), and a guy from the stage, a Paul Rudd look-alike, shouts, "Let me hear it, *DISSS-RUPPTTT!*," you have heard the voice of Clay Christensen, echoing across the valley.

In 2014, days after the *Times*'s publisher, Arthur Sulzberger Jr., fired Jill Abramson, the paper's executive editor, the *Times*'s "Innovation" report was leaked. It included graphs inspired by Christensen's *Innovator's Dilemma*, along with a lengthy, glowing summary of the book's key arguments. The report explains, "Disruption is a predictable pattern across many industries in which fledgling companies use new technology to offer cheaper and inferior alternatives to products sold by established players (think Toyota taking on Detroit decades ago). Today, a pack of news startups are hoping to 'disrupt' our industry by attacking the strongest incumbent—The New York Times."

A pack of attacking startups sounds something like a pack of ravenous hyenas, but, generally, the rhetoric of disruption—a language of panic, fear, asymmetry, and disorder—calls on the rhetoric of another kind of conflict, in which an upstart refuses to play by the established rules of engagement, and blows things up. Don't think of Toyota taking on Detroit. Startups are ruthless and leaderless and unrestrained, and they seem so tiny and powerless, until you realize, but only after it's too late, that they're devastatingly dangerous: *Bang! Ka-boom!* Think of it this way: the *Times* is a nation-state; *BuzzFeed* is stateless. Disruptive innovation is competitive strategy for an age seized by terror.

EVERY AGE HAS A THEORY of rising and falling, of growth and decay, of bloom and wilt: a theory of nature. Every age also has a theory about the past and the present, of what was and what is, a notion of time: a theory of history. Theories of history used to be supernatural: the divine ruled time; the hand of God, a special providence, lay behind the fall of each sparrow. If the present differed from the past, it was usually worse: supernatural theories of history tend to involve decline, a fall from grace, the loss of God's favor, corruption. Beginning in the eighteenth century, as the intellectual historian Dorothy Ross once pointed out, theories of history became secular; then they started something new—historicism, the idea "that all events in historical time can be explained by prior events in historical time." Things began looking up. First there was that, then there was this, and this is *better* than that. The eighteenth century embraced the idea of progress; the nineteenth century had evolution; the twentieth century had growth and then innovation. Our era has disruption, which, despite its futurism, is atavistic. It's a theory of history founded on a profound anxiety about financial collapse, an apocalyptic fear of global devastation, and shaky evidence.

Most big ideas have loud critics. Not disruption. Disruptive innovation as the explanation for how change happens has been subject to little serious criticism, partly because it's headlong, while critical inquiry is unhurried; partly because disrupters ridicule doubters by charging them with fogyism, as if to criticize a theory of change were identical to decrying change; and partly because, in its modern usage, innovation is the idea of progress jammed into a criticism-proof jack-in-the-box.

The idea of progress—the notion that human history is the history of human betterment—dominated the worldview of the West between the Enlightenment and the First World War. It had critics from the start, and, in the last century, even people who cherish the idea of progress, and point to improvements like the eradication of contagious diseases and the education of girls, have been hard-pressed to hold on to it while reckoning with two world wars, the Holocaust and Hiroshima, genocide and global warming. Replacing "progress" with "innovation" skirts the question of whether a novelty is an improvement: the world may not be getting better and better but our devices are getting newer and newer.

The word "innovate"—to make new—used to have chiefly negative connotations: it signified excessive novelty, without purpose or
end. Edmund Burke called the French Revolution a "revolt of innovation"; Federalists declared themselves to be "enemies to innovation."
George Washington, on his deathbed, was said to have uttered these
words: "Beware of innovation in politics." Noah Webster warned in
his dictionary, in 1828, "It is often dangerous to innovate on the customs of a nation."

The redemption of innovation began in 1939, when the economist
Joseph Schumpeter, in his landmark study of business cycles, used the
word to mean bringing new products to market, a usage that spread
slowly, and only in the specialized literatures of economics and business. (In 1942, Schumpeter theorized about "creative destruction";
Christensen, retrofitting, believes that Schumpeter was really describing disruptive innovation.) "Innovation" began to seep beyond specialized literatures in the 1990s, and gained ubiquity only after 9/11.
One measure: between 2011 and 2014, *Time*, the *Times Magazine*, *The
New Yorker*, *Forbes*, and even *Better Homes and Gardens* published special
"innovation" issues—the modern equivalents of what, a century ago,
were known as "sketches of men of progress."

The idea of innovation is the idea of progress stripped of the aspira-
tions of the Enlightenment, scrubbed clean of the horrors of the twentieth century, and relieved of its critics. Disruptive innovation goes
further, holding out the hope of salvation against the very damnation
it describes: disrupt, and you will be saved.

DISRUPTIVE INNOVATION AS A THEORY of change is meant to
serve both as a chronicle of the past (this has happened) and as a model
for the future (it will keep happening). The strength of a prediction
made from a model depends on the quality of the historical evidence
and on the reliability of the methods used to gather and interpret it.
Historical analysis proceeds from certain conditions regarding proof.
None of these conditions have been met.

The Innovator's Dilemma consists of a set of handpicked case studies, beginning with the disk drive industry, which was the subject of
Christensen's doctoral thesis, in 1992. "Nowhere in the history of busi-

ness has there been an industry like disk drives," Christensen writes, which makes it a very odd choice for an investigation designed to create a model for understanding other industries. The first hard disk drive, which weighed more than a ton, was invented at IBM in 1955, by a team that included Alan Shugart. Christensen is chiefly concerned with an era, beginning in the late 1970s, when disk drives decreased in size from 14 inches to 8, then from 8 to 5.25, from 5.25 to 3.5, and from 3.5 to 2.5 and 1.8. He counts 116 new technologies, and classes 111 as sustaining innovations and 5 as disruptive innovations.

Each of these five, he says, introduced "smaller disk drives that were slower and had lower capacity than those used in the mainstream market," and each company that adopted them was an entrant firm that toppled an established firm. In 1973, Alan Shugart founded Shugart Associates, which introduced a 5.25-inch floppy disk drive in 1976; the company was bought by Xerox the next year. In 1978, Shugart Associates developed an 8-inch hard disk drive; Christensen, who is uninterested in the floppy disk drive industry, classes the company as an entrant firm and credits it with disrupting established firms that manufactured 14-inch hard drives.

In 1979, Alan Shugart founded Shugart Technology, which changed its name to Seagate Technology after Xerox threatened to sue. In 1980, Seagate Technology introduced the first 5.25-inch hard disk drive; Christensen, at this point, classes Seagate as an entrant firm, and Shugart Associates as a failed incumbent, even though Shugart Associates was shifting its focus to what was then its very profitable floppy disk drive business. In the mid-eighties, Seagate—here considered by Christensen to be an established firm—delayed manufacturing 3.5-inch drives, which were valued by producers of portable computers and laptops, because its biggest customer, IBM, didn't want them; IBM wanted a better and faster version of the 5.25-inch drive for its full-sized desktop computers. Seagate didn't start shipping 3.5-inch drives until 1988, and by then, Christensen argues, it was too late.

In his original research, Christensen established the cutoff for measuring a company's success or failure as 1989 and explained that " 'successful firms' were arbitrarily defined as those which achieved more than fifty million dollars in revenues in constant 1987 dollars in any single year between 1977 and 1989—even if they subsequently with-drew from the market." Much of the theory of disruptive innovation rests on this arbitrary definition of success.

In fact, Seagate Technology was not felled by disruption. Between 1989 and 1990, its sales doubled, reaching $2.4 billion, "more than all of its U.S. competitors combined," according to an industry report. In 1997, the year Christensen published *The Innovator's Dilemma*, Seagate was the largest company in the disk drive industry, reporting reve-nues of nine billion dollars. In 2013, Seagate shipped its two-billionth disk drive. Most of the entrant firms celebrated by Christensen as tri-umphant disrupters, on the other hand, no longer exist, their success having been in some cases brief and in others illusory. (The fleet-ing nature of their success is, of course, perfectly consistent with his model.) Between 1982 and 1984, Micropolis made the disruptive leap from 8-inch to 5.25-inch drives through what Christensen cred-its as the "Herculean managerial effort" of its CEO, Stuart Mahon. ("Mahon remembers the experience as the most exhausting of his life," Christensen writes.) But shortly thereafter, Micropolis, unable to com-pete with companies like Seagate, failed. MiniScribe, founded in 1980, started out selling 5.25-inch drives and saw quick success. "That was MiniScribe's hour of glory," the company's founder later said. "We had our hour of infamy shortly after that." In 1989, MiniScribe was inves-tigated for fraud and soon collapsed; a report charged that the compa-ny's practices included fabricated financial reports and "shipping bricks and scrap parts disguised as disk drives."

As striking as the disruption in the disk drive industry seemed in the 1980s, more striking, from the vantage of history, are the conti-nuities. Christensen argues that incumbents in the disk drive industry were regularly destroyed by newcomers. But today, after much con-solidation, the divisions that dominate the industry are divisions that led the market in the 1980s. (In some instances, what shifted was their ownership: IBM sold its hard disk division to Hitachi, which later sold its division to Western Digital.) In the longer term, victory in the disk drive industry appears to have gone to the manufacturers that were good at incremental improvements, whether or not they were the first to market the disruptive new format. Companies that were quick to release a new product but not skilled at tinkering have tended to flame out.

Other cases in *The Innovator's Dilemma* are equally murky. In his account of the mechanical excavator industry, Christensen argues that established companies that built cable-operated excavators were slow to recognize the importance of the hydraulic excavator, which was developed in the late 1940s. "Almost the entire population of mechanical shovel manufacturers was wiped out by a disruptive technology—hydraulics—that the leaders' customers and their economic structure had caused them initially to ignore," he argues. Christensen counts thirty established companies in the 1950s and says that, by the 1970s, only four had survived the entrance into the industry of thirteen disruptive newcomers, including Caterpillar, O&K, Demag, and Hitachi. But, in fact, many of Christensen's "new entrants" had been making cable-operated shovels for years. O&K, founded in 1876, had been making them since 1908; Demag had been building excavators since 1925, when it bought a company that built steam shovels; Hitachi, founded in 1910, sold cable-operated shovels before the Second World War. Manufacturers that were genuinely new to excavation equipment tended to sell a lot of hydraulic excavators, if they had a strong distribution network, and then not do so well. And some established companies disrupted by hydraulics didn't do half as badly as Christensen suggests. Bucyrus is the old-line shovel-maker he writes about most. It got its start in Ohio, in 1880, built most of the excavators that dug the Panama Canal, and became Bucyrus-Erie in 1927, when it bought the Erie Steam Shovel Company. It acquired a hydraulics equipment firm in 1948, but, Christensen writes, "faced precisely the same problem in marketing its hydraulic backhoe as Seagate had faced with its 3.5-inch drives."

Unable to persuade its established consumers to buy a hydraulic excavator, Bucyrus introduced a hybrid product, called the Hydrohoe, in 1951—a merely sustaining innovation. Christensen says that Bucyrus "logged record profits until 1966—the point at which the disruptive hydraulics technology had squarely intersected with customers' needs," and then began to decline. "This is typical of industries facing a disruptive technology," he explains. "The leading firms in the established technology remain financially strong until the disruptive technology is, in fact, in the midst of their mainstream market."

But actually, between 1962 and 1979 Bucyrus's sales grew sevenfold and its profits grew twenty-five-fold. Was that so bad? In the 1980s, Bucyrus suffered. The whole construction equipment industry did: it was devastated by recession, inflation, the oil crisis, a drop in home building, and the slowing of highway construction. (Caterpillar sustained heavy losses, too.) In the early 1990s, after a disastrous leveraged buyout handled by Goldman Sachs, Bucyrus entered Chapter 11 protection, but it made some sizable acquisitions when it emerged, as Bucyrus International, and was a leading maker of mining equipment, just as it had been a century earlier. Was it a failure? Caterpillar didn't think so when, in 2011, it bought the firm for nearly nine billion dollars.

Christensen's sources are often dubious and his logic questionable. His single citation for his investigation of the "disruptive transition from mechanical to electronic motor controls," in which he identifies the Allen-Bradley Company as triumphing over four rivals, is a book called *The Bradley Legacy*, an account published by a foundation established by the company's founders. This is akin to calling an actor the greatest talent in a generation after interviewing his publicist. "Use theory to help guide data collection," Christensen advises.

He finds further evidence of his theory in the disruption of the department store by the discount store. "Just as in disk drives and excavators," he writes, "a few of the leading traditional retailers—notably S. S. Kresge, F. W. Woolworth, and Dayton Hudson—saw the disruptive approach coming and invested early." In 1962, Kresge (which traces its origins to 1897) opened Kmart; Dayton-Hudson (1902) opened Target; and Woolworth (1879) opened Woolco. Kresge and Dayton-Hudson ran their discount stores as independent organizations; Woolworth ran its discount store in-house. Kmart and Target succeeded; Woolco failed. Christensen presents this story as yet more evidence of an axiom derived from the disk drive industry: "two models for how to make money cannot peacefully coexist within a single organization." In the mid-1990s, Kmart closed more than two hundred stores, a fact that Christensen does not include in his account of the industry's history. (Kmart filed for bankruptcy in 2002.) Only in a footnote does he make a vague allusion to Kmart's troubles—"when this book was being written, Kmart was a crippled company"—and then he dismisses this piece of counterevidence by fiat: "Kmart's present competitive struggles are unrelated to Kresge's strategy in meeting the original disruptive threat of discounting."

In his discussion of the steel industry, in which he argues that established companies were disrupted by the technology of minimilling (melting down scrap metal to make cheaper, lower-quality sheet metal), Christensen writes that U.S. Steel, founded in 1901, lowered the cost of steel production from "nine labor-hours per ton of steel produced in 1980 to just under three hours per ton in 1991," which he attributes to the company's "ferociously attacking the size of its workforce, paring it from more than 93,000 in 1980 to fewer than 23,000 in 1991," in order to point out that even this accomplishment could not stop the coming disruption. Christensen tends to ignore factors that don't support his theory. Factors having effects on both production and profitability that Christensen does not mention are that, between 1986 and 1987, twenty-two thousand workers at U.S. Steel did not go to work, as part of a labor action, and that U.S. Steel's workers are unionized and have been for generations, while minimill manufacturers, with their newer workforces, are generally non-union. Christensen's logic here seems to be that the industry's labor arrangements can have played no role in U.S. Steel's struggles—and are not even worth mentioning—because U.S. Steel's struggles must be a function of its having failed to build minimills. U.S. Steel's struggles have been and remain grave, but its failure is by no means a matter of historical record. Today, the largest U.S. producer of steel is—U.S. Steel.

THE THEORY OF DISRUPTION is meant to be predictive. On March 10, 2000, Christensen launched a $3.8 million Disruptive Growth Fund, which he managed with Neil Eisner, a broker in St. Louis. Christensen drew on his theory to select stocks. Less than a year later, the fund was quietly liquidated: during a stretch of time when the Nasdaq lost 50 percent of its value, the Disruptive Growth Fund lost 65 percent. In 2007, Christensen told *BusinessWeek* that "the prediction of the theory would be that Apple won't succeed with the iPhone," adding, "History speaks pretty loudly on that." In its first five years, the iPhone generated a hundred and fifty billion dollars of revenue. In the preface to the 2011 edition of "The Innovator's Dilemma," Christensen reports that, since the book's publication, in 1997, "the theory of disruption continues to yield predictions that are quite accurate." This is less because people have used his model to make accurate predictions about things that haven't happened yet than because disruption has been sold as advice, and because much that happened between 1997 and 2011 looks, in retrospect, disruptive. Disruptive innovation can reliably be seen only after the fact. History speaks loudly, apparently, only when you can make it say what you want it to say. The popular incarnation of the theory tends to disavow history altogether. "Predicting the future based on the past is like betting on a football team simply because it won the Super Bowl a decade ago," Josh Linkner writes in *The Road to Reinvention*. His first principle: "Let go of the past." It has nothing to tell you. But unless you already believe in disruption, many of the successes that have been labeled disruptive innovation look like something else, and many of the failures that are often seen to have resulted from failing to embrace disruptive innovation look like bad management.

Christensen has compared the theory of disruptive innovation to a theory of nature: the theory of evolution. But among the many differences between disruption and evolution is that the advocates of disruption have an affinity for circular arguments. If an established company doesn't disrupt, it will fail, and if it fails it must be because it didn't disrupt. When a startup fails, that's a success, since epidemic failure is a hallmark of disruptive innovation. ("Stop being afraid of failure and start embracing it," the organizers of FailCon, an annual conference, implore, suggesting that, in the era of disruption, innovators face unprecedented challenges. For instance: maybe you made the wrong hires?) When an established company succeeds, that's only because it hasn't yet failed. And, when any of these things happen, all of them are only further evidence of disruption.

The handpicked case study, which is Christensen's method, is a notoriously weak foundation on which to build a theory. But if the handpicked case study is the approved approach, it would seem that efforts at embracing disruptive innovation are often fatal. Morrison-Knudsen, an engineering and construction firm, got its start in 1905 and helped build more than a hundred and fifty dams all over the world, including the Hoover. Beginning in 1988, a new CEO, William Agee, looked to new products and new markets, and, after Bill Clinton's election, in 1992, bet on mass transit, turning to the construction of both commuter and long-distance train cars through two subsidiaries, MK Transit and MK Rail. These disruptive businesses proved to be a disaster. Morrison-Knudsen announced in 1995 that it had lost three hundred and fifty million dollars, by which point the company had essentially collapsed—not because it didn't disruptively innovate but because it did. Time Inc., founded in 1922, auto-disrupted, too. In 1994, the company launched Pathfinder, an early new-media venture, an umbrella website for its magazines, at a cost estimated to have exceeded a hundred million dollars; the site was abandoned in 1999. Had Pathfinder been successful, it would have been greeted, retrospectively, as evidence of disruptive innovation. Instead, as one of its producers put it, "it's like it never existed."

In the late 1990s and early 2000s, the financial services industry innovated by selling products like subprime mortgages, collateralized debt obligations, and mortgage-backed securities, some to a previously untapped customer base. At the time, Ed Clark was the CEO of Canada's TD Bank, which traces its roots to 1855. Clark, who earned a PhD in economics at Harvard with a dissertation on public investment in Tanzania, forswore Canada's version of this disruptive innovation, asset-backed commercial paper. The decision made TD Bank one of the strongest banks in the world. Between 2002 and 2012, TD Bank's assets increased from $278 billion to $806 billion. Since 2005, TD Bank has opened thirteen hundred branches in the United States, bought Commerce Bank for $8.5 billion, in 2008, and adopted the motto "America's Most Convenient Bank." With the money it earned by expanding its traditional banking services—almost four billion dollars a year during the height of the financial crisis, according to the Canadian business reporter Howard Green—it set about marketing itself as the bank with the longest hours, the best teller services, and free dog biscuits.

When the financial services industry disruptively innovated, it led to a global financial crisis. Like the bursting of the dot-com bubble, the meltdown didn't dim the fervor for disruption; instead, it fueled it, because these products of disruption contributed to the panic on which the theory of disruption thrives.

DISRUPTIVE INNOVATION AS AN EXPLANATION for how change happens is everywhere. Ideas that come from business schools are exceptionally well marketed. Faith in disruption is the best illustration, and the worst case, of a larger historical transformation having to do with secularization, and what happens when the invisible hand replaces the hand of God as explanation and justification. Innovation and disruption are ideas that originated in the arena of business but which have since been applied to arenas whose values and goals are remote from the values and goals of business. People aren't disk drives. Public schools, colleges and universities, churches, museums, and many hospitals, all of which have been subjected to disruptive innovation, have revenues and expenses and infrastructures, but they aren't industries in the same way that manufacturers of hard disk drives or truck engines or dry goods are industries. Journalism isn't an industry in that sense, either.

Doctors have obligations to their patients, teachers to their students, pastors to their congregations, curators to the public, and journalists to their readers—obligations that lie outside the realm of earnings, and are fundamentally different from the obligations that a business executive has to employees, partners, and investors. Historically, institutions like museums, hospitals, schools, and universities have been supported by patronage, donations made by individuals or funding from church or state. The press has generally supported itself by charging subscribers and selling advertising. (Underwriting by corporations and foundations is a funding source of more recent vintage.) Charging for admission, membership, subscriptions and, for some, earning profits are similarities these institutions have with businesses. Still, that doesn't make them industries, which turn things into commodities and sell them for gain.

In *The Innovative University*, written with Henry J. Eyring, who used to work at the Monitor Group, a consulting firm cofounded by Michael Porter, Christensen subjected Harvard, a college founded by seventeenth-century theocrats, to his case study analysis. "Studying the university's history," Christensen and Eyring wrote, "will allow us to move beyond the forlorn language of crisis to hopeful and practical strategies for success." On the basis of this research, Christensen and Eyring's recommendations for the disruption of the modern university include a "mix of face-to-face and online learning." The publication of *The Innovative University*, in 2011, contributed to a frenzy for massive open online courses, or MOOCs, at colleges and universities across the country, including a collaboration between Harvard and MIT, which was announced in May of 2012. Shortly afterward, the University of Virginia's panicked board of trustees attempted to fire the president, charging her with jeopardizing the institution's future by failing to disruptively innovate with sufficient speed; the vice-chair of the board forwarded to the chair a *Times* column written by David Brooks, "The Campus Tsunami," in which he cited Christensen.

Christensen and Eyring's recommendation of a "mix of face-to-face and online learning" was drawn from an investigation that involves a wildly misguided attempt to apply standards of instruction in the twenty-first century to standards of instruction in the seventeenth. One table in the book, titled "Harvard's Initial DNA, 1636–1707," looks like this:

Initial Traits	Implications
Small, face-to-face classes	High faculty-student intimacy Low instructional efficiency
Classical, religious instruction	High moral content in the curriculum Narrow curriculum with low practicality for non-pastors
Nonspecialized faculty	Dogmatic instruction High faculty empathy for learners Low faculty expertise

In 2014, there were twenty-one thousand students at Harvard. In 1640, there were thirteen. The first year classes were held, Harvard students and their "nonspecialized faculty" (one young schoolmaster, Nathaniel Eaton), enjoying "small, face-to-face classes" (Eaton's wife, who fed the students, was accused of putting "goat's dung in their hasty pudding") with "high faculty empathy for learners" (Eaton conducted thrashings with a stick of walnut said to have been "big enough to have killed a horse"), could have paddled together in a single canoe. That doesn't mean good arguments can't be made for online education. But there's nothing factually persuasive in this account of its historical urgency and even inevitability, which relies on a method well outside anything resembling plausible historical analysis.

Christensen and Eyring also urge universities to establish "heavyweight innovation teams": Christensen thinks that R&D departments housed within a business and accountable to its executives are structurally unable to innovate disruptively—they are preoccupied with pleasing existing customers through incremental improvement. Christensen argues, for instance, that if Digital Equipment Corporation, which was doing very well making minicomputers in the 1960s and '70s, had founded, in the '80s, a separate company at another location to develop the personal computer, it might have triumphed. The logic of disruptive innovation is the logic of the startup: establish a team of innovators, set a whiteboard under a blue sky, and never ask them to make a profit, because there needs to be a wall of separation between the people whose job is to come up with the best, smartest, and most creative and important ideas and the people whose job is to make money by selling stuff. Interestingly, a similar principle has existed, for more than a century, in the press. The "heavyweight innovation team"? That's what journalists used to call the "newsroom."

It's readily apparent that, in a democracy, the important business interests of institutions like the press might at times conflict with what became known as the "public interest." That's why, a very long time ago, newspapers like the *Times* and magazines like this one established a wall of separation between the editorial side of affairs and the business side. (The metaphor is to the Jeffersonian wall between church and state.) "The wall dividing the newsroom and business side has served The Times well for decades," according to the *Times*'s 2014 "Innovation" report, "allowing one side to focus on readers and the other to focus on advertisers," as if this had been, all along, simply a matter of office efficiency. But the notion of a wall should be abandoned, according to the report, because it has "hidden costs" that thwart innovation. Shortly before the release of the report, the *Times* tried to recruit, as its new head of audience development, Michael Wertheim, the former head of promotion at the disruptive media outfit Upworthy. Wertheim turned the *Times* job down, citing its wall as too big an obstacle to disruptive innovation. The recommendation of the "Innovation" report is to understand that both sides, editorial and business, share, as their top priority, "Reader Experience," which can be measured, following Upworthy, in "Attention Minutes." Vox Media, a digital-media disrupter that is mentioned ten times in the *Times* report and is included, along with *BuzzFeed*, in a list of the *Times*'s strongest competitors (few of which are profitable), called the report "brilliant," "shockingly good," and an "insanely clear" explanation of disruption, but expressed the view that there's no way the *Times* will implement its recommendations, because "what the report doesn't mention is the sobering conclusion of Christensen's research: companies faced with disruptive threats almost never manage to handle them gracefully."

DISRUPTIVE INNOVATION IS A THEORY about why businesses fail. It's not more than that. It doesn't explain change. It's not a law of nature. It's an artifact of history, an idea, forged in time; it's the manufacture of a moment of upsetting and edgy uncertainty. Transfixed by change, it's blind to continuity. It makes a very poor prophet.

The upstarts who work at startups don't often stay at any one place for very long. (Three out of four startups fail. More than nine out of ten never earn a return.) They work a year here, a few months there—zany hours everywhere. They wear jeans and sneakers and ride scooters and share offices and sprawl on couches like Great Danes. Their coffee machines look like dollhouse-size factories.

They are told that they should be reckless and ruthless. Their investors, if they're like Josh Linkner, tell them that the world is a terrifying place, moving at a devastating pace. "Today I run a venture capital firm and back the next generation of innovators who are, as I was throughout my earlier career, dead-focused on eating your lunch," Linkner writes. His job appears to be to convince a generation of people who want to do good and do well to learn, instead, remorselessness. Forget rules, obligations, your conscience, loyalty, a sense of the common-weal. If you start a business and it succeeds, Linkner advises, sell it and take the cash. Don't look back. Never pause. Disrupt or be disrupted.

But they do pause and they do look back, and they wonder. Mean-while, they tweet, they post, they tumble in and out of love, they pon-der. They send one another sly messages, touching the screens of sleek, soundless machines with a worshipful tenderness. They swap novels: David Foster Wallace, Chimamanda Ngozi Adichie, Zadie Smith. *Steppenwolf* is still available in print, five dollars cheaper as an e-book. He's a wolf, he's a man. The rest is unreadable. So, as ever, is the future.

—2014

THE ROBOT CARAVAN

THE ROBOTS ARE COMING. HIDE THE WD-40. LOCK up your nine-volt batteries. Build a booby trap out of giant magnets; dig a moat as deep as a grave. "Ever since a study by the University of Oxford predicted that 47 percent of U.S. jobs are at risk of being replaced by robots and artificial intelligence over the next fifteen to twenty years, I haven't been able to stop thinking about the future of work," Andrés Oppenheimer writes, in *The Robots Are Coming: The Future of Jobs in the Age of Automation*. No one is safe. Chapter 4: "They're Coming for Bankers!" Chapter 5: "They're Coming for Lawyers!" They're attacking hospitals: "They're Coming for Doctors!" They're headed to Hollywood: "They're Coming for Entertainers!" I gather they have not yet come for the manufacturers of exclamation points.

The old robots were blue-collar workers, burly and clunky, the machines that rusted the Rust Belt. But according to the economist Richard Baldwin, in *The Globotics Upheaval: Globalization, Robotics, and the Future of Work*, the new ones are "white-collar robots," knowledge workers and quinoa-and-oat-milk globalists, the machines that will bankrupt Brooklyn. Mainly, they're algorithms. Except when they're immigrants. Baldwin calls that kind "remote intelligence," or RI: they're not exactly robots but, somehow, they fall into the same category. They're people from other countries who can steal your job without ever really crossing the border: they just hop over, by way of the internet and apps like Upwork, undocumented, invisible, ethereal. Between artificial intelligence and remote intelligence, Baldwin warns, "this international talent tidal wave is coming straight for the good, stable jobs that have been the foundation of middle-class prosperity in the US and Europe, and other high-wage economies." Change your Wi-Fi password. Clear your browser history. Ask HR about early retirement. The globots are coming.

How can you know if you're about to get replaced by an invading algorithm or an augmented immigrant? "If your job can be easily explained, it can be automated," Anders Sandberg, of Oxford's Future of Humanity Institute, tells Oppenheimer. "If it can't, it won't." (Rotten luck for people whose job description is "Predict the future.") Baldwin offers three-part advice: (1) avoid competing with AI and RI; (2) build skills in things that only humans can do, in person; and (3) "realize that humanity is an edge not a handicap." What all this means is hard to say, especially if you've never before considered being human to be a handicap. As for the future of humanity, Oppenheimer offers another cockamamie rule of three: "Society will be divided into three general groups. The first will be members of the elites, who will be able to adapt to the ever-changing technological landscape and who will earn the most money, followed by a second group made up primarily of those who provide personalized services to the elite, including personal trainers, Zumba class instructors, meditation gurus, piano teachers, and personal chefs, and finally a third group of those who will be mostly unemployed and may be receiving a universal basic income as compensation for being the victims of technological unemployment."

Readers of Douglas Adams will recognize this sort of hooey from *The Hitchhiker's Guide to the Galaxy*. Long ago, in a galaxy not at all far away, the people of the planet Golgafrincham were divided into three groups: A, "all the brilliant leaders, the scientists, the great artists, you know, all the achievers"; B, "hairdressers, tired TV producers, insurance salesmen, personnel officers, security guards, public relations executives, management consultants" (the group that everyone else considers to be "a bunch of useless idiots"); and, C, "all the people who did the actual work, who made things and did things." The B people, told they must lead an expedition to colonize another planet, rocket away in a starship, having been led to believe that their planet is doomed. "Apparently it was going to crash into the sun or something," the B ship's captain tells Arthur Dent, vaguely wondering why the other ships never followed. "Or maybe it was that the moon was going to crash into us. Something of the kind. Absolutely terrifying prospect whatever it was." Dent inquires, "And they made sure they sent you lot off first, did they?"

This time, notwithstanding Elon Musk's ambition to colonize

Mars, no one's trying to persuade the B people to board a spaceship, because the B people—the hairdressers and the Zumba-class instructors, the meditation gurus and the personal trainers—are supposed to stick around to cater to the A people. No, this time it's the C people, the people who make and do things—things that can now be made and done faster and cheaper by robots—who are being flushed down the cosmic toilet. The historian and sometime futurist Yuval Noah Harari has a name for the C people: he calls them the "useless class." Some futurists suggest that, in our Asimov-y future, these sort of people might wind up spending their empty days playing video games. Otherwise, they'll wage a revolution, an eventuality that the self-proclaimed "cognitive elite"—the A people, who believe themselves to be cleverer than the cleverest robots—intend to wait out in fortified lairs. (Peter Thiel owns nearly five hundred acres of land in New Zealand, complete with its own water supply.) More popular is the proposal to pay the C people for doing nothing, in order to avert the revolution. "It's going to be necessary," Musk said during a summit in Dubai two years ago, joining a small herd of other billionaires, including Mark Zuckerberg, of Facebook, and Stewart Butterfield, of Slack, who endorse universal basic income. It's either that or build a wall.

FEAR OF A ROBOT INVASION IS the obverse of fear of an immigrant invasion, a partisan coin: heads, you're worried about robots; tails, you're worried about immigrants. There's just the one coin. Both fears have to do with jobs, whose loss produces suffering, want, and despair, and whose future scarcity represents a terrifying prospect. Misery likes a scapegoat: heads, blame machines; tails, foreigners. But is the present alarm warranted? Panic is not evidence of danger; it's evidence of panic. Stoking fear of invading robots and of invading immigrants has been going on for a long time, and the predictions of disaster have, generally, been bananas. Oh, but this time it's different, the robotomizers insist.

This thesis has been rolling around like a marble in the bowl of a lot of people's brains for a while now, and many of those marbles were handed out by Martin Ford, in his 2015 book, *Rise of the Robots: Technology and the Threat of a Jobless Future.* In the book, and in an essay in *Confronting Dystopia: The New Technological Revolution and the Future of*

Work, Ford acknowledges that all other earlier robot-invasion panics were unfounded. In the nineteenth century, people who worked on farms lost their jobs when agricultural processes were mechanized, but they eventually earned more money working in factories. In the twentieth century, automation of industrial production led to warnings about "unprecedented economic and social disorder." Instead, displaced factory workers moved into service jobs. Machines eliminate jobs; rising productivity creates new jobs.

"Given this long record of false alarms, contemporary economists are generally dismissive of arguments that technological progress might lead to unemployment as well as falling wages and soaring income inequality," Ford admits. After all, "history shows that the economy has consistently adjusted to advancing technology by creating new employment opportunities and that these new jobs often require more skills and pay higher wages."

That was then. The reason that things will be different this time, Ford argues, has to do with the changing pace of change. The transformation from an agricultural to an industrial economy was linear; the current acceleration is exponential. The first followed Newton's law; the second follows Moore's. The employment apocalypse, when it comes, will happen so fast that workers won't have time to adjust by shifting to new employment sectors, and, even if they did have time to adjust, there would be no new employment sectors to go to, because robots will be able to do just about everything.

It is quite possible that this thesis is correct; it is not possible to know that it is correct. Ford, an advocate of universal basic income, is neither a historian nor an economist. He is a futurist, a modern-day shaman, with an MBA. Everybody thinks about the future; futurists do it for a living. Policymakers make plans; futurists read omens. The robots-are-coming omen-reading borrows as much from the conventions of science fiction as from those of historical analysis. It uses "robot" as a shorthand for everything from steam-powered looms to electricity-driven industrial assemblers and artificial intelligence, and thus has the twin effects of compressing time and conflating one thing with another. It indulges in the supposition that work is something the wealthy hand out to the poor, from feudalism to capitalism, instead of something people do, for reasons that include a search for order, meaning, and purpose. It leaves out of its accounting the largest source of labor in the United States before the Civil War, people held in bondage, and fails to consider how the rise of wage labor left women's work uncompensated. And it ignores the brutal truth that, in American history, panic about technological change is almost always tangled up with panic about immigration. Nineteenth-century populists, those farmers left behind by the industrial revolution, wanted railroad companies to be taxed, but they also wanted to bar African Americans and Asian immigrants from full citizenship. They raged against the machine; they fought for the color line.

FUTURISTS FORETELL INEVITABLE OUTCOMES by conjuring up inevitable pasts. People who are in the business of selling predictions need to present the past as predictable—the ground truth, the test case. Machines are more predictable than people, and in histories written by futurists the machines just keep coming; depicting their march as unstoppable certifies the futurists' predictions. But machines don't just keep coming. They are funded, invented, built, sold, bought, and used by people who could just as easily not fund, invent, build, sell, buy, and use them. Machines don't drive history; people do. History is not a smart car.

In *Temp: How American Work, American Business, and the American Dream Became Temporary*, the historian Louis Hyman argues that in the course of the past century management consultants, taking the wheel, reinvented work by making employers more like machines, turning work into the kind of thing that robots could do long before there were any robots able to do it. His story begins in the 1920s, with the rise of management consulting, and takes a turn in the '50s, with the first major wave of automation, a word coined in 1948. "Machines should be used instead of people whenever possible," a staffer for the National Office Managers Association advised in 1952. To compete, workers had to become as flexible as machines: able to work on a task basis; ineligible for unions; free at night; willing to work any shift; requiring no health care or other benefits, not so much as a day off at Christmas; easy to hire; and easier to fire.

"The rise of computers and the rise of temps went hand in hand," Hyman writes. By 1958, Elmer Winter had founded Manpower Inc., and companies all over the country had come to rely on the services of management consultants to trim their employment costs. Hyman argues, "Beginning in the midst of the postwar boom in the 1950s, American jobs were slowly remade from top to bottom: consultants supplanted executives at the top, temps replaced office workers in the middle, and day laborers pushed out union workers at the bottom. On every step of the ladder, work would become more insecure as it became more flexible."

Gradually, Hyman says, "the key features of the postwar corporation—stable workforce, retained earnings, and minimized risk—became liabilities rather than assets." Beginning in the 1970s, Harvard Business School's Michael Porter introduced the logic underlying outsourcing. By the 1980s, corporations had to get "lean." (I worked for Porter in those days, as a Manpower temp.) By the 1990s, they needed to "downsize." If businesses exist not to make things and employ people but instead to maximize profits for investors, labor can be done by temps, by poorly paid workers in other countries, or by robots, whichever is cheapest.

The robots, though, were mainly for show. In the 1980s, Apple called its headquarters the Robot Factory. "To understand the electronics industry is simple: every time someone says 'robot,' simply picture a woman of color," Hyman advises. One in five electronics companies used no automation at all, and the rest used very little. Seagate's disk drives were assembled by women in Singapore. Hewlett-Packard hired so many temporary workers that it started its own temp agency. The most important technology in the electronics industry, as Hyman points out, was the fingernail.

In the 1980s, the sociologist Patricia Fernandez-Kelly conducted a study of the electronics and garment industries in Southern California. More than 70 percent of the labor force was women of color, and more than 70 percent of those women were Hispanic. In San Diego, Fernandez-Kelly interviewed a woman she called Fermina Calero (a pseudonym, to protect her from deportation). Calero was born in Mexico. In 1980, when she was twenty-one, she began working in Tijuana, soldering filaments of metal for sixty-five cents an hour. In 1983, Calero crossed into the United States, illegally, to work at Kaypro, the maker of the Kaypro II, a personal computer that briefly rivaled the Apple II. In the 1960s and '70s, Andrew Kay, the company's founder, had hired management consultants to help him reimagine his labor force. In the '80s, when people speaking English responded to the company's newspaper Help Wanted ads, they were told that there were no openings; when people speaking Spanish called, they were invited to apply. By the time Calero started working for Kaypro, its workforce consisted of seven hundred people, nearly all undocumented Mexican immigrants. The company's general manager said, "They are reliable; they work hard; they don't make trouble." At Kaypro, Calero earned nearly five dollars an hour. When the Immigration and Naturalization Service raided the factory, she hid in a supply closet. She was not a robot.

IN 1984, THE YEAR THAT CALERO HID in a closet at Kaypro, computer scientists at the annual meeting of the American Association for Artificial Intelligence began warning about the coming of an "AI winter": artificial intelligence had been overhyped by a credulous press and overfunded by incautious investors, and, given these wild and wide-eyed expectations, it had underdelivered. The hype was about to die down, and the funding to dry up. The AI winter lasted for years.

Skeptics of the current robots-are-coming argument predict the arrival of another AI winter. "We have not moved a byte forward in understanding human intelligence," Zia Chishti wrote in the *Financial Times*. "We have much faster computers, thanks to Moore's law, but the underlying algorithms are mostly identical to those that powered machines 40 years ago." That goes back to the time of the Kaypro.

A lot has changed in those forty years, not least in the availability of enormous sets of data that artificial intelligences can use to study and learn. Still, the economist Robert J. Gordon is unconvinced that the robots are coming. In his 2016 book, *The Rise and Fall of American Growth*, he argued that a century of economic expansion that began in 1870—driven by developments like electricity, a public water supply, and the interstate highway system—ended in 1970, and that, since then, inventions have been merely incremental. The telephone was patented in 1876. It changed people's lives, and contributed to a huge rise in productivity. The cell phone, Gordon argues, just isn't that different from a telephone. In a 2016 essay, "Why Robots Will Not Decimate

Human Jobs," Gordon points out that the uses to which smartphones get put are "not a part of the market economy that creates jobs and pays wages." Robots have altered manufacturing, he concedes, but he doesn't think that they've altered the economy, or that they're about to. "I play a game called 'find the robot,'" he writes. "In my daily strolls in and out of supermarkets, restaurants, doctor and dentist offices, my nearby hospital, offices in my own university, and the vast amount of employment involving elementary and secondary teachers, personal trainers, and old age caretakers, I have yet to find a robot."

STILL, EVEN IF THE HYPE about robots is mostly unwarranted, the worry about jobs is real. If the latest jobs numbers look good, the longer-term trends look bad, especially for Americans without a high school diploma, a population whose real wages have been falling for decades. In a downward compression of the labor market, these jobs have been taken not so much by robots as by college graduates: as much as 40 percent of college graduates work at jobs that do not require a college degree, Ellen Ruppel Shell reports, in *The Job: Work and Its Future in a Time of Radical Change*. Four out of every five children born in the United States in 1950 went on to earn more than their parents. For children born in 1980, that ratio had fallen to one in two. Lately, it's down to one in three. Estimates range from the cautious to the entirely hysterical, but one reasonable study predicts that, by 2050, one in four working-age American men will be unemployed, having been replaced by some form of automation. Most imminently threatened are the millions of people who work as drivers of cars and trucks, allegedly soon to be replaced by fleets of self-driving vehicles.

Economic inequality produces political instability and partisan death matches. Everyone worries about jobs, but people who worry about robots and people who worry about immigrants propose very different solutions. Either way, much writing in this field is, essentially, fantasy. In *The Globotics Upheaval*, Baldwin predicts that the march of the robots will have four stages: transformation, upheaval, backlash, and resolution. The resolution will involve what he calls "shelterism." Once white-collar workers realize that their jobs are on the line, too, they'll find ways to protect themselves by "sheltering" certain activities, things that only humans can do. He explains, "This will mean that our work lives will be filled with far more caring, sharing, understanding, creating, empathizing, innovating, and managing people who are actually in the same room. This is a logical inevitability—everything else will be done by globots." The catch is that, historically, caring for, sharing, understanding, and empathizing with people who are in the same room as you are has been the work of women, and is therefore either unpaid, and not recognized as work, or paid very badly. Childcare, elementary school teaching, nursing, geriatric care, and social work will not suddenly become high-paying, high-prestige professions simply because everything else is done by robots. If that were going to happen, it would already be happening, because we already know that these jobs require beings who are human. Instead, something darker is going on, mirrored in the feminizing of robots, from the male robots of the 1960s and '70s—Hal, R2-D2, C-3PO, and Mr. Robinson's robot on *Lost in Space*—to the fembots and sexbots of *Her* and *Ex Machina*, and, not least, the sexy and slavish Alexa. Female workers aren't being paid more for being human; instead, robots are selling better when they're female.

The economist Oren Cass, the author of *The Once and Future Worker: A Vision for the Renewal of Work in America*, much of which originally appeared in *National Review*, is fed up with the robot hysteria. "Technological innovation and automation have always been integral to our economic progress, and in a well-functioning labor market, they should produce gains for all types of workers," he insists. He has no patience with advocates of universal basic income, either. "We have reached a point where the rich think paying everyone else to go away represents compassionate thinking," he writes.

Like Hyman, Cass blames mid-twentieth-century economic thinkers for the current malaise, though he blames different thinkers. In the middle decades of the twentieth century, he argues, economic policymakers abandoned workers and the health of the labor market in favor of a commitment to overall economic growth, with redistribution as an adjustment and consumerism as its objective. That required quantifying prosperity, hence the GDP, a measure that Cass, along with other writers, finds to be disastrous, not least because it values consumers above producers. Cass sees universal basic income as the end-stage scenario of every other redistribution program, whose justification is that the poor will be fine without work as long as they can buy things. Here he mocks the advocates of the current economic arrangement, who are prone to note that the poor are not actually starving, "and so many people have iPhones!"

Reporters are suckers for the hype, Cass maintains, pointing out that after a 2017 study by the National Bureau of Economic Research suggested that, in the next hundred years, robots might eliminate as many manufacturing jobs as were lost in 2001 (presumably, a tolerable loss), the *Times* ran a story with the headline "Evidence That Robots Are Winning the Race for American Jobs," while the *Washington Post* titled its story "We're So Unprepared for the Robot Apocalypse." Cass offers a careful criticism of the robots-are-stealing-our-jobs theory. He cites four of its errors. It overestimates twenty-first-century innovations and underestimates the innovations of earlier centuries. It miscalculates the pace of change. It assumes that automation will not create new sectors. (3D printing might replace a lot of manufacturing workers, but it could also create a lot of new small businesses.) And it fails to appreciate the complexity of many of the jobs it thinks robots can do. The 2013 Oxford study that kept Andrés Oppenheimer up at night Cass finds to be mostly silly. Its authors, Carl Frey and Michael Osborne, rated 702 occupations from least "computerizable" to most. Highly vulnerable are school bus drivers, and, while a self-driving school bus does not seem technically too far off, Cass points out, few parents can imagine putting their kids on a bus without a grownup to make sure they don't bash one another the whole way to school.

Cass's own policy proposals center, very reasonably, on the importance of work and family, but he fails to demonstrate how his proposals—lowering environmental regulations and establishing academic tracking in high schools—will achieve his objectives. And though *The Once and Future Worker* offers a rousing call for an honest reckoning with American economic policy, it also indulges in its own sleight of hand. "The story goes that 'automation' or the 'knowledge economy,' not bad public policy, is to blame," Cass writes. "Historically, economists and policy makers have led the effort to explain that technological innovation is good for workers throughout the economy, even as its 'creative destruction' causes dislocation for some. So why, suddenly, are they so eager to throw robots and programmers under the bus?" One answer might be that, given the current state of American political polarization, it's either throw the robots under the bus or throw the immigrants. Cass, not surprisingly, advocates restricting immigration.

DONALD TRUMP RAN FOR PRESIDENT on a promise to create twenty-five million new jobs in a decade. "My economic plan rejects the cynicism that says our labor force will keep declining, that our jobs will keep leaving, and that our economy can never grow as it did once before," he said in September 2016. Many economists mocked his plan, which included protecting American jobs by imposing tariffs on imports. The *Economist* announced a new political fault line, not between left and right but between open and closed: "Welcome immigrants or keep them out? Open up to foreign trade or protect domestic industries? Embrace cultural change, or resist it?" Barack Obama was an opener. Openers tend to talk about robots. "The next wave of economic dislocation won't come from overseas," Obama said in his Farewell Address, in January 2017, days before Trump's inauguration. "It will come from the relentless pace of automation that makes many good, middle-class jobs obsolete."

Trump is a closer. Closers tend to talk about immigrants. "We're going to fight for every last American job," he promised from the floor of a Boeing plant in South Carolina, weeks after taking office. "I don't want companies leaving our country," he said. "There will be a very substantial penalty to be paid when they fire their people and move to another country, make the products, and think that they are going to sell it back over what will soon be a very, very strong border." That June, Boeing laid off nearly two hundred employees from the South Carolina plant, as part of a 40 percent reduction in its production of 777s. Over the year 2017, the company laid off nearly six thousand workers.

Trump's administration mocked fears of a robot invasion. Closers usually do. "I'm not worried at all," Secretary of the Treasury Steve Mnuchin said two years ago. Nevertheless, some think tankers suggested that Trump's election was "secretly about automation." And a study published in 2018 in the *Oxford Review of Economic Policy*—whose lead author, Carl Frey, is the same guy who made the list of the 702 most computerizable jobs—argued that the robot caravan got Trump elected. Measuring the density of robots and comparing them with election returns, Frey and his colleagues found that "electoral districts that became more exposed to automation during the years running up to the election were more likely to vote for Trump." Indulging in a counterfactual, they suggest that a less steeply rising increase in exposure to robots would have tipped both Pennsylvania and Wisconsin toward voting for Hillary Clinton. According to this line of thinking, Twitter bots and fake Facebook news didn't elect Donald Trump, but robots really might have. Or maybe it was all the talk about the wall.

Heads, the robots are coming! Accept the inevitability of near-universal unemployment! Tails, the Mexicans are coming! Close the borders! So far, the only other choice, aside from helplessly watching the rise of extremism, is to mint a new coin. Heat a forge. Smelt a blank. Engrave two dies. Put your blank in between them. Strike the whole thing with a hammer. Anyone can do it.

—2019

MISSION IMPOSSIBLE

ACEBOOK HAS A SAVE-THE-WORLD MISSION STATEMENT—
"to give people the power to build community and bring the
world closer together"—that sounds like a better fit for a church, and not
some little wood-steepled, white-clapboarded, side-of-the-road number
but a castle-in-a-parking-lot megachurch, a big-as-a-city-block cathedral, or, honestly, the Vatican. Mark Zuckerberg, Facebook's CEO,
announced this mission the summer after the 2016 U.S. presidential
election, replacing the company's earlier and no less lofty purpose: "to
give people the power to share and make the world more open and connected." Both versions, like most mission statements, are baloney.

The word "mission" comes from the Latin for "send." In English,
historically, a mission is Christian, and means sending the Holy Spirit
out into the world to spread the Word of God: a mission involves
saving souls. In the seventeenth century, when "mission" first conveyed something secular, it meant diplomacy: emissaries undertake
missions. Scientific and military missions—and the expression "mission accomplished"—date to about the First World War. In 1962, JFK
called going to the moon an "untried mission." "Mission statements"
date to the Vietnam War, when the Joint Chiefs of Staff began drafting ever-changing objectives for a war known for its purposelessness.
(The TV show *Mission: Impossible* debuted in 1966.) After 1973, and at
the urging of the management guru Peter Drucker, businesses started
writing mission statements as part of the process of "strategic planning," another expression Drucker borrowed from the military. Before
long, as higher education was becoming corporatized, mission statements crept into university life. "We are on the verge of mission madness," the *Chronicle of Higher Education* reported in 1979. A decade later,
a management journal announced, "Developing a mission statement
is an important first step in the strategic planning process." But by the
1990s corporate mission statements had moved from the realm of stra-

tegic planning to public relations. That's a big part of why they're bull-shit. One study from 2002 reported that most managers don't believe their own companies' mission statements. Research surveys suggest a rule of thumb: the more ethically dubious the business, the more grandiose and sanctimonious its mission statement.

Facebook's stated mission amounts to the salvation of humanity. In truth, the purpose of Facebook, a multinational corporation with headquarters in California, is to make money for its investors. Facebook is an advertising agency: it collects data and sells ads. Founded in 2004, it now has a market value of close to a trillion dollars. Since 2006, with the launch of its News Feed, Facebook has also been a media company, one that now employs fifteen thousand "content moderators." (In the U.S., about a third of the population routinely get their news from Facebook. In other parts of the world, as many as two-thirds do.) Since 2016, Facebook has become interested in election integrity here and elsewhere; the company has thirty-five thousand security specialists in total, many of whom function almost like a UN team of elections observers. But its early mantra, "Company over country," still resonates. The company is, in important respects, larger than any country. Facebook possesses the personal data of more than a quarter of the world's people, 2.8 billion out of 7.9 billion, and governs the flow of information among them. The number of Facebook users is about the size of the populations of China and India combined. In some corners of the globe, including more than half of African nations, Facebook provides free basic data services, positioning itself as a privately owned utility.

An Ugly Truth: Inside Facebook's Battle for Domination, by Sheera Frenkel and Cecilia Kang, takes its title from a memo written by a Facebook executive in 2016 and leaked to *BuzzFeed News*. Andrew Bosworth, who created Facebook's News Feed, apparently wrote the memo in response to employees' repeated pleas for a change in the service, which, during the U.S. presidential election that year, they knew to be prioritizing fake news, like a story that Hillary Clinton was in a coma. Some employees suspected that a lot of these stories were being posted by fake users, and even by foreign actors (which was later discovered to be the case). Bosworth wrote:

So we connect more people. That can be bad if they make it negative. Maybe it costs a life by exposing someone to bullies. Maybe
someone dies in a terrorist attack coordinated on our tools. And still
we connect people. The ugly truth is that we believe in connecting people so deeply that anything that allows us to connect more
people more often is *de facto* good. . . . That's why all the work
we do in growth is justified. All the questionable contact importing
practices. All the subtle language that helps people stay searchable
by friends. All of the work we do to bring more communication in.

Bosworth argued that his memo was meant to provoke debate, not
to be taken literally, but plainly it spoke to views held within the company. That's the downside of a delusional sense of mission: the loss of
all ethical bearings.

AN UGLY TRUTH IS THE RESULT OF fifteen years of reporting.
Frenkel and Kang, award-winning journalists for the *Times*, conducted
interviews with more than four hundred people, mostly Facebook
employees, past and present, for more than a thousand hours. Many
people who spoke with them were violating nondisclosure agreements.
Frenkel and Kang relied, too, on a very leaky spigot of "never-reported
emails, memos, and white papers involving or approved by top executives." They did speak to Facebook's chief operating officer, Sheryl
Sandberg, off the record, but Zuckerberg, who had cooperated with a
2020 book, *Facebook: The Inside Story*, by the *Wired* editor Steven Levy,
declined to talk to them.

Zuckerberg started the company in 2004, when he was a Harvard
sophomore, with this mission statement: "Thefacebook is an online
directory that connects people through social networks at colleges."
The record of an online chat is a good reminder that he was, at the
time, a teenager:

> *ZUCK:* i have over 4000 emails, pictures, addresses, sns
> *FRIEND:* what?! how'd you manage that one?
> *ZUCK:* people just submitted it
> *ZUCK:* i don't know why

ZUCK: they "trust me"
ZUCK: dumb fucks

Zuckerberg dropped out of college, moved to California, and raised a great deal of venture capital. The network got better, and bigger. Zuckerberg would end meetings by pumping his fist and shouting, "Domination!" New features were rolled out as fast as possible, for the sake of fueling growth. "Fuck it, ship it" became a company catchphrase. Facebook announced a new mission in 2006, the year it introduced the News Feed: "Facebook is a social utility that connects you with the people around you." Growth in the number of users mattered, but so did another measurement: the amount of time a user spent on the site. The point of the News Feed was to drive that second metric.

"Facebook was the world's biggest testing lab, with a quarter of the planet's population as its test subjects," Frenkel and Kang write. Zuckerberg was particularly obsessed with regular surveys that asked users whether Facebook is "good for the world" (a tally abbreviated as GFW). When Facebook implemented such changes as demoting lies in the News Feed, the GFW went up, but the time users spent on Facebook went down. Zuckerberg decided to reverse the changes.

Meanwhile, he talked, more and more, about his sense of mission, each new user another saved soul. He toured the world promoting the idea. "For almost ten years, Facebook has been on a mission to make the world more open and connected," Zuckerberg wrote in 2013, in a Facebook post called "Is Connectivity a Human Right?" It reads something like a papal encyclical. Zuckerberg was abroad when Sandberg, newly appointed Facebook's chief operating officer—a protégée of Lawrence Summers's and a former Google vice president—established an ambitious growth model. But, Frenkel and Kang argue, "as Facebook entered new nations, no one was charged with monitoring the rollouts with an eye toward the complex political and cultural dynamics within those countries. No one was considering how the platform might be abused in a nation like Myanmar, or asking if they had enough content moderators to review the hundreds of new languages in which Facebook users across the planet would be posting." Facebook, inadvertently, inflamed the conflict; its algorithms reward emotion, the more heated the better. Eventually, the United Nations concluded that social media played a "determining role" in the genocide and humanitarian crisis in Myanmar—with some twenty-four thousand Rohingya being killed, and seven hundred thousand becoming refugees. "We need to do more," Zuckerberg and Sandberg would say, again, and again, and again. "We need to do better."

In 2015, by which time anyone paying attention could see that the News Feed was wreaking havoc on journalism, especially local news reporting, a new hire named Andrew Anker proposed adding a paywall option to a feature called "Instant Articles." "That meant that in order to keep viewing stories on a publication, readers would have to be subscribers," Levy writes. "Publishers had been begging for something like that to monetize their stories on Facebook." But, Levy reports, when Anker pitched the idea to Zuckerberg, the CEO cut him off. "Facebook's mission is to make the world more open and connected," Zuckerberg said. "I don't understand how subscription would make the world either more open or connected."

By the next year, more than half of all Americans were getting their news from social media. During the 2016 presidential election, many were wildly misinformed. Russian hackers set up hundreds of fake Facebook accounts. They bought political ads. "I don't want anyone to use our tools to undermine democracy," Zuckerberg said. "That's not what we stand for." But, as Frenkel and Kang observe, "Trump and the Russian hackers had separately come to the same conclusion: they could exploit Facebook's algorithms to work in their favor." It didn't matter if a user, or a post, or an article approved or disapproved of something Trump said or did; reacting to it, in any way, elevated its ranking, and the more intense the reaction, the higher the ranking. Trump became inescapable. The News Feed became a Trump Feed.

In 2017, Zuckerberg went on a listening tour of the United States. "My work is about connecting the world and giving everyone a voice," he announced, messianically. "I want to personally hear more of those voices this year." He gave motivational speeches. "We have to build a world where every single person has a sense of purpose and community—that's how we'll bring the world closer together," he told a crowd of Facebook-group administrators. "I know we can do this!" And he came up with a new mission statement.

AN UGLY TRUTH IS A WORK of muckraking, a form of investigative journalism perfected by Ida Tarbell in a series of essays published in *McClure's* between 1902 and 1904 about John D. Rockefeller's company, Standard Oil. When Samuel McClure decided to assign a big piece on monopolies, Tarbell suggested the sugar trust, but, as Steve Weinberg reported in his 2008 book *Taking on the Trust*, McClure wanted her to write about Standard Oil. That was partly because it was such a good story, and partly because of Tarbell's family history: she'd grown up near an oil field, and Rockefeller had more or less put her father out of business.

Standard Oil, founded in 1870, had, like Facebook, faced scrutiny of its business practices from the start. In 1872 and 1876, it had been the subject of congressional hearings; in 1879, Rockefeller was called to hearings before committees in Pennsylvania, New York, and Ohio; Standard Oil executives were repeatedly summoned by the Interstate Commerce Commission after its establishment, in 1887; the company was investigated by Congress again in 1888, and by Ohio for more than a decade, and was the subject of a vast number of private suits. Earlier reporters had tried to get the goods, too. In 1881, the *Chicago Tribune* reporter Henry Demarest Lloyd wrote an article for the *Atlantic* called "The Story of a Great Monopoly." Lloyd accused the oil trust of bribing politicians, having, for instance, "done everything with the Pennsylvania legislature except refine it." He concluded: "America has the proud satisfaction of having furnished the world with the greatest, wisest and meanest monopoly known to history."

Lloyd wrote something between an essay and a polemic. Tarbell took a different tack, drawing on research skills she'd acquired as a biographer of Lincoln. "Neither Standard Oil and Rockefeller nor any powerful American institution had ever encountered a journalist like Tarbell," Weinberg writes. She also, in something of a first, revealed her sources to readers, explaining that she had gone to state and federal legislatures and courthouses and got the records of all those lawsuits and investigations and even all those private lawsuits, "the testimony of which," she wrote, "is still in manuscript in the files of the courts where the suits were tried." She dug up old newspaper stories (quite difficult to obtain in those days) and wrote to Standard Oil's competitors, asking them to send any correspondence that might cast light on

Rockefeller's anticompetitive practices. She tried, too, to talk to executives at Standard Oil, but, she wrote, "I had been met with that formulated chatter used by those who have accepted a creed." Finally, she found a source inside the company, Henry Rogers, who had known of her father. As Stephanie Gorton writes in her book *Citizen Reporters*, Tarbell "went to the Standard Oil offices at 26 Broadway regularly for two years. Each time, she entered the imposing colonnaded building and was immediately whisked by an assistant from the lobby via a circuitous and private route to Rogers's office, kept out of sight from Standard Oil employees who might recognize her, and spoken to by no one but Rogers and his secretary." Because *McClure's* published the work serially, the evidence kept coming; even as Tarbell was writing, disgruntled competitors and employees went on sending her letters and memos. As the *Boston Globe* put it, she was "writing unfinished history."

On the subject of John D. Rockefeller, Tarbell proved scathing. " 'The most important man in the world,' a great and serious newspaper passionately devoted to democracy calls him, and unquestionably this is the popular measure of him," she wrote. "His importance lies not so much in the fact that he is the richest individual in the world. . . . It lies in the fact that his wealth, and the power springing from it, appeal to the most universal and powerful passion in this country—the passion for money." In sum, "our national life is on every side distinctly poorer, uglier, meaner for the kind of influence he exercises."

On reading the series, Lloyd wrote to her, "When you get through with 'Johnnie,' I don't think there will be very much left of him except something resembling one of his own grease spots." Critics accused Tarbell of being mean-spirited. A review in *The Nation* claimed, "To stir up envy, to arouse prejudice, to inflame passion, to appeal to ignorance, to magnify evils, to charge corruption—these seem to be the methods in favor with too many writers who profess a desire to reform society." In 1906, Theodore Roosevelt coined the term "muckraking" as a slur. "There is in America today a distinct prejudice in favor of those who make the accusations," Walter Lippmann observed, of Tarbell's form of journalism, admitting that "if business and politics really served American need, you could never induce people to believe so many accusations against them." Few could dispute Tarbell's evidence, especially after she published the series of articles as a book of 406 pages, with 36 appendices stretching across 140 pages.

Tarbell hadn't enjoyed taking down Standard Oil. "It was just one of those things that had to be done," she wrote. "I trust that it has not been useless." It had not been useless. In 1911, the U.S. Supreme Court ordered the dissolution of Standard Oil.

The year *McClure's* published the final installment of Tarbell's series, Rockefeller's son, John Jr., on the threshold of inheriting one of the world's greatest fortunes, suffered a nervous breakdown. Shortly before the breakup of his father's company, Rockefeller Jr., a devout and earnest Christian, stepped away from any role in Standard Oil or its successor firms; he turned his attention to philanthropy, guided, in part, by Ivy Lee, his father's public relations manager. In 1920, at Madison Avenue Baptist Church, before an audience of twelve hundred clergymen, he announced that he had found a new calling, as a booster and chief underwriter of a utopian, ecumenical Protestant organization called the Interchurch World Movement. "When a vast multitude of people come together earnestly and prayerfully," he told the crowd, "there must be developed an outpouring of spiritual power such as this land has never before known." In a letter to his father, asking him for tens of millions of dollars to give to the cause, the younger Rockefeller wrote, "I do not think we can overestimate the importance of this Movement. As I see it, it is capable of having a much more far-reaching influence than the League of Nations in bringing about peace, contentment, goodwill, and prosperity among the people of the earth." The Interchurch World Movement, in short, aimed to give people the power to build community and bring the world closer together. It failed. Rockefeller repurposed its funds for Christian missions.

"OUR MISSION IS TO GIVE PEOPLE the power to build community and bring the world closer together" is a statement to be found in Facebook's Terms of Service; everyone who uses Facebook implicitly consents to this mission. During the years of the company's ascent, the world has witnessed a loneliness epidemic, the growth of political extremism and political violence, widening political polarization, the rise of authoritarianism, the decline of democracy, a catastrophic crisis in journalism, and an unprecedented rise in propaganda, fake news, and misinformation. By no means is Facebook responsible for these calamities, but evidence implicates the company as a contributor to each of them. In 2021, President Biden said that misinformation about COVID-19 on Facebook "is killing people."

Collecting data and selling ads does not build community, and it turns out that bringing people closer together, at least in the way Facebook does it, makes it easier for them to hurt one another. Facebook wouldn't be so successful if people didn't love using it, sharing family photographs, joining groups, reading curated news, and even running small businesses. But studies have consistently shown that the more time people spend on Facebook the worse their mental health becomes; Facebooking is also correlated with increased sedentariness, a diminishment of meaningful face-to-face relationships, and a decline in real-world social activities. Efforts to call Zuckerberg and Sandberg to account and get the company to stop doing harm have nearly all ended in failure. Employees and executives have tried in vain to change the company's policies and, especially, its algorithms. Congress has held hearings. Trustbusters have tried to break the company up. Regulators have attempted to impose rules on it. And journalists have written exposés. But, given how profoundly Facebook itself has undermined journalism, it's hard to see how Frenkel and Kang's work, or anyone else's, could have a Tarbell-size effect.

"If what you care about is democracy and elections," Mark Zuckerberg said in 2019, "then you want a company like us to be able to invest billions of dollars a year, like we are, in building really advanced tools to fight election interference." During the next year's presidential election, Frenkel and Kang report, "Trump was the single-largest spender on political ads on Facebook." His Facebook page was busier than those of the major networks, *BuzzFeed*, the *Washington Post,* and the *New York Times* taken together. Over the protests of many Facebook employees, Zuckerberg had adopted, and stuck to, a policy of not subjecting any political advertisements to fact-checking. Refusing to be "an arbiter of truth," Facebook instead established itself as a disseminator of misinformation.

On January 27, 2021, three weeks after the insurrection at the U.S. Capitol, Zuckerberg, having suspended Trump's account, renewed Facebook's commitments: "We're going to continue to focus on helping millions more people participate in healthy communities, and we're going to focus even more on being a force for bringing people closer together." Neither a record-setting five-billion-dollar penalty for privacy violations nor the latest antitrust efforts have managed to check one of the world's most dangerous monopolies. Billions of people remain, instead, in the tightfisted, mechanical grip of its soul-saving mission.

—2021

Part Seven

The Rule
of History

*The past has a hold: writing is the casting
of a line over the edge of time. But there are no
certainties in history. There are only struggles
for justice, and wars interrupted by peace.*

Black law students picketing outside the Supreme Court, 1984.
AP Photo / John Duricka

THE RULE OF HISTORY

T HE REIGN OF KING JOHN WAS IN ALL WAYS UNLIKELY and, in most, dreadful. He was born in 1166 or 1167, the youngest of Henry II's five sons, his ascension to the throne being, by the fingers on one hand, so implausible that he was not named after a king and, as a matter of history, suffers both the indignity of the possibility that he may have been named after his sister Joan and the certain fate of having proved so unredeemable a ruler that no king of England has ever taken his name. He was spiteful and he was weak, although, frankly, so were the medieval historians who chronicled his reign, which can make it hard to know quite how horrible it really was. In any case, the worst king of England is best remembered for an act of capitulation: in 1215, he pledged to his barons that he would obey "the law of the land" when he affixed his seal to a charter that came to be called Magna Carta. He then promptly asked the pope to nullify the agreement; the pope obliged. The king died not long afterward, of dysentery. "Hell itself is made fouler by the presence of John," it was said. In 2015, Magna Carta turned eight hundred years old; King John was seven hundred and ninety-nine years dead. Few men have been less mourned, few legal documents more adored.

Magna Carta has been taken as foundational to the rule of law, chiefly because in it King John promised that he would stop throwing people into dungeons whenever he wished, a provision that lies behind what is now known as due process of law and is understood not as a promise made by a king but as a right possessed by the people. Due process is a bulwark against injustice, but it wasn't put in place in 1215; it is a wall built stone by stone, defended, and attacked, year after year. Much of the rest of Magna Carta, weathered by time and for centuries forgotten, has long since crumbled, an abandoned castle, a romantic ruin.

Magna Carta is written in Latin. The king and the barons spoke

French. "*Par les denz Dieu!*" the king liked to swear, invoking the teeth of God. The peasants, who were illiterate, spoke English. Most of the charter concerns feudal financial arrangements (socage, burgage, and scutage), obsolete measures and descriptions of land and of husbandry (wapentakes and wainages), and obscure instruments for the seizure and inheritance of estates (disseisin and mort d'ancestor). "Men who live outside the forest are not henceforth to come before our justices of the forest through the common summonses, unless they are in a plea," one article begins.

Magna Carta's importance has often been overstated, and its meaning distorted. "The significance of King John's promise has been anything but constant," U.S. Supreme Court Justice John Paul Stevens aptly wrote, in 1992. It also has a very different legacy in the United States than it does in the United Kingdom, where only four of its original sixty-some provisions are still on the books. In 2012, three New Hampshire Republicans introduced into the state legislature a bill that required that "all members of the general court proposing bills and resolutions addressing individual rights or liberties shall include a direct quote from the Magna Carta which sets forth the article from which the individual right or liberty is derived." For American originalists, in particular, Magna Carta has a special lastingness. "It is with us every day," Justice Antonin Scalia said in a speech at a Federalist Society gathering in 2014.

Much has been written of the rule of law, less of the rule of history. Magna Carta, an agreement between the king and his barons, was also meant to bind the past to the present, though perhaps not in quite the way it's turned out. That's how history always turns out: not the way it was meant to. In preparation for its anniversary, Magna Carta acquired a Twitter username: @MagnaCarta800th. There were Magna Carta exhibits at the British Library, in London, at the National Archives, in Washington, and at other museums, too, where medieval manuscript Magna Cartas written in Latin were displayed behind thick glass, like tropical fish or crown jewels. There was also, of course, swag. Much of it made a fetish of ink and parchment, the written word as relic. The gift shop at the British Library sold Magna Carta T-shirts and tea towels, inkwells, quills, and King John pillows. The Library of Congress sold a Magna Carta mug; the National Archives Museum stocked a kids' book called *The Magna Carta: Cornerstone of the Constitution*. Online, by God's teeth, you could buy an "ORIGINAL 1215 Magna Carta British Library Baby Pacifier," with the full Latin text, all thirty-five hundred or so words, on a silicone orthodontic nipple.

THE REIGN OF KING JOHN could not have been foreseen in 1169, when Henry II divided his lands among his surviving older sons: to Henry, his namesake and heir, he gave England, Normandy, and Anjou; to Richard, Aquitaine; to Geoffrey, Brittany. To his youngest son, he gave only a name: Lackland. In a biography, *King John and the Road to Magna Carta*, Stephen Church suggests that the king might have been preparing his youngest son for the life of a scholar. In 1179, he placed him under the tutelage of Ranulf de Glanville, who wrote or oversaw one of the first commentaries on English law, *A Treatise on the Laws and Customs of the Realm of England*.

"English laws are unwritten," the treatise explained, and it is "utterly impossible for the laws and rules of the realm to be reduced to writing." All the same, Glanville argued, custom and precedent together con-stitute a knowable common law, a delicate handling of what, during the reign of Henry II, had become a vexing question: Can a law be a law if it's not written down? Glanville's answer was yes, but that led to another question: If the law isn't written down, and even if it is, by what argument or force can a king be constrained to obey it?

Meanwhile, the sons of Henry II were toppled, one by one. John's brother Henry, the so-called Young King, died in 1183. John became a knight and went on an expedition in Ireland. Some of his troops deserted him. He acquired a new name: John Softsword. After his brother Geoffrey died, in 1186, John allied with Richard against their father. In 1189, John married his cousin Isabella of Gloucester. (When she had no children, he had their marriage ended, locked her in his cas-tle, and then sold her.) Upon the death of Henry II, Richard, the lion-hearted, became king, went on crusade, and was thrown into prison in Germany on his way home, whereupon John, allying with Philip Augustus of France, attempted a rebellion against him, but Richard both fended it off and forgave him. "He is a mere boy," he said. (John was almost thirty.) And lo, in 1199, after Richard's death by crossbow, John, no longer lacking in land or soft of sword, was crowned king of England.

Many times he went to battle. He lost more castles than he gained. He lost Anjou, and much of Aquitaine. He lost Normandy. In 1200, he married another Isabella, who may have been eight or nine; he referred to her as a "thing." He also had a passel of illegitimate children, and allegedly tried to rape the daughter of one of his barons (the first was common, the second not), although, as Church reminds readers, not all reports about John ought to be believed, since nearly all the historians who chronicled his reign hated him. Bearing that in mind, he is nevertheless known to have levied steep taxes, higher than any king ever had before, and to have carried so much coin outside his realm and then kept so much coin in his castle treasuries that it was difficult for anyone to pay him with money. When his noblemen fell into his debt, he took their sons hostage. He had a noblewoman and her son starved to death in a dungeon. It is said that he had one of his clerks crushed to death, on suspicion of disloyalty. He opposed the election of the new archbishop of Canterbury. For this, he was eventually excommunicated by the pope. He began planning to retake Normandy only to face a rebellion in Wales and invasion from France. Cannily, he surrendered England and Ireland to the pope, by way of regaining his favor, and then pledged to go on crusade, for the same reason. In May of 1215, barons rebelling against the king's tyrannical rule captured London. That spring, he agreed to meet with them to negotiate a peace. They met at Runnymede, a meadow by the Thames.

The barons presented the king with a number of demands, the Articles of the Barons, which included, as Article 29, this provision: "The body of a free man is not to be arrested, or imprisoned, or disseised, or outlawed, or exiled, or in any way ruined, nor is the king to go against him or send forcibly against him, except by judgment of his peers or by the law of the land." John's reply: "Why do not the barons, with these unjust exactions, ask my kingdom?" But in June 1215, the king, his royal back against the wall, affixed his beeswax seal to a treaty, or charter, written by his scribes in iron-gall ink on a single sheet of parchment. Under the terms of the charter, the king, his plural self, granted "to all the free men of our kingdom, for us and our heirs in perpetuity" certain "written liberties, to be had and held by them and their heirs by us and our heirs." (Essentially, a "free man" was a noble-man.) One of those liberties is the one that had been demanded by the barons in Article 29: "No free man is to be arrested, or imprisoned . . . save by the lawful judgment of his peers or by the law of the land."

MAGNA CARTA IS VERY OLD, but even when it was written it was not especially new. Kings have insisted on their right to rule, in writing, at least since the sixth century BC, as Nicholas Vincent points out in *Magna Carta: A Very Short Introduction*. Vincent, a pro-fessor of medieval history at the University of East Anglia, is also the editor of and chief contributor to a new collection of illustrated essays, *Magna Carta: The Foundation of Freedom, 1215–2015*. The practice of kings swearing coronation oaths in which they bound themselves to the administration of justice began in 877, in France. Magna Carta borrows from many earlier agreements; most of its ideas, including many of its particular provisions, are centuries old, as David Carpen-ter, a professor of medieval history at King's College, London, explains in *Magna Carta*, an invaluable commentary that answers, but does not supplant, the remarkable and authoritative commentary by J. C. Holt. In eleventh-century Germany, for instance, King Conrad II prom-ised his knights that he wouldn't take their lands "save according to the constitution of our ancestors and the judgment of their peers." In 1100, after his coronation, Henry I, the son of William the Con-queror, issued a decree known as the Charter of Liberties, in which he promised to "abolish all the evil customs by which the Kingdom of England has been unjustly oppressed," a list of customs that appear, all over again, in Magna Carta. The Charter of Liberties hardly stopped either Henry I or his successors from plundering the realm, butchering their enemies, subjugating the church, and flouting the laws. But it did chronicle complaints that made their way into the Articles of the Bar-ons a century later. Meanwhile, Henry II and his sons demanded that their subjects obey, and promised that they were protected by the law of the land, which, as Glanville had established, was unwritten. "We do not wish that you should be treated henceforth save by law and judgment, nor that anyone shall take anything from you by will," King John proclaimed. As Carpenter writes, "Essentially, what happened in

1215 was that the kingdom turned around and told the king to obey his own rules."

King John affixed his seal to the charter in June 1215. In fact, he affixed his seal to many charters (there is no original), so that they could be distributed and made known. But then, in July, he appealed to the pope, asking him to annul it. In a papal bull issued in August, the pope declared the charter "null, and void of all validity forever." King John's realm quickly descended into civil war. The king died in October 1216. He was buried in Worcester, in part because, as Church writes, "so much of his kingdom was in enemy hands." Before his death, he had named his nine-year-old son, Henry, heir to the throne. In an attempt to end the war, the regent who ruled during Henry's minority restored much of the charter issued at Runnymede, in the first of many revisions. In 1217, provisions having to do with the woods were separated into "the charters of the forests"; by 1225, what was left—nearly a third of the 1215 charter had been cut or revised—had become known as Magna Carta. It granted liberties not to free men but to everyone, free and unfree. It also divided its provisions into chapters. It entered the statute books in 1297, and was first publicly proclaimed in English in 1300.

"Did Magna Carta make a difference?" Carpenter asks. Most people, apparently, knew about it. In 1300, even peasants complaining against the lord's bailiff in Essex cited it. But did it work? There's debate on this point, but Carpenter comes down mostly on the side of the charter's inadequacy, unenforceability, and irrelevance. It was confirmed nearly fifty times, but only because it was hardly ever honored. An English translation, a rather bad one, was printed for the first time in 1534, by which time Magna Carta was little more than a curiosity.

Then, strangely, in the seventeenth century Magna Carta became a rallying cry during a parliamentary struggle against arbitrary power, even though by then the various versions of the charter had become hopelessly muddled and its history obscured. Many colonial American charters were influenced by Magna Carta, partly because citing it was a way to drum up settlers. Edward Coke, the person most responsible for reviving interest in Magna Carta in England, described it as his country's "ancient constitution." He was rumored to be writing a book about Magna Carta; Charles I forbade its publication. Eventually, the House of Commons ordered the publication of Coke's work. (That Oliver Cromwell supposedly called it "Magna Farta" might well be, understandably, the single thing about Magna Carta that most Americans remember from their high school history class. While we're at it, he also called the Petition of Right the "Petition of Shite.") American lawyers see Magna Carta through Coke's spectacles, as the legal scholar Roscoe Pound once pointed out. Nevertheless, Magna Carta's significance during the founding of the American colonies is almost always wildly overstated. As cherished and important as Magna Carta became, it didn't cross the Atlantic in "the hip pocket of Captain John Smith," as the legal historian A. E. Dick Howard once put it. Claiming a French-speaking king's short-lived promise to his noblemen as the foundation of English liberty and, later, of American democracy, took a lot of work.

"ON THE 15TH OF THIS MONTH, anno 1215, was *Magna Charta* sign'd by King John, for declaring and establishing *English Liberty*," Benjamin Franklin wrote in *Poor Richard's Almanack*, in 1749, on the page for June, urging his readers to remember it, and mark the day.

Magna Carta was revived in seventeenth-century England and celebrated in eighteenth-century America because of the specific authority it wielded as an artifact—the historical document as an instrument of political protest—but, as Vincent points out, "the fact that Magna Carta itself had undergone a series of transformations between 1215 and 1225 was, to say the least, inconvenient to any argument that the constitution was of its nature unchanging and unalterable."

The myth that Magna Carta had essentially been written in stone was forged in the colonies. By the 1760s, colonists opposed to taxes levied by Parliament in the wake of the Seven Years' War began citing Magna Carta as the authority for their argument, mainly because it was more ancient than any arrangement between a particular colony and a particular king or a particular legislature. In 1766, when Franklin was brought to the House of Commons to explain the colonists' refusal to pay the stamp tax, he was asked, "How then could the assembly of Pennsylvania assert, that laying a tax on them by the stamp-act was an infringement of their rights?" It was true, Franklin admitted, that there was nothing specifically to that effect in the colony's charter. He cited, instead, their understanding of "the common rights of Englishmen, as declared by Magna Charta."

In 1770, when the Massachusetts House of Representatives sent instructions to Franklin, acting as its envoy in Great Britain, he was told to advance the claim that taxes levied by Parliament "were designed to exclude us from the least Share in that Clause of Magna Charta, which has for many Centuries been the noblest Bulwark of the English Liberties, and which cannot be too often repeated. 'No Freeman shall be taken, or imprisoned, or deprived of his Freehold or Liberties or free Customs, or be outlaw'd or exiled or any otherwise destroyed nor will we pass upon him nor condemn him but by the Judgment of his Peers or the Law of the Land.'" The Sons of Liberty imagined themselves the heirs of the barons, despite the fact that the charter enshrines not liberties granted by the king to certain noblemen but liberties granted to all men by nature.

In 1775, Massachusetts adopted a new seal, which pictured a man holding a sword in one hand and Magna Carta in the other. In 1776, Thomas Paine argued that "the charter which secures this freedom in England, was formed, not in the senate, but in the field; and insisted on by the people, not granted by the crown." In "Common Sense," he urged Americans to write their own Magna Carta.

Magna Carta's unusual legacy in the United States is a matter of political history. But it also has to do with the difference between written and unwritten laws, and between promises and rights. At the Constitutional Convention, Magna Carta was barely mentioned, and only in passing. Invoked in a struggle against the king as a means of protesting his power as arbitrary, Magna Carta seemed irrelevant once independence had been declared: the United States had no king in need of restraining. Toward the end of the Constitutional Convention, when George Mason, of Virginia, raised the question of whether the new frame of government ought to include a declaration or a Bill of Rights, the idea was quickly squashed, as Carol Berkin recounts in her short history *The Bill of Rights: The Fight to Secure America's Liberties*. In Federalist No. 84, urging the ratification of the Constitution, Alexander Hamilton explained that a Bill of Rights was a good thing to have, as a defense against a monarch, but that it was altogether unnecessary in a republic. "Bills of rights are, in their origin, stipulations between kings and their subjects, abridgements of prerogative in favor of privilege, reservations of rights not surrendered to the prince," Hamilton explained:

> Such was MAGNA CHARTA, obtained by the barons, sword in hand, from King John. Such were the subsequent confirmations of that charter by succeeding princes. Such was the PETITION OF RIGHT assented to by Charles I., in the beginning of his reign. Such, also, was the Declaration of Right presented by the Lords and Commons to the Prince of Orange in 1688, and afterwards thrown into the form of an act of parliament called the Bill of Rights. It is evident, therefore, that, according to their primitive signification, they have no application to constitutions professedly founded upon the power of the people, and executed by their immediate representatives and servants. Here, in strictness, the people surrender nothing; and as they retain every thing they have no need of particular reservations. "We, THE PEOPLE of the United States, to secure the blessings of liberty to ourselves and our posterity, do ORDAIN and ESTABLISH this Constitution for the United States of America." Here is a better recognition of popular rights, than volumes of those aphorisms which make the principal figure in several of our State bills of rights, and which would sound much better in a treatise of ethics than in a constitution of government.

Madison eventually decided in favor of a Bill of Rights for two reasons, Berkin argues. First, the Constitution would not have been ratified without the concession to Anti-Federalists that the adopting of a Bill of Rights represented. Second, Madison came to believe that, while a Bill of Rights wasn't necessary to abridge the powers of a government that was itself the manifestation of popular sovereignty, it might be useful in checking the tyranny of a political majority against a minority. "Wherever the real power in a Government lies, there is the danger of oppression," Madison wrote to Jefferson in 1788. "In our Governments the real power lies in the majority of the Community, and the invasion of private rights is *cheifly* to be apprehended, not from acts of Government contrary to the sense of its constituents, but from acts in which the Government is the mere instrument of the major number of the constituents."

The Bill of Rights drafted by Madison and ultimately adopted as twenty-seven provisions bundled into ten amendments to the Constitution does not, on the whole, have much to do with King John. Only four of the Bill of Rights' twenty-seven provisions, according to the political scientist Donald S. Lutz, can be traced to Magna Carta. Madison himself complained that, as for "trial by jury, freedom of the press, or liberty of conscience . . . Magna Charta does not contain any one provision for the security of those rights." Instead, the provisions of the Bill of Rights derive largely from bills of rights adopted by the states between 1776 and 1787, which themselves derive from charters of liberties adopted by the colonies, including the Massachusetts Body of Liberties, in 1641, documents in which the colonists stated their fundamental political principles and created their own political order. The Bill of Rights, a set of amendments to the Constitution, is itself a revision. History is nothing so much as that act of emendation—amendment upon amendment upon amendment.

It would not be quite right to say that Magna Carta has withstood the ravages of time. It would be fairer to say that, like much else that is very old, it is on occasion taken out of the closet, dusted off, and put on display to answer a need. Such needs are generally political. They are very often profound.

In the United States in the nineteenth century, the myth of Magna Carta as a single, stable, unchanged document contributed to the veneration of the Constitution as unalterable, despite the fact that Paine, among many other Founders, believed a chief virtue of a written constitution lay in the ability to amend it. Between 1836 and 1943, sixteen American states incorporated the full text of Magna Carta into their statute books, and twenty-five more incorporated, in one form or another, a revision of the twenty-ninth Article of the Barons: "No person shall be deprived of life, liberty, or property, without due process of law." The Fourteenth Amendment was passed in 1868; it came to be interpreted as making the Bill of Rights apply to the states. In the past century, the due process clause of the Fourteenth Amendment has been the subject of some of the most heated contests of constitutional interpretation in American history; it lies at the heart of, for instance, both *Roe v. Wade* and *Lawrence v. Texas*.

Meanwhile, Magna Carta became an American icon. In 1935, King John affixing his wax seal to the charter appeared on the door of the United States Supreme Court Building. During the Second World War, Magna Carta served as a symbol of the shared political values of the United States and the United Kingdom. In 1939, a Magna Carta owned by the Lincoln Cathedral was displayed in New York, at the World's Fair, behind bulletproof glass, in a shrine built for the occasion, called Magna Carta Hall. As Winston Churchill was vigorously urging America's entry into the war, he contemplated offering it to the United States, as the "only really adequate gesture which it is in our power to make in return for the means to preserve our country." It wasn't his to give, and the request that the British Library send the Lincoln Cathedral one of its Magna Cartas, to replace the one he intended to give to the United States, was not well received. Instead, the cathedral's Magna Carta was deposited in the Library of Congress—"in the safe hands of the barons and the commoners," as FDR joked in a letter to Archibald MacLeish, the Librarian of Congress—where it was displayed next to the Declaration of Independence and the Constitution, with which, once the war began, it was evacuated to Fort Knox. It was returned to the Lincoln Cathedral in 1946.

Magna Carta was conscripted to fight in the human rights movement, and in the Cold War, too. "This Universal Declaration of Human Rights . . . reflects the composite views of the many men and governments who have contributed to its formulation," Eleanor Roosevelt said in 1948, urging its adoption in a speech at the United Nations— she had chaired the committee that drafted the declaration—but she insisted, too, on its particular genealogy: "This Universal Declaration of Human Rights may well become the international Magna Carta of all men everywhere." (Its ninth article reads, "No one shall be subjected to arbitrary arrest, detention or exile.") In 1957, the American Bar Association erected a memorial at Runnymede. In a speech given that day, the association's past president argued that in the United States Magna Carta had at last been constitutionalized: "We sought in the written word a measure of certainty."

Magna Carta cuts one way, and, then again, another. "Magna Carta decreed that no man would be imprisoned contrary to the law of the land," Justice Kennedy wrote in the majority opinion in *Boumediene v. Bush*, in 2008, finding that the Guantánamo prisoner Lakhdar Boumediene and other detainees had been deprived of an ancient right. But on the eight-hundredth anniversary of the agreement made at Runnymede, one in every hundred and ten people in the United States is behind bars. #MagnaCartaUSA?

The rule of history is as old as the rule of law. Magna Carta has been sealed and nullified, revised and flouted, elevated and venerated. The past has a hold: writing is the casting of a line over the edge of time. But there are no certainties in history. There are only struggles for justice, and wars interrupted by peace.

—2015

THE AGE OF CONSENT

I N 1947, KURT GÖDEL, ALBERT EINSTEIN, AND OSKAR Morgenstern drove from Princeton to Trenton in Morgenstern's car. The three men, who'd fled Nazi Europe and become close friends at the Institute for Advanced Study, were on their way to a courthouse where Gödel, an Austrian exile, was scheduled to take the U.S. citizenship exam, something his two friends had done already. Morgenstern had founded game theory, Einstein had founded the theory of relativity, and Gödel, the greatest logician since Aristotle, had revolutionized mathematics and philosophy with his incompleteness theorems. Morgenstern drove. Gödel sat in the back. Einstein, up front with Morgenstern, turned around and said, teasing, "Now, Gödel, are you really well prepared for this examination?" Gödel looked stricken.

To prepare for his citizenship test, knowing that he'd be asked questions about the U.S. Constitution, Gödel had dedicated himself to the study of American history and constitutional law. Time and again, he'd phoned Morgenstern with rising panic about the exam. (Gödel, a paranoid recluse who later died of starvation, used the telephone to speak with people even when they were in the same room.) Morgenstern reassured him that "at most they might ask what sort of government we have." But Gödel only grew more upset. Eventually, as Morgenstern later recalled, "he rather excitedly told me that in looking at the Constitution, to his distress, he had found some inner contradictions and that he could show how in a perfectly legal manner it would be possible for somebody to become a dictator and set up a Fascist regime, never intended by those who drew up the Constitution." He'd found a logical flaw.

Morgenstern told Einstein about Gödel's theory; both of them told Gödel not to bring it up during the exam. When they got to the courtroom, the three men sat before a judge, who asked Gödel about the Austrian government.

"It was a republic, but the constitution was such that it finally was changed into a dictatorship," Gödel said.

"That is very bad," the judge replied. "This could not happen in this country."

Morgenstern and Einstein must have exchanged anxious glances. Gödel could not be stopped.

"Oh, yes," he said. "I can prove it."

"Oh, God, let's not go into this," the judge said, and ended the examination.

Neither Gödel nor his friends ever explained what the theory, which has since come to be called Gödel's loophole, was. For some people, conjecturing about Gödel's loophole is as alluring as conjecturing about Fermat's last theorem.

IN 1949, the year after Kurt Gödel became a U.S. citizen, Linda Colley was born in the United Kingdom, a country without a written constitution. Colley, one of the world's most acclaimed historians, is a British citizen and a CBE, a Commander of the Order of the British Empire. (If there were a Nobel Prize in History, Colley would be my nominee.) She lives in the United States. For the past twenty years or so, she's been teaching at Princeton, walking the same grounds and haunting the same library stacks that Gödel once did, by turns puzzled and fascinated, as he was, by the nature of constitutions. "I came to this subject very much as an outsider," she writes in an incandescent, paradigm-shifting book, *The Gun, the Ship, and the Pen: Warfare, Constitutions, and the Making of the Modern World.* "Moving in the late twentieth century to live and work in the United States, a country which makes a cult out of its own written constitution, was therefore for me an arresting experience." Colley has upended much of what historians believe about the origins of written constitutions. Gödel's loophole is all over the internet; you can find it on everything from Reddit to GitHub. The graver the American constitutional crisis, the greater the interest in the idea that there's a bug in the constitutional code. But, for genuine illumination about the promise and the limits of constitutionalism, consider instead Colley's Rule: follow the violence.

"For the preservation of peace and good order, and for the security of the lives and properties of the inhabitants of this colony, we conceive ourselves reduced to the necessity of establishing A FORM OF GOVERNMENT," New Hampshire's congress pronounced in January 1776, months before the colonies declared their independence from Britain, in one of the first written constitutions in the history of the modern world. After New Hampshire, every other former colony devised its own constitution, and each new constitution, along with the Articles of Confederation, offered another lesson in what worked and what didn't. Eleven years later, James Madison, having dedicated himself to the study of history ever since his years as an undergraduate at Princeton, prepared for a national constitutional convention by writing an essay titled "Vices of the Political System of the United States," and then drafting a constitution. Madison's constitution, much tinkered with during the convention, was signed in September 1787 and ratified in June 1788.

Many of the Founders later had grave doubts about the government they'd erected, as Dennis Rasmussen argues in *Fears of a Setting Sun: The Disillusionment of America's Founders*. Washington regretted partisanship, Hamilton thought the federal government too weak, Adams damned the vices of the people, and Jefferson expected the divide over slavery to doom the Union, writing, a few years before his death, "I regret that I am now to die in the belief that the useless sacrifice of themselves, by the generation of '76, to acquire self government and happiness by their country, is to be thrown away by the unwise and unworthy passions of their sons, and that my only consolation is to be that I live not to weep over it." Still, as the usual story has it, American constitutionalism served as a model for what can be called the age of constitution-making, an era also characterized by the spread of democracy; by 1914, governments on every continent had adopted written constitutions, driven by the force of the idea that the nature of rule, the structure of government, and the guarantee of rights are the sorts of things that have got to be written down, printed, and made public.

Colley doesn't see it this way. First, she finds the origins of constitution-writing elsewhere—all over the place, really, and often very far from Philadelphia. Second, she thinks it's important to separate the spread of constitutionalism from the rise of democracy, not least because many nations that adopted written constitutions rejected democracy, and still do. Third, she isn't convinced that the writing of constitutions was simply driven by the force of an idea; instead, she thinks that the writing of constitutions was driven, in large part, by the exigencies of war. States make war and wars make states, the sociologist Charles Tilly once argued. Colley offers this corollary: wars make states make constitutions.

Laws govern people; constitutions govern governments. Written (or carved) constitutions, like Hammurabi's Code, date to antiquity, but hardly anyone read them (hardly anyone *could* read), and, generally, they were locked away and eventually lost. Even Magna Carta all but disappeared after King John affixed his seal to it, in 1215. For a written constitution to restrain a government, people living under that government must be able to get a copy of the constitution, easily and cheaply, and they must be able to read it. That wasn't possible before the invention of the printing press and rising rates of literacy. The U.S. Constitution was printed in Philadelphia two days after it was signed, in the *Pennsylvania Packet, and Daily Advertiser*, a newspaper that cost fourpence.

Kurt Gödel pored over the four-thousand-odd words of the U.S. Constitution and spotted a logical flaw; Linda Colley has made a meticulous study of constitutions written the world over and discovered patterns in the circumstances in which each was written, distributed, and read. Crucial to the emergence of constitutionalism, she maintains, was the growing lethality, frequency, and scale of war. This began in the mid-eighteenth century, when rulers from China to Persia to Spain found themselves committed to long-distance wars that involved vast armies and navies and cost staggering sums. Early on, Spain paid for these wars with the gold and silver it had plundered from the Americas, on lands stolen from indigenous peoples. The slave trade itself was a feature of the increasing violence and widening scope of early modern warfare. The Yoruba Oyo Empire conscripted more than fifty thousand soldiers. During a period when the Kingdom of Dahomey was invaded seven times, soldiers from Dahomey seized, in a single year, 1724, more than eight thousand captives. The Dutch, the Portuguese, and the English offset the cost of arms and men by buying and selling and exploiting the labor of—stealing the lives of—African men, women, and children. Most of the rest of the world paid for its sprawling, devastating wars by raising taxes.

Those taxes changed the course of history. The magnitude of the sacrifice that rulers demanded of ordinary people—the raiding of their scant savings; the lives, limbs, and livelihoods of sons, fathers, and husbands—gave the people a newly keen and anguished appreciation for the immense powers of those rulers, and for their ruthlessness, too. Increasingly, rulers convinced their people to consent to the terrible costs of yearslong, worldwide wars by promising them rights (sometimes even the right to elect their rulers) and agreeing to limits on their own powers. Constitutionalism didn't burst from the head of James Madison, like Athena from Zeus, simply on account of all the books he'd read. Sure, constitutionalism flew from the pages of those books, but it was also shot out of the barrel of a gun. This argument also explains the UK's lack of a written constitution. Long after it lost thirteen of its American colonies, in 1781, and long after it abolished slavery, in 1833, Britain continued to support its foreign wars and its formidable military by taxing its remaining colonies, and by recruiting soldiers from those colonies. Nineteenth-century Britons celebrated their unwritten constitution. "Our constitution is the air we breathe, the restless blood that circulates in our veins, the food that we eat, the soil that nourishes us," one British journalist gushed in 1832. "Constitutions are not made of paper, nor are they to be destroyed by paper." That was a luxury only the British Empire could enjoy.

THE PRECEPT THAT WARS make states make constitutions held elsewhere. Colley starts her account in 1755, during the very beginnings of a transcontinental conflict that would come to be called the Seven Years' War, when Pasquale Paoli, the thirty-year-old *capo generale politico e economico* of Corsica, wrote a ten-page *costituzione*. Leading a rebellion against the island's rule by the Republic of Genoa, Paoli proposed to erect a state. "The General Diet of the People of Corsica, legitimate masters of themselves," he wrote, "having reconquered its liberty," wished "to give a durable and permanent form to its government by transforming it into a constitution suited to assure the well-being of the nation." Though Corsica's constitution didn't last, it nevertheless quite explicitly bears out Colley's Rule. "Every Corsican must have some political rights," Paoli wrote, because "if the franchise of which he is so jealous is, in the end, but a laughable fiction, what interest would he take in defending the country?"

The Seven Years' War, a so-called umbrella war, putatively between Britain and France, stretched from Prussia to Florida, from New-foundland to India. It became entangled with a series of military cam-paigns waged by the Persian ruler Nadir Shah Afshar, and, after his death, by his generals, in Turkey, Afghanistan, Punjab, Kashmir, and Lahore, even as, in Asia, the Qianlong emperor, the fifth member of the Qing dynasty, sent a hundred and fifty thousand troops to crush the Dzungar-Mongolian Empire. Wars generate misery. "We drain ourselves of men and money," Voltaire wrote in 1751, "to destroy one another in the farther parts of Asia and America." And wars gener-ate all sorts of paperwork, not least maps, for making new territorial claims, and law books, for explaining the nature of rule over newly acquired territories. In the 1750s, the Qianlong emperor tasked more than a hundred scholars with preparing a compendium called *Compre-hensive Treatises of Our August Dynasty*, laying out how the Qing would rule over its new Dzungar dominion.

During the brutal world wars of the eighteenth century, millions of men carried millions of weapons, sailed hundreds of thousands of ships, and marched with thousands of armies. If most of those men demanded political rights, and political equality, in exchange for their sacrifices, they didn't always get them. Some constitutions written in the great age of constitution-writing were, like many constitutions written more recently, instruments of tyranny. But, when constitu-tions did grant rights, it was because people, in wartime, had their governments by the throat.

Constitutions and constitution-like compacts, Colley argues, are one kind of paperwork that wars generate. In 1765, ten years after Paoli drafted Corsica's *costituzione*, and at the close of the Seven Years' War, Catherine the Great, the empress of Russia, began drafting the Nakaz, or Grand Instruction. Having seized the throne in a coup d'état in 1762, and therefore insecure in her rule even as she worked to expand her realm through repeated military campaigns, she sought to provide a framework for government. She relied, in particular, on Montesquieu's 1748 *The Spirit of Laws*, which also greatly influenced James Madison. (Catherine called it "the prayerbook of all monarchs with any common sense.") Montesquieu had denounced the militarization of modern life, surveying kingdoms and empires from Spain and France to China, Japan, and India. "Each monarch keeps as many armies on foot as if his people were in danger of being exterminated," Montesquieu wrote. "The consequence of such a situation is a perpetual augmentation of taxes." He and his intellectual kin had a solution, which Colley describes as an irresistible lure to sovereigns: "that in an age of rampant, expensive and disruptive military violence on land and sea, innovatory and informed legislators might intervene so as to bind up society's wounds, re-establish order, remodel their respective states, *and in the process burnish their own reputations."*

That, as Colley makes clear, was Catherine's plan. Faced with unceasing challenges to her authority—as a foreigner who had seized the throne and as a woman—she nevertheless intended to pursue wide-scale warfare against the Ottoman Empire and its allies in an effort to extend Russia's borders. To that end, she insisted on her sovereignty while guaranteeing her subjects liberty and equality. "The equality of citizens consists in their being all subject to the same laws," she wrote in the Nakaz. She called taxes "the tribute which each citizen pays for the preservation of his own well-being."

Catherine arranged for a multiethnic legislative body, composed of 564 elected representatives, to meet in Moscow, in 1767, in order to consider the Nakaz. Women were able to vote for the representatives. Peasants were able to serve; serfs were not. Muslims were allotted fifty-four seats. Although its work consisted in the main of honoring rather than debating or ratifying the Nakaz, it was still an extraordinary gathering.

The Nakaz circulated well beyond Catherine's realm. By 1770, it had been translated into German, Latin, French, and English; editions in Greek, Italian, Latvian, Romanian, Swiss, and Dutch soon followed. The translator of the English edition called it a "constitution." Colley hints at its influence. In 1772, Gustaf III, the king of Sweden, and Catherine's cousin, had drawn up and printed a new constitution of "fixed and sacred fundamental law." If American scholars interested in the history of constitutionalism have taken very little notice of the Nakaz, it's not so much because the document failed to shore up Catherine's regime as because Americans are provincial—instead of looking to Moscow, all eyes turn, worshipfully, to Philadelphia—and because it was created by a woman.

WARS RAVAGED THE AMERICAS, ruining lives, razing settlements, and halting trade. In the Declaration of Independence, Thomas Jefferson blamed George III for having "plundered our seas, ravaged our coasts, burnt our towns, and destroyed the lives of our people." Independence movements in the Americas—beginning with the revolution in thirteen of Britain's North American colonies and that first written constitution, from New Hampshire in 1776, and continuing through Venezuela's first constitution, in 1811—involved rejecting rulers' demands for war-supporting taxes and erecting new governments with checks on those powers, with mixed success. Haiti's 1805 constitution, drafted for Jean-Jacques Dessalines, a former slave, declared the political equality of Africans and their descendants, who, according to the constitution's preamble, had been "so unjustly and for so long a time considered as outcast children."

The king of France convened the Estates General in 1789—nearly two centuries after it had last been called—for the purpose of levying new taxes, because all those wars had left France bankrupt. The constitution that the revolutionary National Assembly adopted two years later guaranteed, among other things, the equal assessment of all taxes upon all citizens, the right to vote for every man who paid a minimum sum of taxes, "public instruction for all citizens," and "liberty to every man to speak, write, print, and publish his opinions."

Placed in this global context, the constitution drafted in Philadelphia in 1787 looks both less and more original. Colley points out that nine of the first ten *Federalist Papers* concern the dangers of war and two more concern insurrection. Thirty of the fifty-five delegates had fought in the War of Independence. The Connecticut delegate Roger Sherman said that there were four reasons to adopt a new constitution: defense against foreign powers, defense against domestic insurrections, treaties with foreign nations, and the regulation of foreign commerce. One overlooked factor that distinguished the constitution debated in Philadelphia from the Nakaz, Colley suggests, is how quickly, easily, and successfully the American document was circulated. There were no newspapers in Russia, and no provincial presses. By contrast, anyone who wanted a copy of the U.S. Constitution could have one, within a matter of days after the convention had adjourned.

Wars make states make constitutions; states print constitutions; constitutions guarantee freedom of the press. In the nearly six hundred constitutions written between 1776 and about 1850, the right most frequently asserted—more often than freedom of religion, freedom of speech, or freedom of assembly—was freedom of the press. Colley argues, "Print was deemed indispensable if this new technology was to function effectively and do its work, both at home and abroad."

As more states adopted constitutions, the number of published constitutions and collections of constitutions grew. Edmund Burke wrote, in 1796, that a chief architect of the 1791 French constitution had "whole nests of pigeon-holes full of constitutions readymade, ticketed, sorted, and numbered; suited to every season and every fancy." A newspaper in Strasbourg even printed a template for anyone wishing to write a new constitution; all you had to do was fill in the blanks. Norway's 1814 constitution, hastily written in Oslo under threat of an invasion by Sweden, borrowed passages verbatim from the printed constitutions of the United States (1787), France (1791, 1793, and 1795), Poland (1791), Batavia (1798), Sweden (1809), and Spain (1812). The new constitution was then printed and made available in post offices, and, as Colley reports, the government encouraged people to paste copies on the walls of their houses. In the 1820s, keen to stir up interest in constitution-making in India, Ram Mohan Roy and James Silk Buckingham, editors of the *Calcutta Journal*, published translations of proposed constitutions for Peru, Mexico, and Gran Colombia—each of which allowed for equal citizenship of people of different races—while ignoring the U.S. Constitution and all the new constitutions being drafted by American states entering the Union. In the United States, in those years, Americans read the autobiography of William Grimes, a fugitive slave, who'd written, "If it were not for the stripes on my back which were made while I was a slave, I would in my will, leave my skin as a legacy to the government, desiring that it might be taken off and made into parchment and then bind the Constitution of glorious happy and free America."

CONSTITUTIONS GRANT RIGHTS; they can also take rights away. In 1794, Mary Wollstonecraft celebrated the promise of constitutionalism: "A constitution is a standard for the people to rally around. It is the pillar of a government, the bond of all social unity and order. The investigation of its principles make it a fountain of light; from which issue the rays of reason, that gradually bring forward the mental powers of the whole community." But constitutions, Colley says, have nearly always made things worse for women. Before constitutions were written, women had informal rights in all sorts of places; constitutions explicitly excluded them, not least because a constitution, in Colley's formulation, is a bargain struck between a state and its men, who made sacrifices to the state as taxpayers and soldiers, which were different from the sacrifices women made in wartime. Then, too, all that constitutional printing and copycatting spread Western notions of women's very limited sphere around the world. In 1846, a third of the members of Hawaii's House of Nobles were female chiefs; Hawaii's 1850 constitution restricted suffrage to men. Before the Meiji constitution of 1889—the first constitution implemented in East Asia, greatly influenced by Germany's 1871 constitution—prohibited Japanese women from voting, they had, to some degree, participated in politics. As Colley points out, "Once written into law and put into print, female disadvantages became harder to change."

The U.S. Constitution denied political rights to indigenous and enslaved people. And state constitutions adopted in the nineteenth century declared sovereignty over native lands and barred women, Black people, and Chinese immigrants from voting, making it all but impossible for any of these people to use the usual mechanisms of electoral politics to change their status. Colley says that these constitutions inspired constitutions in places like Australia and New Zealand, where invaders had seized the lands of peoples like the Maori. In 1849, California adopted a constitution that guaranteed the right to vote to "every white male citizen" and asserted sovereignty over boundaries that extended to include "all the islands, harbors, and bays, along adjacent to the Pacific Coast." The following year, a Scottish settler in Sydney said, "Look for example at what has recently been going on in California," and declared that the people there had "framed a constitution for themselves, that might serve as a model for any nation upon the face of the earth."

Yet this cut the other way as well. California's 1849 constitution, which prohibited slavery, participated in a global movement to end human bondage which also included the constitutions, in the 1840s and 1850s, of Tunisia, Ecuador, Argentina, Peru, Venezuela, and Hawaii. Sometimes indigenous leaders—especially monarchs, like Chief Pomare of Tahiti and Hawaii's King Kamehameha II—could stave off colonization by adopting constitutions. And constitutions could challenge white supremacy. At Liberia's constitutional convention in 1847, one delegate declared, "The people of Liberia do not require the assistance of 'white people' to enable them to make a Constitution for the government of themselves." Wars make states make constitutions: the rule applies equally to the American Civil War. With the Fourteenth and Fifteenth Amendments, Americans rewrote their constitution, adopting revisions to the Constitution that altered its fundamental principles.

The Meiji constitution of 1889 brought constitution-writing to Asia, which was followed by an acceleration of constitution-writing throughout Latin America. In 1906, China began to study constitutions of the West and of Japan in preparation for writing its own. Constitution-making took a turn after the Great War, which claimed some forty million lives. That was a turn to the arrangement not only of government but of society. Postwar constitutions, many of which didn't last long, have some features in common: an absence of any reference to God; a concern with the social, especially in socialist constitutions. Their authors often consulted collections, like "Select Constitutions of the World," published by the Irish Free State (alongside its own new constitution) in 1922. After the Second World War, newly independent nations in Asia and Africa, and civil wars all over the world, added to the growing heap of often short-lived constitutions. Many constitutions promise much and deliver little. Colley asks, "Why, in the light of the limited longevity of so many constitutions over the centuries, and the limited effectiveness in many cases of these texts as guarantors of responsible rule and durable rights, have multiple societies and peoples kept on investing time, imagination, thought and hope so insistently in this kind of paper and parchment political and legal device?" Because, she argues, "in a deeply uncertain, shifting, unequal and violent world," imperfect constitutions "may be the best that we can hope for."

Or maybe we can hope for more. "No part of a constitution is more important than the procedures we use to change it," Richard Albert writes in *Constitutional Amendments: Making, Breaking, and Changing Constitutions*. Writing a constitution is its own kind of expression. So is amending a constitution, a form of constitutional writing (and printing) that Colley does not consider, even though ninety-six out of every hundred of the world's codified constitutions contain an amendment provision. Constitutions set the rules; amendment provisions set the rules for changing the rules.

The U.S. was the first nation whose constitution provided for its own revision. Article V, the amendment clause, reads, "The Congress, whenever two thirds of both houses shall deem it necessary, shall propose amendments to this Constitution, or, on the application of the legislatures of two thirds of the several states, shall call a convention for proposing amendments, which, in either case, shall be valid to all intents and purposes, as part of this Constitution, when ratified by the legislatures of three fourths of the several states, or by conventions in three fourths thereof, as the one or the other mode of ratification may be proposed by the Congress." Without Article V, the Constitution would very likely have failed ratification. Everyone knew that the Constitution was imperfect; Article V left ajar a constitutional door for making it, and the Union, "more perfect." Federalists cited the amendment provision when arguing for ratification. As James Wilson, a delegate from Pennsylvania, contended, the fact that the people "may change their constitution and government whenever they please, is not a principle of discord, rancor, or war: it is a principle of melioration, contentment, and peace." Without an amendment provision, the only way to change the rules is to overthrow the government, by way of insurrection.

The problem, in the United States, is that it is extremely difficult to amend the Constitution. It's often thought to be structurally impossible these days, but much scholarship suggests that it is, instead, merely *culturally* impossible, because of the very reflexes of veneration of the

Constitution that inspired Linda Colley to undertake the project that became "The Gun, the Ship, and the Pen." The system of government put in place by the Constitution is broken in all sorts of ways, subject to forms of corruption, political decay, and antidemocracy measures that include gerrymandering, the filibuster, campaign spending, and the cap on the size of the House of Representatives. The law professor Sanford Levinson has written, "To the extent that we continue thoughtlessly to venerate, and therefore not subject to truly critical examination, our Constitution, we are in the position of the battered wife who continues to profess the 'essential goodness' of her abusive husband." Or, as Burke noted, "A state without the means of some changes is without the means of its conservation."

The U.S. Constitution has been rewritten three times: in 1791, with the ratification of the Bill of Rights, the first ten amendments; after the Civil War, with the ratification of the Reconstruction Amendments; and during the Progressive Era, with the ratification of the Sixteenth, Seventeenth, Eighteenth, and Nineteenth Amendments. It is time for another reinvention.

Other countries regularly amend their constitutions. Americans don't venerate all constitutions; in fact, they're quite keen to amend state constitutions. Albert reports, "Historically, American state constitutions have been amended over 7,500 times, amounting on average to 150 amendments per state. This paints an unmistakable contrast with the U.S. Constitution, whose average annual amendment rate is an exceedingly low 0.07, while the average across all American state constitutions is 0.35, higher than the average of 0.21 for national constitutions around the world."

Rather than being amended, the Constitution has been betrayed, circumvented, violated, and abandoned, by force of practice. Can a U.S. president compel a foreign leader to interfere in an American election? Apparently. Can a U.S. president refuse to accept the results of a free and fair election and incite a mob to attack Congress in order to prevent the certification of the vote? Apparently. The U.S. Constitution, no less than the UK's unwritten constitution, is more than the sum of its words; it's the accretion of practices and precedents.

Kurt Gödel might have been happy to hear that. Gödel's loophole really isn't anything like Fermat's last theorem, because constitutional scholars are pretty sure of what Gödel had in mind. It's a constitutional version of the idea that, if a genie wafts out of an oil lamp and offers you three wishes, you should begin by wishing for more wishes. In what amounts to a genuine oversight, Article V, the amendment provision, does not prohibit amending Article V. It's very hard to ratify a constitutional amendment, but if a president could amass enough power and accrue enough blindly loyal followers he could get an amendment ratified that revised the mechanism of amendment itself. If a revised Article V made it possible for a president to amend the Constitution by fiat (for example, "The president, whenever he shall deem it necessary, shall make amendments to this Constitution, which shall be valid to all intents and purposes, as part of this Constitution"), he could turn a democracy into a dictatorship without ever having done anything unconstitutional. What Gödel did not realize is that it's actually a lot easier than that.

—2021

BENCHED

ORIGINALLY, THE SUPREME COURT OF THE UNITED States met in a drafty room on the second floor of an old stone building called the Merchants' Exchange, at the corner of Broad and Water Streets, in New York. The ground floor, an arcade, was a stock exchange. Lectures and concerts were held upstairs. For meeting, there weren't many places to choose from. Much of the city had burned to the ground during the Revolutionary War; nevertheless, New York became the nation's capital in 1785. After George Washington was inaugurated in 1789, he appointed six Supreme Court justices—the Constitution doesn't say how many there ought to be—but on February 1, 1790, the first day the Court was called to session, upstairs in the Exchange, only three justices showed up and so, lacking a quorum, court was adjourned.

Months later, when the nation's capital moved to Philadelphia, the Supreme Court met in city hall, where it shared quarters with the mayor's court. Not long after, the chief justice, John Jay, wrote to the president to let him know that he was going to skip the next session because his wife was having a baby ("I cannot prevail on myself to be then at a Distance from her," Jay wrote to Washington), and because there wasn't much on the docket, anyway.

In 2012, the Supreme Court—now housed in a building so ostentatious that Justice Louis Brandeis, who, before he was appointed to the bench, in 1916, was known as "the people's attorney," refused to move into his office—debated whether the Affordable Care Act violates the Constitution, especially with regard to the word "commerce." Arguments were heard in March. The Court's decision would be final. It was expected by the end of the month.

UNDER THE CONSTITUTION, the power of the Supreme Court is quite limited. The executive branch holds the sword, Alexander

Hamilton wrote in Federalist No. 78, and the legislative branch the purse. "The judiciary, on the contrary, has no influence over either the sword or the purse; no direction either of the strength or of the wealth of the society; and can take no active resolution whatever." All judges can do is judge. "The judiciary is beyond comparison the weakest of the three departments of powers," Hamilton concluded, citing, in a footnote, Montesquieu: "Of the three powers above mentioned, the judiciary is next to nothing."

The Supreme Court used to be not only an appellate court but also a trial court. People also thought it was a good idea for the justices to ride circuit, so that they'd know the citizenry better. That meant more time away from their families, and, besides, getting around the country was a slog. Justice James Iredell, who said he felt like a "traveling postboy," nearly broke his leg when his horse bolted. Usually, he had to stay at inns, where you shared rooms with strangers. The justices hated riding circuit and, in 1792, petitioned the president to relieve them of the duty, writing, "We cannot reconcile ourselves to the idea of existing in exile from our families." Washington, who was childless, was unmoved.

In 1795, when John Jay resigned from the office of chief justice to become governor of New York, Washington asked Alexander Hamilton to take his place; Hamilton said no. So did Patrick Henry. Anyone who wanted the job had to be a little nutty. The Senate rejected Washington's next nominee for Jay's replacement, the South Carolinian John Rutledge, whereupon Rutledge tried to drown himself near Charleston, crying out to his rescuers that he had been a judge for a long time and "knew of no Law that forbid a man to take away his own Life."

In 1800, the capital moved to Washington, DC, and the following year John Adams nominated his secretary of state, the arch-Federalist Virginian John Marshall, to the office of chief justice. Adams lived in the White House. Congress met at the Capitol. Marshall took his oath of office in a "meanly furnished, very inconvenient" room in the Capitol Building, where the justices, who did not have clerks, had no room to put on their robes (this they did in the courtroom, in front of gawking spectators), or to deliberate (this they did in the hall, as quietly as they could). Cleverly, Marshall made sure that all the justices rented rooms at the same boardinghouse, so that they could at least have someplace to talk together, unobserved.

Marshall was gangly and quirky and such an avid listener that Daniel Webster once said that, on the bench, he took in counsel's argument the way "a baby takes in its mother's milk." He became chief justice just months before Thomas Jefferson became president. Marshall was Jefferson's cousin and also his fiercest political rival, if you don't count Adams. Nearly the last thing Adams did before leaving office was to persuade the lame-duck Federalist Congress to pass the 1801 Judiciary Act, reducing the number of Supreme Court justices to five—which would have prevented Jefferson from naming a justice to the bench until two justices left. The newly elected Republican Congress turned right around and repealed that act and suspended the Supreme Court for more than a year.

In February 1803, when the Marshall Court finally met, it did something really interesting. In *Marbury v. Madison*, a suit against Jefferson's secretary of state, James Madison, Marshall granted to the Supreme Court a power it had not been explicitly granted in the Constitution: the right to decide whether laws passed by Congress are constitutional. This was such an astonishing thing to do that the Court didn't declare another federal law unconstitutional for fifty-four years.

THE SUPREME COURT'S DECISION about the constitutionality of the Affordable Care Act turned on Article I, Section 8, of the Constitution, the commerce clause: "Congress shall have power . . . to regulate Commerce with foreign Nations, and among the several States, and with the Indian Tribes." In *Gibbons v. Ogden*, Marshall interpreted this clause broadly: "Commerce, undoubtedly, is traffic, but it is something more: it is intercourse." ("Intercourse" encompassed all manner of dealings and exchanges: trade, conversation, letter writing, and even—if plainly outside the scope of Marshall's meaning—sex.) Not much came of this until the Gilded Age, when the commerce clause was invoked to justify trust-busting legislation, which was generally upheld. Then, during the New Deal, the "power to regulate commerce," along with the definition of "commerce" itself, became the chief means by which Congress passed legislation protecting people against an unbridled market; the Court complied only after a protracted battle. In 1964, the commerce clause formed part of the basis for the Civil Rights Act, and the Court upheld the argument that the clause grants Congress the power to prohibit racial discrimination in hotels and restaurants.

In 1995, in *United States v. Lopez*, the Court limited that power for the first time since the battle over the New Deal, when Chief Justice William Rehnquist, writing for the majority, overturned a federal law prohibiting the carrying of guns in a school zone: the argument was that gun ownership is not commerce, because it "is in no sense an economic activity." (In a concurring opinion, Justice Clarence Thomas cited Samuel Johnson's *Dictionary of the English Language*.) Five years later, in *United States v. Morrison*, Rehnquist, again writing for the majority, declared parts of the federal Violence Against Women Act unconstitutional, arguing, again, that no economic activity was involved.

However the Court rules on health care, the commerce clause appears unlikely, in the long run, to be able to bear the burdens that have been placed upon it. So long as conservatives hold sway on the Court, the definition of "commerce" will get narrower and narrower, despite the fact that this will require, and already has required, overturning decades of precedent. Unfortunately, Article I, Section 8, may turn out to have been a poor perch on which to build a nest for rights.

There is more at stake, too. This Court has not been hesitant about exercising judicial review. In Marshall's thirty-five years as chief justice, the Court struck down only one act of Congress. In the first seven years of John G. Roberts Jr.'s chief justiceship, the Court struck down a sizable number of federal laws, including one reforming the funding of political campaigns. It also happens to be the most conservative court in modern times. According to a rating system used by political scientists, decisions issued by the Warren Court were conservative 34 percent of the time; the Burger and the Rehnquist Courts issued conservative decisions 55 percent of the time. Between 2005 and 2012, the rulings of the Roberts Court were conservative about 60 percent of the time.

What people think about judicial review usually depends on what they think about the composition of the Court. When the Court is liberal, liberals think judicial review is good, and conservatives think it's bad. This is also true the other way around. Between 1962 and 1969, the Warren Court struck down seventeen acts of Congress. ("With five votes, you can do anything around here," Justice William Brennan said at the time.) Liberals didn't mind; the Warren Court advanced civil rights. Conservatives argued that the behavior of the Warren Court was unconstitutional, and, helped along by that argument, gained control of the Republican Party and, eventually, the Supreme Court, only to engage in what looks like the very same behavior. Except that it isn't quite the same, not least because a conservative court exercising judicial review in the name of originalism suggests, at best, a rather uneven application of the principle.

The commerce clause has one history, judicial review another. They do, however, crisscross. Historically, the struggle over judicial review has been part of a larger struggle over judicial independence: the freedom of the judiciary from the other branches of government, from political influence, and, especially, from moneyed interests, which is why the Court's role in deciding whether Congress has the power to regulate the economy is so woefully vexed.

EARLY AMERICAN COLONISTS INHERITED from England a tradition in which the courts, like the legislature, were extensions of the crown. In most colonies, as the Harvard Law professor Jed Shugerman points out in *The People's Courts: Pursuing Judicial Independence in America*, judges and legislators were the same people and, in many, the legislature served as the court of last resort. (A nomenclatural vestige of this arrangement remains in Massachusetts, where the state legislature is still called the General Court.)

In 1733, William Cosby, the royally appointed governor of New York, sued his predecessor, and the case was heard by the colony's supreme court, headed by Lewis Morris, who ruled against Cosby, whereupon the governor removed Morris from the bench and appointed James DeLancey. When essays critical of the governor appeared in a city newspaper, Cosby arranged to have the newspaper's printer, John Peter Zenger, tried for sedition. At the trial, Zenger's attorneys objected to the justices' authority, arguing that justice cannot be served by "the mere will of a governor." Then DeLancey simply ordered Zenger's attorneys disbarred.

Already in England, a defiant Parliament had been challenging the royal prerogative, demanding that judicial appointments be made not "at the king's pleasure" but "during good behavior" (effectively, for life). Yet reform was slow to reach the colonies, and a corrupt judiciary was one of the abuses that led to the Revolution. In 1768, Benjamin Franklin listed it in an essay called "Causes of American Discontents," and, in the Declaration of Independence, Jefferson included on his list of grievances the king's having "made Judges dependent on his Will alone."

The principle of judicial independence is related to another principle that emerged during these decades, much influenced by Montesquieu's *Spirit of Laws*: the separation of powers. "The judicial power ought to be distinct from both the legislative and executive, and independent," Adams argued in 1776, "so that it may be a check upon both." There is, nevertheless, a tension between judicial independence and the separation of powers. Appointing judges to serve for life would seem to establish judicial independence, but what power then checks the judiciary? One idea was to have the judges elected by the people; the people then check the judiciary.

At the Constitutional Convention, no one argued that the Supreme Court justices ought to be popularly elected, not because the delegates were unconcerned about judicial independence but because there wasn't a great deal of support for the popular election of anyone, including the president (hence the Electoral College). The delegates quickly decided that the president should appoint justices, and the Senate confirm them, and that these justices ought to hold their appointments "during good behavior."

Amid the debate over ratification, this proved controversial. In a 1788 essay called "The Supreme Court: They Will Mould the Government into Almost Any Shape They Please," one Anti-Federalist pointed out that the power granted to the Court was "unprecedented in any free country," because its justices are, finally, answerable to no one: "No errors they may commit can be corrected by any power above them, if any such power there be, nor can they be removed from office for making ever so many erroneous adjudications." This is among the reasons that Hamilton found it expedient, in Federalist No. 78, to emphasize the weakness of the judicial branch.

Jefferson, after his battle with Marshall, came to believe that "in a government founded on the public will, this principle operates . . . against that will." In much that same spirit, a great many states began instituting judicial elections, in place of judicial appointment. You might think that elected judges would be less independent, more subject to political forces, than appointed ones. But timeless political truths are seldom true and rarely timeless. During the decades that reformers were lobbying for judicial elections, the secret ballot was thought to be more subject to political corruption than voting openly. Similarly, the popular vote was considered markedly less partisan than the spoils system: the lesser, by far, of two evils.

Nor was the nature of the Supreme Court set in stone. In the nineteenth century, the Court was, if not as weak as Hamilton suggested, nowhere near as powerful as it later became. In 1810, the Court moved into a different room in the Capitol, where a figure of Justice, decorating the chamber, had no blindfold but, as the joke went, the room was too dark for her to see anything anyway. It was also dank. "The deaths of some of our most talented jurists have been attributed to the location of this Courtroom," one architect remarked. It was in that dimly lit room, in 1857, that the Supreme Court overturned a federal law for the first time since *Marbury v. Madison*. In *Dred Scott v. Sandford*, Chief Justice Roger B. Taney, writing for the majority, voided the Missouri Compromise by arguing that Congress could not prohibit slavery in the territories.

In 1860, the Court moved once more, into the Old Senate Chamber. When Abraham Lincoln was inaugurated, on the East Portico of the Capitol, Taney administered the oath, and Lincoln, in his address, confronted the crisis of constitutional authority. "I do not forget the position, assumed by some, that constitutional questions are to be decided by the Supreme Court," he said, but "if the policy of the government, upon vital questions affecting the whole people, is to be irrevocably fixed by the decisions of Supreme Court, the instant they are made . . . the people will have ceased to be their own rulers, having to that extent, practically resigned their government into the hands of that eminent tribunal." Five weeks later, shots were fired at Fort Sumter.

In the decades following the Civil War, an increasingly activist

Court took up not only matters relating to Reconstruction, and especially to the Fourteenth Amendment, but also questions involving the regulation of business, not least because the Court ruled that corporations could file suits, as if they were people. And then, beginning in the 1890s, the Supreme Court struck down an entire docket of Progressive legislation, including child labor laws, unionization laws, minimum wage laws, and the progressive income tax. In *Lochner v. New York* (1905), in a 5–4 decision, the Court voided a state law establishing that bakers could work no longer than ten hours a day, six days a week, on the ground that the law violated a "liberty of contract," protected under the Fourteenth Amendment. In a dissenting opinion, Justice Oliver Wendell Holmes accused the Court of wildly overreaching its authority. "A Constitution is not intended to embody a particular economic theory," he wrote.

For a long time, legal scholars agreed with Holmes. But in *Rehabilitating Lochner: Defending Individual Rights Against Progressive Reform*, David E. Bernstein, a law professor at George Mason University, takes issue with the logic by which *Lochner* has become "likely the most disreputable case in modern constitutional discourse." Bernstein's measured plea that *Lochner* be treated "like a normal, albeit controversial, case" is perfectly sensible; less persuasive is his argument that, by favoring individual rights over government regulation, *Lochner*-era rulings protected the interest of minorities.

Lochner led to an uproar. In 1906, Roscoe Pound, the eminent legal scholar and later dean of Harvard Law School, delivered an address before the American Bar Association called "The Causes of Popular Dissatisfaction with the Administration of Justice," in which he echoed Holmes's dissent in *Lochner*. "Putting courts into politics, and compelling judges to become politicians, in many jurisdictions has almost destroyed the traditional respect for the Bench," he warned. Bernstein waves this aside, arguing that Pound didn't wholly comprehend the facts of the case, and insists that any discontent with the Court's ruling in *Lochner* abated almost immediately. It remains, however, that *Lochner*, together with a host of other federal and state court rulings, contributed to a surge of popular interest in judicial independence, including calls for "judicial removal": the firing of judges by a simple majority of the legislature. In 1911, Arizona, preparing to enter the

Union, had a proposed constitution that included judicial recall, the removal of judges by popular vote, which was also a platform of Theodore Roosevelt's Bull Moose campaign. The U.S. Congress approved the state's constitution, but when it went to the White House William Howard Taft vetoed it. He objected to recall. Before he became president, Taft was a judge. He wanted not less judicial power but more. The next year, Taft began lobbying Congress for funds to erect for the Supreme Court a building of its own.

On October 13, 1932, Herbert Hoover laid the cornerstone, at a construction site across from the Capitol. The plan was to build the greatest marble building in the world; marble had been shipped from Spain, Italy, and Africa. At the ceremony, after Hoover emptied his trowel, Chief Justice Charles Evans Hughes delivered remarks recalling the Court's long years of wandering. "The court began its work as a homeless department of the government," Hughes said, but "this monument bespeaks the common cause, the unifying principle of our nation."

In 1906, Hughes had run for governor of New York against William Randolph Hearst; as against Hearst's five hundred thousand dollars, Hughes spent six hundred and nineteen dollars. Miraculously, he won. Once in office, he pushed through the state legislature a campaign spending limit. In 1910, Taft appointed Hughes to the Supreme Court, where, as a champion of civil liberties, he often joined with Holmes in dissent. Hughes resigned from the bench in 1916 to run for president; he lost, narrowly, to Woodrow Wilson. After serving as secretary of state under Warren G. Harding and Calvin Coolidge, he was appointed chief justice in 1930.

Three weeks after Hoover laid the cornerstone for the new Supreme Court Building, FDR was elected president, defeating the incumbent by a record-breaking electoral vote: 472–59. As the New York Law School professor James F. Simon chronicles in *FDR and Chief Justice Hughes: The President, the Supreme Court, and the Epic Battle Over the New Deal*, the president-elect immediately began lining up his legislative agenda. He met with Holmes, who told him, "You are in a war, Mr. President, and in a war there is only one rule, 'Form your battalion and fight!'"

By June of 1933, less than a hundred days after his inauguration,

FDR had proposed fifteen legislative elements of his New Deal, all having to do with the federal government's role in the regulation of the economy—and, therefore, with the commerce clause—and each had been made law. Now the New Deal had to pass muster in Hughes's court, where four conservative justices, known as the Four Horsemen, consistently voted in favor of a Lochnerian liberty of contract, while the three liberals—Louis Brandeis, Benjamin Cardozo, and Harlan Fiske Stone—generally supported government regulation. That left Hughes and Owen Roberts. In early rulings, Hughes and Roberts joined the liberals, and the Court, voting 5–4, let New Deal legislation stand. "While an emergency does not create power," Hughes said, "an emergency may furnish the occasion for the exercise of the power."

In the January 1935, session, the Court heard arguments in another challenge. FDR, expecting an adverse decision, prepared a speech in which he quoted Lincoln's remarks about *Dred Scott*, adding, "To stand idly by and to permit the decision of the Supreme Court to be carried through to its logical, inescapable conclusion" would "imperil the economic and political security of this nation." The speech was never given. In another 5–4 decision, Hughes upheld FDR's agenda, leading one of the horsemen to burst out, "The Constitution is gone!"—a comment so unseemly that it was stricken from the record.

On May 27, 1935—afterward known as Black Monday—the Supreme Court met, for very nearly the last time, in the Old Senate Chamber. In three unanimous decisions, the Court devastated the New Deal. Most critically, it found that the National Recovery Administration, which Roosevelt had called the "most important and far-reaching legislation in the history of the American Congress," was unconstitutional, because Congress had exceeded the powers granted to it under the commerce clause. Four days later, the president held a press conference in the Oval Office. He compared the gravity of the decision to *Dred Scott*. Then he raged, "We have been relegated to the horse-and-buggy definition of interstate commerce." But in the horse-and-buggy days, the Court didn't have half as much power as it had in 1935.

THE SUPREME COURT'S NEW BUILDING opened six months later, on October 7, 1935. A pair of reporters described the place as "a classical icebox decorated for some surreal reason by an insane upholsterer." Nine justices took their seats in the same raggedy assortment of chairs they had used in the Senate Chamber. Asked whether he wanted a new chair, Justice Cardozo had refused. "No," he replied slowly, "if Justice Holmes sat in this chair for twenty years, I can sit in it for a while."

And then the Hughes Court went on a spree. In eighteen months, it struck down more than a dozen laws. Congress kept passing them; the Court kept striking them down, generally 5–4. At one point, FDR's solicitor general fainted, right there in the courtroom.

The president began entertaining proposals about fighting back. One senator had an idea. "It takes twelve men to find a man guilty of murder," he said. "I don't see why it should not take a unanimous court to find a law unconstitutional." That might have required a constitutional amendment, a process that is notoriously corruptible. "Give me ten million dollars," Roosevelt said, "and I can prevent any amendment to the Constitution from being ratified by the necessary number of states."

Meanwhile, the president was running for reelection. A week before Election Day, an attack on the Hughes Court, titled *The Nine Old Men*, began appearing in the nation's newspapers and in bookstores. FDR defeated the Republican, Alf Landon, yet again breaking a record in the Electoral College: 523–8. In February 1937, Roosevelt floated his plan: claiming that the justices were doddering, and unable to keep up with the business at hand, he would name an additional justice for every sitting justice over the age of seventy. There were six of them, including the chief justice, who was seventy-four.

The president's approval rating fell. In a radio address on March 9, 1937, he argued that the time had come "to save the Constitution from the Court, and the Court from itself." Then Hughes all but put the matter to rest. "The Supreme Court is fully abreast of its work," he reported on March 22, in a persuasive letter to the Senate Judiciary Committee. If efficiency were actually a concern, he argued, there was a great deal of evidence to suggest that more justices would only slow things down.

What happened next is clear: starting with *West Coast Hotel Co. v. Parrish*, a ruling issued on March 29, 1937, in a 5–4 opinion written by Hughes, that sustained a minimum wage requirement, the Supreme Court began upholding the New Deal. Owen Roberts had switched sides, a move so sudden, and so crucial to the preservation of the Court, that it has been called "the switch in time that saved nine." Why this happened is not quite as clear. It looked purely political. "Even a blind man ought to see that the Court is in politics," Felix Frankfurter wrote to Roosevelt. "It is a deep object lesson—a lurid demonstration—of the relation of men to the 'meaning' of the Constitution." It wasn't as lurid as all that; it had at least something to do with the law.

On May 18, 1937, the Senate Judiciary Committee voted against the president's proposal. The court-packing plan was dead. Six days later, the Supreme Court upheld the old-age insurance provisions of the Social Security Act. The president, and his deal, had won.

ON EITHER SIDE OF THE SUPREME COURT STEPS, on top of fifty-ton marble blocks, sit two sculpted figures: *Contemplation of Justice*, on the left, and *Authority of Law*, on the right. In the pediment above the portico, Liberty gazes into the future; Charles Evans Hughes crouches by her side. Inside, a bronze statue of John Marshall stands in the Lower Great Hall. Above him, etched into marble, are his remarks from *Marbury v. Madison*: "It is emphatically the province and duty of the judicial department to say what the law is."

Within the walls of that building, Dred Scott is nowhere to be found, and Lochner stalks the halls like a ghost. Portraits of the first chief justices, starting with John Jay, hang in the East Conference Room, and of the later justices, in the West. A portrait of Earl Warren was installed after his death, in 1974. Beginning with the Court's ruling in *Brown v. Board of Education*, in 1954, Warren presided over the most activist liberal court in American history. "I would like this court to be remembered as the people's court," Warren said when he retired, in 1969. He was pointing to the difference between conservative judicial activism and liberal judicial activism: one protects the interests of the powerful and the other those of the powerless.

The Supreme Court has been deliberating in a temple of marble for three-quarters of a century. In March of 2012, it heard oral arguments about the Affordable Care Act. No one rode there in a horse and buggy. There was talk, from the bench, of heart transplants, and of a great many other matters unthinkable in 1789. Arguments lasted for three days. On the second day, the solicitor general insisted that the purchase of health insurance is an economic activity. Much discussion followed about whether choosing not to buy health insurance is an economic activity, too, and one that Congress has the power to regulate. If you could require people to buy health insurance, Justice Antonin Scalia wanted to know, could you require them to buy broccoli? "No, that's quite different," the solicitor general answered. "The food market, while it shares that trait that everybody's in it, it is not a market in which your participation is often unpredictable and often involuntary." This did not appear to satisfy.

The ruling that the Supreme Court eventually handed down—upholding the constitutionality of the Affordable Care Act, but barely—left unanswered questions about the relationship between the judicial and the legislative branches of government, and also between the past and the present. The separation of law from politics for which the Revolution was fought has proved elusive. That's not surprising—no such separation being wholly possible—but some years have been better than others. One of the worst was 2000, when the Court determined the outcome of a disputed presidential election. The real loser in that election, Justice John Paul Stevens said in his dissent in *Bush v. Gore*, "is the Nation's confidence in the judge as an impartial guardian of the rule of law."

For centuries, the American struggle for a more independent judiciary has been more steadfast than successful. Currently, nearly 90 percent of state judges run for office. "Spending on judicial campaigns has doubled in the past decade, exceeding $200 million," Shugerman reports. In 2009, after three Iowa supreme court judges overturned a defense-of-marriage act, the American Family Association, the National Organization for Marriage, and the Campaign for Working Families together spent more than eight hundred thousand dollars to campaign against their reelection; all three judges lost. "I never felt so much like a hooker down by the bus station," one Ohio supreme court justice told the *Times* in 2006, "as I did in a judicial race."

Federally, few rulings have wreaked such havoc on the political process as the 2010 case *Citizens United v. Federal Election Commis-*

sion, whereby the Roberts Court struck down much of the McCain-Feingold Act, which placed restrictions on corporate and union funding of political campaigns. Stevens, in his dissent, warned that "a democracy cannot function effectively when its constituent members believe laws are being bought and sold."

That, in the end, is the traffic to worry about. If not only legislators but judges serve at the pleasure of lobbyists, the people will have ceased to be their own rulers. Law will be commerce. And money will be king.

—2012

THE DARK AGES

O N NOVEMBER 13, 2001, GEORGE W. BUSH, ACTING as president and commander in chief, signed a military order concerning the "Detention, Treatment, and Trial of Certain Non-Citizens in the War Against Terrorism." Under its provisions, suspected terrorists who are not citizens of the United States were to be "detained at an appropriate location designated by the Secretary of Defense." If brought to trial, they were to be tried and sentenced by a military commission. No member of the commission need be a lawyer. The ordinary rules of military law would not apply. Nor would the laws of war. Nor, in any conventional sense, would the laws of the United States. In the language of the order, "It is not practicable to apply in military commissions under this order the principles of law and the rules of evidence generally recognized in the trial of criminal cases in the United States district courts."

"You've got to be kidding me," Attorney General John Ashcroft reportedly said when he read an early draft, in which members of the commissions, as well as attorneys for both the prosecution and the defense, were to be selected by the secretary of defense. As Jess Bravin, the *Wall Street Journal*'s Supreme Court correspondent, reports in *The Terror Courts: Rough Justice at Guantanamo Bay*, Ashcroft expected the prosecution of people involved in 9/11 to be handled criminally, by his department, as had been done, successfully, with earlier terrorism cases. Other senior advisers had not been consulted. Condoleezza Rice and Colin Powell learned that Bush had signed the order only when they saw the news reported on television. In the final draft, the Department of Justice was left out altogether. Suspected terrorists could be imprisoned without charge, denied knowledge of the evidence against them, and, if tried, sentenced by courts following no previously established rules.

"Now, some people say, 'Well, gee, that's a dramatic departure from traditional jurisprudence in the United States,'" Vice President Dick Cheney said the next day, "but there's precedent for it." Furthermore, "We think it guarantees that we'll have the kind of treatment of these individuals that we believe they deserve."

This all happened not very long ago, but it can seem like something from another age. Beginning in the fall of 2001, hundreds of men were taken into custody and interrogated, all around the world, but especially in Afghanistan, where the U.S. military dropped flyers offering, in exchange for information about men with ties to Al Qaeda and the Taliban, bounties of millions of dollars. "This is enough money to take care of your family, your village, your tribe for the rest of your life," one flyer read. Detainees later said that they were sold for between five thousand and twenty-five thousand dollars. (The average annual income in Afghanistan at the time was less than three hundred dollars.) The flyers fell, Defense Secretary Donald Rumsfeld said, "like snow-flakes in December in Chicago."

Lakhdar Boumediene was arrested in Sarajevo. Boumediene, a thirty-five-year-old native Algerian, had once worked at an orphan-age in Pakistan run by an organization whose leader had ties to at least one member of Al Qaeda. In 2001, Boumediene was living in Bosnia with his wife and two young daughters, and working as a director of humanitarian aid for the Red Crescent, a Red Cross affiliate. He was charged with plotting to bomb the U.S. and British Embassies. A Bos-nian court, finding no evidence of this, dropped all charges and released him. Boumediene was then taken into American custody. Meanwhile, the Bush administration prepared a document defining the procedures by which the military commissions would operate. In lieu of rights, the term of art was "Procedures accorded to the Accused."

There remained the question of where to imprison the men. Send-ing them to Leavenworth and reopening Alcatraz were both con-sidered but were rejected, because holding suspected terrorists on American soil might allow them to appeal to American courts and U.S. law. Diego Garcia, an island in the Indian Ocean, was considered, too, but it is a British territory, and therefore subject to British law. As Jonathan M. Hansen explains in *Guantánamo: An American History*, the U.S. naval base, which occupies forty-five square miles on the south-eastern end of Cuba, is an imperial leftover, a Cold War discard, a remnant. As a matter of sovereignty, it isn't part of Cuba, and it isn't part of the United States. It's one of the known world's last no-man's-lands, an island out of time, a place without a state. Haitian refugees held there in the 1990s, pleading that their forced repatriation would be unlawful, brought their case to the Supreme Court, which ruled, 8–1, that, absent congressional action, people held at Guantánamo had no recourse to U.S. refugee laws. The case influenced John Yoo, the Bush administration lawyer whose interpretation of American and international law lay behind the administration's counterterrorism policy. Guantánamo, one administration official said, was the "legal equivalent of outer space."

The selection of Guantánamo as the place to imprison men captured in the "global war on terror" was announced on December 27, 2001. The administration's attention then shifted from the prisoners' detention to their treatment. On January 9, 2002, Yoo and a colleague submitted to the general counsel of the Department of Defense one of the first of what came to be called the "torture memos." In the January 9 memo, Yoo concluded that international treaties, such as the Geneva conventions, "do not apply to the Taliban militia," because, although Afghanistan had been a party to the Geneva conventions since 1956, it was a "failed state"; moreover, international treaties "do not protect members of the al Qaeda organization, which as a non–State actor cannot be a party to the international agreements governing war."

Two days later, the first twenty prisoners, shackled, hooded, and blindfolded, arrived at Guantánamo. Their names were not released. They were confined in Camp X-Ray, which you could see right through: its eight-by-eight-foot, concrete-floored cages were made of chain-link fence, and the floodlights were never turned off. More camps were soon built to house more prisoners, eventually 779, from 48 countries. They weren't called criminals, because criminals have to be charged with a crime. They weren't called prisoners, because prisoners of war have rights. They were "unlawful combatants," who were being "detained," in what the president called "a new kind of war," although, really, it was very old.

THE MILITARY ORDER, the location of the prison, and the memos all evaded a variety of legal instruments designed to protect prisoners from torture. But another obstacle remained: the Convention Against Torture and Other Cruel, Inhuman or Degrading Treatment or Punishment, a treaty that the United States had signed in 1988 and ratified in 1994. This objection was addressed in August 2002, in a fifty-page memo to the White House counsel Alberto Gonzales—signed by the Justice Department's Jay S. Bybee but reportedly drafted by Yoo—which attempted to invent a distinction between acts that are "cruel, inhuman, or degrading" and acts that constitute torture. "Severe pain," a threshold for torture, was defined as pain like that associated with "death, organ failure, or permanent damage resulting in a loss of significant body function." ("If the detainee dies, you're doing it wrong," Jonathan Fredman, the chief counsel for the CIA's counterterrorism center, advised, according to meeting minutes later released by the Senate Armed Services Committee.)

Methods described in the torture memos include stripping, exposure to extremes of temperature and light, false threats to family members, and the use of dogs. Lakhdar Boumediene, who arrived in Guantánamo on January 20, 2002, said that, in one sixteen-day period, he was questioned night and day. ("I was kept awake for many days straight," he later wrote. "I was forced to remain in painful positions for hours at a time. These are things I do not want to write about; I want only to forget.") In the memos, these techniques have names like "Fear Up Harsh" and "We Know All," and are daubed with the greasy paint of the bureaucrat. "Sleep Adjustment" is "adjusting the sleeping times of the detainee (e.g., reversing sleep cycles from night to day). This technique is NOT sleep deprivation." Waterboarding: "the individual is bound securely to an inclined bench, which is approximately four feet by seven feet. The individual's feet are gently elevated. A cloth is placed over the forehead and eyes. Water is then applied to the cloth in a controlled manner. As this is done, the cloth is lowered until it covers both the nose and mouth." In this fashion, "water is continuously applied from a height of twelve to twenty-four inches," so that the individual experiences the sensation of drowning. After a break of three or four breaths, "the procedure may then be repeated."

Many of these forms of torment, including subjecting prisoners to stress positions, sleep disruption, semi-starvation, and extreme cold, came from a 1957 study, conducted by the air force, called "Communist Attempts to Elicit False Confessions from Air Force Prisoners of War." It was an investigation of interrogation methods used by Chinese Communists, who tortured American prisoners during the Korean War. Bush's top security advisers, including Rice and Powell, were consulted about what the White House called "enhanced interrogation techniques." Powell objected to defying the Geneva conventions. Ashcroft urged discretion. "Why are we talking about this in the White House?" he is said to have asked at one meeting, warning, "History will not judge this kindly."

The spread of such torture around the world is the subject of *Habeas Corpus After 9/11: Confronting America's New Global Detention System*, by Jonathan Hafetz, who teaches at Seton Hall, and of *The Guantánamo Effect*, which is based on interviews with sixty-two former detainees, conducted by Laurel E. Fletcher, the director of the International Human Rights Law Clinic, at Berkeley, and Eric Stover, the director of Berkeley's Human Rights Center. In Afghanistan alone, procedures authorized in the torture memos were used by the CIA at several sites, including a facility in Kabul known as the Dark Prison (where prisoners were not allowed to see the light) and Bagram Air Base, where, in 2002, two men were tortured to death: both died while chained to the ceiling of their cells. Eliza Griswold, writing in the *New Republic*, quoted a former interrogator who described Bagram as echoing with "medieval sounds." The medieval dungeon: the scrape of shackles, the screams of agony, the groans of despair.

For a time, Americans interrogating suspected terrorists were not answerable to any rules, except those made, ad hoc, by the Bush administration. The White House's answer to terrorism, which is an abandonment of the law of war, was the abandonment of the rule of law.

"THERE'S PRECEDENT FOR IT," Cheney had said. In fact, the history of the trial is inseparable from the histories of evidence, torture, and punishment. An ancient form of adjudication known as trial by ordeal became commonplace after AD 500; its heyday lasted from AD 800 to 1200. In trial by ordeal, a defendant submits to a grueling physical test, the outcome of which is taken as a sign from God, an indication of guilt or innocence. In the end, man is judged by God alone. Trial by ordeal was practiced throughout Latin Christendom. It was a favorite device for trying traitors, slaves, and foreigners. In medieval English law, the ordeal was an appropriate trial for "the foreigner or friendless man." It took many forms. A dispute between conflicting testimonies might be resolved by the trial of the cross: two men were ordered to stand with arms raised; he who could hold them up the longest was found to be telling the truth. Trial by fire involved grasping an iron bar. A plea was offered to God: "If this man is innocent of the charge from which he seeks to clear himself, he will take this fiery iron in his hand and appear unharmed; if he is guilty, let your most just power declare that truth in him, so that wickedness may not conquer justice but falsehood always be overcome by the truth."

The church's sanction for trial by ordeal was withdrawn in 1215, by order of the Fourth Lateran Council. The legal historian John H. Langbein has argued that the abolition of trial by ordeal led to a judicial crisis: placing the fate of men in the hands of other men, rather than in the hands of God, proved to be a difficult adjustment. In continental Europe, trial by ordeal was replaced by judicial torture: torture authorized by the court for the purpose of gathering evidence that could achieve a state of certainty. The jurisprudence of torture, which derived from Roman canon law, was essentially a law of proof: a defendant could be convicted of a serious crime only if his guilt was "full proof," which meant either that he had voluntarily confessed or that there were two eyewitnesses to his crime. In cases of "half proof" (for instance, one eyewitness, or two quarter-proof pieces of circumstantial evidence, added together), the defendant would be tortured. Because people who are tortured will confess to anything, many laws required that a confession extracted by torture include details that "no innocent person can know."

In England, trial by ordeal was replaced not by judicial torture but by trial by jury. Why this happened isn't quite clear; possibly, it had something to do with limits placed on English monarchs, especially those relating to what's now called due process. In 1215, the year the church effectively abolished trial by ordeal, King John signed Magna Carta, pledging certain liberties to the people, including that "no Freeman shall be taken or imprisoned . . . but by lawful judgment of his Peers, or by the Law of the land." Also codified in thirteenth-century England was the writ of habeas corpus, an order requiring a jailer to bring a prisoner before a court and explain the cause of his imprisonment. (At first, the writ was chiefly used by the king, to establish his jurisdiction, rather than by prisoners.) The first criminal jury trial took place in Westminster, in 1220. It included elements of ordeal. Swearing an oath was a means of bringing God's judgment into the proceedings. And there remained the threat of pain. The accused had to consent to trial by jury. The other choice, according to a thirteenth-century treatise, was *prisone forte et dure:* "let their penance be this, that they be barefooted, ungirt and bareheaded, in the worst place in the prison, upon the bare ground continually night and day, that they eat only bread made of barley or bran, and that they drink not the day they eat; nor eat the day they drink, nor drink anything but water, and that they be put in irons." Most people chose trial by jury.

The sixteenth and seventeenth centuries witnessed a revolution in punishment: blood sanctions (maiming and execution) began to be replaced by forms of bondage (galley slavery and indentured servitude) and of confinement (short- and long-term imprisonment). The availability of punishments short of corporal and capital punishment gave courts far more discretion in handling evidence. Defendants for whom evidence was something less than full-proof could be given lighter sentences: shorter terms of bondage or imprisonment. Judicial torture was abandoned. Meanwhile, in England, habeas corpus became a remedy for prisoners seeking relief for arbitrary imprisonment, even in times of war. Five noblemen imprisoned by Charles I for refusing to lend the king money to pay for the Thirty Years' War sought writs of habeas corpus; they argued that, without charges, "imprisonment shall not continue for a time, but for ever." The Five Knights case led to the 1628 Petition of Right, which turned habeas corpus from a privilege to a right and then, in 1641, Parliament passed the Habeas Corpus Act, whose power was expanded in 1679 in a piece of legislation that William Blackstone called a "second Magna Carta."

The law of nations is the rule of law over war. Its most influential theorist, the Dutch jurist Hugo Grotius, wrote *On the Law of War and Peace* (1625) during a time of political and legal ferment that saw the end of judicial torture, the yielding of blood sanctions to bondage and imprisonment, and a revolution in the law of evidence. Holy war was said to have ended with the Middle Ages. In time, the rule of law, revulsion at torture, the abolition of blood sanctions, and the law of evidence became the means by which the nations of the West came to distinguish themselves from the rest of the world (including, not least, non-states like the Taliban insurgency and terrorist organizations like Al Qaeda). Nobody, not even a king, could imprison someone without cause. Torture wasn't a form of jurisprudence; torture was a species of obscenity. War could not be justified by mere appeal to God, and waged by any means, but must be justified by law, and waged with restraint. War, like crime and punishment, was to be ruled not by God, not by men, but by law.

Or so the story goes. In seventeenth-century New England, English colonists ruled that "lawful Captives taken in just Wars" could be sold into slavery. In practice, this meant that, so long as you called a war you waged just, you could enslave your enemies at the end of it. At the close of King Philip's War (1675–1676), in which Algonquian Indians had tried to oust the English from New England, governors sent signed certificates on ships that conveyed prisoners of war to islands in the Caribbean, to be sold as slaves, explaining that they had "perpetrated many notorious barbarous and execrable murthers, villanies and outrages . . . without giving any account of their controversys and refusing (according to the manner of civill nations) an open decision of the same." They had been declared, in effect, unlawful combatants. In 1741, when New Yorkers suspected that the city's slaves were plotting to burn the city down, and murder all the free men (at the time, one in five New Yorkers was enslaved), more than a hundred men in the city were arrested and thrown into a dungeon in the basement of city hall, where they were interrogated for months. Under duress, most confessed; those who didn't were brought to trial. Nearly all the evidence against the accused came from statements extracted from other slaves, which were admissible in court only because a long-standing ban against "Negro Evidence" had been lifted, to cover just such cases of slave conspiracy. Seventeen men were found guilty, and hanged; thirteen were burned at the stake. Most of the rest were shipped to the Caribbean, to islands known, at the time, as graveyards.

The laws of war can be debased and made, even, into weapons of war. The rule of law can be made a travesty. Still, sometimes laws are all that stands in the way of imprisonment, torture, trials, and executions conducted at the king's pleasure.

IN 2001, when the Bush administration talked about precedent for the military commissions, it meant the Second World War. Yoo, in his memos, cited a case involving a military order signed by FDR in 1942, providing for the establishment of a military commission to try eight Nazi saboteurs who had entered the United States; the order's constitutionality was upheld in a Supreme Court case known as *Ex Parte Quirin*. Felix Frankfurter called *Quirin* "not a happy precedent." The reason for the 1942 military tribunal appears to have been that the FBI bungled the prosecution of the sabotage: a military commission was meant to provide the agency with cover. In any case, a number of features distinguish Roosevelt's military order from Bush's. FDR's was backed by legislative authority, during a declared war, and the prisoners were held and the trial conducted in the United States. None of these conditions applied to the Bush order. And, as Neal Katyal and Laurence Tribe argued in the *Yale Law Journal* in 2002, the Bush order "makes the jurisdictional question (whether someone is subject to a military trial at all) the very same one as the question on the merits (whether the person is guilty of a war crime)." The Nazi saboteurs were tried immediately, in a single trial. But, as Bravin writes in *The Terror Courts*, "the Bush administration envisioned creating for the first time a permanent legal structure under the president's sole command."

Among the strongest protests lodged against the commissions and the use of torture were those from members of the military. Bravin profiles Stuart Couch, a lieutenant colonel in the Marine Corps, who in late 2003 joined the prosecution staff. While preparing cases, Couch grew concerned that most of the evidence in the files he saw was paraphrased from detainees' statements. Many of the prisoners at Guantánamo seemed to be ordinary men caught in a dragnet that trained fighters—Al Qaeda's leaders—had been able to escape. "The joke we used to have at commissions is, we'd call them the butcher, the baker, and the candlestick maker," one prosecutor, Air Force Major Rob Preston, said. Couch and others worried that men who were guilty and dangerous either had got away or couldn't be convicted, because the evidence against them was limited to confessions and accusations extracted during brutal interrogations. Then there was the matter of the commissions. Military prosecutors began formally stating their objections. "I sincerely believe that this process is wrongly managed, wrongly focused and a blight on the reputation of the armed forces," Preston wrote in an email, in 2004, the year the first military commission met. Couch refused to participate in the prosecution of cases in which, he believed, the evidence had been obtained through torture. "As an ethical matter, I opine that the interrogation techniques utilized with this detainee are discoverable by defense counsel, as they relate to the credibility of any statements given by him," Couch wrote to his superior. "As discoverable material, I have an ethical duty to disclose such material to the defense."

Meanwhile, reporters, lawyers, and human rights activists had been investigating the conditions under which the prisoners were being held. *The Guantánamo Lawyers: Inside a Prison, Outside the Law*, edited by Mark P. Denbeaux and Jonathan Hafetz, is an anthology of reminiscences by more than a hundred lawyers who defended the detainees. "I would have confessed to anything to get my leg back," a prisoner named Abdul Aziz Naji told his attorney, Ellen Lubell, "but I didn't know what they wanted me to say." Naji lost his leg to a land mine, and his prosthetic was broken by U.S. soldiers at Bagram. At Guantánamo, he was given a replacement that didn't fit; he pulled his stump out of it, to show Lubell, leaving the prosthetic, outfitted with a white sneaker, still shackled to the floor. "I knew I had come to the heart of a new kind of irony," Lubell writes.

Stories began to emerge about the abuse of prisoners. Photographs from Abu Ghraib were broadcast on *60 Minutes II* on April 28, 2004, eight days after oral arguments were heard in the Supreme Court in *Rasul v. Bush*, a case concerning the jurisdiction of the federal courts over the habeas claims of fourteen Guantánamo prisoners. Opposition grew, especially after the Bush administration memos were published in *The Torture Papers*, edited by Karen J. Greenberg and Joshua L. Dratel, and the chilling story behind them was reported by Jane Mayer in her book *The Dark Side*. Doubts were raised about whether many of the men sent to Guantánamo should have been arrested at all. In 2006, a team from Seton Hall School of Law released a study of the 517 prisoners then remaining at Guantánamo; according to Department of Defense data, only 5 percent of these men had been captured by U.S. troops; at least 47 percent had been arrested by Pakistani or Northern Alliance forces during the months when the U.S. government was offering bounties.

"The military commissions were a crude parody of a justice system," Muneer Ahmad, a defense attorney, wrote. "The rules changed constantly." In June 2006, in *Hamdan v. Rumsfeld*, the Supreme Court ruled that, without congressional authorization, the president lacked the power to establish the military commissions, which violated both the Geneva conventions and the Uniform Code of Military Justice. Three months later, Congress reauthorized the commissions under the Military Commissions Act of 2006. A habeas petition filed on behalf of Lakhdar Boumediene was rejected by a lower court, a district court, and an appeals court. In 2006, Boumediene began a hunger strike. (By now, prisoners had begun trying to kill themselves. In 2006, three deaths were declared suicides.) Like other hunger strikers, Boumediene was force-fed through the nose, twice daily. His appeal, *Boumediene v. Bush*, was decided by the Supreme Court in 2008. A 5–4 majority struck down part of the 2006 Military Commissions Act, and ruled that all prisoners confined at Guantánamo had a right to habeas recourse through the U.S. courts.

In 2009, two days after Barack Obama's inauguration, the president released a directive ordering the closing of Guantánamo and issued executive orders banning torture and mandating adherence to the Geneva conventions. On May 15, Lakhdar Boumediene, who had been imprisoned for seven and a half years, was released, and flown to Paris, where he went out for pizza with his wife and two daughters, and cried.

ON JANUARY 28, 2013, a week after Obama began his second term, the State Department shut down the office of Daniel Fried, whose job had been to close Guantánamo. A hundred and sixty-six men remain imprisoned at Guantánamo, and, until their release into the hands of Afghan authorities during the past year—the last slated for transfer just this month—many more were held, some for years, at Bagram. Meanwhile, the *New York Times* reported that the Obama administration held "Terror Tuesdays," meetings in which the president and his national security advisers discussed which suspected terrorists, remaining at large, should be assassinated by drones. In about a third of these cases, the president alone took responsibility for naming the targets, which included American citizens.

In February 2013, NBC News released a confidential, undated Justice Department memo, titled "Lawfulness of a Lethal Operation Directed Against a U.S. Citizen Who Is a Senior Operational Leader of Al Qa'ida or an Associated Force." It explains, in sixteen pages, how it is that the president of the United States has the power to order not imprisonment without charge but the killing of men without anyone bringing evidence before any judicial body, not even an unconstitutional military commission.

There were no unmanned aerial vehicles in the Middle Ages; a drone was a honeybee. But there were assassins. "Assassin" is, in fact, a medievalism; the word gained currency during the Crusades; it derives from "hashish." It meant a Muslim sent on a mission to kill.

The past is often figured as dark, a prison, a tomb; the future, bright, blue sky, a spaceship. This is an inheritance of the Enlightenment, with its faith in progress and reason and law. Part of the terror of September 11 was the gleaming skyscraper become a tomb, the seeming backward march of time, the horror of the unreasonable. What, then, of the assassin become an unmanned flying machine?

—2013

Postscript: As of the middle of 2022, the prison at Guantánamo has not been closed. Thirty-six men remain imprisoned there.

DRAFTED

BEGINNING IN THE SUMMER OF 2022, WOMEN IN about half of the United States may be breaking the law if they decide to end a pregnancy. This will be, in large part, because Supreme Court Justice Samuel Alito appears to have been surprised that there is so little written about abortion in a four-thousand-word document crafted by fifty-five men in 1787. As it happens, there is also nothing at all in that document, which sets out fundamental law, about pregnancy, uteruses, vaginas, fetuses, placentas, menstrual blood, breasts, or breast milk. There is nothing in that document about women at all. Most consequentially, there is nothing in that document—or in the circumstances under which it was written—that suggests its authors imagined women as part of the political community embraced by the phrase "We the People." There were no women among the delegates to the Constitutional Convention. There were no women among the hundreds of people who participated in ratifying conventions in the states. There were no women judges. There were no women legislators. At the time, women could neither hold office nor run for office, and, except in New Jersey, and then only fleetingly, women could not vote. Legally, most women did not exist as persons.

Because these facts appeared to surprise Alito, abortion appeared likely to become a crime in at least twenty states in spring of 2022. "The Constitution makes no reference to abortion, and no such right is implicitly protected by any constitutional provision," Alito wrote, in a leaked draft of the Supreme Court's majority opinion in *Dobbs v. Jackson Women's Health Organization*. The draft decision, which *Politico* published, would overturn *Roe v. Wade*, the 1973 decision legalizing abortion. Chief Justice John Roberts, promising an investigation, denied its authenticity. Five justices reportedly voted in accordance with the draft: Alito, Brett Kavanaugh, Amy Coney Barrett, Clarence Thomas, and Neil Gorsuch. Justices Stephen Breyer, Sonia Sotomayor, and Elena Kagan were sure to dissent. Roberts was not likely to concur. One theory had it that whoever disclosed the draft is trying to make it more difficult, if not impossible, for Roberts to recruit a defector from the majority. But of course at the time of the leak, this remained unknown.

About as wholly speculative as the question of who leaked this decision was the history offered to support it. Alito's opinion rested almost exclusively on a bizarre and impoverished historical analysis. "The Constitution makes no express reference to a right to obtain an abortion, and therefore those who claim that it protects such a right must show that the right is somehow implicit in the constitutional text," he argued, making this observation repeatedly. *Roe*, he wrote, was "remarkably loose in its treatment of the constitutional text" and suffers from one error above all: "it held that the abortion right, which is not mentioned in the Constitution, is part of a right to privacy, which is also not mentioned."

Women are indeed missing from the Constitution. That's a problem to remedy, not a precedent to honor.

Alito cited a number of eighteenth-century texts; he does not cite anything written by a woman, and not because there's nothing available. "The laws respecting woman," Mary Wollstonecraft wrote in *A Vindication of the Rights of Woman*, in 1791, "make an absurd unit of a man and his wife, and then, by the easy transition of only considering him as responsible, she is reduced to a mere cypher." She is but a part of him. She herself does not exist but is instead, as Wollstonecraft wrote, a "non-entity."

If a right isn't mentioned explicitly in the Constitution, Alito argued, following the so-called history test, then it can only become a right if it can be shown to be "deeply rooted in this Nation's history and tradition." As I have argued, the history test disadvantages people who were not enfranchised at the time the Constitution was written, or who have been poorly enfranchised since then. Especially important is the question of who was enfranchised at the time of the ratification of the Fourteenth Amendment, in 1868, the nation's second founding, since many arguments defending abortion rights (and many other rights, too) turn on the equal protection and due process clauses of that amendment. Here, too, Alito was baffled to discover so little about abortion and women. Referring to the advocates for Jackson Women's Health Organization and to amicus briefs like one signed by the American Historical Association, Alito wrote, "Not only are respondents and their *amici* unable to show that a constitutional right to abortion was established when the Fourteenth Amendment was adopted, but they have found no support for the existence of an abortion right that predates the latter part of the 20th century—no state constitutional provision, no statute, no judicial decision, no learned treatise."

He might have consulted the records of the U.S. Senate from the debate over the Fourteenth Amendment, when Jacob Howard, a Republican senator from Michigan, got into an argument with Reverdy Johnson, a Democrat from Maryland. Howard quoted James Madison, who had written that "those who are to be bound by laws, ought to have a voice in making them." This got Johnson terribly worried, because the Fourteenth Amendment uses the word "person." He wanted to know: Did Howard mean to suggest that women could be construed as persons, too?

MR. JOHNSON: Females as well as males?

MR. HOWARD: Mr. Madison does not say anything about females.

MR. JOHNSON: "Persons."

MR. HOWARD: I believe Mr. Madison was old enough and wise enough to take it for granted that there was such a thing as the law of nature which has a certain influence even in political affairs, and that by that law women and children are not regarded as the equals of men.

Alito, shocked—shocked—to discover so little in the law books of the 1860s guaranteeing a right to abortion, had missed the point: hardly anything in the law books of the 1860s guaranteed women anything. Because, usually, they still weren't persons. Nor, for that matter, were fetuses.

I don't happen to think *Roe* was well argued. I agree with Ruth Bader Ginsburg's early analysis—that grounding the right in equality rather than privacy might have been a sounder approach. I'm not even a hard-liner on the question of abortion; I find it morally thorny. But when Samuel Alito says that people who believe abortion is a constitutional right "have no persuasive answer to this historical evidence," he displays nothing so much as the limits of his own evidence. "The page of history teems with woman's wrongs," as Sarah Grimké once put it. It does not teem with women's rights. To use a history of discrimination to deny people their constitutional rights is a perversion of logic and a betrayal of justice. Would the Court decide civil rights cases regarding race by looking exclusively to laws and statutes written before emancipation?

At the close of the opinion, Alito congratulated both himself and the Court that, with this ruling, they are enfranchising women. "Our decision . . . allows women on both sides of the abortion issue to seek to affect the legislative process by influencing public opinion, lobbying legislators, voting, and running for office," he writes. "Women are not without electoral or political power." True, women are no longer without electoral power. But they were without it for almost the entirety of the history on which Alito grounds his analysis of the Constitution and its provisions. You don't need a leaked document to learn that.

—2022

Postscript: In June 2022, the Supreme Court issued its final Dobbs ruling, overturning Roe v. Wade. *Alito's draft remained virtually unchanged in the final opinion.*

Part Eight

The Parent Trap

There's a rock, and a hard place,
and then there's a classroom.

Students protesting a banned books list in Pennsylvania, 2021.
© *Dan Rainville–USA TODAY NETWORK*

BACK TO THE
BLACKBOARD

BEFORE SUNRISE ON A MORNING JUST AFTER LABOR
Day 1977, Humberto and Jackeline Alvarez, Felix Hernandez, Rosario and Jose Robles, and Lidia and Jose Lopez huddled together in the basement of the United States Courthouse in Tyler, Texas, the Rose City, to decide just how much they were willing to risk for the sake of their children, for the sake of other people's children, and for the sake, really, of everyone. Among them, the Alvarezes, Hernandez, the Robleses, and the Lopezes had sixteen children who, the week before, had been barred from entering Tyler's public schools by order of James Plyler, Tyler's school superintendent. On the first day of school, Rosario Robles had walked her five children to Bonner Elementary, where she was met by the principal, who asked her for the children's birth certificates, and, when she couldn't provide them, put her and the kids in his car and drove them home.

This hadn't been the principal's idea, or even Plyler's. In 1975, when Texas passed a law allowing public schools to bar undocumented immigrants, Plyler ignored it. "I guess I was softhearted and concerned about the kids," he said. Also, there weren't many of them. About sixteen thousand children went to the schools in the East Texas city of Tyler, which considered itself the rose-growing capital of America and was named for John Tyler, the president of the United States who had pushed for the annexation of Texas in 1844, which led to a war with Mexico in 1846. Of those sixteen thousand students, fewer than sixty were the children of parents who had, without anyone's permission, entered the United States from Mexico by crossing a border established in 1848, when the war ended with a treaty that turned the top half of Mexico into the bottom third of the United States. Jose Robles worked in a pipe factory. Humberto Alvarez worked in a meatpacking plant. They paid rent. They owned cars. They paid taxes. They grew roses.

Nevertheless, in July of 1977 Tyler's school board, worried that Tyler would become a haven for immigrants driven away from other towns, insisted that undocumented children be kicked out of the city's schools unless their parents paid a thousand dollars a year, per child, which few of them could afford, not even the Robleses, who owned their own home. Turned away from Bonner Elementary, the Robleses sent some of their kids to a local Catholic school—Jose did yard work in exchange for tuition—but they were put in touch with the Mexican American Legal Defense and Educational Fund, which sent an attorney, Peter Roos, who filed a lawsuit in the U.S. Eastern District Court of Texas. It was presided over by a judge whose name was Justice. "There were two judges in Tyler," Roos liked to say. "You got Justice, or no justice."

Participating in a lawsuit as an undocumented immigrant is a very risky proposition. In a closed-door meeting, Roos asked that the parents be allowed to testify in chambers and so avoid revealing their identities, which could lead to deportation. They had come to the courthouse knowing that, at any moment, they could be arrested, and driven to Mexico, without so much as a goodbye. Judge William Wayne Justice refused to grant the protective order. "I am a United States magistrate and if I learn of a violation of the law, it's my sworn duty to disclose it to the authorities," he said. Roos went down to the basement, near the holding cells, to inform the families and give them a chance to think it over. They decided to go ahead with the suit, come what may. Justice did make efforts to protect them from publicity, and from harassment, decreeing that the proceeding would start before dawn, to keep the press and the public at bay, and that the plaintiffs' names would be withheld.

Roos filed a motion requesting that the children be allowed to attend school, without paying tuition, while the case unfolded, which was expected to take years. "An educated populace is the basis of our democratic institutions," his brief argued, citing *Brown v. Board of Education*. "A denial of educational opportunities is repugnant to our notions that an informed and educated citizenry is necessary to our society." The case was docketed as *Doe v. Plyler*. "This is one that's headed for the United States Supreme Court," Justice told his clerk. Five years later, the appeal, *Plyler v. Doe*, went to Washington.

SOME SUPREME COURT DECISIONS ARE FAMOUS. Some are infamous. *Brown v. Board*, *Roe v. Wade*. But *Plyler v. Doe*? It's not any kind of famous. Outside the legal academy, where it is generally deemed to be of limited significance, the case is little known. (During testimony before Congress, Betsy DeVos, Donald Trump's secretary of education, appeared not to have heard of it.) The obscurity of the case might end soon, though, not least because the Court's opinion in *Plyler v. Doe* addressed questions that are central to ongoing debates about both education and immigration and that get to the heart of what schoolchildren and undocumented migrants have in common: vulnerability.

Plyler is arguably a controlling case in *Gary B. v. Snyder*, a lawsuit filed against the governor of Michigan, Rick Snyder, by seven Detroit schoolchildren, for violating their constitutional right to an education. According to the complaint, "illiteracy is the norm" in the Detroit public schools; they are the most economically and racially segregated schools in the country and, in formal assessments of student proficiency, have been rated close to zero. In *Brown*, the Court had described an education as "a right which must be made available to all on equal terms." But the Detroit plaintiffs also cite *Plyler*, in which the majority deemed illiteracy to be "an enduring disability," identified the absolute denial of education as a violation of the equal protection clause, and ruled that no state can "deny a discrete group of innocent children the free public education that it offers to other children residing within its borders."

Plyler's reach extends, too, to lawsuits filed this summer on behalf of immigrant children who were separated from their families at the U.S.-Mexico border. In June 2018, the Texas State Teachers Association called on the governor of the state to make provisions for the education of the detained children, before the beginning of the school year, but has so far received no reply. Thousands of children are being held in more than a hundred detention centers around the country, many run by for-profit contractors. Conditions vary, but, on the whole, instruction is limited and supplies are few. "The kids barely learn anything," a former social worker reported from Arizona.

Court watchers have tended to consider *Plyler* insignificant because the Court's holding was narrow. But in *The Schoolhouse Gate: Public*

Education, the Supreme Court, and the Battle for the American Mind, Justin Driver, a law professor at the University of Chicago, argues that this view of *Plyler* is wrong. "Properly understood," Driver writes, "it rests among the most egalitarian, momentous, and efficacious constitutional opinions that the Supreme Court has issued throughout its entire history."

Driver is not alone in this view. In *No Undocumented Child Left Behind* (2012), the University of Houston law professor Michael A. Olivas called *Plyler* "the apex of the Court's treatment of the undocumented." In *Immigration Outside the Law* (2014), the UCLA law professor Hiroshi Motomura compared *Plyler* to *Brown* and described its influence as "fundamental, profound, and enduring." Even people who think the case hasn't been influential wish it had been. "*Plyler v. Doe* may be irrelevant in a strictly legal sense," the legal journalist Linda Greenhouse wrote, "but there are strong reasons to resurrect its memory and ponder it today." Because, for once, our tired, our poor, our huddled masses—the very littlest of them—breathed free.

LAURA ALVAREZ, TEN YEARS OLD, rode in the family's battered station wagon to the courthouse in Tyler, for a hearing held on September 9, 1977, at six in the morning. (During a related Texas case—later consolidated with *Plyler*—a nine-year-old girl spoke to the judge in chambers and told him that, since being barred from school, the only learning she was getting came from poring over the homework done by a younger sibling—an American citizen.) In Tyler, the assistant attorney general for the State of Texas showed up wearing blue jeans. She'd flown in late the night before, and had lost her luggage. After an attorney from the Carter administration said that the Justice Department would not pursue the litigants while the trial proceeded, during which time the students would be able to attend school, Judge Justice issued the requested injunction.

Witnesses presented testimony about economies: educating these children cost the state money, particularly because they needed special English-language instruction, but not educating these children would be costly, too, in the long term, when they became legal residents but, uneducated, would be able to contribute very little to the tax base. The judge had a policy preference: "The predictable effects of depriving an undocumented child of an education are clear and undisputed. Already disadvantaged as a result of poverty, lack of English-speaking ability, and undeniable racial prejudices, these children, without an education, will become permanently locked into the lowest socio-economic class." But the question didn't turn on anyone's policy preferences; it turned on the Fourteenth Amendment.

The Fourteenth Amendment, ratified in 1868, guarantees certain rights to "citizens" and makes two promises to "persons": it prohibits a state from depriving "any person of life, liberty, or property, without due process of law," and prohibits a state from denying "any person within its jurisdiction the equal protection of the laws." Before *Plyler*, the Supreme Court had established that the due process clause applied to undocumented immigrants, who are, plainly, "persons," but it had not established that the equal protection clause extended to them, and the State of Texas said that it didn't, because undocumented immigrants were in the state illegally. Judge Justice disagreed. "People who have entered the United States, by whatever means, are 'within its jurisdiction' in that they are within the territory of the United States and subject to its laws," he wrote.

But how to apply that clause? The courts bring a standard known as "strict scrutiny" to laws that abridge a "fundamental right," like the right to life, liberty, and property, and to laws that discriminate against a particular class of people, a "suspect class," like the freed slaves in whose interest the amendment was originally written—that is, any population burdened with disabilities "or subjected to such a history of purposeful unequal treatment, or relegated to such a position of political powerlessness as to command extraordinary protection from the majoritarian political process."

Is education a fundamental right? The Constitution, drafted in the summer of 1787, does not mention a right to education, but the Northwest Ordinance, passed by Congress that same summer, held that "religion, morality, and knowledge, being necessary to good government and the happiness of mankind, schools and the means of education shall forever be encouraged." By 1868 the constitutions of twenty-eight of the thirty-two states in the Union had provided for free public education, open to all. Texas, in its 1869 constitution, provided for free public schooling for "all the inhabitants of this State," a provision that was revised to exclude undocumented immigrants only in 1975.

Justice skirted the questions of whether education is a fundamental right and whether undocumented immigrants are a suspect class. Instead of applying the standard of "strict scrutiny" to the Texas law, he applied the lowest level of scrutiny to the law, which is known as the "rational basis test." He decided that the Texas law failed this test. The State of Texas had argued that the law was rational because undocumented children are expensive to educate—they often require bilingual education, free meals, and even free clothing. But, Justice noted, so are other children, including native-born children, and children who have immigrated legally, and their families are not asked to bear the cost of their special education. As to why Texas had even passed such a law, he had two explanations, both cynical: "Children of illegal aliens had never been explicitly afforded any judicial protection, and little political uproar was likely to be raised in their behalf."

In September 1978, Justice ruled in favor of the children. Not long afterward, a small bouquet arrived at his house, sent by three Mexican workers. Then came the hate mail. A man from Lubbock wrote, on the back of a postcard, "Why in the hell don't you illegally move to mexico?"

THE SCHOOLHOUSE GATE IS THE FIRST book-length history of Supreme Court cases involving the constitutional rights of schoolchildren, a set of cases that, though often written about, have never before been written about all together, as if they constituted a distinct body of law. In Driver's view, "the public school has served as the single most significant site of constitutional interpretation within the nation's history." Millions of Americans spend most of their days in public schools—miniature states—where liberty, equality, rights, and privileges are matters of daily struggle. Schools are also, not incidentally, where Americans *learn* about liberty, equality, rights, and privileges. "The schoolroom is the first opportunity most citizens have to experience the power of government," Justice John Paul Stevens once wrote.

The Supreme Court paid relatively little attention to public schools until after the Second World War, but, since then, it has ruled on a slew of cases. Do students have First Amendment rights? In *Tinker v. Des Moines Independent Community School District* (1969), the Court said yes. Three students had sued when they were suspended for wearing black armbands to school to protest the Vietnam War. In a 7–2 opinion, the Court sided with the students, affirming that students do not "shed their constitutional rights to freedom of speech or expression at the schoolhouse gate," and that public schools, though not democracies, "may not be enclaves of totalitarianism," either. Justice Hugo Black issued a heated dissent. "It may be that the Nation has outworn the old-fashioned slogan that 'children are to be seen not heard,'" he wrote, but he hoped it was still true that we "send children to school on the premise that at their age they need to learn, not teach." A still more strident version of Black's position was taken by Justice Clarence Thomas, in *Morse v. Frederick* (2007), a case involving a student who, when a parade passed in front of the school, waved a banner that read "BONG HITS 4 JESUS." Writing for the majority, Chief Justice John Roberts marked an exception to the free-speech rights established in *Tinker*: students are not free to endorse drug use, but Thomas, concurring, used the occasion to wax nostalgic: "In the earliest public schools, teachers taught, and students listened. Teachers commanded, and students obeyed."

Just because the courts have recognized students' First Amendment rights, it doesn't follow that students have other rights. Do students have Fourth Amendment protections against "unreasonable searches and seizures"? Do they have Fifth Amendment protections against self-incrimination? Do they have Eighth Amendment protections against "cruel and unusual punishment"? In *Goss v. Lopez* (1975), the Court ruled that students cannot be suspended or expelled without at least some form of due process, but, two years later, in *Ingraham v. Wright*, it said that schools could punish children, physically, and without any procedure at all. This shift took place amid a growing conservative reaction that viewed the Court's schoolhouse opinions as an example of judicial overreach, as a violation of states' rights, and as part of the rise of permissiveness and the decline of order. *Lopez* had extended to students a Fourteenth Amendment right to due process, partly on the back of the argument that granting students rights is a way of teaching them about citizenship, fairness, and decency. "To insist upon fair treatment before passing judgment against a student accused of wrong-doing is to demonstrate that society has high principles and the conviction to honor them," the legal scholar William G. Buss wrote, in an influential law review article in 1971.

Plenty of teachers and school administrators think that students don't have any rights. "I am the Constitution," Joe Clarke, the principal of a high school in Paterson, New Jersey, liked to say, roaming the hallways with a Willie Mays baseball bat in the 1980s. This was an era that Driver describes as marking a Reagan Justice Department campaign for "education law and order." The era produced a 1985 decision, *New Jersey v. T.L.O.*, in which the Court ruled that schools require only reasonable suspicion, not probable cause, to search students and their backpacks and lockers and other belongings.

Together, the education law-and-order regime and the rise of school shootings, beginning with Columbine in 1999, have produced a new environment in the nation's schools, more than half of which, as of 2007, are patrolled by police officers. It was a police officer's closed-door questioning of a seventh grader, taken out of his social studies class in Chapel Hill, that led to the Court's 2011 decision, in *J.D.B. v. North Carolina*, establishing that only in certain circumstances do students have Fifth Amendment rights. Do students have Second Amendment rights? Not yet. But in 2016 a Kentucky congressman introduced a Safe Students Act that would have repealed the 1990 Gun-Free School Zones Act, and allowed guns in schools. Meanwhile, more and more schools are surveilled by cameras, and bordered by metal detectors. If the schoolhouse is a mini-state, it has also become, in many places, a military state.

FEW DISCUSSIONS OF *PLYLER* are more keenly sensitive to its ambiguities than Ana Raquel Minian's *Undocumented Lives: The Untold Story of Mexican Migration*, a revealing study that, because "undocumented lives" are nearly impossible to trace in the archives, relies on hundreds of oral histories. For Minian, *Plyler*, by its very casting of undocumented children as innocents, underscored the perception of undocumented adults as culpable—criminals to be arrested, detained, prosecuted, and deported.

As Texas appealed to the Fifth Circuit, Woodrow Seals, a district judge in Houston, ruled for the children in a related case. Seals didn't agree that the undocumented children were a suspect class, but he didn't need to, because he believed the Texas statute was not rational, and, in any case, he thought that absolute denial of an education was so severe a harm that, on its own terms, it required strict scrutiny. Public school is "the most important institution in this country," Seals wrote, and "the Constitution does not permit the states to deny access to education to a discrete group of children within its border." Seals handed down his opinion in July 1980, just months before the presidential election. He wrote in a letter, "I hate to think what will happen to my decision if Governor Reagan wins the election and appoints four new justices to the Supreme Court."

Carter's Justice Department had supported the plaintiffs. Reagan's did not. The Supreme Court heard oral arguments in *Plyler v. Doe* on December 1, 1981. The Mexican American Legal Defense and Educational Fund considered the case to be as important as *Brown v. Board of Education*, which, in 1954, Thurgood Marshall, then the head of the NAACP Legal Defense and Educational Fund, had argued before the Court. Marshall had presented *Brown* as a Fourteenth Amendment, equal protection case. The plaintiffs in *Plyler* were making, essentially, the same argument. Conceivably, their case could realize the promise of *Brown* by establishing a constitutional right to an education. They could even press the claim that undocumented immigrants were not only persons under the equal protection clause of the Fourteenth Amendment but also, doctrinally, a suspect class. None of these objectives were politically within their reach, however, given the makeup of the bench.

During oral arguments, Marshall peppered John Hardy, representing Plyler, about what the State of Texas did and did not provide for undocumented immigrants:

MARSHALL: Could Texas deny them fire protection?

HARDY: Deny them fire protection?

MARSHALL: Yes, sir. F-i-r-e.

HARDY: Okay. If their home is on fire, their home is going to be protected with the local fire services just—

MARSHALL: Could Texas pass a law and say they cannot
be protected?

HARDY:—I don't believe so.

MARSHALL: Why not? If they could do this, why couldn't they
do that?

HARDY: Because . . . I am going to take the position that it is an
entitlement of the . . . Justice Marshall, let me think a second.
You . . . that is . . . I don't know. That's a tough question.

MARSHALL: Somebody's house is more important than his child?

Later, Marshall came back at him, asking, "Could Texas pass a law
denying admission to the schools of children of convicts?" Hardy said
that they could, but that it wouldn't be constitutional. Marshall's reply:
"We are dealing with children. I mean, here is a child that is the son of
a murderer, but he can go to school, but the child that is the son of an
unfortunate alien cannot?"

Three days later, the justices held a conference. According to notes
made by Justice Lewis F. Powell Jr., Chief Justice Warren Burger
said, "14A applies as they are persons but illegals are not entitled to
E/P." Marshall said, "Children are *not* illegals. . . . E/P means what it
says." Five justices wanted to uphold the lower court's opinion, four
to reverse it. Justice William J. Brennan Jr. volunteered to write the
majority opinion. He circulated a draft that called for strict scrutiny,
deeming the children "a discrete and historically demeaned group."
Powell said that he couldn't sign it.

Powell, appointed by Nixon in 1971, had been, for a decade, the
chair of the school board of Richmond, Virginia. Sometimes known
as "the education justice," he was deeply committed to public schools.
But, because he was also committed to judicial restraint, he was
opposed to declaring education to be a constitutional right. "It is not
the province of this Court to create substantive constitutional rights in
the name of guaranteeing equal protection of the laws," he had written
in 1973, in *San Antonio Independent School District v. Rodriguez*, a case
that was widely seen as having shut the door on the idea. For Powell, establishing education as a fundamental right invited claims: Are
health care, food, and shelter fundamental rights, too?

Powell was unwilling to sign Brennan's first draft, not only because it went against his opinion in Rodriguez but also because the draft contained language "that will be read as indicating that all illegal aliens, adults as well as children, may be 'discrete and insular minorities for which the Constitution offers a special solicitude.'" Brennan wrote a second draft; Powell once again asked him to narrow his opinion. But other justices, who wanted to uphold the lower court's decision, sought to move Brennan further to the left. After reading a draft of Burger's dissent ("The Constitution does not provide a cure for every social ill," the chief justice wrote, "nor does it vest judges with a mandate to try to remedy every social problem"), Justice Harry Blackmun circulated a proposal for issuing a different opinion, arguing that education has a special status because it's foundational to all other political rights, being necessary "to preserve rights of expression and participation in the political process, and therefore to preserve individual rights generally." Marshall, Brennan, and Stevens were prepared to join that opinion. But Blackmun needed Powell to make five. And Powell wouldn't sign on. "As important as education has been in the life of my family for three generations," he wrote to Blackmun, "I would hesitate before creating another heretofore unidentified right."

In the end, Brennan crafted a compromise. Education is not a constitutional right, he wrote, "but neither is it merely some governmental 'benefit.'" Undocumented migrants are not a suspect class, but their children are vulnerable, and laws that discriminate against them, while not subject to strict scrutiny, deserved "heightened scrutiny." Powell wrote to Brennan after reading the draft, "Your final product is excellent and will be in every text and case book on Constitutional law."

And yet its interpretation remains limited. "Powell wanted the case to be about the education of children, not the equal protection rights of immigrants, and so the decision was," Linda Greenhouse once remarked in a careful study of the Court's deliberations. For many legal scholars, *Plyler* looks like a dead end. It didn't cut through any constitutional thickets; it opened no new road to equal rights for undocumented immigrants, and no new road to the right to an education. It simply meant that no state could pass a law barring undocumented children from public schools. But that is exactly why Driver thinks that *Plyler* was so significant: without it, states would have passed those laws, and millions of children would have been saddled with the disability of illiteracy.

In 1994, when Californians were contemplating Proposition 187, which would have denied services to undocumented immigrants, a reporter for the *Los Angeles Times* was able to track down thirteen of the original sixteen *Plyler* children. Ten had graduated from high school in Tyler. Two worked as teacher's aides. Laura Alvarez and all six of her brothers and sisters stayed in Tyler after Judge Justice issued his opinion in *Plyler*. She became a legal resident of the United States under the terms of the 1986 Immigration Reform and Control Act, graduated in 1987 from John Tyler High School, and spent a decade working for the Tyler school district. "Without an education, I don't know where I'd be right now," she said.

"I'm glad we lost," James Plyler said in an interview in 2007, when he was eighty-two, and long since retired, and enjoying his grandchildren, who are themselves of Mexican descent.

Lewis Powell retired from the Court in 1987. He was replaced by Anthony Kennedy. In another opinion, Powell had written that children should not be punished for the crimes of their parents. "Visiting this condemnation on the head of an infant is illogical and unjust," because "legal burdens should bear some relationship to individual responsibility or wrongdoing." It's hard to know what Kennedy's replacement, Brett Kavanaugh, would say about whether the Constitution guarantees undocumented migrant children the equal protection of the law. Before joining the Court, he never cited *Plyler* in his scholarship and, in opinions issued from the bench, cited it only once. He hasn't written much about equal protection, either, though he has said, in passing, that he finds the equal protection clause ambiguous. As for undocumented migrant children, he issued one important opinion, a dissent in *Garza v. Hargan*, from 2017, that, while not citing *Plyler*, described the plaintiff in the case, an undocumented immigrant minor in Texas, as particularly vulnerable.

"The minor is alone and without family or friends," Kavanaugh wrote. "She is in a U.S. Government detention facility in a country that, for her, is foreign. She is 17 years old." The reason for her vulnerability? "She is pregnant and has to make a major life decision." She wanted to have an abortion; Kavanaugh had earlier joined a decision ruling that she must first leave detention and find a sponsoring foster family. When, in a further appeal, the DC court vacated that ruling, Kavanaugh dissented, arguing that the court had acted on "a constitutional principle as novel as it is wrong: a new right for unlawful immigrant minors in U.S. Government detention to obtain immediate abortion on demand." Her name was kept out of the proceedings. She was another Doe. It is not clear whether she ever finished her education.

—2018

TO HAVE AND TO HOLD

W HEN LOUISE TRUBEK AND HER HUSBAND, DAVE, drove from New Haven to Washington to listen to oral arguments before the Supreme Court in *Trubek v. Ullman*, she was pregnant. The Trubeks had met at the University of Wisconsin, Madison, and married in 1958. The next year, while they were both students at Yale Law School, they filed a complaint against the State of Connecticut about a statute that prevented their physician, C. Lee Buxton, the chief of obstetrics and gynecology at Yale Medical School, from discussing contraception with them. They wanted to have children one day, according to the complaint, but "a pregnancy at this time would mean a disruption of Mrs. Trubek's professional education." By the time that *Trubek v. Ullman* reached the Supreme Court, in the spring of 1961, Louise Trubek had graduated from law school and was ready to start a family. The case was dismissed, without explanation.

Spring of 2015 marked the fiftieth anniversary of the case that went forward instead: *Griswold v. Connecticut*. ("We became the footnote to the footnote," Trubek told me.) In *Griswold*, decided in June 1965, the Supreme Court ruled 7–2 that Connecticut's ban on contraception was unconstitutional, not on the ground of a woman's right to determine the timing and the number of her pregnancies but on the ground of a married couple's right to privacy. "We deal with a right of privacy older than the Bill of Rights," Justice William O. Douglas wrote in the majority opinion. "Marriage is a coming together for better or for worse, hopefully enduring, and intimate to the degree of being sacred."

In the half century since *Griswold*, Douglas's arguments about privacy and marriage have been the signal influence on a series of landmark Supreme Court decisions. In 1972, *Eisenstadt v. Baird* extended *Griswold*'s notion of privacy from married couples to individuals. "If the right of privacy means anything," Justice William Brennan wrote, "it is the right of the individual, married or single, to be free from unwarranted governmental intrusion into matters so fundamentally affecting a person as the decision whether to bear or beget a child." *Griswold* informed *Roe v. Wade*, in 1973, the Court finding that the "right of privacy . . . is broad enough to encompass a woman's decision whether or not to terminate her pregnancy." And in *Lawrence v. Texas*, in 2003, Justice Anthony Kennedy, writing a 6–3 decision overturning a ban on sodomy, described *Griswold* as "the most pertinent beginning point" for the Court's line of reasoning: the generative case.

Fifty years after *Griswold*, the Supreme Court heard oral arguments in *Obergefell v. Hodges*, a consolidation of the petitions of four couples seeking relief from state same-sex-marriage bans in Kentucky, Michigan, Ohio, and Tennessee. The federal Defense of Marriage Act was struck down by the Court in 2013, in *United States v. Windsor*, a ruling in which Kennedy cited and quoted his opinion in *Lawrence*. But bans still stand in thirteen states. In 2004, Ohio passed a law stating that "only a union between one man and one woman may be a marriage valid in or recognized by this state." The Ohioans James Obergefell and John Arthur had been together for nearly twenty years when Arthur was diagnosed with ALS, in 2011. In 2013, they flew to Maryland, a state without a same-sex-marriage ban, and were married on the tarmac. Arthur died three months later, at the age of forty-eight. To his widower, he was, under Ohio law, a stranger.

The coincidence of the fiftieth anniversary of the Court's ruling in *Griswold* and its decision in *Obergefell* makes this, inescapably, an occasion for considering the past half century of legal reasoning about reproductive and gay rights. The cases that link *Griswold* to *Obergefell* are the product of political movements that have been closely allied, both philosophically and historically. That sex and marriage can be separated from reproduction is fundamental to both movements, and to their legal claims. Still, there's a difference between the arguments of political movements and appeals to the Constitution. Good political arguments are expansive: they broaden and deepen the understanding of citizens and of legislators. Bad political arguments are as frothy as soapsuds: they get bigger and bigger, until they pop. But both good and bad constitutional arguments are more like blown-in insulation: they fill every last nook of a very cramped space, and then they harden. Over time, arguments based on a right to privacy have tended to weaken and crack; arguments based on equality have grown only stronger.

ESTELLE GRISWOLD BECAME THE DIRECTOR OF the Planned Parenthood League of Connecticut in 1953, the year that Vern Countryman, a professor at Yale Law School and a former law clerk of Justice Douglas, bought a box of condoms from a drugstore in Hamden and then went to the police and asked them to arrest the druggist for violating an 1879 statute banning the sale of contraceptives. Countryman and several of his colleagues at the law school, including Fowler Harper, were interested in challenging the ban by concocting a test case. So was Griswold, who was tired of driving around Connecticut with boxes of diaphragms in the trunk of her car. By 1957, they'd teamed up with Buxton, who agreed to identify patients who could serve as plaintiffs, and with a civil liberties attorney named Catherine Roraback. In 1958 and 1959, Roraback filed complaints on behalf of four married couples, a set of plaintiffs that, like the petitioners in 2015's same-sex-marriage cases, were carefully selected. All but the Trubeks, whose complaint was filed separately, chose anonymity. Jane Doe had suffered a stroke near the end of a pregnancy; the child had been stillborn, and Doe had been partially paralyzed; another pregnancy might end her life. Pauline and Paul Poe had three children born with multiple congenital abnormalities; all three had died shortly after birth. Harold and Hannah Hoe had a genetic incompatibility that led their doctor to strongly recommend against having children.

Banning contraception at a time when the overwhelming majority of Americans used it was, of course, ridiculous. (Justice Potter Stewart, who dissented in *Griswold*, called the Connecticut statute "an uncommonly silly law.") The law was little enforced. Condoms were openly sold in drugstores, and people of means could get other forms of contraception out of state. (Estelle Griswold once asked whether the police intended to "put a gynecological table at the Greenwich toll station" and examine every woman who crossed the state line.) The ban was a real hardship, though, for the poor, and especially for poor women in relationships with men who refused to use condoms. And if the law was ridiculous it was also intransigent. For decades, Planned Parenthood had tried to get it overturned in the Connecticut legislature, to no avail. So the question was: What legal argument could be used to challenge its constitutionality?

The Constitution never mentions sex, marriage, or reproduction. This is because the political order that the Constitution established was a fraternity of free men who, believing themselves to have been created equal, consented to be governed. Women did not and could not give their consent: they were neither free nor equal. Rule over women lay entirely outside a Lockean social contract in a relationship not of liberty and equality but of confinement and subjugation. As Mary Astell wondered, in 1706, "If all Men are born free, how is it that all Women are born Slaves?"

Essentially, the Constitution is inadequate. It speaks directly only to the sort of people who were enfranchised in 1787; the rest of us are left to make arguments by amendment and, failing that, by indirection. Historically, people who were originally left out of the Constitution or who have wanted to make constitutional arguments about things not originally in the Constitution have most often grounded their arguments in the Bill of Rights. This is a disadvantage. During the debates over the ratification of the Constitution, Federalists warned that if a bill of rights was adopted it would severely constrain constitutional argument. Bills of rights prevent kings from abusing the liberties of the people, but in the United States the people are sovereign, and in the Constitution the people grant to the government certain powers, and no others. Alexander Hamilton argued that it was therefore not only unnecessary to make a list of rights held by the people—"Why declare that things shall not be done which there is no power to do?"—but also dangerous, because once such a list was written down it would imply that those were the people's *only* rights.

By the time that Roraback and Harper set about crafting arguments on behalf of their plaintiffs, the Constitution had been much amended. Roraback and Harper chose to base their argument on the Fourteenth Amendment, which lies at the heart of the 2015 same-sex-marriage cases, too. The briefs submitted by the petitioners in *Obergefell v. Hodges* raise two questions: "Does the Fourteenth Amendment require a state to license a marriage between two people of the same sex?" And "Does the Fourteenth Amendment require a state to recognize a marriage between two people of the same sex when their marriage was lawfully licensed and performed out of state?"

The Fourteenth Amendment was first discussed by Congress in 1865; its purpose, in the aftermath of Emancipation, was to guarantee citizenship, due process of the law, and equal protection of the law for all Americans. With this gain came a loss. Section 1 prohibited discrimination by race. Section 2 mandated discrimination by sex: it guaranteed the right to vote not to all citizens but to all "male inhabitants." When Elizabeth Cady Stanton and Susan B. Anthony, who had been fighting for universal suffrage, learned about that language, they straightaway began petitioning Congress for language that would, instead, specifically "prohibit the several States from disenfranchising any of their citizens on the ground of sex." When that failed—the amendment was ratified in 1868—they tried to get universal suffrage incorporated into the Fifteenth Amendment; that failed, too. In 1869, Stanton and Anthony introduced into Congress a proposed Sixteenth Amendment, guaranteeing women the right to vote. And, when that failed, Anthony went to the polls and in 1872 tried to vote, insisting that the privileges and immunities clause of the Fourteenth Amendment had, in fact, enfranchised women. The Court rejected that claim.

The nature of those rejections proved fateful. In dismissing the claims of suffragists, opponents cited their own right to privacy. As one senator put it in 1881, the enfranchisement of women constitutes a breaking in "through a man's household, through his fireside . . . to open to the intrusion of politics and politicians that sacred circle of the family." In 1884, the House Judiciary Committee rejected the proposed Sixteenth Amendment on the ground that women inhabit and must remain confined to a secluded and private sphere: "To the husband, by natural allotment . . . fall the duties which protect and provide for the household, and to the wife the more quiet and secluded but no less exalted duties of mother to their children and mistress of the domicile."

Connecticut's 1879 anti-contraception law, a "little Comstock law"—so called because it's a state version of the federal Comstock Act of 1873—is swathed in the same concern for female chastity, privacy, and seclusion. And so is the constitutional "right to privacy" first defined by Louis Brandeis and Samuel Warren, in a law review essay in

1890 in which they described a violation of that right as any "intrusion upon the domestic circle." The notion of privacy that Justice Douglas, in *Griswold*, said was "older than the Bill of Rights" was actually devised in the Victorian era, and is bound up with the idea that the home lies outside the sphere of politics, and that women, therefore, ought not to be allowed to vote.

It took suffragists decades of sweat and ink to counter that idea. "To get the word male . . . out of the Constitution cost the women of the country fifty-two years of pauseless campaign," Carrie Chapman Catt said after the Nineteenth Amendment was ratified, more than half a century after the Fourteenth.

All amendments are not created equal. As the Yale legal scholar Reva B. Siegel argued in a brilliant *Harvard Law Review* article called "She the People," the Court at first understood the Nineteenth Amendment as making a foundational change by providing grounds for countering discrimination on the basis of sex. But then that interpretation was abandoned, and the Nineteenth Amendment was left, jurisprudentially, to wither.

PEOPLE WHO WANT TO MAKE ARGUMENTS against laws that discriminate against women tend to reach for awkward and imperfect analogies: sex discrimination is like racial discrimination; women are to men as Blacks are to whites. In the appeal that Harper submitted to the U.S. Supreme Court in *Trubek v. Ullman* and *Poe v. Ullman*, he followed *Brown v. Board of Education*, in which, in 1954, the Court had found that segregated schooling violated the Fourteenth Amendment's equal protection clause. In 1961, the Court issued no formal ruling in *Trubek*, but in *Poe*, Justice Felix Frankfurter, writing for a 5–4 majority, ignored the hardships faced by the Poes, and more or less waved the complaint aside, since neither Buxton nor his patients had been arrested. In a dissent three times the length of the majority opinion, Justice John Marshall Harlan hinted that Harper might have been better advised to pursue a different argument. In 1944, the Court had affirmed the existence of constitutional protections for a "private realm of family life which the state cannot enter." (Privacy, in this sense, is figured as a form of liberty, freedom from the intrusion of the state; when people talk about liberty and due process they are talking about this notion of privacy.) In his *Poe* dissent, Harlan wrote that the plaintiffs' "most substantial claim . . . is their right to enjoy the privacy of their marital relations."

That suggestion did not go unheard. Five months after the decision, Estelle Griswold opened a Planned Parenthood clinic in New Haven, with Buxton as its medical director, so that they could get themselves arrested for dispensing birth control—which, in short order, they did. Privacy was the argument that the Yale Law School professor Thomas Emerson stressed in his appeal of their conviction. (Harper died just before the case reached the Supreme Court; Emerson took his place.) *Griswold*, unlike *Trubek* and *Poe*, involved no married couples and certainly no claims like Louise Trubek's equal rights interest in contraception as a means of gaining an education. It did, however, involve an argument about privacy. "The Constitution nowhere refers to a right of privacy in express terms," Emerson argued in his brief. "But various provisions of the Constitution embody separate aspects of it." During oral arguments in March 1965, the justices asked Emerson what part of the Fourteenth Amendment his argument relied on:

JUSTICE HUGO L. BLACK: You're abandoning your idea of any argument under equal protection as such?

MR. EMERSON: We have never made any argument on equal protection as such, Your Honor.

BLACK: You pitch it wholly on due process, with the broad idea that we can look to see how reasonable or unreasonable the decision of the people of Connecticut has been in connection with this statute.

EMERSON: We pitch it on due process in the basic sense, yes, that it is arbitrary and unreasonable, and in the special sense that it constitutes a deprivation of right against invasion of privacy.

In the opinion issued by the Court in June, Douglas, citing Harlan's dissent in *Poe*, insisted that although a "right to privacy" is not mentioned either in the Constitution or in the Bill of Rights, it is nevertheless there, not in words but in the shadow cast by words. He wrote, mystically, that "specific guarantees in the Bill of Rights have penumbras, formed by emanations from those guarantees that help give them life and substance." No one mentioned the Nineteenth Amendment, or the idea of equal rights for men and women.

"There is nothing in the United States Constitution concerning birth, contraception, or abortion," Jay Floyd told the Court in *Roe v. Wade*, when the case was first argued, in 1971. Floyd spoke on behalf of the Dallas County prosecutor, Henry Wade, defending Texas's anti-abortion statutes. When Sarah Weddington, representing Jane Roe, a Texas woman who sought an abortion, was asked by Justice Stewart where in the Constitution she placed her argument against the Texas statutes, she said, in so many words: anywhere it would stick.

> MS. WEDDINGTON: Certainly, under the *Griswold* decision, it appears that the members of the Court in that case were obviously divided as to the specific constitutional framework of the right which they held to exist in the *Griswold* decision. I'm a little reluctant to aspire to a wisdom that the Court was not in agreement on. I do feel that the Ninth Amendment is an appropriate place for the freedom to rest. I think the Fourteenth Amendment is equally an appropriate place, under the rights of persons to life, liberty, and the pursuit of happiness. I think that in as far as "liberty" is meaningful, that liberty to these women would mean liberty from being forced to continue the unwanted pregnancy.
>
> JUSTICE POTTER STEWART: You're relying, in this branch of the argument, simply on the Due Process clause of the Fourteenth Amendment?
>
> WEDDINGTON: We had originally brought this suit alleging both the Due Process clause, Equal Protection clause, the Ninth Amendment, and a variety of others.
>
> STEWART: And anything else that might be applicable?
>
> WEDDINGTON: Yes, right.

But in the Court's decision Justice Harry Blackmun, writing for the majority, located the right to an abortion in a right to privacy, wherever in the Constitution or amendments anyone cared to find it.

Roe, of course, incited protest on the right. But by the 1980s the Court's opinion was being criticized on the left, too, as a failure of

legal reasoning and even as a betrayal of the idea of equality, especially after the Equal Rights Amendment, first introduced in Congress in 1923, and passed by Congress in 1972, fell short of passage in
the states before its ratification deadline, in 1982. "A right to privacy
looks like an injury got up as a gift," the feminist legal theorist Catharine MacKinnon argued in 1983, since "privacy doctrine reaffirms and
reinforces what the feminist critique of sexuality criticizes: the public/
private split." In 1984, Ruth Bader Ginsburg, then on the U.S. Court
of Appeals in the District of Columbia, regretted that the Supreme
Court had "treated reproductive autonomy under a substantive due
process/personal autonomy headline not expressly linked to discrimination against women." Ginsburg found the Court's opinion in *Roe*
wanting for a number of reasons; among them was its failure to pay any
attention to discrimination against women, or to a woman's "ability to
stand in relation to man, society, and the state as an independent, self-
sustaining, equal citizen."

In *Bowers v. Hardwick*, in 1986, the Court refused to overturn a
ban on sodomy in Georgia, disagreeing with the assertion of Bowers's
attorney that the law was a violation of a right to privacy established
by the chain of cases that began with *Griswold*, because "no connection between family, marriage, or procreation, on the one hand, and
homosexual activity, on the other, has been demonstrated," and therefore the case turned on an asserted "fundamental right to engage in
homosexual sodomy," which, the Court determined, did not exist.
But in a stinging dissent Justice Blackmun countered that the case
did indeed turn on a right to privacy, because "if that right means
anything, it means that, before Georgia can prosecute its citizens for
making choices about the most intimate aspects of their lives, it must
do more than assert that the choice they have made is an 'abominable
crime not fit to be named among Christians.'"

The year after Bowers, Harvard Law School's Martha Minow wrote
an essay called "We, the Family," in which she argued that, despite
the Court's claim that it was relying on a long-standing tradition, the
privacy doctrine it had fashioned from *Griswold* to *Bowers* was new,
incoherent, and unpredictable. "The family is not mentioned in the
Constitution," Minow pointed out, adding that Douglas's language

about "a right of privacy older than the Bill of Rights" was the language of fiction.

In the 1980s and '90s, while the reproductive rights movement struggled against efforts to overturn or roll back *Roe*, the gay rights movement, fighting AIDS, grew. "Privacy" remained a watchword of the reproductive rights movement—and abortion became more hidden, and more difficult to procure—but LGBT activists insisted on the importance and the urgency of visibility, of pride, and of coming out. The legal reasoning employed by these two movements began to split. Privacy arguments, long troubling to feminists, were especially troubling to gay rights activists. And the divide widened when the fight to overturn anti-sodomy laws became a fight for same-sex marriage, a movement whose watchword is "equality." In many ways, this split made sense: sexuality and reproduction may be private but, as the historian Nancy F. Cott demonstrated in the book *Public Vows*, marriage is public. (Cott, a colleague of mine, has been an expert witness in many same-sex-marriage cases.) Still, contraception and abortion don't lie entirely outside the state, either, as the continued agitation over public funding of health care for women has made abundantly clear.

Feminist legal scholars began trying to put the equality back into reproductive rights cases, not least as a matter of historical analysis, pointing out that, in *Griswold* and *Roe*, amicus briefs submitted on behalf of the plaintiffs by organizations that included the ACLU and Planned Parenthood made equality arguments that the Court simply ignored, preferring to base its opinion in these cases on privacy. (The same was true in *Bowers*: organizations like the Lambda Legal Defense and Education Fund submitted amicus briefs arguing equal protection, but the Court talked about privacy.) The gay rights movement learned from that dilemma.

Meanwhile, privacy doctrine left reproductive rights vulnerable. In *Burwell v. Hobby Lobby*, in 2014, the Supreme Court ruled that the religious liberty of a for-profit corporation, Hobby Lobby, had been infringed upon by the Affordable Care Act's mandate that employers provide their employees with health insurance that covers contraception. (Similar religious liberty claims have been and will continue to be made against same-sex marriage.) The Department of Health and

Human Services argued against Hobby Lobby's objections, but the Court found its argument wanting: "HHS asserts that the contraceptive mandate serves a variety of important interests, but many of these are couched in very broad terms, such as promoting 'public health' and 'gender equality.'" Justice Ginsburg, in a sharply worded dissent, quoted the Court's opinion in a 1992 reproductive rights case, *Planned Parenthood v. Casey*: "The ability of women to participate equally in the economic and social life of the Nation has been facilitated by their ability to control their reproductive lives." Justices Breyer, Sotomayor, and Kagan joined in Ginsburg's dissent, though, obviously, they failed to convince their brethren on the bench. Counterfactuals are famously foolish, not to mention futile. Still, it's hard not to ask: If the Nineteenth Amendment had been a broadway in constitutional law, instead of a dead end, and if, beginning with, say, *Trubek v. Ullman*, reproductive rights cases had proceeded from arguments for equality, rather than for privacy, would Justices Scalia, Alito, Kennedy, Thomas, and Roberts still have been able to rule in favor of Hobby Lobby?

THE FORK IN THE CONSTITUTIONAL ROAD that led the reproductive rights movement to *Hobby Lobby* and the gay rights movement to *Obergefell* came in 2003. In June of that year, in *Lawrence v. Texas*, the Supreme Court overruled *Bowers* by declaring a Texas sodomy law unconstitutional. Presented with two Fourteenth Amendment arguments, a due process privacy argument and an equal protection argument, Justice Kennedy, in the majority opinion, explained that the Court had decided the case on the strength of the Griswoldian privacy argument. In a concurring opinion, Justice Sandra Day O'Connor said that she based her decision on the equal protection argument, asserting that the Texas law constituted sex discrimination: a man could not be prosecuted for engaging in a particular activity with a woman but could be prosecuted for engaging in that same activity with a man. O'Connor's reasoning, not Kennedy's, marked the way forward for LGBT litigation that turned, increasingly, to marriage equality.

In November 2003, five months after the ruling in *Lawrence*, the Massachusetts Supreme Judicial Court issued a decision in *Goodridge v. Department of Public Health*. Mary Bonauto, a lawyer for GLAD, the Gay and Lesbian Advocates and Defenders, argued on behalf of seven couples that Massachusetts' marriage licensing law "violates the equality rights" guaranteed in the state's constitution. Bonauto cited privacy doctrine, but she based her argument on equal protection, telling the court, "To deny individuals the right to seek personal fulfillment through marriage is, at the most basic level, a denial of the equal citizenship of gay and lesbian people." Chief Justice Margaret Marshall agreed. In a ruling that established Massachusetts as the first state to guarantee same-sex marriage as a constitutional right, Marshall, following Bonauto, discussed the private nature of intimate family relationships but stressed their civil and public role in communities:

> Barred access to the protections, benefits, and obligations of civil marriage, a person who enters into an intimate, exclusive union with another of the same sex is arbitrarily deprived of membership in one of our community's most rewarding and cherished institutions. That exclusion is incompatible with the constitutional principles of respect for individual autonomy and equality under law.

Marshall also cited *Loving v. Virginia*, the 1967 Supreme Court case that struck down a ban on interracial marriage, drawing an analogy between racial discrimination (if a Black person can marry a Black person but cannot marry a white person, that is discrimination by race) and sex discrimination (if a man can marry a woman but cannot marry a man, that is discrimination by sex).

The marriage bans passed in Kentucky, Michigan, Ohio, and Tennessee, whose constitutionality the U.S. Supreme Court considered in 2015, were passed in reaction to Marshall's decision. The best predictor of how the Court might think about *Obergefell* is Justice Kennedy's majority opinion in *Windsor*, in which he found that the Defense of Marriage Act violated "the Constitution's guarantee of equality"— specifically, the equal protection clauses of the Fifth and the Fourteenth Amendments. He did not utter the word "privacy."

Mary Bonauto made the case for the petitioners in *Obergefell*. The Fourteenth Amendment's equal protection clause provides "enduring guarantees" against discrimination, she said. The justices ignored her constitutional arguments and wandered around in ancient history. Justice Kennedy talked about life thousands and thousands of years ago.

He mentioned the Kalahari, anthropology, "ancient peoples." Bonauto talked about the Constitution. Justice Alito invoked Plato. Bonauto talked about American history. "When our nation did form into this union in 1787 and then when it affirmed the Fourteenth Amendment in 1868," she told the Court, "that's when we made—our nation collectively made—a commitment to individual liberty and equality."

"You're not seeking to join the institution," Chief Justice John Roberts told her. "You're seeking to change what the institution is." Justice Ginsburg interjected that marriage was hardly changeless. "You wouldn't be asking for this relief if the law of marriage was what it was a millennium ago," she said, pointing out the indebtedness of the gay rights and marriage equality movements to the movements for reproductive and women's rights. "There was a change in the institution of marriage, to make it egalitarian. When it wasn't egalitarian, same-sex unions wouldn't fit into what marriage was." Bonauto had a kind of refrain: "Times can blind." Justice Alito said that marriage had been defined as being between a man and a woman for centuries; Bonauto said, "Times can blind."

Donald B. Verrilli Jr., the solicitor general, followed Bonauto and also argued for marriage equality. Privacy didn't come up. Gay men and lesbians "deserve the equal protection of the laws, and they deserve it now," Verrilli said. A protester shouted, "Homosexuality is an abomination!" As the police escorted the protester out of the courtroom, the cry "Burn in hell!" could be heard from the hall.

THE BABY THAT LOUISE TRUBEK was carrying the day she sat in the Supreme Court to listen to oral arguments in *Trubek v. Ullman* was born in September 1961. Her name is Jessica. The Trubeks had two more daughters. Louise Trubek stayed home to take care of them when they were young. In 1970, she went back to work, as a public interest lawyer. "One of the first cases I was involved in had to do with equal rights," she told me. "Myself, I never was that interested in the privacy argument."

There is a lesson in the past fifty years of litigation. When the fight for equal rights for women narrowed to a fight for reproductive rights, defended on the ground of privacy, it weakened. But when the fight for gay rights became a fight for same-sex marriage, asserted on the ground of equality, it got stronger and stronger.

Jessica Trubek is fifty-three and lives in Brooklyn with her wife, Margie Rubins, and their young daughter. "I didn't think that we were going to be able to get married in our lifetime," Trubek told me. They met in 1998, when they were both working at Long Island University. Trubek, who has a PhD, used to teach social studies, but she's now a social worker, attending to low-income families in East New York. Right after Vermont began allowing civil unions, Trubek and Rubins had a ceremony there, but after Massachusetts began allowing same-sex marriage, and some of their friends got married in Province-town, they decided to wait for federal recognition, even though they were under some pressure at home. "Our daughter wanted us to get married," Trubek says. The Court issued its ruling in *Windsor*, striking down the Defense of Marriage Act, in June 2013; Trubek and Rubins married that September. Their daughter was ten. They had a Jewish wedding in Prospect Park, in front of a tree they'd had planted there when their daughter was born.

It was a beautiful day. All the family was there. Louise and Dave Trubek read one of the seven blessings. Trubek and Rubins's daughter sang "Lean on Me," a song about love, and solace. *I'll be your friend,* that little girl sang. *I'll help you carry on.*

—2015

Postscript: In Obergefell, *in 2015, the Supreme Court decided in favor of the plaintiffs.*

THE RETURN OF
THE PERVERT

IN SEPTEMBER 1937, IN THE *NEW YORK HERALD TRI-
bune*, J. Edgar Hoover declared "War on the Sex Criminal!"
Urging an end to "the present apathy of the public to known perverts,"
the director of the FBI insisted that "the sex fiend is a progressive
criminal," that "every sex criminal is a potential murderer," and that,
therefore, any man arrested for committing a sex crime, of any scale,
beginning with the writing of obscene letters, should be examined by
a psychiatrist, possibly isolated from society, and considered for surgical treatment. Criminal sex offenses, at the time, included sodomy,
often described as degeneracy. In 1938, Hoover opened a file on "Sex
Degenerates and Sex Offenders" and by 1942 had begun compiling a
list of "Sex Perverts in Government Service." The press eagerly joined
the war. Newspaper coverage of the plague of perverts grew so fast that
by the end of 1937, the *New York Times* had added a new category to
its index: "sex crimes." Citizens answered Hoover's call, too. In Ohio,
driven by a series of exposés in the *Cleveland Plain Dealer*, they pressed
legislators to pass a new law, confining alleged sex offenders to mental
hospitals, indefinitely. "Burn them alive," one Iowan wrote to Hoover.
Before the end of the decade, Michigan, Illinois, Minnesota, and California had passed "sexual psychopath laws," too. By 1956, twenty-
four states had sexual psychopath laws, and by 1965, thirty, punishing
"sexual misconduct," with indefinite commitment, the sexual psychopath having been defined as "any person, not insane, who by a course
of repeated misconduct in sexual matters has evidenced such lack of
power to control his sexual impulses as to be dangerous to other persons because he is likely to attack or otherwise inflict injury, loss, pain,
or other evil on the objects of his desire." That could mean just about
anything, though what it mainly meant was that it gave law enforcement a license to round up men suspected of sodomy, on the theory
that one type of sexual misconduct would, inevitably, lead to another.

The #MeToo movement that emerged, decades later, was not the same as Hoover's War on the Sex Criminal. It's not fair to compare gay men targeted by the FBI, police vice squads, and citizens' pervert elimination campaigns in the middle decades of the twentieth century to men accused by their long-silenced coworkers, employees, students, or former sexual partners of sexual harassment and sexual assault in the early decades of the twenty-first. #MeToo, which was started in 2006 by activist Tarana Burke, was a political movement driven by, and driving, shifting norms about sex and dominance, power and desire, and it hoped to usher in fundamental change: a new sexual ethic of restraint and a new judicial era of long-sought and long-denied equality before the law. Still, the version that exploded on Twitter starting in 2017, had an uncomfortable amount in common with Hoover's war, especially in sensibility, and ruthlessness.

Like Hoover's war, the #MeToo movement was very difficult to criticize, publicly. Activists of the late 2010s suggested that anyone who questioned the movement was silencing women. When writers from Margaret Atwood to Susan Faludi raised concerns about the possible unintended consequences of the movement's tactics, #MeToo activists, who were often younger women, answered with mockery, invoking a never-trust-anyone-over-forty generational divide: older women just don't get it, and should get out of the way. And maybe that was true, and even fair. But the problem of the past remained: the annals of history, which contain an endless chronicle of stories that could have been written by Shirley Jackson, demonstrate that women are no less likely than men to become convinced of their matchless righteousness, form a mob, lambaste anyone who calls for caution, and commit grave injustices in the name of sexual purity. That makes it worth considering to what degree, for all the movement's origins in a certain strain of feminism and notwithstanding its earnest and determined pursuit of justice for women who have been harassed, assaulted, and abused, #MeToo was also a sex panic.

SEX PANICS, WHICH ARE THE PRODUCTS of changing ideas about sex, are expressions of political power, or, equally often, of political helplessness. They generally begin with a single, terribly disturbing case, sensationally reported, that purports to cast light on an unseen but widespread and longstanding epidemic, behavior that has always been there, but about which the public is apathetic. Hoover's 1937 campaign was set off by the murder of a ten-year-old boy, kidnapped from his family's living room in Tacoma, Washington, in 1936, two days after Christmas. In January 1937, the boy's horribly brutalized body was found, naked and bound, by the side of a road, "the victim of a degenerate." The FBI considered twenty-four thousand possible suspects; the murder was never solved. Newspapers and magazines widened and deepened readers' fears, running endless stories like "Can We End Sex Crimes?" and "Are Sex Crimes Due to Sex?"

Sex panics obscure the actual object of a culture's fears. The late 1930s "war on the sex criminal," like all sex panics, bore little relationship to any actual "sex-crime wave," because there wasn't one. Instead, the panic was a consequence of a Depression-driven rise in the number of aimless men and an attendant crisis of masculinity; the growing influence of psychiatry on the law; a backlash against the anti-Victorian idea, widely expressed in the 1920s, that women have sexual desires of their own; and the interest of a newly bureaucratized federal government in a newly medicalized, and criminalized, notion of homosexuality. As Stanford historian Estelle Freedman has argued, "the concept of the sexual psychopath provided a boundary within which Americans renegotiated the definitions of sexual normality." In practice, prosecuting "aggressive male sexual deviance," mainly involved defining gay men as "perverts," language that has enjoyed a resurgence since the rise of the #MeToo movement. "TODAY'S PERV," ran one front-page headline in the *New York Daily News*. In December 2017, the *New York Post* announced a "pervnado."

The panic that began in 1937 died down during the Second World War but flared back up after the peace. (Unsurprisingly, by the 1940s, it had turned on Hoover himself, when rumors of his homosexuality began to circulate.) In 1946, after the murder of a girl in Chicago led to the rounding up of suspected homosexuals, one gay man wrote to another, "why they don't round us all up and kill us I don't know." New institutes for the study and treatment of sex deviates opened, including the New York State Sex Delinquency Research Project; fifteen states formed commissions to study sex deviance. "How Safe is Your Daughter?" Hoover asked in a magazine essay in 1947, deploying data from the FBI's Sex Offenders File and recommitting the nation to the war on sex crime. "Should wild beasts break out of circus cages, a whole city would be mobilized instantly," Hoover wrote. "But depraved human beings, more savage than beasts, are permitted to rove America almost at will." The beasts, then, were gay men, one step away from becoming pedophiles, two steps away from becoming murderers, and as likely to attack women and girls as men and boys. "The homosexual is an inveterate seducer of the young of both sexes," reported the author of *The Sexual Criminal* in 1949, the year *Colliers'* ran a thirteen-part series called "The Terror in Our Cities." *The New Yorker* published Shirley Jackson's story "The Lottery" in 1948, right when citizens were busy forming scapegoating brigades, like DC's Pervert Elimination Campaign. "Every mother of a daughter—and I am one—can not rest with sex perverts at large," one woman wrote to her governor in 1950. "Dee-Vees," short for "deviates," became a schoolyard taunt.

"The Lottery," in which the residents of a small New England town engage in a ritual stoning, seemed so true to life to so many readers of *The New Yorker* that they took it for truth. (At the time, as Jackson's biographer Ruth Franklin has pointed out, the magazine didn't distinguish reported pieces from short stories.) Jackson got so many letters asking so many questions that an assistant at *The New Yorker* sent out a stock reply, explaining that she'd made it all up: "She has chosen a nameless little village to show, in microcosm, how the forces of belligerence, persecution, and vindictiveness are, in mankind, endless and traditional and that their targets are chosen without reason." But, in fact, she hadn't entirely made it up. The forces of persecution and vindictiveness were everywhere.

SEX PANICS SUBVERT JUDICIAL PROCESSES. From the late 1930s through the 1950s, as the number of states with sexual psychopath laws grew, the evidence required for commitment shrank. (Black men brought up on charges of sexual misconduct were generally sent to prison; white men were more usually sent to insane asylums.) "Such factors as the presumption of innocence, proof beyond a reasonable doubt and all of the other valuable and ancient safeguards by which the person accused of crime has been surrounded are perfectly proper in their correct application," one Nebraska judge remarked in 1949. "Still they have no more logical place in the investigation of a known or suspected corrupter of the minds and bodies of little children than in the case of the insane person before the insanity board." In the 2010s, the believe-the-women rhetoric of #MeToo, and of Title IX investigations, took a not unrelated position: women, like "little children," seemed to have become so powerless, relative to men, that standards like the presumption of innocence and proof beyond a reasonable doubt had little place in any confrontation with a man who is a known or suspected perpetrator of a sex crime. Historically, this is always a devil's bargain.

The modern sex panic's signature characteristic is an inability and unwillingness to distinguish between degrees of misconduct. "You know, there's a difference between, you know, patting someone on the butt and rape or child molestation, right?" the actor Matt Damon said in 2017, in a television interview. "Both of those behaviors need to be confronted and eradicated without question, but they shouldn't be conflated, right?" For this, Damon was denounced by #MeToo activists. Eventually, he gave another television interview, to issue a public apology. This aversion to distinctions derived, in part, from mid-twentieth-century psychiatry's belief in homosexuality as a form of progressive degeneracy, an inevitable descent into the final debauchery. Under the sexual psychopath laws passed beginning in 1937, whether the sex was violent or nonviolent, consensual or nonconsensual mattered not at all, since the theory was that even nonviolent, consensual sex, if deviant, will always lead to something worse. "Once a man assumes the role of homosexual, he often throws off all moral restraints," according to a story published in *Coronet* magazine in 1950. "Some male sex deviants do not stop with infecting their often-innocent partners: they descend through perversions to other forms of depravity, such as drug addiction, burglary, sadism, and even murder."

THE POSTWAR SEX PANIC WAS CHIEFLY a campaign against gay men, carried out at a time of tremendous anxiety about the American family and about U.S. national security, but it was also part of a campaign of the rising conservative movement to replace the domestic welfare commitments of the New Deal, seen by critics as feminine, with a muscular and masculine display of the power of the national security state. In 1947, a year in which Hoover warned that "depraved human beings, more savage than beasts, are permitted to rove America almost at will," thirty-one homosexuals employed by the U.S. Department of State were fired under the terms of a set of "security principles" dictating the dismissal of people known for "habitual drunkenness, sexual perversion, moral turpitude, financial irresponsibility or criminal record." Twenty-eight more gay men were fired in 1948, and thirty-one in 1949. This policy set the stage for McCarthyism. On February 7, 1950, in Wheeling, West Virginia, Joseph McCarthy warned of "known communists" in the employ of the federal government. He said, "I have here in my hand a list of two hundred and five . . . names that were known to the Secretary of State and who nevertheless are still working and shaping the policy of the State Department."

McCarthy's warning gained credibility when, days after his Wheeling speech, John Peurifoy, deputy undersecretary of state, said that while there weren't any communists in the State Department, ninety-one men, homosexuals, had been fired because they were deemed to be "security risks." Both the sequence of events and these two lists—McCarthy's list of 204 communists and Peurifoy's actual list of 91 homosexuals fired between 1947 and 1949, were so widely confused in the press that one Republican representative from Illinois praised McCarthy for the earlier purge: "He has forced the State Department to fire 91 sex perverts."

The compiling of public and private lists of suspected perverts, a notable feature of the #MeToo movement, in the form of lists like 2017's Shitty Media Men Google spreadsheet, a crowdsourced list of allegations and rumors, drove the postwar panic as well. (And questioning of these methods led, invariably, to charges of disloyalty, and of harboring sympathy for the enemy, a form of compassion derided as "himpathy.") In 1950, a week after Peurifoy's statement, Roy Blick, head of the DC police's Morals Division, testified during classified hearings on "the infiltration of subversives and moral perverts into the executive branch of the United States Government" that there were five thousand homosexuals in Washington and that of these nearly four thousand worked for the federal government; the story was leaked to the press. Blick called for a national task force. He said, "There is a need in this country for a central bureau for records of homosexuals and perverts of all types." By April, Blick had forwarded to Hoover a list of 393 federal employees who had been arrested in Washington since 1947 "on charges of sexual irregularities." Hoover began compiling his own list, in what was known, internally, as the FBI's Sex Deviates Program.

On the night of March 31, 1950, as the crusade blazed on, Harvard literature professor F. O. Matthiessen, Matty to his friends, had dinner at a colleague's house and then, instead of heading home, checked into a hotel in Boston. Matthiessen, a brilliant literary critic best known for his 1941 book *American Renaissance: Art and Expression in the Age of Emerson and Whitman*, had lived for a quarter century with his partner, the artist Russell Cheney. Despite grieving Cheney's death in 1945, Matthiessen had rallied. "Our age has had no escape from an awareness of history," he'd said at a lecture in 1947. "Much of that history has been hard and full of suffering. But now we have the luxury of an historical awareness of another sort, of an occasion not of anxiety but of promise. We may speak without exaggeration of this occasion as historic, since we have come here to enact anew the chief function of culture and humanism, to bring man again into communication with man." But by April 1950, Matthiessen expected to be persecuted as a communist and had begun to fear exposure of his homosexuality. He took an elevator to a room on the twelfth story of that Boston hotel and threw himself out the window. He was forty-eight.

And still burned the fire. That summer, North Carolina senator Clyde Hoey launched a congressional investigation into the "Employment of Homosexuals and Other Sex Perverts in Government." The confidential Hoey report applied the language of the sexual psychopath to the demands of the Cold War. "Those who engage in overt acts of perversion lack the emotional stability of normal persons," it declared, and "the lack of emotional stability which is found in most sex perverts and the weakness of their moral fiber, makes them susceptible to the blandishments of the foreign espionage agent."

As with #MeToo, the postwar pervert-elimination campaign looked to Hollywood and tapped into the public's fascination with celebrities, as well as its preference for the erotic blandishments of public shaming, immediate and satisfying, over the toil and delay of criminal prosecution. Hollywood heartthrob Tab Hunter, who had been arrested on a morals charge in 1950, was outed by *Confidential* magazine. So was the MGM movie star Van Johnson, in a September 1954 story titled "The Untold Story of Van Johnson." In 1956, *Confidential* ran a story called "When Harvard Was Home Sweet Homo," about an allegedly all-gay male dorm whose residents "wore enough rouge, lipstick and eyebrow pencil to pass as short-haired coeds from neighboring Radcliffe College for Women." Colleges, by its logic, were good places to hunt for perverts, too.

SEX PANICS ARE POLITICS by other means; they achieve political ends by methods other than elections. #MeToo, which exploded in October 2017, was, among many other things, a resistance movement aimed at toppling the then newly elected American president, Donald Trump. Trump's litany of alleged and proven abuses of women, spanning decades, included accusations of rape by one of his former wives; the frequent and persistent use of language meant to diminish and demean women and women's bodies; the hiring of prostitutes; authorizing a blackmail payment to a porn star; dozens of charges of sexual harassment and assault; and, not least, his own boasting about attacking women. Republicans and Democrats tended to fall on different sides of the issue, and the #MeToo movement was generally seen as helping Democrats—in January 2018, looking ahead to the midterm elections, the *New York Times* asked, "Can Democrats Follow #MeToo to Victory?"—and answered, more or less, yes, unless it hurts them, in the form of a voter backlash. The movement, at its height, took down leading Democrats, from Minnesota senator Al Franken—guilty of seemingly very little at all but who, pressured by his party, resigned— and New York governor Andrew Cuomo, forced from office in the wake of a series of allegations by former members of his staff. Yet it remained chiefly a crusade of the left.

Decades earlier, the politics of the postwar purge of perverts had gone in the other direction, a conservative attack on liberals. It aimed, in part, to eliminate intellectuals in the federal government, men and women who were often derided as "eggheads." The term, inspired by the Illinois Democrat Adlai Stevenson, was coined in 1952 by Louis Bromfield to describe "a person of spurious intellectual pretensions, often a professor or the protégé of a professor; fundamentally superficial, over-emotional and feminine in reactions to any problems." The term connoted, as well, a vague homosexuality. One congressman described leftover New Dealers as "short-haired women and longhaired men messing into everybody's personal affairs and lives." In 1953, after Stevenson, the Democratic nominee, lost the presidency to Dwight Eisenhower, *Confidential*, in "How That Stevenson Rumor Started" ("By phone, on planes and trains, from the racket of factory assembly-lines to the quiet of hospital rooms, from the big-town sharpies to unsophisticated villagers, it burned the ears of a nation"), reported that Stevenson "was well known as Adeline" and said his ex-wife, Ellen, had told a reporter that the "real reason" for their divorce "reflected on the manhood of the father of her three sons."

Three developments together ended the purge of "perverts": the gay liberation movement, the due process revolution, and the sexual revolution. The gay rights movement emerged as a response to the criminal prosecution of homosexuals. For years, men arrested on "morals charges" pled guilty, so as to avoid the spectacle of a trial. In 1949, the Los Angeles Police arrested 74 men for sodomy, 351 men for sex perversion, and 1,319 men for "lewd vagrancy." The next year, the city required all men arrested on such charges to register as sex criminals. In 1952, Dale Jennings, a thirty-four-year-old veteran arrested in Los Angeles, refused to plead guilty. The Mattachine Society, founded in Los Angeles in 1950 and the nation's first homosexual rights organization, raised money for his defense. His lawyer argued that being homosexual was not a crime. The trial resulted in a hung jury. Jennings wrote about his experience in *ONE: The Homosexual Magazine* the next year, urging, "Were all homosexuals and bisexuals to unite militantly, unjust laws and corruption would crumble in short order and we, as a nation, could go on to meet the really important problems which face us." That movement saw one of its first successes in 1958 when, in *One Inc. v. Olesen,* the Supreme Court refused to classify *ONE* magazine as obscenity. By the middle of the 1960s, gay activists were protesting criminal statutes as forms of discrimination.

The due process revolution, under the Warren Court, made applicable to the states the due process clause of the Fourteenth Amendment and elements of the Bill of Rights, including the guarantee against cruel and unusual punishment, the right to a trial by jury, and protection against self-incrimination. The due-process-violating sexual psychopath statutes began to be dismantled, state by state, critics having observed, for instance, that under these statutes, "the truly dangerous offender is usually subjected to the criminal sanction, and the minor offender is caught up in the sex-psychopath procedures." Crimes should be prosecuted as crimes, critics charged, and people who are mentally ill should receive medical treatment. "The Sexual Psychopath Act should be abolished," wrote one legal scholar about DC's statute in 1970. "It is a repressive anachronism [and] . . . violates the basic constitutional concepts of liberty and due process."

The sexual revolution decriminalized and destigmatized all manner of behavior, from premarital sex and adultery to anal and oral sex to pornography and contraception. New penal codes, like one adopted in Connecticut in 1971, abandoned the category of "sexual psychopath" but replaced it with new categories of "sexual misconduct," a term that escaped the courts and entered popular culture during the Watergate hearings, when it emerged that the Campaign to Re-elect the President had paid a California lawyer named Don Segretti to commit political dirty tricks, work Segretti dubbed "ratfucking," that included producing fake letters about Edmund Muskie—on stolen Muskie stationery—that contained allegations of what newspapers delicately described as sexual misconduct.

Hoover's Sex Deviates Program ended at his death in 1972; the FBI soon afterward destroyed the files. In 1973, the American Psychiatric Association declassified homosexuality as a mental illness. By 1977, the term "sexual misconduct" had begun to be overtaken by "sexual harassment." That year, in *Alexander v. Yale*, three female students sued the university. Advised by Catherine MacKinnon, a twenty-eight-year-old graduate of the Yale Law School who was at the time preparing a book called *Sexual Harassment in the Workplace*, they alleged that the harassment was illegal because it was a form of sex discrimination, and therefore in violation of Title IX of a 1972 equal opportunity in education act.

New sex panics followed in the 1980s and 1990s, not least in a movement that aimed to recover the memories of victims of incest and childhood sexual abuse, and in the feminist campaign against pornography, which was led by MacKinnon, the beginning of the sexual counterrevolution. As the gay rights movement gained strength, even as gay men were felled by the AIDS epidemic, the discredited sexual psychopath (no longer a cover term for homosexual) was reimagined as the "sex offender" (closely associated with both pedophilia and pornography), who became the subject of new medical fascination and criminal restriction. While the LGBTQ movement saw signal victories in the first two decades of the twenty-first century, sex offenders, as more than one historian has argued, became "the new queers," men whose sexual conduct leads not only to criminal prosecution but also to public denunciation (including the sordid voyeurism that begins with the television series *To Catch a Predator*), the deprivation of civil liberties, and even the wearing of badges. Public notices outside their homes announced, "A Convicted Sex Offender Lives at This Location."

MacKinnon took a bow. "The #MeToo movement is accomplishing what sexual harassment law to date has not," she wrote in the *Times* in 2018. Did it? Or did it, instead, or also, add yet one more chapter to the sorry history of political terror? Either way, the eradication of the pervert—the counterrevolutionary crusade against the degenerate sex fiend—is a campaign that will be waged and waged again, and, as a proxy for politics, it will never be won.

—2018, FOR A PANEL DISCUSSION AT THE
RADCLIFFE INSTITUTE FOR ADVANCED STUDY

THE PARENT TRAP

IN 1925, LELA V. SCOPES, TWENTY-EIGHT, WAS TURNED down for a job teaching mathematics at a high school in Paducah, Kentucky, her hometown. She had taught in the Paducah schools before going to Lexington to finish college at the University of Kentucky. But that summer her younger brother, John T. Scopes, was set to be tried for the crime of teaching evolution in a high school biology class in Dayton, Tennessee, in violation of state law, and Lela Scopes had refused to denounce either her kin or Charles Darwin. It didn't matter that evolution doesn't ordinarily come up in an algebra class. And it didn't matter that Kentucky's own anti-evolution law had been defeated. "Miss Scopes loses her post because she is in sympathy with her brother's stand," the *Times* reported.

In the 1920s, legislatures in twenty states, most of them in the South, considered thirty-seven anti-evolution measures. Kentucky's bill, proposed in 1922, had been the first. It banned teaching, or countenancing the teaching of, "Darwinism, atheism, agnosticism, or the theory of evolution in so far as it pertains to the origin of man." The bill failed to pass the House by a single vote. Tennessee's law, passed in 1925, made it a crime for teachers in publicly funded schools "to teach any theory that denies the story of the Divine Creation of man as taught in the Bible, and to teach instead that man has descended from a lower order of animals." Scopes challenged the law deliberately, as part of an effort by the ACLU to bring a test case to court. His trial, billed as the trial of the century, was the first to be broadcast live on the radio. It went out across the country, to a nation, rapt.

A century later, the battle over public education that afflicted the 1920s has started up again, this time over the teaching of American history. Since 2020, with the murder of George Floyd and the advance of the Black Lives Matter movement, seventeen states have made efforts to expand the teaching of one sort of history, sometimes called anti-racist history, while thirty-six states have made efforts to restrict that very same kind of instruction. In 2020, Connecticut became the first state to require African American and Latino American history. In 2021, Maine passed An Act to Integrate African American Studies into American History Education, and Illinois added a requirement mandating a unit on Asian American history.

On the blackboard on the other side of the classroom are scrawled what might be called anti-anti-racism measures. Some ban the *Times*'s 1619 Project, or ethnic studies, or training in diversity, inclusion, and belonging, or the bugbear known as critical race theory. Most, like a bill recently introduced in West Virginia, prohibit "race or sex stereo-typing," "race or sex scapegoating," and the teaching of "divisive concepts"—for instance, the idea that "the United States is fundamen-tally racist or sexist," or that "an individual, by virtue of his or her race or sex, is inherently racist, sexist or oppressive, whether consciously or unconsciously."

While all this has been happening, I've been working on a U.S. his-tory textbook, so it's been weird to watch lawmakers try their hands at writing American history, and horrible to see what the ferment is doing to public school teachers. In Virginia, Governor Glenn Youn-gkin set up an email tip line "for parents to send us any instances where they feel that their fundamental rights are being violated . . . or where there are inherently divisive practices in their schools." There and elsewhere, parents are harassing school boards and reporting on teachers, at a time when teachers, who earn too little and are asked to do too much, are already exhausted by battles over remote instruction and mask and vaccine mandates and, not least, by witnessing, without being able to repair, the damage the pandemic has inflicted on their students. Kids carry the burdens of loss, uncertainty, and shaken faith on their narrow shoulders, tucked inside their backpacks. Now, with schools open and masks coming off, teachers are left trying to figure out not only how to care for them but also what to teach, and how to teach it, without losing their jobs owing to complaints filed by parents.

There's a rock, and a hard place, and then there's a classroom. Con-sider the dilemma of teachers in New Mexico. In January 2022, a month before the state's Public Education Department finalized a new social studies curriculum that includes a unit on inequality and justice in which students are asked to "explore inequity throughout the history of the United States and its connection to conflict that arises today," Republican lawmakers proposed a ban on teaching "the idea that social problems are created by racist or patriarchal societal structures and systems." The law, if passed, would make the state's own curriculum a crime.

Evolution is a theory of change. But in February—a hundred years, nearly to the day, after the Kentucky legislature debated the nation's first anti-evolution bill—Republicans in Kentucky introduced a bill that mandates the teaching of twenty-four historical documents, beginning with the 1620 Mayflower Compact and ending with Ronald Reagan's 1964 speech "A Time for Choosing." My own account of American history ends with the 2021 insurrection at the Capitol, and "The Hill We Climb," the poem that Amanda Gorman recited at Joe Biden's inauguration. "Let the globe, if nothing else, say this is true: / That even as we grieved, we grew."

Did we, though? In the 1920s, the curriculum in question was biology; in the 2020s, it's history. Both conflicts followed a global pandemic and fights over public education that pitted the rights of parents against the power of the state. It's not clear who'll win this time. It's not even clear who won last time. But the distinction between these two moments is less than it seems: what was once contested as a matter of biology—can people change?—has come to be contested as a matter of history. Still, this fight isn't really about history. It's about political power. Conservatives believe they can win midterm elections, and maybe even the presidency, by whipping up a frenzy about "parents' rights," and many are also in it for another long game, a hundred years' war: the campaign against public education.

BEFORE STATES BEGAN DECIDING what schools would require—from textbooks to vaccines—they had to require children to attend school. That happened in the Progressive Era, early in the past century, when a Progressive strain ran through not only the Progressive Party but also the Republican, Democratic, Socialist, and Populist Parties. Lela and John Scopes grew up in Paducah, but they spent part of their childhood in Illinois, which, in 1883, became one of the first states in the Union to make school attendance compulsory. By 1916, nearly every state had mandated school attendance, usually between the ages of six and sixteen. Between 1890 and 1920, a new high school opened every day.

Some families objected, citing "parental rights," a legal novelty, but courts broadly upheld compulsory education laws, deeming free public schooling to be essential to democratic citizenship. "The natural rights of a parent to the custody and control of his infant child are subordinate to the power of the state, and may be restricted and regulated by municipal laws," the Indiana Supreme Court ruled in 1901, characterizing a parent's duty to educate his children as a "duty he owes not to the child only, but to the commonwealth." As Tracy Steffes argues in *School, Society, and State: A New Education to Govern Modern America, 1890–1940* (2012), "Public schooling was not just one more progressive reform among many but a major—perhaps *the* major— public response to tensions between democracy and capitalism." Capitalism divided the rich and the poor; democracy required them to live together as equals. Public education was meant to bridge the gap, as wide as the Cumberland.

Beginning in the 1890s, states also introduced textbook laws, in an attempt to wrest control of textbook publishing from what Progressives called "the book trust"—a conglomerate of publishers known as the American Book Company. Tennessee passed one of these laws in 1899: it established a textbook commission that selected books for adoption. The biology book Scopes used to teach his students was a textbook that Tennessee had adopted, statewide, at a time when it made high school compulsory.

"Each year the child is coming to belong more and more to the state, and less and less to the parent," the Stanford professor of education Ellwood Cubberley wrote approvingly in 1909. Progressives fought for children's welfare and children's health, establishing children's hospitals and, in 1912, the U.S. Children's Bureau. Mandatory school attendance was closely tied to two other Progressive reforms that extended the state's reach into the lives of parents and children: compulsory vaccination and the abolition of child labor.

By 1912, twenty-seven states either required vaccination for children attending school or permitted schools to require it. Parents' objections met with little success. In one New Jersey school district, in 1911, three hundred and fifty parents challenged the school board, pledging that "we will, one and all of us . . . move out of Montclair and out of the State of New Jersey before we allow our children to be vaccinated. There are other suburbs of New York which have not this fetish of forcing vaccination on children." The school board backed down. But, beginning in 1914, with a widely cited case called *People v. Ekerold*, parents could be prosecuted for failing to vaccinate their children. "If a parent may escape all obligation under the statute requiring him to send his children to school by simply alleging he does not believe in vaccination," the court ruled, "the policy of the state to give some education to all children, if necessary by compelling measures, will become more or less of a farce."

Before compulsory schooling, many American children worked, in farms or factories. You might think that stopping parents from sending their children to work was a consequence of requiring that they send them to school, but the opposite was true: requiring parents to send their children to school was one way reformers got parents to stop sending their children to work. In 1916, Congress passed a law discouraging the employment of children younger than fourteen in manufacturing and the employment of children younger than sixteen in mines and quarries. When this and other laws targeting child labor were deemed unconstitutional by a laissez-faire Supreme Court, reformers drafted a Child Labor Amendment, granting Congress the "power to limit, regulate, and prohibit the labor of persons under eighteen." It passed Congress in 1924 and went to the states for ratification. Progressive organizations, including the National Association of Colored Women, sent orders to their members to lobby state legislatures to pass the bill.

"Please remember, dear sisters, that unless two-thirds of the state legislators pass the Child Labor Amendment, it will not be incorporated into the Constitution of the United States," the group's former president Mary Church Terrell warned members, "and that will certainly be a calamity." Businesses, not least the southern textile industry, objected. And rural states, especially, objected—Kentucky was among those states which failed to ratify—since the amendment, which was badly written, could be construed as making it a crime for families to ask their children to do chores around the farm. The Ohio

Farm Bureau complained, "The parents of the United States did not know that the congress was considering taking their parental authority from them."

Parenthood, as an identity, and even as a class of rights bearers, is a product both of Progressive reform and of those who resisted it. The magazine *Parents* began publishing in 1926. "Devoted but unenlightened parenthood is a dangerous factor in the lives of children," its editor said, maintaining that parents weren't to be trusted to know how to raise children: they had to be taught, by experts. This doesn't mean that experts usually prevailed; people don't like to be told how to raise their kids, particularly when experts seek the power of the state. Like the Equal Rights Amendment, the Child Labor Amendment became one of only a handful of amendments that passed Congress but have never been ratified.

Anti-evolution laws, usually understood as fundamentalism's response to modernity, emerged from this conflict between parents and the state. So did the teaching of biology, a new subject that stood at the very center of Progressive Era public education. At the time, parents, not schools, paid for and provided schoolbooks, so they had a close acquaintance with what their kids were being taught. The textbook that John Scopes used in Tennessee was a 1914 edition of George William Hunter's *A Civic Biology*, published by the American Book Company. More than a guide to life on earth, *Civic Biology* was a civics primer, a guide to living in a democracy.

"This book shows boys and girls living in an urban community how they may best live within their own environment and how they may cooperate with the civic authorities for the betterment of their environment," the book's foreword explained. *Civic Biology* promoted Progressive public health campaigns, all the more urgent in the wake of the 1918 influenza pandemic, stressing the importance of hygiene, vaccination, and quarantine. "Civic biology symbolized the whole ideology behind education reform," Adam Shapiro wrote in *Trying Biology: The Scopes Trial, Textbooks, and the Antievolution Movement in American Schools* (2013). It contained a section on evolution ("If we follow the early history of man upon the earth, we find that at first he must have been little better than one of the lower animals"), but its discussion emphasized the science of eugenics. Hunter wrote, of alcoholics and the criminal and the mentally ill, "If such people were lower animals, we would probably kill them off to prevent them from spreading."

At bottom, *Civic Biology* rested on social Darwinism. "Society itself is founded upon the principles which biology teaches," Hunter wrote. "Plants and animals are living things, taking what they can from their surroundings; they enter into competition with one another, and those which are the best fitted for life outstrip the others." What did it feel like, for kids who were poor and hungry, living in want and cold and fear, to read those words?

When anti-evolutionists condemned "evolution," they meant something as vague and confused as what people mean more lately when they condemn "critical race theory." Anti-evolutionists weren't simply objecting to Darwin, whose theory of evolution had been taught for more than half a century. They were objecting to the whole Progressive package, including its philosophy of human betterment, its model of democratic citizenship, and its insistence on the interest of the state in free and equal public education as a public good that prevails over the private interests of parents.

IN THE 1920s, Lela and John Scopes were students at the University of Kentucky, in Lexington, when he took a course on evolution taught by a professor named Arthur (Monkey) Miller. That course caught the attention of people who thought the state was spending too much money on the university. In the summer of 1921, Frank McVey, the university's president, had pressed the legislature for funding to expand the university. In January 1922, in a move widely seen as a response, the legislature introduced a bill to ban the teaching of evolution at any school, college, or university that received public funds.

McVey occupied an unusually strong position, partly because of the way he'd handled the recent pandemic. Born in Ohio, the child of Progressive Republicans, McVey had earned a PhD in economics at Yale, where he wrote a dissertation on the Populist movement, and in 1904, after a stint writing for the *Times*, he published *Modern Industrialism*, an argument against laissez-faire economics. He arrived at the University of Kentucky in 1917. A year later, during an influenza outbreak that took the lives of fourteen thousand Kentuckians, McVey made the decision, extraordinary at the time, to shut down the campus for nearly a month. Of twelve hundred students, four hundred became infected and only eight died, rates that were low compared with those at other colleges and universities. The achievement was all the more impressive because young adults, worldwide, suffered particularly high death rates.

The Kentucky anti-evolution campaign drew national attention. William Jennings Bryan, a three-time presidential candidate and a former secretary of state, hastened to offer support, predicting that "the movement will sweep the country and we will drive Darwinism from our schools." In January, Bryan, a barnstorming, larger-than-life showman, traveled to Kentucky to speak before the House and the Senate.

McVey weighed his options: he could fight, or he could sit tight and hope that the law, if passed, would be found unconstitutional. He decided to fight. He wrote to Woodrow Wilson for support, but Wilson refused to take a stand that would have pitted him against a former member of his cabinet. McVey sent telegrams to some fifty people. "Bill has been introduced in Kentucky Legislature with heavy penalty to prohibit teaching of evolution," he cabled. "Wire collect your opinion." Forty-seven fiery replies arrived within four days. The reverend of the First Christian Church of Paducah maintained that the law "contravenes the spirit of democracy." "Universities must be left free to teach that which the best scholarship believes to be true," a pastor wrote from St. Louis. The president of Columbia University suggested that the legislature do one better and prohibit the publication of any books that "use any of the letters by which the word evolution could be spelled." The head of the First Christian Church in Frankfort, the state capital, called the bill "unwise, unamerican and contrary to the spirit of Jesus Christ." Before the bill was considered, McVey had arranged for the responses to be published in newspapers across the state. Finally, he addressed both the House and the Senate and published an open letter to the people of Kentucky. "I have an abiding faith in the good sense and fairness of the people of this State," he wrote. "When they understand what the situation means and when they come to comprehend the motives underlying this attack upon the public schools of the State they will hold the University and the school system in greater respect than ever before."

He said that the university was bound to teach evolution "since all the natural sciences are based upon it," but he hoped Kentuckians could agree that evolution wasn't what its opponents had made it out to be: "Evolution is development; it is change, and every man knows that development and change are going on all the time." He took pains to distinguish the theory of evolution from social Darwinism, regretting the law's conflation of the two. Above all, he pointed out, banning the teaching of evolution "places limitations on the right of thought and freedom of belief," and is therefore a violation of the Kentucky Bill of Rights.

Four days later, the bill was killed in the Senate, and the following month the House voted it down, 42–41. McVey had won, but, as he remarked, "it may be that the fight here in Kentucky is really the fore-runner of a conflict all over the nation."

IN 1924, JOHN SCOPES MOVED from Lexington, Kentucky, to Dayton, Tennessee, to take a job as a high school coach. The next year, Tennessee passed an anti-evolution bill. Black intellectuals and Black reporters didn't think the new law had anything to do with evolution; it had to do with an understanding of history. All Tennessee's lawmakers know about evolution, the *Chicago Defender* suggested, "is that the entire human race is supposed to have started from a common origin. Therein lies their difficulty." If they were to accept evolution, then they would have to admit that "there is no fundamental difference between themselves and the race they pretend to despise." The president of Fisk University, a Black institution, wrote to the governor, "I hope that you will refuse to give your support to the Evolution Bill." But the president of the University of Tennessee, fearful of losing the university's funding, declined to fight the bill, and the governor signed it, declaring he was sure it would never be enforced.

In Dayton, Scopes had briefly subbed for the biology teacher, using the state-mandated textbook, *A Civic Biology*. He agreed to test the law and was arrested in May. William Jennings Bryan joined the prosecution, defending the rights of parents. The month before the trial, he delivered a statement asking, "Who shall control our schools?" To defend the twenty-four-year-old Scopes, the ACLU retained the celebrated Clarence Darrow, who, that year, took on another case at the request of the NAACP. As Darrow and the ACLU saw it, Tennessee's anti-evolution law violated both the state's constitution and the First Amendment. "Scopes is not on trial," Darrow declared. "Civilization is on trial."

During the trial, H. L. Mencken ridiculed Bryan (a "mountebank") and fundamentalists ("poor half wits"): "He has these hillbillies locked up in his pen and he knows it." But W. E. B. Du Bois found very little to laugh about. "Americans are now endeavoring to persuade hilarious and sarcastic Europe that Dayton, Tennessee, is a huge joke, and very, very exceptional," he wrote. "The truth is and we know it: Dayton, Tennessee, is America: a great, ignorant, simple-minded land."

Scopes, in the end, was found guilty (a verdict that was later reversed on a technicality), but Tennessee had been humiliated in the national press. Five days after the trial ended, Bryan died in his bed, and with him, many observers believed, died the anti-evolution campaign. The number of bills proposed in state legislatures dwindled to only three, in 1928 and 1929. But the battle was far from over. "The Fundamentalists have merely changed their tactics," one commentator observed in 1930. They had given up on passing laws. "Primarily, they are concentrating today on the emasculation of textbooks, the 'purging' of libraries, and above all the continued hounding of teachers." That went on for a long time. It's still going on.

LELA SCOPES, AFTER LOSING OUT on that job teaching math in Paducah because she refused to denounce her brother, left Kentucky to take a job at a girls' school in Tarrytown, New York. Then, in 1927, she moved to Illinois, where she taught at the Skokie School, in Winnetka. She never married, and helped raise her brother's children—they lived with her—and then she paid for them to go to college.

In the 1950s, when Lela Scopes retired from teaching and moved back to Paducah, southern segregationists resurrected Bryan's parental rights argument to object to the Supreme Court's 1954 decision in *Brown v. Board of Education*. "Free men have the right to send their children to schools of their own choosing," Senator James Eastland, of Mississippi, insisted after the decision. All-white legislators in southern states repealed Progressive Era compulsory education laws: rather than integrate public schools, they dismantled public education, as Jon

Hale reports in his book *The Choice We Face: How Segregation, Race, and Power Have Shaped America's Most Controversial Education Reform Movement*. The South Carolina governor George Bell Timmerman Jr., signing one such bill in 1955, declared, "The parental right to determine what is best for the child is fundamental. It is a divine right. It is a basic law of nature that no man, no group of men, can successfully destroy." The following year, all but 26 of the 138 southern members of the U.S. House and Senate signed a statement known as the Southern Manifesto, warning that "outside mediators are threatening immediate and revolutionary changes in our public schools systems." Two states in the West—Nevada, in 1956, and Utah, in 1957—passed measures making it legal for parents to keep their children home for schooling.

By the end of the 1950s, segregationists had begun using a new catchphrase: "school choice," maybe because it would have been confusing to call for "parents' rights" when they were also arguing for "states' rights." In Mississippi, opponents of segregation founded Freedom of Choice in the United States, or FOCUS. Advocates for "choice" sought government reimbursement for private school tuition costs, in the name of allowing the free market to drive educational innovation. The free market, unsurprisingly, widened the very inequalities that public education aims to narrow. Between 1962 and 1966, for instance, Louisiana distributed more than fifteen thousand tuition vouchers in New Orleans; in 1966, 94 percent of the funds went to white parents. In the 1970s and '80s, court-mandated busing strengthened calls for choice, and Ronald Reagan pressed for the federal government to invest in vouchers; in the 1990s, Bill Clinton fought for funding for charter schools. Between 1982 and 1993, homeschooling became legal in all fifty states. Philanthropies, from the Bill & Melinda Gates Foundation to the Friedman Foundation for Educational Choice (now EdChoice), later joined the movement in force, funding research and charter schools. And yet, in *Making Up Our Mind: What School Choice Is Really About*, the education scholars Sigal R. Ben-Porath and Michael C. Johanek point out that about nine in ten children in the United States attend public school, and the overwhelming majority of parents—about eight in ten—are happy with their kids' schools. In the name of "choice," a very small minority of edge cases have shaped the entire debate about public education.

A century ago, parents who objected to evolution were rejecting the entire Progressive package. Today's parents' rights groups, like Moms for Liberty, are objecting to a twenty-first-century Progressive package. They're balking at compulsory vaccination and masking, and some of them do seem to want to destroy public education. They're also annoyed at the vein of high-handedness, moral crusading, and snobbery that stretches from old-fashioned Progressivism to the modern kind, laced with the same contempt for the rural poor and the devoutly religious.

But across the past century, behind parents' rights, lies another unbroken strain: some Americans' fierce resistance to the truth that, just as all human beings share common ancestors biologically, all Americans have common ancestors historically. A few parents around the country may not like their children learning that they belong to a much bigger family—whether it's a human family or an American family—but the idea of public education is dedicated to the cultivation of that bigger sense of covenant, toleration, and obligation. In the end, no matter what advocates of parents' rights say, and however much political power they might gain, public schools don't have a choice; they've got to teach, as American history, the history not only of the enslaved Africans who arrived in Virginia in 1619 and the English families who sailed to Plymouth on the Mayflower in 1620, but also that of the Algonquian peoples, who were already present in both places, alongside the ongoing stories of all other Indigenous peoples, and those who came afterward—the Dutch, German, Spanish, Mexican, Chinese, Italian, Cambodian, Guatemalan, Japanese, Sikh, Hmong, Tunisian, Afghan, everyone. That's why parents don't have a right to choose the version of American history they like best, a story of only their own family's origins. Instead, the state has an obligation to welcome children into that entire history, their entire inheritance.

Lela Scopes insisted that her brother's trial had never been about evolution: "The issue was academic freedom." Twentieth-century Progressives defeated anti-evolution laws not by introducing pro-evolution laws but by defending academic freedom and the freedoms of expression and inquiry. This approach isn't available to twenty-first-century progressives, who have ceded the banner of free speech to conservatives. And, in any case, teachers don't have much academic freedom: state school boards and school districts decide what they'll teach. Still, there are limits. Biology and history offer accounts of origins and change, and, when badly taught, they risk taking on the trappings of religion and violating the First Amendment. Biology teachers have to explain evolution, but they can't teach that God does not exist, just as public schools can't preach social justice as a gospel, a dogma that can't be disputed, and, equally, they can't ban it.

That's because history as doctrine is always dangerous. "Probably no deeper division of our people could proceed from any provocation than from finding it necessary to choose what doctrine and whose program public educational officials shall compel youth to unite in embracing," the Supreme Court ruled in 1943, in *West Virginia State Board of Education v. Barnette*, when the Court struck down, as a violation of the First Amendment, a statute that required schoolchildren to salute the flag and recite the Pledge of Allegiance. "Those who begin coercive elimination of dissent soon find themselves exterminating dissenters. Compulsory unification of opinion achieves only the unanimity of the graveyard." History isn't a pledge; it's an argument.

John Scopes died in 1970. Lela Scopes buried him in Paducah, and had his headstone engraved with the words A MAN OF COURAGE. She died in 1989, and is buried nearby, under a stone that reads A GRACIOUS AND GENEROUS LADY. She was ninety-two. She always said she thought the idea of evolution was even more beautiful than Genesis, evidence of an even more wonderful God. But she understood that not everyone agreed with her.

—2022

Part Nine

The Isolation Ward

Loneliness is grief, distended.

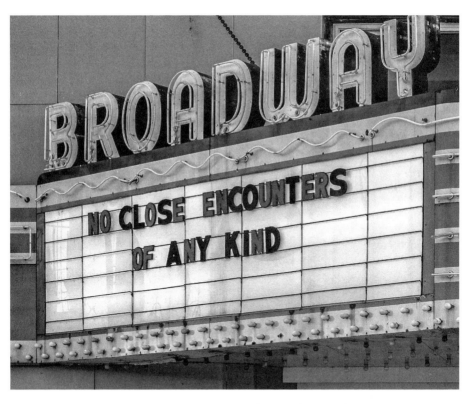

A shuttered theater during the pandemic, 2020.
Photograph by Dan Gaken

PLAGUE YEARS

WHEN THE PLAGUE CAME TO LONDON IN 1665, Londoners lost their wits. They consulted astrologers, quacks, the Bible. They searched their bodies for signs, tokens of the disease: lumps, blisters, black spots. They begged for prophecies; they paid for predictions; they prayed; they yowled. They closed their eyes; they covered their ears. They wept in the street. They read alarming almanacs: "Certain it is, books frighted them terribly." The government, keen to contain the panic, attempted "to suppress the Printing of such Books as terrify'd the People," according to Daniel Defoe, in *A Journal of the Plague Year*, a history that he wrote in tandem with an advice manual called *Due Preparations for the Plague*, in 1722, a year when people feared that the disease might leap across the English Channel again, after having journeyed from the Middle East to Marseille and points north on a merchant ship. Defoe hoped that his books would be useful "both to us and to posterity, though we should be spared from that portion of this bitter cup." In 2020, that bitter cup came out of its cupboard.

In 1665, the skittish fled to the country, and alike the wise, and those who tarried had reason for remorse: by the time they decided to leave, "there was hardly a Horse to be bought or hired in the whole City," Defoe recounted, and, in the event, the gates had been shut, and all were trapped. Everyone behaved badly, though the rich behaved the worst: having failed to heed warnings to provision, they sent their poor servants out for supplies. "This Necessity of going out of our Houses to buy Provisions, was in a great Measure the Ruin of the whole City," Defoe wrote. One in five Londoners died, notwithstanding the precautions taken by merchants. The butcher refused to hand the cook a cut of meat; she had to take it off the hook herself. And he wouldn't touch her money; she had to drop her coins into a bucket of vinegar. Bear that in mind when you run out of Purell.

"Sorrow and sadness sat upon every Face," Defoe wrote. The government's stricture on the publication of terrifying books proved pointless, there being plenty of terror to be read on the streets. You could read the weekly bills of mortality, or count the bodies as they piled up in the lanes. You could read the orders published by the mayor: "If any Person shall have visited any Man known to be infected of the Plague, or entered willingly into any known infected House, being not allowed: The House wherein he inhabiteth shall be shut up." And you could read the signs on the doors of those infected houses, guarded by watchmen, each door marked by a foot-long red cross, above which was to be printed, in letters big enough to be read at a distance, LORD, HAVE MERCY UPON US.

Reading is an infection, a burrowing into the brain: books contaminate, metaphorically, and even microbiologically. In the eighteenth century, ships' captains arriving at port pledged that they had disinfected their ships by swearing on Bibles that had been dipped in seawater. During tuberculosis scares, public libraries fumigated books by sealing them in steel vats filled with formaldehyde gas. During the COVID-19 pandemic, you could find out how to disinfect books on a librarians' thread on Reddit. Your best bet appeared at first to be either denatured-alcohol swipes or kitchen disinfectant in a mist-spray bottle, although if you stuck books in a little oven and heated them to 160 degrees Fahrenheit there was a bonus: you also killed bedbugs. ("Doesn't harm the books!") Or, as happened during the coronavirus closures, libraries could shut their doors, and bookstores, too.

But, of course, books are also a salve and a consolation. In the long centuries during which the plague ravaged Europe, the quarantined, if they were lucky enough to have books, read them. If not, and if they were well enough, they told stories. In Giovanni Boccaccio's *Decameron*, from the fourteenth century, seven women and three men take turns telling stories for ten days while hiding from the Black Death—that "last Pestilentiall mortality universally hurtfull to all that beheld it"—a plague so infamous that Boccaccio begged his readers not to put down his book as too hideous to hold: "I desire it may not be so dreadfull to you, to hinder your further proceeding in reading."

The literature of contagion is vile. A plague is like a lobotomy. It cuts away the higher realms, the loftiest capacities of humanity, and leaves only the animal. "Farewell to the giant powers of man," Mary Shelley wrote in *The Last Man*, in 1826, after a disease has ravaged the world. "Farewell to the arts,—to eloquence." Every story of epidemic is a story of illiteracy, language made powerless, man made brute.

But, then, the existence of books, no matter how grim the tale, is itself a sign, evidence that humanity endures, in the very contagion of reading. Reading may be an infection, the mind of the writer seeping, unstoppable, into the mind of the reader. And yet it is also—in its bidden intimacy, an intimacy in all other ways banned in times of plague—an antidote, proven, unfailing, and exquisite.

STORIES ABOUT PLAGUES RUN THE GAMUT from *Oedipus Rex* to *Angels in America*. "You are the plague," a blind man tells Oedipus. "It's 1986 and there's a plague, friends younger than me are dead, and I'm only thirty," a Tony Kushner character says. There are plagues here and plagues there, from Thebes to New York, horrible and ghastly, but never one plague everywhere, until Mary Shelley decided to write a follow-up to *Frankenstein*.

The Last Man, set in the twenty-first century, is the first major novel to imagine the extinction of the human race by way of a global pandemic. Shelley published it at the age of twenty-eight, after nearly everyone she loved had died, leaving her, as she put it, "the last relic of a beloved race, my companions, extinct before me." The book's narrator begins as a poor and uneducated English shepherd: primitive man, violent and lawless, even monstrous. Cultivated by a nobleman and awakened to learning—"An earnest love of knowledge . . . caused me to pass days and nights in reading and study"—he is elevated by the Enlightenment and becomes a scholar, a defender of liberty, a republican, and a citizen of the world.

Then, in the year 2092, the plague arrives, ravaging first Constantinople. Year after year, the pestilence dies away every winter ("a general and never-failing physician"), and returns every spring, more virulent, more widespread. It reaches across mountains, it spreads over oceans. The sun rises, black: a sign of doom. "Through Asia, from the banks of the Nile to the shores of the Caspian, from the Hellespont even to the sea of Oman, a sudden panic was driven," Shelley wrote. "The men filled the mosques; the women, veiled, hastened to the tombs, and carried offerings to the dead, thus to preserve the living." The nature of the pestilence remains mysterious. "It was called an epidemic. But the grand question was still unsettled of how this epidemic was generated and increased." Not understanding its operation and full of false confidence, legislators hesitate to act. "England was still secure. France, Germany, Italy and Spain, were interposed, walls yet without a breach, between us and the plague." Then come reports of entire nations, destroyed and depopulated. "The vast cities of America, the fertile plains of Hindostan, the crowded abodes of the Chinese, are menaced with utter ruin." The fearful turn to history too late, and find in its pages, even in the pages of the Decameron, the wrong lesson: "We called to mind the plague of 1348, when it was calculated that a third of mankind had been destroyed. As yet western Europe was uninfected; would it always be so?" It would not always be so. Inevitably, the plague comes, at last, to England, but by then the healthy have nowhere left to go, because, in the final terror of pandemic, there is "no refuge on earth": "All the world has the plague!"

If, in *Frankenstein*, Shelley imagined the creation of a man by the stitching together of body parts, in *The Last Man* she imagined the dismemberment of civilization. Death by death, country by country, the human race descends, rung by rung, down a ladder it had once built, and climbed. Shelley's narrator, the erstwhile shepherd, bears witness to the destruction and abandonment of all the "adornments of humanity" that had adorned his own naked self: law, religion, the arts, science, liberal government ("The nations are no longer!"), freedom, commerce, literature, music, theater, industry, transportation, communication, agriculture. "Our minds, late spread abroad through countless spheres and endless combinations of thought, now retrenched themselves behind this wall of flesh, eager to preserve its well-being only." As the pestilence lays waste to the planet, those few who survive are reduced to warring tribes, until only one man, our narrator, is left, shepherd once more. Wandering amid the ruins of Rome, he enters the home of a writer and finds a manuscript on his writing table: "It contained a learned disquisition on the Italian language." The last book is a study of language, humanity's first adornment. And what does our narrator do, alone in the world? "I also will write a book, I cried—for whom to read? to whom dedicated?" He calls it *The History of the Last Man*, and dedicates it to the dead. It will have no readers. Except, of course, the readers of Shelley's book.

THE GREAT DREAM OF THE ENLIGHTENMENT was progress; the great dread of epidemic is regress. But in American literature such destruction often comes with a democratic twist: contagion is the last leveler. Edgar Allan Poe's 1842 tale "The Masque of the Red Death" is set in a medieval world plagued by a contagious disease that kills nearly instantly. "There were sharp pains, and sudden dizziness, and then profuse bleeding at the pores, with dissolution," Poe wrote. "The scarlet stains upon the body and especially upon the face of the victim, were the pest ban which shut him out from the aid and from the sympathy of his fellow-men." In particular, the rich have no sympathy for the poor. (Not irrelevantly, Poe's rich stepfather had entirely cut him off, leaving Poe penniless, and his wife was dying of consumption.) A haughty prince and his noblemen and women retire "to the deep seclusion of one of his castellated abbeys," where they live in depraved luxury until, one night, at a masked ball, a figure arrives wearing a mask "made so nearly to resemble the countenance of a stiffened corpse that the closest scrutiny must have difficulty in detecting the cheat." The visitor is the Red Death itself. Everyone in the abbey dies that night. The nobility cannot escape what the poor must endure.

Poe's red death becomes a pandemic in Jack London's novel *The Scarlet Plague*, serialized in 1912. (The disease is the very same: "The whole face and body turned scarlet in an hour's time.") The plague had come in the year 2013, and wiped out nearly everyone, the high and the low, the powerful nations and the powerless, in all corners of the globe, and left the survivors equal in their wretchedness, and statelessness. One of the handful of survivors had been a scholar at the University of California, Berkeley, a professor of English literature. When the disease hit, he hid out in the chemistry building, and turned out to be immune to the virulence. For years, he lived alone in an old hotel at Yosemite, availing himself of its stores of canned food, until, emerging, he joined a tiny band—the Chauffeurs, led by a brute who had once been a chauffeur—and even found a wife. When the novel opens, in the year 2073, the professor is a very old man, a shepherd, dressed in animal hide—"about his chest and shoulders hung a single, mangy garment of goat-skin"—and living like an animal. He tells the story of the scarlet plague to his grandsons, boys who "spoke in monosyllables and short jerky sentences that was more a gibberish than a language," but who are very handy with a bow and arrow. Their primitivism distresses the professor, who sighs, as he looks out across what was once San Francisco: "Where four million people disported themselves, the wild wolves roam to-day, and the savage progeny of our loins, with prehistoric weapons, defend themselves against the fanged despoilers. Think of it! And all because of the Scarlet Death."

London stole the red death from Poe and took the plot of *The Scarlet Plague* from *The Last Man*—except that London's argument, about the decline and fall of humankind, is far less subtle than Shelley's. "The human race is doomed to sink back farther and farther into the primitive night ere again it begins its bloody climb upward to civilization," the professor explains. For London, it's industrial capitalism and imperialism, not the Enlightenment's engine of moral progress, that drive the climb from savagery to civilization and from scarcity to abundance. London's descent of man is a descent into a very particular age-of-empire heart of darkness: the professor's grandsons have "brown skin." Before the plague came, capitalists and imperialists amassed staggering fortunes. "What is money?" the boys ask their grandfather, when he uses that word to describe a coin they find, minted in 2012. ("The old man's eyes glistened, as he held the coin.") All this—the white skin, the fortunes—was lost! The professor's greatest distress concerns the onetime chauffeur's having wed, by force, the former wife of a magnate: "There she was, Vesta Van Warden, the young wife of John Van Warden, clad in rags, with marred and scarred and toil-calloused hands, bending over the campfire and doing scullion work—she, Vesta, who had been born to the purple of the greatest baronage of wealth the world had ever known." Equally distressing, having conquered the continent, the white man has, in the end, lost the West, and the East, too. The professor attempts to describe to his savage grandsons the fall of American cities, whose fate he learned of in the earliest days of the pandemic, when news could still reach California from other parts of the country, before the last telegraph operators died:

New York City and Chicago were in chaos. . . . A third of the New York police were dead. Their chief was also dead, likewise the mayor. All law and order had ceased. The bodies were lying in the streets un-buried. All railroads and vessels carrying food and such things into the great city had ceased running, and mobs of the hungry poor were pillaging the stores and warehouses. Murder and robbery and drunkenness were everywhere. Already the people had fled from the city by millions—at first the rich, in their private motor-cars and dirigibles, and then the great mass of the population, on foot, carrying the plague with them, themselves starving and pillaging the farmers and all the towns and villages on the way.

All the cities burned. Even the dirigibles of the rich exploded into flames, the world a Hindenburg.

The Scarlet Plague, published right before the Great War, also contains a warning about the cost of world war, the cost, even, of living in a world. "Long and long and long ago, when there were only a few men in the world, there were few diseases," the professor explains. "But as men increased and lived closely together in great cities and civilizations, new diseases arose, new kinds of germs entered their bodies. Thus were countless millions and billions of human beings killed. And the more thickly men packed together, the more terrible were the new diseases that came to be." His grandsons cannot fathom any of this. "The census of 2010 gave eight billions for the whole world," he tells them. They can hardly believe him, and have no idea what a billion could be, or a census, or a world.

"Ten thousand years of culture and civilization passed in the twinkling of an eye," the professor says. He has made it his life's work to become a librarian, to archive those ten thousand years. In a cave on Telegraph Hill, he has stored all the books he could find, even though he is the only man living who knows how to read. "In them is great wisdom," he tells his grandsons, in the novel's final chapter, explaining that he has left, as well, a key to the alphabet. "Some day men will read again," he promises them. They have no idea what he is talking about. Still, the reader does.

THE STRUCTURE OF THE MODERN PLAGUE NOVEL, all the way to Stephen King's *The Stand* and beyond, is a series of variations on *A Journal of the Plague Year* (a story set within the walls of a quarantine) and *The Last Man* (a story set among a ragged band of survivors). Within those two structures, though, the scope for storytelling is vast, and so is the scope for moralism, historical argument, and philosophical reflection. Every plague novel is a parable.

Albert Camus once defined the novel as the place where the human being is abandoned to other human beings. The plague novel is the place where all human beings abandon all other human beings. Unlike other species of apocalyptic fiction, where the enemy can be chemicals or volcanoes or earthquakes or alien invaders, the enemy here is other humans: the touch of other humans, the breath of other humans, and, very often—in the competition for diminishing resources—the mere existence of other humans.

Camus, in *The Plague* (1947), sets the story within the walls of a quarantined French-Algerian town during the Second World War (the year is given as "194–"). With all its omens, prophecies, and scapegoats, it might as well have been London in 1665. Dr. Bernard Rieux, along with everyone else, at first fails to read the signs. (The novel purports to be written from Rieux's notebooks, his journal of a plague year.) He watches a rat stumble, at his doorstep:

> It moved uncertainly, and its fur was sopping wet. The animal stopped and seemed to be trying to get its balance, moved forward again toward the doctor, halted again, then spun round on itself with a little squeal and fell on its side. Its mouth was slightly open and blood was spurting from it. After gazing at it for a moment, the doctor went upstairs.

Rats come out from cellars and die on the streets, in heaps. And yet neither the doctor nor anyone else does anything at all, until after the first human death, of a concierge. Then remorse dawns: "Reviewing that first phase in the light of subsequent events, our townsfolk realized that they had never dreamed it possible that our little town should be chosen out for the scene of such grotesque happenings as the wholesale death of rats in broad daylight or the decease of concierges through exotic maladies."

Soon, we learn, "the whole town was running a temperature." The number of cases rises, and then it leaps. Eleven deaths in forty-eight hours, then more. The government health committee wishes to avoid using the word "plague," but unless it is used emergency measures cannot be put in place. Notices are posted, but only in obscure places, and in very small type, and, as the doctor observes, "it was hard to find in these notices any indication that the authorities were facing the situation squarely." Finally, in desperation, the government adopts a policy of "deratization" and, when thirty people die in a single day, closes the town.

The plague is, of course, the virus of fascism. No one in the town gives much thought to the rats until it's too late—even though the plague "rules out any future, cancels journeys, silences the exchange of views"—and few pay sufficient attention to the rats even after it's too late. This is their folly: "They fancied themselves free, and no one will ever be free so long as there are pestilences."

The Plague does not chronicle a pandemic, in the sense that the plague never escapes the town, and yet Camus's plague is a plague without end. But Rieux learns, from reading history, that there really is only one plague, across all of human history, traveling from place to place, through the passage of time, from "Chinese towns cluttered up with victims silent in their agony" to "the damp, putrefying pallets stuck to the mud floor at the Constantinople lazar-house, where the patients were hauled up from their beds with hooks," to "cartloads of dead bodies rumbling through London's ghoul-haunted darkness— nights and days filled always, everywhere, with the eternal cry of human pain." Next on the list? Auschwitz, Dachau, Buchenwald. The plague is man.

Haunted by this knowledge, Rieux, locked in an unwanted asylum, suffers from an extremity of solitude and from the alienation and brutality of modernity:

Sometimes at midnight, in the great silence of the sleep-bound town, the doctor turned on his radio before going to bed for the few hours' sleep he allowed himself. And from the ends of the earth, across thousands of miles of land and sea, kindly, well-meaning speakers tried to voice their fellow-feeling, and indeed did so, but at the same time proved the utter incapacity of every man truly to share in suffering that he cannot see.

For those in isolation, there is no world: "the plague had swallowed up everything and everyone." They are saved, at the last minute, by a serum, and the town erupts in joyful celebration. In the novel's closing words, the doctor thinks of his reading. "He knew what those jubilant crowds did not know but could have learned from books: that the plague bacillus never dies or disappears for good . . . and that perhaps the day would come when, for the bane and the enlightening of men, it would rouse up its rats again and send them forth to die in a happy city." Men will always become, again, rats.

Camus's observation about "the utter incapacity of every man truly to share in suffering that he cannot see" is the subject of José Saramago's brilliant and devastating reimagining of the plague tale, *Blindness*, from 1995, in which the Defoe-like doctor is an ophthalmologist and the disease that reduces humans to animals is the inability to see. As historical parable, *Blindness* indicts the twentieth-century authoritarian state: the institutionalization of the vulnerable, the ruthlessness of military rulers. When the disease strikes, the government rounds up all the blind and locks them up in a mental asylum, where, blindly, they go to war with one another. They steal, they rape. "The blind are always at war, always have been at war," Saramago writes, in the novel's darkest observation.

But *Blindness* is far darker than any history lesson. For Saramago, blindness isn't a disease; blindness is the human condition. There is, in the novel, only one person left with sight. She reads to the blind, which, for them, is both a paradise and an exasperation: "This is all we are good for, listening to someone reading us the story of a human mankind that existed before us." And that, in the modern plague novel, is the final terror of every world-ending plague, the loss of knowledge, for which reading itself is the only cure. It is this realization that grips Saramago's ophthalmologist, at the very moment that he loses his sight, before the disease is known: the understanding of the preciousness, beauty, and fragility of knowledge. Puzzled by a patient who has come to his office after being stricken suddenly and inexplicably blind—he sees not black but only a milky whiteness—the eye doctor goes home and, after dinner, consults the books in his library. "Late that night, he laid aside the books he had been studying, rubbed his weary eyes and leaned back in his chair," Saramago writes. He decides to go, at last, to bed. "It happened a minute later as he was gathering up the books to return them to the bookshelf. First he perceived that he could no longer see his hands, then he knew he was blind."

Everything went white. As white as a blank page.

—2020

THESE FOUR WALLS

PORCUPINES LIKE TO LIVE ALONE, BUT IN WINTER they sometimes hole up in long-snouted little gangs inside hollow trees and logs, in cavities made by cracks in boulders, beneath piles of brush, or under your front porch, as sneaky as thieves. A gang of porcupines is called, magnificently, a prickle. They hardly ever venture out. Inside, in the damp and ratty dark, fallen-out quills carpet the floor. In spring, female porcupines raise their babies in those dens. A baby porcupine is called a porcupette. There isn't a word for a porcupine den, but I humbly propose calling it a quiver, except when it's a nursery; then it's a pokey.

The animal kingdom is a densely settled city-state of hives, burrows, lairs, nests, webs, caves, pits, and dens. Lodgings come in all sizes and for every length of stay, no security deposit required, from a grotty single bed for the night to fancy permanent quarters for a colony. Quivers are, generally, a mess. Porcupines are rodents, an order of mammals that are, as a rule, unkempt. The celebrated insouciance of the honey badger, a weasel, is nothing to the equanimity of the porcupine. Porcupines are fully armed, near-blind, and imperturbable. They leave their scat outside their front door, piling up. They don't care who sniffs them out. Maine, New Hampshire, and Vermont used to offer bounties to hunters, fifty cents a snout, forty cents for a pair of ears, twenty-five cents for every pair of feet. But since that practice ended, decades ago, porcupines have had few predators, aside from the sort of dog that's too dunderheaded to know any better, which, I confess, forlornly, describes every cur of my acquaintance. Porcupines, in their dens, aren't really hiding; they're just staying snug, in homes they haven't so much built as come by, like squatters, or Goldilocks, or Airbnbers, lovers of the great indoors.

In the encyclopedia of animal accommodations, the most admirable architect is the beaver. Beavers build lodges out of sticks and mud, complete with ventilation and underground entrances. Domesticated animals live in houses built by people (etymologically, that's what it means to be domesticated), from cow barns to pigpens. One reason some people don't eat meat is that on big farms animals are forced to spend so much time crowded together indoors. Factory-farmed chickens, raised in giant sheds stacked with thousands of cages—ten to a cage the size of a file drawer—don't even have room to spread their wings, and most spend every last, miserable moment of their lives inside. That only started in the 1950s, and, recently, lots of people have been going back to raising their own chickens. Since the quarantine, there has been a rush on chicks and back-yard coops. (Enthusiasts who have never met a hen are well advised to read Betty MacDonald's 1945 memoir, *The Egg and I*, in which she recounts, "By the end of the second spring I hated everything about the chicken but the egg.") A DIY coop consists of a roof, a roost, and nesting boxes. Translucent roofing is recommended, the idea, apparently, being that if chickens can see the sky they'll forget that they're indoors. Chickens like to roost inside at night, but among the many reasons for letting them out during the day is that otherwise they might peck one another to death. That's what it means to be cooped up. The Italians call free-range chickens *polli ruspanti*. A wandering chicken is a happy chicken. People are no longer *ruspante*. We build lean-tos and huts and shanties and houses and motels and condominiums and apartment buildings. During the COVID-19 pandemic, we were stuck in them, like a prickle in a quiver, chickens in a coop, bears in a den, waiting out our desolate hibernation.

EVEN BEFORE THE QUARANTINE, Americans and Europeans spent about 90 percent of their time indoors, as Joseph G. Allen and John D. Macomber report, in *Healthy Buildings: How Indoor Spaces Drive Performance and Productivity* (2020). Homes, cars, prisons, schools, buses, factories, trains, airplanes, offices, museums, hospitals, stores, restaurants: how much of your life have you spent indoors, not counting the quarantine? Multiply your age by 0.9. If you're forty, you've spent thirty-six of your years indoors. About a third of that is time spent sleeping, but still. Most humans who live in the United States and Europe spend more time indoors than some species of whale spend underwater. It may be that the minutes you spent walking to and from the subway on a Tuesday in January tallied up to fewer minutes than a whale spent on the surface, filling its lungs, that same day.

This trend wasn't expected to reverse itself after the pandemic ends. "Unlike the outdoor world, the indoor world is expanding," the journalist Emily Anthes reports, in *The Great Indoors: The Surprising Science of How Buildings Shape Our Behavior, Health, and Happiness* (2020). "Over the next forty years, the United Nations estimates, the total amount of indoor square footage will roughly double worldwide." Nevertheless, the indoors is the poor stepchild of the outdoors, at least in terms of environmental activism and regulation. Staying indoors, long before our present woes, was not always and not even very often a choice, including for schoolchildren, prisoners, factory and office workers, and hospital patients. Entire cities sometimes shut down. In 2018, China issued "stay indoors" warnings for seventy-nine cities, owing to air pollution. And from Los Angeles to Shanghai air quality has sometimes been so bad that the elderly are advised to stay inside, and, at schools, recess is canceled. But how much better is it behind closed doors? For all the attention paid to outdoor pollution, Allen and Macomber point out, most people experience outdoor pollution while they're inside—it seeps in—and yet the indoor environment, which produces its own toxins, is subject to very few rules.

Allen teaches at Harvard's T. H. Chan School of Public Health and Macomber teaches at Harvard Business School. Lately, they've been preparing reports and providing advice on whether and how to safely reopen schools. *Healthy Buildings* advises businesses about how to make their buildings more salubrious, on the back of the investor-directed argument that healthier buildings make for more productive employees and more profitable companies. One report from Allen's lab, "The 9 Foundations of a Healthy Building," advocates close control over air quality, dust and pests, lighting and views, moisture, noise, safety and security, thermal health, ventilation, and water quality. Allen and Macomber want to establish national standards, and they make a series of precise and persuasive recommendations for everything from insulation and window shades to water filters and vacuum cleaners.

Given that most pollution is produced by the burning of fossil fuels, and that climate change is a major force in driving people indoors (where they still get sick from the burning of fossil fuels outdoors),

Allen and Macomber also extoll the green building movement. One study they cite shows that in six countries within the span of twenty years, green buildings, compared with their non-green counterparts, averted 54,000 respiratory symptoms, 21,000 lost days of work, 16,000 lost days of school, 11,000 asthma exacerbations, up to 405 premature deaths, and 256 hospital admissions, a savings that amounted to "$4 billion in health and climate co-benefits, on top of the $6.7 billion in energy savings, for a total benefit of $10.7 billion." (Better ventilation uses more energy, but they insist that this is offset by the energy savings of green-building practices.) Still, *Healthy Buildings* also offers a vision of the future that many readers will find disturbing:

Optimizing indoor conditions is going to require a future of hyper-personalization and hyperlocalization of thermal conditions to create zones of "personalized indoor health" that satisfy the unique preference of each person. This is already starting to happen. Some buildings have systems where each workstation has controls for its own temperature and airflow, and systems that disaggregate ventilation from temperature control. The future of personalized indoor health is not far off.

That future is here! Anthes tells us that "Comfy, a California-based company, makes an HVAC-linked mobile app that allows office workers to tinker with the temperature of their own workspaces." One can see the benefits, but this sounds like something out of *WALL-E*. It's also hard not to hear holier-than-thou Henry David Thoreau preaching from across the duck-blind stillness of Walden Pond:

It costs me nothing for curtains, for I have no gazers to shut out but the sun and moon, and I am willing that they should look in. . . . A lady once offered me a mat, but as I had no room to spare within the house, nor time to spare within or without to shake it, I declined it, preferring to wipe my feet on the sod before my door. It is best to avoid the beginnings of evil.

It is hard living with masks and scarcely ever touching anyone. But, reading these books, you begin to see how methods of separation are likely to proliferate, in the form of products and practices being sold not to stop a pandemic but to sell panic, for profit. Is it too late to avoid a world where only the poor go outdoors while the rich live in zones of personalized indoor health, each with its own temperature and moisture controls, earbuds and light visors and HEPA filters, its own customized light-diffusing curtains and dust-catching doormat? Will there be no room left by the post-pandemic threshold for a cheap, recycled rubber, one-size-fits-all welcome mat?

HAVING A ROOF OVER YOUR HEAD is one thing: a home is a human right. Living almost entirely indoors is something else. The Great Confinement varies by place and by wealth, and, historically, it's new. "Over several millennia, humans have evolved from an outdoor species into an indoor one," Allen and Macomber write. Citing E. O. Wilson, they explain, "We evolved in the African savannah's wide-open expanses, intimate with nature and seeking protection under tree canopies," and so "our genetic hardwiring, built over millennia, still craves that connection to nature." To satisfy this craving, photographs of redwoods adorn hospital waiting rooms; you can pop into the Grand Canyon via Zoom. I used to think these dodges were better than nothing, but I've changed my mind. Zoom is usually not better than nothing.

Velux, a Danish company, calls twenty-first-century humans the Indoor Generation, and ascribes a plague of depression and disease to the stuffiness and dampness and mold and darkness of living indoors. (The company sells skylights, the kind of thing you're supposed to put in chicken coops to stop your chickens from going stir-crazy.) Its website features a spooky, M. Night Shyamalan–style video of a pale and sickly little girl explaining, "It all started the day we left nature behind." We feathered our nests, with espresso machines and flat-screen televisions and Spotify. "Our homes became places you would never want to leave," the girl says, the shadows under her eyes grown darker. "But we had closed ourselves in, to a point where nothing could get out." We started getting sick. Itchy, cough-y, sleepless. "Many of us even started to feel sad." And that was in the beforetime.

Benjamin Franklin, who was forever advising his friends to crack their windows open, would have agreed. "It has been a great Mistake, the Sleeping in Rooms exactly clos'd and in Beds surrounded by Curtains," he wrote to a lady friend. At the time, this went against the advice of much medical thought and many books of learning, some dating to the plague years of the fifteenth and sixteenth centuries. For the many who believed disease to be caused by miasmas, the best solution was to keep "bad air" out. Even Franklin had succumbed to the prejudice that he called "Aerophobia," "and clos'd with extreme Care every Crevice in the Rooms I inhabited," he recalled. But "experience has convinced me of my Error," he explained. Shutting up the sick made sense in order to keep them from infecting other people, but shutting them up from the outdoors often only made them sicker.

During and after the yellow fever epidemics of the 1790s (five thousand people died in Philadelphia, then the U.S. capital, in 1793 alone), doctors and scientists, observing the patterns of diseases in cities, began studying the relationship between housing density and epidemics, with many subscribing to a contagion theory of disease. Cities installed public water and sanitation systems, and also designed parks, to encourage people to spend more time outdoors, in fresh air and sunlight. Living indoors itself became a sign of disease. Edgar Allan Poe's "The Fall of the House of Usher," published in 1839, is an indictment of medieval architecture. The narrator, on arriving at Usher's house, notices that "dark draperies hung upon the walls," and that it was impossible even to open the windows: "The windows were long, narrow, and pointed, and at so vast a distance from the black oaken floor as to be altogether inaccessible from within." In a vault inside that building, Usher seals his sickly sister in a coffin, unaware that she is still alive.

In the second half of the nineteenth century, American cities like Denver and Phoenix and rural resorts in states like Montana boasted that they offered, along with fresh air and sunlight, relief from such diseases as asthma, hay fever, and tuberculosis, as the historian Sara Jensen Carr explains in *The Topography of Wellness* (2021). Informed by the British Garden City movement, which urged the setting aside of green space, cities across the country planted trees. A promotional tract for Santa Barbara, published in 1878, promised a change from the consumptive conditions in cities: "The absence of sunlight is a frightful cause of the prevalence of the disease. The streets are so narrow and the houses so high that sunlight seldom reaches the sitting rooms.

The schoolhouses are so situated that children can scarcely ever see the sun." In much the same spirit, Victorian-era builders added "sleeping porches" to the backs of houses (sleeping outdoors was thought to prevent tuberculosis), and hospitals, schools, and asylums were built on rural estates, where patients might be encouraged, or required, to grow their own food, at places like Vermont's Brattleboro Retreat.

Much of the reform of hospitals came at the direction of Florence Nightingale, who argued that "to shut up your patients tight in artificially warmed air is to bake them in a slow oven." She also advocated windows, for the sake of light. But, Anthes reports, these reforms didn't last: "As germ theory and the concept of antisepsis gained ground, hospitals sealed themselves off from the natural world, relying on antibiotics and chemical disinfection, rather than sunlight and fresh air, to reduce the spread of disease."

Carr states the nature of this reversal more baldly. Where "miasma was an affliction of the public realm and consequently encouraged an era of social ethics and responsibility," the advent of germ theory "suddenly shifted the burden of health from the external to the internal, and more implicitly, from the state to the individual." In the age of the microbe and the antiseptic, "health became the burden of the individual, associated with personal exposure and responsibility." Instead of addressing the urban pollution caused by automobiles, architects built skyscrapers set back from the smell of the street. Le Corbusier, in *The Radiant City* (1933), advocated replacing the actual (that is, pestilential) street with streetlike features inside buildings—corridors and hallways and elevators—and treating inhabitants with doses of light and air. Postwar white flight and concern about urban "blight" led to suburban sprawl. Later, New Urbanists celebrated cities for their "walkability." More recently, architects have been engaged in "active design," trying to encourage, for instance, the use of stairs, by making stairwells wider and more brightly lit, and piping music into them, while making elevators slower.

IF "INDUSTRY" WAS THE WATCHWORD of building design in the nineteenth century, and "efficiency" the watchword in much of the twentieth, "wellness" has been the watchword of the twenty-first century. Wellness is a swindle. Many of the architectural experiments chronicled and the building-design reforms advocated in *The Great Indoors* and *Healthy Buildings* advance an anti-universal, hyper-individualized medical model, in which architecture is seen as therapeutic, building by building and person by person. Allen and Macomber date the origin of their field to the 1980s, when people began talking about "sick building syndrome," defined in the dictionary as "a set of symptoms (such as headache, fatigue, and eye irritation) typically affecting workers in modern airtight office buildings that is believed to be caused by indoor pollutants (such as formaldehyde fumes or microorganisms)." Anthes, who describes herself as "unapologetically indoorsy," embraces the possibility of building design as a cure-all: "The promise of improving our health and extending our life spans, even just a little, without ever leaving the house? Well, I found that idea irresistible." She visits schools and apartment buildings specially designed to address aging, obesity, and depression. She gamely reports on smart offices and smart homes and floating cities and proposed villages on the moon and the new field of "indoor ecology" (the study of subjects like the mites to be found in your pillow). "The more I read about the world of indoor microbes, the more I found myself obsessing over my own invisible roommates. I contemplated fungi as I cooked, bacteria as I bathed," she writes. "I began to feel like a stranger in my own home, humbled by how little I knew about what was happening under my roof." The recommendations of that research? "Open a window. Get a dog."

Building design is also increasingly driven by personal data, collected and held as a commodity, and used to improve business performance and productivity. Ethical objections to this type of data collection, suspended during the pandemic, are unlikely to recover their strength when it's over, which means that, if you ever go back to the office, you may be monitored in ways you used to consider a violation of your rights. Anthes profiles an analytics company called Humanyze, which "makes software and hardware that enables companies to analyze their employees' digital and in-person interactions." Among its products is the "sociometric badge," which is worn on a lanyard around your neck, and can detect conversations between two coworkers. The badge "contains a microphone, an accelerometer, and Bluetooth and infrared sensors, which can track the badge-wearer's location as well as the direction that he or she is facing," she writes. "When two badge-wearers are in close proximity, facing each other and engaged in an alternating pattern of speaking, they're probably having a chat." Humanyze uses the data gathered on its badges to produce reports for its clients. It has suggested, for instance, that people who sit near one another in an office are more likely to have face-to-face conversations than those who sit at a distance from one another, and made recommendations for the division of departments between floors and the size of lunch tables. More recently, the company's president has been writing about how working remotely has reminded many of us of the importance of all those casual office interactions that we took for granted, and now sorely miss. A sociometric badge sounds terrible to me. But a lunch table sounds so good.

Anthes also recounts the work of Daniel Davis, "WeWork's slight and stylish director of research," who uses his company's data to fix office problems. A Washington, DC, WeWork featured a "funky, bright yellow wallpaper" that elicited a lot of negative comments, perhaps even from readers of Charlotte Perkins Gilman's 1892 story "The Yellow Wallpaper," about a woman whose husband, a physician, hopes to make her well but instead drives her insane by locking her in a yellow-papered room. ("The color is repellant, almost revolting; a smouldering, unclean yellow, strangely faded by the slow-turning sunlight.") Anthes reports: "Armed with that Feedback, WeWork can switch out or paint over that wallpaper and make a note not to use it again." The woman in "The Yellow Wallpaper" peels it all off with her bare hands.

Are better-designed buildings the solution to all that ails the Indoor Generation? The wellness model is not without its critics, who include Giovanna Borasi and Mirko Zardini, the curators of a 2011 exhibit at the Canadian Centre for Architecture, in Montreal, and the editors of an accompanying book of essays, called *Imperfect Health: The Medicalization of Architecture*. "An ever increasing number of urban, environmental and architectural problems are treated as medical, and remedies are sought for increasingly specific solutions," Borasi and Zardini write. "Tailoring requirements to particular groups of ill, or presumably ill individuals leads to conflicting, contradictory solutions, and finally to even greater segregation of various demographic groups." Fighting disease is a public health crusade; leading a healthier life is, very often, a private one. Or, rather, it was. It isn't anymore.

A PANDEMIC UPENDS EVERYTHING, including the relationship between the private and the public, the rich and the poor, the city and the country, and the outdoors and the indoors. The coronavirus acts like a miasma and a germ, all at once. It's in the air, it's on surfaces, it's inside us. There is nothing so wild as a virus and yet no creature so relentless in its search for a home, no matter how unwelcoming the host. Meanwhile, living indoors all the time is driving people crazy, staring at the wallpaper, peering out windows, craving nature, and one another, whimpering and howling inside.

No one knows for certain where the COVID-19 virus came from, but one murky, unconfirmed theory has it that a pangolin, dragged from its den, caught in a snare, or tracked by a dog, contracted the virus from a live bat, a winged mammal that sleeps, upside down, in places where even the days are dark: chimneys, caverns, crevices in rocks. A colony of bats is sometimes called a camp, as if they'd pitched tents. Pangolins are anteaters, nocturnal and reclusive; scaly, long-snouted, near-blind, and solitary, they are not altogether unlike porcupines. Their scales protect them from stings and bites, and when a lion or a tiger comes near they curl up into a ball, like a prickly burr. Females give birth in dens; pangolin babies cling to their mothers' tails with their sharp-clawed, five-toed paws, much the way a koala joey clutches its mother's shoulders. Before China shut down the Huanan Seafood Wholesale Market, in Wuhan Province, in January 2020, a wildlife section there sold live porcupines, beavers, snakes, badgers, and, possibly, pangolins. Maybe a pangolin, or some other wild animal, contracted the virus from a bat in that market, where peddlers stacked all sorts of animals in cages, cramped, wretched, filthy, desperate, in stall after stall, as if they had built a little city, half outdoors, half indoors, a mayhem.

—2020

THE ISOLATION WARD

T HE FEMALE CHIMPANZEE AT THE PHILADELPHIA Zoological Garden died of complications from a cold early in the morning of December 27, 1878. "Miss Chimpanzee," according to news reports, died "while receiving the attentions of her companion." Both she and that companion, a four-year-old male, had been born near the Gabon River, in West Africa; they had arrived in Philadelphia in April, together. "These Apes can be captured only when young," the zoo superintendent, Arthur E. Brown, explained, and they are generally taken only one or two at a time. In the wild, "they live together in small bands of half a dozen and build platforms among the branches, out of boughs and leaves, on which they sleep." But in Philadelphia, in the monkey house, where it was just the two of them, they had become "accustomed to sleep at night in each other's arms on a blanket on the floor," clutching each other, desperately, achingly, through the long, cold night.

The Philadelphia Zoological Garden was the first zoo in the United States. It opened in 1874, two years after Charles Darwin published *The Expression of the Emotions in Man and Animals*, in which he related what he had learned about the social attachments of primates from Abraham Bartlett, the superintendent of the Zoological Society of London:

Many kinds of monkeys, as I am assured by the keepers in the Zoological Gardens, delight in fondling and being fondled by each other, and by persons to whom they are attached. Mr. Bartlett has described to me the behavior of two chimpanzees, rather older animals than those generally imported into this country, when they were first brought together. They sat opposite, touching each other with their much protruded lips; and the one put his hand on the shoulder of the other. They then mutually folded each other in their arms. Afterwards they stood up, each with one arm on the shoulder of the other, lifted up their heads, opened their mouths, and yelled with delight.

Mr. and Miss Chimpanzee, in Philadelphia, were two of only four chimpanzees in America, and when she died human observers mourned her loss, but, above all, they remarked on the behavior of her companion. For a long time, they reported, he tried in vain to rouse her. Then he "went into a frenzy of grief." This paroxysm accorded entirely with what Darwin had described in humans: "Persons suffering from excessive grief often seek relief by violent and almost frantic movements." The bereaved chimpanzee began to pull out the hair from his head. He wailed, making a sound the zookeeper had never heard before: *Hah-ah-ah-ah-ah.* "His cries were heard over the entire garden. He dashed himself against the bars of the cage and butted his head upon the hard-wood bottom, and when this burst of grief was ended he poked his head under the straw in one corner and moaned as if his heart would break."

Nothing quite like this had ever been recorded. Superintendent Brown prepared a scholarly article, "Grief in the Chimpanzee." Even long after the death of the female, Brown reported, the male "invariably slept on a cross-beam at the top of the cage, returning to inherited habit, and showing, probably, that the apprehension of unseen dangers has been heightened by his sense of loneliness."

Loneliness is grief, distended. People are primates, and even more sociable than chimpanzees. We hunger for intimacy. We wither without it. And yet, long before the present pandemic, with its forced isolation and social distancing, humans had begun building their own monkey houses. Before modern times, very few human beings lived alone. Slowly, beginning not much more than a century ago, that changed. In the United States, more than one in four people now lives alone; in some parts of the country, especially big cities, that percentage is much higher. You can live alone without being lonely, and you can be lonely without living alone, but the two are closely tied together, which makes lockdowns, sheltering in place, that much harder to bear. Loneliness, it seems unnecessary to say, is terrible for your health. In 2017 and 2018, the former U.S. Surgeon General Vivek H. Murthy declared an "epidemic of loneliness," and the UK appointed a Minister of Loneliness. To diagnose this condition, doctors at UCLA devised a Loneliness Scale. Do you often, sometimes, rarely, or never feel these ways?

I am unhappy doing so many things alone.
I have nobody to talk to.
I cannot tolerate being so alone.
I feel as if nobody really understands me.
I am no longer close to anyone.
There is no one I can turn to.
I feel isolated from others.

In the age of pandemics and quarantines, does one disease produce another?

"LONELINESS" IS A VOGUE TERM, and like all vogue terms it's a cover for all sorts of things most people would rather not name and have no idea how to fix. Plenty of people like to be alone. I myself love to be alone. But solitude and seclusion, which are the things I love, are different from loneliness, which is a thing I hate. Loneliness is a state of profound distress. Neuroscientists identify loneliness as a state of hypervigilance whose origins lie among our primate ancestors and in our own hunter-gatherer past. Much of the research in this field was led by John Cacioppo, at the Center for Cognitive and Social Neuroscience, at the University of Chicago. Cacioppo, who died in 2018, was known as Dr. Loneliness. In *Together: The Healing Power of Human Connection in a Sometimes Lonely World* (2020), Murthy explains how Cacioppo's evolutionary theory of loneliness has been tested by anthropologists at the University of Oxford, who have traced its origins back fifty-two million years, to the very first primates. Primates need to belong to an intimate social group, a family or a band, in order to survive; this is especially true for humans (humans you don't know might very well kill you, which is a problem not shared by most other primates). Separated from the group—either finding yourself alone or finding yourself among a group of people who do not know and understand you—triggers a fight-or-flight response. Cacioppo argued that your body understands being alone, or being with strangers, as an emergency. "Over millennia, this hypervigilance in response to isolation became embedded in our nervous system to produce the anxiety we associate with loneliness," Murthy writes. We breathe fast, our heart races, our blood pressure rises, we don't sleep. We act fearful, defensive, and self-involved, all of which drive away people who might actually want to help, and tend to stop lonely people from doing what would benefit them most: reaching out to others.

The loneliness epidemic, in this sense, is rather like the obesity epidemic. Evolutionarily speaking, panicking while being alone, like finding high-calorie foods irresistible, is highly adaptive, but more recently, in a world where laws (mostly) prevent us from killing one another, we need to work with strangers every day, and the problem is more likely to be too much high-calorie food rather than too little. These drives backfire.

Loneliness, Murthy argues, lies behind a host of problems—anxiety, violence, trauma, crime, suicide, depression, political apathy, and even political polarization. Murthy writes with compassion, but his everything-can-be-reduced-to-loneliness argument is hard to swallow, not least because much of what he has to say about loneliness was said about homelessness in the 1980s, when "homelessness" was the vogue term—a word somehow easier to say than "poverty"—and saying it didn't help. (Since then, the number of homeless Americans has increased.) Curiously, Murthy often conflates the two, explaining loneliness as feeling homeless. To belong is to feel at home. "To be at home is to be known," he writes. Home can be anywhere. Human societies are so intricate that people have meaningful, intimate ties of all kinds, with all sorts of groups of other people, even across distances. You can feel at home with friends, or at work, or in a college dining hall, or at church, or in Yankee Stadium, or at your neighborhood bar. Loneliness is the feeling that no place is home. "In community after community," Murthy writes, "I met lonely people who felt homeless even though they had a roof over their heads." Maybe what people experiencing loneliness and people experiencing homelessness both need are homes with other humans who love them and need them, and to know they are needed by them in societies that care about them. That's not a policy agenda. That's an indictment of modern life.

In *A Biography of Loneliness: The History of an Emotion* (2019), the

British historian Fay Bound Alberti defines loneliness as "a conscious, cognitive feeling of estrangement or social separation from meaningful others," and she objects to the idea that it's universal, transhistorical, and the source of all that ails us. She argues that the condition really didn't exist before the nineteenth century, at least not in a chronic form. It's not that people—widows and widowers, in particular, and the very poor, the sick, and the outcast—weren't lonely; it's that, since it wasn't possible to survive without living among other people, and without being bonded to other people, by ties of affection and loyalty and obligation, loneliness was a passing experience. Monarchs probably *were* lonely, chronically. (Hey, it's lonely at the top!) But, for most ordinary people, daily living involved such intricate webs of dependence and exchange—and shared shelter—that to be chronically or desperately lonely was to be dying. The word "loneliness" very seldom appears in English before about 1800. Robinson Crusoe was alone, but never lonely. One exception is *Hamlet*: Ophelia suffers from "loneliness"; then she drowns herself.

Modern loneliness, in Alberti's view, is the child of capitalism and secularism. "Many of the divisions and hierarchies that have developed since the eighteenth century—between self and world, individual and community, public and private—have been naturalized through the politics and philosophy of individualism," she writes. "Is it any coincidence that a language of loneliness emerged at the same time?" It is not a coincidence. The rise of privacy, itself a product of market capitalism—privacy being something that you buy—is a driver of loneliness. So is individualism, which you also have to pay for.

Alberti's book is a cultural history (she offers an anodyne reading of *Wuthering Heights*, for instance, and another of the letters of Sylvia Plath). But the social history is more interesting, and there the scholarship demonstrates that whatever epidemic of loneliness can be said to exist is very closely associated with living alone. Whether living alone makes people lonely or whether people live alone because they're lonely might seem to be harder to say, but the preponderance of the evidence supports the former: it is the force of history, not the exertion of choice, that leads people to live alone. This is a problem for people trying to fight an epidemic of loneliness, because the force of history is relentless.

BEFORE THE TWENTIETH CENTURY, according to the best longitudinal demographic studies, about 5 percent of all households (or about 1 percent of the world population) consisted of just one person. That figure began rising around 1910, driven by urbanization, the decline of live-in servants, a declining birth rate, and the replacement of the traditional, multigenerational family with the nuclear family. By the time David Riesman published *The Lonely Crowd*, in 1950, 9 percent of all households consisted of a single person. In 1959, psychiatry discovered loneliness, in a subtle essay by the German analyst Frieda Fromm-Reichmann. "Loneliness seems to be such a painful, frightening experience that people will do practically everything to avoid it," she wrote. She, too, shrank in horror from its contemplation. "The longing for interpersonal intimacy stays with every human being from infancy through life," she wrote, "and there is no human being who is not threatened by its loss." People who are not lonely are so terrified of loneliness that they shun the lonely, afraid that the condition might be contagious. And people who are lonely are themselves so horrified by what they are experiencing that they become secretive and self-obsessed—"it produces the sad conviction that nobody else has experienced or ever will sense what they are experiencing or have experienced," Fromm-Reichmann wrote. One tragedy of loneliness is that lonely people can't see that lots of people feel the same way they do.

"During the past half century, our species has embarked on a remarkable social experiment," the sociologist Eric Klinenberg wrote in *Going Solo: The Extraordinary Rise and Surprising Appeal of Living Alone* (2012). "For the first time in human history, great numbers of people—at all ages, in all places, of every political persuasion—have begun settling down as singletons." Klinenberg considers this to be, in large part, a triumph; more plausibly, it is a disaster. Beginning in the 1960s, the percentage of single-person households grew at a much steeper rate, driven by a high divorce rate, a still-falling birth rate, and longer lifespans overall. (After the rise of the nuclear family, the old began to reside alone, with women typically outliving their husbands.) A medical literature on loneliness began to emerge in the 1980s, at the same time that policymakers became concerned with, and named, "homelessness," which is a far more dire condition than being a single-person household: to be homeless is to be a household that does not hold a house. Cacioppo began his research in the 1990s, even as humans were building a network of computers, to connect us all. Klinenberg, who graduated from college in 1993, is particularly interested in people who chose to live alone right about then.

I suppose I was one of them. I tried living alone when I was twenty-five, because it seemed important to me, the way owning a piece of furniture that I did not find on the street seemed important to me, as a sign that I had come of age, could pay rent without subletting a sub-let. I could afford to buy privacy, I might say now, but then I'm sure I would have said that I had become "my own person." I lasted only two months. I didn't like watching television alone, and also I didn't have a television, and this, if not the golden age of television, was the golden age of *The Simpsons*, so I started watching television with the person who lived in the apartment next door. I moved in with him, and then I married him.

This experience might not fit so well into the story Klinenberg tells; he argues that networked technologies of communication, beginning with the telephone's widespread adoption, in the 1950s, helped make living alone possible. Radio, television, internet, social media: we can feel at home online. Or not. Robert Putnam's *Bowling Alone* came out in 2000, four years before the launch of Facebook, which monetized loneliness. Some people say that the success of social media was a prod-uct of an epidemic of loneliness; some people say it was a contributor to it; some people say it's the only remedy for it. Connect! Disconnect! The *Economist* declared loneliness to be "the leprosy of the 21st cen-tury." The epidemic only grew.

This is not a peculiarly American phenomenon. Living alone, while common in the United States, is more common in many other parts of the world, including Scandinavia, Japan, Germany, France, the UK, Australia, and Canada, and it's on the rise in China, India, and Brazil. Living alone works best in nations with strong social supports. It works worst in places like the United States. It is best to have not only an internet but a social safety net.

Then, in 2020, the great, global confinement began: enforced isola-tion, social distancing, shutdowns, lockdowns, a human but inhuman zoological garden. It was a terrible, frightful experiment, a test of the human capacity to bear loneliness. Did you pull out your hair? Did you dash yourself against the walls of your cage? Did you, locked inside, thrash and cry and moan? Sometimes, rarely, or never? More today than yesterday?

—2020

BURNED

B URNOUT IS GENERALLY SAID TO DATE TO 1973; AT least, that's around when it got its name. By the 1980s, everyone was burned-out. In 1990, when the Princeton scholar Robert Fagles published a new English translation of the *Iliad*, he had Achilles tell Agamemnon that he doesn't want people to think he's "a worthless, burnt-out coward." This expression, needless to say, was not in Homer's original Greek. Still, the notion that people who fought in the Trojan War, in the twelfth or thirteenth century BC, suffered from burnout is a good indication of the disorder's claim to universality: people who write about burnout tend to argue that it exists everywhere and has existed forever, even if, somehow, it's always getting worse. One Swiss psychotherapist, in a history of burnout published in 2013 that begins with the usual invocation of immediate emergency—"Burnout is increasingly serious and of widespread concern"— insists that he found it in the Old Testament. Moses was burned-out, in Numbers 11:14, when he complained to God, "I am not able to bear all this people alone, because it is too heavy for me." And so was Elijah, in 1 Kings 19, when he "went a day's journey into the wilderness, and came and sat down under a juniper tree: and he requested for himself that he might die; and said, It is enough."

To be burned-out is to be used up, like a battery so depleted that it can't be recharged. In people, unlike batteries, it is said to produce the defining symptoms of "burnout syndrome": exhaustion, cynicism, and loss of efficacy. Around the world, three out of five workers say they're burned-out. A 2020 U.S. study put that figure at three in four. A 2020 book claims that burnout afflicts an entire generation. In *Can't Even: How Millennials Became the Burnout Generation*, the former *Buzz-Feed News* reporter Anne Helen Petersen figures herself as a "pile of embers." The earth itself suffers from burnout. "Burned-out people are going to continue burning up the planet," Arianna Huffington warned in 2021. Burnout is widely reported to have grown worse during the pandemic, according to splashy stories that have appeared on television and radio, up and down the Internet, and in most major newspapers and magazines, including *Forbes*, the *Guardian*, *Nature*, and the *New Scientist*. The *New York Times* solicited testimonials from readers. "I used to be able to send perfect emails in a minute or less," one wrote. "Now it takes me days just to get the motivation to think of a response." When an assignment to write this essay appeared in my inbox, I thought, Oh, God, I can't do that, I've got nothing left, and then I told myself to buck up. The burnout literature will tell you that this, too—the guilt, the self-scolding—is a feature of burnout. If you think you're burned-out, you're burned-out, and if you don't think you're burned-out you're burned-out. Everyone sits under the shade of that juniper tree, weeping, and whispering, "Enough."

But what, exactly, is burnout? The World Health Organization recognized burnout syndrome in 2019, in the eleventh revision of the International Classification of Diseases, but only as an occupational phenomenon, not as a medical condition. In Sweden, you can go on sick leave for burnout. That's probably harder to do in the United States because burnout is not recognized as a mental disorder by the *DSM-5*, published in 2013, and though there's a chance it could one day be added, many psychologists object, citing the idea's vagueness. A number of studies suggest that burnout can't be distinguished from depression, which doesn't make it less horrible but does make it, as a clinical term, imprecise, redundant, and unnecessary.

To question burnout isn't to deny the scale of suffering, or the many ravages of the pandemic: despair, bitterness, fatigue, boredom, loneliness, alienation, and grief—especially grief. To question burnout is to wonder what meaning so baggy an idea can possibly hold, and whether it can really help anyone shoulder hardship. Burnout is a metaphor disguised as a diagnosis. It suffers from two confusions: the particular with the general, and the clinical with the vernacular. If burnout is universal and eternal, it's meaningless. If everyone is burned-out, and always has been, burnout is just . . . the hell of life. But if burnout is a problem of fairly recent vintage—if it began when it was named, in the early 1970s—then it raises a historical question. What started it?

HERBERT J. FREUDENBERGER, the man who named burnout, was born in Frankfurt in 1926. By the time he was twelve, Nazis had torched the synagogue to which his family belonged. Using his father's passport, Freudenberger fled Germany. Eventually, he made his way to New York; for a while, in his teens, he lived on the streets. He went to Brooklyn College, then trained as a psychoanalyst and completed a doctorate in psychology at N.Y.U. In the late 1960s, he became fascinated by the "free clinic" movement. The first free clinic in the country was founded in Haight-Ashbury, in 1967. "'Free' to the free clinic movement represents a philosophical concept rather than an economic term," one of its founders wrote, and the community-based clinics served "alienated populations in the United States including hippies, commune dwellers, drug abusers, third world minorities, and other 'outsiders' who have been rejected by the more dominant culture." Free clinics were free of judgment, and, for patients, free of the risk of legal action. Mostly staffed by volunteers, the clinics specialized in drug-abuse treatment, drug crisis intervention, and what they called "detoxification." At the time, people in Haight-Ashbury talked about being "burnt out" by drug addiction: exhausted, emptied out, used up, with nothing left but despair and desperation. Freudenberger visited the Haight-Ashbury clinic in 1967 and 1968. In 1970, he started a free clinic at St. Marks Place, in New York. It was open in the evening from six to ten. Freudenberger worked all day in his own practice, as a therapist, for ten to twelve hours, and then went to the clinic, where he worked until midnight. "You start your *second* job when most people go home," he wrote in 1973, "and you put a great deal of yourself in the work. . . . You feel a total sense of commitment . . . until you finally find yourself, as I did, in a state of exhaustion."

Burnout, as the Brazilian psychologist Flávio Fontes has pointed out, began as a self-diagnosis, with Freudenberger borrowing the metaphor that drug users invented to describe their suffering to describe his own. In 1974, Freudenberger edited a special issue of the *Journal of Social Issues* dedicated to the free-clinic movement, and contributed an essay on "staff burn-out" (which, as Fontes noted, contains three footnotes, all to essays written by Freudenberger). Freudenberger describes something like the burnout that drug users experienced in his experience of treating them:

Having experienced this feeling state of burn-out myself, I began to ask myself a number of questions about it. First of all, what is burn-out? What are its signs, what type of personalities are more prone than others to its onslaught? Why is it such a common phenomenon among free clinic folk?

The first staff burnout victim, he explained, was often the clinic's charismatic leader, who, like some drug addicts, was quick to anger, cried easily, and grew suspicious, then paranoid. "The burning out person may now believe that since he has been through it all, in the clinic," Freudenberger wrote, "he can take chances that others can't." The person exhibits risk-taking that "sometimes borders on the lunatic." He, too, uses drugs. "He may resort to an excessive use of tranquilizers and barbiturates. Or get into pot and hash quite heavily. He does this with the 'self con' that he needs the rest and is doing it to relax himself."

The street term spread. To be a burnout in the 1970s, as anyone who went to high school in those years remembers, was to be the kind of kid who skipped class to smoke pot behind the parking lot. Meanwhile, Freudenberger extended the notion of "staff burnout" to staffs of all sorts. His papers, at the University of Akron, include a folder each on burnout among attorneys, childcare workers, dentists, librarians, medical professionals, ministers, middle-class women, nurses, parents, pharmacists, police and the military, secretaries, social workers, athletes, teachers, veterinarians. Everywhere he looked, Freudenberger found burnouts. "It's better to burn out than to fade away," Neil Young sang, in 1978, at a time when Freudenberger was popularizing the idea in interviews and preparing the first of his cowritten self-help books. In *Burn-out: The High Cost of High Achievement*, in 1980, he extended the metaphor to the entire United States. "WHY, AS A NATION, DO WE SEEM, BOTH COLLECTIVELY AND INDIVIDUALLY, TO BE IN THE THROES OF A FAST-SPREADING PHENOMENON—BURN-OUT?"

Somehow, suddenly, burning out wasn't any longer what happened to you when you had nothing, bent low, on skid row; it was what happened to you when you wanted everything. This made it an American problem, a yuppie problem, a badge of success. The press lapped up this story, filling the pages of newspapers and magazines with each new category of burned-out workers ("It used to be that just about every time we heard or read the word 'burnout' it was preceded by 'teacher,'" read a 1981 story that warned about "home-makers burnout"), anecdotes ("Pat rolls over, hits the sleep button on her alarm clock and ignores the fact that it's morning. . . . Pat is suffering from 'burnout'"), lists of symptoms ("the farther down the list you go, the closer you are to burnout!"), rules ("Stop nurturing"), and quizzes:

> Are you suffering from burnout? . . . Looking back over the past six months of your life at the office, at home and in social situations. . . .
>
> 1.　Do you seem to be working harder and accomplishing less?
> 2.　Do you tire more easily?
> 3.　Do you often get the blues without apparent reason?
> 4.　Do you forget appointments, deadlines, personal possessions?
> 5.　Have you become increasingly irritable?
> 6.　Have you grown more disappointed in the people around you?
> 7.　Do you see close friends and family members less frequently?
> 8.　Do you suffer physical symptoms like pains, headaches and lingering colds?
> 9.　Do you find it hard to laugh when the joke is on you?
> 10.　Do you have little to say to others?
> 11.　Does sex seem more trouble than it's worth?

You could mark questions with *X*'s, cut out the quiz, and stick it on the fridge, or on the wall of your cubicle. See? See? This says I need a break, goddammit.

Sure, there were skeptics. "The new *IN* thing is 'burnout,'" a *Times-Picayune* columnist wrote. "And if you don't come down with it, possibly you're a bum." Even Freudenberger said he was burned-out on burnout. Still, in 1985 he published a new book, *Women's Burn-*

out: *How to Spot It, How to Reverse It, and How to Prevent It*. In the era of anti-feminist backlash chronicled by Susan Faludi, the press loved quoting Freudenberger saying things like "You *can't* have it all."

Freudenberger died in 1999 at the age of seventy-three. His obituary in the *Times* noted, "He worked 14 or 15 hours a day, six days a week, until three weeks before his death." He had run himself ragged.

"EVERY AGE HAS ITS SIGNATURE AFFLICTIONS," the Korean-born, Berlin-based philosopher Byung-Chul Han writes in *The Burnout Society*, first published in German in 2010. Burnout, for Han, is depression and exhaustion, "the sickness of a society that suffers from excessive positivity," an "achievement society," a yes–we–can world in which nothing is impossible, a world that requires people to strive to the point of self-destruction. "It reflects a humanity waging war on itself."

Lost in the misty history of burnout is a truth about the patients treated at free clinics in the early seventies: many of them were Vietnam War veterans, addicted to heroin. The Haight-Ashbury clinic managed to stay open partly because it treated so many veterans that it received funding from the federal government. Those veterans were burned-out on heroin. But they also suffered from what, for decades, had been called "combat fatigue" or "battle fatigue." In 1980, when Freudenberger first reached a popular audience with his claims about "burnout syndrome," the battle fatigue of Vietnam veterans was recognized by the *DSM-III* as post-traumatic stress disorder. Meanwhile, some groups, particularly feminists and other advocates for battered women and sexually abused children, were extending this understanding to people who had never seen combat.

Burnout, like PTSD, moved from military to civilian life, as if everyone were, suddenly, suffering from battle fatigue. Since the late 1970s, the empirical study of burnout has been led by Christina Maslach, a social psychologist at the University of California, Berkeley. In 1981, she developed the field's principal diagnostic tool, the Maslach Burnout Inventory, and the following year published *Burnout: The Cost of Caring*, which brought her research to a popular readership. "Burnout is a syndrome of emotional exhaustion, depersonalization, and reduced personal accomplishment that can occur among individuals who do 'people work' of some kind," Maslach wrote then. She emphasized burnout in the "helping professions": teaching, nursing, and social work—professions dominated by women who are almost always very poorly paid (people who, extending the military metaphor, are lately classed as frontline workers, alongside police, firefighters, and EMTs). Taking care of vulnerable people and witnessing their anguish exacts an enormous toll and produces its own suffering. Naming that pain was meant to be a step toward alleviating it. But it hasn't worked out that way, because the conditions of doing care work—the emotional drain, the hours, the thanklessness—have not gotten better.

Burnout continued to climb the occupational ladder. "Burnout cuts across executive and managerial levels," *Harvard Business Review* reported in 1981, in an article that told the tale of a knackered executive: "Not only did the long hours and the unremitting pressure of walking a tightrope among conflicting interests exhaust him; they also made it impossible for him to get at the control problems that needed attention. . . . In short, he had 'burned out.'" Burnout kept spreading. "College Presidents, Coaches, Working Mothers Say They're Exhausted," according to a *Newsweek* cover in 1995. With the emergence of the web, people started talking about "digital burnout." "Is the Internet Killing Us?" *Elle* asked in 2014, in an article on "how to deal with burnout." ("Don't answer/write emails in the middle of the night. . . . Watch your breath come in and out of your nostrils or your stomach contracting and expanding as you breathe.") "Work hard and go home" is the motto at Slack, a company whose product, launched in 2014, made it even harder to stop working. Slack burns you out. Social media burns you out. Gig work burns you out. In *Can't Even*, a book that started out as a viral *BuzzFeed* piece, Petersen argues, "Increasingly—and increasingly among millennials—burnout isn't just a temporary affliction. It's our contemporary condition." And it's a condition of the pandemic.

In March 2021, Maslach and a colleague published a careful article in *Harvard Business Review*, in which they warned against using burnout as an umbrella term and expressed regret that its measurement has been put to uses for which it was never intended. "We never designed the MBI as a tool to diagnose an individual health problem," they explained; instead, assessing burnout was meant to encourage employers to "establish healthier workplaces."

The louder the talk about burnout, it appears, the greater the number of people who say they're burned-out: harried, depleted, and disconsolate. What can explain the astonishing rise and spread of this affliction? Declining church membership comes to mind. In 1985, 71 percent of Americans belonged to a house of worship, which is about what that percentage had been since the 1940s; in 2020, only 47 percent of Americans belonged to an institution of faith. Many of the recommended ways to address burnout—wellness, mindfulness, and meditation ("Take time each day, even five minutes, to sit still," *Elle* advised)—are secularized versions of prayer, Sabbath-keeping, and worship. If burnout has been around since the Trojan War, prayer, worship, and the Sabbath are what humans invented to alleviate it. But this explanation goes only so far, not least because the emergence of the prosperity gospel made American Christianity a religion of achievement. Much the same appears to apply to other faiths. A website called productivemuslim.com offers advice on "How to Counter Workplace Burnout" ("There is barakah in earning a halal income"). Also, actually praying, honoring the Sabbath, and attending worship services don't seem to prevent people who are religious from burning out, since religious websites and magazines, too, are full of warnings about burnout, including for the clergy. ("The life of a church leader involves a high level of contact with other people. Often when the church leader is suffering high stress or burnout he or she will withdraw from relationships and fear public appearances.")

You can suffer from marriage burnout and parent burnout and pandemic burnout partly because, although burnout is supposed to be mainly about working too much, people now talk about all sorts of things that aren't work as if they were: you have to work on your marriage, work in your garden, work out, work harder on raising your kids, work on your relationship with God. ("Are You at Risk for Christian Burnout?" one website asks. You'll know you are if you're driving yourself too hard to become "an excellent Christian.") Even getting a massage is "bodywork."

Burnout may be our contemporary condition, but it has very particular historical origins. In the 1970s, when Freudenberger first started looking for burnout across occupations, real wages stagnated and union membership declined. Manufacturing jobs disappeared; service jobs grew. Some of these trends have lately begun to reverse, but all the talk about burnout, beginning in the past few decades, did nothing to solve these problems; instead, it turned responsibility for enormous economic and social upheaval and changes in the labor market back onto the individual worker. Petersen argues that this burden falls especially heavily on millennials, and she offers support for this claim, but a lesson of the history of burnout is that every generation of Americans who have come of age since the 1970s have made the same claim, and they were right, too, because overwork keeps getting worse. In earlier eras, when companies demanded long hours for low wages, workers engaged in collective bargaining and got better contracts. Starting in the 1980s, when companies demanded long hours for low wages, workers put newspaper clippings on the doors of their fridges, burnout checklists. Do you suffer from burnout? Here's how to tell!

Burnout is a combat metaphor. In the conditions of late capitalism, from the Reagan era forward, work, for many people, has come to feel like a battlefield, and daily life, including politics and life online, like yet more slaughter. People across all walks of life—rich and poor, young and old, caretakers and the cared for, the faithful and the faithless—really are worn down, wiped out, threadbare, on edge, battered, and battle-scarred. Lockdowns, too, are features of war, as if each one of us, amid not only the pandemic but also acts of terrorism and mass shootings and armed insurrections, were now engaged in a Hobbesian battle for existence, civil life having become a war zone. May there one day come again more peaceful metaphors for anguish, bone-aching weariness, bitter regret, and haunting loss. "You will tear your heart out, desperate, raging," Achilles warned Agamemnon. Meanwhile, a wellness site tells me that there are "11 ways to alleviate burnout and the 'Pandemic Wall.'" First, "Make a list of coping strategies." Yeah, no.

—2020

Part Ten

In Every Dark Hour

There's a point at which political communication speeds past the last stop where democratic deliberation, the genuine consent of the governed, is possible.

Trump supporters storming the Capitol, January 6, 2021.
Photograph by Tyler Merbler

POLITICS AND THE
NEW MACHINE

"I AM WHO I AM," DONALD J. TRUMP SAID IN AUGUST, on the eve of 2015's first GOP presidential debate, and what he meant by that was this: "I don't have a pollster." The word "pollster," when it was coined, was meant as a slur, like "huckster." That's the way Trump uses it. Other candidates have pollsters: "They pay these guys two hundred thousand dollars a month to tell them, 'Don't say this, don't say that.'" Trump has none: "No one tells me what to say."

Every election is a morality play. The Candidate tries to speak to the People but is thwarted by Negative Campaigning, vilified by a Biased Media, and haunted by a War Record. I am who I am, the Candidate says, and my Opponents are flunkies. Trump makes this claim with unrivaled swagger, but citing his campaign's lack of a pollster as proof of his character, while fascinating, is utterly disingenuous. The Path to Office is long. To reach the Land of Caucuses and Primaries, the Candidate must first cross the Sea of Polls. Trump is a creature of that sea.

Lately, the Sea of Polls is deeper than ever before, and darker. From the late 1990s to 2012, twelve hundred polling organizations conducted nearly thirty-seven thousand polls by making more than three billion phone calls. Most Americans refused to speak to them. This skewed results. Mitt Romney's pollsters believed, even on the morning of the election, that Romney would win. A 2013 study—a poll—found that three out of four Americans suspect polls of bias. Presumably, there was far greater distrust among the people who refused to take the survey.

The modern public opinion poll has been around since the Great Depression, when the response rate—the number of people who take a survey as a percentage of those who were asked—was more than ninety. The participation rate—the number of people who take a survey as a percentage of the population—is far lower. Election pollsters sample only a minuscule portion of the electorate, not uncommonly something on the order of a couple of thousand people out of the more than two hundred million Americans who are eligible to vote. The promise of this work is that the sample is exquisitely representative. But the lower the response rate the harder and more expensive it becomes to realize that promise, which requires both calling many more people and trying to correct for "non-response bias" by giving greater weight to the answers of people from demographic groups that are less likely to respond. Pollster.com's Mark Blumenthal has recalled how, in the 1980s, when the response rate at the firm where he was working had fallen to about 60 percent, people in his office said, "What will happen when it's only twenty? We won't be able to be in business!" A typical response rate is now in the single digits.

Meanwhile, polls are wielding greater influence over American elections than ever. In May 2015, Fox News announced that, in order to participate in its first prime-time debate, hosted jointly with Face-book, Republican candidates had to "place in the top ten of an average of the five most recent national polls." Where the candidates stood on the debate stage would also be determined by their polling numbers. (Ranking in the polls had earlier been used to exclude third-party candidates.) Scott Keeter, Pew's director of survey research, is among the many public opinion experts who found Fox News's decision insupportable. "I just don't think polling is really up to the task of deciding the field for the headliner debate," Keeter told me. Bill McInturff doesn't think so, either. McInturff is a cofounder of Public Opinion Strategies, the leading Republican polling organization; with its Democratic counterpart, Hart Research Associates, he conducts the NBC News/*Wall Street Journal* poll. "I didn't think my job was to design polling so that Fox could pick people for a debate," McInturff told me. Really, it's not possible to design a poll to do that.

Even if more people could be persuaded to answer the phone, polling would still be teetering on the edge of disaster. Few American adults any longer had landlines, and the 1991 Telephone Consumer Protection Act bans autodialing to cell phones. (The law applies both to public opinion polling, a billion-dollar-a-year industry, and to market research, a twenty-billion-dollar-a-year industry.) In 2015 Gallup Inc. agreed to pay twelve million dollars to settle a class action lawsuit filed on behalf of everyone in the United States who, between 2009 and 2013, received an unbidden cell phone call from the company seeking an opinion about politics. (Gallup denies any wrongdoing.) The FCC issued a ruling reaffirming and strengthening the prohibition on random autodialing to cell phones. During congressional hearings, Greg Walden, a Republican from Oregon, who is the chair of the House Subcommittee on Communications and Technology, asked FCC chairman Tom Wheeler if the ruling meant that pollsters would go "the way of blacksmiths." "Well," he said, "they have been, right?"

Internet pollsters have not replaced them. Using methods designed for knocking on doors to measure public opinion on the internet is like trying to shoe a horse with your operating system. Internet pollsters can't call you; they have to wait for you to come to them. Not everyone uses the internet, and, at the moment, the people who do, and who complete online surveys, are younger and leftier than people who don't, while people who have landlines, and who answer the phone, are older and more conservative than people who don't. Some pollsters, both here and around the world, rely on a combination of telephone and internet polling; the trick is to figure out just the right mix. So far, it isn't working. In Israel in March 2015, polls failed to predict Benjamin Netanyahu's victory. That May in the UK, every major national poll failed to forecast the Conservative Party's win.

"It's a little crazy to me that people are still using the same tools that were used in the 1930s," Dan Wagner told me when I asked him about the future of polling. Wagner was the chief analytics officer on the 2012 Obama campaign and is the CEO of Civis Analytics, a data-science technology and advisory firm. Companies like Civis have been collecting information about you and people like you in order to measure public opinion and, among other things, forecast elections by building predictive models and running simulations to determine what issues you and people like you care about, what kind of candidate you'd give money to, and, if you're likely to turn out on Election Day, how you'll vote. They might call you, but they don't need to.

Still, data science can't solve the biggest problem with polling, because that problem is neither methodological nor technological. It's political. Pollsters rose to prominence by claiming that measuring public opinion is good for democracy. But what if it's bad?

A "poll" used to mean the top of your head. Ophelia says of Polonius, "His beard as white as snow: All flaxen was his poll." When voting involved assembling (all in favor of Smith stand here, all in favor of Jones over there), counting votes required counting heads; that is, counting polls. Eventually, a "poll" came to mean the count itself. By the nineteenth century, to vote was to go "to the polls," where, more and more, voting was done on paper. Ballots were often printed in newspapers: you'd cut one out and bring it with you. With the turn to the secret ballot, beginning in the 1880s, the government began supplying the ballots, but newspapers kept printing them; they'd use them to conduct their own polls, called "straw polls." Before the election, you'd cut out your ballot and mail it to the newspaper, which would make a prediction. Political parties conducted straw polls, too. That's one of the ways the political machine worked.

Straw polls were usually conducted a few days or weeks before an election. In August 2015, to cull the field for the first GOP debate, Fox News used polls conducted more than four hundred and sixty days before the general election. (These early polls have become so unreliable that neither Gallup nor Pew conducts them.) The question asked ordinarily takes the form of "If the election were held tomorrow . . ." The circumstances under which the next U.S. presidential election would actually be held tomorrow involve, essentially, Armageddon. Trump won. All flaxen was his poll.

A century ago, newspapers that wanted to predict the outcome of a presidential election had to join forces. In 1908, the *New York Herald*, the *Cincinnati Enquirer*, the *Chicago Record-Herald,* and the *St. Louis Republic* tallied their straws together. William Randolph Hearst's newspapers did the same thing. But the best predictions were made by a national magazine, the *Literary Digest*, beginning in 1916. It regularly miscalculated the popular vote, but for a long time it got the Electoral College winner right. In 1920, the *Digest* mailed out eleven million ballots. By 1932, its mailing list had swelled to twenty million. Most of those names were taken from telephone directories and automobile-registration files. George Gallup was one of the few people who understood that the *Digest* risked underestimating Democratic votes, especially as the Depression deepened, because its sample, while very big, was not very representative: people who supported FDR were much less likely than the rest of the population to own a telephone or a car.

Gallup was borrowing from the insights of social science. Social surveys, first conducted in the 1890s, had been a hallmark of Progressive Era social reform. In 1896, W. E. B. Du Bois went door to door in Philadelphia's Seventh Ward and interviewed some five thousand people in order to prepare his study *The Philadelphia Negro*. In the 1930s, social scientists argued for the merits of a shortcut that relied on statistical science: surveying a tiny but representative sample of a population.

Gallup had always wanted to be a newspaper editor, but after graduating from the University of Iowa, in 1923, he entered a PhD program in applied psychology. In 1928, in a dissertation called "An Objective Method for Determining Reader Interest in the Content of a Newspaper," Gallup argued that "at one time the press was depended upon as the chief agency for instructing and informing the mass of people" but that newspapers no longer filled that role and instead ought to meet "a greater need for entertainment." He therefore devised a method: he'd watch readers go through a newspaper column by column and mark up the parts they liked, so that he could advise an editor which parts of the paper to keep printing and which parts to scrap.

In 1932, when Gallup was a professor of journalism at Northwestern, his mother-in-law, Ola Babcock Miller, ran for secretary of state in Iowa. Her late husband had run for governor; her nomination was largely honorary and she was not expected to win. Gallup had read the work of Walter Lippmann. Lippmann believed that "public opinion" is a fiction created by political elites to suit and advance their interests. Gallup disagreed, and suspected that public opinion, like reader interest, could be quantified. To get a sense of his mother-in-law's chances, Gallup began applying psychology to politics. The year of the race (she won), Gallup moved to New York, and began working for an advertising agency while also teaching at Columbia and running an outfit he called the Editors' Research Bureau, selling his services to newspapers. Gallup thought of this work as "a new form of journalism." But he decided that it ought to sound academic, too. In 1935, in Princeton, he founded the American Institute of Public Opinion, with funding provided by more than a hundred newspapers.

In 1936, in his syndicated column Gallup predicted that the *Literary*

Digest would calculate that Alf Landon would defeat FDR in a land-slide and that the *Digest* would be wrong. He was right on both counts. This was only the beginning. "I had the idea of polling on every major issue," Gallup explained. He began insisting that this work was essential to democracy. Elections come only every two years, but "we need to know the will of the people at all times." Gallup claimed that his polls had rescued American politics from the political machine and restored it to the American pastoral, the New England town meeting. Elmo Roper, another early pollster, called the public opinion survey "the greatest contribution to democracy since the introduction of the secret ballot."

Gallup's early method is known as "quota sampling." He determined what proportion of the people are men, women, Black, white, young, and old. The interviewers who conducted his surveys had to fill a quota so that the population sampled would constitute an exactly proportionate mini-electorate. But what Gallup presented as "public opinion" was the opinion of Americans who were disproportionately educated, white, and male. Nationwide, in the 1930s and '40s, Blacks constituted about 10 percent of the population but made up less than 2 percent of Gallup's survey respondents. Because Blacks in the South were generally prevented from voting, Gallup assigned no "Negro quota" in those states. As the historian Sarah Igo has pointed out, "Instead of functioning as a tool for democracy, opinion polls were deliberately modeled upon, and compounded, democracy's flaws."

Ever since Gallup, two things have been called polls: surveys of opinions and forecasts of election results. (Plenty of other surveys, of course, don't measure opinions but instead concern status and behavior: Do you own a house? Have you seen a doctor in the past month?) It's not a bad idea to reserve the term "polls" for the kind meant to produce election forecasts. When Gallup started out, he was skeptical about using a survey to forecast an election: "Such a test is by no means perfect, because a preelection survey must not only measure public opinion in respect to candidates but must also predict just what groups of people will actually take the trouble to cast their ballots." Also, he didn't think that predicting elections constituted a public good: "While such forecasts provide an interesting and legitimate activity, they probably serve no great social purpose." Then why do it? Gallup conducted polls only to prove the accuracy of his surveys, there being no other way to demonstrate it. The polls themselves, he thought, were pointless.

DONALD TRUMP DIDN'T HAVE a campaign pollster, but in 2015, while he was leading them, his campaign loved polls. Polls admitted Trump into the first GOP debate and polls handed him a victory. "Donald J. Trump Dominates *Time* Poll," the Trump campaign posted on its website following the August debate, linking to a story in which *Time* reported that 47 percent of respondents said that Trump had won. *Time's* "poll" was conducted by PlayBuzz, a viral-content provider that embeds quizzes, polls, lists, and other "playful content" items onto websites to attract traffic. PlayBuzz collected more than seventy-seven thousand "votes" from visitors to *Time's* website in its instant opt-in internet poll. *Time* posted a warning: "The results of this poll are not scientific."

Because most polls do not come with warnings, many reporters and news organizations have been trying to educate readers about polling methods. The day after the first GOP debate, *Slate* published a column called "Did Trump Actually Win the Debate? How to Understand All Those Instant Polls That Say Yes." This, though, didn't stop *Slate* from conducting its own instant poll. "TV talking heads won't decide this election," *Slate's* pollster promised. "The American people will."

The statistician Nate Silver began explaining polls to readers in 2008; the *Times* ran his blog, FiveThirtyEight, for four years. Silver makes his own predictions by aggregating polls, giving greater weight to those which are more reliable. This is helpful, but it's a patch, not a fix. The distinction between one kind of poll and another is important, but it is also often exaggerated. Polls drive polls. Good polls drive polls and bad polls drive polls, and when bad polls drive good polls they're not so good anymore.

Laws govern who can run for office and how. There are laws about who can vote, and where, and when. Seven constitutional amendments and countless Supreme Court cases concern voting. But polls are largely free from government regulation, or even scrutiny. (This is not true in other countries; Canadian election law, for instance, regulates the disclosure of election polls.)

This wasn't always the case. In the 1930s and '40s, motions were regularly introduced in Congress calling for an investigation into the influence of public opinion polling on the political process. "These polls are a racket, and their methods should be exposed to the public," Walter Pierce, a Democratic member of the House, wrote in 1939, the year *Time* first called George Gallup a "pollster." One concern was that polls were jury-rigged. In the presidential election of 1944, George Gallup underestimated Democratic support in two out of three states. When Congress called him in for questioning to answer the charge that "the Gallup poll was engineered in favor of the Republicans," Gallup explained that, anticipating a low turnout, he had taken two points off the projected vote for FDR. In another instance, a congressman voiced concern that polls "are in contradiction to representative government": pollsters appeared to believe that the United States is or ought to be a direct democracy.

Social scientists began criticizing pollsters, too. In 1947, in an address to the American Sociological Association, Herbert Blumer argued that public opinion does not exist, absent its measurement. Pollsters proceed from the assumption that "public opinion" is an aggregation of individual opinions, each given equal weight—an assumption Blumer demonstrated to be preposterous, since people form opinions "as a function of a society in operation." We come to hold and express our opinions in conversation, and especially in debate, over time, and different people and groups influence us, and we them, to different degrees.

Gallup got his back up. In 1948, the week before Election Day, he said, "We have never claimed infallibility, but next Tuesday the whole world will be able to see down to the last percentage point how good we are." He predicted that Dewey would beat Truman. He was quite entirely wrong.

Gallup liked to say that pollsters take the "pulse of democracy." "Although you can take a nation's pulse," E. B. White wrote after the election, "you can't be sure that the nation hasn't just run up a flight of stairs."

In the wake of polling's most notorious failure, the political scientist Lindsay Rogers published a book called *The Pollsters: Public Opinion, Politics, and Democratic Leadership*. Rogers, the Burgess Professor of Public Law at Columbia, had started out as a journalist, and, as a scholar, he was a humanist at a time when most students of government had turned away from the humanities and toward social science. (Amy Fried, in an essay about what was lost in that abandonment, has called him "the Forgotten Lindsay Rogers.") He had drafted *The Pollsters* before the election debacle; his concern had very little to do with miscalculation. Where Blumer argued that polling rests on a misapplication of social science, Rogers argued that it rests on a misunderstanding of American democracy. Even if public opinion could be measured (which Rogers doubted), he believed that legislators' use of polls to inform their votes would be inconsistent with their constitutional duty. The United States has a representative government for many reasons, among them that it protects the rights of minorities against the tyranny of a majority. "The pollsters have dismissed as irrelevant the kind of political society in which we live and which we, as citizens, should endeavor to strengthen," Rogers wrote. Polls, Rogers believed, are a majoritarian monstrosity.

The alarms raised by Blumer and Rogers went unheeded. Instead, many social scientists came to believe that, if the pollsters failed, social science would fail with them (not least by losing foundation and federal research money). Eight days after Truman beat Dewey, the Social Science Research Council appointed an investigative committee, explaining that "extended controversy regarding the preelection polls among lay and professional groups might have extensive and unjustified repercussions upon all types of opinion and attitude studies and perhaps upon social science research generally." The committee concluded that the problem was, in part, quota sampling, but, in any case, the main work of the report was to defend the sample-survey method, including a landmark project founded at the University of Michigan in 1948, which became the most ambitious and most significant survey of American voters: the American National Election Survey.

In 1952, Eisenhower unexpectedly defeated Stevenson. "Yesterday the people surprised the pollsters, the prophets, and many politicians," Edward R. Murrow said on CBS Radio. "They are mysterious and their motives are not to be measured by mechanical means." But politicians don't want the people to be mysterious. Soon, not only political candidates but officeholders—including presidents—began hiring pollsters. Meanwhile, pollsters claim to measure opinions as elusive as

Americans' belief in God, as the sociologist Robert Wuthnow points out in a compelling and disturbing book, *Inventing American Religion: Polls, Surveys, and the Tenuous Quest for a Nation's Faith*. In 1972, when Congress debated a Truth in Polling Act, longtime pollsters like Gallup attempted to distance themselves from campaign and media pollsters. Called to testify, Gallup supported the bill, objecting only to the requirement that pollsters report their response rates. That same year, in *Public Opinion Does Not Exist*, the French sociologist Pierre Bourdieu revisited arguments made by Herbert Blumer. As these and other critics have demonstrated again and again, a sizable number of people polled either know nothing about the matters those polls purport to measure or hold no opinion about them. "The first question a pollster should ask," the sociologist Leo Bogart advised in 1972, is "'Have you thought about this at all? Do you *have* an opinion?'"

Despite growing evidence of problems known as non-opinion, forced opinion, and exclusion bias, journalists only relied on Gallup-style polling more, not less, and they began, too, to do it themselves. In 1973, in *Precision Journalism*, Philip Meyer urged reporters to conduct their own surveys: "If your newspaper has a data-processing department, then it has key-punch machines and people to operate them." Two years later, the *Times* and CBS released their first joint poll, and we've been off to the races ever since, notwithstanding the ongoing concerns raised by critics who point out, as has Gallup Poll's former managing editor David Moore, that "media polls give us distorted readings of the electoral climate, manufacture a false public consensus on policy issues, and in the process undermine American democracy." Polls don't take the pulse of democracy; they raise it.

BY THE END OF AUGUST 2015, Trump, faltering, revealed that he was of course obsessed with his standing in the polls. "I won in every single poll of the debate," he boasted. "I won in *Time* magazine." Trump's lead in the polls had taken so many political reporters by surprise that some people who cover polls—"data journalists" is, broadly, the term of art—began turning to data-science firms like Civis Analytics, wondering whether they, too, saw Trump in the lead.

If public opinion polling is the child of a strained marriage between the press and the academy, data science is the child of a rocky marriage between the academy and Silicon Valley. The term "data science" was coined in 1960, one year after the Democratic National Committee (DNC) hired Simulmatics Corporation, a company founded by Ithiel de Sola Pool, a political scientist from MIT, to provide strategic analysis in advance of the upcoming presidential election. Pool and his team collected punch cards from pollsters who had archived more than sixty polls from the elections of 1952, 1954, 1956, 1958, and 1960, representing more than a hundred thousand interviews, and fed them into a UNIVAC. They then sorted voters into four hundred and eighty possible types (for example, "Eastern, metropolitan, lower-income, white, Catholic, female Democrat") and sorted issues into fifty-two clusters (for example, foreign aid). Simulmatics' first task, completed just before the Democratic National Convention, was a study of "the Negro vote in the North." Its report, which is thought to have influenced the civil rights paragraphs added to the party's platform, concluded that between 1954 and 1956 "a small but significant shift to the Republicans occurred among Northern Negroes, which cost the Democrats about 1 percent of the total votes in 8 key states." After the nominating convention, the DNC commissioned Simulmatics to prepare three more reports, including one that involved running simulations about different ways in which Kennedy might discuss his Catholicism.

In 1964, a political scientist named Eugene Burdick wrote a novel called *The 480*, about the work done by Simulmatics. He was worried about its implications:

There is a benign underworld in American politics. It is not the underworld of cigar-chewing pot-bellied officials who mysteriously run "the machine." Such men are still around, but their power is waning. They are becoming obsolete though they have not yet learned that fact. The new underworld is made up of innocent and well-intentioned people who work with slide rules and calculating machines and computers which can retain an almost infinite number of bits of information as well as sort, categorize, and reproduce this information at the press of a button. Most of these people are highly educated, many of them are Ph.D.s, and none that I have met have malignant political designs on the American public. They may, however, radically reconstruct the

American political system, build a new politics, and even modify revered and venerable American institutions—facts of which they are blissfully innocent. They are technicians and artists; all of them want, desperately, to be scientists.

Burdick's dystopianism is vintage Cold War: the Strangelovian fear of the machine. (Burdick also cowrote *Fail-Safe*, in which a computer error triggers a nuclear war.) But after 1960 the DNC essentially abandoned computer simulation. One reason may have been that LBJ wasn't as interested in the work of MIT scientists as Kennedy had been. For decades, Republicans were far more likely than Democrats to use computer-based polling. In 1977, the Republican National Committee (RNC) acquired a mainframe computer, while the DNC got its own mainframe in the eighties. The political scientist Kenneth Janda speculates that the technological advantage of the Republican Party during these years stemmed from its ties to big business. Democratic technological advances awaited the personal computer; the RNC is to IBM as the DNC is to Apple. In the internet era, beginning with the so-called MoveOn effect, technology at least briefly favored Democrats but, as Matthew Hindman argued in *The Myth of Digital Democracy*, it has not favored democracy.

DOUGLAS RIVERS IS A PROFESSOR of political science at Stanford and the chief scientist at YouGov. He started trying to conduct public opinion surveys via the internet in the nineties, and has done much of the best and most careful work in the field. When he cofounded Knowledge Networks and conducted polls through Web TV, he used probability sampling as an alternative to quota sampling. The initial response rate was something like 50 percent, but over time the rate fell into the single digits. After the dot-com crash, "we slimmed down," Rivers told me when I visited him in Palo Alto. "I went back to teaching."

Rivers then started a company called Polimetrix, which he sold to YouGov for an estimated thirty-five million dollars. There he developed a method called "matched sampling": he uses the U.S. Census Bureau's American Community Survey, which surveys a million people a year, to generate a random sample according to "fifteen variables of representativeness" and to determine who will participate in polls. "You get a million people to take the poll, but you only need a thousand, so you pick the thousand that match your target population," he explained to me.

Sometimes when political scientists are hired by corporations their research becomes proprietary. "When I say I don't know the secret sauce, I really don't know it," Arthur Lupia says of political scientists who sell their research to businesses rather than publish it in journals that would require them to reveal their methodologies. Lupia is a professor of political science at the University of Michigan, a former director of the American National Election Survey, and the lead author of "Improving Public Perceptions of Political Science's Value," a 2014 report prepared by a task force established by the American Political Science Association. Where once social scientists avidly defended the polling industry, many have grown alarmed that media-run horse-race polls may be undermining the public's perception of the usefulness of social science surveys. (Lupia jokes that horse-race polls ought to have a warning label that reads FOR ENTERTAINMENT PURPOSES ONLY.) Like Rivers, Lupia ardently believes in the importance of measuring public opinion. "It is critical for a nation that cherishes its democratic legitimacy to seek credible measures of how citizens think, feel, and act in electoral contexts," Lupia and the political scientist Jon Krosnick have written. Otherwise, "there will be no strong evidentiary basis for differentiating propagandistic tall tales from empirically defensible and logically coherent readings of electoral history."

It's an important point. But it may be that media-run polls have endangered the academic study of public opinion and of political behavior. Public disaffection with the polling industry has contributed to a plummeting response rate for academic and government surveys.

Those surveys are invaluable, the political scientist Sidney Verba has argued. "Surveys produce just what democracy is supposed to produce—equal representation of all citizens," Verba said in a presidential address before the American Political Science Association in 1995. "The sample survey is rigorously egalitarian; it is designed so that each citizen has an equal chance to participate and an equal voice when participating." Verba sees surveying public opinion not only as entirely consistent with democratic theory but as a corrective to democracy's flaws. Surveys, Verba argues, achieve representativeness through science.

The best and most responsible pollsters, whether Democratic, Republican, or nonpartisan, want nothing so much as reliable results. Today, with a response rate in the single digits, they defend their work by pointing out that the people who do answer the phone are the people who are most likely to vote. Bill McInturff, of Public Opinion Strategies, told me, "The people we have trouble getting are less likely to vote." But the difficulty remains. Surveying only likely voters might make for a better election prediction, but it means that the reason for measuring public opinion, the entire justification for the endeavor, has been abandoned. Public opinion polling isn't enhancing political participation. Instead, it's a form of disenfranchisement.

"There are all kinds of problems with public opinion research, as done by surveys," Lupia admits. "But a lot of the alternatives are worse. A lot of what we'd have would be self-serving stories about what's good for people. 'When given a clear choice between eggs and bananas, ninety-eight percent of the people prefer one or the other.' Prior to the polls, I can say that, and you have no check on me. But if there's a poll you have a check."

That's a good point, too, except that there isn't much of a check on political scientists who don't reveal their methods because they've sold their algorithms to startups for millions of dollars. Whether or not they're making money, people who predict elections want to be right, and they believe, as fiercely as Lupia does, that they are engaged in a public good. I asked Doug Rivers what role the measurement of public opinion plays in a democracy. He said, "The cynical answer is 'Once the rockets are up, who cares where they come down.'" (He was quoting a Tom Lehrer song.) But Rivers isn't cynical. He believes that polling "improves the quality of representation." I asked him to give me an example. He said, "You couldn't have had the change in gay marriage without the polling data." Everyone cares where the rockets come down.

THE DAY I VISITED CROWDPAC, at the back of a one-story office building in Menlo Park, the staff was having a debate about what kind of takeout to order during the GOP debate. "What is GOP food? BBQ?" A piece of computer hardware labeled "Hillary's Hard Drive: HEAVY USE: Now Perfectly Clean" rested on a coffee table. There were Bernie Sanders posters on the walls and cutouts of Rand Paul's head popping out of a jar of pencils. Crowdpac is the brainchild of Steve Hilton, a former senior adviser to David Cameron, and Adam Bonica, a young Stanford political scientist. Their idea is to use data science to turn public opinion polling upside down. "There had been an explosion in the use of data, all structured to advance campaigns," Bonica says. "They'd take information from voters and manipulate it to the politicians' advantage. But what if it could go the other way?" The company's unofficial motto on its website used to be "Now you can get the data on them!"

Crowdpac is just getting off the ground, but it has provided an interactive Voter's Guide for several federal, state, and citywide elections from Philadelphia to San Francisco and encouraged people to run for office. Liz Jaff, Crowdpac's Democratic political director (she has a Republican counterpart), showed me a beta site she'd set up, whereby visitors who supported Planned Parenthood could look up all the unopposed GOP candidates who have promised to defund Planned Parenthood and then pledge money to anyone who would run against them. The pledges would be converted to donations automatically, as soon as someone decided to run. Candidates could see how much money they would have, right out of the gate, and their opponents could see, too. "If you get a tweet saying you just got five hundred thousand dollars pledged against you, that sends a message," Jaff said.

"We are trying to figure out what drives people to be interested in politics," Hilton told me. "We are working on tools that help people get engaged with particular issues. If you care about fracking—for or against—what should you do? What candidate should you give money to? What people should you urge to run for office? We are uncovering the hidden political wiring of politics."

I asked him if that wasn't the role of the press.

"Maybe once," he said.

Data science may well turn out to be as flawed as public opinion polling. But a stage in the development of any new tool is to imagine that you've perfected it, in order to ponder its consequences. I asked Hilton to suppose that there existed a flawless tool for measuring public opinion, accurately and instantly, a tool available to voters and politicians alike. Imagine that you're a member of Congress, I said, and you're about to head into the House to vote on an act—let's call it the Smeadwell-Nutley Act. As you do, you use an app called iThePublic to learn the opinions of your constituents. You oppose Smeadwell-Nutley; your constituents are 79 percent in favor of it. Your constituents will instantly know how you've voted, and many have set up an account with Crowdpac to make automatic campaign donations. If you vote against the proposed legislation, your constituents will stop giving money to your reelection campaign. If, contrary to your convictions but in line with your iThePublic, you vote for Smeadwell-Nutley, would that be democracy?

A worried look crossed Hilton's face. Lindsay Rogers has long since been forgotten. But the role of public opinion measurement in a representative government is more troubling than ever.

Hilton shook his head. "You can't solve every problem with more democracy," he said.

TO WINNOW THE FIELD OF CANDIDATES who would hold the main stage in the second GOP debate, in September 2015, CNN had intended to use the average of national polls conducted over the summer. But after Carly Fiorina's campaign complained that the method was unfair, CNN changed its formula. The decision had very little to do with American democracy or social science. It had to do with the practice of American journalism. It would make better television if Fiorina was on the same stage as Trump, since he'd made comments about her appearance. ("Look at that face!" he said.)

"No one tells me what to say," Trump had said in August. By September, on the defensive about Fiorina, he insisted—he knew—that he had the will of the people behind him. "If you look at the polls," he said, "a lot of people like the way I talk."

Donald Trump is a creature of the polls. He is his numbers. But he is only a sign of the times. Turning the press into pollsters has made American political culture Trumpian: frantic, volatile, shortsighted, sales-driven, and antidemocratic.

He kept his lead nearly till the end of October. "Do we love these polls?" he called out to a crowd in Iowa. "Somebody said, 'You love polls.' I said that's only because I've been winning every single one of them. Right? Right? Every single poll." Two days later, when he lost his lead in Iowa to Ben Carson, he'd grown doubtful: "I honestly think those polls are wrong." By the week of the third GOP debate, he'd fallen behind in a national CBS/NYT poll. "The thing with these polls, they're all so different," Trump said, mournfully. "It's not very scientific."

—2015

Postscript: In 2016, all major polling organizations predicted Hillary Clinton would defeat Donald Trump.

THE WAR AND THE ROSES

CLEVELAND

They perched on bar stools, their bodies long and lean, like eels, the women in sleeveless dresses the color of flowers or fruit (marigold, tangerine), the men in fitted suits the color of embers (charcoal, ash). Makeshift television studios lined the floor and the balcony of the convention hall: CNN, Fox, CBS, Univision, PBS. MSNBC built a pop-up studio on East Fourth Street, a square stage raised above the street, like an outdoor boxing ring. "Who won today? Who will win tomorrow?" the networks asked. The guests slumped against the ropes and sagged in their seats, or straightened their backs and slammed their fists. The hosts narrowed their eyes, the osprey to the fish: "Is America over?"

Americans had been assassinating one another, in schools and in churches, in cars and in garages, in bars, parks, and streets, insane with hate—hate whites, hate Blacks, hate Christians, hate Muslims, hate gays, hate police. A certain number of Americans, bearing arms, had lost their minds, their souls, the feel of the earth beneath their feet. Dread fell, and lingered, like mud after rain. At the 2016 Republican National Convention, in Cleveland, Ohio, gas masks were banned, body armor was allowed. "Write any or all emergency phone numbers somewhere on your body using a pen," a security memo urged reporters. "Best to write your name, too," came a whisper over a stall in a women's room, a Sharpie skittering along the tiled floor, as if it had traveled all the way from 1862, when twenty-one-year-old Oliver Wendell Holmes Jr., wounded at Antietam and afraid he was about to die, scratched a note and pinned it to his uniform, Union blue: "I am Capt. O. W. Holmes," hoping his body would find its way home.

"Has America ever before been so divided?" the television hosts asked their guests on street-side sets, while the American people, walking by, stopped, watched, and listened, a tilt of the head, a frown, a selfie. "Wash yourselves! Make yourselves clean!" evangelicals advised, by megaphone, placard, and pamphlet. "Judgment is coming!" T-shirts stating the significance of life came in black and blue or pink (for fetuses). Past the chain-link gate at the entrance to the Quicken Loans Arena, a line of delegates and reporters snaked across an empty parking lot and into security tents—conveyor belts, wands, please place your laptop in the bin—as if we were about to board an airplane, take off, and fly to another country, a terrible country, a land of war. "There are a lot of people who think the whole purpose of all this turmoil is to create martial law," Hal Wick, a delegate from South Dakota, told me, musing darkly on the shootings. Wick doesn't believe that the United States will last much longer if Hillary Clinton is elected. "If you do the research and the reading," he said, "you find out that, if you get to a point where more than half the people are on the dole, the country doesn't exist. It descends into anarchy." It won't take as long as four years. "I give it two or three," Wick said. "Tops."

A parking garage attached to the arena had been converted into a media production center, cubbies for radio and television and Snapchat and Twitter, like cabins on a ship, the floor a tangle of cables like the ropes on deck. Don King stood astride its bow, dressed like a Reagan-era Bruce Springsteen (faded jean jacket; swatches of red, white, and blue). He'd wanted to speak at the convention, but he'd been snubbed; this was his chance to testify. An audience of reporters and photographers flocked around him, seagulls to a mast. He drew himself up. He threw his head back. He roared, as if he were introducing a matchup: "Donald Trump is for *the people*!"

Every tyrant from Mao to Perón rules in the name of the people; his claim does not lessen their suffering. Every leader of every democracy rules in the name of the people, too, but their suffering, if they suffer, leads to his downfall, by way of their votes (which used to be called their "voices"). Still, "the voice of the People" is a figure of speech. "Government requires make-believe," the historian Edmund S. Morgan once gently explained. "Make believe that the king is divine, make believe that he can do no wrong or make believe that the voice of the people is the voice of God. Make believe that the people *have* a voice or make believe that the representatives of the people *are* the people."

Cast back to a time long past. In the thirteenth century, the king of England summoned noblemen to court and demanded that they pledge to obey his laws and pay his taxes, and this they did. But then they, along with other men, sent by counties and towns, began pretending that they weren't making these pledges for themselves alone but that they represented the interests of other people, that they parleyed, that they *spoke* for them; in 1377, they elected their first "Speaker." In the 1640s, many of those men, a Parliament, wished to challenge the king, who claimed that he was divine and that his sovereignty came from God. No one really believed that; they only pretended to believe it. To counter that claim, men in Parliament began to argue that they represented the People, that the People were sovereign, and that the People had granted them authority to represent them, in some time immemorial. Royalists pointed out that this was absurd. How can "the People" rule when "they which are the people this minute, are not the people the next minute"? Who even are they? Also, when, exactly, did they grant Parliament their authority?

In 1647, the Levellers, hoping to remedy this small defect, drafted An Agreement of the People, with the idea that every freeman would assent to it, granting to his representatives the power to represent him. That never quite came to pass, but when, between 1649 and 1660, England had no king, and became a commonwealth, it got a little easier to pretend that there existed such a thing as the People, and that they were the sovereign rulers of . . . themselves. This seed, planted in American soil, under an American sun, sprouted and flourished, fields of wheat, milled to grain, the daily bread. ("The fiction that replaced the divine right of kings is our fiction," Morgan wrote, "and it accordingly seems less fictional to us.") When Parliament then said, "We, the People, have decided to tax you," the colonists, meeting in their own assemblies, answered, "No, *we're* the People." By 1776, what began as make-believe had become self-evident; by 1787, it had become the American creed.

We the people are, apparently, grievously vexed. Around the corner from Don King, NBC News was running a promotional stunt called Election Confessions ("Tell us what you really think"), asking passersby to write on colored sticky notes and shove them in a ballot box; the confessions were displayed, anonymously, on a wall monitor. Blue: "I can't believe it got this far." Orange: "I get to vote for the first time, and now I don't want to." Green: "<u>THESE ARE OUR CHOICES?</u>" I wandered down an aisle and sat next to Johnny Shull, a delegate from North Carolina who used to teach economics at the Charles Koch Institute and helps run a conservative talk-radio hour, *The Chad Adams Show.* Sitting beside him was Susan Phillips, a warm and friendly woman who was a guest that day on the show. I told Shull what Wick had said, about the end of America. "That's silly," he said. Shull had originally supported Rand Paul and was now a Trump delegate. He thinks America is resilient and will bounce back, no matter who wins. Phillips agrees with Wick. She loves Trump because he says all the things she wants to say and can't; because he speaks her thoughts about the half of America that's living off the other half, and about the coming lawlessness. (Mitt Romney's "47 percent," which is the same figure that the Nixon campaign complained about in 1972, has very lately risen, in the populist imagination, to 49 percent.) I asked Phillips what happens if Trump loses. She said, "Then we've got to build our compounds, get our guns ready, and prepare for the worst." Half of the people believe that they know how the other half lives, and deem them enemies.

WE THE PEOPLE WELCOME YOU TO CLEVELAND, banners declared, hanging from street lamps along the road to the city's Public Square, a granite-and-steel plaza with fountains and patches of grass, trough and pasture. Parts of Ohio used to belong to Connecticut, and the New Englanders who settled Cleveland, in the eighteenth century, set aside land for a commons, a place for grazing sheep and cattle and for arguing about politics: the public square, the people's park.

"God hates America!" a wiry man was shouting from the soundstage. "America is doomed!" Most of the protesters came in ones and twos. Oskar Mosco, who told me that he was a pedicab driver from California, carried a poster board on which he'd written, WHY VOTE? He said, "Democracy, lately, is just a fiction." *Make believe the people rule.* I sat down on a step next to Amy Thie, a twenty-two-year-old student at the University of Cincinnati. She'd made a T-shirt that read,

"I know shirts. I make the best shirts. Mexico will pay for them. It's terrific. Everyone agrees I have baby hands," to which she'd affixed a pair of pink plastic doll hands, one clutching a miniature American flag. "Some people really hate Trump," she said. "I don't hate him. I think he's bringing to light aspects of our society that need to come to light." She's worried about the world, but she's not that worried about Trump. "People are too reasonable for this movement to win."

Thie's faith in the people is a faith in the future. It dates to the era of Andrew Jackson, when the idea of the people got hitched to the idea of progress, especially technological progress—the steam engine, the railroad, the telegraph. Ralph Waldo Emerson, awed by the force of American ideas, American people, and American machines, called the United States "the country of the future." If the people can be trusted to be reasonable, all things are possible, the historian George Bancroft argued, in an 1835 speech called "The Office of the People." Bancroft was writing at a time when poor men were newly enfranchised, and a lot of his friends thought that these men were too stupid to vote. Bancroft offered reassurance. If you lock a man in a dark dungeon for his whole life and finally let him out, he may be blinded by the light, but that doesn't mean he lacks the faculty of sight; one day, he will see. Let him add his voice:

> Wherever you see men clustering together to form a party, you may be sure that however much error may be there truth is there also. Apply this principle boldly, for it contains a lesson of candor and a voice of encouragement. There never was a school of philosophy nor a clan in the realm of opinion but carried along with it some important truth. And therefore every sect that has ever flourished has benefited Humanity, for the errors of a sect pass away and are forgotten; its truths are received into the common inheritance.

The voice of the People became a roar and a rumpus. Year after year, the People convened, to write and revise and ratify state constitutions, to vote on party rules and platforms, to pick candidates. The men who drafted the Constitution had been terrified of an unchecked majority; events in France had hardly quieted their concerns. John Adams and

James Madison, old men, hobbled into constitutional conventions in Massachusetts and Virginia, where they sat, stiffly, and endured the declamations of long-whiskered shavers and strivers, the lovers of the People. Americans had grown convention-mad. In 1831, they even began nominating candidates for the presidency in convention halls. The People must exist: they climbed the rafters.

By the time I got to my seat in the Quicken Loans Arena, the chairman of the Republican National Committee, Reince Priebus, was ordering delegates to file out, sending them off to this committee meeting or that: Rules, Platform, Credentials. When he stepped down from the podium, the jumbo teleprompter that he'd been reading from flickered, went black, and then turned back on. I stared, wide-eyed. "They put that up there whenever the stage is empty," a reporter from *The Nation* told me, helpfully. Up there, in LED, was the Gettysburg Address. *Four score and seven years ago our fathers brought forth on this continent, a new nation, conceived in liberty, and dedicated to the proposition that all men are created equal. Now we are engaged in a great civil war, testing whether that nation, or any nation so conceived and so dedicated, can long endure.*

Lincoln stopped in Cleveland in 1861, on the way to his inauguration as the first Republican president. Down on the convention floor, George Engelbach, a delegate from Missouri, was dressed as Lincoln: top hat and suit, whiskers. I asked him why he admired Lincoln. "If it were not for him, we would have a divided country," he said. Engelbach has been a Trump supporter from the start, because "Trump's the only one who can put it back together again." That night, the speakers at the convention talked about dead bodies: the bodies of Americans killed by undocumented immigrants, of Americans killed by terrorists in Benghazi, of Americans killed by men who supported Black Lives Matter. A grieving mother blamed Hillary Clinton for her son's death. Soldiers described the corpses of their fallen comrades. "I pulled his body armor off and checked for vitals," one said. "There were no signs of torture or mutilation," another said. *We have come to dedicate a portion of that field, as a final resting place for those who here gave their lives that that nation might live.* But this wasn't Gettysburg. This battle isn't over. "Our own city streets have become the battleground," the Homeland Security Committee chair, Mike McCaul, said. The Milwaukee County sheriff, David A. Clarke Jr., said, "I call it anarchy."

The next day, in Public Square, Vets vs. Hate took the stage. "Please stop using our veterans as props," Alexander McCoy, an ex-marine, begged the Trump-Pence campaign. I went to see a ten-foot-tall American bald eagle, made entirely out of red-white-and-blue Duck Brand duct tape, on display in a parking lot. (Hope is, always, the thing with feathers.) Then I got a ride out to the Cleveland History Center, where Lauren R. Welch gave me a tour of a collection of memorabilia from earlier GOP conventions, the buttons and the bunting. Welch, twenty-eight and African American, has lived in Cleveland nearly all her life. She's an activist, a supporter of Black Lives Matter. I asked whether either of the two major presidential candidates could bring about a better future. "Even Obama couldn't bring people together," she said, searchingly. No, she said. "Hope comes from the people."

After the Civil War, the idea of the People and the idea of progress got uncoupled, an engine careering away from its train. This was the work of the late nineteenth-century People's Party, a left-wing movement of farmers and workers who found out the hard way that progress sometimes mows men down; they wanted to use democracy to limit certain kinds of technological progress, for the sake of equality. Historians have tended to consider Populism muddleheaded: America looked forward, Populists looked backward. "The utopia of the Populists was in the past, not the future," Richard Hofstadter wrote, disapprovingly. Many historians have said the same thing about conservatism, especially the Trump variety, whose followers, like their leftier, Populist forebears, have found out the hard way that progress mows some men down. I talked to Jimmy Sengenberger, a young conservative who thinks a lot about this question. "Looking back at the founding principles of this country is the best way to look forward," he told me. Sengenberger, twenty-five, was an alternate delegate from Colorado. He's polite and ambitious, a Jimmy Olsen look-alike. He works in a law office during the week and hosts a talk-radio show on Saturday nights. "Progressivism is regressive," he said. "Conservatism is the only truly forward-looking political philosophy."

Newt Gingrich is a historian, so on the third day of the convention, before he was due to speak, I figured I'd ask him whether he was worried that the right had ceded all talk of progress to the left. "No. Listen to my speech," he told me. "I'm going to talk about safety." When

I suggested that making America safe again isn't exactly forward-looking, he assured me that he was going to talk about the future. Back inside the convention hall, after yet another speech by yet another made-for-television Trump child, Ted Cruz was doing a mic check, not by reading the Gettysburg Address from the teleprompter, as others did, but by reciting Dr. Seuss: "I do not like green eggs and ham, I do not like them, Sam-I-am"; ode to an ornery man. That night, Cruz was booed off the stage. Gingrich, who followed him, did talk about the future: he warned of a coming apocalypse.

ON THE LAST DAY of the GOP convention, I went back to Public Square. They came and they came, the protesters, one by one, and two by two. A mother of nine named Samia Assed wandered by. She owns two New York–style delis in Santa Fe. Her family is originally from Palestine. She had driven to Cleveland in a caravan organized by the Grassroots Global Justice Alliance. I asked her if she thought that either Trump or Clinton could bridge the divide. She looked at me as if I were nuts. "They *are* the divide," she said. Erika Husby, another protester, had blond hair piled in a messy bun and was wearing a poncho painted to look like a brick wall. It read WALL OFF TRUMP. She's twenty-four and from Chicago, where she teaches English as a second language. She liked Sanders but was willing to vote for Clinton. Black Lives Matter is "changing the country for the better," she said. Joshua Kaminski, twenty-eight, originally from Michigan, was wearing a Captain America T-shirt and a silver cross on a silver chain. He works for Delta Airlines. He and Oskar Mosco got to talking, each keen, each curious. "I've seen conservatism and Christianity separate," Kaminski told Mosco. "I'm not going to vote against my morals anymore." He's pretty sure he'll vote for Johnson-Weld. Meanwhile, he was giving out water bottles labeled ELECT JESUS.

The rule inside the convention was: Incite fear and division in order to call for safety and union. I decided that the rule outside the convention was: No kidding, it's really awfully nice out here, in a beautiful city park, on a sunny day in July, where a bunch of people are arguing about politics and nothing could possibly be more interesting, and the Elect Jesus people are giving out free water, icy cold, and the police are playing Ping-Pong with the protesters, and you can take a nap in the grass if you want, and you will dream that you are on a farm because the grass smells kind of horsy, and like manure, because of all the mounted police from Texas, wearing those strangely sexy cowboy hats; and, yes, there are police from all over the country here, and if you ask for directions one of them will say to you, "Girl, I'm from Atlanta!" and you have to know that, if they weren't here, who knows what would happen; there are horrible people shouting murderous things and tussling, that's what they came here for, and anything can blow up in an instant; and, yes, there are civilians carrying military-style weapons, but, weirdly, they are less scary here than they are online; they look ridiculous, honestly, and this one lefty guy is a particular creep, don't get cornered; but, also, there's a little Black girl in the fountain rolling around, getting soaked, next to some white guy who's sitting there, just sitting there, in the water, his legs kicked out in front of him, holding a cardboard sign that reads TIRED OF THE VIOLENCE.

I climbed up the steps of the park's Civil War Soldiers' and Sailors' Monument, not far from the spot where Lincoln's casket was put on display, in 1865, on his way home. It was as if he had pinned a note to his suit: *We here highly resolve that these dead shall not have died in vain—that this nation, under God, shall have a new birth of freedom, and that government of the people, by the people, for the people, shall not perish from the earth.*

I trudged back to the arena for the final night's speakers.

"No one has more faith in the American people than my father," Ivanka Trump said. She called him "the people's champion." She was wearing a sleeveless dress the color of a grapefruit, the pinkest of peonies.

Trump took the stage, in a suit as black as cinder. "The American people will come first again," he thundered.

"*I am your voice,*" he said. His face turned as red-hot as the last glowing ember of a fire, dying.

PHILADELPHIA

Welcome to the city of love. "What love, what care, what service, and what travail hath there been to bring thee forth," William Penn said, in 1684, praying for a tiny, frail settlement huddled along the banks of the Delaware River. "O that thou mayest be kept from the evil that would overwhelm thee." In the Wells Fargo Center, LOVE TRUMPS HATE signs fluttered on the floor of the convention hall like the pages of a manuscript scattered by a fierce wind. It was a book of antonyms: the future, not the past; love, not hate. "We are the party of tomorrow!" John Lewis hollered to the crowd. "What the world needs now is love," the Democrats sang, holding hands, leaning, listing. And still the signs fluttered and scattered, the book of antonyms ripped up by Sanders delegates, who tore at its pages and yanked at its binding, its brittle glue. Anne Hamilton, a delegate from North Carolina, got out a marker and doctored her LOVE TRUMPS HATE sign to read LOVE BERNIE OR TRUMP WINS. She was determined. "They said they were going to replace me with an alternate," she told me. "And I just kept repeating, 'Freedom of speech, freedom of speech!'" And a future under Clinton or Trump? "It's like a windshield after a rock hits it," she said. "The glass looks like a spider's web, and you can see through it, but not really, and then, all at once, in a flash, it cracks, and it shatters, and there's nothing left." Slivers of glass and the rush of an unshielded wind.

Philadelphia was to Cleveland the zig to its zag, the other half of the zipper. The Democrats recycle. They provide compost bins. They speak Spanish in the security lines. They serve kosher food. They offer a "Gluten-Free Section." They have blue-curtained breastfeeding and pumping areas. The Democrats run out of coffee. They run out of seats. They run out of food. They run out of *water*. They talk for too long; they run out of time. During breaks between speakers, the Republicans played the Knack's "My Sharona" ("When you gonna give me some time, Sharona / Ooh, you make my motor run"); the Democrats played Prince's "Let's Go Crazy" ("Dearly beloved / We are gathered here today / To get through this thing called 'life'"). Try to get through a night at a Democratic convention, early in the week, with nothing more than M&M's and the voice of the People to jolt you awake. It's like being at a sleepover and trying to stay up until midnight for the candlelit séance, the conjuring of a spirit: *Speak, speak!*

Dearly beloved. "There is tension and dissension in the land," Cynthia Hale, of the Ray of Hope Christian Church, in Decatur, Georgia, said, leading the invocation on the convention's first day. And there was tension and dissension in the hall. "It's time that the people took the power back," Rebecca Davies, a delegate from Illinois, told me. I asked her if she supported Clinton. "God, no!" she said, mock-affronted. She was wearing a pointy hat, made of green felt, with a red feather tucked in its brim. She'd got the hat at a gathering that morning, when Sanders tried to persuade his followers to support Clinton, and they balked. People all over the arena were wearing Robin Hood hats, as if it were 1937 and Warner Bros. was holding auditions for an Errol Flynn film. Davies was cheerful, but she was disappointed; the People, spurned.

The proceedings began. But when Barney Frank got up to speak the crowd booed him. "Thank you, or not, as the case may be," Frank said, grimly. Frank, no fan of Bernie Sanders, co-chaired the Rules Committee, whose decisions Sanders supporters had protested—a protest strengthened by the release, the day before, of hacked Democratic National Committee emails. (Hacked by Russia? Hack more! Trump taunted.) The People had been betrayed by the party, corrupted. "The DNC thinks it's better to keep people ignorant," Robyn Sumners told me, angry, astonished. She was a precinct inspector in California's District 29, where Sanders lost by a smidgen. She blames the press and the DNC. "They don't want people involved," she said. "They don't trust us. They're afraid of Bernie because you know what Bernie does? He wakes people up. I learned in this election: They don't want us to vote." Some Sanders people covered their mouths with blue tape, on which they'd written SILENCED. The People, muffled, stifled, muzzled, unloved.

Carl Davis, a delegate from Texas, works in the mayor's office in Houston. He's African American and a long-standing Clinton supporter. He was a Clinton delegate in 2008, too. "The Democratic Party brings hope to this nation," he told me. "We, we are the ones looking out for the people of this country." Not Trump, not Trump, not Trump. "My name isn't Sucker Boone," Emily Boone, a Kentucky delegate, snapped, when I asked her what she thought of the Republican nominee. When Democrats on the floor talked about Trump, wincing, shuddering, they tended to talk about a political apocalypse possibly even darker than the one conjured by Trump supporters when they imagined a Clinton presidency: fascism, the launch codes, the end of days.

"Donald Trump knows that the American people are angry—a fact so obvious he can see it from the top of Trump Tower," Elizabeth Warren said from the lectern, undertaking the sober, measured work of arguing that Trump did not speak for the American people, that he had misjudged if he thought that he could make the American people angry with one another. "I've got news for Donald Trump," Warren said. "The American people are not falling for it!"

The People are easy to invoke but impossible to curb. A spirit can't be bottled. "If you look at our platform, all the way through it talks about trying to lift people up, people who have been left behind," Chris McCurry told me. This was McCurry's first convention. He was a delegate from South Carolina, where he works as an IT guy in the state's Department of Transportation. He was wearing a hat decorated with red-white-and-blue tinsel and a vest pinned with eleven Hillary buttons. "She's spent her whole life trying to lift up women and children, and when we do that we lift up the nation, when you do that you get gay rights, you fight racism," he said. "You *always* progress."

The Democratic Party's argument is that it is the only party that contains multitudes. What happens when the people are sovereign? "The dangerous term, as it turned out, was not sovereignty," as the historian Daniel T. Rogers once put it. "It was the People." When white men said, "We are the People and therefore we rule," how were they to deny anyone else the right to rule, except by denying their very peoplehood? "We, too, are people!" shouted women, Blacks, immigrants, the poorest of the poor. And, lo, the People did say, "No, you are not people!" That worked for only so long. And, when it failed, the People passed new immigration and citizenship laws, and restricted voting rights, and made corporations honorary people, to give themselves more power. And, lo, a lot of Americans got to worrying about what viciousness, what greed, and what recklessness the People were capable of. These people called themselves Progressives.

In the early decades of the twentieth century, the left lost its faith in the People but kept its faith in progress. Progressives figured that experts, with the light of their science, ought to guide the government in developing the best solutions to political and economic problems. In the 1940s, populism began to move from the left to the right, not sneakily or stealthily but in the shadows all the same, unnoticed, ignored, demeaned. In Christopher Lasch's grumpiest book, *The True and Only Heaven*, from 1991, he argued that a big problem with post-war liberalism was liberals' failure to really listen to the continuing populist criticism of the idea of progress. "Their confidence in being on the winning side of history made progressive people unbearably smug and superior," Lasch wrote, "but they felt isolated and beleaguered in their own country, since it was so much less progressive than they were." That went on for decades.

In 1992, the year Bill Clinton was elected, a letter to the editor appeared in a small newspaper in upstate New York. "The American Dream of the middle class has all but disappeared, substituted with people struggling just to buy next week's groceries," the letter writer argued. "What is it going to take to open up the eyes of our elected officials? AMERICA IS IN SERIOUS DECLINE." It was written by a young Timothy McVeigh.

And still, after Oklahoma City, and Waco, and the militia movement, all through the 1990s, progressive politicians and intellectuals continued to ignore the right-wing narrative of decline, even as it became the hallmark of conservative talk radio. And they ignored Sanders's warnings about decline, too, when he talked about the growing economic divide, the widening gap between the rich and the poor, and the stranglehold of corporate interests over politics. "There is a war going on in this country," Sanders said, in an eight-and-a-half-hour speech from the floor of the Senate, in 2010. "I am talking about a war being waged by some of the wealthiest and most powerful people against working families, against the disappearing and shrinking middle class of our country." He spoke alone. Progressives and liberals talked about growth, prosperity, globalization, innovation.

Dearly beloved. "Don't let anyone ever tell you that this country isn't great," Michelle Obama said, in an uplifting speech on the first night of the Democratic convention. But then Sanders got up and said it: "This election is about ending the forty-year decline of our middle class, the reality that forty-seven million men, women, and children live in poverty." A sea of blue signs waved at him, as if in rebuke: A FUTURE TO **BELIEVE IN**. Sanders, and only Sanders, talked that way about decline and suffering. Meanwhile, outside, a sudden summer storm battered the city, the rain falling like dread.

FUTURE IS BRIGHT was stamped in white on hot-pink sunglasses that Planned Parenthood gave out to volunteers. Cecile Richards, the head of the Planned Parenthood Action Fund, sat next to Bill Clinton the night Michelle Obama addressed the convention. "Look, it was amazing to be there," Richards said, when I talked to her the next morning. "The passing of the torch, from one incredible woman to another incredible woman." Richards thinks that the Republicans are fighting a kind of progress they can't stop. "If I were trying to lead a party that believed in rolling back LGBTQ rights and women's rights, and denying climate change, that would be a very tough agenda to sell to young people in this country," she said. Downtown, a dozen volunteers wearing pink pinnies gathered in front of a Planned Parenthood clinic on Locust Street to help escort women into the clinic, intending to steer them clear of pro-life protesters, who never turned up. The idea that love conquers all entered American political rhetoric by way of the gay rights and the same-sex-marriage movements, in which activists, following the model of the civil rights and the reproductive rights movements, largely bypassed the People and took their case, instead, to the Supreme Court. A few blocks down Locust Street, hundreds of people had gathered for the Great Wall of Love, a rally for unity in front of the Mazzoni Center, an LGBTQ clinic. They sang "Seasons of Love," from *Rent*. They waved white placards that read, in rainbow-colored letters, LOVE WINS.

That night, Sanders, seated with the delegation from Vermont, called for Clinton's nomination by acclamation. The People shouted, but not with one voice. Hundreds of Sanders delegates and supporters rose from their seats and walked out. "We will not yield," Alyssa DeRonne, a delegate from Asheville, North Carolina, said. "I want to see my children philosophizing and inventing new things, not blowing up another country." Anne Hamilton walked out, too. So did Sanders delegates from Hawaii. Carolyn Golojuch, a seventy-year-old Clinton delegate from Honolulu, was disgusted by the walkout. "I have stood on the streets by the state capitol for eighteen years, working for same-sex-marriage rights, for my son, for everyone," she told me. "I have lost jobs. I have fought and I have fought. These Sanders people, they haven't learned how to compromise. And you know what? They don't own the word 'progressive.'" Golojuch's husband, Mike, was wearing a rainbow ALL YOU NEED IS LOVE button, but neither of them had any illusions that love always wins.

What wins? I asked Elizabeth Warren. "The last three or four years that I have been in the Senate, it's been like climbing a sheer rock wall," she said. "And all I do is try to find a finger hole or a toe hole, somewhere, somewhere." People are right to be angry, she said. They should be angry. They're not wrong that the system is rigged. "The rich and the powerful have all kinds of money and all kinds of weapons, to make the country, and the government, just the way they want it," she said. "And the rest of us? All we've got are our voices and our votes, and the only way those have any strength is if we use them together and aim them perfectly."

Two protests were happening by LOVE Park, across the street from city hall, in the shadow of a thirty-foot-tall sculpture called *Government of the People*: naked bodies smushed into the shape of a clenched fist. If you stood in the middle of the park, you could listen to both protests at the same time:

"We, the people, can solve our ills, if we work together—"
"—patriarchy is woven into the fabric—"
"Yesterday we took some action—"
"That is fucked up!"

At one end of the park, a very small audience listened to the Revolution Club; at the other end, by the main stage, hundreds of people, including a lot of Sanders delegates, had gathered for an Occupy DNC rally. They were young, and they were mad, and they were undaunted. They wore Bernie masks and waved Bernie puppets. They chanted, "Hell no, DNC, we won't vote for Hillary." They were waiting for the Green Party's Jill Stein to come and speak. "Jill not Hill," they cried. A woman in a red-white-and-blue cowboy hat raised a sign to the sky: THIS IS NOT A RIOT. They wanted to boycott the Democratic Party. They wanted to ban the oligarchy. "I need that 'Power to the People' right now!" Bruce Carter, of Black Men for Bernie, called from the Occupy stage. "We ain't in no dance mode, we in a fighting mode," he said. "I don't want to dance right now. I want to be mad as hell." The music started. *Power to the people, power to the people, power to the people.* The people began to sway.

Something was slipping away, leaching out, like rainwater. The People had lost their footing, their common ground, muddied. Maybe it was a problem that the Levellers had never managed to get everyone in seventeenth-century England to sign on to that Agreement of the People, because the people I talked to in Cleveland and Philadelphia didn't quite seem to believe in representation anymore. Either they were willing to have Trump speak in their stead (*"I am your voice"*), the very definition of a dictator, or else they wanted to speak for themselves, because the system was rigged, because the establishment could not be trusted, or because no one, no one, could understand them, their true, particular, Instagram selves. They hated and were hated; they wanted to love and be loved. They could see, even through a broken windshield, that the future wasn't all dark and it wasn't all bright; it was as streaked as a sky at twilight.

"Let love rule," Lenny Kravitz sang, a choir behind him, the night before the Democratic convention ended. "We are not a fragile people," President Obama insisted, in a beautiful speech as boundless in its optimism as Trump's was in its pessimism. And, when he has faltered, Obama said, something, someone, an idea, had always picked him up. "It's been you," he said. "The American people."

The next morning, Trump's campaign instructed his supporters not to watch Clinton's speech and, instead, to send money, heaps of it, promising that Hillary would hear the amount by 8:00 p.m., so that "before she steps on stage, she'll have stuck in the back of her mind exactly what's coming for her this November: THE AMERICAN PEOPLE!"

That night, the Democrats told a love story. "We are reviving the heart of our democracy," said the Reverend William Barber II, a North Carolina minister, while the people climbed to the rafters. "We must shock this nation with the power of love."

Ivanka Trump had introduced her father; Chelsea Clinton introduced her mother. Daughters are the new political wives. Chelsea wore a red dress with a heart-shaped neckline. She introduced the presidential nominee as a grandmother. "I hope that my children will someday be as proud of me as I am of my mom," she said. Mother love is the corsage pinned to every dress, right or left. "I'm a mom!" said everyone who was one, at both conventions, from Laura Ingraham to Kirsten Gillibrand. "We all hope for a better tomorrow," Morgan Freeman intoned, in his voice-over to a Clinton campaign film. "Every parent knows that your dream for the future beats in the heart of your child." And here, at last, was the resolution, shaky and cynical, of the argument between the people and progress. People + progress = children. In an age of atrocity, the unruliness of the people and a fear of the future have combined with terror, naked terror, to make the love of children an all-purpose proxy for each fraying bond, each abandoned civic obligation, the last, lingering devotion.

Hillary Clinton took the stage in a suit of paper-white. "I am so proud to be your mother," she said to her daughter, addressing the American people not as citizens but as objects of love. "I will carry all of your voices and stories with me to the White House," she promised, the words like lace. "We begin a new chapter tonight." The balloons fell.

And the nation clenched its teeth, the top and the bottom of a jaw, and waited for November.

—2016

YOU'RE FIRED

BIRD-EYED AARON BURR WAS WANTED FOR MURDER in two states when he presided over the impeachment trial of Supreme Court Justice Samuel Chase in the Senate, in 1805. The House had impeached Chase, a Marylander, on seven articles of misconduct and one article of rudeness. Burr had been indicted in New Jersey, where, according to the indictment, "not having the fear of God before his eyes but being moved and seduced by the instigation of the Devil," he'd killed Alexander Hamilton, the former secretary of the treasury, in a duel. Because Hamilton, who was shot in the belly, died in New York, Burr had been indicted there, too. Still, the Senate met in Washington, and, until Burr's term expired, he held the title of vice president of the United States.

The public loves an impeachment, until the public hates an impeachment. For the occasion of Chase's impeachment trial, a special gallery for lady spectators had been built at the back of the Senate chamber. Burr, a Republican, presided over a Senate of twenty-five Republicans and nine Federalists, who sat, to either side of him, on two rows of crimson cloth-covered benches. They faced three rows of green cloth-covered benches occupied by members of the House of Representatives, Supreme Court justices, and President Thomas Jefferson's cabinet. The House managers (the impeachment-trial equivalent of prosecutors), led by the Virginian John Randolph, sat at a table covered with blue cloth; at another blue table sat Chase and his lawyers, led by the red-faced Maryland attorney general, Luther Martin, a man so steady of heart and clear of mind that in 1787 he'd walked out of the Constitutional Convention, and refused to sign the Constitution, after objecting that its countenancing of slavery was "inconsistent with the principles of the Revolution and dishonorable to the American character." Luther (Brandybottle) Martin had a weakness for liquor. This did not impair him. As a wise historian once remarked, Martin "knew more law drunk than the managers did sober."

Impeachment is an ancient relic, a rusty legal instrument and political weapon first wielded by Parliament, in 1376, to wrest power from the king by charging his ministers with abuses of power, convicting them, removing them from office, and throwing them in prison. Some four hundred years later, impeachment had all but vanished from English practice when American delegates to the Constitutional Convention provided for it in Article II, Section 4: "The President, Vice President and all civil Officers of the United States, shall be removed from Office on Impeachment for, and Conviction of, Treason, Bribery, or other high Crimes and Misdemeanors."

It's one thing to know this power exists. It's another to use it. In one view, nicely expressed by an English solicitor general in 1691, "The power of impeachment ought to be, like Goliath's sword, kept in the temple, and not used but on great occasions." Yet in the autumn of 2019, in the third year of the presidency of Donald J. Trump, House Democrats have unsheathed that terrible, mighty sword. Has time dulled its blade?

IMPEACHMENT IS A TERRIBLE POWER because it was forged to counter a terrible power: the despot who deems himself to be above the law. The delegates to the Constitutional Convention included impeachment in the Constitution as a consequence of their knowledge of history, a study they believed to be a prerequisite for holding a position in government. From their study of English history, they learned what might be called the law of knavery: there aren't any good ways to get rid of a bad king. Really, there were only three ways and they were all horrible: civil war, revolution, or assassination. England had already endured the first and America the second, and no one could endorse the third. "What was the practice before this in cases where the chief Magistrate rendered himself obnoxious?" Benjamin Franklin asked at the convention. "Recourse was had to assassination, in which he was not only deprived of his life but of the opportunity of vindicating his character."

But the delegates knew that Parliament had come up with another way: clipping the king's wings by impeaching his ministers. The

House of Commons couldn't attack the king directly because of the fiction that the king was infallible ("perfect," as Donald Trump would say), so, beginning in 1376, they impeached his favorites, accusing Lord William Latimer and Richard Lyons of acting "falsely in order to have advantages for their own use." Latimer, a peer, insisted that he be tried by his peers—that is, by the House of Lords, not the House of Commons—and it was his peers who convicted him and sent him to prison. That's why the House in 2019 prepared articles of impeachment against Trump, acting as his accusers, but it is the Senate that would judge his innocence or his guilt.

Parliament used impeachment to thwart monarchy's tendency toward absolutism, with mixed results. After conducting at least ten impeachments between 1376 and 1450, Parliament didn't impeach anyone for more than a hundred and seventy years, partly because Parliament met only when the king summoned it, and, if Parliament was going to impeach his ministers, he'd show them by never summoning it, unless he really had to, as when he needed to levy taxes. He, or she: during the forty-five years of Elizabeth I's reign, Parliament was in session for a total of three. Parliament had forged a sword. It just couldn't ever get into Westminster to take it out of its sheath.

The Englishman responsible for bringing the ancient practice of impeachment back into use was Edward Coke, an investor in the Virginia Company who became a Member of Parliament in 1589. Coke, a profoundly agile legal thinker, had served as Elizabeth I's attorney general and as chief justice under her successor, James I. In 1621—two years after the first Africans, slaves, landed in the Virginia colony and a year after the Pilgrims, dissenters, landed at a place they called Plymouth—Coke began to insist that Parliament could debate whatever it wanted to, and soon Parliament began arguing that it ought to meet regularly. To build a case for the supremacy of Parliament, Coke dug out of the archives Magna Carta of 1215, calling it England's "ancient constitution," and he resurrected, too, the ancient right of Parliament to impeach the king's ministers. Parliament promptly impeached Coke's chief adversary, Francis Bacon, the lord chancellor, for bribery; Bacon was convicted, removed from office, and reduced to penury. James then dissolved Parliament and locked up Coke in the Tower of London.

Something of a political death match followed between Parliament and James and his Stuart successors Charles I and Charles II, over the nature of rule. In 1626, the House of Commons impeached the Duke of Buckingham for "maladministration" and corruption, including failure to safeguard the seas. But the king, James's son, Charles I, forestalled a trial in the House of Lords by dismissing Parliament. After Buckingham died, Charles refused to summon Parliament for the next eleven years. In 1649, he was beheaded for treason. After the restoration of the monarchy, in 1660, under Charles II, Parliament occasionally impeached the king's ministers, but in 1716 stopped doing so altogether. Because Parliament had won. It had made the king into a flightless bird.

Why the Americans should have resurrected this practice in 1787 is something of a puzzle, until you remember that all but one of England's original thirteen American colonies had been founded before impeachment went out of style. Also, while Parliament had gained power relative to the king, the colonial assemblies remained virtually powerless, especially against the authority of colonial governors, who, in most colonies, were appointed by the king. To clip their governors' wings, colonial assemblies impeached the governors' men, only to find their convictions overturned by the Privy Council in London, which acted as an appellate court. Colonial lawyers pursuing these cases dedicated themselves to the study of the impeachments against the three Stuart kings. John Adams owned a copy of a law book that defined "impeachment" as "the Accusation and Prosecution of a Person for Treason, or other Crimes and Misdemeanors." Steeped in the lore of Parliament's seventeenth-century battles with the Stuarts, men like Adams considered the right of impeachment to be one of the fundamental rights of Englishmen. And when men like Adams came to write constitutions for the new states, in the 1770s and '80s, they made sure that impeachment was provided for. In Philadelphia in 1787, thirty-three of the convention's fifty-five delegates were trained as lawyers; ten were or had been judges. As Frank Bowman, a law professor at the University of Missouri, reports in *High Crimes and Misdemeanors: A History of Impeachment for the Age of Trump*, fourteen of the delegates had helped draft constitutions in their own states that provided for impeachment. In Philadelphia, they forged a new sword out of very old steel. They Americanized impeachment.

THIS NEW GOVERNMENT WOULD HAVE a president, not a king, but Americans agreed on the need for a provision to get rid of a bad one. All four of the original plans for a new constitution allowed for presidential impeachment. When the Constitutional Convention began, on May 25, 1787, impeachment appears to have been on nearly everyone's mind, not least because Parliament had opened its first impeachment investigation in more than fifty years, on April 3, against a colonial governor of India, and the member charged with heading the investigation was England's famed supporter of American independence, Edmund Burke. What with one thing and another, impeachment came up in the convention's very first week.

A president is not a king; his power would be checked by submitting himself to an election every four years, and by the separation of powers. But this did not provide "sufficient security," James Madison said. "He might pervert his administration into a scheme of peculation or oppression. He might betray his trust to foreign powers." Also, voters might make a bad decision, and regret it, well in advance of the next election. "Some mode of displacing an unfit magistrate is rendered indispensable by the fallibility of those who choose, as well as by the corruptibility of the man chosen," the Virginia delegate George Mason said.

How impeachment actually worked would be hammered out through cases like the impeachment of Samuel Chase, a Supreme Court justice, but, at the Constitutional Convention, nearly all discussion of impeachment concerned the presidency. ("Vice President and all civil Officers" was added only at the very last minute.) A nation that had cast off a king refused to anoint another. "No point is of more importance than that the right of impeachment should continue," Mason said. "Shall any man be above Justice? Above all shall that man be above it, who can commit the most extensive injustice?"

Most of the discussion involved the nature of the conduct for which a president could be impeached. Early on, the delegates had listed, as impeachable offenses, "mal-practice or neglect of duty," a list that got longer before a committee narrowed it down to "Treason & bribery." When Mason proposed adding "maladministration," Madison objected, on the ground that maladministration could mean just about anything. And, as the Pennsylvania delegate Gouverneur Morris put it, it would not be unreasonable to suppose that "an election of every four years will prevent maladministration." Mason therefore proposed substituting "other high crimes and misdemeanors against the State."

The "high" in "high crimes and misdemeanors" has its origins in phrases that include the "certain high treasons and offenses and misprisons" invoked in the impeachment of the Duke of Suffolk, in 1450. Parliament was the "high court," the men Parliament impeached were of the "highest rank"; offenses that Parliament described as "high" were public offenses with consequences for the nation. The phrase "high crimes and misdemeanors" first appeared in an impeachment in 1642, and then regularly, as a catchall for all manner of egregious wrongs, abuses of authority, and crimes against the state.

In 1787, the delegates in Philadelphia narrowed their list down to "Treason & bribery, or other high crimes & misdemeanors against the United States." In preparing the final draft of the Constitution, the Committee on Style deleted the phrase "against the United States," presumably because it is implied.

"What, then, is an impeachable offense?" Gerald Ford, the Michigan Republican and House minority leader, asked in 1970. "The only honest answer is that an impeachable offense is whatever a majority of the House of Representatives considers it to be at a given moment in history." That wasn't an honest answer; it was a depressingly cynical one. Ford had moved to impeach Supreme Court justice William O. Douglas, accusing him of embracing a "hippie-yippie-style revolution," indicting him for a decadent life style, and alleging financial improprieties, charges that appeared, to Ford's critics, to fall well short of impeachable offenses. In 2017, Nancy Pelosi claimed that a president cannot be impeached who has not committed a crime (a position she would not likely take today). According to *Impeachment: A Citizen's Guide,* by the legal scholar Cass Sunstein, who testified before Congress on the meaning of "high crimes and misdemeanors" during the impeachment of William Jefferson Clinton, both Ford and Pelosi were fundamentally wrong. "High crimes and misdemeanors" does have a meaning. An impeachable offense is an abuse of the power of the office that violates the public trust, runs counter to the national interest, and undermines the republic. To believe that words are meaningless is to give up on truth. To believe that presidents can do anything they like is to give up on self-government.

The U.S. Senate has held only eighteen impeachment trials in two hundred and thirty years, and only twice for a president. Because impeachment happens so infrequently, it's hard to draw conclusions about what it does, or even how it works, and, on each occasion, people spend a lot of time fighting over the meaning of the words and the nature of the crimes. Every impeachment is a political experiment.

The ordeal of Samuel Chase is arguably the most significant but least studied impeachment in American history. The Chase impeachment was only the third ever attempted. In 1797, the House had impeached the Tennessee senator William Blount, who stood accused of scheming to conspire with the British and to enlist the Creek and Cherokee Nations to attack the Spanish, all with the design of increasing the value of his highly speculative purchase of western lands. ("Whether the scheme was merely audacious or just plain crazy remains debatable," Bowman writes, darkly foreshadowing more recent shenanigans, involving the possible acquisition of Greenland.) The case rested on a letter allegedly written by Blount, describing this plan; after two senators said they recognized Blount's handwriting, the Senate expelled him in a vote of 25–1, and he slinked off to Tennessee. The House had voted to impeach, but Blount's lawyers argued that senators are not "civil officers," and so can't be impeached. ("#IMPEACH-MITTROMNEY," Trump tweeted. The Blount precedent went some way toward establishing that this is an impossibility.) The motion to dismiss was read aloud in the Senate by Jefferson, who was vice president at the time.

Samuel Chase's troubles began when Congress passed the 1798 Sedition Act, aimed at suppressing Republican opposition to John Adams's Federalist administration. Chase, riding circuit, had presided over the most notorious persecutions of Republican printers on charges of sedition, including the conviction of the printer James Callender. The Sedition Act expired on March 3, 1801, the day before Jefferson's inauguration, but, through a series of midnight appointments, Adams had connived to insure that Jefferson inherited a Federalist Supreme Court. Chase had actively campaigned for Adams and spoke intemperately for the bench, denouncing Republicans. In an overheated charge to a grand jury in Baltimore, he attacked Republicanism, describing it as "mobocracy." Jefferson set an impeachment in motion when he wrote to House Republicans, "Ought this sedition and official attack on the principles of our Constitution . . . go unpunished?"

If the proceedings against Blount tested whether senators could be impeached, the proceedings against Chase tested a new theory of executive power—that Supreme Court justices serve at the pleasure of the president. This test came in the wake of *Marbury v. Madison*, in 1803, in which John Marshall's Supreme Court exercised a prerogative not specified in the Constitution: the Court had declared an act of Congress unconstitutional. A Republican leader of the Senate told the Massachusetts senator John Quincy Adams that he hoped to impeach the entire court. Judicial independence? Judicial review? No. "If the Judges of the Supreme Court should dare, AS THEY HAD DONE, to declare an act of Congress unconstitutional . . . it was the undoubted right of the House of Representatives to remove them, for giving such opinions," he said. "A removal by impeachment was nothing more than a declaration by Congress to this effect: You hold dangerous opinions, and if you are suffered to carry them into effect you will work the destruction of the nation."

John Randolph, a steadfast Republican but no lawyer, drafted the articles of impeachment against Chase, which broadly charged him with prostituting his high office to the low purpose of partisanship but, narrowly, rested on all manner of pettiness, including the charge that during Callender's trial Chase had used "unusual, rude, and contemptuous expressions toward the prisoner's counsel" and had engaged in "repeated and vexatious interruptions." Notwithstanding the weakness of the charges, not to say their vexatiousness, the House voted to impeach. The trial in the Senate opened on February 4, 1805.

An impeachment trial is a medieval play, with its mummers and its costumes and its many-colored cloth-covered tables. Chase's trial lasted a month. Burr ran a well-ordered court. He warned the senators not to eat apples and cake while in session. He censured them for leaving their seats. He hushed the spectators in the galleries.

The trial turned less on what Chase had done than on whether he could be impeached for having done those things. John Randolph, though, didn't really have a theory of impeachment. He had a theory of vengeance. His arguments, a distressed John Quincy Adams wrote in his diary, consisted "altogether of the most hackneyed commonplaces of popular declamation, mingled up with panegyrics and invectives." Randolph called eighteen witnesses, few of whom aided his case, and some of whom aided Chase's. "Saw nothing that struck me as remarkable," one witness, who had attended Callender's trial, said. As an observer put it, "I swear if they go on much farther, they will prove Judge Chase an angel."

Chase's defense called thirty-one witnesses, including some of Randolph's. Chase's attorneys said the charges were plainly silly, and they didn't much bother to refute them, especially since Randolph had done that job so well himself. Instead, they argued about the nature of impeachment. One of Chase's younger lawyers, Joseph Hopkinson, insisted that "no judge can be impeached and removed from office for any act or offense for which he could not be indicted." In other words, an impeachable offense has to be an indictable offense: a crime. "High crimes and misdemeanors," Hopkinson argued, meant "high crimes" and "high misdemeanors."

The trial reached its climax on February 23, when a red-faced Luther Martin rose from behind the defense's table. He spoke for a day and a half, expounding on his own theory of impeachment. A judge could commit a crime, like hitting someone, for which he could not be impeached. He could even commit a high crime for which he could not be impeached. All that he could be impeached for were crimes "such as relate to his office, or which tend to cover the person, who committed them, with *turpitude* and *infamy*; such as show there can be no dependence on that integrity and honor which will secure the performance of his official duties." To be impeached, Martin said, a judge had to commit crimes that either derived from his judicial power or were so horrible, so grotesquely unethical, that they disqualified him from holding a position of public trust.

Republicans outnumbered Federalists in the Senate 25–9. On March 1, for each article, Burr asked of each senator, "Is Samuel Chase, Esq., guilty or not guilty of a high crime or misdemeanor in the article of impeachment just read?" A majority voted guilty for three articles. None earned the required two-thirds supermajority. Six Republicans broke ranks on all eight articles. By a vote of 19–15, the Senate came closest to convicting Chase on the article regarding his partisan zeal in his charge to the Baltimore grand jury. Burr stood up. "It becomes my duty to pronounce that Samuel Chase, Esq., is acquitted," he said. Then he bowed to Chase and left the chamber. As for Burr, he was never convicted of killing Alexander Hamilton. (Two years later, in an unrelated incident of amazing sneakiness, he was tried for treason, and acquitted.)

The acquittal of Samuel Chase established the independence of the judiciary. It also established another principle, as Bowman argues: "The price of the independence granted by life tenure is abstention from party politics." It did not, however, establish a lasting theory of impeachment. Brandybottle Martin had stated his case beautifully, and easily defeated the hapless John Randolph, but Martin's argument was wrong. Nothing in American history, from the founding of its earliest colonies, suggests that an impeachable offense has to be an indictable crime, not for the king's men, not for judges and justices, and not for the president of the United States. Presidents can be impeached for actions that are not crimes, not least because the criminal code was not written with presidents in mind. Most of us cannot commit such staggering outrages as to direct the FBI to spy on our enemies or enlist foreign powers to interfere in our elections. The president has powers that only a president can exercise, or abuse. Were these powers beyond the reach of the people's power, impeachment would be a dead letter.

IF THE HOUSE VOTES TO IMPEACH DONALD TRUMP, it is by no means clear that the Senate will hold a trial. And, if the Senate does hold a trial, the likelihood that it will convict is small. Impeachment is a tall and rickety ladder; conviction is a tiny window, barely cracked open. It's difficult and dangerous to climb the ladder, and no one who has made it to the top has ever managed to crawl in through the window.

After the acquittal of Samuel Chase, in 1805, the House, in the next decades, impeached two more judges, one in 1830 and one in 1862; the Senate acquitted the first and convicted the second. The first real attempt to impeach a president came in 1843, when a Virginia congressman accused John Tyler of "corruption, malconduct, high crimes and misdemeanors," but the House voted down a motion to investigate, 127–83.

In 1868, "out of the midst of political gloom, impeachment, that dead corpse, rose up and walked forth again!" Mark Twain wrote. Republicans in the House impeached President Andrew Johnson by a vote of 126–47. They were desperate, as Brenda Wineapple chronicles in *The Impeachers: The Trial of Andrew Johnson and the Dream of a Just Nation*. Johnson, a Tennessee Democrat who didn't free his slaves until 1863, after the Emancipation Proclamation, had been Abraham Lincoln's improbable vice president, and had assumed the office of the presidency after his assassination, in 1865. Lincoln and congressional Republicans had one plan for Reconstruction: it involved welcoming the freedmen into the political community of the nation. Johnson, who believed that, "in the progress of nations, negroes have shown less capacity for government than any other race of people," betrayed that vision. "Slavery is not abolished until the black man has the ballot," Frederick Douglass declared. But granting the franchise to Black men was the last thing Johnson intended to allow. While Congress was out of session, he set in motion a Reconstruction plan that was completely at variance with what Congress had proposed: he intended to return power to the very people who had waged war against the Union, and he readmitted the former Confederate states to the Union. "No power but Congress had any right to say whether ever or when they should be admitted to the Union as States and entitled to the privileges of the Constitution," the Pennsylvania representative Thaddeus Stevens said during Johnson's impeachment proceedings. (Stevens, ailing, had to be carried into the Capitol on a chair.) "And yet Andrew Johnson, with unblushing hardihood, undertook to rule them by his own power alone." Johnson vetoed the 1866 Civil Rights Bill and nearly every other congressional attempt to reassert authority over the law of the United States. But the Republicans' strategy, to pass a law they expected Johnson to break, so that they could impeach him, backfired.

The Senate acquitted Johnson, falling short by a single vote of the two-thirds majority necessary to convict. Stevens died a couple of months later, "the bravest old ironclad in the Capitol," Twain wrote.

The Republicans had tried to save the republic by burying the Confederacy for good. They failed.

EVERY IMPEACHMENT REINVENTS what impeachment is for, and what it means, a theory of government itself. Every impeachment also offers a chance to establish a new political settlement in an unruly nation. The impeachment of Samuel Chase steered the United States toward judicial independence, and an accommodation with a party system that had not been anticipated by the framers. Chase's acquittal stabilized the republic and restored the balance of power between the executive and the judicial branches. The failed impeachment of Andrew Johnson steered the United States toward a regime of racial segregation: the era of Jim Crow, which would not be undone until the Civil Rights Act of 1964 and the Voting Rights Acts of 1965 were passed, a century later, in the administration of another Johnson. Johnson's acquittal undid the Union's victory in the Civil War, allowed the Confederacy to win the peace, and nearly destroyed the republic.

Johnson's acquittal also elevated the presidency by making impeachment seem doomed. Jefferson once lamented that impeachment had become a "mere scarecrow." That's how it worked for much of the twentieth century: propped up in a field, straw poking out from under its hat. A Republican congressman from Michigan called for the impeachment of FDR, after the president tried to pack the Court. Nothing but another scarecrow.

The impeachment of Richard Nixon, in 1974, which, although it never went to trial, succeeded in the sense that it drove Nixon from office, represented a use entirely consistent with the instrument's medieval origins: it attempted to puncture the swollen power of the presidency and to reassert the supremacy of the legislature. Nixon's presidency began to unravel only after the publication of the Pentagon Papers, in 1971—which indicted not Nixon but Lyndon Johnson, for deceiving the public about Vietnam—and the public anger that made impeachment possible had to do not only with Nixon's lies and abuses of power but also with Johnson's. But a new settlement, curtailing the powers of the president, never came. Instead, the nation became divided, and those divisions widened.

The wider those divisions, the duller the blade of impeachment.

Only very rarely in American history has one party held more than two-thirds of the seats in the Senate (it hasn't happened since 1967), and the more partisan American politics the less likely it is that sixty-seven senators can be rounded up to convict anyone, of anything. And yet the wider those divisions the more willing Congress has been to call for impeachment. Since Ronald Reagan's inauguration in 1981, members of the House have introduced resolutions for impeachment during every presidency. And the people, too, have clamored. IMPEACH BUSH, the yard signs read. IMPEACH OBAMA.

Not every impeachment brings about a political settlement, good or bad. The failed impeachment of Bill Clinton, in 1999, for lying about his sexual relationship with Monica Lewinsky, settled less than nothing, except that it weakened Americans' faith in impeachment as anything other than a crudely wrought partisan hatchet, a prisoner's shiv.

Clinton's impeachment had one more consequence: it got Donald Trump, self-professed playboy, onto national television, as an authority on the sex lives of ego-mad men. "Paula Jones is a loser," Trump said on CNBC. "It's a terrible embarrassment." Also, "I think his lawyers . . . did a terrible job," Trump said. "I'm not even sure that he shouldn't have just gone in and taken the Fifth Amendment." Because why, after all, should any man have to answer for anything?

"Heaven forbid we should see another impeachment!" an exhausted Republican said at the end of the trial of Samuel Chase. The impeachment of an American president is certain to lead to no end of political mischief and almost certain to fail. Still, worse could happen. Heaven forbid this republic should become one man's kingdom.

—2019

Postscript: In 2019 and again in 2021, after the insurrection at the Capitol, the House voted to impeach Trump but the Senate acquitted him.

THE TRUMP PAPERS

D ONALD TRUMP IS NOT MUCH OF A NOTE-TAKER, and he does not like his staff to take notes. During his presidency, he had a habit of tearing up documents at the close of meetings. (Records analysts, armed with Scotch tape, have tried to put the pieces back together.) No real record exists for five meetings Trump had with Vladimir Putin during the first two years of his presidency. Members of his staff routinely used apps that automatically erase text messages, and, before he was banned from Twitter, Trump often deleted his own tweets, notwithstanding a warning from the National Archives and Records Administration that doing so contravenes the Presidential Records Act.

Trump cannot abide documentation for fear of disclosure, and cannot abide disclosure for fear of disparagement. For decades, in private life, he required people who worked with him, and with the Trump Organization, to sign nondisclosure agreements, pledging never to say a bad word about him, his family, or his businesses. He also extracted nondisclosure agreements from women with whom he had or is alleged to have had sex, including both of his ex-wives. In 2015 and 2016, he required these contracts from people involved in his campaign, including a distributor of his MAKE AMERICA GREAT AGAIN hats. (Hillary Clinton's 2016 campaign required NDAs from some employees, too. In 2020, Joe Biden called on Michael Bloomberg to release his former employees from such agreements.) In 2017, Trump, unable to distinguish between private life and public service, carried his practice of requiring nondisclosure agreements into the presidency, demanding that senior White House staff sign NDAs. According to the *Washington Post*, at least one of them, in draft form, included this language: "I understand that the United States Government or, upon completion of the term(s) of Mr. Donald J. Trump, an authorized representative of Mr. Trump, may seek any remedy available to enforce this Agreement including, but not limited to, application for a court order prohibiting disclosure of information in breach of this Agreement." Aides warned him that, for White House employees, such agreements are likely not legally enforceable. The White House counsel, Don McGahn, refused to distribute them; eventually, he relented, and the chief of staff, Reince Priebus, pressured employees to sign them.

Those NDAs haven't stopped a small village's worth of ex-Trump cabinet members and staffers from blabbing about him, much to the president's dismay. "When people are chosen by a man to go into government at high levels and then they leave government and they write a book about a man and say a lot of things that were really guarded and personal, I don't like that," he told the *Washington Post*. In 2019, he tweeted, "I am currently suing various people for violating their confidentiality agreements." That year, a former campaign worker filed a class action lawsuit that, if successful, would render void all campaign NDAs. Trump has only stepped up the fight. Earlier suits were filed by Trump personally, or by his campaign, but in 2020 the Department of Justice filed suit against Stephanie Winston Wolkoff for publishing a book, *Melania and Me*, about her time volunteering for the First Lady, arguing, astonishingly, that Wolkoff's NDA is "a contract with the United States and therefore enforceable by the United States." (Unlike the suit against Trump's former national security adviser John Bolton, relating to the publication of his book *The Room Where It Happened*, there is no claim that anything in Wolkoff's book is or was ever classified. The suit was later dropped.) And Trump hasn't stopped: during the pandemic, he required doctors and staff who treated him at the Walter Reed National Military Medical Center to sign NDAs.

Hardly a day of his presidency passed that Trump did not attempt to suppress evidence, as if all the world were in violation of an NDA never to speak ill of him. He sought to discredit publications and broadcasts that question him, investigations that expose him, crowds that protest him, polls that failed to favor him, and, well past the bitter end, ballots cast against him. None of this boded well for the historical record and for the scheduled transfer of materials from the White House to the National Archives, on January 20, 2021. That morning, even as President-elect Joseph R. Biden Jr. is ascending the steps of the Capitol, staffers from the archives were in the White House, unlocking doors, opening desks, packing boxes, and removing hard drives. What was missing, that day, from file drawers and computer servers at 1600 Pennsylvania Avenue would take months to determine. But records that were never kept, were later destroyed, or were taken, illegally, chronicle the day-to-day doings of one of the most consequential presidencies in American history and might well include evidence of crimes, violations of the Constitution, and human rights abuses. It took a very long time to establish rules governing the fate of presidential records. Trump does not mind breaking rules and, in the course of a long life, has regularly done so with impunity. The Presidential Records Act isn't easily enforceable. The Trump presidency nearly destroyed the United States. Will what went on in the darker corners of his White House ever be known?

"THE TRUTH BEHIND A PRESIDENT'S ACTIONS can be found only in his official papers," Harry S. Truman said in 1949, "and every Presidential paper is official." Truman became an advocate of archival preservation after learning about the fate of his predecessors' papers. When George Washington left office, in 1797, he brought his papers back to Mount Vernon, but, loaned out, they were "extensively mutilated by rats and otherwise injured by damp"; eventually, they were carried by the historian Jared Sparks to Massachusetts, where Sparks threw out anything he didn't like, scrapped what he found worthless, gave away much of the rest, and, beginning in 1837, published what he liked best as *The Writings of George Washington*.

For many years, there was no alternative for a departing president but to take his papers home with him; there wasn't really any place to put them. Thomas Jefferson, "having no confidence that the office of the private secretary of the President of the U.S. will ever be a regular and safe deposit for public papers," took pains to deposit many of his papers with his cabinet departments. In 1810, Congress established a Committee on Ancient Public Records and Archives of the United States. It reported that the records of the federal government were "in a state of great disorder and exposure; and in a situation neither safe nor convenient nor honorable to the nation." Congress took little action. In 1814, the congressional library burned to the ground.

Most of the papers of William Henry Harrison, the log-cabin candidate, succumbed to flames when that log cabin burned down. Those of both John Tyler and Zachary Taylor were largely destroyed during the Civil War. In 1853, when Millard Fillmore left the White House, he had his papers shipped to a mansion in Buffalo. He died in 1874, having made no provisions for the papers. When Fillmore's only son died, in 1889, his will ordered his executors to "burn or otherwise effectively destroy all correspondence or letters to or from my father." Only by the merest miracle were forty-four volumes of Fillmore's presidential letter books found in an attic of a house, in 1908, and only because it was on the verge of being demolished.

Chester Arthur's son had most of his father's presidential papers burned in three garbage cans. "The only place I ever found in my life to put a paper so as to find it again was either a side coat-pocket or the hands of a clerk," Ulysses S. Grant once said. For years after Grant's administration, scholars were able to locate hardly any of his presidential papers. In 1888, Congress urged the Library of Congress to collect the papers of the presidents. In the 1890s, the library established a Manuscript Division, and a historian who later became its chief began lobbying for the establishment of a National Archives; meanwhile, the American Historical Association formed a Public Archives Commission. In 1910, after the commission reported that "many of the records of the Government have in the past been lost or destroyed," the AHA petitioned Congress to build a depository. Congress authorized the funds, but no plan was undertaken until after the close of the First World War.

Grover Cleveland, during his two terms, preferred to communicate in person, leaving no paper trail. He insisted that the records of his presidency were his personal property and, in 1886, refused to turn over papers that the Senate had demanded: "if I saw fit to destroy them no one could complain." (That is what, during the presidency of Dwight D. Eisenhower, came to be called "executive privilege.") Cleveland's contention became a convention: the president's papers belong to the president, who can deny requests for disclosure not only from the public but from other branches of the federal government. William McKinley was assassinated in 1901; his secretary held on to his papers until 1935, when he donated them to the Library of Congress, where they remained under his, and later his son's, tight control until 1954. In 1924, a raft of papers from the Taft, Wilson, and Harding administrations were found in the attic of the White House. Warren Harding's presidency was riven by scandal; after his death, his wife told the chief of the Manuscript Division of the Library of Congress that she had destroyed all his papers, although she had burned only those she thought "would harm his memory." Most of the rest she left to the Harding Memorial Association. The Library of Congress acquired a cache of those and other papers in 1972, on the condition that they be closed to the public until 2014. (They turned out to include a thousand pages of love letters between Harding and his mistress. "Won't you please destroy?" he wrote her in one letter. She did not destroy.) Calvin Coolidge instructed his private secretary to destroy all his personal files; on Coolidge's death, the secretary said, "There would have been nothing preserved if I had not taken some things out on my own responsibility."

In 1933, Herbert Hoover laid the cornerstone of the National Archives Building. "This temple of our history will appropriately be one of the most beautiful buildings in America, an expression of the American soul," he said. A granite, marble, and limestone monument with two forty-foot bronze doors behind seventy-two Corinthian columns, it was built at the height of the Depression, a massive public works project. In 1941, with Hitler in power in Germany and Mussolini in Italy, Franklin Delano Roosevelt spoke at its dedication:

> To bring together the records of the past and to house them in buildings where they will be preserved for the use of men and women living in the future, a Nation must believe in three things. It must believe in the past. It must believe in the future. It must, above all, believe in the capacity of its own people so to learn from the past that they can gain in judgements in creating their own future.

Americans used to believe in those three things. Do they still?

ARCHIVES ARE ANCIENT, but national archives, the official repositories of the records of a nation-state, date to the French Revolution: France established its Archives Nationales in 1790. Britain established what became a pillar of its National Archives in 1838. Newly independent nations have established national archives as part of the project of declaring independence: Argentina established what would become its national archive in 1821, Mexico in 1823, Brazil in 1838.

National archives uphold a particular vision of a nation and of its power, and, during transitions of power in nations that are not democratic, archives are not infrequently attacked. Most attacks involve the destruction of the evidence of atrocity. Brazil abolished slavery in 1888. Two years later, after a military coup, a minister of the new republic ordered the destruction of every document in any archive in the country which related to its history of slavery.

Richard Ovenden's *Burning the Books: A History of the Deliberate Destruction of Knowledge*, is a litany of this sort of tragedy. "The preservation of information continues to be a key tool in the defense of open societies," Ovenden, who runs the Bodleian Libraries, at Oxford, writes. UNESCO's report "Lost Memory" is an inventory of inventories: a list of libraries and archives that were destroyed in the twentieth century, including the widespread devastation of the First and Second World Wars, the burning of some of the collections in the National Library in Phnom Penh by the Khmer Rouge, and the destruction of the National and University Library in Sarajevo, by the Bosnian Serb army, in 1992. Libraries house books: copies. Archives store documents: originals. Archives cannot be replaced. As UNESCO's report puts it, "The loss of archives is as serious as the loss of memory in a human being."

All is not always lost. Officials of the British Empire set fire to entire archives as they left the colonies. In 1961, in Uganda, the objectives of what came to be known as Operation Legacy included the elimination of all documents that might "embarrass" Her Majesty's government. Decades later, some three hundred boxes from Kenya and nearly nine thousand files from more than thirty other former British colonies, including Malta, Malaya, and the Bahamas, were discovered in a top secret government fortress north of London. In 1992, guards from the former Soviet republic of Georgia burned to the ground the State Archive of Abkhazia. But many of its documents had been microfilmed or photocopied, and these records were stored in other buildings. In 2005, Guatemalan officials conducting a safety inspection of a munitions depot came across the long-hidden records of the brutal force that was the National Police—an estimated eighty million pages, described by my Harvard colleague Kirsten Weld as "papers spilling forth from rusted file cabinets, heaped on dirt floors, in trash bags and grain sacks, shoved into every conceivable nook and cranny, moldy and rotting." People have spent more than a decade preserving and organizing them.

Governments that commit atrocities against their own citizens regularly destroy their own archives. After the end of apartheid, South Africa's new government organized a Truth and Reconciliation Commission because, as its report stated, "the former government deliberately and systematically destroyed a huge body of state records and documentation in an attempt to remove incriminating evidence and thereby sanitise the history of oppressive rule." Unfortunately, the records of the commission have fared little better: the archive was restricted and shipped to the National Archives in Pretoria, where it remains to this day, largely uncatalogued and unprocessed; for ordinary South Africans, it's almost entirely unusable. In the aftermath of the Trump administration, the most elusive records won't be those in the White House. If they exist, they'll be far away, in and around detention centers, and will involve the least powerful: the families separated at the border, whose suffering federal officials inflicted, and proved so brutally indifferent to that they have lost track of what children belong to which parents, and how to find them.

In 1950, Truman signed the Federal Records Act, which required federal agencies to preserve their records. It did not require presidents to save their papers, which remained, as ever, their personal property. In 1955, Congress passed the Presidential Libraries Act, encouraging presidents to deposit their papers in privately erected institutions—something that every president has done since FDR, who was also the first president to install a tape recorder in the White House, a method of record-keeping that was used by every president down to Richard M. Nixon.

The presidential libraries are overseen by the National Archives and Records Administration. They were intended to be research centers, and include museums; and they serve, too, as monuments. The Barack

Obama Presidential Library is the first presidential library whose collections will be entirely digital—they will be available to anyone, anywhere, anytime. But the presidential library, which started with FDR, may well end with Obama.

Donald Trump, if he decides that he wants a presidential library, is far more likely to build a presidential museum, or even a theme park, and would most likely build it in Florida. "I have a lot of locations, actually," Trump said on NBC in 2019. In 2020, an anonymous group from New York published its own plans for a Trump library at djtrumplibrary.com. Its exhibits include a Criminal Records Room and a COVID Memorial, just off the Alt-Right Auditorium. But, long before Trump gets around to designing an actual Trump Library, he is likely to run afoul of a struggle over presidential records that began with Watergate and Nixon's tapes.

In 1974, a special prosecutor subpoenaed the Nixon administration for the Watergate tapes. The White House refused to comply. The case went to the Supreme Court. In *United States v. Nixon*, the Court devised a balancing test that measured the argument for executive privilege against the judiciary's interest in criminal justice, and ordered Nixon to turn over the tapes on July 24, 1974. Fifteen days later, Nixon resigned, and proceeded to sign an agreement with the General Services Administration that would have allowed him to destroy the records of his presidency. Congress then passed the Presidential Recordings and Materials Preservation Act, which prohibited Nixon from destroying the tapes. Nixon sued but, in 1977, in *Nixon v. Administrator of General Services*, he lost. Still, his legal battles continued into the 1990s.

To avoid all this happening all over again with another president, Congress in 1978 passed the Presidential Records Act. It puts presidential records in the public domain; the public can see those records five years after the president leaves office, though a president can ask to extend those five years to twelve for material deemed sensitive. No longer are presidential papers the private property of the president. The act also directs every White House to "take all such steps as may be necessary to assure that the activities, deliberations, decisions, and policies that reflect the performance of the President's constitutional, statutory, or other official or ceremonial duties are adequately documented and that such records are preserved and maintained as Presidential records." What counts as "such records" has been much contested. The archivist of the United States is appointed by the president; the archivist cannot tell the president what to do or what to save but can only provide advice, which the president can simply ignore.

The Presidential Records Act was scheduled to go into effect on January 20, 1981, with the inauguration of the next president, who turned out to be Ronald Reagan. Reagan's attorney general, Edwin Meese III, decided to help Nixon, who was still fighting in court for control of the archives of his presidency. The Reagan administration aided the efforts of Nixon's lawyers, who argued that the archivist of the United States has no discretion in evaluating claims of executive privilege but must, instead, defer to them without review. In 1988, in *Public Citizen v. Burke*, the DC Circuit Court ruled against Nixon and the administration. The next year, Reagan left office, and his staff packed up his papers.

Reagan's was the first administration to use email. Preparing to leave the White House, people in the administration tried to erase the computer tapes that stored its electronic mail. The correspondence in question included records of the Iran-contra arms deal, which was, at the time, under criminal investigation. On the last day of Reagan's presidency, the journalist Scott Armstrong (formerly of the *Washington Post*), along with the American Historical Association, the National Security Archive (a nonprofit that Armstrong founded, in 1985), and other organizations, sued Reagan, George H. W. Bush, the National Security Council, and the archivist of the United States. That lawsuit remained unresolved four years later, in 1992, when C. Boyden Gray, a lawyer for the departing president, George H. W. Bush, advised him that destroying things like telephone logs was not a violation of the Presidential Records Act, because, he asserted, the act does not cover "'non-record' materials like scratch pads, unimportant notes to one's secretary, phone and visitor logs or informal notes (of meetings, etc.) used only by the staff member."

Non-record records that the administration sought to destroy also included the White House's digital archive of email, a body of evidence that was the subject of yet another congressional investigation, this time into whether Bush had ordered the State Department to search Bill Clinton's passport records as part of an effort to discredit him during the campaign. A federal judge placed a ten-day restraining order on the Bush White House, banning the destruction of any computer records. "History is full of instances where the outgoing President has decided to erase, burn or destroy all or substantially all Presidential or Executive Office of the President records before the end of his term," the judge declared. But on January 19, 1993, the night before Clinton's inauguration, the Bush administration deleted those computer files, in defiance of the court order. Near midnight, the office of the archivist of the United States, Don W. Wilson, a Reagan appointee, made an agreement with Bush, granting him control over all "Presidential information and all derivative information in whatever form" after leaving office.

Critics of the Presidential Records Act say that, along with the creation of independent counsels, it contributes to endless investigations and the politics of scandal. Lloyd Cutler served as counsel to both Jimmy Carter and Bill Clinton. "Now every congressional committee asks for every scrap of paper under the sun," Cutler said in an oral history conducted in 1999. "Independent counsels ask for every piece of paper under the sun. In this Administration, I would guess ten, fifteen lawyers are kept busy all the time digging up documents by the thousands, literally by the thousands. . . . It stops people from writing memos. Many people came to me and said, 'Can they really look in my diary?' I said, 'I hope you don't keep a diary. Sure, they can look at your diary.'" And so they stopped keeping diaries. And some of them started conducting government business using private email accounts.

In some matters of secrecy, the Clinton administration took its cue from the outgoing Bush administration but promised to archive its emails properly. (A system was eventually set up so that if you tried to delete an email you'd get a message that doing so was in violation of the Presidential Records Act.) Clinton claimed executive privilege again and again, to protect himself from congressional investigation; his staff argued that congressional Republicans were on a mission to destroy him, and so was Kenneth Starr, the independent counsel of the Whitewater investigation. Evading the Presidential Records Act became just another move in the partisan chess game.

Post-Watergate presidential papers are seemingly more formal, more bureaucratic, less intimate, and less candid, as if the less control presidents have over their archives, the less interesting those archives have become. "This is horseshit" is the sort of thing LBJ might scrawl on a memo (or any of us in a self-destructing text). You don't see that as much anymore. Don Wilson, after leaving office, argued that the Presidential Records Act compromised the records of the presidency. Records whose preservation was intended to aid historical research had become, instead, ammunition for prosecutors, creating "a climate for avoiding documentation or perhaps even destroying it." Wilson told me, "Vice President Cheney once said, when I asked him for his papers as chief of staff, 'I didn't keep any.'" And, as Columbia Law School's David Pozen has argued, transparency does not always advance good government: it can interfere with the deliberative process, make dealmaking impossible, and promote a culture of suspicion and mistrust.

Early in George W. Bush's first term, his administration disabled the automated email archive system. Nearly all senior officials in the Bush White House used a private email server run by the Republican National Committee. Then, between 2003 and 2009, they claimed to have lost, and later found, some twenty-two million email messages. Nor has this practice been limited to the White House. Hillary Clinton's use of a personal email account on a private email server to conduct official correspondence while serving as Obama's secretary of state violated the Federal Records Act, which allows the use of a personal account only so long as all emails are archived with the relevant agency or department; Clinton's were not. "The American people are sick and tired of hearing about your damn emails," Bernie Sanders said to Clinton in 2015, during a primary debate, all Larry David–like. But, closer to Election Day, renewed attention on Clinton's emails diminished her chances of defeating Trump.

The evidentiary shell game has been carried over from one administration to the next. Reagan tried to protect Nixon's executive privilege; Bush tried to protect Reagan's. That so many staff members who served in earlier Republican administrations serve again under later presidents has made their commitment to defying the Presidential Records Act even more ardent. This was something keenly felt by George W. Bush, who, after all, was also concerned about protecting his father's legacy (which is yet another argument against political dynasties).

In 2001, when the twelve-year restriction on the Reagan papers expired, they did not all become available to the public, because George W. Bush signed an executive order that had been drafted by his young associate counsel, Brett M. Kavanaugh. During the Clinton presidency, Kavanaugh had served as an aide to Ken Starr. In that capacity, he had argued against executive privilege. But, in the second Bush presidency, Kavanaugh favored executive privilege. Executive Order No. 13233, Further Implementation of the Presidential Records Act, tried to extend executive privilege, in effect, indefinitely. Specifically, it granted to the current president the right to review the declassification of the records of his predecessors before their release to the public: "Concurrent with or after the former President's review of the records, the incumbent President or his designee may also review the records in question, or may utilize whatever other procedures the incumbent President deems appropriate to decide whether to concur in the former President's decision to request withholding of or authorize access to the records." This, of course, allowed Bush to withhold from public view anything in his father's papers that he did not wish to see enter the public record, including documents drafted by members of his own administration who had served in his father's administration or in the Reagan administration. As the archivist Bruce Montgomery observed, "In brief, the Bush order expanded executive privilege beyond the incumbent president to past presidents, their heirs, and even to vice presidents, seemingly in perpetuity."

Historians got angry. At a forum co-sponsored by the PEN American Center, Lyndon Johnson's biographer Robert Caro pointed out, "If you want to challenge the executive order, the historian must ask for specific, detailed things. The Johnson Library has thirty-four million pieces of paper. Unless you've been through it, you can't possibly know what's in there." This raises another delicate point. An archive that holds everything is useless unless you can find your way around it, and that requires money. The entire budget of the National Archives is about the cost of a single C-17 military transport plane. In 2018, when Trump nominated Kavanaugh to the Supreme Court, the National

Archives, with its limited resources, processed twenty thousand pages of documents relating to his service in the independent counsel's office during the Clinton administration but was unable to get through all the requested documents from his work in the Bush administration in time for the Senate to review them. In any case, Kavanaugh's collection was vast: his records included more than six hundred thousand emails alone.

Barack Obama revoked Executive Order No. 13233 on his second day in office. His administration settled a suit filed by the National Security Archive against the Bush administration, for its failure to release visitor logs. Obama's White House published the logs of more than six million visitors, including the head of the National Security Archive. (Shaking his hand, Obama said, "You know, there's gonna be a record of this.") His administration did not require corporate-style NDAs. Nor had any president until Trump. Months before Trump left office, I asked Don Wilson what he expected of the Trump papers, and he said, "What kind of record will we have other than what he dictates will be a record?"

WHEN I VISITED THE OFFICE of the archivist of the United States, David Ferriero, he had three copies of letters that he wrote, as a kid in the 1960s, framed on his office wall. One is to Eisenhower, asking for a photograph. The second is to John F. Kennedy, inquiring about the Peace Corps. The third is to Johnson: "Mr. President, I wish to congratulate you and our country for passing John F. Kennedy's Civil Rights Bill." The originals of those letters ended up in the National Archives, preserved, long before the passage of the Presidential Records Act.

Ferriero, an Obama appointee, says that the PRA operates, essentially, as an honor system. He wishes that it had teeth. Instead, it's all gums. Kel McClanahan, a national security lawyer, told me, "If the president wanted to, he could pull together all of the pieces of paper that he has in his office and have a bonfire with them. He doesn't view the archivist as an impediment to anything, because the archivist is not an impediment to anything."

After Trump's inauguration, in January 2017, the National Archives and Records Administration conferred with the White House to establish rules for record-keeping, and, given the novelty of Trump's favored form of communication, advised Trump to save all his tweets, including deleted ones. Trump hasn't stopped deleting his tweets; instead, the White House set up a system to capture them, before they vanish. On February 22, the White House counsel Don McGahn sent a memo on the subject of Presidential Records Act Obligations to everyone working in the Executive Office of the President, with detailed instructions about how to save and synch email. McGahn's memo also included instructions about texting apps:

> You should not use instant messaging systems, social networks, or other internet-based means of electronic communication to conduct official business without the approval of the Office of the White House Counsel. If you ever generate or receive Presidential records on such platforms, you must preserve them by sending them to your EOP email account via a screenshot or other means. After preserving the communications, you must delete them from the non-EOP platform.

It appears that plenty of people in the White House ignored McGahn's memo. Ivanka Trump used a personal email for official communications. Jared Kushner used WhatsApp to communicate with the Saudi crown prince. The press secretary Sean Spicer held a meeting to warn staff not to use encrypted texting apps, though his chief concern appears to have been that White House personnel were using these apps to leak information to the press.

Ethically, if not legally, what records must be preserved by the White House and deposited with the National Archives at the close of Trump's presidency is subject to more dictates than those of the Presidential Records Act. In 2016, the International Council on Archives, founded with support from UNESCO in 1948, published a working document called "Basic Principles on the Role of Archivists and Records Managers in Support of Human Rights." Essentially an archivists' elaboration of the principles of the 1948 Universal Declaration of Human Rights, it urges governments to preserve archives that contain evidence of violation of human rights.

The rules about record-keeping, like so much about American government, weren't set up with someone like Trump in mind. It's not impossible that his White House will destroy records not so much to cover its own tracks but to sabotage the Biden administration. This would be a crime, of course, but Trump could issue blanket pardons. Yet, as with any administration, there's a limit to what can be lost. Probably not much is on paper, and it's harder to destroy electronic records than most people think. Chances are, a lot of documents that people in the White House might wish did not exist can't really be purged, because they've already been duplicated. Some will have been copied by other offices, as a matter of routine. And some will have been deliberately captured. "I can imagine that at State, Treasury, DOD, the career people have been quietly copying important stuff all the way along, precisely with this in mind," the historian Fredrik Logevall, the author of a biography of Kennedy, told me, in the last months of Trump's presidency.

Other attempts to preserve the record appear to have been less successful. The White House's PRA guidelines, as worked out with the National Archives, forbade the use of smartphone apps that can automatically erase or encrypt text messages. It's possible that the White House has complied with those guidelines, but there's nothing that the National Archives could have done, or could do now, if it hasn't. Watchdog groups sued, concerned about the use of such apps, but the Justice Department successfully argued that "courts cannot review the president's compliance with the Presidential Records Act." In 2019, the National Security Archive joined with two other organizations in a suit against Trump that led to a court's ordering the administration to preserve not only "all records reflecting Defendants' meetings, phone calls, and other communications with foreign leaders" but records having to do with the administration's record-keeping practices. In 2020, the judge in that case dismissed the lawsuit: "The Court is bound by Circuit precedent to find that it lacks authority to oversee the President's day-to-day compliance with the statutory provisions involved in this case."

"I'm very worried," Austin Evers, the executive director of the watchdog group American Oversight, told me, after Trump lost the election. "There are a lot of senior officials in the Trump administration who have been relying on impunity to sleep well at night, and I think it will dawn on them over the coming days and weeks that the records they leave behind will be in the hands of people they do not trust, including career public servants." But, if Jared Kushner set a bonfire in the Rose Garden, Evers thinks that there would be repercussions. "The PRA gets a bad rap," he says. It's difficult to enforce, but it's not unenforceable. And if evidence of document destruction comes out, Evers says, American Oversight is poised to file suit: "We have litigation in the can."

A WEEK AFTER ELECTION DAY, the House Oversight Committee sent strenuously worded letters to the White House and to dozens of federal agencies, warning them not to destroy or remove records during the transition. The letters were signed by the chairs of twenty other House committees. "That letter is the lifeguard whistle from the tower," Tom Blanton, who runs the National Security Archive, told me. " 'Watch out, there are records drowning out there!' "

Trudy Peterson, who served as the acting archivist of the United States under Clinton, helped oversee the packing up of the Ford White House on the day of Carter's inauguration. Crowds were lining the streets, she recalled, while, inside, "people were packing up the president's morning briefing. You have literally the hottest of the hot foreign policy materials in your hands." A convoy of trucks, under military escort, drove from Washington to Michigan. "We lost track of one of the trucks," she told me. "For a matter of moments. But it stopped your heart." Phillip Brady, who served under both Reagan and George H. W. Bush, once recalled what it was like to pack up. People from the White House counsel's office, he said, "would again remind everyone that these are presidential documents; you're not permitted to walk out of the White House with them; these are things that become part of the permanent record." Brady visited the archives at the Bush Library and rummaged through boxes with his name on them. "Some of the messages were a little more candid than you like to recall they were," he said in an interview later. "Because of the hustle of the day, many times you're writing notes to someone: 'I think that's a stupid idea.' . . . An awful lot more is preserved than you would imagine." That's how it's supposed to happen, anyway.

The memo that Don McGahn sent to executive office personnel in February 2017 came with a warning about leaving the White House:

At all times, please keep in mind that presidential records are the property of the United States. You may not dispose of presidential records. When you leave EOP employment, you may not take any presidential records with you. You also may not take copies of any presidential records without prior authorization from the Counsel's office. The willful destruction or concealment of federal records is a federal crime punishable by fines and imprisonment.

Custody of the records of the Trump White House was to be formally transferred to the National Archives at noon on January 20, 2021, the minute that Biden took his oath of office on the steps of the Capitol. Trump, defying tradition, did not attend that ceremony. It was difficult, even, to picture him there. Maybe, earlier, he was in the Oval Office, yanking at the drawers of Resolute, the presidential desk, barking out orders, cornered, frantic, panicked. The obligation, the sober duty, to save the record of this administration fell largely to the people who work under him. It required many small acts of defiance.

The truth will not come from the ex-president. It was clear, even before that day, that, out of a job and burdened by debt, he'd want to make money, billions. He'd need, crave, hunger to be seen, looked at, followed, loved, hated; he'd take anything but being ignored. Would he sell secrets to American adversaries, in the guise of advice and expertise? It wasn't impossible.

"Will you shut up, man?" an exasperated Biden said to Trump during their presidential debate. Donald J. Trump cannot shut up. Aside from the prospect of silencing former White House staffers, shredding papers, deleting files, and burying evidence, another danger, when the sun set on the twentieth of January, wouldn't be what's left unsaid, unrecorded, and unsaved but what Trump would be willing to say, still. And to steal.

—2020

Postscript: It was later discovered that Trump had taken thousands of documents from the White House, in likely violation of the Presidential Records Act, and including a great deal of classified material. As of 2022, a Justice Department investigation is ongoing.

IN EVERY DARK HOUR

THE LAST TIME DEMOCRACY NEARLY DIED ALL OVER the world and almost all at once, Americans argued about it, and then they tried to fix it. "The future of democracy is topic number one in the animated discussion going on all over America," a contributor to the *New York Times* wrote in 1937. "In the Legislatures, over the radio, at the luncheon table, in the drawing rooms, at meetings of forums and in all kinds of groups of citizens everywhere, people are talking about the democratic way of life." People bickered and people hollered, and they also made rules. "You are a liar!" one guy shouted from the audience during a political debate heard on the radio by ten million Americans, from Missoula to Tallahassee. "Now, now, we don't allow that," the moderator said, calmly, and asked him to leave.

In the 1930s, you could count on the Yankees winning the World Series, dust storms plaguing the prairies, evangelicals preaching on the radio, Franklin Delano Roosevelt residing in the White House, people lining up for blocks to get scraps of food, and democracies dying, from the Andes to the Urals and the Alps.

In 1917, Woodrow Wilson's administration had promised that winning the Great War would "make the world safe for democracy." The peace carved nearly a dozen new states out of the former Russian, Ottoman, and Austrian Empires. The number of democracies in the world rose; the spread of liberal-democratic governance began to appear inevitable. But this was no more than a reverie. Infant democracies grew, toddled, wobbled, and fell: Hungary, Albania, Poland, Lithuania, Yugoslavia. In older states, too, the desperate masses turned to authoritarianism. Benito Mussolini marched on Rome in 1922. It had taken a century and a half for European monarchs who ruled by divine right and brute force to be replaced by constitutional democracies and the rule of law. Now fascism and communism toppled these governments in a matter of months, even before the stock market crash of 1929 and the misery that ensued.

"Epitaphs for democracy are the fashion of the day," the soon-to-be Supreme Court justice Felix Frankfurter wrote, dismally, in 1930. The *annus horribilis* that followed differed from every other year in the history of the world, according to the British historian Arnold Toynbee: "In 1931, men and women all over the world were seriously contemplating and frankly discussing the possibility that the Western system of Society might break down and cease to work." When Japan invaded Manchuria, the League of Nations condemned the annexation, to no avail. "The liberal state is destined to perish," Mussolini predicted in 1932. "All the political experiments of our day are anti-liberal." By 1933, the year Adolf Hitler came to power, the American political commentator Walter Lippmann was telling an audience of students at Berkeley that "the old relationships among the great masses of the people of the earth have disappeared." What next? More epitaphs: Greece, Romania, Estonia, and Latvia. Authoritarians multiplied in Portugal, Uruguay, Spain. Japan invaded Shanghai. Mussolini invaded Ethiopia. "The present century is the century of authority," he declared, "a century of the Right, a Fascist century."

American democracy, too, staggered, weakened by corruption, monopoly, apathy, inequality, political violence, hucksterism, racial injustice, unemployment, even starvation. "We do not distrust the future of essential democracy," FDR said in his first inaugural address, telling Americans that the only thing they had to fear was fear itself. But there *was* more to be afraid of, including Americans' own declining faith in self-government. "What Does Democracy Mean?" NBC radio asked listeners. "Do we Negroes believe in democracy?" W. E. B. Du Bois asked the readers of his newspaper column. Could it happen here? Sinclair Lewis asked in 1935. Americans suffered, and hungered, and wondered. The historian Charles Beard, in the inevitable essay on "The Future of Democracy in the United States," predicted that American democracy would endure, if only because "there is in America, no Rome, no Berlin to march on." Some Americans turned to communism. Some turned to fascism. And a lot of people, worried about whether American democracy could survive past the end of the decade, strove to save it.

"It's not too late," Jimmy Stewart pleaded with Congress, rasping, exhausted, in *Mr. Smith Goes to Washington*, in 1939. "Great principles don't get lost once they come to light." It wasn't too late. It's still not too late.

THERE'S A KIND OF LIKENESS you see in family photographs, generation after generation. The same ears, the same funny nose. Sometimes now looks a lot like then. Still, it can be hard to tell whether the likeness is more than skin-deep.

In the 1990s, with the end of the Cold War, democracies grew more plentiful, much as they had after the end of the First World War. As ever, the infant mortality rate for democracies was high: baby democracies tend to die in their cradles. Starting in about 2005, the number of democracies around the world began to fall, as it had in the 1930s. Authoritarians rose to power: Vladimir Putin in Russia, Recep Tayyip Erdoğan in Turkey, Viktor Orbán in Hungary, Jarosław Kaczyński in Poland, Rodrigo Duterte in the Philippines, Jair Bolsonaro in Brazil, and Donald J. Trump in the United States.

"American democracy," as a matter of history, is democracy with an asterisk, the symbol A-Rod's name would need if he were ever inducted into the Hall of Fame. Not until the 1964 Civil Rights Act and the 1965 Voting Rights Act can the United States be said to have met the basic conditions for political equality requisite in a democracy. All the same, measured not against its past but against its contemporaries, American democracy in the twenty-first century is withering. The Democracy Index rates 167 countries, every year, on a scale that ranges from "full democracy" to "authoritarian regime." In 2006, the U.S. was a "full democracy," the seventeenth most democratic nation in the world. In 2016, the index for the first time rated the United States a "flawed democracy," and since then American democracy has gotten only more flawed. True, the United States still doesn't have a Rome or a Berlin to march on. That hasn't saved the nation from misinformation, tribalization, domestic terrorism, human rights abuses, political intolerance, social-media mob rule, white nationalism, a criminal president, the nobbling of Congress, a corrupt presidential administration, assaults on the press, crippling polarization, the undermining of elections, and an epistemological chaos that is the only air that totalitarianism can breathe.

Nothing so sharpens one's appreciation for democracy as bearing witness to its demolition. Mussolini called Italy and Germany "the greatest and soundest democracies which exist in the world today," and Hitler liked to say that, with Nazi Germany, he had achieved a "beautiful democracy," prompting the American political columnist Dorothy Thompson to remark of the fascist state, "If it is going to call itself democratic we had better find another word for what we have and what we want." In the 1930s, Americans didn't find another word. But they did work to decide what they wanted, and to imagine and to build it. Thompson, who had been a foreign correspondent in Germany and Austria and had interviewed the führer, said, in a column that reached eight million readers, "Be sure you know what you prepare to defend."

It's a paradox of democracy that the best way to defend it is to attack it, to ask more of it, by way of criticism, protest, and dissent. American democracy in the 1930s had plenty of critics, left and right, from Mexican Americans who objected to a brutal regime of forced deportations to businessmen who believed the New Deal to be unconstitutional. W. E. B. Du Bois predicted that, unless the United States met its obligations to the dignity and equality of all its citizens and ended its enthrallment to corporations, American democracy would fail: "If it is going to use this power to force the world into color prejudice and race antagonism; if it is going to use it to manufacture millionaires, increase the rule of wealth, and break down democratic government everywhere; if it is going increasingly to stand for reaction, fascism, white supremacy and imperialism; if it is going to promote war and not peace; then America will go the way of the Roman Empire."

The historian Mary Ritter Beard warned that American democracy would make no headway against its "ruthless enemies—war, fascism, ignorance, poverty, scarcity, unemployment, sadistic criminality, racial persecution, man's lust for power and woman's miserable trailing in the shadow of his frightful ways"—unless Americans could imagine a future democracy in which women would no longer be barred from positions of leadership: "If we will not so envisage our future, no Bill of Rights, man's or woman's, is worth the paper on which it is printed."

If the United States hasn't gone the way of the Roman Empire and the Bill of Rights is still worth more than the paper on which it's printed, that's because so many people have been, ever since, fighting the fights Du Bois and Ritter Beard fought. There have been wins and losses. The fight goes on.

Could no system of rule but extremism hold back the chaos of economic decline? In the 1930s, people all over the world, liberals, hoped that the United States would be able to find a middle road, somewhere between the malignity of a state-run economy and the mercilessness of laissez-faire capitalism. Roosevelt campaigned in 1932 on the promise to rescue American democracy by way of a "new deal for the American people," his version of that third way: relief, recovery, and reform. He won forty-two of forty-eight states, and trounced the incumbent, Herbert Hoover, in the Electoral College 472–59. Given the national emergency in which Roosevelt took office, Congress granted him an almost entirely free hand, even as critics raised concerns that the powers he assumed were barely short of dictatorial.

New Dealers were trying to save the economy; they ended up saving democracy. They built a new America; they told a new American story. On New Deal projects, people from different parts of the country labored side by side, constructing roads and bridges and dams, everything from the Lincoln Tunnel to the Hoover Dam, joining together in a common endeavor, shoulder to the wheel, hand to the forge. Many of those public works projects, like better transportation and better electrification, also brought far-flung communities, down to the littlest town or the remotest farm, into a national culture, one enriched with new funds for the arts, theater, music, and storytelling. With radio, more than with any other technology of communication, before or since, Americans gained a sense of their shared suffering, and shared ideals: they listened to one another's voices.

This didn't happen by accident. Writers and actors and directors and broadcasters made it happen. They dedicated themselves to using the medium to bring people together. Beginning in 1938, for instance, FDR's Works Progress Administration produced a twenty-six-week radio drama series for CBS called *Americans All, Immigrants All*, written by Gilbert Seldes, the former editor of the *Dial*. "What brought people to this country from the four corners of the earth?" a pamphlet distributed to schoolteachers explaining the series asked. "What gifts did they bear? What were their problems? What problems remain unsolved?" The finale celebrated the American experiment: "The story of magnificent adventure! The record of an unparalleled event in the history of mankind!"

There is no twenty-first-century equivalent of Seldes's *Americans All, Immigrants All*, because it is no longer acceptable for a serious artist to write in this vein, and for this audience, and for this purpose. (In some quarters, it was barely acceptable even then.) Love of the ordinary, affection for the common people, concern for the commonweal: these were features of the best writing and art of the 1930s. They are not so often features lately.

Americans reelected FDR in 1936 by one of the widest margins in the country's history. American magazines continued the trend from the twenties, in which hardly a month went by without their taking stock: "Is Democracy Doomed?" "Can Democracy Survive?" (Those were the past century's versions of more recent titles, such as *How Democracy Ends, Why Liberalism Failed, How the Right Lost Its Mind*, and *How Democracies Die*. The same ears, that same funny nose.) In 1934, the *Christian Science Monitor* published a debate called "Whither Democracy?," addressed "to everyone who has been thinking about the future of democracy—and who hasn't." It staked, as adversaries, two British scholars: Alfred Zimmern, a historian from Oxford, on the right, and Harold Laski, a political theorist from the London School of Economics, on the left. "Dr. Zimmern says in effect that where democracy has failed it has not been really tried," the editors explained. "Professor Laski sees an irrepressible conflict between the idea of political equality in democracy and the fact of economic inequality in capitalism, and expects at least a temporary resort to Fascism or a capitalistic dictatorship." On the one hand, American democracy is safe; on the other hand, American democracy is not safe.

Zimmern and Laski went on speaking tours of the United States, part of a long parade of visiting professors brought here to prognosticate on the future of democracy. Laski spoke to a crowd three thousand strong, in Washington's Constitution Hall. "Laski Tells How to

Save Democracy," the *Washington Post* reported. Zimmern delivered a series of lectures titled "The Future of Democracy," at the University of Buffalo, in which he warned that democracy had been undermined by a new aristocracy of self-professed experts. "I am no more ready to be governed by experts than I am to be governed by the ex-Kaiser," he professed, expertly.

The year 1935 happened to mark the centennial of the publication of Alexis de Tocqueville's *Democracy in America*, an occasion that elicited still more lectures from European intellectuals coming to the United States to remark on its system of government and the character of its people, close on Tocqueville's heels. Heinrich Brüning, a scholar and a former chancellor of Germany, lectured at Princeton on "The Crisis of Democracy"; the Swiss political theorist William Rappard gave the same title to a series of lectures he delivered at the University of Chicago. In "The Prospects for Democracy," the Scottish historian and later BBC radio quiz-show panelist Denis W. Brogan offered little but gloom: "The defenders of democracy, the thinkers and writers who still believe in its merits, are in danger of suffering the fate of Aristotle, who kept his eyes fixedly on the city-state at a time when that form of government was being reduced to a shadow by the rise of Alexander's world empire." Brogan hedged his bets by predicting the worst. It's an old trick.

The endless train of academics were also called upon to contribute to the nation's growing number of periodicals. In 1937, *The New Republic*, arguing that "at no time since the rise of political democracy have its tenets been so seriously challenged as they are today," ran a series on "The Future of Democracy," featuring pieces by the likes of Bertrand Russell and John Dewey. "Do you think that political democracy is now on the wane?" the editors asked each writer. The series' lead contributor, the Italian philosopher Benedetto Croce, took issue with the question, as philosophers, thankfully, do. "I call this kind of question 'meteorological,'" he grumbled. "It is like asking, 'Do you think that it is going to rain today? Had I better take my umbrella?'" The trouble, Croce explained, is that political problems are not external forces beyond our control; they are forces within our control. "We need solely to make up our own minds and to act."

Don't ask whether you need an umbrella. Go outside and stop the rain.

HERE ARE SOME OF THE SORTS OF PEOPLE who went out and stopped the rain in the 1930s: schoolteachers, city councillors, librarians, poets, union organizers, artists, precinct workers, soldiers, civil rights activists, and investigative reporters. They knew what they were prepared to defend and they defended it, even though they also knew that they risked attack from both the left and the right. Charles Beard (Mary Ritter's husband) spoke out against the newspaper tycoon William Randolph Hearst, the Rupert Murdoch of his day, when he smeared scholars and teachers as communists. "The people who are doing the most damage to American democracy are men like Charles A. Beard," said a historian at Trinity College in Hartford, speaking at a high school on the subject of "Democracy and the Future," and warning against reading Beard's books—at a time when Nazis in Germany and Austria were burning "un-German" books in public squares. That did not exactly happen here, but in the 1930s four of five American superintendents of schools recommended assigning only those U.S. history textbooks which "omit any facts likely to arouse in the minds of the students question or doubt concerning the justice of our social order and government." Beard's books, God bless them, raised doubts.

Beard didn't back down. Nor did WPA muralists and artists, who were subject to the same attack. Instead, Beard took pains to point out that Americans liked to think of themselves as good talkers and good arguers, people with a particular kind of smarts. Not necessarily book learning, but street smarts—reasonableness, open-mindedness, level-headedness. "The kind of universal intellectual prostration required by Bolshevism and Fascism is decidedly foreign to American 'intelligence,'" Beard wrote. Possibly, he allowed, you could call this a stubborn independence of mind, or even mulishness. "Whatever the interpretation, our wisdom or ignorance stands in the way of our accepting the totalitarian assumption of Omniscience," he insisted. "And to this extent it contributes to the continuance of the arguing, debating, never-settling-anything-finally methods of political democracy." Maybe that was whistling in the dark, but sometimes a whistle is all you've got.

The more argument the better is what the North Carolina–born George V. Denny Jr. was banking on, anyway, after a neighbor of his, in Scarsdale, declared that he so strongly disagreed with FDR that he never listened to him. Denny, who helped run something called the League for Political Education, thought that was nuts. In 1935, he launched *America's Town Meeting of the Air,* an hour-long debate program, broadcast nationally on NBC's Blue Network. Each episode opened with a town crier ringing a bell and hollering, "Town meeting tonight! Town meeting tonight!" Then Denny moderated a debate, usually among three or four panelists, on a controversial subject (Does the U.S. have a truly free press? Should schools teach politics?), before opening the discussion up to questions from an audience of more than a thousand people. The debates were conducted at a lecture hall, usually in New York, and broadcast to listeners gathered in public libraries all over the country, so that they could hold their own debates once the show ended. "We are living today on the thin edge of history," Max Lerner, the editor of *The Nation,* said in 1938, during a *Town Meeting of the Air* debate on the meaning of democracy. His panel included a communist, an exile from the Spanish Civil War, a conservative American political economist, and a Russian columnist. "We didn't expect to settle anything, and therefore we succeeded," the Spanish exile said at the end of the hour, offering this definition: "A democracy is a place where a 'Town Meeting of the Air' can take place."

No one expected anyone to come up with an undisputable definition of democracy, since the point was disputation. Asking people about the meaning and the future of democracy and listening to them argue it out was really only a way to get people to stretch their civic muscles. "Democracy can only be saved by democratic men and women," Dorothy Thompson once said. "The war against democracy begins by the destruction of the democratic temper, the democratic method and the democratic heart. If the democratic temper be exacerbated into wanton unreasonableness, which is the essence of the evil, then a victory has been won for the evil we despise and prepare to defend ourselves against, even though it's 3,000 miles away and has never moved."

The most ambitious plan to get Americans to show up in the same room and argue with one another in the 1930s came out of Des Moines, Iowa, from a one-eyed former bricklayer named John W. Studebaker, who had become the superintendent of the city's schools. Studebaker, who after the Second World War helped create the G.I. Bill, had the idea of opening those schools up at night, so that citizens could hold debates. In 1933, with a grant from the Carnegie Corporation and support from the American Association for Adult Education, he started a five-year experiment in civic education.

The meetings began at a quarter to eight, with a fifteen-minute news update, followed by a forty-five-minute lecture, and thirty minutes of debate. The idea was that "the people of the community of every political affiliation, creed, and economic view have an opportunity to participate freely." When Senator Guy Gillette, a Democrat from Iowa, talked about "Why I Support the New Deal," Senator Lester Dickinson, a Republican from Iowa, talked about "Why I Oppose the New Deal." Speakers defended fascism. They attacked capitalism. They attacked fascism. They defended capitalism. Within the first nine months of the program, thirteen thousand of Des Moines' seventy-six thousand adults had attended a forum. The program got so popular that in 1934 FDR appointed Studebaker the U.S. Commissioner of Education and, with the eventual help of Eleanor Roosevelt, the program became a part of the New Deal, and received federal funding. The federal forum program started out in ten test sites—from Orange County, California, to Sedgwick County, Kansas, and Pulaski County, Arkansas. It came to include almost five hundred forums in forty-three states and involved two and a half million Americans. Even people who had steadfastly predicted the demise of democracy participated. "It seems to me the only method by which we are going to achieve democracy in the United States," Du Bois wrote, in 1937.

The federal government paid for it, but everything else fell under local control, and ordinary people made it work, by showing up and participating. Usually, school districts found the speakers and decided on the topics after collecting ballots from the community. In some parts of the country, even in rural areas, meetings were held four and five times a week. They started in schools and spread to YMCAs and YWCAs, labor halls, libraries, settlement houses, and businesses, during lunch hours. Many of the meetings were broadcast by radio. People who went to those meetings debated all sorts of things:

Should the Power of the Supreme Court Be Altered?
Do Company Unions Help Labor?
Do Machines Oust Men?

Must the West Get Out of the East?
Can We Conquer Poverty?
Should Capital Punishment Be Abolished?
Is Propaganda a Menace?
Do We Need a New Constitution?
Should Women Work?
Is America a Good Neighbor?
Can It Happen Here?

These efforts don't always work. Still, trying them is better than talking about the weather, and waiting for someone to hand you an umbrella.

WHEN A TERRIBLE HURRICANE hit New England in 1938, Dr. Lorine Pruette, a Tennessee-born psychologist who had written an essay called "Why Women Fail," and who had urged FDR to name only women to his cabinet, found herself marooned at a farm in New Hampshire with a young neighbor, sixteen-year-old Alice Hooper, a high school sophomore. Waiting out the storm, they had nothing to do except listen to the news, which, needless to say, concerned the future of democracy. Alice asked Pruette a question: "What is it everyone on the radio is talking about—what is this democracy—what does it mean?" Somehow, in the end, NBC arranged a coast-to-coast broadcast, in which eight prominent thinkers—two ministers, three professors, a former ambassador, a poet, and a journalist—tried to explain to Alice the meaning of democracy. American democracy had found its "Yes, Virginia, there is a Santa Claus" moment, except that it was messier, and more interesting, because those eight people didn't agree on the answer. Democracy, Alice, is the darnedest thing.

That broadcast was made possible by the workers who brought electricity to rural New Hampshire; the legislators who signed the 1934 federal Communications Act, mandating public interest broadcasting; the executives at NBC who decided that it was important to run this program; the two ministers, the three professors, the former ambassador, the poet, and the journalist who gave their time, for free, to a public forum, and agreed to disagree without acting like asses; and a whole lot of Americans who took the time to listen, carefully, even though they had plenty of other things to do. Getting out of our current jam will likely require something different, but not entirely different. And it will be worth doing.

A decade-long debate about the future of democracy came to a close at the end of the 1930s—but not because it had been settled. In 1939, the World's Fair opened in Queens, with a main exhibit featuring the saga of democracy and a chipper motto: "The World of Tomorrow." The fairgrounds included a Court of Peace, with pavilions for every nation. By the time the fair opened, Czechoslovakia had fallen to Germany, though, and its pavilion couldn't open. Shortly afterward, Edvard Beneš, the exiled president of Czechoslovakia, delivered a series of lectures at the University of Chicago on, yes, the future of democracy, though he spoke less about the future than about the past, and especially about the terrible present, a time of violently unmoored traditions and laws and agreements, a time "of moral and intellectual crisis and chaos." Soon, more black bunting was brought to the World's Fair, to cover Poland, Belgium, Denmark, France, Luxembourg, and the Netherlands. By the time the World of Tomorrow closed, in 1940, half the European hall lay under a shroud of black.

The federal government stopped funding the forum program in 1941. Americans would take up their debate about the future of democracy, in a different form, only after the defeat of the Axis. For now, there was a war to fight. And there were still essays to publish, if not about the future, then about the present. In 1943, E. B. White got a letter in the mail, from the Writers' War Board, asking him to write a statement about "The Meaning of Democracy." He was a little weary of these pieces, but he knew how much they mattered. He wrote back, "Democracy is a request from a War Board, in the middle of a morning in the middle of a war, wanting to know what democracy is." It meant something once. And, the thing is, it still does.

—2020

THE AMERICAN BEAST

Trump is going to do some crazy shit.
—Steve Bannon, October 31, 2020

THE GOVERNMENT PUBLISHING OFFICE'S 845-PAGE report of the Select Committee to Investigate the January 6th Attack on the United States Capitol is divided into eight chapters, makes eleven recommendations, attaches four appendices, and includes 4,285 endnotes. Its executive summary, which at nearly two hundred pages can hardly be called a summary, provides a numbered list of seventeen key findings, the first eleven of which have, as the subject of the predicate, the forty-fifth president of the United States:

1. Donald Trump purposely disseminated false allegations of fraud. . . .

2. Donald Trump refused to accept the lawful result of the 2020 election. . . .

3. Donald Trump corruptly pressured Vice President Mike Pence to refuse to count electoral votes. . . .

4. Donald Trump sought to corrupt the U.S. Department of Justice. . . .

5. Donald Trump unlawfully pressured State officials and legislators. . . .

6. Donald Trump oversaw an effort to transmit false electoral certificates. . . .

7. Donald Trump pressured Members of Congress to object to valid slates of electors. . . .

8. Donald Trump purposely verified false information filed in Federal court. . . .

9. Donald Trump summoned tens of thousands of supporters to Washington for January 6th. . . .

10. Donald Trump purposely sent a social media message publicly condemning Vice President Pence. . . .

11. Donald Trump refused repeated requests over a multi-

ple hour period that he instruct his violent supporters to
disperse and leave the Capitol. . . .

In a foreword to the report, Bennie G. Thompson, the committee's chairman, stresses the importance of "accountability at all levels," but although the word "conspiracy" appears both in finding
No. 12—"Each of these actions by Donald Trump was taken in support
of a multi-part conspiracy to overturn the lawful results of the 2020
Presidential election"—and more than a hundred times elsewhere in
the document, the report is less an account of a conspiracy than a very
long bill of indictment against a single man.

Two years ago, the president of the United States attempted to overturn an election for no reason other than that he had lost. A mere
handful of Republican officeholders denounced him; for months,
nationally prominent members of the GOP refused to acknowledge
that Joseph Biden had won the presidency. On January 6, 2021, at
Trump's urging, thousands of his supporters staged an armed, lethal,
and yet somehow also inane insurrection at the Capitol, aimed at pre-
venting a joint session of Congress from certifying the results of the
election. They failed. Unless you count being temporarily banned
from Twitter as punishment, the former president has suffered no consequences for his actions; Republicans have refused to hold him to
account, not least because many party leaders have been implicated
in the attempted overthrow of the United States government. Days
after the insurrection, the House voted to impeach the president, but
the Senate then failed to convict him. Months later, the House voted
to establish an independent, 9/11-style commission to investigate the
insurrection, but the Senate blocked that by way of the filibuster. The
House soon voted to hold its own investigation, under the aegis of a
select committee composed of seven Democrats and six Republicans.
Then Nancy Pelosi, the Democratic Speaker of the House, refused to
seat on the committee two Republicans who had supported the insurrection, whereupon Kevin McCarthy, the Republican minority leader,
denounced the committee and pulled his members from it, after which
the GOP, declaring the attack on the Capitol to have been "legitimate
political discourse," censured the two Republicans who did serve on
the committee, Liz Cheney and Adam Kinzinger, both of whom left

office this month. (Cheney lost her bid for reelection, and Kinzinger declined to run.)

Congress established the January 6th Committee on June 30, 2021. The committee's report is the fullest record yet of the conspiracy to overturn the results of the 2020 presidential election, much of it deriving from the dauntless work of earlier reporters, much of it newly gathered by the committee itself. In the course of eighteen months, the committee reviewed thousands of pages of evidence and presented testimony from more than seventy witnesses during ten televised hearings produced with the aid of the former president of ABC News and illustrated with taped video interviews, Facebook posts, text messages, YouTube clips, and surveillance footage, all of it easily snipped and posted on social media. The hearings made for great television and, probably more important, great memes, the TikTokification of testimony. "Like our hearings, this report is designed to deliver our findings in detail in a format that is accessible for all Americans," Liz Cheney, the committee's vice-chair, writes in a foreword to the written report. But the report, unlike the hearings, is dreary, repetitive, and exhausting. In that sense, it's like Trump himself. It's also surprisingly scanty in the key elements of storytelling—setting, character, and plot. It's as if the committee found itself unable to surmount Trump's madness and senselessness, trapped in his very plotlessness.

The report doesn't lack for details, which consist mainly of running down and debunking bogus claims about dead voters, shredded ballots, dumped votes, voting machines linked to Hugo Chávez, a faked water-main rupture, suitcases full of ballots, USB drives, truckloads of ballots in garbage bins, unmarked vans, a Dominion voting machine connected to China by way of a smart thermostat, and some guy meddling with the election from inside a prison in Italy. There are inconsequential but *Veep*-worthy revelations: an Oath Keeper calling followers of QAnon "Q-tards," and Lieutenant General Michael Flynn, at the rally at the Ellipse on January 6, asked whether he would march to the Capitol, answering, "Hell, no. It's freezing." Antics abound: Rudy Giuliani (who is now facing disbarment) holding a press conference at Four Seasons Total Landscaping; Ivanka and Jared fretting, uselessly; a Proud Boys subcommittee calling itself the Ministry of Self-Defense entertaining a proposal from South Florida cryptocurrency investors that refers to the planned attack on the Capitol as operation Storm the Winter Palace, a reference to the 1917 Bolshevik Revolution (leading the report's authors to huff, "No historical event has been less American"). At one point, Trump supporters in Michigan plan to hide out in the state's capitol overnight, so that, in the morning, they can sign an elector certificate that, by law, has to be signed in that building. Not for nothing did William Barr, the attorney general at the time, refer to Trump's legal team as the "clown car." It's all so madcap and vaudevillian that, if the stakes weren't so high, and the matter at hand not so grave, it would be the Marx Brothers in *Night at the White House*.

But the stakes *are* high; they tower. Trump might get reelected. Or he might get indicted. Both could happen. Even if he were to die tomorrow, the attempt to overturn the election would require an accounting of its deeper roots in American political behavior and discourse, of the anti-government takeover of the GOP, and of the role played by the 147 Republicans who, in the early morning of January 7, 2021, only hours after the Capitol had been cleared of rioters, voted against certifying the results of the election. The siege of the building is, in the end, the least of it. The Department of Justice has so far filed criminal charges against more than nine hundred people who participated in the insurrection, of whom nearly five hundred have either pleaded guilty or been convicted. The January 6th Report makes eight criminal referrals, recommending that the Department of Justice prosecute the former president (and in some cases other people) for crimes that include obstruction of an official proceeding, conspiracy to defraud the United States, and incitement or assistance of insurrection, the charge for which Trump was impeached in January 2021. Much turns on the reception of this report. As a brief for the prosecution, it's a start. As a book, it's essential if miserable reading. As history, it's a shambles.

INVESTIGATORY COMMITTEES AND COMMISSIONS began to multiply about a century ago, with the rise of the administrative state and the extension of executive power. Their purpose is chiefly to hold bureaucrats and elected officials and, especially, the executive branch accountable for wrongdoing. It wasn't clear, at first, whether these commissions were constitutional. That question was resolved in 1927, when, in *McGrain v. Daugherty*, the U.S. Supreme Court upheld a conviction for contempt of the brother of the attorney general, who had refused to appear before a Senate committee investigating the Teapot Dome scandal. The investigatory commission proliferated during the Progressive Era, and has origins in "race riot" commissions like the Chicago Commission on Race Relations, established in 1919 by the governor of Illinois "to get the facts and interpret them and to find a way out," or, as Lyndon B. Johnson put it, when charging the Kerner Commission with investigating "civil disorders" half a century later, "What happened? Why did it happen? What can be done to prevent it from happening again and again?"

These same questions animate the January 6th investigation, and a case can be made that the insurrection was, among other things, a race riot—a white race riot. But the committee has not taken as its model the race-riot report. Instead, the report is indebted to earlier investigations into attacks on the United States, a kinship suggested by the committee's preference for the word "attack" over the word "insurrection," as if it came from without. "I don't know if you want to use the word 'insurrection,' 'coup,' whatever," a White House staffer told the committee. The committee knew which word it wanted to use.

Congress ordered the select committee to "investigate and report upon the facts, circumstances, and causes" of the attack on the Capitol. The charge borrows its language from investigations into earlier attacks on the United States. On December 18, 1941, eleven days after the Japanese bombing of Pearl Harbor, FDR appointed a commission "to ascertain and report the facts relating to the attack." In 1963, after John F. Kennedy was assassinated, Lyndon B. Johnson directed the Warren Commission "to evaluate all the facts and circumstances surrounding the assassination," which, at the time, many suspected to have been a covert operation coordinated by the KGB, given that Lee Harvey Oswald had defected to the Soviet Union in 1959. In 2002, Congress charged the 9/11 Commission with determining the "facts and circumstances relating to the terrorist attacks of September 11, 2001." Each investigated failures within the federal government, especially failures of intelligence, but each looked, too, to foreign actors.

If you're going to report on the facts, circumstances, and causes of an event, the natural way to do it is to write a story that is both painstakingly researched and kept kissing-close to the evidence—a story, in other words, that is also a history. A history has to be true, to the best of your knowledge at the time of the writing, and it ought to be riveting. The Warren Commission Report (1964) reads like a mystery novel: "In the corner house itself, Mrs. Barbara Jeanette Davis and her sister-in-law, Mrs. Virginia Davis, heard the shots and rushed to the door in time to see the man walk rapidly across the lawn shaking a revolver as if he were emptying it of cartridge cases." The Starr Report (1998), an investigation of a real estate deal that ended up exposing Bill Clinton's relationship with Monica Lewinsky, often reads like porn: "In the course of flirting with him, she raised her jacket in the back and showed him the straps of her thong underwear, which extended above her pants." The 9/11 Commission Report (2004) reads like an international thriller: "Tuesday, September 11, 2001, dawned temperate and nearly cloudless in the eastern United States. . . . In Sarasota, Florida, President George W. Bush went for an early morning run. For those heading to an airport, weather conditions could not have been better for a safe and pleasant journey. Among the travelers were Mohamed Atta and Abdul Aziz al Omari, who arrived at the airport in Portland, Maine." The January 6th Report reads like a prosecuting attorney's statement to a jury: "President Trump's decision to declare victory falsely on election night and, unlawfully, to call for the vote counting to stop, was not a spontaneous decision. It was premeditated." A page-turner it is not.

The reports of earlier investigatory commissions have been mixed successes. The Warren Report, which concluded that Oswald acted alone, is notorious, since it did little to halt the flowering of conspiracy theories involving everything from the Mafia to Martians. "We are looking to you, not to approve our own notions, but to guide us and to guide the country through a thicket of tension, conflicting evidence, and extreme opinion," LBJ told the Kerner Commission. But, when the report came in, the president refused even to accept a copy. The Starr Report is just plain embarrassing.

Reports of investigatory commissions don't age well: as is the case with all historical analysis, more evidence always comes out later. Still, some reports are better than others. The 9/11 Commission Report was a finalist for the National Book Award. In an "authorized" edition published by W. W. Norton, the report was also an unexpected bestseller. As with the January 6th Report, which is available from several different publishers as a book, you could get the 9/11 report free online, but people bought it anyway. *Time* described it as "one of the most riveting, disturbing and revealing accounts of crime, espionage and the inner workings of government ever written." The *Times Book Review* called it "an improbable literary triumph."

Families of the victims, not members of Congress, had demanded the formation of the 9/11 Commission, which consisted of five Democrats and five Republicans (none of whom were current members of Congress). The architects of the report were two professors of history—the commission's executive director, Philip D. Zelikow, and a senior adviser, Ernest R. May—who had taught courses together and had also collaborated on a book, *The Kennedy Tapes*. May, a Harvard professor (and a colleague of mine until his death, in 2009), wanted to reinvent the genre. "Typically, government reports focus on 'findings' and array the evidence accordingly," he explained. "None, to our knowledge, had ever attempted simply to produce professional-quality narrative history." This is what May set out to do—he wanted to create "enduringly readable history"—and it's not only the report's narrative structure but also its sense of historical time that endows it with both immediacy and lastingness.

The historical narrative is the first eleven chapters of a thirteen-chapter report. There is no two-hundred-page executive summary. There is no executive summary at all, or any list of findings. There is, instead, a taut, three-page preface, and then the story begins, the "story of eccentric and violent ideas sprouting in the fertile ground of political and social turmoil."

The 9/11 report has plenty of flaws, as May was the first to admit. "For one thing, the report skirts the question of whether American policies and actions fed the anger that manifested itself on September 11," he wrote in the *New Republic* in 2005. For another, because some members of the commission and its staff had worked at national security agencies, "collective drafting led to the introduction of passages that offset criticism of an agency with words of praise. Not all these words were deserved." Both Bill Clinton and George W. Bush got off even easier than the CIA, the FBI, and the NSA. What May was hinting at is illustrated in a thirty-one-page document declassified only this fall, a "memorandum for the record" of a meeting between Bush and the commissioners in which the commissioners repeatedly pressed

Bush on whether he knew, in the summer of 2001, about the threat posed by Al Qaeda. Bush said he'd been briefed only about "threats overseas." This was a lie. He'd been warned about specific threats to the United States. Nowhere in the commission's final report—released in July 2004, less than four months before a presidential election— is the president implicated. If he had been, he might not have been reelected. "Our aim has not been to assign individual blame," reads the preface, written by the bipartisan commission's co-chairs. Instead, they hoped to provide an explanation.

May wanted the 9/11 report to "transcend the passions of the moment," and it did. He hoped it might serve as a model for future reports. "In these perilous times, there will surely be other events that will require the principles of historiography allied to the resources of government, so that urgency will sometimes become the friend of truth." This is the bar that was set for members of the January 6th Committee. Their report does not clear that bar. Not because the report isn't accurate but because it hasn't achieved escape velocity from the leaden passions of the present.

HERE, RADICALLY REDUCED—forty gallons of sap to one gallon of maple syrup—is a very un-executive summary of the report. Donald Trump never said he'd abide by the outcome of the election. In May of 2020, fearing that Biden might win in November, he tweeted, "It will be the greatest Rigged Election in history!" He understood that he would likely lose but that, owing to an effect known as the Red Mirage, it would look, for a while, as if he had won: more Democrats than Republicans would vote by mail and, since mail-in ballots are often the last to be counted, early counting would favor Republicans. "When that happens," Roger Stone advised him, "the key thing to do is to claim victory. . . . No, we won. Fuck you, Sorry. Over."

That was Plan A. In September, the *Atlantic* published a bomb-shell article by Barton Gellman reporting that the Trump campaign had a scheme "to bypass election results and appoint loyal electors in battleground states where Republicans hold the legislative majority." That was Plan B. Plan A ("Fuck you") was more Trump's style. "He's gonna declare victory," Steve Bannon said. "But that doesn't mean he's the winner. He's just gonna say he's a winner." On Election Night,

November 3, Trump wanted to do just that, but his campaign team persuaded him not to. His patience didn't last long. "This is a fraud on the American public," Trump said on November 4. "We were getting ready to win this election. Frankly, we did win this election." The next day, he tweeted, "*STOP THE COUNT!*" On November 7, CNN, NBC, MSNBC, ABC, the Associated Press, and Fox News all declared that Joseph Biden had won. The election was not close. Counting the votes just took a while.

After Biden won, Trump continued to insist that widespread fraud had been committed. Bill Stepien, Trump's campaign manager, told the January 6th Committee that the campaign became a "truth telling squad," chasing allegations, discovering them to be unfounded, and telling the president, "Yeah, that wasn't true." The Department of Homeland Security looked into allegations, most of which popped up online, and announced, "There is no evidence that any voting system deleted or lost votes, changed votes, or was in any way compromised." The Justice Department, too, investigated charges of fraud, but, as Barr informed the committee, he was left telling the president, repeatedly, "They're not panning out."

For Plan C, the president turned to Rudy Giuliani and a group of lawyers that included Sidney Powell. They filed sixty-two lawsuits challenging election results, and lost all but one of these suits (and that one involved neither allegations of fraud nor any significant number of votes). Twenty-two of the judges who decided these cases had been appointed by Republicans, and ten had been appointed by Trump.

On December 11, the Supreme Court rejected a suit that had challenged the results in Pennsylvania, Georgia, Michigan, and Wisconsin. Trump had had every right to challenge the results of state elections, but at this point he had exhausted his legal options. He decided to fall back on Plan B, the fake-electors plan, which required hundreds of legislators across the country to set aside the popular vote in states won by Biden, claiming that the results were fraudulent, and appointing their own slate of electors, who would cast their Electoral College votes for Trump on December 14. According to Cassidy Hutchinson, an aide to Trump's chief of staff, Mark Meadows, the White House counsel determined that, since none of the fraud allegations had been upheld by any court, the fake-electors plan was illegal. But one deputy assistant to the president told Trump that it didn't matter whether there had been fraud or not, because "state legislators 'have the constitutional right to substitute their judgment for a certified majority of their constituents' if that prevents socialism."

Plan B required Trump to put pressure on a lot of people. The committee counted at least two hundred attempts he made to influence state or local officials by phone, text, posts, or public remarks. Instructing Trump supporters to join in, Giuliani said, "Sometimes it even requires being threatened." A Trump campaign spreadsheet documents efforts to contact more than 190 Republican state legislators in Arizona, Georgia, and Michigan alone.

Barr resigned. "I didn't want to be part of it," he told the committee. Plenty of other people were happy to be part of it, though. Ronna McDaniel, the RNC chair, participated and provided Trump with the assistance of RNC staffers. On December 14, certified electors met in every state. In seven states that Biden had won—Arizona, Georgia, Michigan, Nevada, New Mexico, Pennsylvania, and Wisconsin—fake electors also met and produced counterfeit Electoral College certificates for Trump. Five of these certificates were sent to Washington but were rejected because they lacked the required state seal; two arrived after the deadline. None were accepted.

Trump then launched Plan D, which was not so much a plan as a pig's breakfast of a conspiracy, a coup, and a putsch. Everything turned on January 6, the day a joint session of Congress was to certify the results of the Electoral College vote. To stop that from happening, Trump recruited members of Congress into a conspiracy to overturn the election by rejecting the certified votes and accepting the counterfeits; he asked the vice president to participate in a coup by simply declaring him the winner; and he incited his supporters to take over the Capitol by force, in a poorly planned putsch, which he intended to lead. On December 17, Kayleigh McEnany said on Fox News, "There has been an alternate slate of electors voted upon that Congress will decide in January." Two days later, Trump tweeted, "Big protest in D.C. On January 6th. Be there, will be wild." The legal architect of the Pence part of the pig's breakfast—"a coup in search of a legal theory," as one federal judge called it—was a lawyer named John Eastman. The Trump lawyer Eric Herschmann recalled a conversation he had with Eastman:

You're saying you believe the Vice President, acting as President of the Senate, can be the sole decisionmaker as to, under your theory, who becomes the next President of the United States? And he said, yes. And I said, are you out of your F'ing mind?

Trump pressed the acting attorney general, Jeffrey Rosen, and other members of the Department of Justice to aid the conspiracy by declaring some of the voting to have been fraudulent. Rosen refused. "The DOJ can't and won't snap its fingers and change the outcome of the election," he told Trump. Trump replied, "I don't expect you to do that. Just say the election was corrupt and leave the rest to me and the Republican congressmen." Trump tried to replace Rosen with a lackey named Jeffrey Clark, but, in a tense meeting at the White House on January 3, Rosen and others made clear to him that, if he did so, much of the department would resign. Trump and Eastman met repeatedly with Pence in the Oval Office and tried to recruit him into the conspiracy. Pence refused. At 11:20 *a.m.* on January 6, Trump called Pence and again asked him, and again Pence refused, after which, according to Ivanka, the president called the vice president a pussy.

Trump was slated to speak at his be-wild rally at the Ellipse at noon, but when he arrived he was unhappy about the size of the crowd. The Secret Service had set up magnetometers, known as mags, to screen for weapons. Twenty-eight thousand people went through the mags, from whom the Secret Service collected, among other banned items, "269 knives or blades, 242 cannisters of pepper spray, 18 brass knuckles, 18 tasers, 6 pieces of body armor, 3 gas masks, 30 batons or blunt instruments." Some people had ditched their bags, and presumably their weapons, in trees or cars. In a crowd that included members of white-supremacist and far-right, anti-government extremist groups—including the Proud Boys, the Oath Keepers, America First, and QAnon—another twenty-five thousand people simply refused to go through the mags. "I don't fucking care that they have weapons," Trump shouted. "They're not here to hurt *me*. Take the fucking mags away." The mags stayed. Trump took to the podium and fired up his followers for the march to the Capitol until 1:10 *p.m.*, and then he walked to his motorcade, climbed into the presidential SUV, which is known as the Beast, and demanded to be driven to the Capitol. Secret Service agents persuaded him to return to the White House.

Just before the joint session was to begin, at one o'clock, Pence released a written statement: "I do not believe that the Founders of our country intended to invest the Vice President with unilateral authority to decide which electoral votes should be counted during the Joint Session of Congress." The voting began. By 1:21, Trump had been informed that the Capitol was under attack. He spent the rest of the day watching it on television. For hours, his staff and his advisers begged him to order the mob to disperse or to call for military assistance; he refused. At 1:46, Representative Paul Gosar objected to the count from Arizona, after which Senator Ted Cruz endorsed that objection. Pence was evacuated at 2:12. Seconds later, Proud Boys achieved the first breach of the Capitol, smashing a window in the Senate wing. Eleven minutes later, the mob broke through the doors to the East Rotunda, and Trump tweeted, "Mike Pence didn't have the courage to do what should have been done." The mob chanted, "Hang Mike Pence." Meadows told a colleague, "He thinks Mike deserves it." Kevin McCarthy called the president. "They literally just came through my office windows," he said. "You need to call them off." Trump said, "Well, Kevin, I guess they're just more upset about the election theft than you are." At 4:17 *p.m.*, the president released a video message in which he asked the insurrectionists to go home, and told them that he loved them.

And that, in brief, is the report, which concludes that "the central cause of January 6th was one man, former President Donald Trump." And that, in brief, is the problem: chasing Trump, never quite untethering itself from him, fluttering in the biting wind of his violent derangement, like a ribbon pinned to the tail of a kite during a tornado, and failing, entirely, to see the tornado.

IN THE JANUARY 6TH REPORT, Donald Trump acted alone and came out of nowhere. He has no past. Neither does the nation. The rest of the country doesn't even exist. No one dies of COVID, no one loses a job, no one sinks to her knees in grief upon hearing on the radio the news that Americans—*Americans*—are staging an armed invasion of the Capitol. Among the many reasons this investigation ought to have been conducted by a body independent from the federal government is that there is very little suffering in Congress's January 6th Report, except that of members of Congress running for their lives that day.

The report is organized around the idea of the "Big Lie," which is the title of the report's first chapter. "The Big Lie" is what Democratic politicians and many journalists call Trump's claim that he had won the election. (It is also an expression first notably used by Adolf Hitler.) It is an inept phrase: it turns an attempted coup d'état into something that sounds like a children's book written by Margaret Wise Brown. "The Big Lie" is so ham-handed that, unsurprisingly, it's an expression that Trump adores. "The Fraudulent Presidential Election of 2020 will be, from this day forth, known as *THE BIG LIE!*" he announced at one point. Playing "You lie!" "No, you lie!" with Donald Trump is a fool's game.

"The Big Lie" is not a big lie. It is an elaborate fiction, an artful story, with heroes and villains, exotic locales, and a sinister plot. *The election was stolen by a cabal of Democrats, socialists, immigrants, criminals, Black people, and spies.* This story is vicious and idiotic, and none of it is true, but it is not a Big Lie devised by an orange-haired supervillain born rich in 1946: it is the latest chapter in a fictive counter-history of the United States that has been told by the far right for decades and decades and wretched decades. In 2020, it gained so much speed so fast that it acted something like a stampede. Unfortunately, reading the report is like being in the stampede. "The stolen election narrative has proven to be remarkably durable precisely because it is a matter of belief—not evidence, or reason," the report states. It does not ask why this should be. Why believe? Two in five Americans and three in five Republicans *still* believe. Republicans who most fiercely believe hold the party by the throat. The 9/11 Commission Report asked, "How did Bin Ladin—with his call for indiscriminate killing of Americans— win thousands of followers and some degree of approval from millions more?" The January 6th Committee Report, for all its weight and consequence, never asks why anyone believed Donald Trump, which is why it is unlikely to persuade anyone not to.

WHY BELIEVE? Answering that question would have required a historical vantage on the decay of the party system, the celebration of political intolerance by both the right and the left, the contribution of social media to political extremism, and the predicament of American journalism. Calling the system rigged when you're losing is an old trick. At the end of the Cold War, American zealots turned their most ruthless ideological weapons on one another, Manicheans all. In 1992, Newt Gingrich told Republican candidates to get the message out that the Democrats were going to rig the presidential election. It didn't matter to Gingrich that this wasn't true. "They're going to buy registrations, they're going to buy votes," he warned. "They're going to turn out votes, they're going to steal votes, they're going to do anything they can." After the contested Bush v. Gore election of 2000, sowing doubt about elections became common practice for outsiders in both parties. "The system is rigged" was the watchword of Bernie Sanders's 2016 campaign: primaries rigged against challengers, the economy rigged against working people. Suspecting that things like elections might be rigged, even when that's not true, isn't a crazy conspiracy theory; it is a political product routinely sold to voters in every city and state in the country.

Why believe? In the past two decades, public approval of Congress has fallen from 80 percent to 20 percent. Might it be that Congress has lost any real grip on the American experience, and no longer speaks for a nation and a people that Richard Hofstadter once called a "huge, inarticulate beast"? The report lacks not only a sense of the past but also a meaningful sense of the present. A chronicle that runs from April 2020 to January 2021, it is a story told out of time. The "facts, circumstances, and causes" relating to the insurrection that it fails to investigate and, in most cases, even to note, include COVID-19 deaths, masks, lockdowns, joblessness, farm closures, guns and mass shootings, a national mental health crisis, daily reports of devastating storms and fires, George Floyd, Black Lives Matter, and partisan, and especially congressional, eye-gouging over each and every one of the items in this list. Why believe? Was the election stolen? No. But was 2020 painful? Yes.

Why believe? Nowhere acknowledged in the report is the fact that November 3, 2020, really was a weird Election Day. In the middle of a pandemic, unprecedented numbers of people voted by mail and by absentee ballot, and, even if you trudged out to the polls, you were met with the general misery of masks and loneliness and loss and, for many people, a sense of impending doom. For the entire stretch of time chronicled in this report, it felt to many Americans, not always for the same reasons, as though a great deal was being stolen from them: their jobs, their coworkers, a sense of justice and fairness in the world, predictable weather, the idea of America, the people they love, human touch. The January 6th Report offers no shuddering sense, not even a little shiver, of the national mood of vulnerability, fear, and sorrow. "The assassination of John Fitzgerald Kennedy on November 22, 1963, was a cruel and shocking act of violence directed against a man, a family, a nation, and against all mankind," the Warren Commission Report opens. Nothing in the January 6th report is stated so squarely.

Why believe? During the pandemic, more people spent more time online than ever before. The report fails to examine the way in which Facebook and Twitter profited by spreading misinformation about the election, providing the organizational architecture for the insurrection, and making possible the doxing and harassment of courageous and dedicated public servants who refused to participate in the conspiracy. When Trump staffers tell him that allegations of fraud are unfounded, he replies, "You guys may not be following the internet the way I do." Nor did the committee.

Why believe? Every single television and news outlet that reported live on Election Day, 2020, knew about the Red Mirage, and although some news anchors regularly pointed out that the outcome would not be known for days, they were nevertheless complicit in promoting the fiction of a Trump victory: simply by reporting, second by second, on November 3, 2020, they endorsed the idea that the outcome could be known that night even though they knew it to be untrue. The committee does not remark on this. Nor does it indict the media-run polls and horse-race coverage—vastly greater in number, speed, and influence than ever before—or the growing partisanship of the press. Nor does it inquire into the consequences of an educated national elite of politicians, journalists, and academics increasingly living their lives in a Met Gala to Davos to White House Correspondents' Dinner world, or the degree to which so many of them appear to have so wholly given themselves over to Twitter—knowing the world through it, reporting from it, being ruled by it.

Why believe? The answer to that question—the knowledge of what has happened to America—will have to wait for another day. From beneath the Capitol dome, the January 6th Committee has issued its report. It blames Trump. It explains very little. Outside, the whirling wind heaves and twists and roars.

—2023

Acknowledgments

Heartfelt thanks to Henry Finder at *The New Yorker* and to Bob Weil. I remain forever indebted to David Remnick. At Liveright, thanks to Janet Byrne, Don Rifkin, Steve Attardo, and Haley Bracken. Thanks, as ever, to Tina Bennett. Very special thanks to the many amazing librarians and archivists who helped me research the essays in this book and to all the fact-checkers who checked facts. I've drawn here on material from too many collections to name but they include those of the BBC, the Beinecke Library, and Houghton Library, and historical collections at the Harvard Business School Library, Special Collections at the Harvard Law School, the Library of Congress Manuscripts Division, the Massachusetts Historical Society, the National Archives, the Manuscripts and Archives Division of the New York Public Library, the Schlesinger Library at Radcliffe Institute for Advanced Study, and Manuscripts and Archives at Yale University. To Adrianna Alty, Dan Balz, Elise Broach, Gaby Calvocoressi, Jelani Cobb, Nancy Cott, Sophie Crane, Phil Deloria, Zachary Elkins, Deb Favreau, Benjamin Filene, Beverly Gage, Jamal Greene, Stephen Greenblatt, Elizabeth Hinton, Maya Jasanoff, Jane Kamensky, Elis and Josh Kanner, Lisa Lovett, Ken Mack, Luke Menand, Adelaide Mandeville, Liz McNerney, Benjamin Naddaff-Hafrey, Latif Nasser, Evan Osnos, Dan Penrice, Leah Price, Julie Reuben, Bruce Schulman, Rachel Seidman, Reva Siegel, Ramie Targoff, Sue Vargo, Denise Webb, to the late and much-missed Tony Horwitz, and to all the rest of my friends, colleagues, and family who talked me through essay after essay, love and thanks, always.

Index

Page numbers in *italics* refer to illustrations.

About the Author

Jill Lepore is the David Woods Kemper '41 Professor of American History at Harvard. She's also a staff writer at *The New Yorker*. Her many books include the international bestseller *These Truths: A History of the United States*.